The Melting Pot

A Tale of Three Citizens

by
Isabel Berman

Mazo Publishers

The Melting Pot: A Tale of Three Citizens
Copyright © 2020 Isabel Berman

ISBN 978-1-946124-69-2

Contact The Author
bermanis@gmail.com

Mazo Publishers
Website: www.mazopublishers.com
Email: mazopublishers@gmail.com

The front cover design was created by Studio ER. The photograph of "The Tree of Life" is credited to Shaula Haitner and Wikipedia. The image of the Israeli flag is credited to Oleg Vakhromov and Unsplash.

54321
All rights reserved.

No part of this publication may be translated, reproduced, stored in a retrieval system, or transmitted in any form or by any means, electronic, mechanical, photocopying, recording or otherwise, without prior permission in writing from the publisher.

To my 1000s of students who taught me as much as I taught them

♦ ♦ ♦

*To my niece Ilyse, friends and colleagues
who were my sounding board for this book*

The Author

Isabel Berman grew up in Long Island, New York where she developed her love for literature, music, art, opera, and theatre, as well as the Yankees and the Knicks. She attended university in Philadelphia.

A year after the Six Day War (1967), she enrolled in The Hebrew University of Jerusalem's foreign student program. She fell in love with Israel and returned after completing her Masters degree. With a grant from The Hebrew University, Isabel completed a doctorate at Columbia University.

Now living in Israel for almost 50 years, during the span of her career in English education, Isabel was responsible for developing the examinations for the English sections of many of the higher level university programs, as well as English course instructional material for university students and cadets in the Israeli Foreign Ministry.

She is currently working on a fictionalized biography of her parents.

A Note From The Author

The term "Melting Pot" is a metaphor for a place (such as a city or country) where people of different backgrounds (race, culture, ethnos, religion) come together and gradually assimilate into a cohesive community. The characters in these tales meet each other through David Ben Gurion's "ideal melting pot" – Tzahal, the Israeli Defense Forces (IDF). Based on immigrants known to me, the characters' names and places of origin have been changed and their stories have been embellished. But the historic references are accurate, as are the many place names presented in the stories. If anyone is offended by any of the details in the three tales, I sincerely apologize.

The "Tree of Life" featured on the cover was created by Cubist sculptor Jacques (Chaim Jacob) Lipshitz. This sculpture depicts the biblical figures Noah, Abraham, Isaac, Moses and six flames, perhaps representing six million Holocaust victims, together with Moses' hand converging to form a Menorah. Seen against the background of blue sky and desert behind Hadassah Hospital on Mt. Scopus in Jerusalem, the Tree of Life's sculpted parts seem to be engaged in a struggle to survive: in other words, the history of Israel.

I want to acknowledge both Wikipedia and the IDF for being the source of the historical and military detail that I was able to incorporate in this book, *The Melting Pot: A Tale of Three Citizens*.

Table of Contents

Tale Number 1 ~ Page 7

Dominik/Gabriel's Story

♦ Glossary ~ Page 122

———•●•———

Tale Number 2 ~ Page 125

Lise's Story of Family and Israel

♦ Glossary ~ Page 281

———•●•———

Tale Number 3 ~ Page 285

Alexander's Story

♦ Glossary ~ Page 412

———•●•———

Epilogue

Page 415

———•●•———

♦ *Foreign words or phrases appear in each tale. The reader will find explanations and translations in each glossary as they relate to the story.*

– Tale Number 1 –
Dominik/Gabriel's Story
Prologue: Oxford

He recognized the spiky handwriting instantly, even though he hadn't seen it for 15 years, more than half of his life. He stood next to the open letterbox and stared at the envelope, shifting it from hand to hand as if it might burn him. It was a little bulky. Did it contain documents? It was addressed to him at Balliol College, Oxford University, but some kind person had crossed out the address and sent it to the flat.

What did she want? Money? For God's sake, he was a foreign graduate student whose salary as a teaching assistant covered only a portion of their expenses. He did occasional translation work or tutoring to supplement his income and pay their rent, their bills, buy food; he even tended bar every now and then in order to get a decent meal in the kitchen of a local pub. He had no money to give her, but maybe she was sick and unable to support herself even though she was still a fairly young woman.

He glanced once more at the envelope and for a moment considered writing "Address Unknown. Return to Sender" and leaving it for the postal carrier, but he knew Dani would be disappointed if he did. Instead, he slammed the box shut and raced up the two flights of stairs to their flat. He slammed that door, too, as thoughts of why she'd written and what she wanted tumbled around in his brain. He walked to his workstation and tossed the letter behind his laptop, behind the books and papers that were part of his research. "I'll open it later," he told himself. But the pulse in his neck was throbbing and he kept glancing towards the envelope. "How did she know I'm at Oxford? How did she even know my name?" he asked himself every few seconds. "What can *my mother* possibly want?"

Chapter 1

Fifteen years earlier in Austria…

"Get out of my house!" she screamed. "Get the hell out. If you want to be one of those filthy Christ-killers, you can go to hell with all of them!" She dragged him to the door, pushed him out into the icy sleet and slammed the door. He stood shivering in the December afternoon, tears running down his face. Where could he go in Graz? Fourteen years old, no money, and not even his coat. He ran the fifteen long city blocks to the synagogue, telling himself over and over that at least running was keeping him warm.

The big door into the synagogue's vestibule squeaked, even when it was wet. The rabbi, a tall man in his mid-forties holding reading glasses, came to the door to see who was seeking sanctuary in such weather. He saw the handsome dark-haired, dark-eyed young boy just inside the door, trembling, and dripping water on the floor.

"Stay there," the Rabbi said. "I'll bring some towels." He recognized the boy from a few days before; he was the one who'd come to ask if the Rabbi would answer a few questions. The rabbi had told him to go home, write down the questions, and come back later.

Now he brought the boy two towels and another for the vestibule floor. He then went to bring a blanket and some clothing. "Here," he said when the boy had dried his head and face. "Take off your wet things right here and put these on. I'm sorry I have no shoes for you but the socks will help. Then come into my study where it's warm. I'll get you something hot to drink." When he left the hallway, the Rabbi realized the clothing on the towel was the uniform of the Domkirche, the Graz Cathedral School.

"Come in and sit down. Drink this. Take your time and in a little while we'll talk," the Rabbi said. Too numb to do anything else, the boy sat on the chair near the Rabbi's desk, shivering in the borrowed sweat-suit that was far too big, the blanket wrapped around his narrow shoulders. He still trembled as he slowly sipped the hot, sweet tea. When the boy set the empty mug down, the Rabbi quietly said, "I recognize your uniform. You're from the Domkirche School. What's your name?"

"Dominik Müller, sir, but sometimes my mother calls me Daryush."

"Nice names," the Rabbi said. "Dominik means 'belonging to the Lord' and Daryush or Darius was a great Persian leader. My name is

Chapter 1

Samuel Breitling." The boy politely held out his hand and the Rabbi took it. "Are you hungry, Dominik? I can offer you a sandwich and another cup of tea and then we'll talk. I'll even try to answer some of your questions," the Rabbi said with a smile.

The corner of the boy's mouth quirked in a tiny smile. "Thank you, sir," he said. "I am a little hungry but I'm much warmer now." After the lad had eaten the sandwich and finished a second cup of tea, the Rabbi asked him why he'd come to him for answers, and Dominik replied that one of the priests in his school had told him to go to the Rabbi.

Rabbi Breitling was shocked. "Why me?" he asked.

"The priests were very angry when I asked questions. The monsignor told me my questions were heretical and one of the priests called me an apostate. I know that's bad but I'm not quite sure of what it means. The monsignor told me I was expelled from the church school, and I would be excommunicated and shunned in the church. The priest who called me an apostate shouted at me as I was leaving the church, "There's a synagogue a few blocks away. Go ask the Rabbi to answer your questions. You're more Jew than Christian!"

Hiding his concerns, the Rabbi asked quietly, "Is that where you came from now? The Domkirche School?"

The boy trembled for a moment. "No, sir," he replied. "I came from home. I haven't been back to school since I was there a few days ago."

"What were you doing?" Rabbi Breitling asked.

"I got up each morning and put on my school clothes. I had breakfast with my mother like I do every day and then I left. I kept waiting for her to tell me the school had called to find out where I was, but she didn't say a thing. She's very busy now with a translation she's working on, but if a priest had called, she would have said something. The first day I went to the library at the university and tried to find answers to some of my questions. I went there again yesterday, but the librarian wanted to know why I wasn't in school. So I walked around town, went to the park and sat on a bench until I saw kids coming from school. Then I went home. Today, when the weather got so bad, I went home early. My mother heard me come in and wanted to know why I was home, if I was sick. I took off my coat and went into her study." The boy stopped speaking. He was pale and trembling badly again.

"And?"

"I told her what happened at school. She asked me what questions I'd asked the priests. When I told her, she jumped up from her desk, grabbed me by the collar and started yelling at me. She pulled me to the front door, threw me out and told me never to come back." Tears rolling down his face, his voice shaking, he whispered, "She shouted awful things, too. I didn't know what to do. I didn't know where to go. So I came here."

"It's OK, Dominik," the Rabbi said, kindly. "We'll sort everything out later, maybe tomorrow. Now I'm going to take you to my flat, which is just around the corner. My wife and my two sons live in Zurich, Switzerland, but my nephew and two other students live here with me. My housekeeper will prepare a room for you. So let's go and you can have some quiet time, a rest, and we'll straighten everything out. We'll talk again after you meet the others and after we all have dinner together."

The boy slipped his feet into his sodden shoes and the Rabbi opened a very large umbrella as they stepped out of the synagogue. When they got to the flat and the Rabbi opened the front door, he called out "Sarah". A small middle-aged woman wearing a blue dress the same color as her eyes rushed in, clutching a wooden spoon. "Is something wrong, Rabbi?" she asked.

"Nothing's wrong, Sarah. This young man is Dominik, and he'll be with us for a little while. Please sort out a room for him and see if you can find some clothing that fits him. Unfortunately, I must go back to the synagogue in such foul weather for a meeting. Dominik, this is Frau Sarah Bernhardt, my housekeeper. I'll leave you in her very capable hands and I'll see you later." He left, closing the door quietly behind him.

Frau Bernhardt said, "Come along, young man. We'll find some proper things for you."

He replied, "Yes, ma'am" so sheepishly she knew he'd recognized her name and found it amusing.

"Just like the famous actress, right? Funny, no? But not always." She led him down the hall to a large room containing a bed neatly made up with a plaid spread, a wooden chest of drawers and a large wardrobe, a desk with two chairs, and bookshelves half-filled with books of all kinds. Several pictures of Swiss scenes were on the pale green walls. "If you want a warm shower, the bathroom is right across the hall and there are towels on the shelf." She left him then and he realized she was still holding the spoon.

In his office, Rabbi Breitling placed a call to St. Giles Cathedral and asked to speak to Monsignor Dietrich in the Domkirche School. "Please tell the monsignor this is Rabbi Breitling. I'm calling about

Chapter 1

Dominik Müller."

Instantly the phone line clicked and the monsignor's voice stated, "So the boy did come to you. Maybe the hotheaded young priest who told him to go to you was right. I understand a few runaway teenagers live in your flat."

"Not runaways." The rabbi's tone was equally bristling. "My nephew is one; his mother died several months ago and his father is an engineer deep in Brazil. Not a congenial location for a boy. Two other youngsters are from dysfunctional families. But I really called to talk to you about Dominik."

"Of course, Rabbi Breitling. I apologize for my rudeness. I spoke to the boy's mother a little while ago and she's distraught about his behavior."

"And what about her behavior?" the Rabbi thought, but he controlled the angry retort as the monsignor continued. "The boy has a strange history. He's very bright, of course, but that doesn't alleviate the situation. His mother, Frederica, is a hard-working single parent, and as far as I know his father is unknown, or at least unacknowledged. She became pregnant as a university student in Vienna and her parents, who are devout members of our church, sent her to England to have the baby. He was born in London in 1982 and was in day care while his mother worked as a translator, so his actual first language was English. When the boy was not yet four years old, his mother married a wealthy Armenian businessman she met through her work, and they moved to Yerevan in Armenia.

"I don't know if the husband was a Christian because she's never said, although most Armenians are. In Yerevan, the boy learned both Armenian and Turkish from his nannies and even some Farsi from other servants in the household. He attended a private day school where the language was mostly English. But Frederica had no other children and she said Yerevan is not London, not even Graz, so the marriage broke up after four years and she came back to Austria when the boy was eight years old. They lived in her parents' home at first until Frederica found work. Did I say she's a very talented linguist? She brought the boy to us even though he knew almost no German, but he picked up the language very quickly.

"He also knew nothing about our religion, but as I said he's a very bright boy and learns quickly when he wants to. When he was eleven, he began serving here as an altar boy, but by the time he was thirteen he was refusing to participate in the mass and was beginning to ask questions about our faith that we would not answer. His questioning became impossible and I had no choice but to expel him; his master teacher, Father Erich, told the boy to go to you. His mother, as I've said, is distraught, and she will not allow him back into her home until the boy apologizes to all of us, does some penance, and comes back to the school and our ways."

Although he was annoyed that the priest had not called Dominik by name even once, Rabbi Breitling politely said, "Thank you, Monsignor, for so much relevant information. At this moment, Dominik seems to be in deep shock. He can stay with me for a while, even a few days. As I'm sure you know, Jews do not proselytize, but I do not want to anger his mother and his grandparents. Nor do I want to involve the family services of Graz at this time. Would it be possible for me to speak with Dominik's mother?"

"I'll get in touch with her and get back to you in the morning. Let the boy stay in your home tonight," the Monsignor affirmed, and closed the phone.

◆ ◆ ◆

When he heard voices in the hall, Dominick, now dressed in jeans and a warm sweater, opened his door and stepped out into the hall. He saw Frau Bernhardt collecting umbrellas and damp jackets from three teens. "Shoes here until they dry," she said. "Then go change out of your school clothes and come to the kitchen for a hot drink." She noticed the teens peering over her head and around her. "That's Dominik. He'll be here for a while. David, I'm sure you have an extra pair of running shoes that you can lend Dominik until his shoes are dry. I think you're about the same size."

Certainement, mon capitaine!" the dark-haired, shorter of the two boys said with a small salute; then he clicked his shoeless heels and winked.

"Go on, silly lad. You'll meet Dominik later. Your cocoa's waiting."

"I'd rather have tea," the girl said. "I'm on a diet."

"You'll have cocoa," the housekeeper said. "This is not dieting weather."

The pretty girl with tumbling red curls and flashing green eyes put her arms around Frau Bernhardt, gave her a smacking kiss on the cheek and said "OK" before she pranced off in stocking feet to the flat next door. She gave Dominik a long, cool look before she closed the door. And winked.

The kitchen was bright, warm, inviting. Wonderful smells wafted from pots simmering on the Aga. Dominik sat at the table where four

Chapter 1

mugs and a plate of cookies were waiting.

The first one into the kitchen was David, holding out a pair of Adidas running shoes. "Here, mate. These should fit you. Do you also need socks?'

"Thanks, David…right?" he said, placing the shoes on the floor. "Frau Bernhardt gave me socks and underwear, jeans and a couple of sweaters."

The other boy nodded and said, "I recognize the sweater. It belongs to my cousin Jakob but he's so much taller now and it wouldn't fit him."

"Is he one of the Rabbi's sons? Why don't they live here?"

"Yes, he's the Rabbi's older son; the younger one is Daniel. Deborah, my aunt, is the Rabbi's wife; her parents are Holocaust survivors; you know what that was, right? Her parents are quite old and she's afraid it would kill them if she lived in Austria, especially in Graz because it was such an anti-Jewish city during Hitler's time. So, when the Rabbi came here, she stayed in Zurich. He goes to Zurich often as it's only a 7-hour drive or a short flight. And she comes here quite often, too. The boys used to live here but Jakob's in university now and Daniel's traveling with some friends; in fact, he just visited my dad in Brazil."

"Your dad lives in Brazil? What's he doing there?"

"He's an engineer and he's working on a big project in the jungle there. It probably won't be finished for another two years or so. When my mom was alive, we used to go with him and stay in cities not too far away. But she died almost two years ago, and my dad decided it would be better for me to live here with the Rabbi and finish my schooling here. I miss my dad a lot, but it's OK here and he comes here whenever he has a holiday or when the weather in Brazil gets so bad they can't work. We started sending e-mails, too, but he doesn't always have a computer connection… even when he leaves the jungle and goes to Recife! So, he usually telephones from there."

The girl and the other boy came into the kitchen. "Hi, I'm Ruth. And this is Karl who's tall and 'a pretty' blond, but he doesn't talk. Cat got your tongue, Karlie?" She stuck her tongue out at Karl and stared at Dominik. "What's your story, boy? We want to know, so start talking now!"

"That's enough, Ruth. Honestly, sometimes I think you must have been vaccinated with a phonograph needle, the way you never stop your silly chatter," Frau Bernhardt said with a smile. She brought over the pot of hot chocolate and filled the mugs. "And 'the boy' has a name; he's Dominik!"

"OK, Dominik, so what is your story? And why don't we have several marshmallows in our cocoa, Frau Sarah?" asked Ruth.

"I thought you're on a diet," Karl mumbled as he stood up, opened a kitchen cabinet and took out a bag of small marshmallows."

"Not today. You heard Frau Sarah. The weather doesn't allow dieting."

"How can the weather allow anything, Ruth? It's not a person. It doesn't have opinions." Karl scoffed.

"You know, Karl. Maybe it's better when you don't talk. You have no imagination. And I can't stand what you call your logical mind. So I'll just ignore you, you peasant!" Ruth said, looking down her nose at him, her voice very haughty like a member of the royalty.

Dominik sat through all of this, amazed. Girls and boys didn't have much contact in the Domkirche School; the nuns and priests were always there. He'd never heard kids talking to each other like this. He absolutely loved it. David winked at him. "You'll get used to them. They're always like this, especially Ruth. I'll tell you some things later so you can make fun of her."

"Don't you dare, David. Just because the Rabbi's your uncle doesn't mean you can be a snitch. There are things called privilege and privacy. Rabbis are like doctors, lawyers and priests. They can't tell the things they know."

"That's why he didn't tell me anything. I have my own sources," he claimed in a falsely cynical voice, twirling an imaginary moustache.

"Oh you, you don't know anything, unless you read the diary I 'never' wrote," Ruth laughed.

"If you've finished your cocoa and nonsense, go do your homework," Frau Sarah ordered in a kindly way. "Dominik, you can keep me company, or rest in your room. There are some good books there."

"Wow! Sarah Bernhardt wants you to keep company with her, Dominik," Ruth teased, as the three teens stood up, rinsed their mugs in the sink, and went off to their rooms, giggling and chatting. Dominik also washed his mug, dried his hands, and went to "his" room, deep in thought.

A short time later, the Rabbi came in. "It's wicked out there. How are things here, Sarah?"

Frau Sarah smiled at him. "Not very wicked, except Ruth of course! The kids have all met over mugs of hot chocolate. David told Dominik a little about your situation, the *rabbanit* and your sons in Switzerland, his father in Brazil, about his mother and why he lives here; David misses his father, of course. Ruth was her usual self, teasing Karl,

Chapter 1

trying to question Dominik. But they didn't find out anything. For that matter, neither did I. But the wet clothing you brought home earlier was the uniform from the Domkirche School."

Rabbi Breitling chuckled. "Not much gets past you, Sarah. I think we'll all know the whole story soon enough. I spoke to Monsignor Dietrich at the Domkirche and he told me Dominik was expelled for asking questions they considered heretical. His mother threw him out into the street for the same reason. They called him an apostate and threatened to excommunicate him. They won't let him go back until he apologizes, takes some punishment and promises to ask no more questions. I'm not sure he'll agree to their terms.

I told Monsignor Dietrich I'd like to speak to Frau Müller, Dominik's mother. There's no father in the picture, it seems. I don't really want to involve the state family services yet, so I'll wait until I speak to the mother before I say anything to Dominik or much to the other kids. Dominik's had a strange life with lots of upheaval. It's a pity, because he's obviously very bright."

"Dominik's a nice boy, and very polite, maybe a little too polite, and maybe a little shy. He was excited, exhilarated, after meeting the others. Even if he only stays a few days, I think it will be good for him," Frau Sarah stated, and then added, "Dinner will be ready in an hour or so."

The rabbi appreciated Sarah Bernhardt's wisdom and insight, especially when it came to dealing with young people. She was such a good woman who'd survived enormous personal tragedy with grace. *What a teacher and mother she must have been*, he thought. She'd been a damaged soul when he first met her – a wife, a mother of three teenagers, a physical education teacher who'd lost everything in a flaming car crash ten years earlier. She was the only survivor, living with deep-seated guilt because she'd been driving. The police, the judge at the inquest, the doctors and psychiatrists she'd seen all told her it wasn't her fault, that the driver of the truck swerved into her lane and into her car at high speed and she was lucky to be alive. Lucky, ha! She told all of them she still heard the screams of her children and husband in her dreams almost every night…and then silence. She told all of them – the judge and the doctors – that she should have died with her family. She could no longer teach gymnastics – not physically as one leg had been severely injured and she had a slight limp. And certainly not emotionally, as teaching would bring her into daily contact with far too many healthy young people.

She had been working in the synagogue as a part-time secretary when Rabbi Breitling arrived in Graz. Although she was very quiet and had such sad – even tragic – eyes, the Rabbi couldn't help but be impressed with her organizational skills. Since one of his goals was to increase the size of the synagogue's congregation and involve its membership, children as well as parents, in projects to bolster the synagogue's image and even to welcome Jewish tourists in Graz, he elicited her help constantly. It was only as the festival of *Purim* approached and the Rabbi wanted to organize a carnival and masquerade for the children that Sarah's tragedy was revealed to him. The accident had occurred on Purim as the family was delivering *mishloach manot*. Most of the time, Sarah wore the mask of serenity and graciousness; but on Purim, Sarah wore no mask. She'd never be able to celebrate the joy of Purim; for her, it would always be a day of mourning. The model *seders* on *Passover*, the *Simchat Torah* dancing, the *Chanukah* parties and all the other events she organized – the women's auxiliary, the choir, the book club for teenagers – were outstanding. The only other major project she refused to handle at first was bereavement counseling. Deborah, the Rabbi's wife, a trained social worker, had come to Graz to start the group; Sarah became an active member herself and eventually took on the leadership, and the Rabbi's admiration for his middle-aged helper increased every day.

When the Rabbi's sister was diagnosed with acute myeloid leukemia, she returned to their home in Zurich with her husband and son. But the disease progressed quickly as often happens in adults, the Rabbi often reminded himself; she lasted only a matter of weeks. Eli, his brother-in-law, and his nephew David tried living in Switzerland but after four months it wasn't working despite the deep love between the two. Eli was bored with his job in Zurich; he said it was nothing more than pushing pencils around on paper to plan future projects in the jungle. He missed his work in Brazil and he knew the team needed him there. David understood his father's unhappiness but didn't know how he could help. Eli couldn't take David back to Brazil because he couldn't leave him alone in Rio de Janeiro or Recife, even with a housekeeper, or in a boarding school. They'd discussed it and discussed it, back and forth, back and forth. Finally, the *rabbanit* suggested Eli return to Brazil and David move into his uncle's apartment in Graz. He'd go to school there, continue his Hebrew studies, and both David and the Rabbi would be less lonely. Eli would visit when possible and David would go to Brazil in the school holidays. When it was finally agreed, the Rabbi discussed a few other concerns with his wife. "You know I can 'survive' on the meals you sometimes freeze for me or a

Chapter 1

casserole that Sarah or another woman in the congregation provides, or on dinners in other people's homes – "Invite the Rabbi" has become one of Sarah's pet projects! But that won't work for David; he's only thirteen, a growing boy, and he is really depressed by his mother's death and his father being so far away. He needs more attention as well as full and nutritious meals. My hours are sometimes very long and I often come to Zurich for a few days. What can we do?"

"Why don't you ask Sarah to be your housekeeper as well as part-time general factotum? She can move out of her home where she's surrounded by heartbreaking memories and into the flat next door to yours. She'd probably love it and it might well be the final step in her personal recovery."

Her husband grinned at her and said, "General factotum, eh? At least you didn't call her my 'dogsbody' or say she does my 'donkey work'! It's a great idea, my darling. If anyone can do this, Sarah Bernhardt can." Sarah had accepted the position immediately. And the job itself took on extra depth when teenagers from dysfunctional and problematic families came to stay in the Rabbi's flat for a few days or a few months. It always amazed him how wonderfully she coped with teenagers and they all loved her, even when she was "tough" with them. Simon Gordon, an old American friend, called the Rabbi's home-life in Graz a "win-win" situation.

When Frau Sarah called them all to dinner, the Rabbi and the three teens went to the sink, picked up a 2-handled pitcher, poured some water over their hands, recited a blessing silently and dried their hands. Each then refilled the pitcher and handed it to the next person, including Dominik, who did the same, but without the blessing. When everyone was seated, even Frau Sarah, the Rabbi picked up a basket of warm rolls and said, *'Barukh attah Adonai Eloheinu melekh ha-olam, ha-motzi lechem min ha-aretz'. Amein.*" He sprinkled salt on them and gave everyone a roll, saying "Eat, eat!" after biting his own roll. He said to Dominik, "This *bracha*, or blessing, is called *Hamotzi* and we say it whenever we eat bread."

Dominik thought the dinner was wonderful; salad and a stew with lots of meat and vegetables, fruit and tea and cake at the end. But it was the talk around the table that fascinated him more than the food, talk about what they all did in school, special things they'd learned. Ruth made them laugh when she said, "My biology partner refused to touch the frog we were told to dissect because frogs aren't kosher. And he isn't even Jewish!" David said he'd received an e-mail from Daniel from Sao Paulo; they're on the way to Iguazu Falls and he and his friends will take lots of pictures. The rabbi said he'd received a similar message and Daniel said they'd go to Argentina after the Falls, which would probably be easier than spending additional time in Brazil since they all spoke Spanish. David disagreed, saying Portuguese wasn't so different from Spanish and Daniel had said they'd managed quite well in Brazil. Dominik was amazed to hear David contradicting the Rabbi, even if he was the Rabbi's nephew, even if they disagreed over something trivial like understanding some Portuguese if one spoke Spanish. Dominik knew he could say something about understanding some Georgian because he spoke Armenian, but he really didn't think he wanted to get into this particular argument.

Dominik did contribute a little to the dinner conversation, saying he'd started reading *The Diary of Anne Frank*, which was in his room in English. When Karl asked him if he knew other languages, Dominik said, "I speak English because I was born in London and we lived there until I was four. I also speak Armenian and Turkish because my mother married an Armenian man and we went to live in Yerevan. That's in Armenia. We lived there for four years, but it was boring for my mother, so they got divorced and we came to Austria because my mother's parents live here. I had a Turkish nanny in Armenia and I wasn't bored. I also know some Georgian because Tbilisi is quite close to Yerevan; he smiled shyly at David who instantly noticed the allusion to Spanish and Portuguese and grinned at Dominik. My stepfather had business with men from China and Japan and Iran; they all treated me like a little puppy and I learned quite a lot of their languages. I know Latin from the Church, and some French and Spanish because my mother is a translator for those languages into English and German." The other teens didn't say anything. They just stared at him with their mouths open. The rabbi knew they were astonished and very curious and wanted to know more, but he suggested they hold back all their questions until the next day. When they'd all finished eating, the Rabbi told Dominik they'd now recite the *Birkat Hamazon*, grace after meals. But with four "men" at the table, they'd begin with a different prayer, *Zimun*. Although the only Hebrew word he knew was "Amen", Dominik was mesmerized.

Everyone helped Frau Sarah clear the table and David said it was his turn to stack the dishwasher and he'd join them when he was finished. Ruth and Karl went into the Rabbi's study and he said to Dominik, "We're going to study *Torah* a little tonight. I've spent most of my life studying *Torah* and have barely scratched the surface. But I think you've had a hard day today and should just take it easy

Chapter 1

tonight. Why don't you read some more about Anne Frank. We'll talk tomorrow. OK?"

"OK," Dominik replied. "Thank you for everything, Rabbi. Good night."

In his study, after David joined them, Ruth asked the Rabbi if Dominik would be living with them. "I really don't know yet. We'll see tomorrow or after the weekend," the Rabbi replied. "What did all of you think of him?"

"He's cute," Ruth replied. The rabbi looked at her a bit critically. "OK," she said. "He's very smart and seems very nice and I think he's had a very hard time recently." The boys agreed and Karl said he thought Dominik was brilliant. The three youngsters all wanted to know more about him, but the Rabbi smiled at them and said, "Not tonight. An American writer once wrote 'Tomorrow is another day'."

"Ooh, I know what that's from," Ruth said. "I saw the film. It's from 'Gone with the Wind'."

They then settled down to discuss the weekly *Torah* portion for Shabbat, and the one for the following week, the Shabbat of *Chanukah*, and some of the commentary and interpretations of major scholars. At 10:00, the Rabbi rose and said they'd done a good job; he was proud of them for recognizing that you couldn't *lein Torah* standing on one leg. "Go to bed so you'll be refreshed tomorrow. Have a good night."

After they left, the Rabbi poured a small glass of cognac for himself and then sat for a long time, thinking about Dominik and his difficult situation, about how to approach Dominik's mother and the monsignor and about possible solutions. Finally, he picked up the phone, telephoned Deborah in Zurich, told her about his e-mail from Daniel…and about Dominik.

"He sounds like a special young boy in a sorry position. Just be open to his viewpoint, Shmulik, and don't rush him. Don't give in to the mother and the monsignor unless you think that's what Dominik wants. I'm looking forward to meeting him. Maybe I'll spend some time with him when I come to Graz after my parents leave for Israel next week. My brother wants them to stay the whole winter because his family needs them at this time. At least that's what he told them. He didn't say the weather's so much better in Israel than Switzerland during the winter months."

◆ ◆ ◆

The following morning the Rabbi was in his office working on his sermon for that night's Shabbat service, when Mina, his part-time secretary, rang through. "Monsignor Dietrich is on the phone, Rabbi."

He picked up his extension and said, "Good morning, Monsignor. Have you spoken to Dominik's mother?"

"Yes, Rabbi. She and her parents are willing to speak to you after Mass on Sunday, at 1:00. They're not in a conciliatory mood. They think the boy is incorrigible, and I agree with them. They won't come to you, so we can meet in the Domkirche gatehouse. Is that all right?"

"I'll be there at 1:00 on Sunday, Monsignor."

A little after noon, the Rabbi let himself into his apartment and called out, "Sarah, I'm home. Have you prepared lunch? I'd like Dominik to join me."

The door to Dominik's room was open and he came out. "I heard you, Rabbi Breitling, and here I am."

The two went into the kitchen together and saw Frau Sarah setting out salad and bread and luncheon meat for sandwiches. "I've put the kettle on for tea but hope you'll excuse me. I have some things to do next door." She left quietly and the Rabbi made sandwiches and tea for them.

"Please sit down and eat, Dominik. Afterwards, we have a few things to discuss." When they'd finished the sandwiches, the Rabbi said, "I've spoken to Monsignor Dietrich and he told me a number of things about you and your history. From his point of view, of course. I asked him to arrange a meeting between your mother and me and he set up a meeting for Sunday afternoon. He'll be there; so will your grandparents. Do you want to come?"

Dominik looked like he was about to cry. "Do I have to go? They'll make me go back to the school and the church. I hate it. I can't go back."

"You don't have to go if you don't want to. Are you afraid they'll punish you?" the Rabbi asked with concern. "Have they ever hurt you?"

"I'm not afraid of punishment. They won't hit me. The priests will just make me say some *Pater Nosters* and *Hail Marys*. That's what they always do and that will be the end of it. Except it won't be the end… Rabbi, I have to tell you that yesterday was the most horrible day of my life, but last night was the best night I can remember. I really like David and Karl and Ruth. I think I can learn a lot here. Can I live here and go to the school they attend? Please? I don't know if I want to become Jewish, but I know I feel so good here. I know I'm confused about who I am and what I want to do with my life. But I love it here. I feel like I belong. I've never felt that way before. Not anywhere, not with anyone. If I can stay, I'll get a job. I'll pay rent…!"

Chapter 1

The rabbi smiled. "No rent needed, Dominik. Just calm down and trust me. I'll go to the meeting alone and then we – you and I – will make some decisions. These are not easy decisions when we consider your mother and where you've come from. These are not decisions that can be made standing on one leg. But in the meantime, you can stay here. Tonight is our Shabbat and we attend services at the synagogue and then we have a festive meal. We have services again tomorrow morning and then we enjoy a quiet day. We eat, we read, we discuss some spiritual issues. If the weather's nice, we go for a walk. In the late afternoon, a few people usually come here and we discuss the weekly portion of the *Torah* and argue a little. Shabbat's our day of rest, but that doesn't mean we can't enjoy an intellectual argument. You can join us for Shabbat if you want. I hope you'll think about it. But now, I need you to tell me about the questions that made all the priests and your mother so angry. With some detail, please."

Dominik looked at the Rabbi, the expression on his face changing from hope to despair. "I'm illegitimate, sir. I don't even know who my father is. My mother never claimed to be a virgin; she never said I was the child of God, like Jesus. She got me the usual way, sir. I know she wasn't raped." Dominik couldn't look at the Rabbi. Rabbi Breitling reached across and put his hand on the boy's shoulder. "It's all right, Dominik. Monsignor Dietrich told me. I'm not judging your mother or you."

The boy looked up and the words poured out. "How could Mary have a baby and still claim to be a virgin? The 'Virgin Mother'! Is that a sick joke? And to say her child was the son of God? Wasn't that just an excuse so the people wouldn't stone her? How could she be taken bodily up to heaven when she was old? Up to heaven? Is there a heaven? Do people really go to a place after they die? Then why are their bones still in their coffins? And how could Jesus feed 5000 people with 5 loaves of bread and 2 fishes? Was it mass hypnosis? What happened to the body of Jesus after he died? Did his friends steal the body and then say it was a miracle and that Jesus was resurrected in order to come back and save the world some day? If Jesus was resurrected, how could he do nothing when so many Jews, so many of *his* people – after all, he was a Jew – were massacred in the Crusades and the Inquisition and here in Austria and in Poland and Germany not so long ago? And how could God – if there is a God – allow them to crucify his 'son'?" Dominik stopped speaking, his ragged breathing the only sound in the room. The rabbi handed him a glass of water and he drank it all.

The rabbi thought to himself, *"The lad's amazing. What an intellect!*

What a shame the Church can't acknowledge his brilliance and do something positive instead of feeling threatened. What do they think? That he's another Martin Luther and will start another Reformation?" But all he said aloud was "I can see why they're angry, Dominik. Your questions are very provocative. I don't know enough about fundamental Christian belief and dogma to have answers to those questions. But I do know we sometimes have to accept things just on faith. Judaism also has some miracles – the angel interrupting Abraham when he was binding Isaac on Mount Moriah and letting him sacrifice a ram instead, the voice of God speaking to Moses in the burning bush, the parting of the Red Sea, one small bottle of oil burning for eight days in the Temple. And there are many more."

"But Rabbi, we also read the Old Testament in my Church and there could be logical reasons for those miracles. I read somewhere that the ebb and flow of the tide can part the sea. Maybe the candelabra didn't need a lot of oil or maybe the bottle wasn't small. Other miracles might be symbols or metaphors. Being willing to sacrifice Isaac was a test, and Abraham passed it. Maybe the Holocaust was also a test but the Germans – I should say the Nazis – failed. Not the Jews. The Jews didn't fail, because there's Israel and there are Jews living in Germany now…" He ran out of breath again.

The rabbi responded, "These are huge issues, Dominik. Scholars have been debating them for hundreds of years; many brilliant commentators have reached the same conclusions as you, but others have rejected them. Logic can't always be applied. Some scholars think one question often leads to another and then another. Shakespeare once said, 'There are more things in heaven and earth, Horatio, than are dreamt of in your philosophy'. As for me, even standing on two legs, I have more questions than answers. Your questions are far too big for us to answer right now. Maybe we'll discuss…"

"That's the whole point, Rabbi," Dominik interrupted him, a small grin on his face. "We discuss them. We can even disagree. But you didn't call me a heretic and an apostate and throw me out onto the street!"

◆ ◆ ◆

Dominik decided to go to the Shabbat services. Frau Bernhardt had told him to call her "Frau Sarah" and she'd found a white dress shirt and sweater as well as a warm winter jacket for him; his own shoes and trousers were dry and clean, again thanks to Frau…Sarah. Before leaving the building, the boys went into the flat next door to

Chapter 1

the Rabbi's and watched both Frau Sarah and Ruth light the Shabbat candles. "OK," David said, "Let's go to *shul*."

"*Shul?*" Dominik queried.

"It's another word for synagogue, so much shorter. It's from Yiddish. Do you know what Yiddish is?"

Before Dominik could answer that he knew what Yiddish is, Ruth said, "In Israel they call it '*beit knesset*' which isn't shorter than synagogue. But it means the same thing, house of assembly."

"Have you been in Israel?" Dominik asked.

"Yes, I spent a year at a kibbutz. That's where I decided to convert."

"And she never lets us forget it," Karl blurted out.

Ruth ignored him and said, "I've only been back in Austria three months and I'm so lucky to be living in Frau Sarah's apartment and studying with Rabbi Breitling. If you stay, I'll tell you all about Israel."

"Again and again and again!" David quipped. Everyone laughed.

"I didn't know you converted," Dominik said. "Are you Jewish now?"

"Not yet, but I'm on the way," she said. "You see, my father's Jewish but my mother's not… and you have to have a Jewish mother to be Jewish. My parents are divorced and my father lives in Israel, on the kibbutz. My mom and stepfather and I weren't getting along, so she let me go to live with my dad. But that didn't work out, so I came back. I really want to be Jewish. That's why my mother agreed to let me live here."

By this time, they'd arrived at the entrance to the synagogue and were in good spirits. Ruth went upstairs while the boys sat downstairs. Dominik noticed a lot of people…but only men and boys. "Where are the women?" he asked, a little concerned.

David answered, "Upstairs, like Ruth. I'll tell you more about that later. Do you see the Rabbi?" Dominik saw him sitting in an elaborate chair on a raised platform. He was wearing a white robe and a white hat sort of like the kind chefs wear. Another man, wearing a similar robe and hat, was sitting in a similar chair on the other side of what seemed to be a niche in the wall with an embroidered curtain in front. Dominik found the whole service intriguing. No bells, no organ music, no incense, no one down on their knees repeatedly, although they did have to stand up a few times. The other man, whom David called a *chazzan* had a pleasant singing voice and Dominik noticed the *chazzan*'s chanting was almost operatic, but it wasn't his taste even though it was so different from the boring ritual chanting of the priests and altar boys during Mass at the cathedral. The rabbi led the congregants in their prayer books and then he spoke for a few minutes about the meaning of the coming holiday of *Chanukah*, its message of freedom and its miracles. Dominik felt the Rabbi was speaking directly to him. Towards the end of the service, a few men stood up and recited a prayer. "That's the *Kaddish*, a prayer of sanctification of God's name, it's said at all prayer services by people mourning the death of loved ones – a parent or a wife or a child, even for a brother or sister," David whispered. After announcements from the Rabbi about the next day, the evening service concluded with a hymn that Dominik assumed had deep spiritual meaning.

Outside, Karl asked Dominik what he thought of the service. "It was great! Nothing like my church!" he said quickly. Ruth joined them and they waited quietly for the Rabbi. To answer Dominik's earlier question, David told him men and women are required to sit separately in most synagogues. He also said this synagogue was a renovated temporary one and there were proposals to build a new one in tribute to the old one that the Nazis had destroyed. A few minutes later, the Rabbi came out, accompanied by a young man, a very lovely woman and a set of cute twins.

"This is Jonathan Rosen, his wife Meredith, and their twins, Jeremy and Annie. They're from England and will be joining us for meals this Shabbat. We'll all speak English tonight and you may have to help us out, Dominik, if we aren't sure of some English words. Dominik was born in London," the Rabbi told the Rosens.

"Where?" Jeremy asked. "We live in Finchley. Did you live near us?"

"I really don't know," Dominik said in his beautiful English. "I was only four years old when we left England."

Meredith asked, "Your English is perfect. Did you learn it in Austria?"

"No, we lived in Armenia until I was eight. Then we moved here because my grandparents live here," Dominik replied. He could tell by the look on her face that she didn't believe he'd reached his level of English in his first four years, so he added, "In school in Armenia, we studied in English. My mother's a linguist, so we always speak English …but I do make mistakes."

"Dominik speaks Armenian, Turkish, Georgian, Chinese and Japanese, Spanish, French, Farsi, English, Latin – and German, of course," Karl stated proudly, as if he were reciting his own personal accomplishments.

"Amazing!" Jonathan Rosen exclaimed. "I wish I knew half that

Chapter 1

number of languages. Maybe my children will master a few by the time they're your age, Dominik. What do you say, kids? German? French? Hebrew?"

"Hebrew!" Jeremy shouted.

"French!" Annie said.

"Maybe Hebrew will be my next language," Dominik said quietly.

By that time, they'd arrived at the Rabbi's residence and were greeted by Frau Sarah. She took their coats and then led them into the dining room beautifully set up for the Shabbat meal. Frau Sarah directed everyone to seats and the Rabbi noticed there were two extra place settings. Sarah had known there would be four additional guests for Shabbat meals, but she'd set twelve places and he was a little concerned because she never got it wrong. He would ask her to remove two places after *Kiddush*. But first, as he told Dominik, they had to sing *"Shalom Aleichem"*, the song welcoming Shabbat, and *"Eshet Chayil"*, a paean of praise to the woman of the house. After the singing, the Rabbi picked up the decanted *Kiddush* wine and was getting ready to pour it into a large silver goblet when Annie, between her brother and Ruth, asked if Frau Sarah was Ruth's grandma. "No," Ruth said. "She's the Rabbi's housekeeper and our housemother."

"Is the Rabbi your father?" Annie asked. "Are these boys your brothers?" Holding up her fingers, she said, "Three? I only have one."

Ruth smiled as she responded, "I wish Frau Sarah was my grandma. The rabbi isn't my father and I don't have brothers. David is the Rabbi's nephew, and the rest of us just live here." Annie would have asked more questions but her mother told her to quiet down so the Rabbi could recite *Kiddush*.

Everyone stood up, but just before he started the blessing over the wine, the front door opened and an elegant woman and a tall young man came in. The rabbi was so surprised he almost dropped the goblet of wine. He told the visitors, "My wife and my son Jakob. This is wonderful! Deborah, I thought you were going to spend this Shabbat with your parents, before they leave for Israel." He put down the goblet and walked over to embrace his wife and son and to whisper a special blessing to Jakob.

"Good Shabbos, everyone," Deborah said. "My parents are spending this Shabbat with my cousins in Bern, Samuel. Jakob drove them and since he was knackered from a tough week at university, he decided to relax by driving straight through to Graz, although I don't know how he can call it relaxing to drive for so many hours. I came along as company on the long drive and to meet everyone. And to surprise

my husband! We've been hiding in Frau Sarah's flat, but I was in here earlier to light the Shabbat candles." She and Jakob went to stand by the places set for them, and the Rabbi picked up the *Kiddush* cup again and recited the blessing for wine.

After everyone had sipped a bit of wine, the Rabbi and his family from the *Kiddush* goblet and all the others from tiny glasses, the Rabbi turned to Jonathan and asked, "Would you like to do the *motzi*?"

"I can do it," Jeremy said proudly.

"You know how, Jeremy. But let's give Jakob the honor since he had a hard week and has traveled so far," Jonathan said, smiling at his little son.

Everyone went to the kitchen and performed the same washing of hands as the night before. Then everyone sat quietly – even Annie – until the Rabbi was seated. David and Karl were quietly humming a little tune.

Dominik saw a plate covered with an embroidered cloth. He wondered why, but no one was talking, so he didn't ask. Jakob removed the cloth, used the knife on the board to make small incisions on two loaves of bread and then picked up both, holding them together. He made the same blessing the Rabbi had recited the previous night over bread, tore off a small piece from one, dipped it in the salt dish near him and ate it. Then he tore apart the rest and put the pieces in a basket, sprinkled a little salt on them and passed it to his father, who took a bit and passed it on. When everyone had eaten their bread, Jakob said, "Great *challah*, Frau Sarah. I miss it. Why don't you move to Basel and keep house for me?" Dominik noted that Frau Sarah turned a little pink.

"I also helped make them," Ruth said. "And I set most of the table."

Jakob winked at her. "Of course, because you guessed I was coming."

Karl laughed out loud. "Ruth's got a crush on you, Jakob."

"Do not!"

"Do too!"

"Enough, children!" Rabbi Breitling said. I'd really like to enjoy our meal and spend time with my family and our guests tonight, not listening to your banter. Maybe later. You can stop blushing, Ruth. Karl was just teasing."

Dominik was amazed that everything was so cheerful and relaxed, even though the table and rituals were formal. "Excuse me," he said quietly. "Can I ask why the breads were covered? The rolls weren't last night."

Chapter 1

"That way the *challot* won't be insulted because the wine gets the first *bracha*," David stated.

The rabbi added, "Some scholars interpret the covering of the *challot* allegorically, explaining that just as we go out of our way to protect an inanimate object like bread from being 'insulted' by the blessing over wine coming first, we should display the same sensitivity toward the feelings of other people. And two *challot* also commemorate the double portion of *manna* the Jews received every Friday during their forty years in the desert with Moses so they wouldn't have to gather food on Shabbat."

Dominik was a little confused about each person getting a sip of wine and a bit of bread. Even though the Rabbi had explained the reason for two *challot*, the double ritual of bread and wine reminded him of the Eucharist, the sacrament of Holy Communion. But whose blood and bones underwent transubstantiation? Whose bones and blood did Jews consume? They didn't accept Jesus as their Savior, their messiah. Dominik was confused, but he knew it wasn't appropriate to ask the Rabbi at the Shabbat dinner table.

He thought the whole dinner was marvelous, a little like Sunday dinners in Armenia or at his grandmother's house on Christmas and Easter. The food was different, of course – no ham or pork, no butter or cheese for the bread, no milk for the children or beer for the grownups. There was some kind of paté, or chopped liver, which he didn't like, but he ate it on a piece of *challah*. There was chicken soup with noodles, which he did like.

"Oh look," Jeremy said, "the noodles are Hebrew letters."

Annie poked him in the side, "We have those at home too, silly."

There were so many dishes: roast chicken and dumplings, potatoes and peas, two kinds of salad. There were other differences between this meal and the dinners at his grandmother's house besides the food. There was no silence. The children were allowed, even encouraged, to talk – not that there were ever many children to be silenced at his grandmother's dinners. There were jokes and a discussion of current news in Europe and Israel. Jakob started a friendly argument about a point the Rabbi had raised in his sermon, and the debate got quite heated as the others joined in. Jeremy thumped his spoon on the table and shouted, "I think Jakob's right!" Everyone laughed.

There was singing. Between every course, they sang a song about the holiness, or the spirit, of Shabbat. David leaned over and, in a low voice, told Dominik the songs are called *'zemirot'* and there are different ones for Friday night and Saturday. He reached behind his head and took a small booklet from the sideboard, flipped some pages and handed it to Dominik who noted that it was printed in Hebrew on one side and German on the other. "This is a *bentscher* and here's what we'll probably sing next. You can follow the German translation. Or you can have an English *bentscher*."

The rabbi said anyone who wanted more wine should pass their glass to him. David whispered that the Rabbi couldn't pass the bottle because Ruth and Dominik weren't Jewish and it's forbidden for a non-Jew to touch the bottle of sacramental wine.

"He's doing it in such a polite way that I guess I'm another *challah* at this table," Dominik whispered, and David laughed quietly.

Ruth said, "What's going on? What are you two whispering about?"

David grinned. "Your fashionable green dress, of course!"

"I think it's a beautiful dress," Annie said sincerely, her face revealing a touch of hero worship. Dominik agreed, smiling at both girls.

The rabbi leaned towards his lovely wife. "You're so quiet, Deborah. Are your parents all right? Was the drive difficult? Jakob loves a little speed."

Deborah held up her hands and started counting off on her fingers. "I'm not tired, my parents are fine and they've already packed for their trip, and Jakob remembered his 'old' mother doesn't like speeding so he drove at the proper speed. I'm just enjoying Shabbat with my family and our guests." She smiled at Dominik and winked saucily at her husband.

Karl started singing another Shabbat song in a lovely clear tenor voice. Everyone joined in and Dominik followed it in his *bentscher*. It was lovely and he hoped the translation was accurate. He said, "I like this *zemirot*."

"*Zemir*," David told him, "when it's only one."

"*Zemir*," Dominik echoed.

After the elaborate desserts of fruit sorbet and cakes, most of the plates were removed from the table, leaving only the wine, bread and salt. David handed out the *bentschers* and the Rabbi asked Jonathan Rosen to start the *Zimun*, the extra prayer since there were six men at the table – plus Jeremy, he added with a smile. David opened Dominik's *bentscher* to the proper place so he could follow. The Shabbat Grace after Meals was half singing, half speaking…with a silent part as well. When they'd finished, everyone kissed their *bentschers* and handed them to David who placed them on the sideboard. Then, surprising all the guests, the Rabbi sang in his deep voice "Thank you, Sarah" and

Chapter 1

held the note. Jakob, Karl and David sang "Thank you, Sarah" two notes higher and held their note. And then Deborah and Ruth did the same. For a moment, all the notes lingered in the air like a perfect chord. Although she was used to this custom, Frau Sarah dipped her head in silent appreciation of their gesture.

"Now, young people to the kitchen to help Frau Sarah clean up, adults and twins to the salon," the Rabbi said.

"Am I a young person or am I an adult?" Jakob asked. His father replied. "You'll always be a young person to me, Jakob, but tonight I'd like to hear a little about why you were 'knackered' from your studies and if you've heard anything special from Daniel." He said to the Rosens, "Jakob is studying to be a rabbi and our other son, Daniel, is in South America with friends."

"Wow," Jeremy exclaimed. "I'd like to go to South America."

"You'd like to go everywhere, even to the moon," his sister said.

He glared at her, "Well, maybe I'll be an aster...astronaut when I'm big."

Everyone laughed again and Meredith said gently, "Let's listen to Jakob."

"There really isn't much to tell. A couple of the rabbis and professors are still feuding, and some students are lining up on the opposing sides. Not me. I just like hearing all the viewpoints. Much of the grumbling, of course, is about Israel and the tyrannical power of the *Rabbinut* there compared to the lack of rabbinical power here. Daniel called a few days ago but the connection was so bad and all I know is he's having a fabulous time, but struggling to find kosher food, and on Sunday they're heading to Iguazu Falls. He saw Uncle Eli who misses David constantly and sends his love. Now, Dad, if you don't mind, I'd like to go to Hershel Beckman's house. We haven't gotten together in a long time. I saw him in *shul* and he invited me."

"You were in *shul*?" his father asked, a little stunned. "I didn't see you."

"I know. I was sort of hiding in the back because Mom and I wanted to surprise you. So, please excuse me, I'll see you at *shul* tomorrow. I'll sleep at Hershel's tonight. Good night everyone and Shabbat Shalom."

"If you're staying over at Hershel's, take a clean set of underwear and a fresh shirt for the morning," Deborah told him.

He came over and kissed her cheek. "Stop being such a mom... but I love you anyway," he said, kissing her noisily. The twins giggled.

"Why don't you get together with all your old friends here for

Sunday breakfast?" the Rabbi asked.

"I can't," he said. "I need to be in Basel for a meeting on Sunday. Then I'll pick up *Oma* and *Opa* in Bern and drive them home, even though they said they'd go by taxi or cousin Stephen will drive them. But I want to go or I won't see them before they leave for Israel. Mom has *my* permission to stay longer if she wants," he added with a wink. "Maybe Hersh and I can arrange something with our friends *motzei Shabbat*."

Frau Sarah and the others came into the salon just as Jakob was about to leave. "David, I spoke to Daniel yesterday and he said your Dad misses you like crazy. I told him I'd be here for Shabbat and he said your Dad sends you lots of love. But, sorry cousin, I'm not going to kiss you. That's only for my Mom and Frau Sarah." He hugged Frau Sarah and gave her a noisy kiss on the cheek. The twins giggled again.

The rabbi glared jokingly at his son's foolishness. "Out now!" he said. "Good *Shabbos*."

Deborah smiled at Sarah, "I hope Jakob didn't embarrass you."

"Of course not. He's got me wrapped around his little finger," she said, "He's a fine young man. Both of your sons are, and they always tease me."

"We'll go to our flat now," Meredith said, glancing at her sleepy children. "They've had a full day, flying in this afternoon, getting ready for Shabbat, coming here this evening. Come on, children, let's get your coats."

"I want Ruth to sleep at our flat, Mummy. Please?" Annie said, yawning.

"Maybe tomorrow," her mother said, buttoning their warm coats. "Now let's see if you can remember the words we practiced on the plane."

The twins bowed to the Rabbi. *"Dankeschön, Rabbi. Dankeschön, Frau Sarah. Dankeschön, Rabbanit. Gute Nacht. Auf Wiedersehen."* They bowed again. "Was that right, Mummy?"

Both Deborah and Frau Sarah came over to hug the children. "That was perfect," Deborah said, giving each of them a kiss, which Jeremy rubbed away. Everyone said *"Shabbat shalom"* and the Rosens left.

"Long day for everyone," the Rabbi sighed. "The lights will go off at 11:30. So, good night, everyone." Frau Sarah and Ruth went to their flat, and the boys headed down the hall.

David knew Dominik was probably confused about the lights, so he said, "Jews aren't allowed to work or ride or write or cook on

Shabbat, only if it's a matter of life or death. We're not even allowed to turn lights on and off, so we have a timer and it shuts them off automatically at a set time. It will turn them on again tomorrow afternoon. Interesting religion, right?"

"Very. Very different from mine. I like it a lot," Dominik said. "Thanks for everything tonight, David. You made it so much easier for me."

Dominik got ready for bed and laid down. He still had some time before "Lights Out!" so he picked up *The Diary of Anne Frank*, hoping to finish the book. He found it astonishing that a young girl his age could write so normally about her family's life in hiding. And the tragic end of the family, only her father surviving the Holocaust. But he couldn't concentrate on the book. He had too much to think about. The lights went out and Dominik lay there, too exhilarated and at the same time too confused to sleep. He said to himself, *"Some Jewish people are incredible. So full of life and joy, even when their life was hard, even when they had no joy – like Anne Frank. But so welcoming to strangers. So different from my grandparents, even from my mother. And so very different from the priests and the other kids in my school."* He felt he could speak about anything with Rabbi Breitling, and he wouldn't be judged or excommunicated or condemned to purgatory.

He knew his mother loved him, but his grandfather was a very hard man; he thought his mother was afraid of her father and the priests, especially the Monsignor. He knew his mother had an older brother, but no one ever talked about him or what happened to him, not even his name or if he was still alive. Just like no one ever talked about Dominik's father, not even his name. It was so different here in the Rabbi's house; they could talk about everything. They talked and they argued, but with love. His comments and questions weren't met with anger or total silence. Dominik knew he'd love to be part of a family like the Rabbi's, but he wasn't – and could never be – a real member of the Rabbi's family. Would he like to be Jewish? Did he want to be Jewish? With these questions and *zemirot* – he recalled the Hebrew word – echoing in his head, Dominik finally fell asleep.

In the morning, when he was dressed and ready for *shul*, Dominik was aware of how quiet the house was. He walked into the kitchen and found Karl drinking a glass of juice and eating a piece of cake, reading a prayer book. "*Shabbat shalom*. The others have already gone to *shul*," Karl said. "I've been waiting for you. Rabbanit Breitling said you should eat, a piece of cake or challah, and drink some juice or a cup of tea, and then we'll go to *shul* if you want to go. Today will be fun because there's a *simcha*, a Bar Mitzvah. Do you know what that is? There'll be a reception with a lot of food and drinks. It's pretty special."

Dominik laughed. "*Shabbat shalom* to you, too. Slow down a bit. Ruth says you don't talk much, but she should hear you this morning. I know that a *Bar Mitzvah* is a coming-of-age ritual for a 13-year-old boy, but we don't have them in the Catholic church. And I'm sure a *simcha* is a happy event." He poured a glass of juice and drank deeply. On the closed lid of the Aga, he saw a hot plate with a few pots. "I know you can't cook on Shabbat, so I guess that's keeping dinner warm, but I didn't notice it last night," he said.

"It was empty," Karl said. "I told everyone you're smart, and you're right about a *Bar Mitzvah* and a *simcha*. Whenever you're ready, we can go."

"*Vamanos!*" Dominik said, showing off. "That's Spanish for 'Let's go!'"

The *shul* was very crowded, but David and Jakob had empty seats next to them for Karl and Dominik. After saying *"Shabbat Shalom"*, David said, "It's so crowded today because Matthew, the *Bar Mitzvah* boy, is from a prominent family. His father's a banker and his mother's a famous actress. She's gorgeous!" A boy around Dominik's age, wearing a ritual prayer shawl and a skull cap was sitting next to the *chazzan*. "The shawl is called a *tallit* and the skull cap is a *yarmulke* or *kippah;* the platform they are sitting on is called a *bimah*," David whispered before Dominik could ask. All the men in the *shul* were wearing *tallits* and *yarmulkes*. Karl had handed them to him when they entered the synagogue, so Dominik was wearing them, too; now he was pleased to know what they were called. *"It's funny,"* he thought. *"The Pope, cardinals and archbishops all wear kippahs, but to them it's a 'pileolus' or 'zucchetto'. I wonder why they wear the same kind of hat."* It had become a habit to say to himself *"I'll ask the Rabbi."*

Dominik was following the German in the prayer book, a *siddur*, David whispered. The rabbi called Matthew's grandfather and his father to the *bimah*. Matthew stood up and pulled open the curtain in front of the niche, revealing several *Torah* scrolls wrapped in purple velvet with silver balls or crowns on the handles. His grandfather took out one and held it aloft. Then he passed it to his son who handed it to Matthew. Each of them in turn took the fringes of his *tallit*, touched it to the *Torah* and brought them to his lips. Matthew, holding the *Torah*, sat down, and the Rabbi called two different men – Matthew's other grandfather and an uncle – to remove the crowns and cover of

Chapter 1

the *Torah*; Matthew then brought the *Torah* to the podium and laid it down. The rabbi unrolled it partway and picked up an ebony pointer with a tiny silver hand. Before Matthew even began to chant that week's *Torah* portion and between sections of the reading, the Rabbi called other men to the *bimah* to recite a short blessing in Hebrew. "It's an honor to be called to the *Torah* on Shabbat. It's called an *aliyah* and there are seven *aliyahs* during the reading," David, Dominik's private tutor, said. When Matthew completed his reading, the Rabbi surprised everyone by calling David to the *bimah* to help with the rewrapping and return of the *Torah* to the niche – the *ark*, saying that David, his nephew, had helped Matthew prepare for the *Bar Mitzvah*, something Dominik could easily understand since he was aware of how much David was helping him.

The service continued with the *chazzan* chanting the *Haftarah*. After the *chazzan* returned to his seat, Matthew stood for his *Bar Mitzvah* speech, five minutes of his personal interpretation of his *Torah* portion, and another minute or so in which he commented on why he liked the idea of using the *tzitzit*, the fringes, to kiss the *Torah*. He said if all the people called to an *aliyah* kissed the *Torah* itself, there would be big holes in the parchment. Everyone laughed. Matthew thanked his parents and his grandparents, the Rabbi and the *chazzan*, and David for their help. Everyone shouted *"Mazal tov!"* Candy came flying down from the women's balcony, and children, including Jeremy, scrambled to pick up the sweets.

When everyone settled, the Rabbi led the congregation in the closing prayers and brought the Shabbat morning service to an end. He made a few announcements about the services later in the day and then everyone was invited to the *shul's* large vestibule where tables were set up, laden with drinks and snacks provided by Matthew's parents. One grandfather recited the blessing over the wine, and the other gave the blessing for the large challah that sat on one of the tables. Then everyone "fell" on the cakes and sandwiches, wine and fruit juices. As they offered congratulations to the *Bar Mitzvah* boy and his family, people couldn't help staring at Matthew's very beautiful and very famous mother. "Personally," Jakob quipped to his friends, "I think my mom and Ruth are more beautiful than the actress." Ruth, nearby, blushed, but for once she didn't say anything.

Dominik, who'd been enthralled by the entire service, was standing with his friends and he said to Ruth, "He's right you know. You are beautiful."

"Uh-oh," Karl teased, "Now Dominik has a crush on Ruth!"

Annie and Jeremy came over just then and asked if they could go to the Rabbi's house. "We've got lots of candy in our pockets." Dominik was glad for the distraction from Karl's teasing as the crowd in the *shul* dispersed.

Dominik was quiet during the short walk to the Rabbi's flat. Rabbanit Breitling asked, "What did you think of the services, Dominik?"

He smiled as big a smile as he could. "I think it was awesome, nothing like my church. But a little scary 'cause there's so much to learn. Last night was great, but today, the *Bar Mitzvah*…all I can say is 'Wow!' Is that OK?"

Deborah laughed, "Of course it's OK. It really was a 'Wow Bar Mitzvah'. Matthew did a very good job, and a little English birdy named Annie told me my son thinks Ruth and I are beautiful! So I'll echo your 'Wow!'"

Shyly, David said, "I agree with Jakob. I think you're awesome, too!"

She laughed again. "Awesome, too! Another 'Wow', Dominik. Thank you…but you should know I have faults, just like everyone else."

By this time, they'd reached the flat. Frau Sarah had set up everything for the afternoon meal. After a convivial Shabbat lunch, a similar pattern to the previous evening; only the food was a little different and there were no blessings over the wine and bread because, David told Dominik, they'd heard those blessings at *shul*, everyone went in different directions. The Rosens went back to their rented flat. The rabbi and rabbanit went to rest in their room. Karl went out to meet some friends and discuss their plans for the *Chanukah* party. David and Dominik went to their rooms – David to read, Dominik to read… and to ponder. Frau Sarah and Ruth put away the leftovers and Ruth said, "I'll clean up. It's my good deed for the day."

"Don't do a thing, "Frau Sarah said. "Let it wait until *motzei Shabbat* and everyone will help. You can profit from a little quiet reading time as well."

"I can profit from help in French. I have a test on Tuesday. Maybe I'll ask Dominik to help me."

Frau Sarah looked at her and said seriously, "Don't try out your wiles on him, Ruth. You know you're pretty, funny, and a flirt. He's young and he's had a really hard time. He doesn't need to develop a crush on you."

"OK, Frau Sarah, maybe I'll try my wiles on Karl instead. I'll get him to grow his hair very long and then, like Delilah, I'll make him cut it and give his power to me. Except that wouldn't work on Karl. Too bad I can't use my wiles on Jakob," she said. When they went to their flat, Frau Sarah told Ruth to give it a little time. This time her voice held sympathy.

Dominik lay on his bed, thinking over all the things that had happened since his mother threw him out into the cold. But thinking about his future frightened him.

"Where will I go? What will I do? These people are really awesome… not just the rabbanit. They stick to their traditions but with so much wisdom, and with humor, and love and respect for each other. They treat strangers like old friends. They even encourage children to ask all kinds of questions. They like to be challenged intellectually. Their religious services are different: repeated rituals, but not like ours; women and men not sitting together, no organ music drowning out thoughts."

He thought of the candy flying down from the balcony.

"There's fun even in the middle of a religious ceremony. And they don't pretend to be drinking the blood and eating the bones of their Savior!" he added a little contemptuously.

"I'm sure not every synagogue is like Rabbi Breitling's and not every family is so kind. But do I want to be part of their world? I don't know. Maybe it's just too good to be true. Do I want to go back to my mother's somber world and to my grandparents and the monsignor? And my school? No way! To my mom…sure, but not to everything and everyone else."

His thoughts were beginning to run a little wild, so Dominik took a book from one of the shelves and began to read.

Chapter 2

On Sunday, the Rabbi arrived early at the gatehouse of the Domkirche on Burggasse Street. The door was slightly ajar but no one else was there. He walked in, looked around, and was immediately pleased Dominik had opted not to attend the meeting. The room contained a fairly large table with five chairs arranged on one side and two on the other; there was a tape recorder on the table. *"It looks like an Inquisition,"* he thought. *"Dominik would have been devastated."* He sat down, crossed his legs, and waited.

He didn't wait very long. At 1:00 on the dot, the door opened fully and five people marched in and sat down, all on the same side: the monsignor, a younger priest, Frederica Müller, and her parents. Dominik's resemblance to his attractive, dark-haired mother was unmistakable. Her own mother was an older version of Frederica but she was nervous, perhaps even frightened. Herr Müller was a tall man, gruff not only in physical appearance, but also in the attitude clinging to him. The rabbi smiled at the five people and said pleasantly, "I'm Rabbi Samuel Breitling and I'm pleased we could arrange this meeting. Let me assure you that Dominik is fine." No one said a thing.

Monsignor Dietrich turned on the tape recorder and barely glanced at the Rabbi as he stated introductions weren't really necessary. "But, as a point of information, this is Father Erich who, in a moment of temper caused by the boy's insufferable questions, told the boy to go to the synagogue and ask you his questions. He never thought the boy would actually do that."

The rabbi nodded at the young priest. "When Dominik was not allowed to return to school and his mother made him leave her house as well, he was confused and didn't know where else to go. He was very wet and very cold when he came to me. I couldn't turn him away in that condition, but I called the monsignor almost immediately to tell him where Dominik was."

"Is he ready to apologize and behave properly?" Frederica asked. "It's the only way I'll let him come home."

"What about his father?" the Rabbi asked. "Perhaps he could live with him until some basic decisions are made about Dominik's future?"

Herr Müller burst out, "That rapist? We won't let him take the boy!"

Frederica looked at her father sadly. "Papa, you know he didn't rape me. I loved him, but he had to go back to Iran when he finished his PhD. I didn't even know I was pregnant when he left. But he never called me."

"That's why you sometimes call Dominic 'Daryush', isn't it?" the Rabbi asked. "Couldn't you contact him now?"

"I don't know where he lives, what he's doing, if he has a family, if he'd even be interested," she said quietly.

"Oh, he'd be interested," Monsignor Dietrich scorned. "He'd be interested in his son. Another Moslem. But knowing how incorrigible the boy is and how he asks challenging questions, he wouldn't last long in Iran."

She gulped. "So we are back to my son apologizing…"

"I'm not sure he believes he has to apologize," the Rabbi responded.

"That's what you told him, I suppose," Herr Müller said sarcastically. "His questions were blasphemous. I think he should be dragged back and severely punished until he swears not to insult the Church again."

The monsignor laid a hand on the older man's shoulder. "You know we don't punish sinners physically any more, Friedrich. If the boy apologizes and comes back, we'll supervise all his schoolwork, outside activities and friends. We'll discourage questions. But we won't abuse him."

"Not like the Jews. He's a pretty boy, and probably already their new plaything," Müller said truculently.

"Papa, please," Frederica said, a sad plea in her eyes.

"We offer friendship even to the stranger," the Rabbi said quietly.

"So you say. Why do you have three kids who aren't yours living in your house? The monsignor told us that. And where are your wife and your kids? Did they leave you because you abused them? Or did you just get rid of them?" The old man's hostility seemed to pour out of him.

The rabbi glanced at the two clergymen who sat there passively, looking at their hands, saying nothing. "Why my wife and sons live in Switzerland is a private family matter. But the three youngsters who are in my care have never been abused in any way. One, David Rosenzweig, is my nephew; his mother, my sister, passed away two years ago and it was impossible for David to live alone in Brazil where his father heads a major construction project. We all decided to let David live with me, but he and his father see each other as often as possible. The other boy, Karl Goldsmith, is the grandson of an elderly member of my congregation. He was living with her but associating with a rough group of boys, neglecting his schoolwork. She couldn't control him, so she asked me to take him in; unfortunately, she passed away, leaving Karl in my care. The girl's parents are divorced. Her father's Jewish but her mother endorses no religion. Ruth Segal, as she's called now although her real name is Elspeth, has just returned from almost a year of living and studying at a kibbutz in Israel. She wants to convert to Judaism; that's why she changed her name to Ruth, but she's still a long way from conversion. All three youngsters are excellent students. They attend the *Bundesrealgymnasium* and then study with me in the evening. Ruth doesn't live in my house. She's in the flat next door with my housekeeper."

"They'd all run away if they could, like your wife," Herr Müller stated, pugnaciously.

"Papa, please…" Frederica said again, looking embarrassed. Her mother also looked uncomfortable at this antagonistic turn of the conversation.

The two priests still said nothing. The rabbi glanced at them and then said, "I'd really like to get back to the subject of Dominik. However, for the sake of clarity, I'll tell you my wife and I are Swiss citizens. She and our sons live in Zurich because her parents are Holocaust survivors and it would raise many unpleasant memories for them if their daughter were to live in Austria. But we see each other frequently…usually during the week. My wife is here now and my older son returned to Zurich this morning."

"A likely story," Müller muttered, half under his breath.

Such belligerence towards Jews from older Austrians and Germans was quite common, the Rabbi knew, although he hesitated to call it outright anti-Semitism. He was actually more concerned at the hostility and rigid control of the two clergymen. Like many citizens of Austria and Switzerland, he'd heard rumors that Cardinal Ratzinger, native son of Munich and the former Archbishop of Germany, the monsignor's personal mentor, might be the next Pope. *"Maybe,"* the Rabbi thought to himself as a small joke, *"these Austrian priests believe they have to be 'holier than the Pope' and maintain control over all parishioners, even reluctant ones, and bring 'sinners' back into the fold."* Aloud, he said, "Please let's get back to Dominik's situation."

"I really will not take him back unless he apologizes. If you want, I'll grant you temporary guardianship until then," Frederica announced.

Her father and the priests were appalled. "You can't do that, Frederica," her father shouted, "I'll go with Father Erich and we'll haul the boy home. If you give them permission, the Jews will steal him. You know they do, even without permission, and they use their blood in some rituals." Frau Müller turned very pale at her husband's

Chapter 2

truculent words, but she said nothing.

"We don't steal anyone," Rabbi Breitling said. "And we don't encourage conversion either. In fact, we make it difficult so it's not a hasty decision. But if someone really wants to convert, we won't stop her. Or him."

"I'll let him stay with you until he calms down," Frederica said. "I'm sure he'll give in soon and come home. He's stubborn, but he knows I love him."

"Are you sure that's what you want to do?" an angry Monsignor Dietrich asked. Frederica nodded, visibly stressed by the entire confrontation.

"In that case, I'll leave now," the Rabbi said. "I'll talk to Dominik and present the alternatives. If he decides to stay with us for a while, I'll let you know. In any case, the decision is his. I won't pressure him in any way."

"You'll have to talk to my lawyer. I don't want to see him or talk to him if he chooses you," she said, her tone of voice flat, her face expressionless.

"So be it," the Rabbi said as he left. He drew in a deep breath outside the Domkirche's grounds. He knew Dominik's choice would not be an easy one.

Deborah and Sarah were waiting for him in the flat. Sarah took his coat and hat, and Deborah took his hand. "You look shattered," she said.

"It was awful. It's not a nice thing to say, but I'm glad Dominik didn't come. It would have been excruciating for him. They'll accept nothing but complete capitulation – the family and the priests. His mother seems to be intelligent, but she's intimidated by her father and the monsignor, although she actually stood up to both of them. She said she loves Dominik and wants him to come home, but she'll grant me temporary guardianship if Dominik chooses to stay here. His grandmother's a quiet mouse. Nobody wants to see Dominik or talk to him or even know him if he decides to stay with us, but his mother and grandmother looked very sad. Where is he, by the way?"

Deborah said the three boys had gone for a walk but would be back by 4:00. "Dominik seems to have his mother's intelligence and stubborn spirit, although he's trying very hard to be polite and fit in here. Maybe he's trying too hard to make us like him. By the way, have you noticed that you always refer to him by name?" Sarah nodded quietly at that.

"You're right," the Rabbi said. "Dominik's a very determined lad.

But he's very troubled, confused and hurt right now. I always refer to him by his name because I couldn't stand all of them except his mother only calling him 'the boy'. I'll speak to him when the boys," he grinned, "get back. I had to tell them about the teens living here, Deborah, and why you and our sons live in Zurich. The grandfather and both priests were extremely hostile."

She smiled. "I'm sure you handled it diplomatically; you always do. Look away, Sarah, I'm going to kiss my husband and I don't want to shock you."

The housekeeper laughed and went into the kitchen. "We'll pretend we're English and I'll make us all a cup of tea," she said "They say 'cuppa', don't they? Maybe I'll check that out with 'the boy' called Dominik!"

When the boys came in, they were laughing, but Deborah, sitting on the sofa, sensed the fear behind Dominik's smile. "Is the Rabbi back?" he asked.

"He is, Dominik," she replied. "He's waiting for you in his study."

Dominik knocked on the door and entered the room when the Rabbi said, gently, "Come in and sit down, Dominik. We have a lot to talk about. And you'll have some very difficult decisions to make."

"Do I have to go back? Do you want me to?" he asked in a small voice.

"It's not up to me, Dominik. It's your decision, completely yours. Your mother, your grandfather and the priests insist on a full apology as well as an unconditional promise not to ask any additional provocative questions. They aren't willing to compromise. Your mother has offered me temporary guardianship if you want time to consider your options. That's important because otherwise I'd have some legal difficulties with the state if you're here and your mother lives only a few blocks away. I think her offer is generous. If you decide to stay here, even for a short time while you're making up your mind, you'll go to public school with David, Karl and Ruth. In the meantime, your mother doesn't want to see you or even talk to you until you've reached a decision. These aren't easy options, Dominik, and you have to think very seriously about them. I always say you can't make a difficult decision standing on one leg? When you've made a decision, we'll talk again. Are you all right with that?"

Dominik looked at him very seriously. "Yes, sir," he said. "I still don't think I did anything that requires an apology. And I don't think I can stop asking questions. My head is full of them. Even some for you," he said with a little smile. "I guess I'll have to stay here while

I think about everything. I'm glad that's all right with you. I also think my mother's offer was fair. She won't even talk to me…" His face crumpled and he looked like he was about to cry. But then he straightened up, took a deep breath and sighed. "Thank you, sir. I'd like to go to school with the others."

"That's fine," the Rabbi said. "At dinner, we'll tell them you're staying for a while. And that you'll be going to school with them. My wife will go with you to talk to the headmaster who's not only an excellent educator but also a very nice chap. I'll call your mother's attorney tomorrow and we'll arrange everything. I hope you have something to do for the rest of the afternoon. The others are probably finishing their homework for tomorrow."

After Dominik left, Deborah came in. "How did it go? He didn't look terribly upset. He told me he was going to his room to read. It's interesting that he thinks of it as *his* room."

The rabbi held out his hand and she came over and sat in front of him on his desk. "Dominik's quick and clever. He was extremely upset about his mother not talking to him. He wants to stay here while he thinks about what he should do. He appreciates her gesture about the guardianship, but he also understands, despite the hurt, that he might have to sacrifice his relationship with her if he doesn't capitulate. But I'm not sure he'll be able to grant them his total surrender. I also don't think his attachment to the Church is all that strong, at least not now. He feels betrayed for the crime of intelligence."

"Would you help him convert to Judaism?" Deborah asked, compassion for the boy's plight in her eyes.

"You know I don't encourage anyone to convert, my darling. But if he decides he wants to become Jewish after several years, I'd be willing to steer him into a proper course of study. At the moment, all we can do is follow the old cliché: Take it one day at a time…and be here for him."

Deborah put her arms around him and gave him a hug. "At times like this, I know why I love you," she said.

◆ ◆ ◆

On Monday morning, Rabbi Breitling called Monsignor Dietrich for the phone number of Frederica Müller's lawyer. "I gather the boy has decided to stay with you," the monsignor said, a definite chill in his voice.

"Actually, Dominik hasn't decided anything yet. He wants a little time to think about the situation, his options and the consequences," the Rabbi said, and added, "He's very upset that his mother won't talk to him."

The monsignor stated, "Her lawyer will be upset too. He's a parishioner," He gave the Rabbi the attorney's phone number and ended the call.

The rabbi then called the attorney who was angry more than upset, but he agreed to draft papers for one month and to bring them to the Rabbi's office after his client signed. "Perhaps Frau Müller will send some of Dominik's clothes and other things," the Rabbi suggested.

"Perhaps," the lawyer acknowledged.

The *rabbanit* accompanied the youngsters to *Bundesrealgymnasium* and then went into the headmaster's office with Dominik. "How are you, Frau Breitling? And your sons?" he asked. "It's a pleasure to see you again. It's been quite a long time – since you brought David to us, I think."

"Yes. And you, headmaster, how are you?" Deborah inquired. "We're all fine. Jakob's studying in university and Daniel's travelling in South America with friends, two other graduates from this school." They chatted for a few minutes, but finally, Deborah said, "This is Dominik Müller, headmaster. He's staying with the Rabbi for a while and wants to attend school. He's 14 years old and, in my opinion, very intelligent with an amazing command of languages," she said, smiling at Dominik. "We'll have his documents and transcripts in a day or two, but I don't know how long he'll be staying here."

The headmaster shook hands with Dominik and said, "We'll give you a chance, young man…er, Dominik. Are you by any chance in trouble, a runaway turning to the Rabbi for sanctuary?"

"In a way, I guess," Dominik said shyly. "I've been at the Domkirche School since I was eight years old, but they threw me out. And so did my mother. That's why I came to Rabbi Breitling and he took me in."

The headmaster looked startled. "Please wait outside in the anteroom, Dominik. You'll find information about our courses. I'll finish my talk with Frau Breitling and then we'll work out a schedule of classes for you."

Deborah smiled as Dominik went out. "Very diplomatic, headmaster. It's a long and not very pretty story. As I said, he's very intelligent and he was asking questions that the priests wouldn't – or maybe couldn't – answer. He was expelled and one of the priests suggested in anger that he go to a rabbi to get the answers to his questions. His mother threw him out of their house when she heard what happened and that he wouldn't apologize. He didn't know what to do, so he naïvely followed the priest's suggestion and came to my husband last Thursday, wet and freezing. Since then, my husband spoke to Dominik's mother and to the priests, and they agreed to let the boy stay with the Rabbi for a short time. In fact, at this moment, the Rabbi is receiving temporary guardianship papers from Frau Müller's attorney. There's anger and hostility, especially from the grandfather and Monsignor Dietrich, but at least Dominik's mother has agreed to give him a chance to calm down. In fact, the Rabbi's temporary guardianship was her idea. Obviously, Dominik comes by his intelligence naturally. Will you allow him to attend classes?"

"Wouldn't staying with his father be the best solution for Dominik?" the headmaster inquired.

"His father is not in the picture," Deborah answered. "He lives in Iran. And he may not even know of his son's existence."

"Complications inside complications inside complications…" he mused. "All right, we'll allow him to study here until the Christmas break. I'll place him at his age level in the Humanities track and then we'll see if he should be moved up or down. The other three youngsters living with the Rabbi are older than Dominik, but they're friendly and will probably help him adjust to a state school. Especially the Rabbi's nephew, who's become a favorite here. I'd appreciate receiving Dominik's papers as soon as possible. And I'll speak with Monsignor Dietrich. I'm sure I'll get an earful."

"Thank you, headmaster. I don't think you'll be sorry," Deborah said. "In just a few days, I've become fond of him. I'll leave now. *Auf wiedersehen.*"

"*Auf wiedersehen,*" he responded automatically. "Please send Dominik in on your way out. Warm regards to the Rabbi and your sons." He smiled at her, "*Shalom*, Frau Breitling."

Deborah left the headmaster's office, smiling. She saw Dominik sitting on the edge of a small sofa, holding an unopened brochure and looking very frightened. She walked over to him and sat down. "It's OK, Dominik. The headmaster wants you to go in and both of you will plan a program for the time you're here. He's a really nice person. Compassionate, too."

"I don't know what to say, Rabbanit Breitling."

"Just say thank you. To him."

Dominik went into the headmaster's office and sat in the seat opposite the educator. The headmaster took out a pen and pad and said in English, "I'll be speaking to Monsignor Dietrich in a little while, Dominik. I've asked my secretary to place a call to him. Is that all right with you?"

"Yes, sir," Dominik responded in English. "He'll tell you I'm incorrigible, a disgrace to the church, a heretic, an apostate."

"And does that bother you?" the headmaster asked in French.

"*Oui, mais d'un autre coté pas beaucoup!* I did ask very provocative questions," Dominik replied in French. "What my *maman* thinks of me bothers me more. She won't talk to me or see me…"

"What other languages do you know?" the headmaster interrupted, noting the boy was clearly upset, and now speaking in German.

"Latin, Armenian, Turkish, Spanish. A little Georgian and Farsi. And some Urdu, as well as a few words of Japanese and Chinese. English, of course," Dominik added with a shy smile. "People doing business with my stepfather or working for him came from different places around the world. They all treated me like a puppy, giving me sweets and talking to me in their languages, so I listened. I mostly know only the spoken languages because some of the alphabets are different from German and English."

"I'm very impressed, and I'm not going to test you anymore. I'm sure you'll do well here. I've told Frau Breitling we'll let you study here until Christmas, unconditionally. And after the New Year, we'll talk again about your situation. Now let's think about some of the classes you should take. A course in religion or ethics is a standard requirement in Austrian schools. I think you should choose ethics."

"Does the headmaster have a hidden agenda? Or did the rabbanit say something to him?" Dominik wondered. But all he said was "Thank you, sir" and opened the school brochure. They discussed various classes and programs and the headmaster could see Dominik relaxing a little.

Later that morning the headmaster had quite a long conversation with Monsignor Dietrich about Dominik and did indeed get an earful, mostly controlled rage, he decided, at the potential defection of a brilliant young boy, possibly a future cleric. When the school day ended, a few teachers of the classes Dominik was attending claimed he was too advanced for their classes. Two traditional teachers voiced concern that despite how polite he was – after all it was only his first day – he might prove to be disruptive, especially if he was bored in class.

The headmaster wondered if he'd fallen for the charm of both Dominik and Frau Breitling. He couldn't bring himself to believe this brilliant young boy would cause discipline problems, despite the monsignor's extremely negative opinion. He'd have to work out a

Chapter 2

better program for Dominik – a higher grade level, giving the boy a real challenge. Perhaps the school's most advanced courses in French and Spanish, maybe introductory Italian, German poetry and English literature, metaphysics, ethics from Aristotle to Marcuse and John Rawls, an introduction to German philosophers. *"Lieber Himmel!"* the headmaster thought, laughing, "I'm planning a university curriculum for a 14-year-old." He set the potential program aside and went home to his delightfully "average" family.

In the late afternoon, Dominik, his excitement bubbling over, walked home with David. "What a great place! I know I'm going to love it. Like I love you guys! And the Rabbi and the Rabbanit. And Frau Sarah…and…!"

David laughed, "Slow down. How were your classes? What about other kids? Do they know how smart you are? Or where you came from?"

"The classes weren't hard, and they weren't boring either. Some teachers asked me tough questions and were surprised when I answered, just as the headmaster was surprised when I talked to him in English and French. I'm not bragging when I say my English is better than Herr Bremen's; I make a few mistakes in grammar but he makes more. A couple of the teachers are great; a couple of the others think I may be a problem because I know too much, but I don't want to get into trouble in this school. Most of the kids were OK, but I had a little trouble with one boy; I'm glad no teachers heard it. I was told the headmaster wants to see me again…tomorrow morning. Do you think I'm already in trouble, that he'll make me leave?"

David told him Herr Doktor Schneider was a good guy and wouldn't make him leave, and everyone knew Herr Bremen shouldn't teach English. He asked what the trouble with the boy was about. "He was a pretty big kid, standing near the water fountain with some other boys from my class during recess. He asked me if I'm an Ay-rab. That's how he said it. I said no. He asked if I'm a Turk? Or a Jew? He said, 'You're dark and you look like an Ay-rab, a Turk or a Jew. Or maybe Eye-talian.' I told him my grandparents have lived in Graz almost forever and both my mother and my grandmother have dark hair and dark eyes. Then he asked me why I came to the school so close to Christmas, and I told him I was in the Domkirche School for 6 years but didn't want to continue in a religious school. And then, it was really strange. He said his parents don't like Catholics, so maybe I'm all right since I left that school. And then he left with all his buddies."

"I think I know the boy you mean. He's part of a group of bullies but they back down if you stand up to them, don't fight or report them," David said. He slapped Dominik lightly on the shoulder. "You did good, Dom."

When they got to the Rabbi's flat, Frau Bernhardt had a snack waiting for them. David said he had a lot of homework and was going to his room to do it. He said he didn't know if they'd be *leining Torah* with the Rabbi because his aunt was staying at least one more day. If they were *leining*, Dominik could join them. If they weren't *leining*, maybe he'd come with Karl and him to the recreation center around the corner to shoot a few hoops. He gave Dominik a little salute and went to do his homework.

Dominik was walking down the hall to his room when he heard the Rabbi calling him. "Come in and sit down, Dominik. I have a few things to tell you. And then you'll tell me about school today. First of all, hello. I hope the *Bundesrealgymnasium* was interesting. These documents on my desk are the signed temporary guardianship papers, your birth certificate and some recent transcripts from the Domkirche School. Your mother's lawyer brought them here earlier this afternoon. So now there are no legal issues or problems with you staying here. But don't forget that the guardianship is temporary, just one month, although it can be extended if you decide to stay here. Advocate Obermann also brought a package containing some clothes and books from home. And your mother sent you a little money because she doesn't want you to be dependent on me." He didn't add that the attorney said she didn't want him to be dependent on charity from the Jews. The *rabbanit*, who'd been sitting quietly on the sofa in the study, smiled at Dominik and told him she'd picked up the school uniform and extra shirts for him, so he wouldn't have to borrow David's.

"Thank you both so much for everything. Since I have some money now, I'll be able to pay you back, at least for the uniforms," he said. "School was really different for me and I want to stay. Some lessons were interesting. I don't remember much about my school in Armenia but here – the teachers, the students, the discussions – all of it was so much more open than the Domkirche School." He didn't tell them about the bullying incident.

"I'm glad to hear that, Dominik. But you still have to take things slowly. New situations are exciting but they might not live up to your expectations in the long run. So please don't make any decisions while standing on one leg," the Rabbi reminded him with a smile. "As to paying for your uniform, we 'll discuss that at another time. If by any chance you don't stay after the new year – I'm not saying you won't, but if that happens – we'll find a boy who needs a school uniform. Now why don't you open the packages in your room and we'll see you later at dinner."

In his room, Dominik picked up the envelope on his desk and recognized his mother's spiky handwriting: Dominik Müller. *"Did she really have to use my full name? Did she think there's another Dominik in the Rabbi's flat?"* he wondered. He didn't want to think she might be sending him a message in that way. He opened the envelope: 1500 Austrian schillings. Nothing else. *"I guess she is sending me a message – goodbye but not good luck."* He sat down on his bed for a few minutes, not quite understanding his own feelings. A few minutes later, he opened the large box, noting with a sardonic droop of his shoulders that his name wasn't written on the top of this box. It contained socks, underwear, pajamas, 3 dress shirts, 3 long sleeved T-shirts, 4 sweaters, 2 pairs of jeans and a pair of dress slacks, his ski jacket and his good jacket, a wool cap and scarf, his Sketchers and his other pair of good shoes. There was a toothbrush and a hairbrush. He put away the clothing, thinking it looked like his mother expected him to stay with the Rabbi longer than two weeks. She'd only forgotten his Austrian national football sweatshirt and his favorite sweater. *On purpose?*

When he finished the clothing, he started on the books. He looked at the titles – the Bible; Basic Catechism; *Fundamentals of the Faith*, a copy of Benson's *Come Rack, Come Rope*; St. Augustine's *On Christian Doctrine;* Pope John Paul II's *Crossing the Threshold of Hope*; and *Co-Workers of the Truth: Meditations for Every Day of the Year* by Cardinal Ratzinger – and he started laughing, but not because there was anything funny. His mother hadn't included any of his language dictionaries, the mystery he had been reading before she threw him out, or the biography he wanted to read. *Oh, his mother was really good at sending messages, not just the money without any kind of note…but only Catholic books!* He put the books on the shelf above the desk, next to Hebrew books, even a Hebrew dictionary. *"How ironic!"* he thought. Then he collapsed the box and stored it on the side of his closet, wondering if he'd need it again when the Rabbi's guardianship expired. Finally, he hung up the uniform the *rabbanit* had left on his bed.

He lay down on the bed, totally exhausted. And confused. He'd return the borrowed clothing and running shoes to David when he went to dinner.

It seemed to him that his eyes had been closed for all of 2 minutes when there was a knock on his door. "It's David. Frau Sarah says dinner will be ready in 5 minutes, so we should wash and come to the kitchen."

"Come in for a minute, David," Dominik said. "Let me give back your running shoes and the other things you lent me."

"There's no rush. I don't need the things. Are you OK?" David asked.

"Fine," Dominik answered automatically. "My mother's lawyer delivered a lot of my own things and your aunt bought me the school uniform today."

"That's great," David said. "Now you'll really feel at home."

"I guess so," Dominik replied, but his smile was a little sad.

At dinner, the Rabbi told everyone he'd been granted guardianship by Dominik's mother for one month. That meant Dominik would be staying with them legally for the next few weeks. The youngsters cheered and a rather subdued Dominik thanked them for their support. After dinner, the Rabbi invited everyone including Frau Bernhardt to his study to discuss the coming *Chanukah* festivities at the *shul*. "But before we start, let me tell you the *rabbanit* is going back to Zurich tomorrow afternoon in order to help her parents finish getting ready for their trip to Israel; they'll spend a few weeks there with Deborah's brother and his family. The *rabbanit* will be back on Thursday." There were additional cheers from the teenagers, including Dominik, and the *rabbanit* smiled at all of them. "Now, is there anything else before we talk about *Chanukah*?"

Dominik looked at him a little sheepishly and said, "I hope you won't mind me asking a question, Rabbi. A number of times you've told me I shouldn't make a decision while standing on one leg. What is the basis of that expression?"

The rabbi smiled at him. "Of course I don't mind. It involves the different philosophical positions of two major first century *Torah* sages, Rabbi Hillel and Rabbi Shammai. Despite Rabbi Hillel's careful observance of Jewish law, he usually advocated a more liberal interpretation of Jewish law and tradition, of *Halakha*, than Rabbi Shammai. The difference between the two great teachers is clear in a story about a Gentile, a non-Jew, who wished to provoke the two rabbis. He first approached Rabbi Shammai, asking him to summarize the *Torah* while standing on one leg. The rabbi, enraged by the request, gave the man an angry whack with a rod. But Rabbi Hillel replied, 'That which is hateful to you, do not do to another: This is the whole *Torah*; the rest is commentary. Now go study.' It's a brief statement, but the first half cannot be separated from the second half. Calling the rest of the *Torah* 'commentary' can't be ignored or dismissed. On the contrary, Rabbi Hillel clearly said commentary is crucial and ultimate wisdom lies in it. Although not doing to others what is hateful to yourself may be the *Torah*'s central message, it is not one that can be treated in isolation from the vast body of practice and learning surrounding it. The command to study, of course, demands time and deep concentration, and that's why we say one shouldn't make an important decision while standing on one leg. By the way, Jesus of Nazareth paraphrased Rabbi Hillel when he said, according to the gospel of Matthew, 'Do unto others what you would have them do unto you, for this sums up the Law and the Prophets'. Is it clear now, Dominik?"

"Very clear. Thank you, sir. I'll think a lot before I make my decision. I know I wouldn't be able to stand on one leg that long," he answered with a smile. Dominik was amazed by the explanation, but even more so that the Rabbi could quote the Christian gospels.

Just as they were starting to discuss the *Chanukah* festivities and what each of them would do to make the celebration a success, the phone on the Rabbi's desk rang. He answered and had a brief, low-voiced conversation. Then he said, "I have to go to the hospital. That was Diane Weiss. Her father is very ill and the family needs me. I may be very late, so carry on without me, please. The *rabbanit* and Frau Sarah will help."

"I'll go, too," the *rabbanit* said. "Miriam and Diane may also need me."

They left, but before Frau Sarah could take over the plans for *Chanukah*, Dominik asked, "Is the Rabbi going to administer the Last Rites?"

David answered him, "Jews don't actually have formal last rites. Instead, if Herr Weiss is conscious, he'll say the *Shema*. Religious Jews recite it twice a day as a *mitzvah*. Parents teach their children to say it before they go to sleep. The family might be keeping a vigil at Herr Weiss's bedside, reciting *tehillim*. And both my uncle and my aunt will comfort the family."

"What are the Last Rites in the Catholic Church?" Karl asked Dominik.

Dominik looked at them and then replied automatically, "For Extreme Unction, or Last Rites, the priest puts a long stole with religious symbols around his neck. '*Viaticum*' is Latin for provision for the journey. It's one of the Seven Sacraments initiated by Jesus.

It uses oil blessed by a bishop or archbishop. The priest places his hands on the head of the sick person and then says a prayer over the already blessed oil or, if necessary, blesses the oil himself. The actual anointing of the sick person is done on the forehead, eyelids, ears, nostrils, lips, hands, feet with the prayer 'Per istam sanctam Unctiónem et suam piisimam misericórdiam, indúlgeat tibi Dóminus quidquid per visum, audtiotum, odorátum, gustum et locutiónem, tactum, gressum deliquisti.' If he can, the sick person responds 'Amen'."

Frau Sarah was as astonished as the teenagers. "Thank you, Dominik," she said. "Now let's talk about the Chanukah celebrations."

The next morning the four teens walked to school, and Dominik went to see the headmaster. David said, "Good luck. Remember, he's a nice guy."

Frau Kleiner, the headmaster's secretary, looked up when the door opened. "Go right in, Dominik. He's expecting you," she said with a smile.

"Thank you." He opened the door. "Good morning, sir," he said.

"And good morning to you, Dominik. Come sit down," the headmaster said. He steepled his fingers on his desk and looked at the nervous boy who sat at the very edge of his chair. "Dominik Müller, what am I going to do with you? Even if you're only with us for a short time, I'd like learning to be a challenge for you; I'm sure you feel the same way. A few teachers thought the classes you attended yesterday were far too easy for you. So I'm putting together a different program. Maybe English literature and since you're so good with languages, an Arabic class where you'll learn to read as well as speak. You'll continue grammar and writing in German, of course. Are you interested in a music appreciation course? Austria has produced some great composers – Mozart, Schubert, Mahler, but our course includes German composers, too: Bach, Beethoven, Brahms, Mendelssohn."

The headmaster could see Dominik was thrilled at the possibilities. He'd relaxed, sitting deeper in his chair. "That will be wonderful, sir," he said.

"Good. Now there's space for 'Ethics from Aristotle to the Present' which we couldn't fit in yesterday. I think you'll learn a lot, although they've gone past Aristotle at this point," the headmaster added. "I'll print the schedule and write a note to each teacher and you'll be able to join the next class this morning – the Ethics class. Good luck, Dominik, I hope this turns into a worthwhile experience for you – and for us."

Dominik was almost walking on air when he entered the room of the Ethics class. He handed the note from the headmaster to Herr Gottfried, the instructor, and looked at the students filing into the room. David was one of the students. Herr Gottfried introduced Dominik and then said, "Gunther, please move elsewhere so Dominik can sit next to David. Thank you."

Not only the Ethics class, but the rest of the day passed like a dream. Even though his friends weren't in any of his other classes, Dominik knew he had so much to learn, and he'd very gladly accept the challenges. After his last class of the day, his ears were ringing with the rich tones of Bach's "Chaconne". Frau Hummell told them the 15-minute Chaconne was usually considered the pinnacle of the violin repertoire as it covered every aspect of the violin known in Bach's time. She said it was rewritten numerous times for other instruments after Bach, and she played parts of several different versions – flute, guitar, piano and a full orchestra version – but Dominik liked the violin solo best. He couldn't pinpoint one particular highlight of his day, but he felt elated by everything. When his friends met him outside after school, Dominik was smiling broadly and Karl teased, "Look at him. Where is Dominik and who has taken over his body?"

Dominik laughed and said, "This has been such a fantastic day that I don't know what to say."

"Don't say anything," Karl joked. "We'll get it out of you later. Let's go, or as Dom would say, *'Vamanos!'*" They all laughed as they made their way home. Dominik was shocked to realize he was beginning to think of the Rabbi's flat as home.

Frau Sarah had snacks on the table when they arrived home, joking and laughing. She was delighted to see Dominik so happy, but she was also concerned he might be too euphoric. The change from his previous situation to the current one was so extreme he might not realize he was in danger of totally breaking all ties, not only with the Church but also with his mother. She made a mental note to discuss her worries with the Rabbi. "Dinner in two hours," she said as the teenagers went to their rooms to change out of their uniforms and start their homework. She heard Dominik ask David if he could borrow the book for their Ethics assignment.

After dinner, they all sat in the Rabbi's study and finalized their jobs for the *Chanukah* celebration. When they'd all said their goodnights, the Rabbi asked Dominik to stay. "How did everything go today, Dominik?"

"I can't even begin to tell you how fabulous it was…like something out of a fairy tale," Dominik replied, a huge smile on his face. "The headmaster, my classes, the Bach 'Chaconne' ... everything was perfect!"

"Frau Sarah said you were bubbling with excitement when you came home. And she's worried, as am I," the Rabbi said seriously. "I have an American friend who's taught me many of their expressions. One I always remember is 'Don't rain on my parade!' I don't want to rain on your parade, Dominik, and I'm pleased today was 'perfect'. But I also don't want you to forget you have a mother who loves you even though she's angry right now. And a grandmother. And a different school and social structure. Enjoy what today was and tomorrow will be. But you have a major decision to make. I don't want you to think for even a minute that I would ask you to leave, but I also don't want you to put the decision too far back in your mind. OK?"

"I won't forget, sir," Dominik said in an equally serious tone, but added cheekily, "You were the one who told me not to make a major decision while standing on one leg! Good night, Rabbi."

The rabbi laughed heartily as Dominik left. "Saucy lad!" he thought. After a minute, he picked up the phone to call Deborah's parents in Zurich. When his father-in-law answered the phone, he said, "I want to wish you a very good trip, Papá. And *'Chag Chanukah Sameach!'* Please give my warm regards to Aaron and Rena and the children. And, last but not least, enjoy the warmth of Eretz Yisrael and forget the winter of Switzerland. We'll miss you, of course, but we know you're in good hands." He exchanged similar words with Deborah's mother and then asked if his wife was there. "She left a few minutes ago. She'll call you when she gets home. Happy Chanukah, Samuel. We'll see you next month, *baruch ha shem*."

The rabbi sat in his study with a small glass of cognac, pondering the enigma of Dominik as he waited for Deborah's call. A few minutes later, the phone rang and she said, "Hello my darling. Please tell me everyone is well and then tell me the latest news about your 'temporary resident'."

They spoke for more than half an hour and the Rabbi told her all about Dominik's "perfect" day. "I reminded him he mustn't forget he has a serious decision to make. And he, cheeky lad, reminded me I'd told him not to make a serious decision while standing on one leg."

Deborah laughed, "Cheeky indeed, which I like, given his situation at the moment! He has a good head on those thin shoulders, so I know he'll make the right decision. Not necessarily what we'd like or what his mother wants, but what's right for him. We'll talk again tomorrow and I'll be back in my second home on Thursday by noon.

Chapter 2

Is everything set? I have a *Chanukah* treat for all the children attending the party."

"Of course everything's set. We've got the extremely efficient Frau Sarah Bernhardt organizing everything, even though it's so difficult for her when it involves so many young people. Good night, my love."

For Dominik the next day was a wonderful repeat of the previous day. He enjoyed his classes, his friends…even the weather. But in the evening, after dinner with the Rabbi, Frau Sarah and the other teens, he spent a long time thinking about his situation. Although he was still very upset about his mother, he missed her a lot. He wondered, *"If I go back, will it ever be the same? Will she make me go back to the Domkirche School? I know I want to be with her, but I also know I don't want to go back to that school! And not to the Catholic church. It's parochial and bigoted. The rabbi says it's only dogma, and all religions have to accept many things on faith. But the monsignor and the priests are not just dogmatic; they're narrow-minded and totally closed to someone who isn't sure of what he should believe. I know this is my dilemma, and I know I'll find my way…but not tonight."* He picked up the Ethics book he'd been reading earlier to prepare for the next day's lesson on Maimonides and St. Francis of Assisi.

Thursday's school day was as gratifying for Dominik as the previous day. He learned about Maimonides and he answered questions about St. Francis; his Ethics instructor was satisfied. He recognized Bach's "B-Minor Mass" from the Domkirche, but when he listened to it in his music class, it seemed special. He corrected Herr Bremen's English twice, not nine times. *"Maybe he'll do **his** homework more carefully,"* Dominik thought, *"and I won't have to correct him at all."* He didn't like showing off in class, and he liked it even less when his corrections made other students laugh at the teacher, but he couldn't let the mistakes stand in a class trying hard to learn English.

When the youngsters returned from school, the *rabbanit* was there. She greeted them and said, "We don't have a lot of time before we must be at the synagogue…so have your snack, dash to change out of your uniforms, and we'll be off. The rabbi and Frau Sarah are already there."

At the *shul*, Dominik noticed the seven-branched brass menorah had been moved to the corner of the *bimah*; and the Rabbi was standing near a larger menorah with one tall branch in the middle and four branches on each side. David told him this menorah was a *chanukiah*, and it represented the eight days of Chanukah, with the tall branch in the center standing for the one bottle of oil that lasted eight days. The rabbi greeted them and told them Frau Sarah needed them downstairs in the Hebrew school's auditorium where the party after the candle-lighting would be held. The teens went downstairs to a lot of noise and bustling as several people set up tables while others moved chairs around the walls. Frau Sarah was placing a few hotplates heated by candles on tables and mothers were unpacking boxes of powdered-sugar and jelly donuts. Ruth said she'd arrange the donuts, telling the boys in her cheeky way, "I'll do this because you'll eat them all before they're even on the tables. Ask Frau Sarah what she wants you to do." Each of the boys grabbed a donut and then asked Frau Sarah what they should do. She handed David a box of drawings and a roll of masking tape and pointed to *chanukiot* made by children in the Hebrew classes. She told them to hang the drawings around the room and to put the *chanukiot* on the shelf along the back wall, taping the name of the child who made it in front of each.

While they were hanging the drawings, Dominik said, "I don't know much about *Chanukah* except that it's a happy holiday. Can you fill me in?"

"Sure," David answered. "In 198 BCE, the land of Israel became part of the Seleucid Empire. At first, the king, Antiochus III, allowed the Jews to be autonomous, but later he began a program of Hellenization that would force the Jews to abandon monotheism for paganism. He backed down when the Jews objected to idols in their temples, but Antiochus IV, who inherited the throne in 176 BCE, issued a decree forbidding all religious practice. Jewish worship was forbidden, Torah scrolls were burned, Sabbath as a day of rest, circumcision and *kashrut* were prohibited under penalty of death. Rabbi Eliezer, 90 years old, was ordered by Antiochus's servants to eat pork so others would do the same. When he refused, they killed him. A Jewish family known as the Maccabees – Mattathias, a priest, and his five sons – refused to worship the idols and sparked a revolt in 167 BCE. After Mattathias' death a year later, his son Judah led an army of Jews to victory over the Seleucids. The Maccabees destroyed pagan altars, circumcised boys and sent Hellenized Jews into exile. In two years, the Maccabees succeeded in many battles by using guerrilla tactics."

Karl interrupted, "The Maccabees were great and Judah was brilliant!"

"Anyway," David continued, "after their victory, the Maccabees entered Jerusalem in triumph, ritually cleansed the Temple, removed the idols and reestablished traditional Jewish worship. Jonathan

Chapter 2

Maccabee became High Priest. Since the golden Menorah had been stolen, the Maccabees had a new one made. But when they went to light it, they found only one small bottle of pure olive oil with the seal of the former High Priest – enough for only one day. Somehow it burned for eight days, until they were able to acquire new oil. Later, the Maccabees established the Hasmonean dynasty which ruled the Land of Israel from 164 to 63 BCE."

"Wow!" Dominik said. "That's some story."

"Yes, it is. And because of it, and to remember it, our sages made it an eight-day celebration every year, lighting candles and eating oily food like donuts, *sufganiyot* in Hebrew, and potato *latkes*," David added. "Frau Sarah serves those with applesauce and they're delicious." By the time David had finished the story, they'd hung all the drawings and Frau Sarah was placing *latkes* on the hotplates while Ruth put bowls of apple sauce on the tables. The *rabbanit* came downstairs and placed a few packages under a table. She said it all looked wonderful, but it was time for candle-lighting upstairs.

The sanctuary was filled with families sitting together. Dominik saw the Rabbi had placed 2 candles in the *chanukiah*. After welcoming everyone, he removed the tall center candle, accepted a long match from the *chazzan* and lighted the candle; then he used it to light the first candle on the right. "The candle the Rabbi is holding is called the *shamash*," David whispered.

"I guess the *shamash* represents the one bottle of oil that lasted all eight days," Dominik said. "Fantastic!"

The rabbi then chanted the three *Chanukah* blessings, and the *chazzan* and the congregation began to sing *"Maoz-Tzur"*, which Dominik knew as "Rock of Ages", even though he didn't understand the Hebrew words. When they'd finished singing, the Rabbi invited everyone to the Chanukah party downstairs. After everyone filled their plates with *latkes* and *sufganiyot*, and they were drinking hot cider, the *rabbanit* opened the packages she had brought from Zurich and distributed little bags of chocolate coins. Proud parents walked around the room looking at their children's drawings and *chanukiot*. Older children were sitting at tables in the back playing with *dreidels* and "gambling" with raisins. Once Karl explained all the rules, Dominik collected a mountain of raisins. "I'm just lucky," he said, although he wasn't referring only to the game. At 9:00, the Rabbi announced, "Good night, everyone. Tomorrow's a school day. *Chag Chanukah Sameach.*"

The *rabbanit* told the teens to walk home and finish their

homework. "Frau Sarah and I, with the Rabbi and the *chazzan*, will straighten up down here. Good night and *Chag Chanukah Sameach*," she added.

Walking back to the Rabbi's flat, Ruth asked Dominik what he thought of the party. "Fabulous!" he said. "There's nothing like it in my church."

"Not even Christmas?" Ruth asked. "All the beautiful decorations and gifts? Some people call *Chanukah* the 'Jewish Christmas'!"

"It's not very special in my family. Church services on Christmas Eve and Christmas day are very long…too long. We have a tree and dinner, but not like Shabbat here. And no one challenges my grandfather's opinions."

The other teens were quiet as they went into the flat, all feeling a little sad. "We've got school tomorrow, so let's do our homework," David said.

They had ten days before the Christmas break and Dominik was in love. He loved every minute in school, especially the challenges in some classes, and he loved most of his classmates, even the bully who was now a friend. He loved going to the synagogue every night during the remaining days of *Chanukah* to light the candles, and then coming home for potato *latkes* or jelly donuts. He loved the atmosphere, especially the evenings in the Rabbi's study, even though there were so many things he didn't understand about how one studies *Torah*. He loved Frau Sarah, her obvious caring, and, of course, the meals she prepared. He loved Rabbi and Rabbanit Breitling. He loved his close friends, David, Karl and especially Ruth. Whenever he thought about his deadline, he missed his mother, so he tried to ignore it.

During the school holidays, the *rabbanit* took the teens on a skiing trip to Modriach, an hour away from Graz. David was a good skier but the others were beginners; Dominik loved skiing, and knew he would welcome any opportunity in the future to ski. The *rabbanit* then took them to Vienna for three days, where they stayed in the luxurious home of the Breitlings' good friends, the Goldblums. They were sightseers every day, ogling the vibrant Christmas decorations; exploring the Museum of Art, the Imperial Treasury in Hofburg Palace, the national library, and city hall. The first evening, the Goldblums took them to *Die Josefstadt*, the oldest theatre still functioning in Vienna; Saul Goldblum told them Beethoven had performed there. They had dinner in two kosher restaurants: *Alef-Alef*, where Ruth was delighted to find Israeli foods on the menu. She said they'd love *felafel* – deep-fried chickpea balls; the second restaurant, Novellino's, was more elegant. After dinner, they toured Schoenbrunn Palace and attended a concert of Mozart and Schubert music. All of them enjoyed the entire trip, but Dominik felt guilty knowing how much it cost. The *rabbanit* refused to take any money. "It's an early Christmas gift," she said with a smile. Dominik thanked her profusely. After a final lunch with the Goldblums, they drove back to Graz, sorry to leave Vienna, but far more cheerful when the *rabbanit* said Jakob would be staying until New Year's Eve and they'd have fun in Graz.

On Christmas Day, Dominik called his grandparents' house to speak to his mother, but his grandfather hung up as soon as he recognized Dominik's voice. Recalling all the *rabbanit*'s Christmas gifts to him – the ski trip, the museums, the theatre and concert, the restaurants, he was distraught when he told her what had happened. "I know it was terrible, Dominik, but they're all still waiting for your decision. As our American friend would say, 'the ball is in your court'." Although he'd tried so hard to ignore his situation, Dominik knew he'd have to decide soon, especially after the Christmas Day fiasco. He weighed what was more important: on one side, in order to live with his mother, he would apologize to Monsignor Dietrich and return to the Domkirche, and not question the dogma of the Church; on the other side, he would study in classes that offered challenges to him and live with people who allowed him to voice his opinions. He knew that the Rabbi was willing to discuss all this with him, but he also knew that the Rabbi wanted him to make his own decision.

At last, on New Year's Day 1997, Dominik tapped on the Rabbi's study door. "Come in," the Rabbi said. When he saw Dominik, he added, "Happy New Year. This isn't the Jewish new year, *Rosh Hashanah*, but I know that you've always celebrated the new year on the first of January."

Looking very pale and a little sad, Dominik said quietly, "Thank you, Rabbi. I've reached a decision, and not standing on one leg." He grinned.

"Cheeky lad," the *rabbanit* said with a smile. "Do you want to speak to the Rabbi alone? I can find something to do elsewhere."

"No, please stay. I know you also want to know what I've decided. I love my mother and I really miss her. She's always been good to me… until now. But I can't go back to the Domkirche or apologize for just asking questions. Here we can disagree and no one is called a heretic. I love a challenge, like some of my classes. Will you let me stay?" He brushed away a few tears.

"If it were only up to me, of course," the Rabbi said. "But you know we'll have to discuss this with your mother and Monsignor Dietrich."

The next morning the Rabbi telephoned Dominik's mother. "Happy New Year, Frau Müller," he said. "I'm phoning to tell you Dominik has made a decision about his future after careful deliberation. We'd like to meet with you to discuss everything. I think Dominik should be at this meeting and he won't go into the church at this time. There's a café down the block from the synagogue. Can we meet there later this afternoon?"

"All right," she said a little hesitantly. "But I won't come alone. I'll ask my attorney and the monsignor, if he can make it. Is 4:00 acceptable?"

"That's fine. We'll see you there at four o'clock," the Rabbi said.

◆ ◆ ◆

A few minutes before 4:00, Rabbi Breitling and Dominik walked into the café and took a secluded table for six people. The rabbi ordered coffee for himself and a hot chocolate for Dominik. A few minutes later, Frederica Müller, Advocate Obermann, and the young priest who'd been at the first meeting with Rabbi Breitling arrived. Dominik went to embrace his mother, but she backed away, looking sad. He sat down, clearly disappointed. The attorney spoke first. "Have you reached a decision, Dominik?"

"I have, sir." Dominik replied. "I can't go back to the Domkirche school and I can't stop asking questions."

"Then I have no son!" Frederica said.

At the same time, the priest burst out, "I knew you were an apostate, maybe even the Antichrist. You will be excommunicated, you know, and you'll end your life in Hell!" Frederica gasped at the priest's words.

The rabbi put his hand on Dominik's arm and said quietly, "Everything will be all right, Dominik."

"Maybe for you, Rabbi, because you'll have another convert. But not for Dominik, not for his mother – and certainly not for God!" the priest said.

Adv. Obermann said, "This is a sad day for all of us, Father Erich, but I know Rabbi Breitling is not looking for another convert. Frau Müller, we'll have to give the Rabbi full legal guardianship until Dominik is 18 and we'll work out some financial assistance for the boy. The court will insist on that. Rabbi Breitling, I'll get back to you when the legal work is completed." He looked at Frederica and the priest, and added, "We should go now."

Chapter 2

After they left, the Rabbi looked at Dominik and said, "I know this is very hard, but trust me. In time, things will work out. Now finish your chocolate or drink some water and let's go home. You have school tomorrow."

"She couldn't even look at me. She's my mother and we really only have each other. How can she be like that?"

The rabbi smiled. "She's in shock, too, Dominik. Give her time. She's an intelligent woman and she'll come around. If she can't accept your decision today, at least she'll recognize your right to decide your own future."

Neither of them would have believed it would be fifteen years before Dominik and his mother saw or spoke to each other again.

◆ ◆ ◆

At dinner that night, the Rabbi told all of them that Dominik would be living there permanently. Frau Sarah smiled and the teens started to cheer before noticing the sadness on Dominik's face. Then, even Ruth refrained from teasing, but their broad smiles showed how happy they were.

Four unusually quiet teens returned to school the next day, accompanied by Rabbi and Rabbanit Breitling. In his office, the headmaster stood up, and shook hands with them, saying, "Since both of you have come, I assume we have a permanent new student."

"Good morning, Herr Doktor Schneider," the Rabbi said. "Yes, Dominik will be staying on. I have legal guardianship, and it will be made permanent until he's 18. I'm also responsible for any school expenses you require."

"And I'm responsible for Dominik's proper uniforms and anything else he needs," the *rabbanit* added.

"I'll have his fees waived. I'm sorry we can't send the bill for everything to Monsignor Dietrich. I couldn't believe how he verbally attacked 'the boy' when I spoke with him, never calling Dominik by name.

The rabbi didn't say anything but remembered how annoyed he'd been in his conversations with the monsignor. "I'm sure this will work out well for all of us," he said, "especially for Dominik."

"I agree, Rabbi. The *Bundesrealgymnasium* is fortunate to have him as a student. I just hope Dominik doesn't challenge some of the teachers into leaving, although I wouldn't be too upset if a few of them opt for early retirement," the headmaster said with a smile.

♦ ♦ ♦

The next four years seemed to pass quickly for the Rabbi's "family". His older son, Jakob, completed his rabbinical studies and moved to Israel in order to improve his conversational Hebrew and to look into the possibility of making *Aliyah*. His younger son, Daniel, returned from his adventures in South America and began studying medicine at the University of Zurich, UZH. Ruth, David, and Karl, all a year older than Dominik, graduated from high school in 1999, after normal teenage experiences – success in sports and clubs: football, chess and debating for David; choir, school musicals, and basketball for Karl, drama club costumes, the school's newspaper and yearbook for Ruth. There were parties, romances ending with a "broken heart" which somehow healed quickly, synagogue activities, and *leining Torah* with the Rabbi. After graduation, they pursued individual academic paths quite far away from Graz, although they visited frequently. Ruth had completed her studies with the Rabbi and converted to Judaism; in her last two years in *Bundesrealgymnasium*, she'd concentrated on French and was studying jewelry design at La Cambre Ecole Nationale Supérieure des Arts Visuels in Brussels and working part-time with a fashion reporter of a local newspaper. David was at the Medical University of Vienna, one of Europe's oldest medical faculties. Karl was studying music, both classical and jazz, at University Mozarteum in Salzburg; he was also in their choir. Living away from the Rabbi's house, the synagogue and each other was hard for all of them, but they stayed in touch by e-mail and they coordinated their visits home for holidays. Dominik missed them enormously; there was no one else to pal around with, no one to laugh with, no one to tease. Frau Sarah told the Rabbi she thought Dominik was almost as depressed as he'd been when he first came to the Rabbi's home. The *rabbanit* said that was natural in a way. After the separation from his mother, his great "loss", the other teens became his "siblings" psychologically.

When he was seventeen, Dominik started the conversion process under the tutelage of Rabbi Breitling. One evening, when they were in the Rabbi's study, the Rabbi asked Dominik if he ever thought about finding his father. "It shouldn't be too difficult," he said. "How many young Iranians were studying for a PhD in philosophy at the University of Vienna in the early 1980s?" It was surprisingly easy, just a few phone calls and they located him. Darian Sarkohi was a philosophy professor at Tabriz University, one of the top schools in Iran, a frequent contributor to the Iranian magazine, *Adineh*, married and the father of two daughters. Dominik said he'd like to meet his father, grandmother, stepmother, half-sisters – his Iranian family.

On one of his visits to Zurich, the Rabbi contacted Professor Sarkohi who was shocked to learn about Dominik. He said he remembered Frederica, of course; he had tried to contact her after he returned to Iran, but her father wouldn't allow him to speak to her; the last time he called, Herr Müller said she was dead. The rabbi suggested a meeting in Zurich during Dominik's school holidays. Professor Sarkohi said he would arrange to give a lecture at UZH and he would book a flight and a room at Hotel Schweizerhof. They agreed to meet during Dominik's next school break. The rabbi accompanied Dominik to their first meeting, a bit surprised by the strong resemblance between father and son, although he thought Dominik resembled his mother as well. The rabbi introduced himself, chatted for a few minutes and left. The meeting was strained for only a few minutes; then neither Dominik nor his father, thrilled at encountering each other, could stop talking. Professor Sarkohi was impressed with Dominik's facility with languages, even a little Farsi. "Of course I shouldn't be surprised," he said, "Your mother is a very good linguist so you come by your talent naturally. Those years in Armenia also offered many other languages to you, and your stepfather sounds like a good man, but I can understand that Yerevan wasn't the right place for your mother. Still, it's remarkable that you picked up so many languages at such a young age. Chess and debating, hmm? We'll have to play sometime. And maybe we'll correspond in Farsi. My mother, your *mâdarbozorg*, will be thrilled to talk to you in Farsi even though her English is outstanding!" He was sorry to hear about Dominik's problems with the Domkirche priests and his total estrangement from his mother. "Although we live in Tabriz and it's several hundred miles away from Tehran, fortunately for us, we're familiar with religious dogma and fanatics who rigidly accept the tenets and biases of Islam. I know that your grandfather was rigid and domineering and your mother was afraid of him. It's sad. Rabbi Breitling seems to be a fine man, so open to new ideas, and I'm happy that you have enjoyed living with him and your friends in Graz. I'm not even surprised that you want to convert to Judaism. Judaism doesn't sound extreme in any way," he said with a wink, "and I know that Rabbi Breitling wouldn't let you make such a decision while standing on one leg!"

Dominik told his father he planned to go to Israel for at least a year after he graduated from high school and to go through a second conversion in the Holy Land. But he hoped they'd meet again soon. "We can stay in touch by e-mail. I'll open an account from the Rabbi's home," he said, and explained why the Rabbi's synagogue was in Graz but his 'real home' was in Zurich. "The rabbi's wife is wonderful; she's like a second mother to all of us. And their sons, Jakob and Daniel, are like brothers to me. But David, the Rabbi's nephew, is my 'real' older brother."

His father said, "Dominik. I'm proud to call you my son, and I'll try to arrange opportunities for us to see each other here, perhaps by setting up additional meetings at the university, but it isn't easy given what life is like in Iran now. Maybe next time I'll be able to bring your *mâdarbozorg* for 'special medical treatment' in Switzerland; she'll be delighted to meet her only grandson." They did meet twice more before Dominik went to Israel; he met his grandmother who was warm and open, so different from what he remembered of his Austrian grandmother. That meeting took place shortly after Dominik completed his conversion to Judaism, and his grandmother wanted to know all about it. He described his studies with the Rabbi and how much he'd learned, the test administered by the Rabbinical Court, and the *Mikveh*, but he didn't tell her about his circumcision; although he'd been circumcised at birth in London, he was still required to undergo a symbolic ritual, *hatafat dam brit*. His grandmother was fascinated by Judaism; she told him that true Islam welcomed Jews as older brothers; unfortunately, the extremists in Iran hated Jews and Israel. At their final meeting in Zurich, his father said he wished he and his family could leave Iran, but he knew it was an impossible dream. Before they parted, his father said, "Fare thee well, my dear son. We'll meet again, but who knows when or where."

Chapter 3

On Dominik's 18th birthday, the Rabbi's legal guardianship ended, as did the allowance from his mother who still refused to see him. He had saved most of his allowance because the Breitlings wouldn't let him contribute to the household expenses. When he'd insisted, the *rabbanit* hugged him and said, "My dear Dominik, you've become as precious to us as David; we wouldn't take money from him, and we won't accept any from you."

After graduating from the *Bundesrealgymnasium* in June, 2000, Dominik decided to work until his 18th birthday in order to add more to his savings for Israel. Two young boys from dysfunctional families came to live with the Rabbi, and Dominik tutored them in their schoolwork and Hebrew. Herr Doktor Schneider, who'd always appreciated Dominik's intelligence and talent for languages, offered him several paid tutoring assignments, and his bank account – his "Israeli nest-egg" – increased significantly. Even though Dominik's teenage comrades were all studying in different places, they all managed to come to Graz between Rosh Hashanah and Yom Kippur 2000 and the Breitling *"mishpacha,"* except for Jakob who was in Israel, spent the High Holy Days together; since he'd be moving to Israel shortly, this was particularly meaningful for Dominik as he didn't know when he would see all his friends again. He wanted to improve his proficiency in spoken Hebrew, so he decided to go to Kibbutz Sde Eliyahu, where the conversion studies were in Hebrew. In keeping with Sde Eliyahu's philosophy that a *giur*'s values and identity were influenced by the conversion process, it had to be experienced not only intellectually but also emotionally, personally, socially and nationally. The Jewish way of life had to be lived; therefore, conversion wasn't limited only to studying Judaism. Chuckling, Dominik thought, *"Like with every other thing in my life, I won't be able to make the decision to convert a second time to Judaism while standing on one leg!"*

In November, Dominik moved to Israel. Since he didn't know anyone in Israel except Jakob Breitling, he called Jakob and asked to stay with him for a couple of days in order to prepare all the documents that he would require. Jakob met him at the airport and told him they were going on Dominik's first tour of Jerusalem, the eternal city. "We'll have to be careful about where we go because, as you know, what has become known as the Second Intifada has caused a lot of violence on both the Israeli and Palestinian sides. But I know you've seen pictures of Jerusalem, Dom, yet there's nothing like being there and seeing it yourself." From the entrance to the city, Jakob drove them straight to the observation area on Mount Scopus. They got out of the car and walked to the low wall; Jakob started pointing out the walls around the Old City, the golden Dome of the Rock and the almost black dome of al-Aksa mosque. He pointed to Hebrew University behind them and the magnificent building of the nearby Mormon Center as well as Augusta Victoria Hospital with its tall bell-tower built in the early 20th century by the German Kaiser in honor of his wife. Dominik just stood there, agog, with tears pouring down his face. "Let's go around to the other observation point and if we're lucky, we'll be able to see the Dead Sea," Jakob said. "Then, if the security services will allow us, we'll drive past Augusta Victoria and over to the Mount of Olives. OK?" Speechless, Dominik just nodded. It wasn't clear enough to see the Dead Sea, but they were able to discern the Moav Mountains on the other side, in Jordan. Nobody stopped them, so Jakob then drove past Augusta Victoria and straight through to the observation point on the Mount of Olives; they parked and stepped out of the car. There were a few tourists focusing their cameras on the panoramic view directly in front of them, one middle-aged Arab man with a camel, and two soldiers with guns. The Arab man asked them if they wanted a ride on the camel for five US dollars and Dominik answered, "Not today, thank you" in perfect Hebrew. As they stood at the railing, Jakob pointed out the Jewish cemetery right below them and then the astonishing view of the Old City with its surrounding walls and the Temple Mount, the Dome of the Rock and al-Aksa mosque, the sealed Golden Gate, the stairs leading up into the Jewish Quarter, and in the distance, modern Jerusalem. "We can't see the Kotel (Western Wall) from here but maybe we'll be able to go there tomorrow or the next time you come to Jerusalem," Jakob said. As they drove down Sultan Suleiman Street, the long road from the Mount of Olives to West Jerusalem that bordered the Old City walls on one side and mostly Arab-inhabited East Jerusalem on the other, Jakob pointed out the magnificent British colonial style white limestone Rockefeller Museum – the initial location of the Dead Sea Scrolls – on the right, and first the New Gate and then the Damascus Gate into the Old City on the left. As they passed the beautiful old Notre Dame Church known for its comfortable guesthouse and superb restaurant and approached Jaffa road, Jakob asked, "Are you hungry?" He turned right onto Jaffa Road and headed into downtown Jerusalem when Dominik said he was. They parked the car in a lot on Hillel Street next to a movie theatre and crossed the street to Ta'ami

– the best humus and falafel restaurant in Jerusalem according to Jakob. Dominik told Jakob that he'd eaten humus and falafel when Jakob's mother had taken him and the other kids staying with Rabbi Breitling to Vienna on vacation and Ruth had insisted that they eat in Vienna's only Israeli restaurant; he added that he loved the food then, but this was infinitely better. After their meal, they went to Jakob's flat on Bustenai Street and settled in for the evening with some chat and some prayer.

Jakob had arranged to take a couple of days off from work, so he gave Dominik a personal tour of Jerusalem. In the morning after breakfast, they drove to the Old City and parked in the big lot across from the Jaffa Gate. As they entered the square inside the gate, Jakob said they would get to the Christian Quarter and the Holy Sepulchre if they took the road to the left, to the Armenian Quarter if they went to the right past David's Tower, and to the Muslim Quarter and the Jewish Quarter and finally to the Kotel if they went straight ahead. Dominik chose the last option and they walked down the colorful "shuk" with its many shops selling souvenirs, jewelry, clothing, trinkets and spices of all kinds. At the bottom they passed by the grand fountain and columns in the Muristan area and the Lutheran Church of the Holy Redeemer and then turned into the Jewish Quarter, passing Crusader ruins. Dominik was astounded at how crowded the quarter was until they finally reached the bottom of the stairs and the area opened into the enlarged plaza of the Kotel. They passed through a security barrier and both young men approached the men's side of the ancient wall.

Dominik closed his eyes and then took a deep breath; when he opened his eyes he reached into his pocket and took out a small note he had written the previous night and stuffed it into a small crevice above his head in the Kotel. Then both of them spent a few minutes in prayer. Jakob asked Dominik if he wanted to go into the tunnel under the Temple Mount and he instantly agreed. They entered the tunnel's southern entrance, walked the tunnel's entire length and exited from the northern end on the Via Dolorosa in the Muslim Quarter. Chuckling, Dominik thought, *"How many of the hypocritical priests in my old Domkirche School would believe that I'm walking up the street where Jesus carried his cross on the way to his crucifixion?"* He winked at Jakob but didn't say anything. At the top of the ancient stair-like road, after passing numerous stations of the cross, Jakob asked Dominik if he wanted to go into the Holy Sepulchre, but he declined, so they found their way through the Christian Quarter back to the Jaffa Gate and then to the car. As they drove away, Dominik said, "That was exciting, exhilarating and exalting and I for one expect an expresso after that exhausting experience," Jakob, knowing that Dominik had been deeply affected by his first sight of the Kotel, nevertheless teased his friend for his alliterative ability and said that, without exaggeration, they had barely touched the surface of what there was to see in the Old City, but they would leave it for another day, grab that extremely strong cuppa, and explore some of the extraordinary sights of modern Jerusalem. In good spirits they drove to Caffit, one of Jakob's favorite cafés in the Germany Colony, where they enjoyed coffee and a pastry as Dominik came down from his emotional high in the Old City. Then they drove up to Rehov Palmach, passed the Islamic Museum and the Jerusalem Theatre complex and continued to Fichman and Tchernichovsky Streets and through the Valley of the Cross to the Knesset, the building housing Israel's Parliament.

"It's very impressive," Dominik said. "And the tall buildings near here and all the trees are impressive, too. So different from the tightly closed-in feeling in Old City. The Knesset itself looks sort of like the Parthenon in Greece – but it's closed in, not open pillars." Jakob told him that was the idea when the Rothschilds commissioned the building – to make it resemble the cradle of democracy. But at a party in the penthouse of one of those tall buildings you mentioned, someone remarked that a person with a high-powered rifle would be able to see right into the plenum of the Knesset. A few days later, full-grown trees were brought in and planted in order to block that view. He said there are Knesset tours on Sundays, Mondays and Tuesdays – and that the Chagall tapestries are really worth seeing. They couldn't get really close to the Knesset right then for security reasons but they were able to stop near the huge bronze menorah in the rose garden opposite the entrance. Jakob said it was based on the gold menorah in the Temple in Jerusalem and the branches are engraved with the history of the Jewish people. After allowing that very brief stop, the soldier on duty told them to move. They did and after pointing out all the government office buildings opposite, Jakob drove across the main road to the Israel Museum.

"Let's go in," he said. "You'll be fascinated." They started their tour with the Shrine of the Book, the unusual white-domed building with its displays of facsimiles of the Isaiah scroll, dating from the second century BCE, the most intact of the Dead Sea Scrolls, and the Aleppo Codex, dating from the 10th century CE, the oldest existing Hebrew Bible; the originals being too fragile to be exposed even in the temperature-controlled environment of the Shrine. They then walked through the Billy Rose Art Garden, designed by Japanese-American sculptor Isamu Noguchi. Reading the Museum's brochure, Dominik learned that the uniqueness of the garden was its resemblance to a Zen garden with its ground covered in gravel, its small rock gardens with indigenous plants and its terraces reminiscent of the ancient agricultural activity in the Judean Hills. With more than 50 works from Billy Rose's collection, many of them of heroic size, including outstanding pieces by Rodin, Maillol, Daumier. Jacques Lipshitz and Sir Jacob Epstein, the garden is considered one of Noguchi's masterpieces – a synthesis of the cultures of the Far East, the Near East, and the West, against the backdrop of Jerusalem's dramatic landscape. Before they entered the museum itself, Jakob told Dominik that Billy Rose had donated the sculptures because he didn't want his greedy sisters to inherit them; they actually tried to have the will broken, but they lost and Israel kept the treasures. Inside the Museum itself, Dominik was astounded by the four full-sized synagogues – the elegant Italian Baroque synagogue from Vittorio Veneto that was built in 1700; the wooden synagogue from Horb in Germany built in the early 18th century, its walls and ceiling covered with paintings and inscriptions; the 18th century Tzedek ve-Shalom synagogue from South America, built by Spanish-Portuguese Jews who came from Holland to the New World; and the Kadavumbagam synagogue from the town of Cochin in southern India, built in the 16th century, a wooden structure with an exquisitely carved and painted ceiling influenced by the decorations of Hindu temples. He was amazed by the Torah niche from Isfahan, the Yemenite bride, as well as the extraordinary display of Torah cases and finials, Torah ark curtains, Torahs, Megillahs, Haggadot and Mezuzzahs from around the world. He marveled at the grandeur of the Rothschild salon from their family home in Paris that later became part of the American Embassy. When President and Mrs. Kennedy visited Paris, Jackie Kennedy was enthusiastic about the Rococo elegance of the 18th century salon but asked why so many of its furnishings, and objects d'art were replicas, not originals. The current Baron Edmond de Rothschild claimed the family had donated the contents of the room in memory of an earlier Baron Edmond de Rothschild known in Zionist history as HaNadiv (The Benefactor). As they walked away from that ornate room, Dominik said, "Enough! My head is exploding! It's on sensory overload!"

Jakob laughed and said, "OK. Let's go next door to Hebrew University. We'll walk around the Givat Ram campus and have a snack in the cafeteria and then we'll go to the sad but very significant finale of your Grand Tour of Jerusalem – Yad Vashem, Israel's Holocaust memorial." And that's what they did, with a half-hour stop at the Holyland Hotel in Beit Vegan to see the 1:50 scale model of the city of Jerusalem in the late Second Temple period (circa 66 CE at the height of the Jewish revolt against the Romans). Measuring 2,000 square meters (22,000 square feet), it was commissioned by the owner of the Holyland Hotel in memory of his son, an IDF soldier killed in the War of Independence in 1948. The model, which included a replica of the Herod's Temple, was designed by Israeli historian Michael Avi-Yonah based on the writings of Flavius Josephus and other historical sources. Born Yosef ben Matityahu in Jerusalem and fighting in the Jewish revolt until 67 CE, Josephus defected and was granted Roman citizenship, becoming an advisor and friend of the Emperor Vespasian's son Titus, serving as his translator when Titus led the Siege of Jerusalem in 70 CE. Since the siege proved ineffective at stopping the Jewish revolt, the city's destruction and the looting of Herod's Temple soon followed. Josephus recorded Jewish history, with special emphasis on the first century CE and the First Jewish-Roman War (66-70 CE), including the Siege of Masada.

From the Holyland Hotel, Jakob and Dominik went to Mount Herzl and Yad Vashem. A monument to the names of the murdered, Yad Vashem means "monument and name" in Hebrew; it took its name from Isaiah 56:5, "To all of them I erect a monument in my house and in my walls, I give them a name worth more than sons and daughters: I give them an eternal name that will never be erased."

Inside Yad Vashem, they walked around the Garden of the Righteous Among Nations, an impressive yet simple site of many trees integrated into the natural surroundings of the hill; the Garden also consists of a series of walls creating open rooms, where the names of all the Righteous who had no trees planted in their honor are engraved on the walls according to their countries of origin. By the time the Garden was dedicated in 1996, almost 14,000 Righteous had been honored, with new names added every year. Dominik and Jakob then entered the extremely imposing Hall of Remembrance with its walls made of basalt from the Sea of Galilee area, and an angular roof, giving it a tent-like shape. The names of 22 of the most infamous Nazi murder sites are engraved on the mosaic floor – symbolic of the hundreds of extermination and concentration camps, transit camps and killing sites throughout Europe. The Eternal Flame, that burns from a base resembling a broken bronze goblet, illuminates the Hall, its smoke exiting the building through an opening at the highest point of the ceiling. In front of the Eternal Flame, there's a stone crypt containing the ashes from the extermination camps of Holocaust victims, The official Holocaust Martyrs and Heroes Remembrance Day ceremony, had been held in front of the Hall of Remembrance until they created a large plaza, a more suitable venue for the large audience and televised ceremony. At one end of the large plaza there is a copy of Nathan Rapoport's Monument to the Warsaw Ghetto (the original is in Warsaw). The monument is composed of two bronze reliefs mounted on a red brick wall, symbolizing the ghetto walls. Between the reliefs is an inscription from Ezekiel 16:6 – *"bedamaich chayi"* (In your blood you shall live). The relief on the right, The Last March, depicts the mass deportation of Jews to the extermination camps – elderly people, children, women and men – emphasizing the indiscriminate nature of the deportation and extermination of European Jewry. The other relief portrays the Warsaw Ghetto Uprising. It shows men and women of all ages holding a range of weapons – a rifle, a stone, a dagger, a grenade. Their penultimate visit was to the Pillar of Heroism, a 21-meter-high pillar, its inscription stressing the concept of both the physical heroism of the fighters and the spiritual heroism of the martyrs. Finally, almost wiped out by emotion and exhaustion, they went to the Children's Monument. Funded by Abraham and Edith Spiegel of California, whose two-year-old son Uziel perished in Auschwitz, Yad Vashem had commissioned Moshe Safdie to design a memorial to the one-and-a-half million children murdered in the Holocaust. In the entrance area on a low hill, there are several white, broken off stelae of different heights, symbolizing the children whose lives were cut down at different ages by the murder madness of the Nazis. From there, a long, narrow passage leads to an iron door; next to it is Uziel Spiegel's face in relief. The door opens to a dark subterranean room. At its entrance there are black-and-white photographs of 9 children – 5 boys, including Uziel Spiegel, and 4 girls. In the center of the room, a glass case contains five lit candles. The flames are reflected by mirrors and prisms in the ceiling and the floor, producing innumerable dots of brilliant light in the glass walls, reminiscent of a starlit sky. While the spectators move through the room along a hand railing in the sparse light of the sky, somber music plays in the background, and voices in Hebrew, English and Yiddish recite the names, ages and places of origin of the youngest victims of the Third Reich's mania on an endless tape recording, which takes about three months to repeat all the names. To many visitors to Yad Vashem, these murders of babies, school-age youngsters and early teenagers are probably the most shocking extermination acts of the Shoah. Dominik and Jakob emerged from the Children's Memorial, weeping and white-faced, walked silently to the car and went home to Jakob's flat.

The following morning, after breakfast, the two young men said farewell. As he gave Jakob a brotherly bear hug, Dominik said, "The Talmud said, 'Ten measures of beauty were given to the world; Jerusalem received nine, while the rest of the world received one.' I've seen beautiful places, like Vienna, but nothing like Jerusalem. The Talmud was right. I know there is still so much more to see in this magical city – and I will – but I'll never forget these two days with you as my guide."

Taking his luggage with him, Dominik went to the Ministry of the Interior in the Generali Building in downtown Jerusalem. Since he'd already converted to Judaism under the authority of the Austrian Rabbinate, with the help of one of Rabbi Breitling's friends, he'd been allowed to enroll late in Kibbutz Sde Eliyahu's eight-month *Ulpan Giur*, which officially began in October immediately after *Sukkoth*. Named after Rabbi Eliyahu Guttmacher, an early leader of Religious Zionism, Sde Eliyahu, was one of three religious kibbutzim in the Jordan Valley, together with Ein Hanatziv and Tirat Zvi. It was founded in May 1939 as a Tower and Stockade settlement by refugees escaping from Nazi Germany. The establishment of new Jewish settlements was legally restricted by the Mandatory Palestine authorities, but the British generally gave tacit approval to the Tower and Stockade settlements as a means of countering the Arab Revolt. During the revolt from 1936 to 1939, these settlements provided safe havens on land purchased officially by Keren Kayemet LeIsrael, the Jewish National Fund (KKL-JNF). They protected the Jewish population, particularly in remote areas, and they established "facts on the ground", a matter of great importance to the leadership of the *Yishuv*. Eventually these settlements would become fortified agricultural settlements, *kibbutzim* and *moshavim*, serving the main need for defense against Arab raiders while simultaneously creating contiguous regions of Jewish population, which would later help determine the secure borders of the United Nations Partition Plan for Palestine.

Between the founding of the State of Israel in 1948 and the Six-Day War in 1967, the Jordan Valley kibbutzim were constantly bombarded by Jordan; kibbutz children slept in shelters every night. From its very beginning, Sde Eliyahu produced dates, grapes, pomegranates and other field crops, as well as poultry. The regional high school was in

Sde Eliyahu, serving religious students from the surrounding area, and there was a *beit midrash* for former Israel Defense Forces soldiers who wanted to combine Jewish studies and farm work. And, of course, *Ulpan Giur*, Dominik's reason for choosing to study at Sde Eliyahu was there. The kibbutz supplied room and board, and Dominik was assigned to a dormitory apartment with three other students. *Ulpan Giur*'s schedule included four rotating hours of classroom study: Jewish Law, Prayer, the Jewish Lifecycle, Shabbat and Holidays, Torah, Jewish Philosophy and History. Four hours of work on the kibbutz each day based on the needs of the kibbutz were also required. And extra-curricular activities – tours, sports, social programs with *kibbutznikim* – were offered.

As Dominik was not an *Oleh Chadash*, he had to supply a number of important documents: (1) a letter of recommendation from the Chief Rabbi of Austria about his participation in the Austrian Jewish community; (2) a resumé with his reasons for applying to *Ulpan Giur*; and (3) authorization from a special committee in the Ministry of the Interior allowing him to participate in the Conversion Ulpan.

Upon arrival at Sde Eliyahu by taxi, Dominik presented all 3 documents. He considered the *Ulpan*'s fees reasonable; if he were an *Oleh Chadash*, the Jewish Agency would have paid all his tuition and living expenses, but since he was still a tourist, he had to pay his fees – $500 for tuition, room and board; 110 New Israeli Shekels (NIS) per month for medical insurance, and 100NIS for library services. Dominik thought six-months at that price was a bargain. He was assigned to a host family so he wouldn't be alone on Shabbat; the Katzes were friendly *kibbutznikim*, but nothing like his buddies in Graz, and he always felt a little alone and forlorn on Shabbat. The rest of the time he was too busy to be sad. Having already studied most of the same subjects with Rabbi Breitling, the *Ulpan*'s courses were simple and he could fulfill his own goal of acquiring an excellent command of Hebrew by reading the newspaper every day and conversing with the *kibbutznikim*. In the middle of the program and again towards the end, Rabbi Dotan, a representative from the *Bet Din*, came to the Kibbutz to interview and open a file on each prospective convert. At his first meeting with Dominik, he asked, "Why are you doing conversion again when you converted in Austria last year?"

"For two reasons, Rabbi Dotan, and I hope you won't think me foolish," Dominik replied. "The main reason is that something in my heart and my head said that I *must* convert in Israel to link my life with the entire history of the Jewish people, and I can do that only in

Israel. The second reason is to master the Hebrew language, and I also can do that only in Israel." The rabbi smiled at Dominik and shook hands. Rabbi Dotan came again before the *Ulpan* ended to prepare the converts for their official meeting with the Bet Din, and to let them know he'd be one of the three rabbinical judges.

Part of the official Bet Din hearing was to verify a convert's knowledge of Judaism, *Elohim*, *Shabbat*, *Torah*, the *mitzvot*. Dominik answered all his questions accurately in perfect Hebrew. Because he'd already converted via an accepted Rabbinical authority in Austria, he was exempted from another circumcision and immersion in a *mikveh*. Just before the final signing of his conversion papers, Dominik asked for a moment of their time. "I know in ancient times, most converts brought sacrifices or offerings to the Temple in Jerusalem. I know this practice was dropped after the destruction of the Temple, and Jewish law today doesn't require an offering. However, I'd like to give a donation to orphans as a symbolic offering. I felt like an orphan at one time and Rabbi Breitling helped me overcome my problems; now I'd like to help children living through similar difficult situations." Dominik had to choose a Hebrew name before signing the conversion oath which was then officially signed and stamped by the Bet Din rabbis. There was a connection between the meaning of his birth name Dominik – belonging to God – and the name of the Archangel Gabriel – God's strength, so he chose Gabriel as his Hebrew first name. And since a convert's parents are not Jewish, *ben Avraham Avinu* is often used as the convert's surname, but Dominik told the Bet Din rabbis that he wanted his last name to honor his spiritual father, Rabbi Samuel – in Hebrew, Shmuel – Breitling. He asked them to change his surname to "ben Shmuel". The three rabbis agreed and welcomed Gabriel ben Shmuel with a smile and a blessing.

An announcement of successful conversions is not mandatory, but it's a popular custom at Sde Eliyahu. After Shabbat services, the converts stand and tell the congregation why they converted or about lessons learned in the *Ulpan*. Although Dominik had visited Jakob Breitling in Jerusalem several times, Jakob hadn't told him the Rabbi and Rabbanit would be visiting after *Shavuot*, when the ceremony for the converts was to be held; Dominik was elated when they all came to Sde Eliyahu that Shabbat. They were equally delighted when Gabriel ben Shmuel explained the significance of his name, acknowledging the presence in the congregation of his "spiritual father". It was a marvelous reunion; it would have been an even happier event if his father, grandmother, and close friends were there as well. Sadly, on

Chapter 3

such a momentous day, he wouldn't allow himself even to think of his mother.

Two days later, while packing to leave the kibbutz and spend a few days in Jerusalem with the Breitlings, he heard an announcement on the kibbutz loudspeaker: "Gabriel ben Shmuel, you have a visitor in the dining hall". He laughed, telling himself to get used to his name. His "guest", Lieutenant Avi, was a *Tzahal* recruitment officer who said the IDF was very interested in him because of his language skills, and he wanted to know if Gabriel was interested in the IDF. "But I'm not an Israeli," Gabriel said.

With typical *sabra* bluntness, the officer said, "So become one. You're Jewish now and you can easily and quickly become an Israeli."

"OK," Gabriel responded. "I'm interested." And thus the next chapter in the life of Gabriel ben Shmuel, formerly Dominik Müller, began.

Chapter 4

Jakob Breitling was an assistant rabbi in the Yakar Center in Jerusalem. *Yakar, the Center for Tradition and Creativity*, was established in London in 1978 by Rabbi Mickey Rosen and in Jerusalem in 1992. An acronym in honor of Rabbi Rosen's father, Yaakov Kopul Rosen, *Yakar*'s concept was unique: it integrated traditional Jewish learning with social action, interfaith dialogue and the arts. This appealed to Jakob Breitling's modern ideas when he made *Aliyah*, and he became a rabbi in Yakar Jerusalem. He rented an elegant 3-bedroom semi-furnished flat in a neighborhood called the Greek Colony, close to Yakar. Jakob loved the spacious flat because it meant his parents and grandparents, his brother and his friends would be able to visit. Dominik stayed with him when he first arrived in Israel and a few Shabbats during his time at *Ulpan Giur*; after leaving Sde Eliyahu, now permanently known as Gabriel, he moved in as a semi-permanent resident, using Jakob's flat as his official address for the IDF.

The day after settling his possessions in Jakob's apartment, Gabriel began the process of becoming an Israeli. He brought his current Austrian passport and the visa slip he'd received upon entry into Israel, his conversion papers from the Bet Din, and three passport photos to the Ministry of the Interior Since he'd been in the same Ministry office to receive his authorization for participation in the *Ulpan*, the process this time was relatively short, just a few hours of being patient with Israeli bureaucracy. He received his *Teudat Zehut* and ended the day as an *Oleh Chadash*, with a small booklet from the Jewish Agency, outlining the rights and privileges he would receive as a new immigrant. The friendly clerk who gave him his ID card suggested that he visit the Jewish Agency before going into the IDF; she also advised him to open an account in the Jerusalem branch of a major Israeli bank. Gabriel opened a bank account and went to the Jewish Agency the next day. He was told to register with the IDF's Lone Soldier division and his *Mashkit Tash* would work with the Jewish Agency to guarantee and maintain his rights. Gabriel was amazed at how much financial, social and even psychological aid was extended to a lone soldier.

Back in Jakob's flat, he took out the card Lieutenant Avi had given him and telephoned the recruiter; the lieutenant invited Gabriel to the Induction Center at Tel HaShomer, a very large IDF base not far from Tel Aviv, the following day at 1100 hours. "That's eleven o'clock in civilian time," Avi said. Then he added, "There's an office here to help *Olim Chadashim* and Lone Soldiers. We'll consider this your *tzav rishon*, and you'll meet your *Mashkit Tash*, who'll work with you every step of the way. There are two elements in the *tzav rishon*: a physical examination and a *KABA* test. The physical fitness and health exam determine if you're capable of serving in a combat unit. You'll receive a profile ranging from 24 to 97, any score above 72 means you're fit for combat. The next part is the *KABA*, a psychometric test and interview to determine your IQ and to evaluate the quality of your high school education in order to decide whether you, a new recruit, are suitable for elite combat, reconnaissance or a non-combat position. Given your many language skills, Gabriel, I'm quite sure the IDF will make an exception and place you in *Modi'in*, although they usually want someone who's lived here for at least two years. You'll need security clearance, but that shouldn't be a problem either, even though your father and his family live in Iran. Any questions? If not, I'll see you tomorrow at 1100 hours."

Gabriel had a few questions but decided he'd ask his *Mashkit Tash* the next day. So he said, "Thank you, sir. I'll be there at 1100 hours."

When Jakob came home later, he found a very excited Gabriel in the flat. "Let's go out to eat," Jakob said, "and you'll tell me what you expect. I'll tell you about some of my own *Tzahal* experiences. A year after I made *Aliyah*, I did six months in the IDF, one month of basic training and five months in the Chaplain's Corps; I was assigned to *Modi'in*. Now I volunteer two days each month as a chaplain, wherever they need me. By the way, I'm free tomorrow morning, so I'll drive you to Tel HaShomer."

Jakob left Gabriel at Tel HaShomer at 10:45; he was immediately sent to *Bakum* where a pretty young woman was waiting. She greeted him, said she was Sergeant Michal, his *Mashkit Tash*, and that Lieutenant Avi was at a meeting but would join them shortly. "In the meantime, I'll tell you about the rights and benefits you're entitled to as a Lone Soldier. You'll receive a monthly stipend double to your unit's standard monthly salary. You'll also receive a food stipend to Supersal that will appear on your *Teudat Choger*, your IDF identification card. The IDF – in your case, me – coordinates all your benefits with the Ministry of Immigrant Absorption and you'll soon receive the Absorption Basket that all *Olim Chadashim* receive in their first six months and, as a lone soldier, for at least one year an additional monthly stipend equal to the salary of an IDF private. The Ministry of Immigrant Absorption will also suspend deadlines on certain rights, such as purchasing a car tax-free, until you've completed your army service. You'll receive rental assistance, an extra monthly stipend, from the *Ministry of Housing*. This service needs to be renewed every six months, so you'll have to bring your IDF identification card, the lone soldier letter issued by the IDF and your *Teudat Zehut* to the *Ministry of Housing*. The IDF will cover the cost of one flight home to Austria or Switzerland during your period of service. Where will you live? Do you want the IDF to provide housing for you, a room at a kibbutz or a hostel for soldiers or a shared furnished flat?"

"No, ma'am," Gabriel said. "I have a permanent residence in Jerusalem for as long as I need it, with Rabbi Jakob Breitling who's like an older brother. It's a large flat and I have my own room, but I'd like to pay him monthly rent, so I'm really pleased about all the stipends. In fact, ma'am, I'm overwhelmed at Israel's generosity to a lone soldier."

"Please don't call me 'ma'am'! *'Ma'am'* is my mother," Michal laughed. "After all, I'm only a year or two older than you."

"OK, ma'…er, Sergeant Michal," Gabriel said, also laughing.

At that point, Lieutenant Avi came into the room. "I'm glad to see you two getting along so well. It's important for the next two years, Gabriel. I should say your *Mashkit Tash* is important since she'll be looking out for you. Do you have any questions for me now?"

"Thousands," Gabriel said, still laughing. "But I don't know where to start. So I'll just begin by asking what happens now?"

"What happens now," the lieutenant said, "is a physical examination, then the *KABA* test and another interview or two. The meeting I came from was about you and it was agreed that your language skills, especially Urdu and Farsi, will be very useful to *Modi'in* if you can receive security clearance. So, today really is your *tzav rishon*. Sergeant Michal will take you for your physical examination now and they'll deal with you afterwards. Good luck."

Michal took a detour to one of the canteens at Tel HaShomer. "Let's get something to eat and then you'll fill out this medical questionnaire to help the army doctor determine your physical classification," she said, indicating a form in the folder she was carrying. They chose sandwiches, small salads and iced tea; Michal paid for their lunch with coupons. After lunch, Gabriel filled out the medical questionnaire and Michal gave him the folder. There were several other documents inside, including a card of stickers he would have to give them to move through the stations of the various examinations. Another was an enormous list of "personal" items recruits should bring to make basic

Chapter 4

training more comfortable.

When he finished reading the list, he replaced it in the folder and looked at Michal, bemused. "They're kidding, right? There must be fifty things on this list! Wow!" Grinning and shaking her head, Michal walked with him to the Medical Unit where she wished him good luck and said she'd see him again soon. The clerk at the Medical Unit desk told Gabriel they had been expecting him and ushered him into a cubicle where an army doctor was waiting. Gabriel handed the doctor the questionnaire in his folder and was told to undress while the doctor read it. His physical exam consisted of a general check-up, a urine test, and a blood test. The doctor said he'd receive his profile later that afternoon, but he assumed it would be very high. They X-rayed his teeth; he was told this was only for identification in case of an accident. The clerk then directed Gabriel to the area for testing his Hebrew proficiency. He was handed an exam, told the time allotment, and that he'd do a Hebrew *ulpan* if his score was below 5; Gabriel scored 9, the highest score. He laughed, *"It seems my time at Sde Eliyahu paid off."*

The next step was a personal interview with Lieutenant Moshe, in which Gabriel was asked questions about his history, educational background, the languages he knew and where he'd learned them, in which language he was most fluent, what he knew about Islam and Christianity, why he'd converted to Judaism twice. Then he was sent to the *KABA*, a computerized psycho-technical IQ test checking his analytical abilities. He was told he could take the test in English, Spanish, French or Russian, but since his Hebrew was so good – that 9 on the Hebrew exam – they'd like him to do the 2-hour test in Hebrew. His score would weigh heavily in deciding which units the army would offer him. Less than 90 minutes later, Gabriel had completed the *KABA* exam. He was sent back to the interview room where Lieutenant Moshe was seated alongside Lieutenant Avi and another officer, Captain Yair, who told him his physical profile had come through: it was 97, so he was physically fit for every IDF unit, combat or non-combat. Less than a minute later, a clerk came into the room with a note for the captain. It was Gabriel's *KABA* score. Captain Yair looked at the note, handed it to the other two officers who nodded, and then smiled at Gabriel. He said, *"Kol haKavod!* We'd still like you in *Modi'in*, but your combined score is so high you can go for the paratroopers or pilot training if you can pass the *gibush*. Do you know what that is?"

"Yes, sir. I know it's the selection tryout for the special units. I also know it's been called a survival course. Or 'hell week'. But I really want to be in *Modi'in*. I think that's where I can contribute the most."

Captain Yair smiled. "Great! On behalf of my fellow officers, I'm proud to welcome you to *Tzahal*. You'll hear from us very soon about induction procedures and basic training. I live in Jerusalem and I'm leaving now, after what's been a longer day for you than for me. Would you like a ride home?"

"Thank you, sir." Gabriel shook hands with the other officers. Lieutenant Avi winked and said, "I'll tell Sergeant Michal".

The next day Gabriel purchased a backpack and many of the items on the list his *Mashkit Tash* had given him. Two days later, he received the letter informing him to report to *Bakum* at Tel HaShomer, at 800 hours on Sunday, July 9th. With about 100 other new recruits, he was given a close haircut and then received his uniforms, underwear, socks, boots, a shaving kit, a toothbrush, a towel, a sewing kit, a mess kit and cutlery, and a kitbag to hold all of them. He was told to check everything and if there were any problems, to exchange those items immediately. He was photographed badly, given a cash advance on his stipend which, he was told, would be transferred automatically every month to his bank account. His *tironut* was at *Mifrasit*, a base in *Modi'in*'s southern branch near Beersheva. In many units, *tironut* was often the most difficult period in a soldier's life, after *gibush*, which Gabriel hadn't attended, but his *tironut* in *Modi'in* was quite different. It had only two objectives: to teach new recruits the essentials of being a soldier and to help individuals from many different cultures work together; it was rigorous, and recruits often learned their own capabilities, those of their fellow soldiers, and a great deal about human nature under stress. Gabriel's *tironut* lasted only one month and consisted of shooting practice, a little guard duty, inspections, and some physical training like hikes and field exercises. Lectures and training films offered a welcome diversion from the more exhausting daily routine. His group was warned never to let their weapons out of sight or possession as loss of a weapon was a major offense in the IDF and carried a heavy penalty. During *tironut*, Gabriel tried to become friends with the other recruits, even if they weren't anything like his old friends whom he sorely missed in this new stage of his life. He understood that laughter and jokes were important, and all recruits had to learn to support each other – friends or not – especially if they were in difficult circumstances.

Tzahal, primarily a Jewish army, allowed every soldier, regardless of the faith, to practice his or her religion freely, and special

Chapter 4

accommodation was provided; this was important to Gabriel, and he was given sufficient time to perform his daily rituals. The food on all bases was kosher, but there were problems involving the mixing of dairy and meat utensils, especially out in the field. At *Bakum*, he'd received one mess kit and one set of cutlery, but he was told he could request an additional set; so he did. During *tironut*, he wore the "all-army" olive drab fatigues and beret; however, at the *Modi'in* swearing-in ceremony, he received the unit's shoulder tag and beret pin for his dress uniform. Jakob attended the *tekes* so that Gabriel wouldn't feel totally alone among the recruits and their families.

He was assigned to Urim, Unit 8200's base in the Negev, for specialized training; his knowledge and facility with many languages – Urdu, Farsi and Turkish in particular – was so important to Modi'in that security clearance came through rapidly. After the swearing-in *tekes*, he had a few days off, and he spent them in Jerusalem with Jakob before reporting to Urim.

On the first day, Gabriel and the other recruits were told Urim was the IDF's main Unit 8200 location, responsible for collecting signal intelligence (SIGINT), code decryption, analysis and evaluation of counterintelligence and information security. On that first day, officers made a point of telling the recruits Unit 8200 played a pivotal role in *Tzahal*. The recruits would learn the four major phases of intelligence: data collection, data analysis, data processing and data dissemination. They'd collect and analyze foreign communications – chatter, maps, pictures and other types of information crucial to the safety of Israel. Like other Intel agencies, the only function of some groups was to study maps; since useful intelligence can be gathered from photo-interpretation of high-altitude pictures of a country, Unit 8200 had catalogs of munitions factories, military bases and even the design of crates and containers in order to interpret shipments and inventories. Their studies at Urim included the operational environment of hostile, friendly and neutral forces, the civilian populations of combat areas, and the reading of maps. Gabriel was fascinated by operational intelligence focused on both the verification and the denial of collected data. Many facts were gathered from public sources: newspapers, radio, TV. The recruits were told that data collection of this type was known as open source intelligence because while population, ethnic make-up and main industries of a region were extremely important, this information was usually public and readily available. All intelligence about critical threats, however, was kept in high priority files, with important enemy capabilities analyzed on a scale based on estimation of the enemy's preparation time. Threats and the vulnerability of enemies was reported to Israel's decision-makers; these were a crucial part of Unit 8200's responsibility. Secret information – encryption keys for scrambling and/or unscrambling data, diplomatic message traffic, battle orders – were restricted to senior analysts with very high security clearance in order to protect the sources and actual methods of data collection. The recruits were instructed in the strategic importance of many different issues – economics, political assessments, military capabilities and the real intentions of foreign nations as well as non-state actors like Hezbollah and Al-Qaeda. Sometimes intelligence in these areas was scientific, technical, sociological, diplomatic, tactical – but all of it was analyzed in combination with known facts about the area, such as its history, industrial capacities, geography, demographics. Some recruits received additional instruction in specific languages.

Almost immediately, Gabriel began studies in specific dialects of Arabic, Farsi and Urdu. Being the only one studying these languages he often felt lonely, isolated from his fellow recruits. He knew Al-Qaeda communication might originate in Saudi Arabia, Afghanistan, Iran or Pakistan and it was vital for Unit 8200 to understand and evaluate all their communication, but he still felt very alone. Some days he knew his brain was overloaded from information thrown at him in different languages and he would eat a quick evening meal and then collapse on his bunk. Early the next morning, he'd shower, dress, eat breakfast and report to his squad room for another day of diverse instruction – all alone. Until Yaniv arrived.

All Unit 8200 intelligence activities, from the tactical to the strategic in peacetime and wartime, were conducted in pairs, with one member of the team handling most of the language analysis and the other dealing with the technical elements. Gabriel's partner was Yaniv Hofman from Ramat Aviv who'd been assigned to Urim two weeks after him. Tactical intelligence in SIGINT focused on communication with decision-makers involving actual and potential operations; Gabriel knew this would be Yaniv's realm with crucial information disseminated through database systems, Intel bulletins and, assuming he had the very highest security clearance, even by verbal briefings to senior military and government personnel. Gabriel knew that although he and Yaniv didn't do the same type of work, at least having a partner would make his Unit 8200 experience far less lonely.

They enjoyed working together and they shared breaks, quiet time and a lot of conversation. Although Gabriel didn't say anything

Chapter 4

specific about his mother, he told Yaniv in perfect Hebrew without a trace of a foreign accent that he was illegitimate, that his birth name was Dominik Müeller which he'd changed when he converted, that his Catholic school in Austria had expelled him and his mother had disowned him because he questioned Christian dogma, so he had gone to live with a remarkable rabbi and a few teenagers, and that he had converted to Judaism twice – first in Vienna and then at Kibbutz Sde Eliyahu. He told Yaniv that an IDF recruiter came to Sde Eliyahu two days before he left and urged him to make *Aliyah* and join Unit 8200. He told Yaniv that his father was a philosophy professor in Iran, and the Rabbi, a Swiss citizen, arranged for him to meet his father in Zurich.

Yaniv told Gabriel that he believed in coincidence and asked if Gabriel did. "One of my grandmothers – I have three – calls it *bashert*, a Yiddish word for 'destiny' or fate'. But to me it is all just coincidence. Here's the first coincidence: my *Ema,* a well-known artist, was born in Germany but she was raised in Denmark, until she went to study art in Paris and met my *Aba*, a PhD student at the Sorbonne. My parents had two weddings – the first in Paris and the second in Tel Aviv after my *Ema* converted to Judaism, but she converted only once, in Israel, even though she started the conversion process in Paris. My family name is 'Hofman' with one 'f' and one 'n', the way Israelis spell a name in English, and here's the second coincidence: my *Ema*'s maiden name was also 'Hoffmann', but with two 'fs' and two 'ns' in the German way. And coincidence number 3: both your father and mine are philosophy professors, yours in Iran and my dad at Tel Aviv University. Our house is a gathering place for family and friends from all over the world; maybe someday my father will invite yours to a conference and your Iranian family will be able to come here. Come home with me our first free Shabbat, meet everyone and let my sister Dani fall in love with you. You can ask my grandparents who are usually at our house on Shabbat to tell you their stories that are also full of coincidences. During World War Two, both my Israeli grandfathers and my German grandfather were at El Alamein – on opposite sides; my German grandpa deserted to the British and spent most of the war in a POW camp. That's coincidence number three." Yaniv added, "I don't think I've talked so much in a very long time."

Gabriel exclaimed, "This is really weird, especially if your *Ema* is Lise Hofman! I've seen her paintings – one in the home of my 'remarkable rabbi' in Zurich, another one in Vienna in the home of his good friends, and there is a painting of a Purim party in the home of the Rabbi's son in Jerusalem. I can't wait to tell them I know the artist's son."

Yaniv laughed. "You see, coincidences upon coincidences. My *Ema*'s name is Lise, and after you come for Shabbat at our house, you'll be able to tell all your friends that you met the artist, not just her son! I told you we were *bashert* to be buddies."

Only one month after Gabriel came to Urim, the World Trade Center and the Pentagon in the United States were attacked on 9/11 by terrorists. Like every Israeli – and especially Unit 8200 – Gabriel was appalled. In order to bolster Unit 8200's mastery of tactical intelligence and provide the United States with urgently needed data in its war on terror, all leave was cancelled and Gabriel and Yaniv worked an enormous number of extra hours.

A few weeks later, when both were finally free for Shabbat, Gabriel and Yaniv took two buses to Ramat Aviv on Friday afternoon, stopping only to buy flowers for Yaniv's mother. They walked into a house full of people, noise, laughter, and delicious cooking aromas. Gabriel said, "Am I in Israel or in Austria? This is exactly what it was like in the Rabbi's flat in Graz on Friday as we were getting ready to go to *shul* – noise, laughter, Karl singing and the terrific smells of Frau Sarah's tasty meals. All I can say is 'Wow!'"

Yaniv teased Gabriel about still more coincidences, just as a beautiful barefoot lady with messy blonde hair came into the hallway. She grabbed Yaniv in a bear hug and said, "Let me look at you, my love. Grandma Anna will say you're getting too skinny. Now introduce me to your good-looking friend and tell me about all these coincidences. Then let's go outside."

Hugging her, Yaniv said, "*Ema*, this is Gabriel, my partner and friend at Urim. Grandma Anna always says I'm too skinny and wants to fatten me up. I'll enjoy it this Shabbat because the food she makes is so much better than what the cooks at Urim have the *chutzpah* to call 'food'. You wouldn't believe how awful it is and sometimes Gabriel and I just have PB&J that we get at the kiosk or halvah on challah. As for all the coincidences, you'll just have to wait to hear them until we 'stow our gear' and have a snack. There's a lot of noise here. Who's outside? Grandma Anna and Grandpa Richard? *Savta*? *Saba*? Kobi? Keren? Dani? And that new guy Uncle Ted sent here? What's his name again? Alex?"

"*Ema?*" Gabriel couldn't get over his first sight of this gorgeous woman or that she was Yaniv's mother! He handed her the flowers he'd bought at a local florist, and said, "It's a pleasure to meet you,

Chapter 4

Ma'am. One coincidence is that I've seen some of your fabulous paintings!"

"*Shalom*, Gabriel. Welcome to our noisy abode. Thank you for these gorgeous flowers. Yaniv, why does every new friend who comes here call me 'Ma'am'? It makes me feel really old. Gabriel, my name is Lise as you know since you've seen some of my paintings. You'll have to tell me which ones and where you've seen them. He's a charmer. I already like him," she said to Yaniv, smiling broadly at both young men. "But your *Aba* says I like anyone who appreciates my paintings. We have a really full house this Shabbat. All the grandparents, all your siblings. And three – I should say four – surprises! Alex is here and so are Uncle Ted and Aunt Shani who are staying with *Savta* and *Saba*, but they're here now; so is Tammy, of course. I'm sure you'll remember Simon Gordon, our friend from Harvard. Wait, that's five! Now come out to the deck and eat your fill of snacks. You can 'stow your gear', as you put it, later. In the meantime, I'll put the flowers in water."

She put her free arm around Yaniv's shoulder and led the two young men towards the deck. "Look who's here, everyone. This handsome young man is Yaniv's buddy, Gabriel. He brought me these lovely flowers and he says he knows and likes my paintings."

Gabriel knew his mouth was agape, but he couldn't get over Yaniv's *Ema*! A young man on the deck laughed and said, "You can close your mouth now, Gabriel…right? I had the same reaction not long ago when I met Lise for the first time. Did she tell you not to call her 'Ma'am'? That's what she told me. She's always like this—beautiful and bubbly. Fortunately, David doesn't get jealous; he just loves her. By the way, I'm Alex."

A tall dark-haired, slightly older man laughed and came over to the two young men. He hugged Yaniv, shook Gabriel's hand and said, "I'm David, Lise's non-jealous husband and Yaniv's *Aba*. Welcome to The Happy Hofman Madhouse! I'll introduce everybody and test you on their names later," he added, winking at his son.

"He'll do that, too," a very pretty young girl sitting on the floor with three other girls, said. "I'm Dani. My *Ema*'s right. You are handsome!" Everyone laughed – and Gabriel loved the extraordinary atmosphere on the crowded enclosed deck. When Yaniv and Gabriel had eaten some brownies, David introduced everyone, but there was no test. After they took their duffels to Yaniv's room, changed out of their uniforms, and went downstairs, Yaniv asked if anyone was going to the *beit knesset* as he was sure Gabriel would want to go. Ted

Hoffman and his daughter Tammy, Simon Gordon, Alex and Dani all stood.

"Let's go," Dani said.

"Not like that, young lady," her father said. "If you really want to go to the *beit knesset*, you have to put on a dress. Do that now and join everyone later. I'm sure Tammy will wait for you."

"Aye, aye, cap'n!" she said with a salute and a cheeky smile. "But I'd rather have 'handsome Gabriel' wait for me. I can show him the way."

By early Sunday morning, when the two soldiers had to return to Urim, Gabriel knew he'd never experienced a Shabbat quite like this one, even when everyone was at the Rabbi's home. "OK," he admitted, "Frau Sarah's Shabbat meals are comparable to Grandma Anna's and Savta Aya's, but the people…" It was the people, the conversation and the banter that made the weekend truly exceptional. They kept drawing him into all the discussions, even into political arguments and the sad stories about the casualties of 9/11 and the heroism of the people on United Airlines flight 93 who brought the plane down in Pennsylvania, not far away from Ted Hoffman's home in Pittsburgh. Lise asked Gabriel again where he had seen her paintings and when he said one was in Rabbi Breitling's home in Zurich and another was in Jakob Breitling's flat in Jerusalem, Simon Gordon asked if he was talking about Samuel and Deborah Breitling. "Yes," he said. "They sort of adopted me when my mother disowned me and I was expelled from the Catholic school. They became my family and probably saved my life!"

"I know about that boy, but his name wasn't Gabriel. Samuel Breitling is an old friend, ever since we were both counselors in Camp Ramah in the States, and we've always stayed in touch. I know his entire family, both boys, and even Deborah's family here in Israel."

"I was Dominik Müller when I came to Rabbi Breitling. I changed my name to Gabriel Ben Shmuel when I converted to Judaism here in Israel. I chose Ben Shmuel to honor him, because he was—and is—my spiritual father. Are you the American friend who taught them expressions like 'win-win' and 'the ball is in your court'?" Professor Gordon admitted his guilt for conveying American slang to Rabbi Breitling and his family.

"This is another one of those odd coincidences, *bro*," Yaniv said. That led to a long conversation about coincidences: Lise and David meeting in a Paris gallery when he wanted to buy her *Little Mermaid* painting for his sister who'd always loved the story, both Lise's father and David's fighting at El Alamein in World War II on opposite sides, Alex being sponsored by David's cousin Ted Hoffman who sent him to the Israeli Hofmans, and both David and Gabriel's biological fathers being professors of philosophy.

Yaniv's older brother Kobi and his sister Dani pouted a little at being left out of the conversation, but even their pretended "petulance" was just added fun. Gabriel was attracted to Dani whose cheeky teasing reminded him of Ruth when he'd first moved into the Rabbi's flat in Graz, but he told himself Dani, a gorgeous blonde with green eyes and a cute dimple near her smiling mouth, was Yaniv's little sister and she was only sixteen, far too young for him, and absolutely off limits, no matter how much he enjoyed her flirting.

On the bus to Urim, Gabriel couldn't stop talking about the fabulous Shabbat, the fabulous ambiance and the even more fabulous people. "Are you having vocabulary trouble, Gabriel? A language scholar who knows only one word – fabulous!" Yaniv teased, "It was just like I told you, and both my *Em*a and *Ab*a said you're welcome there whenever you want. There are more people in our family, my aunt, uncle, their kids. You should get to know Kobi and Keren; they're wonderful although they'll never hear me saying that. And there's Dani…" He stopped talking as he saw a slight blush on Gabriel's cheeks. *"Uh-oh!"* he thought, but he didn't say anything.

Despite the gravity and tension of his job at Urim, time passed quickly for Gabriel. Many Shabbats were spent with his "second – or maybe it was his third – family" in Ramat Aviv, or in Jerusalem with Jakob, his "older brother". He went on a few dates with Michal, his *Mashkit Tash,* and while he found her company pleasant and enjoyed their dates and the sex she'd initiated, he knew their relationship couldn't last, not because he wasn't as attracted to her as he was to Yaniv's sister Dani, but because Michal wanted something permanent and he wasn't ready for that. He also dated Maya, the younger sister of one of Keren Hofman's friends, but they were usually part of a group going to clubs and parties in Tel Aviv; they were nice but not as meaningful as his friends in Graz who were always on his mind.

In December 2002, Gabriel used his Lone Soldier right to a free ticket home and flew to Zurich for two weeks. To be reunited with the Rabbi and Rabbanit and his old friends who had Christmas breaks from their various universities was, to quote an old cliché, a dream come true. They stayed up late every night, talking and drinking wine, at first in the Breitling home in Zurich, where Frau Sarah even joined them the first Shabbat, eager to see her beloved young people. Then they went to Davos, less than two hours away from Zurich and close to the Parsenn funicular linking Davos with the ski slopes in the Weissfluhjoch ridge.

During the day, they skied; each night they sat around the huge open fireplace in the hotel's lounge, drinking *glug*, dipping toast into fondue and sampling delectable Leonidas chocolates Ruth had brought from Brussels, basking in the pleasure of being together again. They had missed each other so much and now had so much to share: David loved studying medicine but had recently decided to transfer from MUV in Vienna to Tel Aviv University's Sackler School of Medicine if he could be accepted; Gabriel said he'd put in a good word with the father of a friend, a TAU professor.

Ruth loved designing jewelry and her college, but she also talked about her friends among Belgium's fashion journalists; without these friends, she said, Brussels was really boring – its most famous attractions were the *Manneken Pis*, the statue of a little boy peeing in a fountain, and Belgian chocolate. She looked gorgeous in her après-ski outfits, and Ruth was teased by all the young men that she'd turned into the "fashionista" she always wanted to be. Ruth told them about her plans to relocate to Israel in the near future to bring her revolutionary jewelry designs to the diamond exchange in Ramat Gan. Karl was only able to join them for a few days because he was principal tenor in Salzburg's University Mozarteum Choir, with two solos in upcoming concerts. He sang one solo and although they'd known he had a wonderful singing voice, they were agog at how much his talent had developed. Daniel, the Breitlings' younger son, had switched his major from medicine to systems engineering; he tried explaining that it was interdisciplinary, combining technical tools and human-centered processes in order to reduce risk management and optimize methods. All the others stared at him, totally silent. Finally Karl asked, "Dom – er, Gabriel, is he speaking Greek? Is Greek one of your many languages?"

"I'll start learning it tomorrow," Gabriel said, grinning. "I may need it in the future." Little did he know he was predicting a language he'd need in his graduate studies, but then it would be ancient, not modern, Greek. When it was Gabriel's turn to talk about himself, he told them about his conversion at Kibbutz Sde Eliyahu, and his initial despair despite knowing that he was doing the right thing for himself and learning so much; he told them about feeling so lonely and that Shabbat visits to Jakob in Jerusalem were his only consolation during those months. And he told them about his friend Yaniv, the Hofmans and their home in Ramat Aviv always filled with family and fabulous

Chapter 4

people. He asked if they remembered the Lise Hofman paintings at the Rabbi's home in Zurich and the Goldblum home in Vienna, and then he told them Yaniv's mother was the artist who'd painted them. He told them Lise Hofman was as warm and beautiful as Rabbanit Breitling. But when they asked about Unit 8200, he joked, "If I tell you, I'll have to kill you!" David asked when the IDF had turned him into James Bond, quoting lines from "Dr. No".

When their extraordinary Swiss reunion ended and they had to return to their everyday lives, they hugged and said goodbye wistfully.

Chapter 5

Just before he completed his military service at the end of June 2004, Gabriel's CO asked if he'd be interested in Unit 8200 as a career, but he opted out of the IDF. He was involved in his first serious relationship, with Rina Brenner, a Hebrew University Social Work student in Jerusalem, one of Yaniv's high school friends. In the fall term, Gabriel began studying at Hebrew University for a BA in Philosophy and Theoretical Linguistics; he also seriously increased his Arabic studies. At first, he continued to live in Jakob's flat, but Jakob had met and married Rebecca Berns, a lovely young American, a *chozeret b'teshuva*. When Jakob and Rebecca returned from their wedding in Chicago and honeymoon in Switzerland, they both assured Gabriel he was welcome to stay in the flat as there was plenty of room, but he felt like the quintessential "third wheel". During the short break between semesters, he found a semi-furnished apartment in French Hill, quite close to Hebrew University's Mount Scopus campus; it had fairly new appliances in the kitchen and a large salon with French doors opening onto a terrace. Each of the two bedrooms had a double bed, a desk and bookshelves, and a closet with sufficient space, although Gabriel didn't need that much. Using his *Oleh Chadash* rights that had been deferred during his IDF service, he purchased an automobile at a reduced tax rate, making his life easier despite his horror at the reckless driving on Jerusalem's narrow roads.

Rina soon moved out of her dorm and into Gabriel's flat, even though her wealthy, secular parents objected to her living with a religious convert from Austria. Her conservative father refused to think about his "baby daughter" having sex with anyone – especially with Gabriel. Her family's prejudices slowly seeped into Rina's consciousness, and with the promise of a fully paid summer vacation in Italy, she moved back into the Hebrew University dorm until she completed her BA. At first, Gabriel was devastated by their breakup, but as he became more deeply immersed in his studies, he realized Rina had not been the love of his life. He continued going to the Hofmans on weekends and holidays, and Lise assured him he'd probably have quite a few broken relationships before finding 'The One'. "In other words," she giggled, "you'll kiss a lot of frogs before you finally meet your princess."

"Thanks a lot," he laughed. "Just what I've always wanted: froggy kisses followed by a breaking heart again and again. Mine, I mean."

Yaniv, now a captain in Unit 8200, would complete his 4-year military career, except for reserve duty, in the fall and he'd begin studying Computer Science and Counter-terrorism at IDC, the Interdisciplinary Center Herzliya. At home for a few days, gulping down a glass of juice, he jumped into the discussion. "Gabe, you know that Dani's finishing the IDF – or the IDF is finishing with her very soon; unlike me, she's going to do a real post-army trip with some friends. Then, after her 'mis-adventures', she'll begin her BA at Hebrew University, which means she'll be living in Jerusalem, too," he said with a grin. Lise picked up a special vibe between the two friends and she wondered about it, but they said nothing more.

In July 2005, Ruth made *Aliyah*, but she wasn't sure about where her future lay. On arrival, she went directly to David Rosenzweig's large flat because she had a few appointments at the Diamond Exchange in Ramat Gan with a few jewelry manufacturers she'd met in Brussels. In Antwerp, Belgium's diamond center, she'd also met members of Israel's diamond community, but most of the Israelis were ultra-religious and they looked disdainfully at her fashionably short skirts if they looked at her at all. She knew *Haredi* men would never accept the ideas of a "mere" woman, so she would have to find less narrow-minded manufacturers who'd appreciate her un-Orthodox designs, or unless she wore a very long skirt, send a male to present her craft! At a fine gems fair in Milan, she'd met a young woman who was studying jewelry design in Italy; Yael, her new friend, gave Ruth the phone number of her uncle, CEO of a prestigious jewelry firm in Israel. Both Gabriel and David assured her that it was with her talent, not the length of her skirts, that she'd find her niche in the jewelry world. And Gabriel added that he hoped she wouldn't be kissing any "frogs". Ruth, his first "crush" from his early days in Graz, proved to be a better distraction for Gabriel than thinking about Dani, Rina or any additional "frogs" in his future. She thought his comment about kissing frogs was crazy until he told her about his failed relationship with Rina and Lise's theory about "kissing lots of frogs before finding 'The One'!". Ruth laughed and told him about all the "frogs" she had kissed during her years in Belgium; then she croaked like a frog, and with a loud smacking sound, puckered her lips and kissed him. Gabriel burst out laughing, "You'll never be a frog, Ruth. You're far too fashionable and besides, green's a great color on you!"

He'd taken a little time off from studying to relax with his old friends, but David had exams, so Gabriel told Ruth she was welcome to share his flat if she wanted to check out opportunities in Jerusalem. She accepted his offer when her appointments in the Diamond Center in Ramat Gan and at Yael's family's firm were fruitless and she decided to look into possibilities in Israel's capitol. In between exams, Gabriel toured the Holy City with Ruth. They went to the Israel Museum and saw the jewelry in the museum's shop, but she was told that most of their jewelry was imported from abroad, from the Metropolitan Museum in New York and other museums. In the Malcha Mall and on Ben Yehuda Street, they explored jewelry shops and Ruth's trained eye caught work by a few artisans whose designs were in the same creative realm as hers; she asked the shopkeepers for the names and phone numbers of those jewelry craftsmen, and showed them a few of her designs. The owner of a fashionable boutique on Ben Yehuda Street told a delighted Ruth and a happy Gabriel that he would sell her work if she could provide a substantial number of items.

Ruth stayed in Gabriel's flat in August when he was in *milu'im* for three weeks. She contacted the artists she appreciated, but all of them worked in Tel Aviv. She met them individually, discussed their designs and showed them her jewelry; each of them immediately offered her a job. She declined, stating that she wanted to create new designs and produce jewelry she could sell on consignment. She told them she'd brought semi-precious and a few precious stones as well as beading pliers, files, sizing gauges and measures, calipers, tweezers, ring mountings, loupes and several other jewelry tools from Belgium, and she'd declared everything at Customs in Ben-Gurion airport. So all she needed from them was to know where she could purchase sheets of gold and silver, wire, mountings, pearls, crystal beads. All the artisans mentioned Pasternak Findings in Ramat Gan, and one told her to contact the Jewish Agency for financial aid; as an *olah chadasha*, she was entitled to receive assistance and other benefits.

Since Gabriel wasn't home for Shabbat during his *milu'im*, Ruth went to Jakob Breitling's home. She liked his wife Rebecca, and she was happy that she was completely over her teenage "crush" on Jakob. She also liked the Shabbat services at Yakar. To her surprise, after Shabbat, Rebecca showed her a room above their garage with large windows on all sides and excellent ventilation; Jakob told her it could be a perfect studio. By the time Gabriel returned from *milu'im*, Ruth had installed a long worktable and a few chairs in *her* studio, and before her appointment at the Jewish Agency, she bought all the supplies she'd need to produce jewelry. When Rebecca informed her that a neighbor was going abroad for a year and wanted to sublet her lovely apartment, Ruth rented it on sight.

Chapter 5

♦ ♦ ♦

Rosh Hashanah began on the evening of October 3rd, 2005. Gabriel, David and Ruth were all invited to the Hofmans for the holiday. She was staying at David's flat, a short walk to the synagogue and to the Hofmans, but Gabriel bunked with Yaniv. He was sorry Alex who was visiting his family in Slovakia wasn't there. Gabriel absolutely "knew" Ruth and Alex would be a perfect match. *"Oh well,"* he said to himself, *"I'm sure Alex will be back for Sukkoth, and I'll find other ways to help Ruth in the meantime!"*

In many ways, *Sukkoth* was a repeat of *Rosh Hashanah*; Gabriel, David and Ruth were all invited to the Hofmans, but this time Alex was there. Noting a mutual attraction with Alex constantly staring at Ruth who often gazed at him as well, Gabriel leaned towards Ruth sitting next to him at the table and whispered, "He's not a frog!" She laughed but refused to share the joke, even though both Yaniv and Dani told her she wasn't being fair. Lise, who also noticed Alex and Ruth eying each other a lot, lifted a thumb and winked at Gabriel. Since Alex would be starting a BA at Hebrew University after all the *chagim*, and since Ruth also lived in Jerusalem, Gabriel invited Alex to share his flat.

On Shabbat during *Sukkoth*, Gabriel met Tamar Rejwan, one of Dani's friends, a very pretty brunette with brown eyes flecked with gold. Like Dani, she was about to begin her BA at Hebrew University, but in an odd combination of studies – Art History and Political Science. Tamar told him she was from a family of wealthy Persian Jews with a very long history in London, in Great Neck, New York, in Beverly Hills, California, and, of course, in Israel. Gabriel told her about his Iranian family and that he'd met his father in Switzerland, thanks to Rabbi Breitling; he also told her he'd found out via e-mail sent through the Rabbi that somehow his father and his family had managed to leave Shiraz for London, but their life in England as Iranian émigrés was far from easy as despite his father's reputation as a philosopher and writer, he had not been able to find a position in a British university; Dani's *Aba* affirmed that Gabriel's father was well-known in philosophy circles. Tamar was sympathetic about the plight of Gabriel's family, and said *motzei chag* she'd tell her *Aba*, a professor in SICSA, the Sassoon International Center for the Study of Antisemitism at Hebrew University, about the Sarkohi family's difficult situation.

Professor Rejwan contacted his cousin, Vidal Sassoon, the famous hairdresser, who at that time was president of the American Friends of

Hebrew University in California and had acquaintances on the Board of Governors of UCLA. Through them, Professor Sarkohi was offered a tenured position at that university beginning in January 2006, and Vidal Sassoon arranged the expensive move of Gabriel's family's to Los Angeles. When his father telephoned with the good news, he said in a choked voice, "When I first met you in Zurich, Gabriel, I knew I was lucky and had a remarkable son, but this help through your friends is beyond imagination. I don't know how I can ever thank you, Tamar, her father, the Sassoons."

Gabriel responded, "You're my family, and it's what families do for each other. It's something I learned from the Rabbi. I'm sorry my mother doesn't know, or care, about any of this. Believe it or not, I still miss her a lot."

"Of course you miss her," his father said, "You were very close at one time. Maybe someday…"

Gabriel interrupted his father. "Don't even go there, *bâbâ*," he said sadly. "I've waited for so many years and there's been absolutely nothing."

Shortly after the academic year began, Gabriel and Tamar started dating exclusively, but within a few months she accepted the sad reality that she and Gabriel were not soul-mates; she knew neither of them was one of the "frogs" he'd told her about, but neither were they 'The One' for each other. During the semester break, she invited both Gabriel and Dani to meet her for coffee at Café Atara. When they arrived, separately, they saw Tamar at a table near the back. "We have to talk," she said. "I know how much the two of you care for each other; in fact you've been in love with each other for years and I'm in the way! I've seen the way you try not to look at each other and I've seen the sparks between you. I've never set off those sparks in Gabriel and he didn't set them off for me, but I've ignored the truth. When we double-dated with you and your boyfriend of the moment, Dani, there was always something between you and Gabriel. None of those other guys lasted long, and some of them were really nice. I remember the first time we met Gabriel; we were still in high school and you fell for him then."

Dani flushed and swallowed. "We've never…"

"I know that, Dani," Tamar said quietly. "I know you, so I know you'd never move in on a friend's territory. But Gabriel's not 'my territory'. Don't say anything, Gabriel. I know you're grateful to me for what my father and relatives in California did for your father and his family. But do you want to know something? That's not enough for me. I deserve a lot better. I know you care for me, but like a sister, like you care for your friend Ruth. Don't say anything. Just answer this: Do you love each other? A simple nod will do." Without looking at each other, Dani and Gabriel each nodded 'Yes'.

"OK," Tamar said. "Truth is good, and since we're being truthful, I can tell you I still love you – both of you – as my very best friends. But I have a secret, Dani, one I'm willing to bet you've never guessed. When we were growing up, I had a crush on your brother – on Yaniv, not Kobi. But your 'brother the nerd' never looked at me; he was always too wrapped up in his computers. But enough of all this maudlin conversation! Let's just finish our coffee and go home to our own rooms."

Gabriel finally spoke. "You're the best, Tamar, and you deserve the best. I'm sure you'll find 'The One' someday. If it's Yaniv, I'll be very happy for both of you."

"Me, too," Dani said, sniffing a bit. "Now if I can find a way to get my dear brother to shut off his computers for a while…"

"Don't even think about it, Dani," Tamar said. "What's that old song? Oh yes! *'Que Sera, Sera';* if it's meant to be, it will be. Yaniv believes in fate or coincidence, so we'll see…"

"But sometimes even a nerd needs a jump-start or a kick in the pants!" Dani added with a smile before Tamar said anything. "OK, I'll keep quiet."

After that incredibly honest evening, Gabriel and Dani were inseparable. They didn't make love their first full night together. They kissed deeply for hours, and they decided to move slowly into the deeper world of sex – they would wait until their second night! The next night, after the most ecstatic and the longest and most sweaty lovemaking of his life, Gabriel looked at Dani with all his feelings in his eyes. He said, "I never believed all those stories about the earth moving or someone's heart standing still; they were romantic words, song lyrics. But now I know they're true. I never felt those things when I was making love with anyone else. I guess I was only 'having sex' until now."

Still, he was a tiny bit disappointed that Dani hadn't been a virgin, and he told her he would have loved to have been her first. She burst out laughing. "This is the 21st century, my dearest true love. Do you really think many girls my age are still virgins?"

"Have there been a lot of guys? You're so beautiful, so full of life and…I don't know what to call it…verve? Vitality? *Chutzpah?*" At that last one, she punched him in the arm playfully. "I know you've dated a lot, so you can tell me the truth. I can take it."

"Only two," she said quietly. "The first one was just after high school, and I was the one who pushed for it. I had a crush on you and I wanted to be 'a sophisticated *femme fatale*' if you and I ever got together. He was my *Aba*'s teaching assistant, nice, smart, a few years older; he was very gentle that first time, but there were no other times. He was so afraid *Aba* would find out and fire him. Obviously, he didn't really know my *Aba*."

"Is he still working with your *Aba*? I don't have the right to be jealous, but if he's around, I'd punch him in the face." That bought another punch on the arm, this one a little stronger. "Stop making me your personal punching bag, Dani," he said. "I may not have the right to be jealous, but I hate the idea of anyone hitting, but in his case not hitting, on the woman I love."

"I love you, too, Gabriel. Danny, yeah, the same name, graduated and is now doing a PhD in the States. Do I have the right to be jealous of all the other women in your life? Not Tamar, because I love her. Not Rina, as she was stupid and let you go. But maybe all the others…"

Gabriel laughed. "There haven't been so many others. Between *Tzahal* and keeping my grades high for scholarships, I haven't had that much time. Besides, I was suffering from unrequited lust! Yes lust; I didn't know then that it was love for a flirtatious 15-year-old. Or were you 16? I had to get rid of my frustration somehow, although I'm religious and I'm supposed to believe sex should follow marriage. Right?"

This time, Dani didn't punch him. She moved onto his lap, grabbed his face and gave him noisy, open-mouthed kisses…a lot of them, until they were both breathless, hot and ready for another round of passion. Not just having sex; making love. This time Dani was on top, touching every inch of him with her hands and mouth; he was so aroused and knew he couldn't hold on to his control much longer, so he flipped Dani onto her back, kissed his way down her body from her engorged nipples to the sweet indentation of her naval and finally into the glorious wetness below, until she shrieked his name again and again as she welcomed her climax. "Never… never… never… I've never felt anything like this," she whispered as Gabriel donned a condom, and quickly entered her while she was still convulsing, bringing both of them quickly to an earthshaking climax, what the French call *"le petite mort"*, the little death. When they had both caught their breath and were cuddling in his bed after Gabriel disposed of the condom, he asked, "What about the second guy? And why only two? I've met some of your boyfriends and they've been pretty nice guys. Don't get mad at me for asking. I just want to know everything about you…even that."

"I'm not mad. The second one was someone in the army. And it was just sex, sex that wasn't even satisfactory. Despite my very limited experience, I knew more about sex than he did, so our 'love affair' – if I can even call it that – was very short. As for all the guys I've dated… after the one in the army, I knew I had to have strong feelings for a person to have sex with him, and I never had strong feelings for any of them. I wouldn't let them go beyond 'first base', so they gave up on me after only one or two dates." She grinned at him in her cheeky way and she whispered, "I really was saving myself for you all that time."

Dani didn't move into Gabriel's flat because she knew she was still young and she was afraid her parents would be disappointed. But they weren't. No one in the Hofman family – not even her older brothers – disapproved of her loving relationship with Gabriel. One Friday afternoon, a few minutes after they arrived in Ramat Aviv for the weekend, Lise pulled Dani aside and said to her, "If you remember our stories, you know that your father and I fell in love when we were still in university and we started making love after knowing each other for a week; I understand the same thing was true of Gabriel's parents after two weeks. So move his things into your room and sleep with each other, and make love if you wish, every night."

Dani's face turned red. "In your house?" she asked, barely breathing.

"It's your house, too, my darling daughter. And you know both your *Aba* and I already love Gabriel like another son."

Dani hugged her mother and went to find Gabriel.

◆ ◆ ◆

In July 2006, Gabriel, Dani and Alex had completed only a few of their final exams when Gabriel received a *tzav shmoneh* summoning him to *milu'im* at Urim, Unit 8200's command base, a week before the outbreak of the Second Lebanon War. Hugging and saying goodbye to a frightened Dani before he left, he said in a very strange American drawl, "A man's gotta do what a man's gotta do!" She laughed of course and quipped, "And what does a woman gotta do? Sit back and worry? Get pregnant and stay barefoot? John Wayne was always a 'male chauvinist pig'!" Then she kissed him again and again before he left. As usual at Urim, he translated online chatter and hundreds of Farsi codes trying to ascertain the depth of Iran's unprecedented military support for Hezbollah. Hezbollah had fired Iranian-made rockets into northern Israel, and ambushes resulted in the death of five IDF soldiers along with the kidnapping of two others. Two days after Gabriel's *tzav shmoneh*, Yaniv and Alex were called up and Dani was summoned on July 12th, the first day of the war; she held briefings with the foreign press covering the war. Gabriel, who'd never been in Israel during a war, admitted he was a little frightened, not so much for himself but for the comrades who had come to mean almost as much to him as his "family" in Graz, especially Alex whose *Sayeret Matkal* unit had to engage the paramilitary forces of Hezbollah in more than a few covert attacks, and Kobi, "a flying cat" whose Unit 669 rescued many injured soldiers. Lise and David, all of the grandparents, and Ruth were glued to TV and radio, worrying about their loved ones until the ceasefire on August 14th. But like the majority of Israelis, the Hofman family had mixed feelings about this short but emotionally devastating war, believing there had not been a decisive victory in this conflict; 121 soldiers and 45 civilians were killed by Hezbollah rockets as well as an unreported number of Lebanese and at least 600 Hezbollah fighters. Dani, Gabriel and Alex, slightly depressed, returned to Hebrew University for their remaining exams, and Yaniv went back to IDC Herzliya. A few weeks later, when exam results were published, all of them had aced the exams. That was when Dani informed her parents that she was moving in with Gabriel.

After he received his BA from Hebrew University in 2007, Gabriel was offered scholarships for an MA-PhD at Oxford, Harvard, UCLA, Tel Aviv and Hebrew Universities. "I'll bet some of those offers were made because of my dad and your father and their friends," he said to Dani, shocked at the accolades in the acceptance letters. She disagreed, and with a kiss, proudly said it was because he was so clever, and his work combining esoteric language and extremist philosophy was essential, not just fascinating.

Although he really wanted to go to Oxford, Dani was at the stage in her studies in Jerusalem where it was impossible for her to transfer. They knew that working on their degrees made it impossible for either of them to take the flight between Israel and the UK frequently; nor would they be able to concentrate if they were e-mailing and phoning constantly during the long separations. Since Dani was the most important part of his life – far more important than a degree from Oxford, however prestigious – Gabriel opted for an MA in philosophy from Hebrew University, and hoped for an Oxford PhD in the future. When they graduated in June 2008, with a BA for Dani and an MA for Gabriel, Dani's parents, grandparents, sister, brothers, aunts and uncles attended the MA ceremony, as did Jakob and Rebecca

Breitling. Gabriel's MA thesis, based on John Locke's opinions on the misuse of language, proved that extremist Islamic scholars used words loosely or intentionally to obfuscate meaning, thus leading to new interpretations of the Qur'an; he proved that deviations stemming from the misinterpretation of Islamic text and flawed translations were truly radical and could be very dangerous when widely disseminated. His professors were so impressed by Gabriel's thesis that he was recognized as Hebrew University's outstanding MA graduate of 2008. After receiving his diploma, a plaque and a standing ovation from the audience, Gabriel looked at Dani and then almost fell off the stage when he saw his father standing next to her father. Outside the auditorium, after many hugs and congratulations, Dani's father said, "Lise reminded me that my father and hers surprised me by attending my PhD defense at the Sorbonne. It was one of the great moments of my life…not quite as momentous as my two weddings and the birth of my children, but nonetheless a fabulous moment. I contacted your father and invited him to give a few lectures at Tel Aviv University; and that's how we arranged for him to come here today."

With tears in his eyes, Gabriel said, "Thank you, David, and you, Lise. I don't know what to say. The two of you are the best. This is indeed a very great moment. Dad, *bâbâ*, have you met Dani, the love of my life?"

Gabriel and Dani moved to Oxford in August for him to pursue a DPhil. When they arrived at Heathrow, he was sure he'd feel anxious about being back in the country of his birth. But he and his mother had left England when he was only four years old, so although he felt some unease, his angst wasn't about the UK. In fact, he was just happy to be in Oxford with Dani. Because of her IDF work and her English skills, Dani was offered a PR position in the Israeli Embassy. They had found a small flat not far from the Oxford train station so Dani could work on her laptop during the 75-minute commute and reduce her workload to four days. Everything in Oxford was focused on the university and Gabriel enjoyed his commute to and from his tutorials at Balliol College or the Bodleian Library, a 15-minute walk. He loved meeting Dani for dinner at Holywell Manor, the graduate center's medieval building; the inexpensive but superb meals were prepared by an award-winning chef. Afterwards Gabriel and Dani would meander slowly through Oxford's quaint streets, but by the time they reached the flat, they'd race up the two flights of stairs, pulling off clothing and tossing them onto the floor the minute they opened the door. They'd make love against the door, or on the striped rug from Jerusalem's Arab *shuk* or in the enameled clawfoot tub surprisingly large for such a small flat, or in their double bed, and most of the time in more than one site before they finally succumbed to sleep. Their passion for each other was endless, and Gabriel often marveled at how far that desperately sad young boy who'd been thrown out into the street by his mother had come.

Gabriel knew he'd been given an extraordinary opportunity by Oxford; its philosophy faculty was considered one of the best in the world with more than 150 major philosophers and distinguished visiting luminaries, covering the vast range of philosophy. He appreciated their tutorial system which allowed him to discuss his research not only one-to-one with his personal tutor but with some outstanding philosophers and linguists. For the DPhil, Gabriel was required to write a 75,000 word dissertation on his research into the earliest translations of the Qur'an from Arabic into Persian in the 8th century, into Greek and Sindhi (Pakistani) in the 9th century, and later into Urdu, Turkish, Armenian, Bengali, Russian, French, English, German, even Hebrew – and how so many translations altered and distorted not only the real meaning of the text linguistically but also the intent of the Qur'an. This led him into evaluating the potential danger of such egregious misinterpretation and misuse of the Qur'an by extremist Islamic groups. The treasured Islamic manuscripts in the Bodleian Library, dating back to the 17th century, were fascinating. He arrived at the Bodleian early one day to meet with his tutor, and – for some unknown reason – he looked up both Dani's father and his in the library's catalog; he was amazed at the list of books and articles by both professors. Laughing, he said to himself, "It looks like being suspicious of dogma is in my genetic makeup, from my father abhorring Iran's fanaticism, to me questioning the priests in the Domkirche about Catholic mysticism and challenging Rabbi Breitling about Jewish miracles, to debating Dani's *Aba*'s contradictions of famous French philosophers' interpretations of contemporary protests, and even to doubting Dani's grandfathers' so-called coincidences. It's just too bad my very clever mother doesn't know how much her linguistic input in my DNA has given me – not only an inquisitive mind but also a potentially gratifying career!"

When Operation Cast Lead, a three-week conflict between Israel and the Palestinians broke out in Gaza at the end of December 2008, both Gabriel and Dani immediately volunteered to rejoin their units, but both were told by the IDF that they weren't needed at that time. They knew Yaniv and Kobi had both been called in, and they worried up until yet another brief, calamitous war ended, and Dani's brothers were released safe and sound, at least physically.

Dani and Gabriel lived frugally in England because they didn't want to be dependent on her family or his father, so they refused to take money for daily living. Dani's Embassy salary helped defray some expenses, as did Gabriel's tutoring and occasional stint as a bartender in a pub where they enjoyed a meal. They accepted airline tickets from her parents so they could join the family for holidays and major celebrations like Passover, summer break, the Weizmann Institute's retirement party for Dani's illustrious grandfather.

In 2009, instead of staying in Israel through the High Holy Days, they returned to Oxford in August after three fun-filled weeks; Gabriel had accepted a TA job and had to prepare his assignments as well as meet with his tutor to organize his own research. His salary was sufficient to meet their basic needs, especially with tutoring on the side, and Dani quit her Embassy job. In mid-September they flew to Graz to spend *Rosh Hashanah* and the 10-day *Yamim Noraim* with the Rabbi's family and Gabriel's old friends, except Jakob, David and Ruth who all lived in Israel. Karl, taking a brief holiday away from his touring Klezmer band came, as did Daniel on a break after an engineering project in Nigeria with David's father. Dani, who'd met the Breitlings, except Daniel, when they visited Jakob's family in Jerusalem, was absolutely delighted to meet him and Frau Sarah; Frau Sarah, Karl and Daniel were just as pleased with her, especially when they recalled how very broken Gabriel had been when he first stumbled into the Rabbi's home.

During the summer, they'd spent some time with David, Gabriel's "brother", a pediatric cardiology resident at Schneider Children's Medical Center. Dani knew David well, having met him many times when he was at TAU's Sackler School of Medicine and dating her sister Keren; he'd helped Dani and her friends plan the itinerary for their post-army trip to South America. But Keren went to Denmark for her PhD, thus putting an end to her relationship with David. Gabriel and Dani took him to the café on Milano Square that her parents had frequented when they first came to Israel; her cousin Yael, Alon and Dina's daughter, who was studying medicine, joined them. Dani hoped something romantic would happen between the two doctors because these "relatives" deserved the same kind of happiness that she'd found with Gabriel. David had been crushed when Keren "deserted" him for her PhD, but Keren merely liked him – or so Dani thought. And unfortunately, it seemed that David and Yael were just destined to be good friends.

In October, when the British academic year began, Dani enrolled as a candidate for an MA in Art History at the Courtauld Institute of Art, the semi-independent school within the University of London, located inside Somerset House in the Strand. Her BA studies at Hebrew University had been so extensive and her grades so high that Dani's only requirements were two seminars in subjects she'd barely knew, French Impressionist and Post-Impressionist art. As each seminar met only once a week, going to London wasn't a problem, and she could do her research in Oxford's library. She told Gabriel The Courtauld's collection was very impressive, and they both laughed at her unintentional "almost-pun". Both seminars were interesting and having coffee and "nibbles" with fellow students in the Somerset House café was an added pleasure. MA students at The Courtauld, as it was always called, had to choose an area of specialized research – from antiquity to modern or futuristic art. During Orientation, Dani found she was intrigued by the conservation of antique mosaics, and Gabriel teased her about "going antique" so she wouldn't step on her mother's toes by choosing to specialize in contemporary art; she secretly admitted he might be right. The Courtauld, a major world center for art conservation, admitted only eight students each year into the 18-month program. Dani was accepted into the program for two reasons – her superb record at Hebrew U and the unique opportunity to save recently unearthed mosaics and wall paintings near the Sea of Galilee. The Courtauld's program focused on diagnosis of the deterioration of the ancient works, strategies to control additional decay and respect for the integrity of the object and its context. Always a brilliant student, Dani had never been so excited about any project since the *chanukiah* she made at the JCC in Brookline, Massachusetts, when her *Aba* was a visiting professor at Harvard. Knowing how supportive Dani always was of him, Gabriel was truly elated with her enthusiasm. He knew she had liked her BA courses at Hebrew U, and she had succeeded brilliantly, but he had never seen her like this – except in relation to him. So he promised to help her with this degree in any way that he could.

The next year and a half passed quietly and rather quickly. They both worked hard on their research, but they also took long walks along the Isis, Oxford's segment of the River Thames. They continued to enjoy excellent dinners in Holywell Manor, which "certainly beat shopping and cooking when there are so many other pleasures to enjoy, like making love with my future husband," Dani claimed. Gabriel swatted his cheeky future wife's rear – and took her home to bed. They were both enchanted by the legend of Rosa, Oxford's "Comrade

Tortoise" named after a notorious Marxist, Rosa Luxemburg; the tortoise resided at Balliol College for 43 years. Each June, tortoises from other Oxford colleges took part in a race – a very slow race – which Rosa won many times. But she disappeared in 2004; numerous conspiracy theories were offered although none were proved true. A Christ Church graduate donated two new tortoises, one to his college and one to Balliol. "Keeper of the Tortoise" was a task given to a new student every year, even when there was no "resident tortoise". Gabriel and Dani loved this eccentricity, and they both wondered if any Israeli university would ever be so lighthearted.

Occasionally they defected from Oxford. They went to Swansea to visit one of Gabriel's first dons, giving them the opportunity to see Wales and the Cotswolds. They went to Stratford-on-Avon and were enthralled by the Royal Shakespeare's *Macbeth*. They went to Bath but despite its connection to Jane Austen, they found it neither as unique nor anywhere as charming as Cornwall. They had spent a long weekend at a B&B in St. Ives, exploring nearby Truro's famed smugglers' coastline and its quaint shops. Their hosts, on hearing Dani was studying art conservation, insisted she would enjoy a different kind of conservation – the Screech Owl Sanctuary in St. Columb Major, where they learned about captive breeding programs and efforts to reintroduce the birds into the wild, and where they were even allowed to touch the owls. They visited Penzance, with Dani singing the music from the Gilbert and Sullivan comic opera about the area's pirates; Gabriel didn't say he was glad it was only a 20-minute drive since, unlike Karl, singing wasn't Dani's forte. Sadly, they couldn't afford to buy a painting Dani loved by one of the many artists who flocked to Cornwall every year. "It's OK, Dani," Gabriel said. "Not one of those artists is as good as your *Ema*."

Both of them as children had loved Beatrix Potter's stories so they had to go to the Lake District before returning to Israel. They spent a weekend at Buckle Yeat, a B&B just a minute away from Hill Top, Potter's home; their cottage was illustrated in a few of her stories, according to the owners. They went to Dove Cottage, Wordsworth's home in Grasmere, but there were no golden daffodils "fluttering and dancing" in the breeze. With a picnic lunch in knapsacks on their backs, they hiked the Windermere Way, the 10.5-mile circular walk around the lake. Stopping for lunch halfway through, lying on a blanket from Gabriel's knapsack, he said, "That's it. I'm really ready to go home – to Israel, not to Oxford." Dani heartily agreed.

Chapter 6

Even though his dissertation had been submitted and his students' papers had all been marked, Gabriel was depressed on April 12th, 2011, the day he received the letter from his mother. Oxford had been severely criticized by the British press for not paying attention to plagiarism, and one of Gabriel's undergraduate students had been caught with a purloined paper, but not for his course. The Council of Dons voted to expel the student, not just fail him in the course where he'd cheated. But neither Oxford's plagiarism problem nor his mother's letter was the reason for Gabriel's mood; he was so morose because Dani was in Israel and his loneliness overwhelmed him. She'd gone home to finish her MA project on the deterioration and conservation of the Galilee mosaics and wall paintings; she had to evaluate the potential effects of her preservation methods and produce written, graphic and photographic documentation so The Courtauld could publish her thesis. Gabriel had been offered a teaching position in both linguistics and philosophy at Tel Aviv University, so Dani was also trying to find an apartment. More important in her opinion, with her parents' help, she was finalizing the plans for their wedding. Gabriel would join them in Tel Aviv for Passover, so he decided not to let himself open the letter from his mother until they were together.

The minute Dani saw him at the airport, she realized something was very wrong. "What is it?" she asked, after kissing him. "Did some idiotic professor reject your dissertation?"

"Of course not, my wonderful silly girl, whom I love to distraction and missed desperately," he said. "I don't know what the professors think as I haven't heard from anyone but my tutor. I'm upset because you were not there when I received a very long letter from my mother."

"That's why you're upset? What did she say?" Dani, inquired.

"I don't know," Gabriel answered. "I haven't opened it. I want to read it at your parent's house with the people I love. OK?"

Dani said with a smile, "Of course it's OK. I would have ripped it open and read it immediately. But I know you, so we'll wait until we're home." She drove to Ramat Aviv as quickly as the law allowed.

The entire family greeted him with hugs, kisses and shoulder slaps; Anna had prepared snacks and drinks, but Gabriel put his untouched plate and cup down on a side table. He took his mother's letter out of his pocket, unfolded the 5 pages, and began to read it aloud.

Chapter 6

21 March 2011

My dearest Daryush,

I know I should address you as Gabriel, but to me, my darling son, you will always be Dominik or Daryush. I am sure you are curious about how I found you and how I know your name is now Gabriel. I went to see Rabbi Breitling a few months ago and he told me about you – rather reluctantly I'll say, to his credit. Since then, I've been trying to work up the courage to write to you...

I live with so much guilt for the way I treated you; I live with it every day. You should know that I have never stopped thinking about you, never stopped loving you, never stopped hoping I would see you again...never stopped knowing how much I hurt you.

Dominik, my dearest, you know my father was a hard man, and very domineering. I was always intimidated by him, as was my mother. Every time I tried to rebel against his harshness, that worked to my detriment. One of those times was when I fell in love with your father and another, of course, when I gave birth to you, the only two real loves of my life besides my brother. My father basically threw me out when I was pregnant, and I was alone when you were born. I can't say life in London where you were born was easy, but my love for you sustained me.

Marrying Ara and moving to Yerevan when you were 4-years-old was a mistake for me, but it wasn't a mistake for you. Ara was – and still is – a good man, and he cared very deeply for you. I was the problem. I disliked my life in Armenia; I was bored and churlish – maybe even childish. I was unfriendly to Ara's business associates and friends. If I'd had another child or two to care for, it would have been different – but that never happened.

After Ara and I divorced, I knew you needed to have a family – so we moved to Graz, even though it frightened me to be living under my father's thumb again. Since I've always been fortunate to have a profession which allows me to be independent, in time you and I were able to live in our own home. But my father insisted you follow the same educational path as my brother and I if I wanted us to live in Graz. At first the Domkirche did seem to be a good educational choice for you. But when you began to question many of the beliefs of the Church, my father was furious, claiming he saw the same streak of rebellion in you that he used to see in me.

And he had a strong ally in Monsignor Dietrich, a priest so rigid we'd label him an extremist today. I was truly shocked by your behavior – and perhaps if I'm completely honest with myself now, even a little envious of your courage. But once again my father intimidated me, as did Monsignor Dietrich, and my only bit of courage was when I stopped them from going to Rabbi Breitling's home and physically dragging you back to the Church. You can't imagine how painful it was for me to surrender custody of you to the Rabbi. The only thing that kept me sane was knowing I couldn't allow myself to communicate with you, although I cried every day for years and years. And all these years, I have missed you every minute. It was like living forever with a chronic heartache, so much self-inflicted pain.

But now so many things have happened, and it is your right to know all of them. First of all, my father died a few months ago, and little by little, things that I never knew were revealed. My sweet but timid mother told me she had been born Jewish; her parents were killed in a riot in 1938, when their synagogue was dynamited and burned on November 10, (Kristallnacht, the "Night of the Broken Glass"). Only 5-years-old, she was saved by a Catholic family, the Müllers, whose oldest daughter was her babysitter that awful night. The Müllers took my mother into their home and told everyone she was a niece whose parents had died in a fire. To their credit, they were always kind to her – and they did save her from the Nazis and certain death. Friedrich, the Müllers' oldest son, and my mother were married in 1953 and a year later, in 1954, my brother Friedrich Jünger was born. My poor mother suffered three miscarriages before I was born in 1960. I worshipped my big brother and he adored me.

The only other man I ever loved was Darian Sarkohi, your father, an Iranian PhD student at the university in Vienna. We were lovers for quite a long time, but I never took him home because I knew my father would not accept a foreign son-in-law – no matter how brilliant he was. Darian had to return to Iran after graduation, but he promised he'd be in touch with me very soon and we could find a way to be together. I had completed my BA and was home in Graz waiting to hear from Darian. But he never called. And then I found out I was pregnant. So did my father when he heard me vomiting in the bathroom several

Chapter 6

mornings in a row. He confronted me and demanded to know who the father was. I told him the father of my baby was the man I loved, an Iranian graduate student. My father slapped me very hard. He screamed that he'd never accept a foreigner's bastard as his grandchild, he would not be shamed in the eyes of the Church or gossiped about by all the neighbors.

My darling Dominik, there are so many ironies in our history – incredible ironies inside ironies. My mother told me a young man whose name she thought was Darren called a few times after I returned from Vienna, but when he wouldn't give my father any details about who he was, my father wouldn't let him speak to me. The Rabbi told me it wasn't difficult for him to locate an Iranian student who'd been studying for a PhD in Vienna in the 1980s – and I know you've met your father several times; you've even met your grandmother, and through you, your father and his family were able to relocate to California. How ironic! My love, you know the man whose name I never told you, and you see him whenever you can while I, who loved you with all my heart from the moment you were born, haven't seen you for fifteen years.

Dominik, my darling, please don't feel guilty about anything. I know it was all my fault – but I hope you can see the tragic irony of this situation. Rabbi Breitling told me you converted to Judaism – TWICE!! – and that's why you changed your name to Gabriel. Well, since my mother was born Jewish, I'm also Jewish; if we had known, you would never have had to convert even ONCE! As I said, ironies inside ironies! After my father died, my mother stopped going to church; she said there was no reason since she isn't Catholic. A few weeks after the funeral, Monsignor Dietrich came to see her when he noticed she wasn't attending Mass. He didn't believe her when she told him she was born Jewish and the Müllers, and her husband Friedrich in particular, destroyed all her memories of her childhood and her parents with their lies; they crushed her self-confidence and she didn't even remember that her real name was Esther. Friedrich broke up her family, sabotaged her daughter's possibility of marriage to the father of her son and later her relationship with her brilliant son. She told the monsignor that Friedrich demolished her own contact with her son and grandson. She even told him that she blamed him, Monsignor Dietrich, for encouraging Friedrich's hostility and prejudices. I couldn't believe it. The monsignor was absolutely furious and told my mother he was excommunicating her from the Church and she would burn in hell. Before he left the house, my mother asked why he would excommunicate someone who wasn't even Catholic and then she said, "Good riddance!"

She's a different person now, warm and open, even though she's getting on in years. We share a nice flat in Graz; I still do a lot of translation and I went back to university for an MA degree. I teach two linguistics courses.

And here are two more ironies. My mother does some volunteer work with teenagers who are at risk, and they just love her. When I met Rabbi Breitling and told him everything and even what my mother was doing, he thought she might like to meet Sarah Bernhardt; they have become friends and Frau Sarah has told her a lot about you. The Rabbi told me a little about your life in Israel, that you're currently working towards a PhD at Oxford, and that you have a lovely fiancée named Daniella Hofman. I'm so happy for you, but so envious of your close relationship with the Rabbi's family and with Daniella and her family.

Dominik, my dear, dear love, would it be possible for us to meet? I can come to London or Oxford – wherever you want, if you agree.

I'm longing to hear from you.

All my love always,

Mother

Nobody said a word when he'd finished reading. Gabriel said, "There are three additional documents One is an Austrian birth certificate for 'Esther, female, Jewish, born 7 August 1933 to Eliakim and Miriam Weiss'. The second one is dated 10 September 1939; it's a legal affidavit for adoption by Hermann and Johanna Müller née Waldheim of Elke Waldheim, female, 6 years of age, Catholic, born 7 August 1933 to Ernst and Ilse Waldheim, parents deceased'. The third is a certificate for 'marriage between Friedrich and Elke Müller née Waldheim, 15 May 1953, in the Domkirche Cathedral, Graz, Austria'." He said, laughing a bit cynically, "One long letter and three documents. My mother is thorough and organized! Talk about irony!"

"Gabriel, honey," Lise said. "Don't be bitter. She's hurting. And so are you. You've been hurting for many years, but maybe now's the time to let it go. She didn't know her mother was Jewish until her father died. It won't be easy for either of you to put all this behind you, but at least think about it."

David nodded, as did Yaniv, Kobi, and Lise's father. Grandma Anna, a Holocaust survivor herself, had been weeping quietly while Gabriel read his mother's letter, but she nodded along with all the others. Dani, who'd been sitting close to him the whole time, kissed him. "I think *Ema*'s absolutely right, Gabriel. *Saba* says the great Yiddish writer, Sholem Aleichem, in one of his stories, tells a drunk man 'if three people tell a man that he's drunk, he should go to sleep'. You're not drunk, but now seven people have told you to try to forgive your mother. So do it! Let's invite her to Oxford. Now let's talk about something important – our wedding!" Everyone laughed as usual at Dani's cheeky comment, including Gabriel; as she'd intended, the tension in the room dissipated.

Later, when they were all sitting quietly, drinking wine, Lise said, "I did conversion lessons twice, and I have no regrets at all. I love being Jewish, my family and life here, and celebrating all the holidays. Gabriel, do you think your life would've been better or at least easier if you'd always known you were Jewish by birth?"

He burst out laughing. "Easier, maybe, and I wouldn't have lost fifteen years with my mother. But I also wouldn't have had the special experiences I've had with the Breitlings and my close friends. I wouldn't have met Yaniv and all of you. I wouldn't have fallen in love with Dani and I wouldn't have decided to spend my life in Israel. So no, in no way am I sorry that I didn't know I was born Jewish. Grandma Anna, you always say a lot of things in life are *bashert* – and I think my life is a perfect example."

◆ ◆ ◆

Gabriel and Dani returned to Oxford and met his mother at Gloucester Green, Oxford's bus station, three weeks later. She'd told them she knew parking at Heathrow was a hassle, so she'd take the direct bus to Oxford. The second she stepped off the bus, Gabriel recognized her and she knew him. But after mutual "hellos", neither of them knew what to say. So, as usual, gregarious Dani stepped into the awkward breach, asking about Frederica's flight from Graz, if she was hungry, if there was anything she couldn't eat as they'd be picking up some things at the market just two minutes away. Frederica, smiling at Dani, said, "I don't fly very well, and the flight from Graz to London is not non-stop, so I flew from Vienna. They fed us decently on the plane, so I'm not hungry. I'm not fussy at all about food, but maybe you'll let me take you out."

Dani, trying to make everything seem normal, squeezed Gabriel's hand and suggested, "Let's have coffee at Combibos and get to know each other. It's very nearby. Then we'll take you to Rewley House where we've booked a room for you because our flat is really tiny and can't accommodate guests except my brothers who don't mind sleeping on the floor. Rewley House is halfway between our flat and Balliol College, Gabriel's domain, and I'm sure you'll enjoy walking around the area. Rewley House is really close to the Bodleian Library and the Ashmolean, Oxford's museum, which I know well from my own work and I can tell you it's marvelous. Oxford is so charming with quaint shops and... I'm talking too much as usual."

Gabriel laughed and really looked at his mother for the first time. "Dani has a knack for breaking the tension in any room by talking non-stop. It's best just to ignore her." Dani punched him lightly on the arm. "Or," he grinned, "agree with her! Actually, Mo..." He stopped speaking. "I don't know what to call you," he said awkwardly, coughing and blinking rapidly.

"How about 'Madame Monster' or Madame Ogre'? I really deserve those names!" She smiled sadly. "Call me 'Frederica or nothing. You'll call me 'Mother' only if, or when, you're ready."

"I started to say 'Mother' yesterday at Holywell Manor, Balliol's dining hall, when I reserved a table for tonight. The chef there is quite famous."

With the ice between mother and son melting slightly, the three of them sat down in Combibos. Dani went to place their order, leaving Gabriel and Frederica alone. His mother looked at him with eyes full of love. "I know we have to take this reunion slowly, but I'm so proud of you and of all you've accomplished without my family. And Dani is absolutely adorable as well as beautiful. Lucky, lucky you!"

"I know I'm really lucky," Gabriel said. "It was very difficult for me at first. But Rabbi Breitling's home became my home, and his family became my family along with the other teenagers living there. It was hard again when I first came to Israel. My only friend was the Rabbi's son Jakob. And the army was just as bad, because boot camp was such a new experience and the other recruits were so different from me. My translation work left me even more isolated. So the day I met Dani's brother was one of the luckiest days of my life. Yaniv and I were partners in our army unit, and through him I found another special family, Dani of course, her parents and grandparents, her sister Keren

Chapter 6

and her other brother Kobi, and so many new friends, like Tamar whose family helped my father and his family get to California. By the way, Yaniv's brilliant; he's a 'techie' in computers and cryptography, but if I told you anything about the work we did together in the army, I'd have to kill you."

Dani came back as Frederica, laughing, said, "Even at eight-years-old, you were a James Bond fan! I won't ask about things I shouldn't know and I'll try to call you Gabriel, but it might take a while for me to get used to it."

He responded with a smile, "It took me a while to get used to it, too."

As they waited for their coffee, Dani noted how relaxed, even convivial, the atmosphere was. She squeezed Gabriel's hand under the table. "I called him 'handsome Gabriel' the day I met him," she said. "And I still call him that, sometimes!" After the coffee, they took his mother to Rewley House, her hotel, on Wellington Square and St. John Street, in one of Oxford's most picturesque neighborhoods. Walking back to their flat, Dani asked, "I'm so proud of how you handled that. It wasn't really too bad, was it?"

"It could have been a lot worse. I was worried, maybe even scared, about seeing her again after so many years. But at least our first meeting is over," Gabriel admitted.

Later, at Holywell Manor, Frederica said she'd enjoyed walking around the area near Rewley House. "As you said, Dani, Oxford is charming. It's funny. I've been in the UK so many times since Domer-Gabriel and I lived here. London, of course, Yorkshire, Leeds, Edinburgh, Glasgow, and even Belfast and Derry. I did a course at Cambridge, but for some unknown reason, I've never been here although Oxford's so close to London."

"You've waited for Gabriel to give you a reason," Dani said with a grin.

"Right! I had an unconscious, or perhaps a subconscious reason. Or maybe I'm just psychic!" Frederica said, returning Dani's smile.

The remainder of the evening passed pleasantly for all of them. Frederica asked Gabriel many questions about his research and dissertation, and he answered in detail because he knew she would understand, given her expertise in linguistics. As they lingered over coffee before walking back to Rewley House, they exchanged cell phone numbers and said they'd be in touch the next day. Gabriel said he had some work to finish and he wanted to start packing his books and papers, but he promised they'd get together in the evening. Dani offered to 'play tour guide' at the Ashmolean, and Frederica jumped at the opportunity to get to know her vivacious future daughter-in-law. On their way home, holding hands as was their custom, Dani said, "I like her."

"I always liked her. And not just because she was my mother," Gabriel responded. "But it hurt so much when she threw me out and it will take me a while to get over that. I can say that I liked her a lot this evening."

The following morning, he received a call from the chairman of Balliol's philosophy division, Professor David Wallace, asking Gabriel to come to his office as soon as possible. Even though he knew his research had been thorough and his dissertation well-written, Gabriel was nervous as he dressed and walked to the college. When he arrived, Professor Wallace's secretary said, "Go right in. They're expecting you." He opened the door and saw several faculty members standing with Professor Wallace, who smiled and said "Congratulations, *Doctor* Ben-Shmuel! I wanted to be the first to tell you the Faculty Board not only approved your dissertation, but they acclaimed it: *summa cum laude*. I wish we could keep you here, but unfortunately there are no openings now. Maybe sometime in the future… I hope Tel Aviv University knows what an asset you are. In the meantime, you must order full academic dress for the ceremony."

Gabriel stammered his thanks, shaking hands with all the professors, each expressing regret that Gabriel couldn't stay at Oxford, stating it was their loss. Professor Wallace offered a toast to Gabriel's continued academic success; completely flabbergasted, he drank the glass of champagne. In the secretary's office, after receiving her congratulations, he called Dani and asked, "Is my mother with you?"

"I left her in the Ashmolean. I had to take an important call. Gabriel…"

"Wait a second. I have to tell you something. Wallace called me to his office and all the professors in the department were there. My dissertation was approved *summa cum laude*. I am now officially Dr. Ben-Shmuel, or I will be after graduation. You had to be the first to know, and all I can say right now is 'Wow!' Please don't tell my mother. I'll tell her later. Right now, I'm going to call your father. And then, although I'll wake him up in the middle of the night, I'm calling my father, too. Now Dani, my darling, what was your important call?"

"Ohmigod!" Dani blurted. "Congratulations, my dearest love! And here's another 'Wow!' It's for me! My call was from The Courtauld. My thesis has been approved and it will be published. I'll tell your

Chapter 6

mother about me when I'm back in the Ashmolean, but I want to tell my parents myself. The little girl they once thought was a changeling has 'done them proud!' Do you believe it? Both of us getting the fabulous news on the same day! Yaniv will be thrilled; it's another coincidence!"

She was upset by the total silence on his end of the phone until she heard Gabriel gasping, "What a day! We'll celebrate our success in style tonight, my darling, with champagne! And then you'll have to tell me all about being a 'changeling'."

They celebrated at one of Oxford's best restaurant, a French-style bistro. They splurged on an expensive bottle of champagne when Gabriel told his mother they were enjoying a double celebration, Dani's and his. He shocked himself before the evening ended when he heard himself inviting his mother to graduation. "It's in two weeks, so please stay."

Frederica started crying. "To have a relationship with you after all these years, and to share this achievement! It's a dream come true! I know I don't deserve it. I can't stay here in Oxford that long; I'll go to London and then to Cambridge as there's something I must do, but I will come back for your commencement. In fact, I'll book a room in Rewley House tonight. God, I'm so excited… Pinch me please, just to prove I'm not dreaming."

Gabriel said, "I have to tell you that I spoke to my father earlier and he'll be at the ceremony. Are you OK with that? Dani's parents and grandparents are also coming. Her ceremony at The Courtauld is two days after mine."

"I haven't seen your father for almost thirty years, but I can handle it if he can. It's worth it just to be here for the remarkable double celebrations."

"And it will give you the opportunity to meet my family before you come to Israel for our August wedding," Dani tossed out the invitation casually, holding Gabriel's hand tightly. "And you must bring your mother; Rabbi Breitling's son Jakob will officiate and we hope Frau Sarah will also come."

Frederica blinked, tears in her eyes. "Now I know I'm dreaming! I don't know what to say!"

Gabriel smiled, and teased, "Just say 'Yes!' It's a 3-letter word, so simple even a linguist like you can say it!"

Before Frederica left for London, Gabriel suggested, "Why don't you go to the Medical School in Graz to find out about your brother? Someone there probably transferred his records, his transcripts, to another place. And if he left Austria, they would know where he went."

Frederica beamed. "You're brilliant. I tried a few government ministries, but no one could help me. Why didn't I think of the Graz Medical School?"

Dani met Frederica at Rewley House when she returned to Oxford for Gabriel's graduation, and took her to the Old Schools Quadrangle of the Bodleian Library, opposite Christopher Wren's 17th century Sheldonian Theatre, where families and guests were gathering prior to the ceremony. Frederica knew the Breitlings would be there, but she was amazed that so many of Dani's relatives had come to Oxford for Gabriel. Dani's parents were absolutely charming and Frederica understood her son's extraordinary relationship with them; Lise and David found her equally charming. When Frederica wondered aloud if Oxford and The Courtauld could accommodate so much family, David responded, "I'm sure Oxford can, but we might have to capture the London Eye and hold it hostage to seat everyone for Dani's graduation. Our family loves to party, so just wait until you see the size of the wedding. Gabriel's friends and our family will come from all over the world. We'll probably need a circus tent for the event!" Frederica was very grateful that after her disastrous treatment of her son, he'd had the good fortune to grow up with Rabbi Breitling's "family" in Graz and then to be welcomed into Dani's loving family. She was grateful that she could openly share a laugh with Dani's loving family, and Dani's loving family breathed a sigh of relief that Gabriel's reconciliation with his mother had gone so well. Frederica know that never in her life had she used the word "loving" so frequently.

Her meeting with Gabriel's father, who was there with his mother and his younger daughter, took place in a quiet corner of the Old School Quad, and it wasn't awkward. Gabriel thought he'd have to introduce them again, but the minute Frederica saw Darian, she said Gabriel looked just like him.

He disagreed. "No, I think he looks more like you, Frederica."

His daughter Shirin, called Sharon – a less ethnic name – in Los Angeles, jumped into the friendly dispute. "I think my brother looks like himself."

Frederica and Darian laughed, and Frederica said, "And who do you look like, young lady. You're absolutely beautiful."

"She's the image of her mother," Darian replied, "while Darla, my other daughter, resembles my side of the family."

"Your wife couldn't come?" Frederica inquired.

"Soraya, Susie in California, is a successful real estate broker in LA, and she isn't shy, but she was very apprehensive about meeting you. She adores Gabriel, and now that we've met again and there's no visible bloodshed," he grinned, "I'll be able to convince her to attend the wedding. What do you think, Shirin?"

"I know both Mom and Darla want to be at the wedding," she responded.

Shirin and Gabriel left them at that point, she to join her grandmother, he to don his formal academic outfit – a scarlet robe and hood with a navy blue insert, and a scarlet cap with both blue and scarlet tassels denoting a DPhil with honors. Dressed, he hurried to the Sheldonian for the ceremony.

"I called you several times from Iran," Darian said. "At first your father wouldn't let me talk to you, but the last time I called, he told me you were dead, and it was my fault. I loved you so much, Frederica, and I mourned for two years. Then I met Soraya and my life changed, especially when our daughters were born. And then, you can imagine my astonishment when Rabbi Breitling found me so many years later and I learned I had a son. And such a wonderful son! So thank you for giving me Gabriel."

Frederica smiled. "Actually I should thank you. I named him Dominik but usually called him 'Daryush' because of you, Darian. I was so hurt that you never got in touch. I only found out about your phone calls after my father died and my mother told me someone named 'Darren' had called a few times, but my father wouldn't let him talk to me. I didn't know he told you I was dead. My brother had a huge fight with him when I refused to have an abortion, and both of us left my parents' house. My mother gave me a little money and I went to London, but I don't know where my brother went. I haven't seen him since that dreadful night. I don't even know if he's still alive, but I'm following a suggestion from Gabriel and trying to find him through the medical school he attended in Graz. I was only half-alive after his school expelled him and I threw Dominik, er- Gabriel, out into the cold; I was as horrible as my father. Thank heavens Rabbi Breitling took him in and helped him become such a wonderful young man. Dani and her family are marvelous to him and for him, so at least he's grown to manhood with loving families – the Rabbi's, Dani's, yours. I'm so glad he met you and has a relationship with his real father. I don't know if I'll ever get over my guilt, but Gabriel – I'm still not used to calling him that – has forgiven me, and that means the world to me. Now tell me, how did you and your family get out of

Iran? I know it's such a repressive regime."

"I brought my mother to London for a 'surgical procedure'," he said with a smile. "While we were here, my cousin was able to sneak Soraya and the girls out of Tabriz into – this is a bit ironic – Armenia, and then to London with help from an Armenian businessman...possibly your ex-husband, but I never knew his name. We left everything behind and life in London wasn't easy for penniless Iranian refugees. We worked hard, and since the girls' level of English was excellent, school wasn't a problem. Then suddenly our luck changed – thanks to Gabriel. He had Israeli friends who'd originally come from Iran – Persia to them – and they had family in London and in California, the Sassoons. Yes, Vidal, the famous hairdresser! Through him, I attained my post at UCLA and we moved to the 'good life' in LA."

Frederica smiled, "As Shakespeare said, 'All's well that ends well'!" She walked over to Darian's mother and said, "I'm so happy to meet you, Mrs. Sarkohi. I hope you don't hate me for how I mistreated Gabriel in the past."

"How could I hate you?" the old woman said. "You gave me my beloved grandson." She patted Frederica's cheek and added, "I think we should leave the past in the past and look only to the future. And please call me Fara."

"Right on, Grandma!" Shirin said, "You're a smart old lady!"

"And you're a fresh kid, but I love you anyway," her grandmother said.

Dani called everyone together for the Oxford formal commencement ceremony. Someone outside was playing a tape recording of "Pomp and Circumstance" as the crowd entered the theatre. "Why aren't they playing that inside during the processional that fits Elgar's title?" David wondered.

Anna answered. "Because Oxford's Degree Day is older than Edward Elgar's march. It dates from the second half of the twelfth century and still retains all the essential features of its ancient predecessors, including all proceedings conducted in Latin. By the way, Shakespeare actually was the first one to use the words 'pomp and circumstance', in *Othello*."

"How does she know all that?" David asked and his father-in-law joked that his wife sometimes had to prove that she was a great librarian, not just a great cook! Anna laughed with the others at Richard's teasing.

The solemn event lasted more than two hours and then the new Oxford graduates carrying their diplomas marched out of the

Chapter 6

Sheldonian Theatre. As Gabriel passed them, David whispered to his father, "You and Richard thought my PhD ceremony at the Sorbonne was impressive, but only the British, maybe only Oxford, can put on an extravaganza like this!"

After Gabriel rejoined them and everyone congratulated him, the entire family went to Wadham College, where Dani and Gabriel had organized a festive meal in one section of the 400-year old Hall, including a kosher meal for the Breitlings. Gabriel's father insisted on paying for the dinner. As the well-fed group left the Hall, Dani's grandfather said they should walk off all the calories before driving to London for Dani's smaller graduation ceremony two days later. Tipsy after too much excellent wine, Frederica walked to Rewley House, arms entwined with Gabriel and Dani. She knew she'd never been happier.

Before leaving Oxford, Gabriel's affable grandmother had told Frederica she wasn't going back to California until after the wedding. She'd be staying in London with Iranian expatriate friends before embarking on a senior citizen tour of the Holy Land. "I want to see al-Aksa before I die."

"I don't believe you're anywhere near death's door," Frederica said with a smile. "Look at Dani's grandfather, Richard. He's over 90 and he's so spry. Next to him, you're a young chick! You know, my mother wants to see Israel when she goes for the wedding. Maybe we can book the same tour for her. She's lively and funny; I think the two of you will get along very well."

"Does she speak English?" Fara asked. When Frederica nodded, the older woman said, "Yes, please do that. Of course we'll get along – we share a grandson. And it will be better not to be one old lady, all alone on a tour."

◆ ◆ ◆

"Fantastic! Absolutely fabulous!" Those were the words everyone who attended Gabriel and Dani's wedding said. During their summer vacation in Israel in 2010, they'd investigated hotels and events centers in Tel Aviv and Jerusalem as venues for the wedding; they'd chosen Jerusalem's Mount Zion Hotel and booked it for late August 2011. The stunning 19th century hotel had unique features: the Banquet Garden, on tiers near the pool, could seat 500 guests, with a breathtaking view from every seat of the biblical Hinnom Valley and the Old City from the Jaffa Gate and the Tower of David to the clock tower of the Dormition Abbey. Jerusalem evenings in the summer were always cool no matter how hot the day, nor was there any chance of rain, so an outdoor wedding was feasible. As soon as the date was set, Lise started planning a *chuppah*. She had made several geometrical ones: the one above the bed she and David shared, another for David's sister, and she'd made one more for Ted Hoffman's daughter Tammy's wedding. But she wanted to make something unique for Dani and Gabriel; she decided to create a patchwork quilt incorporating special moments in both their lives on the reverse side of a geometric *chuppah*. She selected photos and other mementos: Dani as an infant with her green eyes wide open; Dani rolling around in autumn leaves in Brookline; Dani on her first bicycle with Kobi holding the seat; Dani with her JCC *chanukiah*; Dani on skis in Vermont and the Andes; Dani, thumb in her mouth, enthralled as David read her a Beatrix Potter story; a red wool tassel from a hat Dani loved; a bit of navy satin from a party dress; Dani in her IDF uniform; Dani dancing a tango in Buenos Aires; Dani in a gaucho outfit riding a Criollo horse. She had no mementos of Gabriel's early years because of the estrangement with his mother, but Deborah Breitling sent a few photos after he became, as she said, a 'member' of the Rabbi's family at age 14, and Lise had a few photos taken in Israel: Gabriel wearing his first *kippa* and *tallit*; Gabriel standing on one leg, "Yes? No? Yes? No?" in a bubble above him; Gabriel stuffing a *sufgania* into his mouth and Ruth shaking a finger at him; Gabriel *leining Torah* with the Rabbi in his study; Gabriel, at the sink in Graz, a dishtowel on his shoulder, kissing Frau Sarah's cheek; Gabriel and Yaniv in their Unit 8200 uniforms; Gabriel handing Hebrew U's Outstanding Graduate of 2008 plaque to his father; Gabriel with a few versions of the Qur'an on his desk in Oxford. Lise had photos of Gabriel and Dani together: playing water polo in the Hofman pool; studying in the Bodleian Library; relaxing on the Arab rug in their Oxford flat; cheering Balliol College's tortoise Rosa in her last very slow race; petting wild creatures in Cornwall's Screech Owl Sanctuary; reading side-by-side on a window seat at Buckle Yeat, near Beatrix Potter's home; looking over recipes with Grandma Anna; drinking champagne with Alex and Ruth at their wedding at the Hofman's home. Gabriel and Dani up to their necks in bubbles and laughing in their huge clawfoot tub would be the centerpiece of the quilt. After Gabriel reconciled with his mother, Lise called Frederica and asked if she had any mementos of Gabriel's childhood. Two days later, a DHL package arrived, with a sweet photo of Gabriel as an infant asleep in his mother's arms; Gabriel with arms raised as he took his first tottering steps; Gabriel on a pony in Regents Park; Gabriel

Chapter 6

in Armenia on a see-saw with Ara, his stepfather; Gabriel scribbling words that he said were Chinese; Gabriel hugging a scruffy one-eyed stuffed camel; a bronzed baby shoe; Gabriel in the national football jersey of Austria.

Dani and Gabriel knew nothing about Lise's special project. As another surprise, she'd asked Gabriel to send her a list of what he wanted to include in the *ketubah* and she'd make it for their wedding; she didn't tell him she was sending the details to the friend in Yafo who'd made the *ketubah* for her own wedding. Her friend's calligraphy and illuminated borders rivaled those of Italian masters.

♦♦♦

Guests arrived from all over the world for the wedding: Gabriel's father and his family from Los Angeles, his mother from Austria, his friend Karl from Salzburg, Ruth and Alex from Washington with their year-old twins to be "guests" of their tenants in Ruth's old flat, and Eli Rosenzweig arrived from Brazil to see Gabriel, his son David's "brother", marry adorable Dani. Both of Gabriel's grandmothers were already in Israel on a senior-citizen tour with Frau Sarah. The Breitlings were in Jerusalem, enjoying a summer holiday with their grandchildren. As for Dani's family, her grandmother came from Sweden with her husband; her Uncle Jonas and his family came from Denmark and her Aunt Marta's family came from Germany. All the Hoffmans from Pittsburgh were staying at the King David Hotel. Claude and Mignon, Chloe, Henri and Marcel, "*Our* French Connection" in David's words, were at a charming hotel near the Jaffa Gate and Claude was already checking out Israeli artists. The Boston contingent – the Gordons, Aliza, Gil and their children had all come for the wedding.

Frederica had an astonishing surprise for both her mother and Gabriel; she had found her brother! The authorities in Vienna had told her Friedrich left Austria two days after her; however, they didn't know his destination. But a retired medical professor in Graz told her he'd forwarded her brother's transcripts to the Monash Faculty of Medicine in Melbourne, Australia. He had changed his name from Friedrich Müller to Ted Miller and married a young Jewish attorney. Their son and daughter, twins, would begin their university studies in February, but they were active members of Habonim Dror, a worldwide Jewish youth movement, and as volunteers on a kibbutz, they were teaching English to Israeli teenagers. Ted and his wife Judy were currently visiting them and touring Israel, just in time for

Gabriel's wedding and Ted's grand reunion with his family. He was thrilled to see his mother again, now that she was no longer a timid, mouse-like creature. Ted was even delighted to meet Darian Sarkohi, since his own alienation from his family was the result of his father's horrendous treatment of Frederica when she refused to abort Darian's son. And he said it was a miracle to see his adored sister again and meet his brilliant nephew.

Gabriel was in total shock, to go from basically "no family" at the age of 14 to so much family: his mother, grandmother, uncle, aunt and cousins; his father and his other grandmother, his stepmother and half-sisters; all of the Breitlings, David, Karl, Ruth, his 'family' from the Rabbi's home in Austria; and, of course, Dani's family – Lise, David, Keren, Kobi, Yaniv, and even Alex. He found it impossible to believe that he now had so many loving people in his life, his world, after that agonizing experience at age 14!

Immediate families and some close friends arrived at the Mt. Zion Hotel the day before the wedding and for an Israeli version of a rehearsal dinner that evening. Lise told everyone she'd booked the King David Hall because her husband was her personal "King David"; she also felt the stone walls and Middle Eastern décor of the hall offered a unique start to the upcoming festivities. She claimed the dinner itself was a test to see if the cuisine lived up to the standard of the samples they'd tasted when they booked the hotel. The meal was sumptuous. After dinner, the young men took Gabriel out for a pseudo-stag party in downtown Jerusalem; they drifted into clubs and bars but they didn't find a place they liked; there was too much noise, too many young kids out for the evening, even a few drug-deals going on. Then Alex remembered *Tmol Shilshom*, a bookstore-café known for excellent coffee and cakes. Meanwhile, the girls held an informal hen-party for Dani around the pool. Older family members sat in another area or retired to their rooms. When Keren noticed Dani yawning, she said in the "big-sister voice" she'd used when Dani was little, "Time for 'beddy-bye', 'Danny-Tanny'!" Lise grinned, Dani hugged Keren, said good night and went up to her room – all alone in a big bed, no Gabriel until the next night. An hour later, she heard a quiet tap on her door; Gabriel was there. He smiled and said, "We believe in coincidences, not superstitions. I can't sleep without you and we both need to be rested for tomorrow. I'll leave early; no one will know I've been here."

He didn't leave early. After they made love and fell asleep, the next thing they heard was loud banging on the door and Lise ordering them to wake up because they had a lot to do. She told Dani to let her in and tell Gabriel to stay under the covers if he was naked. Gabriel half-choked, half-laughed at her words and called out, "I'll be completely dressed by the time Dani opens the door." He was, earning a loving hug from his soon-to-be mother-in-law.

"How did you know he was here, *Ema*?" Dani asked.

"*Aba* went to wake him and Yaniv, and your brother told him Gabriel hadn't come back to their room last night. But don't hit Yaniv for being a snitch! I knew Gabriel wasn't sleeping in a deck chair near the pool, so this room was the logical conclusion," Lise said, laughing. "Now get dressed and come downstairs for your 'last breakfast as free people'!"

"I don't think I've been a 'free person' since the first time Yaniv brought me to your house and I laid eyes on Dani, after first having a 'crush' on you!" he told Lise, squeezing her shoulder softly. "Let's go downstairs. I'm so hungry I could eat a horse if it were kosher! Join us soon, Dani!"

◆ ◆ ◆

The wedding day was gorgeous, and the wedding was as spectacular as the day. The only hitch was Gabriel's struggle to break the glass and end the ceremony; everyone laughed and applauded when he finally accomplished that feat. Jakob Breitling, now one of the main rabbis of Jerusalem's Yakar Center, officiated. The four tall poles supporting Lise's beautiful geometric *chuppah* were held by Dani's uncle Jonas, her cousin Yoni, Alex, and Gil, her adored babysitter Aliza's husband. Both Dani's father and his walked Gabriel, the *chatan*, to the *bimah*, where Yaniv as best man stood next to the Rabbi. Keren then walked to Jakob's other side. Lise and Frederica, each holding a lighted candle in one hand and Dani's arm with the other, walked the *kallah* around Gabriel seven times. This was followed by the wedding's legal elements: *kiddushin*, the betrothal *bracha*, the ring ceremony, and the reading of the *ketubah*. Lise's friend in Yafo had created a dazzling *ketubah* filled with Gabriel's humor – if they ever divorced, a court would decide who owned the paintings Lise had given them and the first edition Beatrix Potter books from Buckle Yeat, or the 30 rescued screech owls he was sponsoring as a special gift for his conservationist wife. The rabbi laughed several times as he read the *ketubah* aloud, joined by Dani and the guests. The next part of the ceremony was *nissuin*, the *sheva brachot*. Gabriel and Dani had thought very hard about the order of reciting the seven blessings, the heart of a Jewish wedding ceremony. Rabbi Samuel Breitling chanted the first, and a smiling Gabriel recalled the Rabbi reciting the same blessing over wine on his very first Shabbat in Graz, with his "brother", David R, explaining the Hebrew words. Aya and Ephraim, Dani's *Savta* and *Saba* were called to the *chuppah* to give the second blessing. The next one went to Grandma Anna and Grandpa Richard, followed by Kobi and then Dina and Alon. David R was called to recite the sixth blessing. Dani and Gabriel had agreed that the seventh blessing had to go to Karl because his trained voice would enhance the beauty of the longest *brachah*. Finally it was time to break the glass and end the ceremony, but Gabriel found it difficult to stomp on the glass which kept slipping out of the silk napkin wrapped around it. When he succeeded, there was laughter followed by shouts of *"Mazal Tov"*. Then the Rabbi told Gabriel to kiss his bride and he invited everyone to join Dr. and Mrs. Ben Shmuel in the Banquet Garden for the reception and festivities.

Without telling anyone why, Lise and David stayed behind for several minutes to detach the *chuppah* from its poles so the hotel staff could then reverse it and place it on a table downstairs in the Banquet Garden. When that was in place, David called over Gabriel and Dani, followed by all the family and guests. Dani burst into tears when she saw Lise's exquisite and unusual wall hanging. "My wedding gown is the most gorgeous dress I've ever seen, and the *ketubah* is brilliant, but this – this is Gabriel and me, this is our lives. This is us! I have no other words!"

"I do!" Gabriel said again, but this time his words were barely more than an emotional whisper. "We'd better never get divorced, my love; because you'll have the fight of your life over who keeps this fabulous work of art, even though Lise is *your Ema*!" He hugged a silently weeping Dani and added, "I don't think we'll ever have to worry about that happening!" Then he hugged Lise and said "Thank you, *Ema*" as a tear rolled down his cheek.

Everyone exclaimed over the uniqueness, completely astounded by Lise's extraordinary *chuppah*-cum-wall-hanging. Claude demanded one just like it for his gallérie, but Lise told him it was so time-consuming that she'd only undertake the task again for the weddings of her other children. "*Alors!*" Claude said, "maybe I can talk Gabriel and Dani into selling theirs to me for a really good price." David, standing proudly next to Lise as she received so many accolades, smiled at Claude and said he doubted Claude would be more successful than he was in getting Richard to sell his diptych of the Little Mermaid or

Dina to part with *Le Petit Sirène*. Their French friend sighed, gave a very Gallic shrug and said, "*C'est la vie!*".

Guests were overheard saying "Scrumptious food!" and one of Gabriel's half-sisters stated: "Finger-licking good!" Dancing was non-stop before and after Gabriel's old friends and Dani's siblings entertained everyone with a comic skit about the bridal couple. When the celebration was flagging and guests were getting ready to leave, David called all the single women to the front and Dani climbed to a higher tier in the Banquet Garden to throw her bouquet. She noted where each young women was standing, and mentally focusing on her sister's position, tossed the bouquet over her shoulder and directly into the Keren's hands. "That means you're next, Keren," she said, and glanced with a wink at David R who wiggled his dark eyebrows like Groucho Marx and winked suggestively at a blushing Keren. Gabriel then helped Dani down and everyone went back to the dancing which probably continued most of the night, although Dani and Gabriel left soon after.

They wanted only one *sheva brachot* party and explained that they had been sleeping with each other for years, so they just wanted to spend some relaxed quality time with their visiting families. At a barbecue for families and friends two days later, Gabriel's half-sisters asked about the custom, and Deborah Breitling said in the old days a bride was a very young virgin whose first sexual experience was painful, so the bridal couple was given festive dinners every night for seven nights until they were so tired they couldn't do anything but sleep, and the bride could heal. Both girls giggled, and then enjoyed flirting with a lot of young men.

Ten days after the wedding, Dani and Gabriel were finally alone, on the *Golden Iris* for a 7-day cruise to the Greek islands. Despite more than 1000 people aboard the luxury liner, they felt like they were on their own with no required tasks for the first time in a very long time, sight-seeing during the day, shopping for trinkets when the ship stopped at various islands, and reveling in their total privacy at night as they made love in their opulent stateroom. Yaniv met them at the port in Haifa when they returned; he hugged them, lifted some luggage, and said, "You two look relaxed and happy, but not very tan. Where did you spend most of your time? In your cabin?" When they just grinned at him, he added, "Are you ready to take up the challenge of your new lives as a mature married couple?"

"Absolutely!" they said simultaneously, and they laughed a little.

Glossary
Mostly Hebrew Words and Phrases
Chapter 1

rabbanit – Rabbi's wife

mishloach manot – gifts of food, snacks, wine on **Purim**, the Jewish holiday that commemorates Queen Esther saving the Jewish people in ancient Persia from Haman, the evil prime minister who was planning to kill them

seder – the ritual feast that marks the beginning of *Passover* (*Pesach*), the Jewish holiday celebrating the exodus from Egypt of the Jews led by Moses

Simchat Torah – the conclusion and the beginning of the cycle of Torah readings

Chanukah – the Jewish holiday commemorating the rededication of the Temple in Jerusalem at the time of the Maccabean Revolt against the Seleucid Empire.

bracha – a blessing, recognition of the good that God has given to us.

Ha Motzi (or just *Motzi*) – the blessing on bread: *Blessed are You, Oh Lord our God, King of the Universe, who brings forth bread from the earth. Amen.*

Birkat Hamazon – blessing or grace after meals

Mezuman – When three or more adult men eat a meal that includes bread they are obligated to begin *Birkat Hamazon* with a "*zimun*" based on Biblical verses.

Torah – the Pentateuch, the first five books of the Hebrew Bible [the source of the Christian Old Testament]; the *Torah* usually includes rabbinical commentaries; studying and analyzing the *Torah* is called *leining* (reading) *Torah*

Pater Noster (the Lord's Prayer in Latin) and **Hail Mary** – a prayer to the Virgin Mary, used by Roman Catholics; from Luke 1:28.

kashrut – kosher

shul, beit knesset – synagogue

Kiddush – the blessing over wine on Shabbat: *Blessed are You, Oh Lord our God, King of the Universe, Creator of the fruit of the vine. Amen.*

challah – bread, usually braided, eaten on Shabbat and holidays. [plural: *challot*]

manna – an edible substance provided for the Israelites during their forty years in the desert following their flight from Egypt; it is defined in *Exodus* as a flake-like thing which could be baked into a cake

zemirot – Hebrew songs for Shabbat and Jewish holidays [singular: *zemir*]

bentscher – a booklet for reciting Grace after Meals, as well as other prayers and songs usually recited on Shabbat or a holiday [Yiddish name for *Birchon*]

Rabbinut – the Chief Rabbinate of Israel

Oma and *Opa* – grandmother and grandfather [German]

motzei Shabbat – after Shabbat, Saturday evening after sundown

Haftarah – sections from the books of *Nevi'im* ("Prophets") of the *Tanakh* (the Hebrew Bible), following the *Torah* reading on Shabbat, Jewish holidays and fast days. The *haftarah* is thematically linked to the *parasha* (*Torah* portion).

Glossary

Chapter 2

"Oui, mais d'un autre coté pas beaucoup!" – Yes, but not that much! [French]
"Lieber Himmel!" Good heavens! Or Goodness gracious! [German]
Halakha – body of Jewish religious laws, from the Written and Oral Torahs.
Shema – Judaism's most sacred prayer, recited morning and evening by observant Jews: *"Sh'ma Yisrael, Adonai Eloheinu, Adonai Echad"* (Hear, O Israel, the Lord is our God, the Lord is one).
mitzvah – commandment or a good deed [plural: 613 ***mitzvot*** for religious Jews]
tehillim – psalms
"Viaticum" – Latin for Last Rites
"Chag Chanukah Sameah!" Happy Chanukah holiday!
"Baruch ha shem" (Blessed be God) – the religious Jewish way of thanking God
sufganiyot – jelly donuts
latkes – potato pancakes fried in oil
chanukiah – a 9-branched candelabra, with one candle (called a ***shamas***h) at a different height than the others; plural: ***chanukiot***
"Maoz-Tzur", a liturgical poem sung on *Chanukah*, after lighting the candles
dreidel – a four-sided spinning top [Yiddish; a *sevivon* in Hebrew]. Each side has a Hebrew letter: נ (Nun), ג (Gimel), ה (Hei), ש (Shin), the acronym for *"Nes Gadol Haya Sham"* (a great miracle happened there). These letters stand for the rules of the gambling game – Nun is for the Yiddish word *nisht* ("nothing"), Hei for *halb* ("half"), Gimel for *gants* ("all"), and Shin for *shtel ayn* ("put in"). The fourth side of the dreidel is inscribed with the letter פ (Pei) for *"Poh"* (here) in Israel because the miracle of Chanukah occurred in the Land of Israel.
Aliyah – literally, ascend; used to acknowledge immigrating to Israel
mâdarbozorg – grandmother [Farsi]
hatafat dam brit – a small prick, a single drop of blood, a symbolic ritual according to Jewish law for a convert who had already been circumcised.

Chapter 3

mishpacha – family
giur – conversion; ***Ulpan Giur*** – Conversion School
Sukkoth – holiday; observant Jews eat all meals in a *sukkah* – a temporary hut
moshavim – cooperative agricultural villages
beit midrash – a study hall located in a synagogue, yeshiva, or even on a religious kibbutz; literal meaning: House of Learning
kibbutznikim – members of the kibbutz
Oleh Chadash – new immigrant (plural: *Olim Chadashim*)
Bet Din – Rabbinical Court
Elohim – a name for God used frequently by observant Jews
mikveh – ritual bath
ben Avraham Avinu – son of Abraham our father
Shavuot – holiday commemorating the giving of the Torah to Moses on Mt. Sinai

Glossary

Tzahal – acronym: *"Tsva haHagana le Yisrael"*, Israel's Defense Forces (the IDF)
sabra – anyone born in Israel, literally: a prickly pear – tough outside, soft inside

Chapter 4

yakar – precious or worthy
Teudat Zehut – personal identity card that every Israeli has
Mashkit Tash – the army equivalent of a social worker or counselor who helps with the social and financial concerns of a lone soldier
tzav rishon – first call-up or draft
kaba – acronym for *kivutzat aicut* (quality group); based on the kaba score, the IDF determines a recruit's IQ and suitability for a particular unit. The kaba score has 3 parts: psychometric tests worth 50%; an interview, 33%; formal education, 17% of the kaba – the higher the quality of education, the better the score.
Bakum – the Induction or Conscription Center for all new recruits at Tel HaShomer
Teudat Choger – IDF identification card
Modi'in – the Military Intelligence Corps
"Kol haKavod!" – All the Honor, the Hebrew equivalent of "Well Done!"
tironut – basic training or "boot" camp
tekes – ceremony
SIGINT – acronym for signal intelligence
bashert – meant to be, fated or destined [Yiddish]
Ema and ***Aba*** – mother and father
Savta and ***Saba*** – grandmother and grandfather
glug – Glühwein or mulled wine (Norwegian)

Chapter 5

chozeret b'teshuva – a woman who renews her faith in Judaism
milu'im – reserve duty
Haredi – an ultra-Orthodox Jew
Yamim Noraim – literally, Days of Awe; the High Holy Days (*Rosh Hashana* and *Yom Kippur*) and the interim days between them
chutzpah – nerve, audacity, cheekiness
femme fatale – sometimes called a "maneater", a seductive woman [French]
tzav shmoneh – the Israeli army's emergency call-up order
bâbâ – dad or papa; more affectionate than father [Farsi, Arabic]

Chapter 6

summa cum laude – with the highest distinction [Latin]
chuppah – the canopy beneath which Jewish marriage ceremonies are performed
kallah – the bride
chatan – the groom
kiddushin – betrothal: sanctification and blessing, sipping a glass of wine
ketubah – ceremonial prenuptial agreement: the groom's responsibilities

– Tale Number 2 –
Lise's Story of Family and Israel
Prologue: July 1957

"*Mutti* wants to speak to you, Lise," Jonas said as he handed his five-year-old sister the old-fashioned telephone.

"*Guten Morgen*, Lise. We're going to go on a little holiday before you start school. Pack your little suitcase – pajamas, underpants, socks, another dress, two pairs of shorts and two shirts, a sweater, your toothbrush, your hairbrush and the book you're reading. Jonas will help you and then you and Jonas will come to me. Don't tell *Oma*. You know she worries. You and Jonas should come while she's resting. OK, Lise?"

"Where are you, *Mutti*? Are you far away?" Lise asked, a little frightened as she tried to understand her mother through the static in the phone.

"That doesn't matter, Lise. Jonas knows where I am. Do what I told you."

"Can I bring Hansel and Gretel?" Lise inquired.

"Only if they fit into your case…or you can carry them. I'll see you later, Lise," she replied.

Three hours later, when their grandmother was resting, Jonas picked up his and Lise's small suitcases and said, "Let's go." They left the house quietly and walked to the bus stop. They boarded the rickety bus to the main bus terminal; then they boarded another bus to Checkpoint Charlie, the well-known crossing point between East and West Berlin. The following year East German police would monitor checkpoints, but in 1957 two children – a 10-year-old boy and a 5-year-old girl – just walked through; no one stopped or questioned them. They found a taxi and Jonas told the driver, "Kempinski Hotel, *bitte*."

"Who will pay my fare?" the driver asked the young boy.

"We're meeting our aunt and she'll pay you. If she's not there, you can take us back and I'll pay you." Jonas replied, glaring at Lise who didn't say a word.

As they drove through West Berlin streets, Lise stared at the buildings and activity all around. She had never been on this side of the city and she'd never seen so many people – men, women, children – dressed in colorful outfits. To her eyes, everything looked new and shiny; near their house, everything was grey and shabby.

At the hotel, Jonas murmured, "Stay here a minute, Lise." He opened the door, but before he'd taken more than a step, Lise ran out to her mother.

"Is Papa here?" she asked.

"Shh," *Mutti* whispered. "We'll see him later." Then, in a voice that Lise didn't recognize as her mother's, she asked the cab driver, "How much do they owe you?" She paid him and they watched the taxi drive away.

Since travel out of West Berlin by train or by bus involved going back to the East side where papers and passports were checked, Richard had told Marlene that she and the children must travel by air. The United States, England and France guaranteed air service to other cities in Germany for Berliners, even East Berliners who managed to cross into the west. Because he was worried the *Stasi* would discover that he, Marlene and two of his three children were missing, Richard had devised diversionary methods of travel for them.

In front of the Kempinski Hotel, Marlene signaled another cab. "Tempelhof Airport," she told the driver. She then said to the children, "We're flying to Hamburg and we'll stay there tonight. Papa will meet us tomorrow."

"We're going in an airplane?" Lise asked, her eyes filled with excitement.

"Of course, silly, how else can we fly? We aren't birds," Jonas said, but Lise knew he was also thrilled because neither of them had ever been on an airplane before. She didn't know if this was also a new experience for *Mutti*. The flight was quite short, but both children enjoyed every minute on the plane. Richard had arranged a small hotel for them in Hamburg, and he'd bought presents for them before he left, a book about the Danish physicist Niels Bohr for Jonas whose interest in science was unusual for a child, and a fairly large sketchbook and pastel sticks for Lise who loved to draw. Marlene gave them the gifts when she opened her case, and thus both children were occupied. They had an early dinner in an inexpensive restaurant near the hotel; when they returned to their room, Marlene saw the children drooping with tiredness. "It's been a busy day for you two," she said, "so let's have an early night." They gave in after only a short protest. Marlene herself was mentally exhausted; still fearful about the outcome of their departure, she took a headache tablet and retired as well.

Prologue

In the morning, they breakfasted in the same restaurant and Marlene bought sandwiches and fruit. Then they went to the bus station where they boarded an express bus for the two-hour trip to Kiel. At the railroad station in Kiel, she purchased first-class tickets on the train to Copenhagen. "Isn't first-class very expensive?" Jonas asked.

"It is," she answered, "Papa gave me the money; he wanted the two of you to enjoy the trip." She didn't tell them Richard had planned this for a long time and thought the *Stasi* would be less likely to discover their destination if they traveled first-class.

"Are we really going to Copenhagen?" the children queried.

"I told you this would be exciting. We'll cross bridges over canals and go through tunnels, and Papa will be waiting at the end," she said.

"I read about Copenhagen in the book about Niels Bohr. That's where he was born and he still lives there," Jonas said.

"I'll draw pictures of the bridges and canals for Papa," Lise added.

Marlene marveled at the innocence of her children; they were so absorbed in this new adventure and totally unaware of the potential danger in what they were doing. She was far more stressed, her head pounding and her mouth dry, but for the children's sake, she hid her anxiety.

Richard was at the train station when they arrived, nervously pacing up and down. When she saw her father, Lise threw herself into his arms. Jonas hugged him and Richard tousled the boy's hair. "Richard, people are staring!" she said as she looked at her husband cuddling the children.

"That's OK," he said. "Let people look. I haven't seen these two for over a week, and we're in Denmark where it's OK for people to see us."

"You didn't see Marta for four years," Marlene criticized.

"I wasn't exactly in a position to spend time with her, was I? But my older daughter and I are close now," Richard responded quietly, not willing to have a public argument with his wife.

Lise looked over at her mother and asked, "Are you tired, *Mutti*?"

"Yes," her mother answered. "I have a headache, but I'll get over it."

Jonas looked at both his parents, and said, "We're not going back, are we?"

Richard ruffled his son's straight blond hair affectionately and said quietly, "I'll tell you later." They took a taxi to the Copenhagen Strand Hotel. "It's not the Kempinski, but it's clean," Richard said, winking at his children.

By the time their cases were unpacked and Lise had explained her drawings to her father, the little girl was tired and both children were hungry. "There's a family restaurant around the corner," Richard said. "Let's go." When they were seated at a corner table and the waiter had taken their order, Richard looked at the two youngsters and said, "I have something to tell you. You were right, Jonas. We're not going back to Berlin. We're going to live here in Copenhagen. You'll go to school here and we'll all learn to speak Danish."

Both children spoke at the same time. "I don't want to live here. I don't like it here. I don't like Danish. I want to go home," a very cranky Lise said.

"But what about *Oma* and Marta?" Jonas asked. "Will they come here too?"

"I'll answer all of your questions, but one at a time," Richard said. "I'm not sure *Oma* would be able to come. She's not young anymore and her health isn't very good now. Marta and I had a long talk before I went to the conference in Prague and she decided to stay with *Oma*. She has only one more year left in gymnasium and she's really looking forward to studying medicine at Humboldt University. She wouldn't be able to learn a new language and win a place in a medical school if she came here with us. And she's very close to *Oma*. Now here's a little secret for you, Lise. After you go on some rides in the Luna Park at Tivoli Gardens and you see the statue of the Little Mermaid, I know you'll love Copenhagen." This was too much for the children to absorb, so they just ate their meals quietly.

Finally, Jonas asked, "Where will we live? We can't always stay in a hotel."

Richard smiled at his young son. "I'm not sure. I have a meeting tomorrow and then I'll know more. You and Lise will see a little of Copenhagen with *Mutti* while I'm at my meeting. OK?"

Lise fell asleep almost instantly when they were back in their hotel room, but Jonas stayed up a while, talking to his parents. "Why didn't we fly straight to Copenhagen, Papa? Were you afraid the *Stasi* would find us?" Jonas asked. "And how were you able to get here undetected?"

"Are you sure you aren't 50 years old, Jonas? You're much too smart for a 10-year-old," Richard said, smiling. "The *Stasi* is exactly why *Mutti* brought you here the way she did. We planned this before I went to Prague. After I gave my talk about my projects at the conference, a colleague and I left Prague in the middle of the night. We drove quickly to Vienna and an old friend from my days as a British POW met us there. He had a false passport for me and an airline ticket to Copenhagen. Fortunately, no official at the airport in Vienna or here checked my passport very carefully, so here I am. Now we're all here."

"Not all," Jonas said. "Won't the *Stasi* question Marta and *Oma*?"

"Probably," Richard answered. "But Marta and *Oma* don't know where we are. When I talked to Marta, she told me she knew how much I hated the Hitler Youth who betrayed their parents to the Gestapo when I was young, so she asked me not to tell her our plans or our destination. All she'll be able to tell the *Stasi* is that I didn't come back from my conference in Prague and she has no idea where *Mutti*, Lise and you have gone."

"Will we ever see Marta and *Oma* again?" Jonas asked very quietly.

"I'm sure we will…" Richard said, "Someday."

After breakfast the next morning, Richard went to his meeting and Marlene took the children to Tivoli, the Danish amusement park. The lines for the rides were very long with so many visitors; Jonas and Lise wanted to ride everything and taste everything. After an hour's wait to get on the *Rutsjebanen*, the famed wooden roller coaster, and then standing in a longer line at the *Vaffelbageriet*, they ate ice cream in waffle cones as they marveled at the Tivoli Boy Guards with their red and white uniforms, bearskin hats and brass instruments for the daily Pipe and Drums parade. Looking at her two rather dirty children with excited faces, Marlene asked, "Do you still want to see the Little Mermaid?"

Both children cried "Yes!" and she said, "OK. I'm sure we'll come to Tivoli many times. Papa says it's one of Copenhagen's special things. It's a long walk from here to the Little Mermaid, so let's see if there's a bus or we'll go by taxi."

Jonas looked at his mother and said, "By bus. Or we'll run out of money."

For the first time in days, Marlene laughed and said, "Don't worry about that today, Jonas. Your papa's been saving for this for a long time."

At the Langelinie Pier where the renowned statue sat perched on her rock in the harbor, the sun was beginning to set. Streaks of bright orange and crimson, pink and purple were reflected in the old bronze of the small statue and in the water. Lise just stood there with her mouth and eyes wide open, dazzled. At last she said, "*Wunderbar*! I've never seen anything so wonderful!"

"When he bought the book about Niels Bohr for Jonas, Papa bought you the Hans Christian Anderson story. We'll read it later," Marlene told Lise.

"Let's go right now," Lise said, her face alight with excitement. "I want you to read it to me, *Mutti*, and I'll draw pictures of her. She's the most beautiful thing ever and I want to know all about her!" Marlene and Jonas smiled as they walked to a taxi stand, a no longer tired Lise skipping ahead of them.

Richard was waiting for them, looking more relaxed. Marlene assumed his meeting had gone well; she'd ask later. Both children started telling Richard about their day even before he said hello. They told him about all the rides at Tivoli, the parade of 100 boys with fur hats and lots of drums and about the huge ice cream cones. "Mine was so big I couldn't finish it, so *Mutti* ate some," Lise said. Jonas showed his father a map of Tivoli and explained the shortest route for their next visit to the famous park. Then Lise said the very best part of the day was the Little Mermaid. "Someday I'll paint you a special picture of her. Please, Papa, read me the story," she begged, gazing up into the smiling face of her adored Papa as she opened her sketchbook and the box of pastel sticks. Richard smiled at Marlene over the children's heads, trying to tell her with his eyes that their new homeland would be good for them, but he could see she wasn't convinced.

Chapter 1

Thirteen years later...

The dean announced "Lise Hoffmann" and she walked quickly up to the stage to receive her award. It was May 1970, the graduation ceremony of the Jutland Arts Academy at Aarhus University. Lise had only completed her first year of studies in the Danish arts college but her diptych, *"The Little Mermaid: Two Images"* had taken first prize in the annual art contest. The left side of her painting showed the famous statue at sunset with glorious red, orange, purple and pink streaks reflected in the bronze of the statue and in the sea. The right side, hinged to the left panel, was headless with blood dripping down her neck; she held her bloody head in her hand, but the face wasn't that of the famous statue. It was Lise's face! Because she was receiving an award, her father and Anna, his second wife, were there; so was Jonas with Brigitte, his fiancée. Her mother was with a man she introduced as Albert Halverson; it seemed Marlene had a new lover and Lise hoped this relationship was serious. After the dean handed Lise a certificate and a cheque, and kissed her on both cheeks, she held up the diptych to thunderous applause, especially from her family. When Lise sat down next to her father, she whispered, "I told you I'd paint her for you someday. This is my gift to you."

"I remember," he said. "It was your first day in Copenhagen. But why the Little Mermaid with no head?" Richard asked. "Is that because the criminals who vandalized it a few years ago said no one would ever find her head?" Lise nodded. "But why does the severed head have your face?"

Anna looked first at Lise and then at her husband as he studied the brilliant diptych. She said very quietly, "Lise's had so much turmoil in her young life and I'm sure she sometimes thinks her own head is gone, that it's been cut off. Richard, you know your divorce was very hard on her. Jonas lives in his own scientific world, but he was aware of the tension between you and Marlene, so it was easier for him. You were the center of Lise's universe, and then you were gone. She was only seven-years-old, still adjusting to a new country, a new life, and suddenly there was another upheaval." She lowered her voice, almost to a whisper. "Marlene was bitter and made it so difficult for you to see the children whenever you wanted even though you were providing as much as you could for them. Think about it from your lovely, sensitive Lise's point of view. Marlene doesn't exude warmth and for so many years now, most of the sunlight has been gone from Lise's world."

"From mine too," he said." I adored her and I missed our little daily chats, her sweet explanations of her drawings. I missed reading to her as she sat on my lap, even when she could read so well herself. I missed her so much. The only thing that got me through those years without my children was you."

"I know, and your love has helped me cope with my guilt about the break-up of your marriage. I love both Jonas and Lise, but I know I also contributed to her loss of her beloved Papa, to her loneliness." She reached over and squeezed Lise's hand, noting the tears in her eyes. "I understand why you cut off her head in your glorious painting and put your own head in her hand, Lise. But yours is such a good head, 'bloody but unbowed' like Henley's *Invictus*. Your 'unconquerable soul' will always bring you to the right place. Like a female version of his famous poem, you are the 'mistress of your fate'."

Lise smiled at her stepmother, knowing the widowed Dutch librarian, who'd come into her father's life in Copenhagen, understood her so much better than her own mother ever did. And Anna could explain everything so well. "Thank you, Anna. I love you, too. And you make my Papa so very happy."

So much had happened to the Hoffmann family in their almost thirteen years in Denmark. After careful and thorough investigation into the family's history, asylum was granted. Richard's staunch anti-Nazi background, resulting in two years of imprisonment in Dachau Concentration Camp on fictitious charges of being a "Communist student agitator", was in his favor, as was his desertion to the British at the first battle of El Alamein. Conscripted into Rommel's *Afrika Korps* after his release from Dachau, he wouldn't – couldn't – support the mad desires of his homeland's *Führer* to take over the world; he defected as soon as possible. After three years as a British prisoner of war, Richard had an almost perfect command of the English language. The Danish were equally impressed with his rise to a fairly high position in East Germany's Ministry of Culture and his intense disillusionment with the rigid bureaucracy and growing corruption of the *GDR* leadership. Richard's work had involved checking the texts of popular songs for anti-state messages – mostly lyrics translated from British and American rock'n'roll songs; it was an absurd task, almost like a throwback to Nazi paranoia in Richard's estimation. Such control was a major insult to the intelligence of the German people and led to Richard's strong desire to leave, especially for the sake of his younger children. Despite his mother and older daughter living

Chapter 1

in East Berlin, Richard was able to convince the Danes that he loved his family in Germany and in Denmark, but his belief in freedom for his children was absolute. The Danes believed he was trustworthy, and at first he was given a rather low-level position in the Ministry of Culture, updating the Danish library system. Later, when he was transferred to the Justice Ministry with security clearance, Jonas asked if he was a spy; Richard just laughed.

Shortly after they had arrived in Copenhagen, the Hoffmanns moved to a small but comfortable apartment in the "Latin Quarter", a neighborhood close to the university. The children were enrolled in the local school and all of them began to study Danish. Jonas's teachers recognized his prodigious ability in science and Lise's teacher noticed her rare talent in art, and since the Danish education system encouraged gifted children, both of them were given special instruction. Less than two years later, they moved to a larger flat and Richard enrolled in an MA-PhD program in Political Science in the nearby university. Marlene started working at Illums, a major department store.

In the coffee shop in the university library, Richard met Anna, a Holocaust survivor who had lost her parents, sisters, grandparents, husband, and baby son who was bayonetted by a sadistic Nazi guard at the gate of Bergen-Belsen (Star Camp – *Sternlager*), perhaps one of the most diabolical of all horrors of that cruel time. Although she didn't understand why, Anna survived; but she couldn't return to her family home near Amsterdam after her liberation from the camp. Instead, she moved to Copenhagen where she found work as a translator. Eventually she enrolled in the university's Library Science program for an MA. At first, because the coffee shop was crowded, Anna and Richard just sat at the same table; later it was because they liked each other's company. Richard soon realized he had far more in common with Anna than with Marlene; he loved her openness and warmth – despite the tragedies she'd endured – as much as he appreciated her intelligence. Near the end of 1959, Marlene's animosity to Richard deepened along with an unsubstantiated belief that he was unfaithful; at that time, he and Anna were just good friends.

Despite her success at Illums, Marlene never felt at home in what she considered Denmark's hostile society. After they decided to separate, Richard moved in with Anna, although he supported Marlene and the children financially and tried to see the children as often as possible. Two months after he left, Marlene divorced him.

Marlene was extremely resentful of Richard's obvious happiness with Anna; she claimed he brought her to a strange country and then abandoned her. Since Richard provided her with a good home and everything she asked for, the only way she could manifest her bitterness was by depriving him of what he loved most – his children. She canceled scheduled visits with the children at the last minute; she filled the children's few hours of free time with so many activities that they had little time for Richard. When Lise complained about not seeing her beloved papa, Marlene said he was very, very busy; then she would ask Lise, knowing the answer would be 'No', if she wanted a very short visit with her father instead of a full afternoon of art lessons.

Marlene had always been a beautiful woman with an innate sense of fashion trends; within a comparatively short time, she became the manager of the haute couture boutique at Illums. She dressed stylishly and attracted men, especially manufacturers and buyers. She started dating after the divorce; before, she had been afraid that she would lose her alimony if Richard could prove she'd been unfaithful. In Illums, she met Albert Halverson, a successful businessman with boutiques in Aarhus in the north of Denmark and in Gothenberg and Malmo in Sweden; he was a good man and cared so deeply for Marlene that within a few years, her antagonism towards Richard and Anna dissipated.

The late 1960s and early 1970s were a very turbulent period throughout the world, except Denmark. It was the time of "The Troubles" in Northern Ireland; it was the time of worldwide student unrest – of "Danny the Red" Cohn-Bendit in the Sorbonne in Paris, Mario Savio at Berkeley in California, the SDS and Mark Rudd at Columbia in New York; it was the time of increasingly violent protests against America's war in Vietnam. It was the time of Woodstock, it was the time of Muhammed Ali refusing to serve in the American Army, and of John Lennon and Yoko Ono posting a billboard stating "The war is over" in New York's Times Square. It was the time of full-frontal nudity for the first time in Off-Broadway's "Hair". It was the time of Women's Lib, Betty Friedan and Gloria Steinem; it was the time of bra-burning. It was the time of the Black Panthers. Despite her artistic achievements at Jutland Academy, Lise knew she was stagnating in Copenhagen, a basically complacent nation in a tempestuous world. She sent an application and a portfolio to Le École Nationale Superieure des Beaux-Arts, the famous fine arts school in Paris, with a copy of the letter about her award in the Aarhus University art contest; a day before the Jutland ceremony, she received a letter of acceptance from Beaux-Arts. She knew she had to go to Paris, and she was thrilled to see the pride in her father's eyes after the

Chapter 1

award ceremony when she told the family her special news.

It was almost a relief for Lise to leave for Paris two months later. Marlene fatuously promised Lise they'd see each other frequently, but Lise was happy that her mother was now totally free to pursue her life with Albert Halverson; he could give Marlene the kind of life she'd always wanted. Lise's father and Anna were far more sincere as they hugged and kissed Lise at the airport and told her how much they'd miss her. Richard slipped an envelope of francs into her hand just before she joined the boarding passengers, "to tide you over until you're settled," he said. Jonas, so involved in his PhD studies and in Brigitte, arrived out of breath as Lise was about to enter the plane, but she heard him calling her and she fought her way back through the other passengers to share a few parting words and a hug with her beloved brother, her best friend.

◆ ◆ ◆

July 1972

It was very quiet in the Pierné Gallérie in Saint-Germain-de-Prés that July evening. Paris had been sweltering all day, but it was finally beginning to cool down. Couples were coming out, strolling in the lovely square across from the gallérie or along the quays on both sides of the Seine, sipping cool drinks and aperitifs in the cafés. Tourists stood at the railings of the dinner cruise boats, enjoying the sights of Paris before heading to their tables and very expensive gourmet meals. Lise sighed. Maybe a few buyers or browsers would come into the gallérie later. She went into the gallérie's tiny office and picked up her pad, staring at the outline of a possible final year project. It was hard to believe she had been in Paris two years, honing her craft at the École de Beaux-Arts, and working in the gallérie to supplement her stipend and the monthly allowance that Richard sent her. Living in Paris was expensive; she shared a flat in the 5th Arrondissement with two other students, Chloe Laurent who was also a student in the Beaux-Arts, and Marcel Roux, an MA student in linguistics and semantics at the Sorbonne. She and Marcel had been lovers for a time after she moved into the flat, but perhaps because his intensity reminded her of Jonas and the idea of a relationship with her brother was absurd, she ended their brief affair and now they were good friends. Quite melancholy, Lise sighed again. She really loved Paris…but so often she felt deeply lonely.

Her somber mood was broken by the tinkling of the bell as someone opened the door of the gallérie. Lise went to greet her customer, a tall, very handsome young man standing half in, half out of the doorway. "The little painting in the corner of the window is *The Little Mermaid* in Copenhagen, isn't it? Although the painting's partly abstract, I recognize it. Do you know the artist? Is it for sale?" he asked in excellent French with a slight accent she didn't recognize.

"Yes, and yes, and yes," she began, but before she could continue with her explanation, he interrupted. "If it's not too expensive, I'd like to buy it for my sister. Her birthday's next month and I'll be home in Tel Aviv by then, and the painting would be a terrific gift," he finished, breathless. He knew that he was babbling, but he'd never seen a more gorgeous woman – so tall, so slim, a true Nordic beauty; he just wanted to bask as long as possible in her presence. In all his 25 years, he'd never experienced anything quite like this feeling.

Lise laughed, as intrigued by this young Israeli as he seemed to be with her. "I'm the artist and Claude, the owner of the gallérie, allowed me to place it in the corner of the window. Yes, it's for sale. And no, it's not very expensive. I'd like to sell it to you for your sister. How old is she?"

"Twenty-one. She has always loved Hans Christian Andersen's stories, and *The Little Mermaid* in particular. She'll love this. I knew it was the mermaid even though I've never been in Denmark, but at the same time it's much more sophisticated than the photos I've seen. I think your combination of the abstract and the realistic is superb. And the colors are fabulous. Why did you paint it?"

"The first time I saw the statue, I was five years old, and it was my first day in Copenhagen," Lise said. "The sun was just beginning to set and marvelous red, pink, purple and orange streaks were reflected in the bronze statue and in the water. I've never forgotten it. And I've painted her many times."

"Are you Danish?" he inquired, intrigued by this young woman who spoke excellent French with almost no accent. Her long blonde hair in a braid down her back made her look both cool and sophisticated.

"Yes, I am," she responded. "And, of course, both the *Little Mermaid* and Hans Christian Andersen are the iconic treasures of Denmark. I was actually born in Germany; we moved to Copenhagen the day before I saw the *Little Mermaid*. I promised my father I would paint her for him one day…and I did. Because of *her* – a painting I did of her – I was accepted into the Beaux-Arts, where I've just finished my second year. By the way, my name is Lise." She was shocked that she'd revealed so much of herself to a stranger. But he knew so much about art and the *Little Mermaid*, and he was interested in her work

Chapter 1

and her motivation. She knew she was babbling, but this young Israeli was the most beautiful man she'd ever seen – so tall, so slim, with remarkable very light blue eyes like…oh, yes, Paul Newman's famous feature. She just wanted to bask as long as possible in the presence of this handsome stranger; she often worked with nude male models at the Beaux-Arts, but in all her 20 years, she'd never experienced anything quite like this feeling.

They continued to discuss her painting and haggled playfully over the price. As she was wrapping the small painting, he asked what time the gallérie closed and if she'd have a drink with him afterwards. She agreed quickly, surprising herself yet again; he said he'd return at closing time. "By the way, my name's David. I'm a PhD student at the Sorbonne," he said, tossing the words casually over his shoulder as he left the gallérie.

That was the beginning. They met after she locked the gallérie and went to a nearby café where they sat until the owner let them know it was closing time; then they walked to another café on the Seine, shuttered and dark, and waited on a bench across the street. They shared experiences, humorous stories about their families, deeper thoughts, anything so they wouldn't have to say goodbye. They watched the sunrise, the first pink and gray rays breaking through the darkness, turning blackness to purple and then to red and orange, the streaks reflected in the iron lattice of the Eiffel Tower. Lise said, "The flashing colors remind me of that first day in Copenhagen and the *Little Mermaid* at sunset," she laughed, "but *Le Petit Sirène* was far more glorious than *L'eiffel*, at least in the eyes of a five-year-old!"

David laughed, "You really have a thing for that little statue, don't you? But I'm so glad you do… because she's what brought you to Paris and to me." Lise just smiled and rested her shining blond head on his shoulder.

When the proprietor lifted the heavy metal security grill on the closed café and brought out a few small tables and chairs, he spotted them and beckoned them over. He brought them freshly made coffee and buttery croissants with *confiture de pêches* and said, in a manner surprising for a practical Frenchman, and laughing, "You're my first customers of the day and such a beautiful young couple so much in love, *c'est la tournée du patron!*" He added, "You will bring me good luck all day!" Laughing as well, Lise and David thanked him and then couldn't stop staring into each other's eyes.

They saw each other every evening and whenever they could in the daytime and after one very long week, they started seeing each other all night as well. They usually made love in his apartment near the Sorbonne, not far from the gallérie. At first they made love tentatively, very gently, and then vigorously and passionately, tasting, touching everywhere. They murmured their needs and feelings in hushed tones in French or in English, and laughed ecstatically afterwards. They laughed at the coincidence of having the same surname, even though hers was spelled Hoffmann with two 'fs' and two 'ns' while his was Hofman with one 'f' and one 'n'. They laughed even harder when he told her his American relatives combined both, spelling Hoffman with two 'fs' and one 'n'. They laughed when she tried to pronounce a few Hebrew words and he experimented with Danish; they laughed at each other's atrocious accents. They laughed a lot – at silly things and at strange things.

Lise had never laughed so much in her life; in fact, she couldn't remember ever having been so happy. During the day, David usually worked on a seminar paper he had to submit before he flew to Tel Aviv for the remainder of his summer break, and since the Beaux-Arts was on its summer break and she had no classes, Lise painted or worked in the gallérie. In the evening, if she wasn't working, they joined the couples walking along the Seine and kissing in the shadows, until they'd race to his flat to fall into bed and make ecstatic love again and again. Sometimes they didn't even make it to the bed, ripping off their clothes and falling on the sofa or the rug, even standing against the door the minute he locked it; their passion for each other was boundless. David loved Lise's flawless skin; he loved kissing every inch of her body from her toes to the top of her head but he especially loved her small, beautifully shaped breasts – sometimes sucking one nipple noisily while he played with the other while Lise's small but strong hands clutched him tightly. "You are undoubtedly the most beautiful woman I've ever seen," he told her so frequently that she began to believe him.

"So are you…the most beautiful man, I mean," running her hands up his chest; she touched a scar on his shoulder and asked what it was. He said he'd landed wrong after a parachute jump in the army, but it wasn't a major injury.

His penis intrigued her because she'd never seen a circumcised male; none of the models at the Beaux-Arts was Jewish. One night she examined him very thoroughly, laughing when he became fully aroused. "Did it hurt when they cut off that little piece of skin?" she asked, rubbing the head of his penis gently.

"I don't remember," he laughed. "I was only eight days old and

Chapter 1

I was drunk; I was sucking a piece of cotton-wool soaked in sweet wine that they'd given me so I wouldn't feel the pain. But it hurts now with you teasing me, so let's change places and I'll touch you." He kissed her lightly and then ardently. He parted her thighs with his knees and touched the small bud near the opening of her sex; it swelled immediately. He used his fingers to judge her readiness and then reached for a condom; she used her fingers to arouse him further as she sheathed him in latex. He smoothly entered the wetness and warmth that was *his* Lise. But she was still in a playful mood and said with a grin, "*Achtung! Vait* a minute. Your maleness belongs to me and *ve vill do this my vay!*"

David allowed Lise to reverse their positions again and with Lise straddling him, he was barely able to contain his chuckles as he sputtered, "*Jawohl mein schöne junge Frau!* I'm standing at full attention and I salute you!" Both of them were laughing until she slid down and took him into her mouth. He said, "Not like that tonight, Lise; I can't hold out much longer." David pulled her up and, kissing deeply, their lovemaking was as fulfilling as ever. David was not inexperienced, but he'd never known making love could be so filled with fun and laughter; his fascinating Lise was quickly becoming the major joy in his life. This amusing young woman, bold and never too shy to initiate passionate lovemaking, was the same young woman who told him she'd grown up totally lacking in self-confidence; she'd believed she was too tall and too skinny, too awkward, too stupid to make friends, and a constant embarrassment to her very beautiful mother. She told him her father and stepmother tried to convince her she wasn't any of those things, but by court order she'd been required to live with her mother until she went away to college, the mother who never stopped criticizing her. David didn't say it aloud, but he was furious, "*Her mother is a piece of work! Beautiful, maybe, but totally self-absorbed and belittling. How could she make Lise feel so insecure? Was she so afraid of competition from a beautiful and very talented daughter? At least now Lise's far away from her mother's influence and she's finding out how very wrong her mother was.*"

They avoided talk about their imminent departures, his to Tel Aviv and hers to Denmark, although they both knew their days together were quickly running out; neither of them wanted to think about being apart. But they did talk, on the day before he left. "I'll only be gone for six weeks," he said. "Then I'll be back, and we'll be together, my darling. I'll call you as often as I can, here before you leave, and later at your father's home. I'll write as well, but in what language? French?

English? Lise, I've rented my flat for another year, so I'll ask you now if Chloe and Marcel would be upset if you moved in with me? My flat is so much closer to the Beaux-Arts and to the gallérie...no need to ride the Metro."

Lise tried not to show how much his words thrilled her. "So many questions, my love. Let's see," she said, holding up her fingers one by one. "English or French, as we always use both since you can't speak Danish and I can't manage Hebrew. About the flat: Chloe and Marcel won't be upset; in fact, the opposite. Chloe's been talking about moving in with her boyfriend Henri, and Marcel's going back to Nice as soon as he finishes his final papers. Both of them have been worried about what I would do, so now, with no qualms, we'll give up our flat when the lease is up. Your flat is close to the gallérie and the Beaux-Arts, but..." she hesitated, "I'm in love with you and I'm sure you love me, but what are you really asking me, David?" she asked with her usual candor.

"I love you and I think I'm asking you to marry me," he answered solemnly. "I know we've only known each other three weeks, but it feels right. It's been special from the first moment I saw you in the gallérie. I've never felt this way about anyone. I've had girlfriends before and even lived with one for several months, but this is different. Of course, I'd say that in any case, but I mean it. You're so talented, Lise. I know you'll love living and painting in Tel Aviv; the light is special there. I'm not just saying that. You're so aware of color and light and all Israeli artists love the light in Tel Aviv. And the beach is wonderful. I don't want an answer now, my love, because I'm babbling. We'll be apart for a few weeks," he groaned, "so let's see if we still feel the same way when we're back." He quirked his mouth to one side, doing a very bad imitation of Bogart in *Casablanca*, "If it doesn't work out...'*we'll always have Paris, Lise*'," he stated with a grin.

Lise burst out laughing. "I really do love you. I'm quite sure my answer will be 'Yes!' if you still want me next month. But what about your family, David? I'm not Jewish. Would they accept me?"

"They'll probably accept you a lot sooner than the state of Israel will," he said. "Just seeing how happy you make me will absolutely be enough for my parents and grandparents. But maybe while you're in Denmark, you can think about becoming Jewish. You said you've never followed any religion and your stepmother is Jewish. Will you talk to her about converting?" She promised she would, and he said, "Let's stop talking and you should start kissing me." She burst out laughing again and enthusiastically did as he suggested.

Chapter 1

◆ ◆ ◆

Back in Paris two days earlier than he'd anticipated, David couldn't wait to see Lise and went directly from the airport to her flat. "She's at the gallérie," Chloe said. "She's a little nervous about whether you still feel the same way, and if you still want her to move in with you. So am I. Here I am, packing my things to take to Henri's place. Marcel's already back in Nice, and we have to be out of here in less than two weeks."

"Are you both crazy? You know I don't really mean that. Lise isn't crazy and neither are you! I absolutely want her to move in with me. I want to marry her. My mother gave me my grandmother's engagement ring if Lise agrees to marry me. I'll run to the gallérie this minute if I can leave my things here. *Au revoir*, Chloe. We'll meet again…so it's not goodbye. It's just *bonne chance* and good luck…to both of us." He smiled, giving her a quick peck on the cheek.

Not willing to waste a precious minute, David ignored the Metro and did run all the way to the gallérie. And there she was. He could see his "beautiful little mermaid" through the window, talking to a hesitant customer about an obviously expensive painting. She turned and saw him before he opened the door; she gestured to Claude, the gallérie owner, to take over the customer and went to David who pulled her outside and into his arms. They shared a very long kiss. "God, how I missed you!" he said. "I'm back early because I couldn't wait any longer. We can't be separated for such a long time ever again. I love you, Lise, and now I am asking you the question I said I was thinking of asking you before we went home. Lise, my beloved, will you marry me? I'll get down on one knee if you want."

"My darling idiot, you don't want the dirt of *La Rive Gauche*, the Left Bank of the Seine, on your pants. So don't even think of kneeling! Besides, I hate the idea of a man, any man, kneeling at my feet. Of course I'll marry you. I love you, and these few weeks away from you have been torture for me, too," she exclaimed, kissing him boldly again and again.

Claude and the customer had been watching the emotional reunion through the window, the woman oohing and aahing about young love and Paris, even if it wasn't April or springtime. Claude opened the door and came outside with the customer just when David took a small box out of his pocket and slipped a ring on Lise's finger. "It was my *savta*'s, my grand-mère's. She wants you to have it, but we'll get another one if you don't like it…"

"*Félicitations!*" Claude cried, embracing both of them – and kissing them on each cheek even before Lise could tell David she loved the ring.

"Congratulations!" the woman, an American tourist, echoed, giving Claude a pointed look. "I'll buy the painting you showed me, Lise, as a gift to such a charming couple because that way I'm sure the commission Monsieur Pierné will give you should help you start your life together in the best possible way!" Claude immediately invited them back inside the gallérie and said he'd open a bottle of the best champagne to celebrate their "brilliant" news!

"Just a moment please, Claude," David said. "I have to know what Lise thinks of my grand-mère's ring!" She loved the old-fashioned rose cut of the not-so-small diamond of course; it suited her perfectly. They went back into the shop, where they drank champagne with Claude and the American tourist, and then Claude waved them off, slipping some large franc notes into David's hand. "Go celebrate! It's a cliché, *bien sûr*, but Paris really is a city for lovers!"

They raced to David's flat, desperate for each other after their separation. They stripped, tossing clothing everywhere the moment he closed the door and fell onto the small rug near the entrance. With no gentleness this time, they made love furiously, passion soaring to previously unknown heights – kissing, tasting, biting lips and necks and shoulders and finally, gasping for breath, they fell back, shattered. "I guess I missed you!" David whispered through bruised and swollen lips. He struggled onto his elbows to look at Lise who lay on her back, eyes closed. "I've never been so wild. God, did I hurt you, my darling?"

Lise blinked. "That was incredible!" she gasped. "I was just as wild, so I guess I missed you, too. But I do hurt, because I probably have rug burn! And this floor is so hard, even with the carpet!"

David chuckled, stood and picked Lise up gently, carrying her to his bed where they spent the afternoon, making love more leisurely, telling each other about their time apart, how boring Israel was for him, how boring Denmark was for her. And then making love again. Finally, they realized they were both famished and they laughed when they realized there wasn't a thing to eat in his flat, so they agreed to spend Claude's largesse on a dinner cruise on the Seine. "But where's your luggage? Did you bring anything back from Israel besides my gorgeous ring?" Lise asked casually.

"I did," he replied, "but I went straight from the airport to your flat and then to the gallérie. I guess I know where we'll sleep tonight."

Lise laughed, "If we sleep at all! And then tomorrow morning, we can pack my things and move them here so Chloe and I can give up the flat."

They picked up their clothing from the entranceway, showered together, and hurried to the Pont de l'Alma, the embarkation point for the Bateaux Mouche cruise on the Seine. Musicians played French songs as mostly tourists, but also a few local passengers, milled around, sipping cocktails and hanging over the rails, waving to the people on the dock. David asked the *Maître d' hôtel*, the host, for a bottle of fine – but not the most expensive – champagne so that they could celebrate their *fiançailles* in true French style. "We shall take care of everything," the Frenchman said, smiling at them as David passed quite a few francs into his hand. "*Félicitations, mademoiselle la belle et monsieur.* Tonight you 'll have the best table on board and *le banquet magnifique! Bon voyage!*" He led them to a table overlooking the right bank of the Seine and they laughed joyously when the cork popped loudly out of the bottle of champagne the waiter brought them, a far better vintage than David had requested. They toasted each other, they toasted their good luck in meeting at the gallérie, they toasted the Little Mermaid, they toasted Claude and his American client, they toasted the Bateaux Mouche and its debonair *Maître d'*. David, slightly bemused but unsure if it was the wine or just being with Lise, claimed, "*Le Français sont de tels romantiques!* Or at least the Parisiens are!" The strolling musicians stopped near their table to play romantic music, the smiling waiters served each gourmet dish with a flourish, and the jovial people at nearby tables toasted them on their engagement, *"L'amour toujours!"*

"Should we be red-faced with embarrassment?" Lise asked David.

"Of course not, *mon amour*," he laughed, a bit tipsily. "This is Paris, we are in love and, as Claude aptly told us, 'Paris is a city for lovers!' Undoubtedly it's a cliché, but it's also undoubtedly true!"

When they disembarked at 10:30, so many of the other passengers offered congratulations that Lise's cheeks burned. Rather than taking their usual stroll along the Seine, they rushed to Lise's flat so they could telephone first Richard and Anna and then David's parents to tell them the news; no one was surprised after the way the two had moped while they'd been apart. Richard said if Lise wanted, he'd call both Marlene and Jonas; Lise agreed, and David told her he was glad because although he wouldn't mind speaking to her brother, he wasn't too keen about even a short conversation with her mother. "She's not so bad now," Lise said, a little defensively. "Albert really makes her happy. I spent a few days with them in Malmö and she was like a different person. She didn't criticize me at all, and we went out together to shops and to restaurants, even to the theatre with

Albert and some of their friends. She bought me the dress I'm wearing now and some other things. She didn't even say anything nasty about Richard and Anna. So, while I don't expect her to say she's overjoyed, I think she will be pleased for us."

"That's good. And it's a very pretty dress, such a perfect color for you. It's like your eyes," he said, his gaze exploring the stylish cobalt blue dress from its fairly modest scoop neck to its less than modest short skirt. "You've always said she had good taste. And so do you… after all, you chose me! But now I want to get you out of that pretty dress as fast as I can!" Lise laughed at his absurdity. In Lise's room, they found David's things and a note from Chloe taped on the mirror, wishing them *"Félicitations!"* Later, lying in Lise's bed after another round of lovemaking, she suddenly said, "Oh, I forgot to tell you. I spoke to Anna about becoming Jewish."

David kissed her brow. "And what did that wise lady say?"

"She said I should do it if it's important to your family or if it would make it easier for me to live in Israel. My family always celebrated Christmas with a tree and presents, but we didn't go to church. In my whole life, I haven't been inside many churches, except here in Paris to study their art. What Anna said was really interesting. She said she remembered being Jewish and happy when she was a little girl in Amsterdam. But after the War, she hated God and the Jewish religion; she even cursed God. She couldn't believe a "merciful God", which was what she'd been taught in the Jewish religion, would allow grown men to torture and kill an innocent baby in front of his mother's eyes…and then keep the mother alive with that horrible image for the rest of her days. She said she'd read that Holocaust survivors either became observant, turning to God for comfort, or like her, they turned completely away from religion.

"I think my father tried to lessen Anna's angst, because he said if Jesus, who was born Jewish and died Jewish, had known about the crimes that would be perpetrated in his name, he would have killed himself! I laughed, but she didn't. Anna said Jews don't commit suicide even when they want to. Her voice was full of sadness, but then she smiled at me and said now she was glad that she'd survived, so she could meet and marry my father and fall in love with his children. You know I love her, too, as does Jonas. Did I tell you his baby daughter is named Annalise? For the two women he says he loves most after Brigitte. A few times Anna said solemnly that I should convert if life in Israel would be easier for me if I am Jewish and so my future children will grow up where they'll always be safe," Lise said, her voice

Chapter 1

breaking a little.

David said, "Now I know that Anna truly is a very wise lady. Do you think she and your father never had a baby because of the one who was killed?"

"I don't know," Lise answered. "Neither one of them was young when they married and Anna occasionally suffers from depression. What sane person wouldn't feel despair as well as hatred with a history like hers? She lost her parents, her grandparents, her sisters, her husband, everyone she knew and loved. I think what they did to her baby and making her stand there watching has to be one of the most horrible things I've ever heard! I don't think she can ever forget such an atrocity. Besides, my father already had three children…"

She thought she felt him smiling into her hair as he said, "And how very glad I am about that, especially about the one here with me right now. You know, Lise, Claude has Jewish friends and clients. Let's ask your boss about who we should see to start the conversion process. I'd like our children to be born in Israel, always safe."

"Our children…" she murmured sleepily. "Boys? Girls?"

"Does it matter?" he asked. "All I know right now about our future children is that they'll have blue eyes, either like yours that turn a tumultuous blue-grey like the Mediterranean in a storm when you're angry or upset, or bland, light blue ones like mine. And I also know our children will have fascinating stories to tell their children about their parents and grandparents and great-grand…" He stopped speaking when he glanced down and saw that Lise was already asleep. "Dream about our blue-eyed children, my lovely little mermaid," he said before turning off the lamp and closing his own eyes.

Two days later Claude sent them to *Le Consistoire Central Israélite de France*, established by Napoleon in 1808 to deal with all religious issues concerning and of concern to Jews. Between Lise moving all her things into David's flat and working daily in the gallérie, and David setting deadlines for completing his dissertation according to his supervisor's schedule, they still found time to attend a preliminary meeting with a rabbi recommended by the Consistoire. Rabbin René Bonfils first asked Lise why she wanted to convert. He told them many potential converts were in romantic relationships with Jews and hoped to combine their lives, while others were on a spiritual search and learned about Judaism through reading, attending a Jewish religious ceremony, and so on. Whatever their motivation, the first step in conversion for everyone was to explore why they wanted to convert. Lise told him her reason was the first one – she wanted to marry

David, an Israeli; and the second was that she wanted their children to be raised Jewish, and safely, in Israel. Hearing her sincerity, Rabbin Bonfils agreed to instruct Lise in conversion.

The next few months were incredibly busy. Classes at the Beaux-Arts were intense, with several new projects; she worked at the gallérie and met regularly with Rabbi Bonfils, completing specific study assignments – reading about Jewish beliefs and religious practices, prayer services, *kashrut*, candle-lighting, the Jewish holidays; and the history of the Jewish people, the Holocaust, and Israel. A little Hebrew was also included. When he had time, David attended sessions with Lise; he enjoyed hearing her trying to learn Hebrew, especially when Rabbin Bonfils told her to imitate David's accent and not his since the Rabbin's Hebrew had a definite French lilt.

Following the Rabbin's advice, they went to a few kosher restaurants in the Jewish neighborhood of Le Marais. Some of the restaurants served authentic but kosher French cuisine, but many were either Eastern European bland or North African spicy, and not very appealing, particularly to David who was a surprisingly good amateur chef. On the other hand, they appreciated the famed historic district itself – far more than the food. One afternoon while they were exploring Le Marais, they realized it was the closest they'd ever get to seeing medieval Paris with its pre-revolutionary buildings, narrow, winding streets and ancient cobblestoned alleys. Le Marais had once been an aristocratic area, but over time, it became so seedy it was almost razed. After the nobility moved to far more fashionable Faubourg Saint-Germain district, Le Marais became the center of Paris's Jewish population. They met a delightful old man who told them so many Eastern European Jews, including his grandparents and parents, moved into Le Marais during the first half of the 20th century, and the area became known as "the Pletzel". He took them to the corner of Rue des Rosiers and Rue Ferdinand Duval and showed them a plaque installed by the City of Paris. The plaque (in translation) stated:

> "Fleeing persecution, Ashkenazi Jews flooded into Paris beginning in 1881. They found places living among their co-religionists already established in the Marais. By 1900, about 6,000 had arrived from Rumania, Russia and Austria-Hungary; 18,000 more arrived in the years preceding the First World War. Installed in considerable numbers in the Rue des Écouffes, the Rue Ferdinand Duval (named Rue des

Chapter 1

Juifs – Street of Jews – until 1900), and the Rue des Rosiers, they constituted a new community, "the Pletzel", the "little place" in Yiddish, and they created the École Israelite du Travail (Israelite Trade School) at 4B Rue des Rosiers. The life of this community was evoked in Les Eaux Mêlées ("Agitated Waters"), a novel by Roger Ikor [which won the Prix Goncourt in 1955]. More than half of the Jewish population of the Pletzel perished in Nazi death camps."

Moises, their elderly guide and new friend, told them he was born in the *Pletzel* and still lived nearby, and that Rue de Rosiers was a major center for Parisian Jews – with bookshops selling Jewish books, kosher grocery shops, chacuteries and pâtisseries, restaurants, and notices of Jewish events posted on kiosks. He took them to the Pavee Synagogue, close to Rue de Rosiers. Lise was delighted to learn it had been designed in 1913 by Hector Guimard, one of the foremost representatives of the French Art Nouveau style. Moises told them the building was dynamited along with six other synagogues on Yom Kippur in 1941, but it was later restored to its previous glory. Lise and David noticed he was growing tired although he loved showing them Le Marais. He refused to take money from them for the impromptu tour, so they took him to a café for cognac and pastries, and they listened raptly to more anecdotes about Le Marais that he related. Before leaving, Moises philosophically suggested that they should return to Le Marais, sit in a café and read Sartre or Camus, or the most famous book ever written – the Bible. They laughed at his humor and gave him a donation for a Jewish charity. In a state of euphoria, they went back to their everyday lives. Lise told David she thought being Jewish might not be a bad thing.

David was proceeding quite rapidly with his supervisor's suggestions for revisions in his PhD *thèse* on the influence of the leftist, post-structuralist philosophies of Marcuse, Foucault and Derrida on contemporary economics. On the one hand, he was eager to finish his dissertation, but on the other, he knew he'd have to go back to Tel Aviv when he completed his doctorate. And he didn't want to leave Lise.

◆ ◆ ◆

One evening, as they were sharing an omelet, a baguette and the remainder of half a bottle of Lise's favorite Chardonnay, David looked at her across the small table, and blurted, "Lise, let's get married now!

Here, in Paris!"

"How?" she asked, startled. "I haven't converted yet, and I think it will be quite a while before I'll be able to do so."

David smiled, "I was in the library at the Sorbonne and I looked it up. You don't have to convert to get married here. Only civil marriage ceremonies are legal in France. If we want a religious wedding, we can only have that after the civil one. At least one of us must have resided in France for 40 days prior to the wedding, and both of us can prove we've lived here much longer than 40 days. Copies of our apartment leases are sufficient proof of our residency in Paris. The wedding would be performed by a state registrar at City Hall; the banns must be published 10 days before the wedding. We have to go to the Danish and Israeli embassies for legal affidavits stating that we are eligible to marry under the laws of our countries – a certificate less than three months old of our single-status, and copies of our birth certificates and passports. Is your birth certificate here, Lise? I brought mine with me when I came to Paris. We also need medical certificates less than 2 months old. I know it sounds like a lot, sweetheart, but we can take care of it in only two or three days. And after the banns are published, I'll bet both our families will come for the ceremony."

"Wow!" she exclaimed. "Aren't you breathless from reciting all that? I am, just from listening. I can't believe you want to do this. I don't have my birth certificate, but Jonas can get it from my mother and send it to me. It may be a silly question, but are you sure you can marry me under Israeli law?"

He laughed. "Yes, because it's a civil ceremony – not really recognized in Israel. We'll get married again by a rabbi when you're 'officially' Jewish. It's easier to start the procedure for recognition of our marriage if we're already married when we arrive in Israel and your first entry is with my family name."

"My family name is the same as yours anyway, even though the spelling is a bit different," Lise reminded him. "But you said it's exactly the same in Hebrew. Let's do it, my darling. Let's get married!" she laughed, jumping to her feet and dancing around the room. She pulled him out of his chair and they continued to whirl until they were both dizzy with excitement.

It took them a few more than three days, but eventually they'd completed all the paperwork and the banns were published. David's parents, his sister Dina, and Sammy and Sara, his father's parents – a wonderful surprise for David – flew in from Tel Aviv the day before the wedding. Lise's father and Anna, her brother Jonas with his wife

Chapter 1

Brigitte and baby daughter, and even her mother and Albert, came the day before the event. The families met at the Villa Saint Germain des Prés – a hotel recommended by Claude. They celebrated at a gourmet dinner in a Belle Époque-style brasserie, *Le Bouillon Racine*, which had once been a soup kitchen. The next morning, at City Hall, Claude and Chloe were their official witnesses at the brief ceremony. The weather was fair and mild – really quite surprising for Paris in mid-January – so Lise and David decided to celebrate with everyone on a Bateaux Mouche luncheon cruise. To their delight, it was the same ship where they had celebrated their engagement four months earlier, and the *Maitre d' hotel* recognized them. He said, "How could I forget such a beautiful couple who were so much in love? I am French." Everyone laughed at his oh-so-typical French romanticism.

Richard and Ephraim, Lise's and David's fathers immediately treated each other like old friends. Concerned about economics, they asked how Claude and his wife Mignon could take so much time away from the gallérie, or if it was closed for a holiday. Claude laughed. "Like the *Maitre d'*, I am also a romantic. Our son lives in Montreal, so Mignon and I think of Lise and David as our children. They met in my gallérie when he bought the painting of *"La Petite Sirène"* for Dina. And he asked Lise to marry him at the gallérie. I was the first person to wish them *félicitations* and I sent them to celebrate their engagement on this very boat! So how can we not rejoice in their happiness? The gallérie is closed only in our hearts; friends are covering for us. Besides, January is not a busy time for *galléries d'art*," he added. "Patrons – Parisians and tourists – are still recovering from their Christmas shopping." Lise and David were thrilled not only by their wedding, but also by the warmth and congeniality among their families and French friends; they both loved – using a French term – the *bonhomie*. They'd enjoyed the visits, but two days later, Lise's family returned to Denmark and Sweden although David's family – his parents, grandparents and sister – spent a few more days in Paris. Then, Lise and David went back to their respective universities and daily tasks.

David had a meeting with the Sorbonne's thesis committee, which met once every 12 months. His revisions had been closely monitored by his supervisor and now it was the role of the thesis committee to confirm that he'd fulfilled all of his obligations with respect to Advanced PhD seminars, and to determine if his research could be integrated into the Sorbonne's highly respected academic landscape. The committee approved and a pre-defense panel was organized for

March; with almost no changes, his thesis was approved for final defense.

On June 4, 1973, David successfully passed the defense of his PhD thesis *summa cum laude*. Faculty, fellow students and even the general public were invited to attend the final defense; the work of a young Israeli researching and writing about French philosophers seemed to be intriguing and the Sorbonne's Salle Bourjac was crowded. Lise, Claude and Mignon, Chloe and Henri, and a few other friends were there to boost David's morale; Marcel even came from Nice to wish him good luck. But the biggest surprise happened just as David was about to begin his defense. Suddenly both his father and Lise's came into the hall, arms linked, and took two vacant seats. David was both shocked and energized by such support. Afterwards, his supervisor stated that David had presented a brilliant defense and congratulated him warmly.

Celebrating his achievement at a bistro near the Sorbonne – enjoying once again champagne provided by Claude, David was only sad because he would be returning to Israel very soon, leaving Lise in Paris for another six or seven months. But once again, the two fathers had a surprise – a round-trip airline ticket for Lise: she would spend July and August in Tel Aviv with David and come back to Paris for the academic year and her final semester. David said it was one of the best days of his life, but not the very best; that was the day he met Lise. Ephraim said, "And they say Israelis aren't romantic!"

Laughing, Richard added, "But they – whoever they are – don't know these two! Maybe it's just the effect Paris has on the young!"

Chapter 2

Unlike Paris or Copenhagen in the summer, it was hot and humid when Lise and David arrived in Tel Aviv. Aya, David's mother, met them at the airport and drove them home, to her modern apartment just off the corner of Yehuda Hamaccabi and Ibn Gvirol Streets. "It's quite close to the beach," Aya told Lise, "but it's impossible to walk to the beach in the summer; it's just too hot!"

"Unlike Europe, Israel has only one TV channel and that's black and white, but, again unlike Europe, we all have air-conditioning! There's even been talk of lowering the cost of auto insurance if the car has air-conditioning!" David told her as they walked into his parents' lovely fourth-floor apartment. "If it cools off tonight, we'll take a walk. This isn't St-Germain-des-Prés but it has its own *joie de vivre*. Tomorrow we'll be tourists; we'll go to the beach and to a museum – so you'll get a sense of Tel Aviv." Aya followed them to the room David used whenever he came home, anticipating his astonishment at all the changes. His freshly painted room, large for an Israeli flat, had a queen-sized bed, a large chest of drawers and a matching armoire, two chairs and a small table. David asked when they'd had time to do so much. Aya said, "As soon as we came back from Paris; since you and Lise are married, we decided to turn your temporary headquarters into a real guest room for the whole summer and afterwards. The bathroom next door isn't an en-suite, Lise, but it's only for the two of you until the whole family descends on us this weekend." Lise was as thrilled as David with the comfort of the room and what his parents had done to make their time together special, although she told him later that she was embarrassed at the thought of making love right next door to his parents; he promised they'd be quiet. After David's father came home from work and his sister Dina popped in from her apartment near Tel Aviv University, the family sat down to a light dinner and Ephraim asked David about his plans.

"First of all, I want to show Lise some of Israel. I know that she'll be very enthusiastic, like all artists, by the light in Tel Aviv. I want her to experience it, so she'll be able to settle here next year and enjoy painting; she has a remarkable talent with color. And I'll start looking for a job. I've contacted two of my professors at Tel Aviv University and although there aren't any openings now, the head of the philosophy department wants to speak to me. Maybe I'll look for something in writing or publishing, but it might not be easy for me to get back into using Hebrew after writing so much in French," David said.

"What about translating?" Dina asked. "I'm sure there's a need for someone who's proficient in both languages, and English as well." David said he'd look into that also. "And we'll start looking for a place to rent or buy so we'll have our own place when Lise comes back in January," he added.

"You two may be in for a surprise," his mother said. "Sammy and Sara – the grandparents you met in Paris, Lise – are getting older and they've been talking about a new kind of housing in Israel, sheltered-living residences for senior citizens. These are not typical old-age homes with one bare room for an elderly couple; rather, they are small apartments in a modern complex that offers many facilities, including medical. Your grandparents saw one not too far from here, and Sara said it's beautiful and intended for English speakers like them. If they decide to make the move, I'm sure they'll offer you their apartment. After all, you're their favorite grandson!"

He laughed, "I'm their only grandson, not their favorite! Just wait until you see their place, Lise; it's on Basel Street, a block away from the sea and it even has a private garden. But I won't pressure them. They'll move into sheltered living only when they're ready." Lise agreed with him, saying she'd been so impressed at how vigorous and full of life the older couple were in Paris. She added she couldn't believe they were ready to move into an old-age residence."

"Sheltered living, not an old-age home," Dina said. "Of course they were full of life in Paris. Their 'favorite grandson' was getting married – in Paris! But the move might not be a bad idea. They both have arthritis, and Grandpa had bypass surgery last year. I think they would enjoy many of the activities advertised by these new senior citizen residences – concerts, lectures, day trips, and even weekends at the Dead Sea. I hope they'll consider it seriously."

Lise smiled at her sister-in-law and said, "Dina, I'm sure you're their favorite granddaughter! I know there are others who I'm looking forward to meeting, but you are really special."

"You'll get your wish soon, Lise," Aya said, laughing. "My parents, Esther and Yaakov – called *Savta* and *Saba* in our family – and my brother Chaim and his family are coming this weekend; Sara and Sammy will be here. Ephraim's sister and brother will probably come as well with their daughters. I don't know if you're in for a treat – or an ordeal! There'll be lots of food, lots of children, and lots of noise."

"I love children," Lise replied, "and we'll get along although I barely know any Hebrew. They can teach me some new words, laugh at my terrible accent, and I'll teach them how to paint. But please don't expect me to remember all their names at this first meeting!"

David grinned at his parents, "I told you last summer that she's unique!" He gave her a quick kiss. "Let's go for a walk, *wife*." The evening was surprisingly comfortable, and David said, "Tel Aviv doesn't usually cool off like this in the evening." They walked down a few streets to Milano Square with a few shops and cafés. "Do you fancy a good cup of coffee?" he asked. Lise was delighted with the ambience at Zorik's, one of the oldest cafés in the square. They drank coffee, shared a rich pastry, and people-watched – one of Lise's most favorite activities. David laughed at her enthusiasm. "Well, no one's ever claimed Tel Aviv is part of a third-world country! In fact, it calls itself the 'city that never sleeps'! You'll see. Believe it or not," he added, "this neighborhood is probably one of the last places in Israel where it's common to see very elegantly dressed, perfectly coiffed 75-year-old ladies – 'ladies', not women – with handbags that match their shoes, sipping tea at eleven o'clock in the morning, and chatting in Hungarian or carefully enunciated, grammatically perfect, but old-fashioned Hebrew. Now, my *petite sirène*, let's go home," he added. "Aren't you tired?"

"A little," she admitted, "but I love being here and I love your family."

During the next two months, they enjoyed their honeymoon. They went to the beach and to museums. They explored the flea market in Old Yafo and bought some odd antiques and knick-knacks. They climbed the snake path in Masada, the Herodian fortification where 2000 years earlier, a group of Jewish rebels barricaded themselves until they were defeated by the Romans and then committed suicide. They stayed overnight not far from Masada, in Ein Gedi, a nature reserve in the Judean Desert across from the lowest spot on earth, the Dead Sea; they had a picnic breakfast near Ein Gedi's waterfall and then went "swimming" in the Dead Sea. Lise thought the buoyancy of the sea, eight times saltier than the ocean, was hilarious as it pushed her into floating whenever she tried to swim. She and David covered parts of each other with natural black Dead Sea mud, relaxed for a while, and then went to the fresh water showers. They hiked two kilometers into Nahal Arugot to watch hundreds of ibexes and even more rock hyraxes – resembling rabbits with very short ears – running to their favorite feeding spots. Exhausted after an exhilarating day, they returned to the Ein Gedi kibbutz hotel to shower, eat dinner, and then fall into their bed.

They went to Yad Vashem, the memorial to the Holocaust in

Jerusalem; it was depressing but Lise understood its significance in Jewish history, and how powerful it would be for Anna when her father and stepmother came to visit them in Israel. David told her that tour guides argued about whether tourists should see all of Jerusalem first and then complete their tour at Yad Vashem, or the opposite. They went to the Israel Museum with its impressive sculpture garden donated by the American theatrical producer Billy Rose and designed by Isamu Noguchi; Lise was so impressed that it seemed to blend Eastern and Western culture – Japanese-type gravel terraces and magnificent European sculptural masterpieces. She was fascinated by the Shrine of the Book housing the Dead Sea Scrolls and the special projects for thousands of children in the Youth Wing. At the Holyland Hotel, they viewed the Second Temple model of Jerusalem, "the city of my namesake, King David, maybe even my ancestor," David said, with the grin she could never resist. They walked through the Old City; Lise slipped a small note with her personal prayer into a crack between stones in the Western Wall. In a shop on the Via Dolorosa, they had tea with an Armenian pottery dealer and bought a few lovely tiles he had produced using age-old designs; in the Jewish Quarter, they had coffee with a modern potter and they purchased a few of his pots. They explored Yemin Moshe, Jerusalem's first neighborhood outside the Old City, now reconstructed for artists and writers. When they left Jerusalem, Lise confessed that she couldn't decide which side in the tour-guide argument about Yad Vashem first or last was the correct one. Although she loved Jerusalem's antiquity and atmosphere, as an artist whose special talent revolved around using color and light, she was more inspired by Tel Aviv and she looked forward to living there, painting her semi-abstract works, and raising a family in the "city that never sleeps".

David went to interviews and received a few translation jobs for French and English. His meeting with the chairman of Tel Aviv U's philosophy department was both challenging and stimulating; with mutual respect, they agreed that David would teach a course in the spring term, when the professor who usually taught that course retired. His grandparents decided to move to the sheltered living complex they liked and they wanted David and Lise to have the Basel Street flat, which Lise loved; they were apologetic about not being able to give it to them as a gift, but they had to buy into the senior citizens' residence and they needed the money. Both Lise and David loved them all the more for their generosity of spirit. Sara and Sammy intended to move in December, giving David time to do some renovations before Lise moved to Israel from Paris. She planned a few changes in the flat and David started looking into the legalities of getting a permit to build a studio for Lise in the private garden.

After their halcyon days, and with her mind teeming with future plans, Lise reluctantly returned to Paris at the end of August. She was upset about leaving David, but she knew she had only one final term at the Beaux-Arts; her job at Claude's gallérie and her conversion lessons with Rabbin Bonfils would help the time pass quickly. She missed David terribly during the next few weeks, but they spoke very frequently.

◆◆◆

At two o'clock p.m. on Saturday, October 6, 1973, Yom Kippur, the holiest day in the Jewish calendar, Egypt and Syria launched simultaneous surprise attacks on Israel. After they heard the warning sirens and turned on the radio, David sat by the phone in his parents' home, barely moving, waiting for the call to join his unit. He'd tried phoning Lise but was unable to get an open line to Paris; when he'd been with his unit for two days of training in August, Lise had seen him in his paratroopers uniform and red beret, a surreal experience for both of them in the middle of their honeymoon. On that Saturday evening in October, David was summoned; his father drove him as close as possible to his base in the North. On the way, they collected others from his unit, all of them angry about the attacks, all of them scared, all of them worried that they weren't sufficiently trained to turn this debacle in Israel's favor. No one knew exactly how bad the attacks from Syria and Egypt had been, but rumors said they had been absolutely devastating. On the other hand, everyone agreed it was fortunate – in an ironic way – that the attacks occurred on Yom Kippur when most Israelis were at home or in synagogue, and the army could be mobilized quickly; had the attacks happened on Rosh Hashanah ten days earlier, Israeli reserve soldiers would have been widely scattered – some camping in Israel, others abroad, and mobilization would have been far more difficult and slow.

During the Six-Day War, David had been a lieutenant in the Paratroopers, part of the brigade that captured the Golan Heights. During the battle, he was injured while helping rescue a wounded soldier deep behind enemy lines; after the war he received a medal for distinguished service. Now he was on his way back to the Golan, for whatever role he was assigned. He'd told Lise that the paratroopers were like a family with very strong bonds built on their shared experiences and, sadly, on the blood they shed in battle. They were a military elite based on individual merit, and their extraordinary camaraderie took away any discrimination of family origin, education and wealth. David explained to Lise that Israelis serve in their IDF units long after their compulsory service, either in the career army or in the reserves; for David, it was the reserves.

In the Golan Heights, although wary and insufficiently trained, the reserves came to the aid and in many cases to the rescue of the beleaguered regular IDF forces. David was given an M16 rifle, a weapon he had never handled before; but he was a quick learner and soon mastered how to use the firearm. By the first ceasefire, October 22nd, IDF paratroopers had pushed all the way into Syria. The IDF controlled the Syrian side of Mount Hermon, the Golan had been reconquered and the paratroopers were like an armored infantry thrust deep into Syria. On November 11th, when the final ceasefire was declared, David's unit was only 40 kilometers outside of Damascus, Syria's capital, and the Israelis on the Egyptian front were only 101 kilometers away from Cairo. The IDF had triumphed, but the price Israel paid was extremely heavy: 2522 dead, 400 taken prisoner, 800 tanks, 115 planes destroyed. David lost several comrades, some known and others unknown, but he mourned mostly for three childhood friends who never returned from the disasters of the first few days at the Suez Canal.

In Paris, Lise was frantic almost all the time; she found it impossible to eat, sleep, or paint; her small radio and TV were tuned 24 hours a day to the news, although the information coming from Israel was sporadic and she suspected it was inaccurate. Not knowing if David was alive or dead, not knowing where he was or what kind of danger he faced, she allowed her imagination full reign. She envisioned horrible scenarios – David directly involved in hand-to-hand fighting with soldiers resembling bearded monsters or David parachuting into the midst of a fierce battle, or David as a POW of the Germans ... Germans? She laughed hysterically when she realized these visions were actually from old World War II films and her father's history. One evening, Chloe found her sitting on the floor, weeping. "Has something happened? Is David okay?" she asked, wrapping her arms around Lise, who replied, "I don't know. I just keep remembering his words before he left for Tel Aviv when we first met; he said *'We'll always have Paris, Lise!'* Chloe, what if that's all we will ever have?"

Chloe burst out laughing. "That was Bogart's terrific line in *Casablanca*, but it's not your reality. David's parents phoned you last night to tell you they had heard from him, and he's all right, and they'll call you again whenever he calls them. Let's hope they'll call you tomorrow. Now eat a little and tell me again about your honeymoon in Tel Aviv. OK?"

Chloe and Henri, Claude and Mignon, her father and stepmother, even her mother, offered Lise as much comfort and support as they could during this awful period in her young marriage. Finally, on November 30th, seven weeks after the war began, David phoned. He was home, but he sounded so distant, so agitated. "Are you OK, my darling? Have they released you yet?" Lise queried. "Can you come to Paris? I think we really need to be with each other now."

David's family and the IDF, or at least David's commanding officer, agreed, and he arrived in Paris three days later. Gaunt, unsmiling, with a haunted look, Lise almost didn't recognize her handsome, gregarious husband. "You've lost so much weight," they both said simultaneously. "And so many friends," David said. But at least they were together, and their love gradually restored both of them to health. Long walks along the Seine helped David, as did seeing Lise return to her lovely, cheerful self. Once, during a walk in the crisp December chill, David told her he'd lost so many friends in this war that he knew a tiny bit – only a tiny smidgeon – of how Anna had felt after the Holocaust; at least Lise and his entire family were safe. Lise, Chloe, Claude and David's Sorbonne supervisor convinced him to write about his experiences and the traumas of the war; they said it would be cathartic even if he never published it. He accepted their advice and thousands of words began flowing from his pen. David began to recover as he wrote in French; Chloe's fiancé Henri had several journalist friends and acquaintances in publishing, and they arranged the sale of David's articles to a few French periodicals for substantial payment – although he didn't really care about the money.

In January, David and Lise went to the Beaux-Arts to speak to her advisors. "Professeur Cardin and Professeur Lambert, my final project is almost done," she said quietly. "You know my husband is Israeli and fought in their recent war. Living here, not having any contact with him when he was at the front, not knowing if he was alive or dead... was the most traumatic experience of my life. I couldn't sleep, I couldn't eat, I couldn't work." Shaking and trying not to cry, she stopped speaking. David reached over and took her hand.

"We understand, my dear. But he's right here in front of us and he's most certainly alive," Professeur Cardin said gently.

"Yes, I know," Lise smiled through her tears. "But I don't think I could survive another separation like that," she finished passionately. "My dear professeurs, you know my work. Please allow me to go to Tel Aviv with my husband. I promise I'll send my completed project to you within two or three months." Having read David's article and understanding what the young couple had lived through, and after hearing her heartfelt plea, the two advisors agreed to allow her to complete her work in Israel.

The owner of their flat was equally sympathetic to Lise's situation and since David had found someone, a graduate student at the Sorbonne who was eager to sublet the apartment, the lease was broken with no penalty. Lise and David packed all her belongings and art supplies for shipment to Israel and then they flew to Copenhagen for a short visit with her family, who were thankful David had come through the war unscathed, at least physically. Everyone promised to come and visit in Israel. "It's really not that far away, just a hop and a skip by plane! And quite safe now, I'm sure," Richard said calmly, hugging his beloved daughter, smiling at his son-in-law, and then hugging David, too.

◆◆◆

In mid-January David's grandparents moved into a charming apartment in Herzliya, 15-minutes away from their old flat. Although both of them were totally fluent in Hebrew, they'd chosen a "Golden Age Community" built for English-speaking senior citizens. Their new flat was smaller than the one on Basel Street, so they gave some furnishings to David's parents, sister and other family members, but they left numerous items for Lise and David, telling them to keep whatever they wanted and discard anything they couldn't use. After several meetings, much haggling and a few compromises on his plans, David received permission from the municipality to build a semi-detached addition to the kitchen as a studio for Lise. In the meantime, they continued to live in his parents' flat while he helped with the major renovations, not just supervising, but also doing some of the work; he said the physical work was therapy for his still somewhat troubled mind. He also worked on Hebrew versions of some of the articles about the Yom Kippur War he'd written in French, and he began an article based on his Sorbonne dissertation for an English academic journal in philosophy. Working simultaneously in all three languages was as exhausting mentally as the physical labor – but David knew "publish or perish" was the unacknowledged motto for advancement in Israeli academia, that esoteric world he was determined to enter. Lise worked diligently on her final project for the Beaux-Arts on the closed-in balcony of her in-laws' home – windows open to let in the sunlight and let out the paint fumes; she had opted to work in oil rather than water-color early in her studies and worried that breathing in the intense smell was harmful for all of them. Lise and David were sometimes so tired after showering off the day's grime and paint before having dinner with his parents that they could barely speak; on those evenings, they practically crawled into bed very early.

To accommodate soldiers returning to university after the Yom Kippur War, the 1973 Israeli academic year began extremely late. David was asked to teach two introductory courses in the late second semester and another in the extra summer term. He was pleased at the result of the late opening, but certainly not by the cause. Still, he felt he was slowly beginning to wedge his foot into the door of Israel's tight academic world. Three days after shipping her project to Paris, Lise and David moved to Basel Street, and Lise began a completely new endeavor – setting up the flat by first deciding which of the furnishings left by his grandparents she wanted to keep, then unpacking the crates that had arrived from France. She explored Tel Aviv's plethora of shops to purchase lamps and linens; she meandered through Yafo's *shuk ha pishpeshim* with David or Dina, finding a small Persian rug, an old picture frame, a Victorian card table and a few other unusual accoutrements, and then arranging everything according to her own taste. All of these were new experiences that she surprisingly enjoyed. When everything was set up, even Lise's studio, they invited David's parents, grandparents and Dina to a dinner party, prepared mostly by David. Despite living in Paris for several years, *haute couture* was much more Lise's forte than *haute cuisine*; but she liked being David's *sous-chef*. He was very proud of his "imported" young wife – learning Hebrew, continuing her conversion lessons with Rabbi Gershon Herman, a friend of her Parisian conversion instructor. And she was experimenting with new paints in her studio, enthralled with the light of Tel Aviv. "Someday she may even find the time to learn how to cook," David told their 'first guests' with a smile; Lise lightly punched his arm.

Ephraim, David's father was a professor of biochemistry at the Weizmann Institute in Rehovot and Aya, his mother was the principal of a junior high school in Tel Aviv; both parents were active participants in the intellectual life of the city, with subscriptions to the Mann Auditorium for concerts and for Habima and the Cameri for theatre. Although much of Israel's cultural life had been curtailed by the Yom Kippur War, Aya and Ephraim often entertained at home. Their friends had seen Lise's work-in-progress for the Beaux-Arts as well as her painting of the Little Mermaid that David had bought Dina, and one of their friends, originally from France and currently the director of L'Institut Français de Tel Aviv, asked Lise if she'd be interested in giving a lecture in French, or even just a short talk, on current trends in the modern art world. She was honored and instantly agreed, assuming her lecture would be *gratis*; she was astounded when he said how much she would be paid. David was excited for her, saying it was yet another new start for his lovely Lise. Her lecture was well attended, and Lise joked that everyone who was there was a friend or an acquaintance of David's parents and had come to check out the bride. She was equally astonished when she received an offer for a similar lecture in German at the Goethe Institute. She accepted again, of course, and this time quipped, "What's next? Danish? English? Maybe they're just checking my linguistic ability and not my knowledge of art. At least they'll never have to worry about me giving a lecture in Hebrew!"

Ephraim replied before David had a chance, "I'm sure someday you'll be proficient in Hebrew as well, my dear daughter-in-law. I think your language skills are almost as extraordinary as your artistic talent, your humor, and your beauty." Lise blushed and ran over to kiss her father-in-law French-style on both cheeks and to thank him for his compliments.

A few days later, she received a phone call from the manager of an art shop in the Hilton Hotel, asking if she was interested in a sales position, even part-time. They needed someone who knew the art world and was fluent in several languages; he'd attended the French lecture and was sure she could do the job. An extra bonus for Lise was that the Hilton was only a short walk from their apartment. She couldn't believe what was happening to her new life in Israel. The lectures at L'Institut Français and the Goethe Institute turned into biweekly art appreciation courses in the two different languages, and Lise was astounded at how much she enjoyed teaching. Fortunately, the courses met in alternate weeks and she was thus only obligated one evening per week. She worked an afternoon shift at the Hilton twice a week; it was exhilarating work because not only was she learning a lot about Israeli art, but she was also meeting wealthy American and European connoisseurs of the various genres sold in the Hilton shop. She was free in the mornings for her conversion lessons and for her own painting; afternoons and evenings when she wasn't at the Hilton,

Chapter 2

she prepared her art lectures while David worked on his lectures and articles. Occasionally they went to see a film or to a concert, and David's old friends began dropping by or meeting them at a café. They usually spent Shabbat with David's family. Dina, who was as tall and slim as Lise, often consulted her about styles and asked how she could develop a chic Parisian look like Lise's; Dina was dating an upcoming doctor and while she wanted him to appreciate her brain and personality, she also hoped he'd be pleased with her appearance. When Lise told him about Dina's fashion requests, David joked that he and Lise were so busy that they'd have to make an appointment when they wanted to make love. "That'll never happen!" Lise exclaimed, sliding her arms around his neck. "I'm ready whenever you're up for it."

David laughed, "How about now? I'm definitely up for it!" he said, placing her hand on his obvious erection as he picked her up and raced to their room. He tossed her on the bed and came down beside her before she could open her mouth to say anything. So he just took her mouth with his and moved in as deeply as ever. They touched and teased; within minutes their clothing was discarded and their game of love intensified, lasting long into the night. One night, after Lise had been in Israel six months, they were lying spoon-fashion in bed, with David's hand lightly stroking her breast after a vigorous hour of passion. Neither of them was ready for sleep and Lise kissed his hand as she softly murmured, "I'd never have believed that my life could be so wonderful and so full. It's all because of you, my darling." David turned her in his arms, kissed her deeply and said she deserved it, but he had some other wonderful thoughts on his mind right then…so would she please stop talking.

Early in 1975 David was offered additional classes at the University, with the promise of *teken*. When two of his articles in English were published by prestigious philosophy journals, the dean of the Faculty of Humanities praised the quality of his work at a department meeting. He phoned Lise immediately to let her know about this. "I remember what you said and turnabout is fair play: all of this is because of you, my darling. You inspire me."

Every summer an art fair was held on the wide median along Tel Aviv's Rothschild Blvd. The first time Lise displayed her work there, she sold a few paintings – three of them to *étudiants* in one of her art appreciation courses. She told them she would have given them a discount at L'Institut Français, but they replied they were delighted to purchase paintings by their "professeure". This gave her the courage to enter her work in other fairs and two art critics mentioned her as one of the best new artists in Israel. She was thrilled; not only did their reviews boost her sales, but they further increased her self-confidence. When she proudly showed David the cheques she had received at the last fair, he laughed and whirled her around. He said, "I have always known how good you are. I purchased the very first painting you sold. And just think how that changed my life!" he added with a wink.

"And mine! Would either of us have believed that evening at the gallérie that I would end up in Tel Aviv married to the handsome Israeli who bought *'La Petite Sirène'*? Claude once said he would never have allowed me to put it in the window if he'd known he would lose me along with the painting!"

"He didn't lose you; he gained a new place to vacation and some new friends and…!" David quipped.

"But he hasn't visited us yet. Maybe he and Mignon will come to our second wedding, the Jewish one!" Lise said. David smiled but he didn't say anything, knowing that event was still quite far away if it was to occur at all.

Lise loved shopping for vegetables, fruit, cheese and spices at the raucous and busy Carmel market, carrying her odiferous purchases home in a plastic basket. She was anxious to learn how to cook because she knew it was unfair to be so dependent on David's skills when his schedule was as heavy as hers; at the very least, she should be able to share the chore with him. Fortunately, Aya was willing to show her how to prepare some dishes, as was Anna. When she and Richard came to visit, Lise prevailed on her stepmother to help her cook the things she'd loved so many years ago in Denmark, only this time they'd be kosher. Since Anna was Jewish, it was easy to adjust the recipes, never mixing meat and milk. No mustardy cream sauce on pepper steak; and for Lyonnaise potatoes to accompany Steak Diane, the thinly sliced potatoes and onions were sautéed in margarine. Aya taught Lise to make the Israeli dishes that David had always loved – casseroles of chicken and vegetables, frittatas with cheese and herbs served with wonderful breads, and *bureka*s along with the pickles and olives that Lise brought home from the outdoor market.

Despite her hectic schedule, she continued conversion lessons with Rabbi Herman, memorizing the material she'd be asked on the test. Her first meeting with the Conversion Court, to open a file and meet the three rabbinical judges who would preside at the final meeting had taken place only three months after she arrived in Israel. The second meeting, at the end of her first year, was an interview with the court coordinator to ascertain her progress. Finally, a little less than two years after opening a file, Lise applied to the Conversion Court and was invited to a final meeting; accompanied by the Rabbi, David and his parents – and both sets of grandparents. Very nervous, Lise dressed modestly for her Conversion Court appearance. She was questioned rigorously in the session – not only about Judaism, but also about her family in Denmark and Germany, about churches she'd attended, and about her reason for converting. Speaking in Hebrew and French, and even English, Lise answered all of their questions truthfully and calmly. At last, the rabbinical judges said they were satisfied and Lise would be referred to a *Mikveh* for the ritual immersion. She was given a conversion certificate and told the process was irreversible; she would never be able to go back to her prior religion. Lise told them being Jewish was totally acceptable to her, and she was told to update her religious status in the Interior Ministry. When she and David had first arrived in Israel, having been married abroad in a civil ceremony, Lise was granted permanent resident status which was necessary for conversion and she had received an *Aliyah* certificate from the Jewish Agency. Now she would be a full citizen and her children would be Jewish. If she and David wished to marry according to *Halakha*, they could have a wedding performed by a rabbi under a *chuppah*. David asked if she really needed to have a second wedding because he thought their French wedding with their families and closest Parisian friends had been wonderful, that it suited them, their courtship, and their life in France so well.

But Lise felt strongly about a Jewish wedding. "I want to do it for our future children. Do you remember that you promised me our children would grow up safe in their own country? I want them to know their parents were married in Israel." Her heartfelt arguments, and her winning ways, persuaded David as usual, and they decided to get married in February 1976, during his semester break. David's mother, grandmothers, sister, aunts and cousins assisted Lise in the wedding preparations; they rented a hall and hired a caterer, a florist, a live band, a photographer, and helped Lise find a dress that wasn't traditional white because, she said, she was an "old married lady!" She knew the significance of each wedding ritual and she wanted to implement all of them. With the help of David's maternal grandmother, Lise designed and made a geometric *chuppah*; on seeing the finished canopy, David said, "God, Lise, you're so unbelievably talented! It's absolutely wonderful, like an Agam or a Vasarely, changing its appearance from every angle."

"Stop showing off your knowledge of modern art, David," Lise teased, but his approval thrilled her. "It's going to hang on the wall above our bed after the wedding." David stated. Dina, getting married the following June, asked for a handmade *chuppah*, too; she knew they'd make one for her in different colors. Dina chose shades of blue as her wedding colors so that Lise, her matron of honor, could wear her gorgeous ice blue wedding dress again.

Richard and Anna came to Tel Aviv, and her father and beloved stepmother would walk her down the aisle. On a surprisingly mild night for Tel Aviv in mid-February, David said they were lucky – with both winter weddings. The ceremony was held outside, and David was worried that it was too cold for Lise and all the other women in their fragile finery as the Jewish religious ceremony was much longer than their French civil wedding. He convinced his two grandmothers and Anna to wear winter coats. Dina's fiancé, Alon, two of David's friends, and Claude held the *chuppah* aloft, each corner attached to a pole wrapped in flowers. David's four grandparents walked to the *chuppah* and stood behind Rabbi Herman who officiated. David's and Lise' fathers escorted him, the *chatan*, to the *chuppah*. Richard stepped to one side of the *chuppah* and Ephraim, one of David's two principal witnesses, moved to the other side. Then Dina walked down the long strip of carpet – the makeshift aisle – and stood next to her fiancé.

Exquisite in her silk gown, her shining blonde hair styled into an elegant knot with loose tendrils around her lovely face and a flower circlet, Lise, the *kallah*, walked to David with Aya and Anna. Aya and Anna, each holding one of Lise's arms circled David seven times as a sign not just of Lise's commitment to David but to his heritage as well. Then, Aya and Anna joined their husbands and Lise stood at David's side, facing the Rabbi. He recited the betrothal blessings and offered a cup of wine which both David and Lise sipped. A Jewish marriage becomes official when the *chatan* gives a ring, usually plain gold, to the *kallah*. Before their two witnesses, David declared to Lise, "Behold, you are betrothed unto me with this ring, according to the law of Moses and Israel" and placed the ring on her finger. Next came the reading of the *ketubah* listing the *chatan*'s responsibilities; David had added several extra promises to the document made by a Jaffa artist Lise had met at the art shop in the Hilton: 50 canvasses, 500 tubes of brilliant oil paints, 100 sable brushes – and an unlimited amount of turpentine.

When the Rabbi finished reading amid laughter at David's additions, David vowed he'd protect Lise and their children with his life. The *ketubah* was signed by the witnesses – David's father and his paternal grandfather, and it became a legal contract to remain in the bride's possession throughout their marriage. The calligraphy and border were so beautiful they knew it had to be displayed in their home. The *Sheva Brachot* – seven blessings – were recited by the Rabbi with the second cup of wine. David's father placed a glass wrapped in a cloth on the floor and David stamped on it, shattering the glass. The guests applauded and shouted "*Mazel Tov*".

Rabbi Herman, who knew that some guests didn't understand the ritual, explained that it was a symbolic reference to the destruction of the Temple in Jerusalem by the Romans in 70 CE, and it connected the newly married couple to the spiritual and national destiny of the Jewish people. When David broke the glass, Alon, Dina's fiancé, holding one end of the *chuppah,* quietly remarked that this was probably the last time David would "put his foot down." David quickly responded, "Speak for yourself, brother-in-law." Dina, standing next to her fiancé, added, "He's right!" The ceremony was complete and David and Lise led their guests back into the hall for the joyous reception: the music, the dancing, the food, the flowers, the photographer circulating unobtrusively, the overall ambiance and the *joie de vivre,* the ecstatic expressions of Lise and David.

The family members who had attended the ceremony in Paris enjoyed a reunion with Claude and Mignon who always closed the gallérie for a holiday mid-winter – this year in Israel with Claude being given the honor of holding the wedding *chuppah*. Mignon had been sitting with David's uncle Jakob who explained the elements of the ceremony to her. "It's so different from a civil marriage or religious one in France, although I have only attended Catholic weddings at home," Mignon said. "It's *enchanté* to be here." And Claude said later there was no way they would have missed this wedding since they'd been part of the union of Lise and David almost from the first moment they had met! Claude told Lise they were going to Jerusalem for two days but would be at the Tel Aviv Hilton when the happy pair returned from their honeymoon. In Eilat? When she nodded, he said he wanted to talk to her about buying Israeli art for the gallérie, including some of her work. But no business talk right then unless her father was willing to sell Claude the diptych of *'La Petite Sirène'*!

"Never!" Richard responded. "It's my most prized possession after my wife, my children (his smile included David) and Annelise, my own *petite sirène,* my gorgeous granddaughter. The only way I'll ever part with the diptych is if Lise asks for it. And since she promised to paint it for me when she was only 5-years-old, I don't think she'll ever do that. Sorry, Claude…"

The Frenchman gave a typical Gallic shrug and said, "*C'est la vie, mes amis*! So let's talk of other things. What is it the British say, 'of cabbages and kings?' *Non*! Let's talk of this wedding. *Magnifique!*" Dina laughed and said since they were enjoying it so much, they must come again in June for her wedding. "I'm so sorry, little one," he responded. "June is not possible. So you and Alon must come to Paris on your *voyage de noces* – honeymoon – and we shall entertain you. As I once said to tonight's bride and groom, it may be a cliché but Paris is the city for lovers!" Dina laughed and said they might take him up on the offer. Alon had never been to Paris so they would start saving their pennies and look forward to being fêted!

She winked at her fiancée and said, "*Alon, mon amour*, start filling the piggy bank right now!"

Alon kissed Dina's hand and laughed, "My sweet joker, I haven't put my foot down on the glass yet! So I follow orders only from my captain in the reserves – and my mother! But a honeymoon in Paris would be great!"

Lise jumped into the teasing conversation at this point. "If anyone is to be fêted, Mignon and Claude, it's the two of you. When you come back to Tel Aviv and we're back home, you must come to dinner at our place. And I'll be cooking!" She noted the odd look on Mignon's face, and smiled, "I've actually learned to cook…some things. Not L*e Cordon Bleu*, but *Le Cordon Anna, Le Cordon Aya* and *Les Cordons Grandmas Esther and Sara*. You might actually enjoy my *cuisine!*" Everyone laughed and after more dancing and laughter and dessert and a few speeches, the festive evening came to an end. Lise and David went home to Basel Street, recapping highlights of the evening. She said, her voice husky with emotion, "David, this has probably been the most wonderful day. I feel like I have everything, but there's something I must ask you. I want our home to be a Jewish home. I'm not saying we have to keep it kosher, even though that's not hard in Israel. I want us to celebrate all Jewish holidays, and I want our children to know not just how much they are loved, but their roots and traditions. Those are the things I missed out on when I was growing up, even though I always knew I was loved by my father, my brother, our dear Anna, and now even by my mother and Albert. I don't remember Marta well from when I was little, or *Oma*. But I'm sure we all loved each other, and yet family history and roots were not talked about," she added a little wistfully.

"Did you think I'd argue about this, my darling?" he asked, his voice deeper than usual. "My family has never been religious, but we always knew who we were, where we came from, our connection to this land. All of us have fought for this country, my parents and grandparents even before there was an Israel. It's the eternal home of the Jewish people…so of course I want our children to know their roots. I didn't think we needed a Jewish wedding, but today has indeed been glorious. My only sadness was the absence of a few of my very best childhood friends who would have enjoyed this extraordinary day in my life, but there's nothing to be done about that. Unfortunately, war's also one of the realities of life in Israel."

"Don't be sad, my love. I'm sure your friends would have wanted you to be happy tonight. Papa told me earlier tonight he didn't want me to be sad, but someone got a message to him from Marta. *Oma* died peacefully in her sleep, and she prayed our family will be reunited with Marta someday. I'm sure we will, and I'll get the chance to know my big sister."

David kissed Lise and said, "Yes, let's not be sad tonight. Let's go to sleep. It's been a long day and we must get up really early to pack for Eilat. It will be stupendous to lie beside you near a pool and do nothing for a few days!"

"Are you mad? Tonight's our wedding night, at least our second one!" Lise exclaimed, grabbing him and giving him a very loud, sloppy kiss. Then she started to undo his silk tie. "We must 'consummate' our marriage tonight; it's a Jewish requirement! Let's make love without protection and maybe we'll make a baby!" She pulled off his tie, and then his jacket and shirt.

"You're insatiable," he laughed, "and I love it!" as he carefully pulled down the long zipper on her lovely dress. When they were both naked, David kissed her all over her gorgeous body, from her toes to her neck, from behind her knees to her perfect breasts. And she eagerly followed suit on his long, lean body. They made love very late into the night and slept so late the following morning that they almost missed their flight to Eilat.

Chapter 3

Lise decided her life was perfect during the next few years. Her world was David, the family, and her art. She was ecstatically happy, falling even more in love with David each day, knowing he brought out the very best in her. He was a toucher; he never passed by Lise without brushing his fingers on her cheek or the back of her neck, giving her a hug, or a kiss or two, sometimes just a quick touch of lips, other times a passionate embrace. And she was learning to do the same to him. Her mother was rarely demonstrative, and she usually frowned when Richard openly showed tenderness for his children. She was enthusiastic about their achievements, but hugging or caressing them was unnatural to her. As a result, at a very young age and despite Richard's and Anna's open signs of affection, Lise had developed the ability to hide her own emotions. She poured her passion into her art until David changed her; he had breached her defensive walls almost from their first meeting. Lise learned to appreciate his teasing. At first she'd been offended by some of his comments, but in time she realized he wasn't criticizing her – he was just trying to lighten her mood and she learned to love his wry sense of humor.

David loved giving her gifts – small ones and large ones, silly tokens and extravagant tributes. She accepted his presents with joy and learned to tease him for a goofy trinket; she even began to find silly gifts for him. She loved his support and obvious pride in her work; he never belittled what she painted, and he encouraged her to try new techniques and styles, praising her openly to family and friends. She loved his warmth and she responded to his esteem. She loved the depth of his devotion to his family, to his parents and his sister, to his grandparents, and cousins – and she loved his feelings of responsibility towards all of them. She loved his intelligence; he challenged her to read more and search for deep meaning so that they would be able to discuss anything and everything. She never felt he was condescending or trying to educate her. She loved his affection for his friends and his concern about their wellbeing; he wasn't an intellectual or social snob, and he never judged the people he liked according to how much money they made or their level of education, but only on their sincerity and generosity. His friends cared as deeply for him; at first Lise was admitted into his circle just because David had chosen her, but eventually their feelings for her and hers for them evolved into real fondness. She loved his passion about humane ideals and politics, and she admired him for participating in protests and

Chapter 3

demonstrations in support of his beliefs. She stayed away from those events, not because she was indifferent to causes and ideals but because she found it impossible to play a role in such activities. David and her father wondered whether the sight of huge shouting crowds triggered unconscious memories of pro-Nazi demonstrations before her father's incarceration in Dachau for anti-Nazi activities, events she had only seen in film. Lise laughed at them, "Papa, you know that I have always been uncomfortable in big crowds. I love both of you, but please stop being amateur 'shrinks'." In short, there wasn't anything about David that Lise didn't love, and she thanked heaven, and Claude, for the remarkable chance that had brought David into the gallérie on the Rive Gauche to inquire about purchasing *Le Petit Sirène* when Claude displayed her painting in the window.

Of course, life for Israel and Israelis wasn't idyllic during Lise's first years in Tel Aviv. There were tragedies as well as triumphs, abysmal lows as well as extraordinary highs. There were appalling terrorist attacks: in Avivim in 1972 a school bus was attacked and 9 children were killed and 24 injured; in 1974, 115 high school students from Safed spending the night in Ma'alot were taken hostage and 25 were murdered; a bus was hijacked on the Coastal Highway in 1978, killing 31 Israelis and wounding 71; in Jerusalem's Zion Square, a bomb planted in a refrigerator exploded, killing 14 and injuring 80.

But there were also high points: the remarkable IDF rescue of hostages at Entebbe Airport in Uganda on July 4, 1976 which overshadowed a little of America's bicentennial celebrations. After Egyptian President Anwar Sadat's surprising 1977 visit to Israel, *Shalom Achshav*, an NGO, was created. Three hundred reserve officers, David among them, wrote to Prime Minister Menachem Begin, advocating a solution to the Israeli-Arab conflict; at a 1978 rally in Tel Aviv, thousands called for Begin to sign a peace treaty with Egypt in exchange for the return of Sinai. Begin and Sadat signed a peace treaty at Camp David in Maryland, and Sinai was back under Egyptian control.

In 1981, Israeli F-16s destroyed Iraq's nuclear reactor in Osirak; the world – with the exception of US Senator Ted Kennedy – condemned Israel's action, but eventually that action was applauded by many. Only one month after Osirak, Israel bombed the Palestine Liberation Organization headquarters in Beirut; Yasser Arafat escaped, but there were 300 civilian deaths, and an angry United States brokered a shaky ceasefire between Israel and the PLO. David, like the majority of his colleagues and all of *Shalom Achshav*, was horrified by what he viewed as an immoral action by Israel.

In June 1982, Israel launched the first Lebanon War, called Operation Peace for Galilee, to remove PLO forces from south Lebanon after ceasefire violations and the attempted assassination of Israel's ambassador in London, Shlomo Argov; Arafat and the PLO leadership fled to Tunisia. In September, hundreds of Palestinians in the Sabra and Shatila refugee camps were killed by Lebanese Phalangists. Despite propaganda blaming Israel for the massacre, the Red Cross verified that almost none of the dead were non-combatants, and not even one Israeli soldier had entered the two camps or was at the horrific event. Even so, David attended a massive protest organized by *Shalom Achshav*. A Commission of Inquiry was opened; it held Defense Minister Ariel Sharon indirectly responsible for the massacre and he was forced to resign. Terrorists opened fire at airports in Vienna and Rome in December 1985, killing 19 and wounding 138. The assumption was that the PLO intention was to hijack two planes, fly them to Tel Aviv and blow them up; six gunmen were killed by El Al and local security.

The first *Intifada* began in December 1987. Israel's response to the violence, riots, general strikes, and civil disobedience across the West Bank and Gaza Strip was tear gas, plastic bullets, and live ammunition. This uprising was perceived by many Israelis as political activism from the Palestinians; *Shalom Achshav* called for negotiations to end Israeli occupation of the West Bank and the Gaza Strip. Prior to the *Intifada*, Egypt's Muslim Brotherhood opposed the PLO and was non-confrontational; the Muslim Brotherhood even had support from Israelis who favored a peaceful solution, and it had refrained from violent attacks. But very soon after the *Intifada* began, Sheikh Ahmed Yassin created Hamas. As an offshoot of the Brotherhood, Hamas gained popularity at first by establishing hospitals, soup kitchens, and an education system – but they were committed to "the liberation of Palestine from Israeli occupation of the entire area, including modern-day Israel, and the creation of an Islamic state." When Hamas began suicide bombings, David was appalled by their attacks on Israeli civilians, especially on children. Despite the United States, Canada, Japan and the European Union labeling Hamas a terrorist organization, *Shalom Achshav* refused to condemn Hamas, and David pulled out of all active participation in the peace movement.

During this same period, Israel's economic success was phenomenal. After the Six-Day War in 1967, Israel embarked on high-tech development in order to exploit its advantage in world-class academic resources and highly skilled labor, in contrast to its relatively poor endowment in natural resources. David told Lise that former Prime Minister Golda Meir once told American leaders that "Israel's only natural resources were sand – and brains!" Motorola, IBM, Intel and Microsoft recognized those "brains" and Israeli ingenuity; they all opened research and development centers in Israel. The first microprocessor for personal computers, the USB flash drive, ICQ-instant messaging, cherry tomatoes, drip irrigation, quasicrystals, thermal imaging night-vision systems, robotic systems and fiber-optics were produced in Israel; stem cell research began in Israel in the 1960s and in the late 1970s, Israeli scientists produced human growth hormones and interferon proteins and the Weizmann Institute developed Copaxone, the leading medication for treating multiple sclerosis.

◆ ◆ ◆

For Lise and David, life was as normal as life in Israel could ever be. They didn't "make a baby" on their second wedding night, but eventually Lise and David had four healthy children – and one tragic loss: Keren, born in 1979; Kobi in 1981; Yaniv 18 months later in 1982; Daniella in 1985. They adored their children and spent as much time as possible with them. Early in her first pregnancy, Lise couldn't stand the smell of paint. She tried watercolors and pastel sticks instead of oil, but she didn't enjoy working in either medium, so she appreciated the stimulation of the Hilton art shop for, as she called it, a soupçon of her professional world. But in the last trimester of her pregnancy, her aversion to the smell of paint abated and she joyfully returned to painting. Both her obstetrician and David objected to her standing on her swollen feet too many hours each day; if the alternatives were working at the Hilton or painting, she had no choice – and Lise gave up the Hilton job in her seventh month. After Keren was born, Lise was thrilled to be a stay-at-home mother; every moment in her baby daughter's presence brought another delight. The first year, Lise painted while Keren slept in an infant seat in the studio; most of her paintings were of Keren. When she was awake, fed, in a dry diaper, Lise would strap her in her stroller and they would go for a walk along the wide sidewalks abutting the beach, and – depending on the weather – glimpsing a placid or turbulent Mediterranean below the luxurious hotels. Weather never deterred Lise from those walks, and David teased her. "Your Danish upbringing is so obvious!" But he joined them whenever he could.

An exquisite child with hair as blonde as her sunny personality, Keren was a miniature Lise. But her big, very light blue eyes, always looking around with curiosity, were more like her father's. She rarely cried and she was cherished by her parents, grandparents, great-grandparents, her aunt and uncle. To David and Lise, it was "absolutely marvelous" that they'd created this delightful baby, and sometimes they were content just to watch her, talk to her quietly, hug and kiss her, or even read to her; during Keren's first few months, Lise loved just cuddling her when she fell asleep while nursing, one of her tiny hands resting on her mother's breast. David bought a new camera and photographed her constantly: Keren sleeping with her rosebud mouth slightly ajar or holding Lise's breast, Keren in her baby bathtub, Keren in her infant seat, Keren in her stroller, Keren giggling while Lise tickled her, Keren with her grandparents, Keren with David being photographed by Lise, later, Keren waving at the camera. Lise teased David; "Keren's baby album will burst its seams before she's even a year old!" But she also painted Keren, totally absorbed and totally in love with her tiny subject. Keren was both an early walker and an early talker, and Lise and David "knew" no other child was as precocious, as bright, as appealing as their toddler. Of course, all of Keren's grandparents agreed, even Richard and Anna, who came to Israel two or three times a year. Marlene and Albert also visited, but never at the same time as Richard and Anna, and all of them cherished this sweet little girl. Lise was astounded at how openly affectionate Marlene was with Keren and attributed the change in her mother to Albert who really was a very nice man. Keren, a clever little girl, basked in the warm glow of so much attention. Before Keren was even two-years-old, Lise was pregnant again; she and David realized they would have to put her in *gan*, nursery school. "She's always surrounded by adults and needs to be with children her age," David said. "We don't want her to resent the new baby, to think she's being replaced."

"You're an amateur Dr. Freud again, David," Lise teased. But secretly, she agreed with him, and with Aya's help, they found an excellent *gan*. Lise used those morning hours while Keren was in *gan* to paint. David usually took his daughter to *gan* and, since it was quite near, Lise collected her at the end of each session; they walked home slowly and Lise told Keren the names and the colors of the flowers they saw. She was worried that she wouldn't be able to continue sharing these special times with Keren if she had to bring the new baby with her and she would have to take the car when David couldn't collect Keren. But as was to happen often, the problem was resolved with a

Chapter 3

gift from Richard and Anna when they came to Israel immediately after Kobi's birth.

David was amazed that Lise, so slender, gave birth to robust infants; each child weighed over three kilograms. Both times David phoned his parents and Lise's family from the hospital as soon as he knew that Lise and the baby were OK after Lise's long hours of labor. Richard adored his grandchildren: Keren and Annalise, Jonas's little daughter, and although he had never seen them, Marta's twin girls whose photographs had been smuggled out of East Berlin and sent to him. But, according to Anna, he was "out of his mind" when his grandson was born; he immediately booked a trip to Israel for them. "Typical male chauvinist!" Lise teased, when she spoke to him after Kobi's birth. Anna agreed. Lise came home from hospital as soon as allowed, the day after Kobi was born; she didn't want her precious little daughter to be frightened by her *Ema*'s absence. David brought Keren home from *gan*, and she climbed onto the big bed where Lise was resting with the baby in her arms. Keren stared at him and smiled. "*Buba!* Mine!" she said. David and Lise grinned at each other; he lifted his infant son gently out of Lise's arms, and she pulled Keren onto her lap, ignoring all the discomfort. She kissed Keren and tickled her a little, and then David placed the baby in Keren's arms with great tenderness. "Not a *buba*," he said, although he knew she was too young to understand. "This is Kobi. He's a baby, a brother, Keren's little brother." He kissed Keren very gently and then gave the infant a similar kiss. Keren leaned over and gave the baby a gentle kiss, too. "*Buba!* Mine!" she repeated. David told his mother Keren was calling the baby her *buba*, and his parents brought Keren a baby doll that cried and wet when given a tiny bottle of water. Ephraim kissed his granddaughter and said, "*Ema* has a baby, and this one is yours." Keren held the doll just like Lise held the baby and gave her *buba* a gentle kiss.

"We have to arrange a *brit milah*," David said to Lise and his parents, "We don't have much time, and I am not sure whom to contact." Lise only knew that Jewish law going back to Abraham, set the *brit milah* on the eighth day after the birth of a healthy boy; it was both a covenant with God and a celebration.

"It's been a very long time since your *brit*," Aya said to David. "But a few of our friends are now grandparents; I'll call them about a *mohel*, a suitable hall, a caterer. So let *Aba* and me arrange this as our gift. We'll do the legwork. Just give me a list of the people you want to invite, and I'm sure Dina will help."

Both Lise and David were delighted with his mother's offer. He hugged her and said, "Just so you know, although I know we're supposed to keep it a secret until the *brit* itself, we're naming the baby Yaakov in memory of your father. We've missed him so much this last year; I think *Savta* will be pleased."

"She'll be as thrilled as I am," Aya said. She turned to Ephraim, "I told you they'd let us make the *brit*, but giving the baby my father's name is so much more than I expected." She looked at her son and daughter-in-law with love and said, "I thought you'd go for a modern name so popular today, a unisex name like Tal or Gal, not a Biblical name, not my father's name." Aya stopped talking, tears welling in her eyes. Ephraim put his arm around her.

David sighed, "Why do women always cry when good things happen?"

"Oh shut up, David," Lise teased. "This is an emotional moment for *your Ema*. So please take your son over to her before he's ready for another feed. I love Biblical names, Aya, and I loved your father; he was another *Saba* to me. But I hope you don't mind that we'll probably call the baby Kobi."

While David placed the infant in his mother's arms, Ephraim answered, "Of course she doesn't mind. Kobi it is."

David said, "*Aba*, we're asking your father – Kobi's great-grandfather – to be the *sandak*. We've also talked to Dina and Alon about being Kobi's godparents. You know that a very short time after Keren was born, Lise and I made official wills; if anything were to happen to the two of us, Dina and Alon will be the legal guardians of our children. What do you think of all this?"

Ephraim, his voice breaking with emotion, said, "I'm just overwhelmed; my father will be, too. I have no words. I'm just… so proud of both of you. And I think this little boy, and his precious big sister, are blessed in their parents."

Keren put down her doll, climbed up on his lap, patted his cheeks, and said, "Don't *cwy*, *Saba*." Everyone smiled at her perspicacity.

Richard and Anna arrived three days after Kobi's birth, in time to help Lise in every possible way and, of course, in time for the *brit*. Among their gifts for Keren and the baby, they brought a lightweight yet very sturdy double stroller from Denmark, which would enable Lise to take both children on their daily walk. "What a fantastic stroller," Lise told them. "I love walking with Keren; the fresh air is healthy and enjoyable for both of us. I've been worried about how I'd walk home with two children, although at least I don't have to worry about

Chapter 3

snow in Tel Aviv; I thought I'd have to drive with both children. Now you've made it possible for me to walk home with them."

On the eighth day after Kobi's birth, everything went smoothly. Aya had found the perfect hall in one of the small hotels across from the Hilton. Dina knew an excellent caterer and she chose the buffet menu with some input from her brother and sister-in-law. The *mohel* David's parents hired came highly recommended. Kobi's *brit milah* began when Lise carried the baby dressed in a little blue sweater, a matching cap, and a diaper, and handed him to David's grandfather, a *Kohen*, in a chair – called the Chair of Elijah – on a platform. Lise didn't watch the actual circumcision, but of course she trembled when the baby began crying. David winked at her and she remembered him saying he didn't remember his *brit* because he'd only been eight days old – and drunk! She smiled as her father-in-law whispered to her father that there aren't many Jewish alcoholics because a baby's first taste of alcohol comes with pain. After the circumcision, David took the baby, now Yaakov, from his grandfather; he and Lise then went into a small room where the *mohel* instructed them on how to care for the baby's penis. The *mohel* shook David's hand, congratulated Lise on a fine boy, accepted a cheque – and left. Lise and David went back into the hall and Lise placed the sleeping baby in his carriage. Then the celebration began; all of the guests enjoyed the extensive buffet of hors d'oeuvres, salads, hot dishes, desserts and drinks ordered by Dina. When only the family and a huge mountain of gifts were still in the hall, Dina whispered to a tired Lise, who was waiting to take the baby home, "I have a secret to tell you."

Lise smiled at Dina and said, "Congratulations! You're pregnant. That's absolutely great!"

"How did you know?" her shocked sister-in-law inquired. "We've only been sure for a few days. We haven't told anyone yet, not even our parents."

"I guessed. I saw your face when a waitress took the lid off a chafing dish and you turned green as the aroma reached you; I thought you'd be sick. And you didn't drink coffee. I was the same during both pregnancies. No coffee, and I couldn't paint for a few months because the smell of paint made me ill. So, my dearest sister-in-law, 2 + 2 = pregnant!" Lise said and hugged Dina.

"Wow!" Dina exclaimed. "I've always known you're a great artist and smart, but now I think you're amazing. Please don't tell anyone except David. Alon and I want to tell our parents and grandparents."

"Of course, I won't say anything," Lise said, yawning. "But now

I absolutely must go home." When Ephraim brought his car to the front of the hotel and asked Lise if she wanted him to drive her home, she said, "No thanks. It's so close. It will be fine if you just bring all the gifts." Then Lise turned to the rest of the family and said, "Thank you all for everything; I'll never forget this. And we'll see you all very soon. *Layla tov!*"

David pushed the carriage with the sleeping baby and they walked the two blocks to their apartment. He said, "You look exhausted, Lise. I wish I could put you in this carriage or carry you home!" As soon as they arrived at their flat, she immediately went to their room to change into a nightshirt and lie down. David brought her the baby a few minutes later so she could feed him. Keren, who'd been in the care of a babysitter, came into their bedroom carrying her baby-doll; she lay down next to her mother, and "nursed" her baby". David, who'd been helping his parents bring in all the gifts, saw his two "girls" as he came back inside and raced for his camera to photograph his wife plus baby and his daughter plus babydoll.

Both children thrived. Kobi was as beautiful and as good as Keren. They repeated the previous pattern of Lise painting in the mornings, this time with Kobi asleep in the infant seat in her studio. When it was time to collect Keren from *gan*, she'd place Kobi in one section of the double stroller. On the way back home, she continued pointing out sights to Keren and, in the spring, flowers, while Kobi – comfortable in the stroller – slept peacefully.

When Kobi was seven months old, Dina gave birth to a 3.5 kilogram boy whom they named Yonatan after Alon's grandfather. The *brit* was almost an exact copy of Kobi's *brit*, same hall, same *mohel*, same caterer. "Kobi's *brit* was the dress rehearsal," Alon quipped. Dina, a social worker studying for a PhD at Tel Aviv University, enjoyed her three-month maternity leave. She and baby Yoni spent a great deal of time with her sister-in-law, niece and nephew. She envied Lise's "stay-at-home-mother" status, and Lise being able to work with the babies nearby in her studio, but Dina returned to work after her legal "vacation" because, given Israel's shortage of social workers, she felt guilty. After soul-searching and investigating various alternatives, Dina and Alon placed Yoni in a day-care facility run by WIZO, the Women's International Zionist Organization, which had an excellent reputation, but Dina was worried about leaving her baby in the care of strangers and tried to spend as many hours as possible with him; therefore her PhD was shelved. After she was physically assaulted at work by a client's husband who claimed Dina was depriving his wife of her rights, Alon suggested she take a break from social work and concentrate on her doctorate, although it would mean irregular hours. Ironically, her PhD topic was the psychological relationship between working mothers and their children, and the interviews had to be conducted at hours convenient for the subjects of her study, which meant in the evening. Alon, a senior cardiology resident at Beilinson Hospital, worked fewer hours than previously and he spent more time at home with the baby, particularly when off-duty. Grandma Aya, who was still the principal of a junior high school, offered to help when she had the time, as did Alon's mother, who managed the gift shops at a large complex of museums in Ramat Aviv. But when she had to meet with her supervisor or conduct a morning interview, Dina brought Yoni to Lise. "Since I'm already coping with two, it's no big deal to take on three, four…" Lise joked. "Seriously," she added, "bring Yoni here every day; when he's asleep, transpose your notes on David's computer. I'm here if he whimpers and when he needs feeding, I'll bring him to you."

Dina agreed although she promised herself, and Lise, it wouldn't be every day. "I can't include myself and Yoni as research subjects," she stated. "We might manifest a negative relationship and skew my results. On the other hand, you're a perfect subject, Lise. Maybe I'll do an ethnographic study and focus on only one mother's relationship with her children, nephews, friends!"

The three children bonded beautifully in Lise's care. Protective of both her "babies", Keren treated Yoni like another brother. With only seven months between the two boys, Kobi and Yoni were almost like twins. "Same blue eyes, but one blond and the other dark-haired, one a bit bigger and more mature than the other – so they're easy to tell apart," Alon teased. A few months later, when Dina's dissertation was submitted to the university, she was required to take a full-time internship in order to receive certification as a clinical psychologist. Through a colleague, she was able to hire Aliza Cohen, an intelligent, trained *metapelet*, but Yoni missed his cousins – especially Kobi – so Yoni was still in Lise's care for several hours almost every day with Aliza there as well. Aliza's help was invaluable when Lise was pregnant again. As a toddler, Kobi was as curious about everything as his sister, but far more adventurous, and Yoni was his crawling sidekick. No cabinet door was closed tight enough for Kobi not to open it and pull out the contents, no chair or table was too high to climb. David "baby-proofed" their house, but Lise insisted on leaving one kitchen cabinet open so the two little boys could pull out pots and beat on them with wooden spoons. "Do you think when the two of them are older they'll do skydiving or rappelling? Or maybe bungee jumping?" David wondered aloud as he rescued a bowl of fruit from the dining room table; Kobi had dragged a small box to the table to use as a stepstool onto one of the chairs, and Yoni had crawled inside the box.

"Probably," Lise laughed. "Or perhaps a new extreme sport that hasn't been invented yet. Kobi's so innovative he'll probably devise new acrobatic feats; I wish he were a little less creative and a little more fearful, not a daredevil. I also hope beating on pots won't make him decide to be a rock band drummer."

When Yaniv – Lise and David's second son – was born, Keren was a lovely 4-and-a-half-old and Kobi a 2-year-old rambunctious imp. Throughout her pregnancy, David and all the family referred to the future infant as "Tuna"; David didn't recall why he'd started the nickname, but it stuck. At birth, Yaniv was slightly jaundiced, and Alon, ever the joker, teased, "Now we can call him 'Yellow fin'!" Yaniv's *brit milah* was delayed until he was three weeks old, but even so: same hall, same caterer, same *mohel*. "This is now a family habit," the *mohel* said, "but I don't mind. More babies, the greater the *mitzvah*!" Like the others, Yaniv was a very good baby, seldom crying, bright blue eyes looking with interest at everything and everyone around him. David said prophetically if his infant son were old enough to smile, the whole world would receive his largesse; he was absolutely as captivated by this new baby as he was by the others. In spite of Lise claiming she could "manage" all of the children with Aliza's help, David insisted on another *metapelet* to help out; his parents, Dina and Alon concurred. Aliza's mother, Miri, was able to come in for a few hours a day and the children all benefitted from the attention of another "*savta*"; Lise benefitted from the older woman's experience. Having both Aliza's and Miri's help was particularly important when Yoni was 3-years-old and Dina gave birth to a little girl, Yael. This time Dina was at home for her full maternity leave plus an additional three months, and she spent most of her time with Lise and the children. She had received her PhD *magna cum laude*, and she was immediately hired by a private clinic where she was allowed to set her own work hours; she arranged her schedule to alleviate Lise's responsibility for so many children: Keren, Kobi, Yoni, Yaniv, and Yael plus the many little friends who came for play dates. Even so, after an afternoon of petty squabbles, lots of tears, spilled drinks, diaper and clothing changes, she said to Lise. "How could we ever have survived through all of this without Aliza and Miri?"

Chapter 3

Lise laughed, "They are indeed wonderful, but you know something, Dina? We would have survived. And so would the children!"

By this time Lise and David had moved to Afeka, a neighborhood of villas within walking or cycling distance of Tel Aviv University – for David's health and fitness, Lise said. Their home was a 6-bedroom house with a very large deck off the kitchen and an enormous fenced-in backyard. They built a studio for Lise and installed an elaborate swing set and a sandbox for the children, all of whom were bright, curious, exuberant and full of good humor. In the back of the house, the children roughhoused and tumbled, argued and made up, and built forts or kicked around a football. Lise continued to walk at least an hour every day, usually early in the morning. This was her method of keeping fit, but she also used her private exercise time as a quiet moment to focus on her plans for the day, and as a way of giving David quality time with their children while he prepared breakfast. They intended to install an in-ground swimming pool – as exercise to maintain David's health – she teased him again, because you're so much older than me! "A whole five years…in my dotage!" he said, laughing. For the children's safety, they delayed installing the pool until the children were old enough; in the meantime, on very hot Tel Aviv summer days they jumped through the sprinkler system on the lawn; then, to save water, Lise bought a few small wading pools. David hung a basketball hoop on the top of the garage at the front of the house; eventually this would be for the children but its immediate use was for him and his friends who wanted a little exercise and a friendly game of pick-up.

Lise gave birth to Shira, their second daughter, in 1983. She was the image of Keren, and obviously of Lise as well, a sweet, happy, gurgling cherub. And everyone adored her, even all the other children. But one morning, a little later than usual, Lise was surprised that the baby monitor was completely silent, and there was no bubbly sound coming from the delightful 7-month old, whom Lise called her personal alarm clock. She told herself that the batteries in the monitor probably died; tragically, it was baby Shira who had died. Lise tiptoed into Shira's room and as soon as she saw the baby, face down on the mattress, panic washed over Lise. She gently pulled Shira up, but her lips were blue and she was ice cold. Lise screamed and David raced into the room.

"Oh my God," he said, as he touched Shira's neck, searching for any trace of a pulse. Lise pushed his hand aside and picked up the tiny girl; she wrapped her in the blanket with its happy red-breasted little robins that always gently covered her at night, and sat down on the floor, rocking back and forth. She kept saying, "Wake up my little angel. Everything is all right!" Keren came into the room and David quietly told her to go back to bed. Then he went to their room, took his phone and called Alon and Dina. He told them, half-choking and with tears pouring down his face, that they had put a healthy baby to bed last night, on her back, but she never woke up. Dina said they were on their way and they would take care of everything, that they would be there in a few minutes, and David went back to Shira's room. He sat down on the floor and put his arms around Lise who was still rocking and crooning to the baby; they sat together, weeping.

The police and paramedics arrived in what seemed like seconds to David, together with Dina and Alon. David's parents, white-faced with shock, came a few minutes later and went directly to the other children. The house became a crime scene – a normal occurrence in sudden death, especially the death of an infant – and it was impossible to dispel the hysteria, the intense pain. At least the police investigator and the forensic pediatrician assigned to their case were extremely considerate during their interviews with the shocked and obviously bereaved parents. With SIDS – sudden infant death syndrome – an autopsy is mandated under Israeli law only when the circumstances are suspicious and an unnatural injury or violence may have happened. After consultation with Alon and Dina, the authorities decided a postmortem wasn't required in this case and a death certificate was issued by the Ministry of the Interior stating that the cause of Shira Hofman's death was acknowledged by the police as unknown but not a result of abuse or negligence. A traumatized David told his parents that the moment his beautiful little daughter was carried away from their home would haunt him forever.

Dina and Alon, Lise's and David's parents, their *metapelet* Aliza and her mother and other friends looked after the other children, prepared all meals, and tried to ease the situation for Lise and David. Lise was as distraught as she had been when David was in the Golan and out of contact with her during the Yom Kippur War. She found it impossible to eat, sleep, paint – and worst of all – she couldn't bear to look at the other children. The family often found her frantically pacing around the garden, pulling at her hair, telling herself out loud that she was having a nightmare and had to wake up Shira. In her head, she knew it wasn't a dream and she heard herself bargaining with God to reverse the abomination; she would do anything to bring back her special angel. The night before Shira's funeral, they all went

Chapter 3

to the cemetery chapel; Lise hadn't really wanted to go, but Dina told her she might regret it for the rest of her life if she didn't. Finally, seeing her lovely baby lying there made the tragedy real, and Lise knew that the pain and sorrow of losing her tiny child would return on every birthday, every holiday and family gathering, or even whenever she saw another bubbly little blond the age Shira would have been had she survived.

Before meeting and loving David, Lise had always guarded her feelings, and now she reverted to her youth, self-conscious about revealing her unshakable grief – but she couldn't help it. The turning point for Lise didn't come from David no matter how hard he tried; it came in an intervention initiated by Dina, when Anna and Aya brought Keren, Kobi and Yaniv to Lise a few days later as she sat in her studio staring vacantly out the window. Looking into Anna's sad eyes when she placed a wriggling Yaniv on Lise's lap, she remembered that her dear stepmother had witnessed the brutal murder of her own baby by a Nazi guard at the entrance to Auschwitz. Somehow Anna had survived and moved on to love her second husband's children, one of whom was Lise; she realized Anna had to be her role model. Lise hugged and kissed the three children who were so happy to have their *Ema*'s attention again. But sometimes, late at night, with David sleeping beside her, his arm holding her, she couldn't help thinking that if she'd done something different that night, Shira might have survived.

It took time, but life returned almost to normal. Even Lise and David's sex life rebounded to the exuberant passion of their youth, full of fun and laughter, at least in bed. They were both stunned, and Lise was very unhappy, when a condom failed, or perhaps they'd simply forgotten to use it in a moment of overwhelming desire; and Lise, almost 34-years-old, gave birth to Daniella, another daughter, in 1985. This pregnancy was the most difficult that Lise had experienced. From the moment she knew she was carrying another child, she had morning sickness, afternoon sickness, evening sickness; maybe it was guilt that she would be replacing her lovely little songbird! Wherever she was, she always had soda crackers and ginger tea with her to ease the nausea. Seeing the other children so content in her presence helped, as did the support of the entire family. One night when she was feeling a bit better, she said to David in her teasing way, "If I didn't love you so much, I'd be furious about you making me pregnant again and I'd say you were the 'Devil Incarnate'!. This baby better not have yellow eyes, or 'it' would be something right out of *Rosemary's*

Baby, that stupid horror film!"

David, lounging next to her near the pool, laughed, "I'm sure that this baby, boy or girl, will have blue eyes like all our other children!" He was wrong; this baby, another little girl, had flashing green eyes.

Unlike her previous births and in contrast to the entire pregnancy, this one had been extraordinarily easy; after only three hours of labor, she gave birth to a healthy green-eyed blond. Her obstetrician and the pediatrician declared both mother and baby in perfect condition, although the pediatrician, a close friend of Alon and Dina, said, "She's beautiful, but also a little unusual since almost all babies, like your other children, are born with blue eyes! It has something to do with not enough melanin in infants and that's why the color of a baby's eyes often changes in the first few months. Although," he smiled, "green eyes are genetically recessive like blue… Sorry, TMI, too much information!"

"At least she wasn't born with yellow eyes!" David said, and Lise laughed a little as she and David shared a private joke while she counted the fingers and toes of this precious infant lying on her stomach.

In contrast to the other children, Dani, even as an infant, was demanding; while the others were content to bask quietly in the love, warmth and attention from the adults around them, she clamored for more. She was very bright but also impulsive and mercurial; quick to take offense, fortunately she was also quick to forgive imagined grievances. Eventually they realized that she was also the only of their children who had even a modicum of Lise's talent, and that was why almost everyone excused her capriciousness. Lise said Dani had inherited her artistic temperament. "Ha!" David scoffed. "You don't have a smidgen of artistic temperament, so how could Dani inherit something you don't have?" Frustrated after a noisy tantrum from his tiny daughter, David said, "She certainly resembles her siblings in looks, despite her green eyes, but she's a changeling, having surreptitiously replaced our 'real' child at birth!" He adored her unconditionally. Aya and Dina, an educator and a psychologist, said Dani's odd mannerisms came from being the family baby, indulged by parents and grandparents, especially by Richard who said she was the image of Lise as a child in spite of the difference in eye color, or from frequent teasing from her siblings, especially Kobi. Or maybe her willfulness was the result of sensitivity to Lise's deep remorse about "replacing" baby Shira with her, another daughter. Laughing at both of them, Lise said Dani was what she was because her *Ema* was an "old lady" when Dani was born.

Chapter 3

◆ ◆ ◆

When Kobi was five years old, his *gan chova* teacher read the class a story about astronauts and he decided he could fly. He flew off the top of his closet and landed on his left shoulder. Both Aliza and Miri had the flu and Lise was handling all the children on her own. She was in the kitchen when she heard the bang and Kobi's loud screams; she raced into his room, closely followed by Keren. Fortunately Lise didn't have to deal with two mischievous boys because Yoni was at home with Alon as he had a slight cold; it had sometimes been necessary to take both scamps to the ER after minor injuries caused by a silly prank. But this time, it was obviously serious. Lise didn't want to complicate his injury by moving Kobi, so she tried to calm her sobbing child while she called *Magen David Adom*. She explained that her son had fallen and probably broken his shoulder or collarbone, and she asked them to send an ambulance. She called David at the university, but she knew he was in class, so she asked the department secretary to tell him what had happened and that the medics would take Kobi to Ichilov Hospital. Then she phoned her mother-in-law and asked her to come over immediately to stay with the younger children who were napping at the moment, so she could go to the hospital with Kobi; Lise said she'd ask a neighbor to come over if the ambulance arrived before Aya. Then she and Keren sat on the floor with Kobi, soothing him; she held his hand on the uninjured side and kissed the weeping boy until the ambulance arrived.

Kobi was lying on a bed and a young doctor had just finished checking the X-rays of his shoulder and clavicle when David rushed into the ER. "We've given him some pain relief and I'll give you a prescription for a painkiller for children that you can safely administer at home if he needs it. There's no sign of a fracture in his clavicle, just dislocation, so this young fellow will have to keep his arm in a sling until it heals," the doctor said. "We'll let him rest here until the pain subsides and then you can take him home. Tell the nurse when he's ready to go home and she'll give you the release papers. Please schedule an appointment with an orthopedist at your *Kupat Holim* next week to check that he's healing properly." He smiled at Kobi, who was already feeling better as the pain medication took effect, and said, "No more flying for a while, Kobi. Maybe when you're older." Then he left to attend to another patient.

"Thank heavens!" Lise said. "The paramedics said they were sure he didn't need surgery, but he was in such pain! He screamed so much when they moved him and sobbed all the way here; it broke my heart. But now he's calm; I guess it's the painkiller." She asked David to call Aya and tell her Kobi was OK and they'd be home soon. Feeling so guilty for allowing Kobi out of her sight long enough for his mischievous soul to leap into this misadventure, Lise told David it was hard enough calling him; how would she have been able to tell Dina and Alon if it had been Yoni, Kobi's "partner-in-crime"? Sitting next to Kobi's bed with his arm around an obviously traumatized Keren, who'd insisted on riding in the ambulance with Kobi and Lise, David said, "Children have accidents all the time, Lise. And we all know Kobi's a daredevil." He paused, winking at his son, who was holding his father's hand in his good one. " Yoni follows Kobi in all their mishaps," he continued. "You can't keep them in sight every minute, especially with other small children at home, and when two *metapelets* are off sick. I don't blame you for Kobi's mishap, and neither would Dina and Alon if it had been Yoni. As it is, all of us are astounded at how fantastically you keep it all together with five children around and sometimes more if their pals come to visit, and still manage to paint. So please don't blame yourself." He squeezed Kobi's hand gently and stroked Keren's shoulder. "*Ema*'s wonderful and what happened to Kobi was his fault, not hers. Isn't that right, Keren?"

"It wasn't *Ema*'s fault. It was mine!" Keren said, her voice breaking. "Kobi told me he was going to fly and I told him he was silly. I said he could only fly if he went on an airplane, like Grandpa and Grandma Anna when they visit us. And then I went to my room to read. I didn't tell *Ema* what he said, so it's my fault that he's hurt." She burst into tears.

Lise grabbed her and gave her a bear-hug. "Oh sweetheart," Lise said. "It wasn't your fault, just like it wasn't mine, as *Aba* said. Nobody would believe Kobi when he said he could fly – not *Aba*, not me, not *Savta* or *Saba*, not Grandpa or Grandma Anna. We all know Kobi does silly things sometimes, and even his very wonderful big sister can't always stop him. Nobody blames you. We just love you to bits. So, no more tears please."

David picked Keren up and sat her on his knees; he took a tissue from the table near Kobi and mopped her face. "This wasn't your fault, my darling girl. *Ema*'s absolutely right, you know…and *Ema*'s always right!" Keren giggled and David kissed her cheek. "Look," he added, "Kobi's almost asleep, so his arm doesn't hurt now and we can take him home. I'll carry him to the car while *Ema* and you tell the nurse we're leaving. OK?" They left the ER with Kobi in David's arms and a much calmer Keren holding Lise's hand.

Chapter 4

Despite all the distractions in her stay-at-home-mother role when she was the principal minder of so many children, Lise's career flourished. She painted constantly and received critical recognition for her work, described as a unique combination of the real and the surreal, and uniquely expressionistic when she was painting the sea's myriad aspects. Her portraits were excellent, capturing her subject's character, often with background scenes unrelated to her subject's reality. Her work was exhibited in galleries and she sold many paintings, but the walls of her own home held paintings of the children, David, his beloved parents and grandparents, her family in Denmark and Sweden; these were not for sale. When Dina and Alon returned from their honeymoon in Paris, Lise had presented them with a splendid painting of them dancing at their wedding, eyes only for each other. "How did you ever do a painting like this so fast? We've only been gone two weeks!" Dina exclaimed. Lise told her she'd been inspired by the beauty of the couple and by their love. Dina and Alon laughed, but secretly believed her; they hung the painting in their living room so that everyone could admire it. Sometimes Aya teased Lise that she was envious of the paintings Dina had, *Le Petite Sirène* and the newer one of Dina and Alon dancing. Lise offered her in-laws their choice of any of her paintings; later, she made portraits of all the children for David's parents and smaller portraits of the entire family for David's grandparents. Maybe it was necessity, or perhaps it was just talent, but Lise had developed new techniques for painting quickly and she was able to produce prodigious amounts of work in a remarkably short time, especially when she switched from oils to fast-drying acrylics.

David's career also flourished; he published numerous articles in prestigious philosophy journals and was granted tenure at Tel Aviv University. He wrote a book about Herbert Marcuse's influence on the student rebel movements of the late 1960s in France and America, stating that these weren't Marxist-type calls for the overturn of capitalism in favor of socialism as many claimed; nor were they mere protests against corporations for funding research into anti-personnel weapons, such as the napalm used by the American in Vietnam. Rather, David suggested, the impetus behind the student movements was Marcuse's belief that Marxism neglected the individual, and that there was a need for individual liberation as well as personal well-being and social transformation. David also believed that the late '60s and early '70s were the halcyon days of individual freedom, particularly for the young. His book was an amazing success in a market whose readers were not usually noted for an interest in philosophy. His next book, an introduction to modern philosophical theory tied to an economic substructure, became a textbook in philosophy and economics courses at many universities around the world. This achievement led to David's promotion to associate professor in 1985. A few months later, he was invited to be a visiting professor by several major American universities – Harvard, Yale and Stanford among them. This was an opportunity too important to refuse, but he and Lise also thought it would be better to wait until the children were older and able to appreciate living in another country; besides, she was pregnant with Dani and they remembered her determination that her children would be born in Israel. By 1989, however, they were ready for a year abroad. "Where would you want to live, Lise? Boston? New Haven? Palo Alto?" David asked, when they were seriously discussing the offers. "You can work anywhere and a new venue will be stimulating. But what about the children? We'll be going with a 10-year-old daughter, 8- and 6-year-old sons, and a frequently obstreperous 4-year-old imp. We can take a *metapelet* with us to make things easier. What do you think?"

"Boston," Lise responded immediately, "although Cambridge isn't actually Boston. The last time we saw him, your cousin Ted said there are wonderful Jewish communities in that area – Newton and Brookline; they'd be great for our children. I'd like them to experience a real winter, to play in snow, maybe even learn to ski and ice-skate. They'd like that and Kobi will probably be a speed-skater by the end of the winter. Nursery school in the States, away from *ganenot* who know her siblings, can probably help Dani come into her own as the special child we know she is. Let's call Ted and see what he thinks."

They had traveled abroad as a family a number of times – to Denmark and Sweden; the children loved being with their "other" grandparents, their uncle Jonas and their older cousin, Annalise. Although Jonas and Brigitte, his actress wife, were divorced, they both adored their daughter and she thrived with their attention and that of all her devoted grandparents. The children loved Tivoli Gardens, especially when Annalise was with them; they were thrilled to see the actual Little Mermaid statue that Lise had painted so many times. They liked crossing by ferry to Malmö to be with Grandma Marlene and Grandpa Albert. On their trips abroad, Lise and David brought a *metapelet* with them, usually a teenager from a special art class Lise

Chapter 4

taught in Old Yafo.

A year before David's sabbatical, they had visited his relatives in America, spending most of their time in Pittsburgh, Pennsylvania, with Ted – Theodore Herzl Hoffman – and his family. A successful attorney, Ted was very active in the Jewish Federation of Greater Pittsburgh and Chairman of the Board of the local Jewish Community Center. He was only two years older than David and, as children, they'd enjoyed many happy vacations together, sometimes in Tel Aviv, other times in the United States. So it was natural for David's family to spend most of that first American vacation with Ted's family. Lise couldn't believe how much the two handsome men resembled each other; both were tall, lean, dark-haired, with light blue eyes. Ted said they often pretended to be the other one when they were kids; David laughed and said no one knew which was which until they heard him trying to speak with Ted's American accent. Ted teased, "I don't have an accent. You're the Israeli. You have the accent."

They visited other relatives in Long Island and Los Angeles, but Pittsburgh was their base. David and Ted took Keren, Kobi and Ethan, Ted's son, to Three Rivers Stadium for the Israeli children's first baseball game, the L.A. Dodgers vs. Pittsburgh's Pirates. Yaniv and Dani sulked at being excluded, as did Ted's daughter, Tammy, but Ted's wife Shani and Lise found other fun activities for them. In California, the whole family went to Disneyland and to Knott's Berry Farm, an extraordinary old West park; later, Lise painted the children enjoying the sights. In late August during that first visit, Lise and David were sitting on the wrap-around porch of Ted and Shani's luxurious home in Squirrel Hill, an upscale Pittsburgh neighborhood with a very large Jewish population, drinking wine and talking quietly; all the children were asleep upstairs. Suddenly, Lise asked, "Why are there so many Hoffmans in the United States and so few in Israel – only Sammy and Sara, their children, grandchildren and now their great-grandchildren, especially when all of you here are such strong Zionists?"

Lazy and relaxed, David looked at Lise and said, "Let Ted explain; he's a far better storyteller than I, especially when it involves Zionism."

"It's a very long story…and probably boring, Lise!" Ted said.

"It's not boring at all, Ted," Shani tossed in. "Lise will be fascinated, and I don't mind hearing it again! I'm sure David doesn't mind either, even though he's almost asleep." Grinning at her husband, she took another sip of wine.

Ted took a sip of his wine and began. "OK. Our great-grandfather

Benjamin and his brother Max were the sons of Jewish immigrants from Germany who had arrived in America in the 19th century. They prospered in real estate and banking – in Chicago and later in Pittsburgh. Unlike many German-Jewish immigrants, they never ignored their Jewish roots and were supporters of the Zionist movement. Ben's sons, my grandfather Daniel, and David's grandfather Sammy, were active in *Hashomer Hatza'ir*, the oldest Jewish youth movement which started in Poland but became a world organization of Zionist youth, the future pioneers in *Eretz Yisrael*. Their ideology blended scouting, Zionist and socialist principles, and visions of a collective lifestyle." He paused, and said, "Are you sure this isn't boring you, Lise?"

"Not at all. Please go on," she said, smiling.

"In the Pittsburgh chapter of *Hashomer Hatza'ir* in 1915, Sammy met Sara Cohen; he was 16 and she was 15. Though still in high school, they promised each other that someday they'd live in a *kibbutz*, working to build the Jewish nation. They were very young, very idealistic, and very much in love."

Lise interjected, "They're in their 90's, and still very much in love."

Ted continued, "In 1918, a year after Britain's Foreign Secretary Sir Arthur Balfour wrote to Baron Rothschild promising to support the establishment of a national home for the Jewish people in Palestine, Sara and Sammy got married; their parents allowed it since they had already been inseparable for three years. The young idealists yearned to go to Palestine with many *Hashomer Hatza'ir* friends, but both families refused to support this desire. Benjamin insisted that Sammy finish his university education; Daniel, studying law, was furious at his brother. 'We planned to be corporate attorneys for the family bank. Dad, Uncle Max, and our cousins are counting on us,' Daniel reminded Sammy who said there were far more important things than university and being a lawyer, like helping to develop *Eretz Yisrael* into a homeland for all Jews. With no family backing for his dream, Sammy continued his studies but didn't relinquish his active participation in *Hashomer Hatza'ir*. In March 1920, Sara gave birth to Ephraim, and two years later to Jacob and then to Judith. By then, Sammy had completed law school; as planned, he and Daniel were the family corporation's attorneys. But everyone, even my grandfather, knew Sammy's heart wasn't in his law career in Pittsburgh. Sara's family, like ours, was wealthy and could provide live-in help, enabling her to study nursing, an inestimable value when she and Sammy would finally fulfill the dream they both refused to abandon. In 1928, Sammy had been working for the bank for five years and Sara was a part-time nurse when finally their parents gave them permission to go to *Eretz Yisrael* for a trial period, hoping they would find the life too harsh and would return home; both families agreed to help them financially. Secretly, Benjamin hoped Sammy would someday open a branch of the family bank in the Jewish homeland, an ambition endorsed by Max and Sammy. On April 25, 1928, Sara and Sammy sailed first-class on the *RMS Mauretania*, with their three children aged eight, six, and five; the *Mauretania*, the world's fastest ship at that time, made the transatlantic crossing in seven days. My grandfather accompanied them to New York; he told me he spoke sincerely to Sammy before going ashore, 'You know I don't wish you bad luck, but I really think you'll come back. Look at this luxurious ship. This is how you've always lived. Do you honestly think you and Sara will be able to cope with malaria, horrible flies, poor sanitation, poor transportation, awful food, shortages of everything, and a shack or tent instead of a house? We've read Mark Twain's *Innocents Abroad* and know the ordeal you're going into. Is it fair to your children? What if they get sick? I'm sorry if my pessimism hurts, Sammy, but I love you and I'm very worried about this move.' Sammy said he understood his brother's misgivings, but he still believed they would succeed."

Ted said, "That's as much as I know. Eventually, our grandfathers made up, and they worked together even before Israel became the Jewish homeland, but my grandfather never told me any more. And my father doesn't know either."

Lise sighed, "I guess I'll just have to beg Sara and Sammy to tell me the rest when we're back home. We'll record their story and send it to you."

David laughed quietly. "You won't have to beg, Lise. They adore you and will do or say anything you ask!"

"They're not the only ones!" Ted stated. Three pairs of startled eyes turned to him. "Hey, don't get jealous," Ted said to his wife and cousin. "I love you, Lise, but I'm not in love with you. I meant that Lise's very special. Ask your sister and brother-in-law, David."

"I know," he said, taking Lise's hand and kissing her palm.

"Well thanks for the compliments," Lise said, blushing a most appealing shade of pink. "Now I think it's time for all of us to say Goodnight."

A week later, when they were back in Israel, Lise said, "I'm inviting your whole family, even Uncle Jake and Aunt Yehudit, for a barbecue next week."

David laughed, "You really are relentless, like a little 'dog with a big bone'. You'll get the whole family history somehow, won't you?"

She smiled and said, "But they'll all have a good time too, with lots of food, lots of stories about family in the States, lots of pictures, lots of children and lots of games. I like your aunts and uncles – lots!" she added, laughing.

"And lots of noise!" David teased. "I can't ever say 'No' to you, my darling. Besides, Grandpa and Grandma will love the day as well. And maybe, just maybe, they'll tell us the rest of the story."

The following Shabbat was a perfect day for a barbecue; everyone came and, as Lise had predicted, with lots of food and lots of children. When they were all sitting around, pleasantly replete after the feast, David's Uncle Jake said, "We're delighted to be here, but is it a special occasion? Rachel and I can't pin down a birthday, anniversary, anything out of the ordinary. So come clean, you two, what's going on? Are you pregnant again, Lise?"

Lise laughed and sent all the cousins out into the yard to play, promising to call them back later for watermelon and ice cream. After a strong denial about being pregnant while sipping a glass of wine, Lise looked at all the adults on the deck, and said, "You know Kobi's curiosity comes from me. In my nosy way, I asked Ted why there are so many Hoffmans in America and so few of you in Israel. He could only tell us the family history up until Grandpa and Grandma sailed to England and his grandfather was so angry and worried. I don't know too much of my own family history, and what I do know is far from nice. So please, Grandpa and Grandma, tell us the rest of the story. That's why I invited everyone today."

"Yes, please." Aya said. "I don't know the whole story either."

"Neither do I, and I was there for a lot of it," Ephraim tossed in.

Yehudit claimed, "I have vague memories of being very hot and very dirty and very thirsty – the wonderful life on a kibbutz in the 1920s!"

Sammy looked around at all of them and then at Sara. "We didn't anticipate this, but we'll tell you. It's a long story, so I'll start and you jump in whenever you feel like it, Sara…and the rest of you can stop us when it gets boring! As Ted told you, we sailed to England in grand style, seven days and not even one storm. We spent a few days in London; then we crossed to Calais on a turbo-steamer, and then went by train to Paris and Marseille. We traveled first-class, but each journey and the interim waiting periods seemed endless. Travel then was not like today, crossing the Atlantic on the Concorde in

Chapter 4

three hours or so. In Marseille there was a further delay for a few days because the ship to *Eretz Yisrael* was quarantined when sailors had what seemed to be cholera but was only dysentery. Finally, we set sail for Palestine. The ship docked in Egypt, in Alexandria, for a few hours, but we weren't allowed to go ashore. Standing on the deck, I noticed workers unloading heavy cargo. A foreman wielding a whip forced them to work faster. 'This is Egypt, not *Eretz Yisrael*,' I told myself. 'We won't see such things in our homeland.' I was glad Sara and the children were in our cabin and hadn't seen the cruel treatment of the dockworkers. When we arrived in Haifa, we passed through customs quickly because I'd arranged our documents for Mandatory Palestine at the British Consulate in New York.

In Haifa, we went to the local offices of *Hashomer Hatza'ir* in a rickety cab, with our luggage following in a horse-drawn cart. You children were cranky, and complaining about the heat and the flies. You were very thirsty but Mama wouldn't let you drink water unless it was boiled; that's your vague memory, Yehudit. Our *Hashomer Hatza'ir* hosts took us to a nearby boarding house for the night; at least it was clean and you could drink the water. Mama soothed you by saying, 'Just think of the adventures we're having. When you're grown up and living in modern *Eretz Yisrael*, you'll be able to tell *your* grandchildren what it was like when *their* grandparents came to Palestine.' At eight-years-old, Ephraim, you understood, but Jake and Yehudit, you were really too young to grasp her meaning, and Yehudit, you just cried yourself to sleep. We set out early the next day for the *Hashomer Hatza'ir* kibbutz between Afula and Beit Shean in the Jezreel Valley; it took us almost a full day to get there, but we were greeted by old friends from Pittsburgh who had made *Aliyah* two years earlier. They brought us into the makeshift dining hall, gave us something to eat and drink, and then, Ephraim, you saw a boy you'd played with at home. You shouted 'Hey Morey, it's good to see you. How do you like it here?' and the boy said, 'It's great. We sleep in a children's house and work in the fields after school. I'm called Moshe now, and we speak only Hebrew.' You seemed excited, Ephraim, but none of you was sure you'd like working in the fields or speaking only Hebrew. Yehudit, you didn't want to sleep in a children's house. After a few days, you all wanted to go home to your old beds, but none of you really complained. In fact, the three of you adapted to kibbutz life much faster than Sara and I; almost from the start we felt this might not be the best way for us to contribute to the future Jewish homeland. Sara was upset that the other women did most of the nursing and she spent more time in the laundry than in the infirmary. The work in the fields was back-breaking as well as boring, and while some of the heartier members ridiculed my 'city-boy ways', others asked me for legal and economic advice. Within a very short time, I was dealing with almost all the administrative work of the kibbutz, and although Sara and I did appreciate the hard work and zeal of our kibbutz friends, we were frustrated. Only a couple of hour-long visits with our children each day was not how we wanted to raise our family; we hated the idea of you in children's houses, not at home with us. Sara actually looked forward to being the night *metapelet* in our children's houses and she often offered to take the turn of others. We decided to give the kibbutz six months; if we still weren't satisfied with our life there, we would move, but not back to Pittsburgh. Six months later, we moved to Tel Aviv. Given my education and experience in America, it was no problem for me to find a position with a foreign bank in Palestine. Both Barclays and the Anglo-Palestine Bank (APB) wanted someone with my expertise and with my connections. I chose the APB, founded by the World Zionist Organization as a commercial bank for the future Jewish nation. Its main office was in London, so the APB was registered as a foreign bank; that didn't bother me since I was looking for investments to enhance the *Yishuv*'s finances… Am I boring you?"

"Not boring, but you look a little tired, Papa," Yehudit said. "Take a drink and maybe Mama will continue with the rest of the story."

Sara agreed. "In Tel Aviv, I was hired as a nurse in one of the 'well-baby' clinics that had been started in 1921. Its primary job was to immunize against smallpox, to measure an infant's growth and development, to treat infections, and to teach mothers about clean water – in other words, preventive medicine. The work was stimulating and challenging, and eventually I was promoted and asked to help train nurses; then I was promoted again to an administrative role combined with the training. I missed direct nursing but I knew my contribution to *Eretz Yisrael* was greater in my new job. My working hours also enabled me to be with my own children after school and, although I felt a little guilty, this was far more rewarding than our life on the kibbutz…or in Pittsburgh. With the financial aid we received from our parents, we purchased an apartment in Tel Aviv, on Basel Street, not far from the beach," she said, smiling at Lise and David, "and you, my beloved children, when you were not attending your excellent school, you frolicked on the beach. The years passed and in each letter home about our 'good life' in Palestine, we surprised our families. They were

Chapter 4

so worried about the 1929 and 1936 Arab attacks, but we assured them that Hebron and Safed were far away from Tel Aviv. We continued to work with *Hashomer Hatza'ir,* supporting young people who came to build *Eretz Yisrael*. Happily we, the Palestine Hofmans, flourished. All three of you…" she paused, smiling proudly at Ephraim, Jake and Yehudit, "were excellent students and popular. You attended Gymnasia Herzliya, the first Hebrew high school in Palestine. It was obvious, Ephraim, that you were brilliant in science, while you, Jacob, were destined for the financial world. Even as a small child, Yehudit, you 'taught' your friends and your dolls, and we knew you'd go into education. You all had dreams of university life and travel, but as so often happens in life, history intervened.

"After the Nuremburg Laws were passed by the Nazi government in 1935, Jews were excluded from everything, expelled from schools, fired from their jobs, stripped of their valuable property and possession. On November 9, 1938, *Kristallnacht,* Jewish homes and shops throughout Germany and Austria were ransacked, hundreds of synagogues were vandalized and burned to the ground, and Torah scrolls were destroyed. We were anxious for the *Yishuv* to ingather as many European Jews as possible, and we appealed to Sammy's brother and to some of our cousins with business interests and assets in Swiss banks who regularly traveled to Europe. They established contacts within Germany and financed the exit of many Jews between 1939 and 1940, but when the British government issued its infamous White Paper, curtailing the number of Jews allowed into Palestine, our American families were no longer able to sponsor immigrants. So we involved our families in the illegal efforts to bring Jews to Palestine!" Sara said, her voice full of emotion.

Ephraim refilled his mother's glass of iced tea and said, "*Ema*, I can tell the story, or at least my part of it, from this point. In September 1939, I was 19, a student at Hebrew University in Jerusalem, when Germany invaded Poland and World War II began; I immediately volunteered for the British army. In 1940, I joined an infantry unit for Jews and Arabs, the Palestine Buffs. As part of the British forces in North Africa, we fought against Rommel's *Afrika Korps* in Tobruk and the two battles of El Alamein."

"Oh my God!" Lise gasped.

Everyone looked at her and David ran to her. Kneeling and touching her forehead with his lips, he asked, "Do you feel sick, Lise? You're so pale."

"I'm all right. I feel sick, but you can't even imagine why," she said quietly. "When my father was released from Dachau in 1942, he was home for a short time, only long enough for my mother to become pregnant. Then, with almost no training, he was sent to Rommel's *Afrika Korps*, to the second battle of El Alamein. *Aba*, you and my father could have killed each other."

Ephraim reached over and patted her hand. "Well, I'm very glad we didn't. I like your father." Everyone laughed, and Lise felt a little better.

"He likes you, too," she said. "Anyway, he deserted as soon as he could and was a British POW until the end of the war."

Ephraim said, "I knew about the POW part, but didn't know he'd been at El Alamein. So that's something else we share, along with our children and our grandchildren. And a relationship of sorts with the British, although I think he appreciated them more than I did. In 1944, the British established the Jewish Brigade, which fought under the Zionist blue and white flag; both Jake and I were among the 5000 Jewish volunteers from Palestine sent to Italy to fight the Germans. When the war ended, some Jewish soldiers worked with the allied commands to establish DP camps, to arrange shelter and classify the displaced persons, mainly Holocaust survivors. Ironically, the United Nations Relief and Rehabilitation Administration, UNRRWA, took full responsibility for running the camps to aid so many Jews. Yes, the same UNRRWA that aids those who cause Israel so much grief today! Ironic! The officials in the DP camps wanted to repatriate the survivors to their countries of origin, and many survivors tried to return to their old homes but found they had been destroyed or other people were living in them. There were no surviving family members and there was no one to help them – no food, no shelter, no work. So most of them returned to the DP camps, where some actually married other survivors in order to find a new way forward, a new family, love – and not just survival. Many Jewish soldiers helping in the DP camps, including Jake, were appalled at the overall situation, and they became involved in efforts to facilitate the clandestine entry of Jewish refugees into Palestine, those efforts which Papa's brother and his cousins had helped organize even before America entered the war.

I chose another way to help my fellow Jews. A long time before the war ended, the *Yishuv*'s leaders decided, despite Britain's recalcitrance, to proceed with the establishment of a Jewish state in Palestine, fulfilling the promise of the Balfour Declaration. They knew every move to implement the creation of a Jewish state would be fiercely resisted by the Arabs, more than two-thirds of the local population.

Chapter 4

By 1946, there was no doubt that armed conflict with the Arabs would immediately break out after Britain's formal withdrawal from its Mandate. British restrictions thwarted all of the *Haganah*'s efforts to purchase weapons, so the *Yishuv* turned again to sources in America. And once again our Pittsburgh family came through; they helped the *Haganah* acquire large amounts of much-needed arms illegally. Uncle Daniel and a few cousins were part of an arms-smuggling scheme devised by a wealthy New York Jew, whose family made its fortune in the oil and chemical business, and by the *Yishuv*'s fiery leader, David Ben-Gurion. Working closely with Ben-Gurion's very close aide, Teddy Kollek, later Jerusalem's famous mayor, I used my Palestine Buffs experience to help gun-runners – the transporters of illegal weapons from the States – circumvent the British blockade. My parents helped a lot; Papa found new ways to funnel money to Ben-Gurion to pay for the arms, and Mama aided the illegal immigrants when they arrived in Tel Aviv."

"My turn," Judith said. "Using only my code name 'Mnemosyne', a Greek word for 'memory', I was active in *Haganah* from the day I was old enough to be accepted into their ranks. Even with so much going on around us, I was still able to introduce Ephraim to Aya Bergstein, a fellow *Haganah* member and a good friend who was also studying at the David Yellin College of Education in Jerusalem; they were married in 1944 before Ephraim was deployed in Italy by the Jewish Brigade. After the war, Aya, Ephraim, Jake and I were involved in the struggles against the British, but Aya had to curtail all her activities in 1947 when David was born. Jake and Ephraim returned to Hebrew University, Jake in economics and Ephraim in biology, but both of them continued clandestine work with the *Haganah*, often disappearing for weeks at a time. My parents rented an apartment for us in Beit Hakerem, near the university; they also hired another student, Rachel Ginsberg, to help with baby David. Aya received her teaching certificate and began teaching at *Leyada*, the high school attached to Hebrew University, and I went back to my parents' home temporarily. Using my code name 'Mnemosyne', I would sneak down to the beach almost every night to rescue 'illegals' and their children; I would escort them to my parents' nearby home, carrying the small ones, so they could avoid detection until we moved them elsewhere. I was almost captured by the British a few times. My parents pleaded with me to stop my activities because I would be hanged if I were caught, as would my parents for harboring illegals. I reluctantly agreed and went back to college. Aya helped me and I started teaching at *Leyada*."

"I know the story from here, so now it's my turn," Aya said. "Israel declared statehood on May 14, 1948, the day the British Mandate officially ended, and seven Arab nations declared war on us the very next day. The fighting in and around Jerusalem was fierce; both Ephraim and Jake were in it. When our War of Independence ended, Israel was bloody but we had survived, although we lost the Old City of Jerusalem. '*Aba* Sammy', once again aided by his family in America and with the support of Ben-Gurion's government, began to develop investment banking in Israel. They had anticipated an enormous surge in the *Aliyah* of Jews from the Arab countries where they had encountered prejudice and brutality during World War Two and continued to suffer during the Arab war with Israel. No one knows the exact number of Jews killed in the *Farhud* in Iraq and the death marches and labor camps in North Africa after the Mufti of Jerusalem, Haj Mohammed Amin al-Husseini, declared that the Arabs were Hitler's 'natural friends'. The *Aliyah* from the Arab countries between 1948 and 1950 was not totally unlike the immigration of Holocaust survivors; the new state welcomed them, but housing and all basic necessities were insufficient, and the majority of North Africans were sent to refugee absorption camps, *ma'abarot*, where poverty was rife as were cultural clashes.

"*Aba* purchased land from Arabs in Jaffa for future development, and *Ema* continued her work with *Tipat Chalav*, the well-baby clinics. She said it was more rewarding to work under Israeli authority than British, even if the Brits were far more efficient. Ephraim and Jake completed their studies at Hebrew University, and Ephraim did an MSc and later a PhD in biochemistry at the Weizmann Institute. With *Aba's* help, as usual, Ephraim, David and I moved to Tel Aviv and I became a teacher and later a guidance counselor in the junior high school where I still work today. In Jerusalem, Jake was employed by the Bank of Israel; he married Aunt Rachel, David's *metapelet*, who graduated *magna cum laude* from Hebrew University's prestigious law school."

Jake interrupted in a teasing tone, "At that time Israel's only law school!"

Aya laughed and then continued. "Yehudit married Uncle Tzachi, also a teacher at *Leyada*, although now he's a supervisor in the Education Ministry. With good jobs, all of them chose to stay in Jerusalem. So *Aba* purchased the Beit Hakerem flat for Yehudit and Tzachi, and Jake and Rachel moved to the flat on Alfassi Street that's not only beautiful, but also close to the city center."

Chapter 4

Sammy added, "Our parents, Sara's and mine, visited us in 1955; they were so proud of *Eretz Yisrael* and all that we'd accomplished. My brother Daniel came often, first with his children and later his grandchildren; that's why David and Ted are so close. The American Hoffmans are committed to helping Israel in every way, but they chose to stay in the *Galut* – the Diaspora – and despite the distance, which is getting smaller all the time, both branches of the family have remained strongly connected. Some of the younger ones have come to Israel to study for a year and they have fallen in love with our country and with our *sabras*. That's why no one was surprised when Ricky, one of my cousin Arthur's grandsons, married Miri and settled in a kibbutz; it's so different from the one we came to – and left. And no one will be surprised if Ted's children, Tammy and Ethan – my brother Daniel's grandchildren – decide to study here and make *Aliyah*. We welcome all of them with open arms, and therefore our Israeli Hoffman branch may get larger in time. How much easier it is for young Americans to make *Aliyah* now than it was for us, but how 'sad' that they will never experience all the 'unique joys of pioneer life' in Israel's early years!" All the family, enthralled, laughed at Sammy's last riposte.

Lise said, "What a remarkable history; it's part of Israel's incredible story. I didn't find it boring in any way, *Saba*. Thank you all so much for sharing it. In fact, let's open another bottle of wine and toast all the Hoffmans, especially *Saba* Sammy and *Savta* Sara. Then we'll call in the children for dessert."

Lise went to bring ice cream and fruit for dessert out to the deck as David rose to shut off the tape recorder. He said,"Lise promised Ted we'd record the full story, and I hope someday all those children waiting impatiently for ice cream will appreciate it as well."

◆ ◆ ◆

David called Ted and told him of the 1989-90 visiting professorship offers from Stanford, Harvard and Yale. Ted said, "Too bad it isn't Pitt, but 'Harvard is Harvard!' It will be a unique experience for all of you."

"What about living in the area?" David asked.

Ted immediately said, "Forget Cambridge. It's too crowded and expensive, and it would be claustrophobic for Lise and the kids, but you want to be close enough so they can visit Harvard. I know Keren loves science; she'll be excited about being so near M.I.T. Both Brookline and Newton are less than half an hour from Harvard; both have a large Jewish community and excellent JCCs. Or there's Swampscott;

it's a little further away, about 45 minutes. Since your children are totally fluent in English thanks to your grandparents as well as Lise's relatives, they can attend public school; Brookline has the best. It's really not worth it to undertake the ridiculous expense of Jewish day schools as your children know Hebrew even better than English, and probably better than the teachers. They wouldn't learn much about Israel, or about the US either. The schools in Brookline have children from 40 or 50 different countries, children whose parents are visiting scholars like you or studying at M.I.T. and Harvard, another bonus. Dani can attend the JCC's *gan*; I have *proteksia* and I'll be able to wangle free membership and her tuition won't cost a penny. By the way, the schools in Newton are also exceptional, but I'd still go with Brookline."

"Sounds good," David said. "Lise's listening and nodding her approval, so we'll go with Harvard and Brookline. But what about housing? With four kids and a *metapelet*, we need a large place. And Lise needs a studio."

"Give me a minute," Ted said, thinking. "I've got a few acquaintances in all three cities and I'll make some calls. If someone is going to Israel for a year, you might do an exchange. I'll get back to you." It worked out exactly as Ted had said. An M.I.T. professor, his wife – a lecturer in history – and their three children were spending a year in Israel; he would be at Technion in Haifa, but she had a part-time job at Tel Aviv University. Their house in Brookline was large and modern, and they preferred Tel Aviv's cultural life to Haifa's, so the Hofman home in Ramat Aviv would be perfect. They even agreed to swap cars and bicycles. Lise's only stipulation was that her studio had to be off-limits; the Americans agreed, and their living conditions for David's sabbatical year were a *fait accomplis*.

Just before they left for America, Lise's father telephoned. "I called to wish you a wonderful year, but I also have marvelous news. With the Berlin Wall coming down soon and lines of communication opening, Jonas was able to find Marta and we've all spoken to her. You know that she's married and has twin daughters; her husband is also a doctor. Just imagine! Your mother and I have decided to bring Marta and her family for a visit in Copenhagen and Malmö as soon as possible. We're all so excited. It's been 33 years since I last saw her, and I can't believe she's 50 years old. In my mind she's still 17, very smart, and willing to protect us from the *Stasi*! Maybe you'll meet her next year on your way back to Israel. *Bon voyage*, my darling. Wish David good luck from Anna and me. Have an awesome year…

all of you!" Lise thought she could hear tears in her father's voice; she thanked him for the exciting news, and said she was so sorry that she wasn't there now to hear more about Marta and her family. Tears pouring down her face, Lise told him to give her love to Anna and to Jonas...to everyone.

David came in with the children, just as she was putting down the phone. "What's wrong, Lise? Is everyone OK?" he asked, pulling her into his arms.

She laughed so the children wouldn't start questioning her, and said, "Great! These are happy tears! Everything's wonderful! My father just called. My sister Marta will be visiting them soon; Papa and Albert are paying for it. I haven't seen her for 33 years, since I was five years old! Wow! My father is so happy! So is my mother, and so am I. It's *wunderbar*!"

"She must be very old, like Grandpa Sammy or like you, *Aba*!" Dani said. Her parents and siblings burst out laughing at her bizarre concept of age.

As predicted, David's sabbatical year at Harvard was superb. His colleagues were intellectually challenging and friendly; they all thought the same of him. Although younger than Israeli students who begin university after completing their compulsory army service, his Harvard students were very intelligent and hardworking and David enjoyed his two undergraduate courses and one MA seminar; he looked forward to each day in Cambridge. Sometimes, when the children were in school, Lise would come to Harvard; they'd stroll along the Charles River, with feelings of *déjà vu* about their own student days in Paris, although instead of the dinner cruise ships on the Seine, they watched rowers practicing for the local Regatta. They appreciated the street music around the university, sometimes a classic violin solo, at other times cool jazz or the rhythm of steel drums; once they even heard students from Peru playing Andean pipes. Cambridge exuded an international aura and a youthful vitality, probably a result of the two prestigious universities dominating the city. Cambridge reminded them in many ways of Tel Aviv, "the city that never sleeps", and that wasn't surprising. In cafes filled with students arguing about philosophy, politics, literature, and art, they often joined David's colleagues. One day a senior professor said, "Cambridge is a city where counter-culture still lives, classic culture thrives, and multi-culture is a way of life." Lisa told him she hoped he wouldn't think her rude, but he sounded like a tourist brochure, so maybe he could sell that sentence to the city as an advertisement. Everyone at the table was amused, including the elderly professor who punched David lightly on the shoulder and remarked, "She's a real corker, isn't she!" Neither David nor Lise knew what a 'corker' was, but they laughed along with all the others.

Aliza, their cherished *metapelet*, had married an army officer when Dani was a baby, but only a year later, he was killed in an automobile accident, not in military action. She still worked for them, and Lise asked her if she'd like to come to the States with them for a change of scene; she immediately agreed. She was indispensable when they were sightseeing, especially because some trips were too exhausting for Dani; Aliza always found a way to amuse the cranky little girl. As a family, the Hofmans explored Boston's history: the red brick Freedom Trail; the wharf where the famous Tea Party had taken place; "Old Ironsides", the world's oldest naval vessel that was still afloat. David said that although America's history wasn't nearly as ancient as Israel's, it was very interesting. They climbed to the top of the lighthouses that had guided ships into Boston Harbor, and they tried to identify the 600 varieties of trees in the Public Garden as they rode in the Swan Boats. In late October, Lise wanted to take a trip to Vermont to see the fall foliage – the natural change in color of the trees from green to orange, to gold, to yellow. To deep red. She was familiar with the phenomenon in Europe, but she'd heard autumn in New England was spectacular and not to be missed; she knew it would be boring for the children, so Aliza minded them while Lise and David enjoyed a weekend on their own. Hotel rooms in Vermont in October are booked years in advance, and she was about to give up when Simon Gordon, a Harvard colleague, offered them his family's cottage for the annual spectacle! Glorying in the array of colors of the trees around the cottage, a memory of that first sunset in Copenhagen as it was reflected in *Le Petite Sirène* flashed through her mind. "I really can't wait to paint this," she said to David.

The Gordons invited them for Thanksgiving and Lise brought a painting of Vermont's fall foliage, realistic and yet expressionistic, in her unique style; the Gordons were not only delighted, but impressed. "This is exquisite, perfect for Thanksgiving as well," Betty Gordon said, placing the painting on a sideboard in the dining room for everyone to admire. The children had been in a holiday pageant: Kobi as a Pilgrim, Keren an Indian, Yaniv a turkey, and Dani, not in a public school where they celebrated the holiday, was a pumpkin; all of them wore charming costumes made by Lise with Aliza's help. They were excited about playing with their new friends, but earlier that Thursday, they'd been glued to the TV as they watched Macy's

Chapter 4

Thanksgiving Parade in New York, fascinated by the giant balloons of Superman, Big Bird, Mickey Mouse and many others floating above the crowd, and high school bands escorting Santa Claus. Both Lise and David knew Macy's spectacular ritual was the "official" opening of America's ultra-commercial Christmas season, but their children were enthralled, reminded of the *Adloyada* in Israel. At the Gordon home, the men and boys were also glued to the TV, cheering and jeering every play in the football game between the Detroit Lions and Cleveland Browns; the women and girls were chatting in the enormous kitchen and dining room, cooking, tossing salad, setting the tables. David smiled at Betty and asked, "Do you have a task for me? I don't care for American football; I prefer the kind where the players don't wear protective body armor and enormous helmets! At home we play World Cup football – what you call soccer – and the players wear shorts, T-shirts and footgear, nothing else! Besides, I think at the moment the gender separation in this house is totally chauvinistic!" Betty Gordon laughed and agreed; she handed David a glass of wine and a big towel to wrap around his waist, gave him a large cutting board and a carving knife and the first of the turkeys. She told him to carve and they'd see if he should have been a surgeon instead of a philosopher! Lise's task was to create a centerpiece; she collected items from the kitchen and made a cornucopia overflowing with colorful fruit and vegetables; Betty took photos of the table, saying it wasn't every year that a famous artist decorated for her, and it was gorgeous! All the women setting the table applauded and Lise, who still was often shy with strangers, felt as relaxed as she did at family dinners.

Thirty people were at the Gordons' home for Thanksgiving, and, as soon as it was clear Cleveland had lost the game, the guests gathered around the huge dining room table laden with the traditional holiday foods: the turkeys David carved with surgical skill, bread stuffing and chestnut dressing, sweet potatoes, cranberry sauce, salads, succotash and pumpkin and pecan pies. Dani, in her precocious way, showed off her bright orange costume, and made them laugh when she asked who'd cut her up and put her in a pie. Winking at his wife, Simon Gordon joked that they had to stuff themselves fast because another football game was coming up and he was going to teach David that it was a better game than Israeli football! But in the end, the discussions around the dinner table were so animated that nobody watched football. The children played board games and charades until a tired Hofman family went home to their own beds. Earlier, Lise had noticed Aliza sitting on a sofa in the living room, with Dani asleep in her lap, chatting to one of Simon's PhD students, an Israeli named Gil Yardeni. "How lovely! I hope something comes of this. She's not just our babysitter; she's our very dear friend and she deserves to be happy again," Lise whispered to Betty Gordon.

Except when David had classes and meetings, family life for the Hofmans revolved around their children, just as it did in Israel. After an early snowfall, they went to Vermont to ski. They knew the children would love the Austrian ambiance of the Trapp Family Lodge although it was a few miles away from the main ski lifts. After checking in, they took the children on a sleigh ride, and after dinner they all viewed a documentary about the Von Trapp family and then the children watched *The Sound of Music* with a babysitter while Aliza joined Lise and David in the Bierhall. Within two hours at the main ski area the next day, athlete-cum-daredevil Kobi quickly moved from a novice to an advanced slope. Despite misgivings, they allowed Kobi to try snowboarding; he mastered that sport just as quickly. Keren was more enchanted with the ice-skating on the pond outside their lodge. As a child in Denmark, Lise had loved skating and she was delighted to be Keren's first instructor. After a fun-filled but strenuous day, the whole family, including Aliza, relaxed in the hot-tub in their luxurious suite. Lise, David and Aliza drank *glug* that David had ordered from Room Service along with hamburgers and lemonade for the children. The next day, Sunday, they skied and skated, and then had a four-hour drive home; Monday was back-to-school for all, including David.

The older children were delighted that school would be closed for Chanukah just as it was in Israel, but David said it was purely by chance that the Jewish holidays coincided with Christmas vacation. Lise promised they'd still receive eight days of presents, and they would spend part of the vacation in New York City. Chanukah began on Friday night, December 22nd, so they spent Shabbat with the Gordons, lighting the first candles, eating potato latkes, and spinning dreidels. On Saturday night, they went to the Brookline JCC for their Chanukah celebration. All around the big hall, they saw *chanukiot*; Dani was one of the "stars" of the evening because her *chanukiah* was one of the official ones used to light the second candle. A few of her paintings were hanging on the wall as well; Lise and David hugged her and told her how proud they were of her, as did Keren and Yaniv. Kobi didn't say anything because teasing his little sister was one of his favorite pastimes and she would have been shocked if he'd said anything nice to her. But when he heard another child stating that his paintings were a lot better than Dani's, Kobi immediately praised

Chapter 4

Dani's talent not just in art, but also on skis. On their way home from the JCC, David said, "Simon Gordon told me about a new American custom for Chanukah. Each child gives up one of his or her eight gifts and donates money to poor children. *Ema* and I would be very proud of all of you if you adopt this custom." The children were very quiet at first, but then Yaniv said he would be happy to do that. The others agreed as well, except Dani who'd fallen asleep on Aliza's lap, her face covered in jam from her jelly donut.

It had snowed before the Christmas vacation, not enough to cancel school, but enough to build snowmen and have snowball fights with their friends. In the evenings before the children's bedtimes, the family drove around Brookline and even into Boston to see the elaborate Christmas displays in shop windows and the fantastic decorations on people's homes. They went ice-skating at the Larz Anderson Outdoor Rink, not far from home, and Lise taught all of them to skate, an easily remembered skill even though she hadn't skated much since she'd left Denmark – except in Vermont with Keren. They learned quickly; the weakest skater was David, and the children laughed at their clumsy *Aba*. "How can an Israeli, even a good athlete like me, ice-skate?" he asked, defending his awkwardness. "We don't have ice rinks?" Lise said she was willing to help him stay on his feet anytime and anywhere. Keren was the best skater in the family, and she begged for figure-skates and lessons as one of her Chanukah presents. "Where would you ice skate at home? Maybe you should try roller skates – on wheels," David suggested.

"There's no regular roller skating rink in Israel either," Keren retorted, "but there is an ice-skating rink in Metulla. We could go there." Kobi said he'd like to go up north to learn how to play ice hockey; he added that he knew he'd be a good player, knocking other kids off balance…the way he had knocked *Aba* down. Yaniv and Dani just kept skating while the discussion between the older siblings and parents continued and Lise objected to Kobi's aggressive attitude.

Finally David said, "We'll see after the holidays. End of discussion." In the end, Keren had skating lessons on ice; Kobi didn't.

Aliza didn't go to New York with them during the Christmas break, and Lise knew she'd be spending time with Gil, the Israeli she'd met at the Gordon home on Thanksgiving and had been dating since then. "Have a wonderful holiday away from this rambunctious bunch," Lise said warmly. "You really deserve it." David gave her some money and told her to indulge herself a little.

On their first evening in New York, at the world-famous Plaza

Hotel, they went to the hotel's main dining room and were surprised when David asked the Maitre d' for the Hofman table. Lise knew he hadn't made a reservation, but as they followed the host into the room, Yaniv spotted Richard and Anna at a large table. He raced to hug his grandparents. "I didn't think I would see you for months and months, but *Aba* and *Ema* knew, didn't they?" the little boy asked. Richard winked and, holding on to a bouncing Dani who'd reached him a minute after her brother, said that his *Aba* knew, but they'd wanted to surprise everyone, even *Ema*. And Anna, hugging Lise, added that five months was too long, that they needed an 'injection' of grandchildren kisses more often. "Did you know that *Savta* and *Saba* came in October and we dressed up in costumes like Purim at home, only here they call it Halloween?" Yaniv asked. "*Ema* and Aliza made us great costumes, not Superman or cowboys like most kids, and we have lots of pictures. I was an astronaut, Kobi was a football player; Keren was a scientist, of course, but Dani's costume was best. She was a turtle with a papier-mâché back she helped *Ema* paint. It was so much fun and much sillier than Purim because people put Jack-O-Lanterns – pumpkins with cut-out faces on their porches and they hung paper witches and skeletons on their doors. It was very exciting, but *Ema* was really mean and she wouldn't let us eat all the candy we got Trick-or-Treating. We collected a lot of money for UNICEF that helps poor children in Africa and Brazil, you know. *Aba* was really proud of us when we also gave up one of our Chanukah presents to help poor children." He ran out of breath and stopped talking. Richard and Anna were amazed that the quiet little boy they adored had become so exuberant. Richard told them he and Grandma Anna knew David's parents had visited around Halloween and they couldn't wait to see the pictures of the children in their costumes.

After dinner, Lise sat in the lobby with her father and Anna and heard about their visit with Marta's family; David took the children up to bed and read them *Eloise: A book for precocious grown-ups* – Kay Thompson's very famous story about the Plaza's most famous "resident", Eloise, the elusive mischief-maker. The book had been charming visitors to the iconic hotel since its publication in 1955, and the children were enthralled with Eloise's antics; Kobi whispered to Dani that maybe they'd pour water down the mail-chute too – like Eloise. "No way," David said, laughing. "You'd all be arrested and Grandpa Richard and I would have to pay all our money to bail you out! So instead, we'll have 'Eloise tea' in the Palm Court tomorrow afternoon. OK?" Downstairs, Anna told Lise that Marta and her girls

Chapter 4

were beautiful. In fact, she said, they all looked very much alike – Marta, her girls, you and your girls. Marlene's genes seem to be strong and healthy…and beautiful. And Marta's charming husband, Philipp, is very interested in research. David's father would really like him.

"You know," Lise said, "I don't really remember Marta at all, but now that I've spoken to her on the phone, I can't wait to meet her. Did you know she was shocked at the painting you gave her? She said she'd heard of an Israeli artist named Lise Hofman but hadn't realized the 'famous' Lise Hofman was the little sister who'd always liked to draw – even though the name was the same."

"I can't begin to tell you how we enjoyed that visit, and not because it was interesting to hear about Germany after so many years," Richard said. "I'm a lucky man. I have a wonderful wife, three brilliant children and their spouses, seven extraordinary grandchildren; and even the in-laws are special. I actually get along with my ex-wife and her husband! Jonas and Brigitte are finally back together; Annalise has always known that both of them love her, and at last they've realized that they still love each other, too. Jonas is so open now, you would never believe it, and that's thanks to Brigitte and Annalise…and maybe Anna." He squeezed her hand. "He doesn't live only in his esoteric scientific world anymore. He actually has fun!" Lise said she was so glad, mostly for Annalise; she knew the separation of her parents had been hard for her niece, even though they never said a word against each other. Lise didn't say she was thinking of her mother, but Richard and Anna caught the undertone.

The family's days in Manhattan were filled with so many activities that they passed too quickly. They walked up and down Fifth Avenue, fascinated by the extravagant decorations in the stores. The children insisted on going to Macy's because of the Thanksgiving parade, but they were very disappointed that it was "just" a store; their favorite shop was F.A.O. Schwartz, the toy "emporium" where Richard and Anna spoiled their grandchildren. As Lise and the children were choosing their new toys, David went next door to Tiffany's and purchased a very beautiful aquamarine bracelet for Lise. Then they all walked to nearby Rumpelmeyer's, the ice-cream parlor in the St. Moritz Hotel; everyone savored hot chocolate with huge mounds of whipped cream. It was *déjà vu* for Lise and David. Angeline's in Paris served the same hot chocolate and Angeline herself was a Rumpelmeyer; that was the original name of the fashionable café on the Rue de Rivoli. As they finished their hot chocolate, David handed Lise the box wrapped in Tiffany's signature blue paper. "I couldn't resist this," he said. "It matches your eyes. I couldn't buy you a ring because you don't even wear your wedding ring since your poor hands are so often covered with paint, washed in turpentine and…!" Lise kissed him and said, "Shhh, the bracelet is gorgeous. And I'll wear it whenever we go out. Thank you, my darling."

They went ice-skating at Rockefeller Center, and Richard and Anna were amazed at the children's proficiency, especially Keren's. "You remind me of your mother when she was a little girl. She loved to skate," Richard said to Keren, who didn't know if she was more thrilled by the compliment from her grandfather or the spectacular skaters on the ice. They had hot chocolate again, at one of the cafes surrounding the famous rink beneath the gigantic Christmas tree. They went to a matinee performance of *The Fantasticks*, and to Madison Square Garden to see the Ice Capades. Lise took the two younger children to a marionette theatre and Anna took Keren ice-skating while David, Richard and Kobi went to an exhibition hockey game between the New York Rangers and the Pittsburgh Penguins. David of course rooted for the Penguins but Kobi and Richard chose the Rangers; Kobi declared he was in heaven. They ate dinner in Chinatown, the children's first taste of dim sum which none of them liked, had pizza on Mulberry Street in Little Italy, and devoured hotdogs and crinkle-cut French fries in Nathan's Famous restaurant on 42nd Street.

Their last excursion was to the Museum of Natural History where the older children were dumbstruck by the immense skeletons of a Tyrannosaurus Rex and a Brontosaurus, and the 94-foot blue whale suspended from the ceiling of the Ocean Life Hall; they were amazed when they were allowed to touch rocks and samples of gems in the Hall of Minerals, and they were mesmerized by the 28 life-like dioramas in the Hall of African Mammals. The enormous Museum was overwhelming and a bit frightening for Dani, so her grandparents sat with her in the cafeteria and she colored dinosaur pictures in a book Richard bought in the gift shop. At LaGuardia Airport, waiting for their flight to Boston, David asked what they'd liked best. "The hockey game," Kobi said, drawing smiles from both his grandfather and father. "Everything, but I really loved the 'Ice Capades' and skating in Rockefeller Center," Keren answered. Yaniv thought for a few seconds and said, "The rocks at the Museum, the blue whale… and hot chocolate at that ice cream place." Dani giggled as she replied, "Eloise! And the Etch-a-Sketch that Grandpa bought me. I love it. It's so much fun."

When David asked Lise, she replied, "I'll echo my older daughter and just say 'Everything'. Being with my family, with Papa and Anna, in this magical city was incredible. In my mind's eye so many images are stored that I can't wait to reproduce them on canvas. What about you, David? And you, Papa? Anna?" David agreed whole-heartedly with Richard and Anna when they said the family being together was the most phenomenal experience, especially the enthusiasm of the children at almost everything they'd seen and done.

The previous evening, after the children were asleep, Richard told them he and Anna were planning to move to Tel Aviv "to be closer to you," he said. Then he added with a twinkle in his eyes, "And to spend our final years in a warmer climate." He knew the Israeli authorities might balk at him settling in Israel but, because of the 'Law of Return', Anna would receive citizenship and all he wanted was permanent residence status. With an Israeli daughter and all the documents explaining his history, he hoped the move would go smoothly. Lise and David both promised to help in every way.

Everyone fell asleep on the short flight to Boston; five amazingly full days and too many experiences to process at once. Aliza was waiting at the door when the limousine arrived. She greeted them with hugs and kisses and took the children to bed with no arguments, no begging for a few minutes of TV, no requests for a glass of water. When she came downstairs, Aliza looked at Lise and David and asked with a smile, "Who are these strange children? What have you done with the boisterous Hofman kids?"

Lise laughed and gave Aliza a quick hug. She said they were all exhausted, but she had to get Richard and Anna settled in the guest room. "Then it's bed for all of us. We'll unpack tomorrow and there's a lot of laundry. We'll tell you all about New York, and you'll tell us what you've been doing. It's still early, so why don't you meet your friend, or friends, somewhere?" she added.

Breakfast the next day was a noisy affair as all of the children told Aliza about the trip – simultaneously. "One at a time, please, or I can't hear you. So let's start with you, Dani, and work our way up to you, Keren," she said, with a wink only the adults saw. Dani was excited to be first for once and started to tell Aliza about Eloise and the 'tea sandwiches' and the big toy store. Then the other children amused Aliza with their anecdotes. When Lise asked, Aliza said she had gone out with Gil and some of his fellow Harvard students a few times and they'd gone to dinner and the theatre with his friends working in the Israeli Consulate in Boston. She said it had been a very different experience for her, and the most special thing was that no one made her feel stupid or inadequate, the way her own family – except her mother – sometimes made her feel since she was *only* a *metapelet*. David stared at her in astonishment and protested, "You're not stupid or inadequate, Aliza. You're quite the opposite!"

Before Aliza could even thank him, Keren exclaimed, "Oh, we forgot. We brought you presents. I'll get them." The children had bought her trinkets and souvenirs of New York City that they picked out themselves. But Keren had also purchased bright red woolen mittens and Richard and Anna gave her the matching hat and scarf. "They'll look great with your black hair and your black coat," Keren said. Aliza was astounded when Keren handed her two additional boxes and said, "These are from *Ema* and *Aba*." Lise and David had bought her a grey cashmere sweater dress with a diagonal red stripe from neckline to hem, and black boots in butter-soft Italian leather. Lise told her the boots were from Macy's, so they could be changed in Boston if they didn't fit, but she hoped they would fit as they'd be gorgeous with the new dress, scarf and hat. Aliza couldn't speak; she just stood there with tears rolling down her face.

Dani stood on a chair to hug her and said, "Don't be sad, Aliza. You can play with my Eloise doll or you can color a picture of a bronto-, a bronto-, a dinosaur in my book." Aliza cried even more, but everyone else chuckled.

Finally David stood up and said, "Enough tears and enough drama. There's a lot of unpacking and *Ema* said something last night about laundry. So I'll help her. Kids, why don't you get dressed and go out for some fresh air. Simon and your friends are coming here later and you can tell them about the trip. Maybe they've never been in New York City, so think about all that you want to tell them. Have a cup of coffee, Aliza, and then try on your gifts. OK?"

On New Year's Eve, Lise and David went to a party at the Cambridge home of the chairman of Harvard's Philosophy Department, his annual "soirée". New Year's Eve was a major date night in the US and babysitters were very hard to find. Richard and Anna said Aliza should go with Gil who'd also been invited to the chairman's party. Aliza said she felt guilty, but Anna told her they were "old folks" who'd attended many New Year parties in Denmark; besides, they wanted to see Aliza in her gorgeous new dress and boots. Lise looked stunning in a V-necked black velvet dress; her only accessories were the aquamarine bracelet and a matching pendant and earrings that she'd found in her jewelry box – old gifts from David that she'd rarely worn. Everyone at the chairman's elegant and formidable residence was also stylishly dressed.

Lise quietly said to David that the chairman's wife looked like her house, elegant and formidable. David whispered in her ear, "The uptight, er-upright '*Mrs. Chairman*' reminds me of those huge dragon-type animals in the Museum of Natural History's dioramas." Simon Gordon overheard David's remark and burst out laughing. "I've always wondered what she reminded me of, and you just nailed her perfectly. Betty," he called to his wife, "You've got to hear this." David was embarrassed, but Simon assured him no one else would know what he had said. "Besides," he added, "they would all probably agree." The whole evening was full of good cheer, good food, good liquor; when the clock struck midnight, every couple kissed in the New Year, and when she and David ended their kiss, Lise noticed Aliza and Gil still standing there with their arms locked around each other. She wasn't surprised when they left a little later, saying they had another party near the Israeli Consulate. When he said goodnight, David added, "Aliza, you know there's no curfew; stay out all night if you want and we'll see you at home tomorrow." Lise, David and the Gordons left the party at 1:00 a.m. with Betty driving. In the Hofman's driveway, Lise invited them in for coffee, but Betty refused, saying their sitter was a neighbor's daughter and she was anxious to check that everything was all right. Simon, however, said Kimmie would have called if she'd had a problem and since her parents were entertaining at home, adults were on hand if needed. Betty gave in and parked the car. Anna and Richard were still awake, so they sat in the kitchen drinking wine, chatting and laughing until 2:30 a.m.

It was completely quiet when they went upstairs, and not being sleepy, Lise locked the bedroom door. David pulled down the zipper on her dress which fell to the carpet as he kissed her breasts, moving from one to the other, and then playfully fingered her clitoris at the same time, arousing her to new heights as he removed what he called her "very sexy black thong". She started to unclasp the pendant and he said, "No, leave it on, and the bracelet, too; they both match your eyes and turn me on!" Lise laughed and did as he asked; then she said it was her turn as she undressed him, touching him boldly as she removed each article of his clothing one by one. "You turn me on, too," she said saucily. She lowered the lights as they touched and tasted each other's heated bodies, at first slowly and then madly – every kiss, every touch, every taste, every possessive gesture, every hungry need – until breathless, clasped tightly in each other's arms, they climaxed together and collapsed on their bed, too exhausted to say a word. David pulled her to his side, kissing her damp hair. They just lay there for a brief time, quietly, not sleeping, catching their breath so they could make exquisite love again and again. "What a perfect way to start the new year," they both said as they awoke after barely an hour of sleep. David added, "No matter how many years we've been married, no matter how many times we've made love, it's always like that first time in Paris. Happy New Year, my darling."

When they came downstairs later that morning, all the children were at the kitchen table drinking orange juice while Anna made pancakes that Richard decorated with raisins eyes, marshmallow noses, and mouths of cherry jam. Dani begged him to let her make the faces. Lise and David were delighted with the merriment and she said, "Good morning, everyone. What a perfect way to start the new year!" Realizing what she'd said, she winked at David.

Dani asked, "Where's Aliza? She makes good pancakes, too. I'll go get her."

With a worried look on his face, Kobi said, "Aliza's not home. Do you think she's OK? My friend Tony says there are always lots and lots of accidents on New Year's Eve, and I'm scared. Maybe she's lying somewhere in a street, all covered in blood! Maybe Aliza's dead!"

Dani started to cry. "I'm scared too. I want Aliza…now!"

David smiled at his children and stated, "Aliza's with Gil and I'm sure she's fine. I told her she could stay out all night. Kobi, when you're as old as Aliza, you can stay out all night. And I won't be worried that you're lying in a street covered in blood. You've scared Dani, and that's not a very nice way to start the new year."

"I'll never be as old as Aliza," Dani said, her tears stopping instantly. "I want to stay with you, *Aba*, and with *Ema* and Grandpa Richard and Grandma Anna and Keren and Yaniv…but not you, Kobi. Maybe you'll stay out all night and have an ax-axerdent! Maybe you'll lie in the street, all covered in blood." She stuck her tongue out at her brother.

"Will not!"

"Will too!"

Richard grinned at Lise who said, "Enough, my bloodthirsty monsters! No one's going to lie in the street all covered in blood! Don't you think you should eat the terrific pancakes Grandma and Grandpa made before they're as cold as the snow outside?" The children started eating. Drinking coffee, Lise thought, *"Another little crisis upsetting Dani and instigated by Kobi – averted!"* Aloud she said, "Hurry. We're going to the Gordons. Betty and I are taking Keren and Sally

Chapter 4

ice-skating, and anyone else who wants to come as well. But before that, we'll watch the Rose Bowl parade on TV, and then *Aba* and Kobi and the 'men' will watch lots of football and eat lots of popcorn!"

As usual, Dani peppered them with questions. "What's a Rose Bowl parade? Will there be big balloons like Macy's parade? Will they throw roses from a big bowl? Will Aliza be there?" Lise laughed and said she couldn't answer any of those questions, but they'd find out at the Gordons. She told them to put on warm things, especially Keren, because it would be cold out on the ice.

◆ ◆ ◆

In February, major sadness pierced the beautiful bubble of their life, with the death of Sammy, David's dear grandfather. He and Ted flew to Israel for the funeral and part of the *shiva;* it was then that David heard his mother had been diagnosed with breast cancer shortly after his parents returned to Israel from their visit to America in October. "How could you keep it from me?" he asked, angry at being left out of the loop. "Even though the disease was caught and treated early and her prognosis for a long life is excellent, you should have told me," he admonished his sister. Ted had gone out for a walk, and Grandma Sara was resting while he and Dina were chatting in his parents' apartment. "Why didn't you call me? I would've come here to be with her and *Aba* while she was going through chemotherapy."

"That's why she made us promise not to tell you," Dina replied. "She didn't want you to disrupt your sabbatical just to hold her hand. Alon was in touch with her doctors right from the start and we all knew that her chances were excellent. She had *Aba*, *Savta* Esther, Uncle Chaim, Aunt Dvora, Grandma Sara; and Grandpa Sammy was still OK then. She had us and her friends, so I think she had enough people holding her hand. Give up? Say 'Uncle'!"

"Uncle!" he said, grinning at his sister, and high-fiving Yoni, his nephew, who was sitting close to him on the sofa.

When David returned to Brookline, the first thing he did was hug and kiss Lise and the children; then he told her about his mother's cancer. She phoned Aya immediately. "I should be angry with you for not letting us know, but I'm just so happy that you're OK," she told her mother-in-law. "This family can't do without you." Aya responded that it wouldn't have to do without her for a long time, thanks to good genes and early treatment of the cancer.

While David had been away, Lise was asked by the JCC to exhibit and sell some of her paintings at a fund-raiser; she quickly agreed, partly to show her appreciation for what the JCC teachers had done to boost her youngest child's confidence. She knew the exhibition was part of a major scholarship drive for disadvantaged children, so she decided to donate 75% of the money received for each painting; the JCC's director was amazed at her generosity. People in the community already knew about Lise's fame – not only in Israel but also in Europe, so interest was high and the paintings would probably fetch very good prices. Lise spent much of February and March choosing and organizing the paintings for the sale scheduled for Sunday, April 1st. She'd set all the prices of the paintings high and she said even though it was April Fool's Day, she was no fool and knew her work would bring in a lot of money, but she was sorry so many paintings were stored in their house in Israel. "More for us when we get home," David teased. "Besides, you've amassed a vast number of extraordinary canvases here. Just wait until the good people of Brookline see those paintings of Vermont's autumn foliage; they'll be gone in minutes and the JCC will be very grateful." His prediction was correct, and all her paintings sold. "I'm glad you held back two from Vermont for us," he said. "I want to remember that gorgeous October weekend and my gorgeous wife's rendering of the gorgeous foliage. Did you know that I once asked Dina to sell me *Le Petite Sirène*? She refused, of course, and said it will someday go to her daughter. I was a little disappointed, just like Claude when he asked Richard to sell him the diptych and your dad said 'No'. I know you're no fool; I wouldn't have married you if you were. Besides, all of us know how gifted you are and love your work!"

A few days after the fundraiser, they flew to Pittsburgh to spend *Pesach* with Ted's family. Easter was a week later, so the children would miss only a few school days. Aliza stayed home with Gil. Lise whispered that things were getting really serious, and David said he was very pleased for them. "Simon told me Gil will complete his PhD next year. So maybe Aliza won't return to Israel; that's fine as long as when they come back, Gil doesn't take my job!"

"You're a nut!" Lise laughed. "I don't think Tel Aviv University would ever think of replacing you. You're really good PR for them, especially since your wife is a very famous artist!"

The *seder* at Ted and Shani's Squirrel Hill home was superb: twenty-five family members around their huge dining room table, everyone taking turns reading the *Haggadah* in English or Hebrew. By the time they'd all had the required four cups of wine, everyone was merry. The meal was outstanding, several guests having brought dishes that were their special forte. While they were all singing *"Chad Gadya"*, Dani fell asleep, almost slipping off her chair. As the youngest child present, she had asked *Mah Nishtanah*, the obligatory four questions, and she had recited them perfectly. David carried her upstairs to bed and when he returned to the table, he was happy they were on the last verse of the song he'd always despised. Then Ted asked for the return of the *afikoman*. Kobi and Ted's son Ethan had found it together and the two boys demanded "a ransom": a remote-control airplane for Kobi and a microscope for Ethan. When Ted promised to buy the gifts after the holiday, they gave him the broken matzah and everyone ate a small piece to end the *seder*. David laughed, "The 'ransom' is exactly what each of them is most interested in, Kobi in flying and Ethan in science. Are you sure Ethan isn't the grandson of my father the scientist?" The next night Pittsburgh's JCC was holding a second *seder*. When Keren asked why, Shani told her Israelis don't have to attend a second one, but the JCC's was a lot of fun. Lise stayed home with Dani, but the others went and loved it. This time Keren "stole" an *afikoman;* she asked for professional ice-skates and David, not at all surprised by her request, promised she'd get them.

On the flight back to Boston, they talked about the special holiday they'd had. "Will you paint pictures of it, *Ema*?" Dani asked. Lise told her she might. "Paint me asking the 4 Questions; I know I was really good!" Dani added. As everyone smiled, Lise agreed to paint the *seder* and said Dani would help her.

The rest of David's sabbatical flew by. He appreciated the approval of his colleagues and students and he received many requests to return. He even had a contract from Harvard University Press for a new book. Lise gave away a few paintings; she packed the others for shipment to Israel with their clothing and purchases. As their departure date approached, they found it very hard to say goodbye to all their new friends…and to Aliza who'd decided to stay with Gil in Cambridge. They left earlier than originally planned so they could spend a few days in Berlin with Marta before the beginning of Israel's school year. Lise said they absolutely had to stay at the Kempinski Hotel because that was where she and Jonas met their mother the day they left Germany; the hotel was even more luxurious than Lise's "child's eye" remembered, especially when she compared it to the dilapidated and drab buildings in East Berlin. "Just wait," Marta's husband Philipp said, "In a few years, East Berlin will be ultramodern and high-tech! And then the Kempinski will look old-fashioned!" Lise loved getting to know her sister and her family, but her own brood was anxious to go back home to Tel Aviv; so they didn't see much of Berlin. The older children feared they had forgotten Hebrew, so David spoke only Hebrew with them. He noticed, even though the children didn't, how the German people on the street looked at him strangely when he was speaking Hebrew, and how they stared at the *Magen David* openly visible on his crewneck tee-shirt. Smiling to himself, although he knew his behavior was childish and unnecessary, David thought he must remember to tell Richard how he flaunted his Jewishness, his Israeli-ness, in the former Nazi homeland. On their last day in Berlin, Lise asked how it was that Marta, Philipp and the girls had learned to speak English so well as she didn't think they taught English in East Germany. Marta replied that German and a little Latin used to be enough to study medicine, but today's doctors had to know English to keep up with the latest developments, so she and Philipp learned English on their own and taught it to their daughters so that someday she'd be reunited with her family. Of course, she added, she didn't expect her mother to be remarried and living in Sweden, or her father and brother to be in Denmark, and her little sister in Israel! So English really was their common language, and Marta's family would keep at it until they met again. The sisters hugged and they both cried when it was time to say *"Auf Wiedersehen"*.

In Tel Aviv, they experienced culture shock. Israel was so much hotter than Brookline; their house which had once seemed so large seemed to have shrunk; they heard only Hebrew all around them. But they had so much to share with family and friends and, as time passed, life returned to normal. School began and the children had no problem reading, writing and speaking Hebrew. Dani was enrolled in a *"gan chovah"* near the school Kobi and Yaniv attended; she informed Lise and David that she was now "all grown up," and they allowed her to walk with her brothers, knowing good-hearted Yaniv would protect her from Kobi's teasing. David was back at Tel Aviv University preparing his new lectures and meeting colleagues and students, researching material for the book he'd contracted with the Harvard University Press. Lise painted in her studio; invited to participate with another artist in an exhibit at a prestigious Tel Aviv gallery, she was busy deciding which of her finished works she'd display and what kind of new ones she wanted to paint. Some mornings, when the children were in school, and if their work could wait, she and David would make love. One morning, David was nuzzling her neck when she said, "Isn't it amazing that after so many years we are still so passionate in bed?"

David chuckled, "Not only in bed, my darling. Last Sunday it was

Chapter 4

in the kitchen, and before that, my office. Maybe tomorrow we'll try out your studio. Wouldn't it be a lot of fun to squish around in paint?" She burst out laughing, and he said, "I'm an idiot! It will be oily, smelly, and probably uncomfortable. But…the shower afterwards would be fun!" He turned over on his back, pulled Lise down on top of him, and joined in her laughter. "Oh well, it was just a random thought. Now kiss me and touch me as if you mean it! We can always share the shower without being covered in paint!"

"What is really amazing," Lise thought, *"is how truly wonderful my life is! A husband I adore and our children, our families… four generations here and abroad, our friends here and abroad, my work, David's work, the recognition we're both getting… Yes, there have been tragedies, like losing our precious Shira. Still, I sometimes wish I'd become a true believer during my conversion lessons. Then I'd be able to thank God for all my blessings!"*

◆◆◆

Israel, however, was not so blessed. It was going through major upheavals in the 1990s, some good, some not so good. In 1993, Prime Minister Yitzhak Rabin and Yasser Arafat signed the Oslo Accords to end the age-old conflict between the Palestinians and the Israelis. President Bill Clinton had brought them to the White House for the official signing of the historic document; in the Rose Garden, Clinton Rabin, Arafat and Israel's Foreign Minister Shimon Peres, the *éminence grise* behind the final drafting of the Oslo Accords, shook hands, although with reluctance on Rabin's part. Nevertheless, the three men received the Nobel Peace Prize jointly in 1994. In his address to the assembled dignitaries in December, Rabin stated:

> *"Military cemeteries in every corner of the world are silent testimony to the failure of national leaders to sanctify human life. There is only one radical means to do so. Not armored plating, nor tanks, nor planes, nor concrete fortifications. The only radical solution is peace."*

Less than a year later, on November 4, 1995, Prime Minister Yitzhak Rabin was assassinated, not by a Muslim terrorist but by a Jewish extremist. Israel was in deep shock, as were leaders from all over the world who came to his funeral. President Bill Clinton's words, "*Shalom, chaver*" were etched forever in David's mind and heart, as they were in Lise's.

On the positive side in the 1990s, innovative Israelis registered more than 5,000 patents in America: in solar energy, in genetic engineering, in computer security, semiconductors and communications. Such a high concentration of high-tech industries in the coastal plain of Israel led to the nickname Silicon *Wadi*, the Arabic word for valley. Mirabilis, started by three young Israelis, created the world's first instant messaging system, ICQ, a homophone for "I seek you"; they sold it to an American corporate giant for more than $400 million. Earlier, an Israeli team working for Oracle created Kindle which was eventually bought by Amazon. Checkpoint, a leading firewall firm, reduced worldwide security complexity with protection against all types of threats. Medical diagnostic equipment was developed and marketed globally – tiny cameras in pills swallowed to find blockages, laser scalpels for less invasive surgery, and a no-touch, no-radiation device designed to prevent crib death called Baby Sense that unfortunately was developed too late to save Lise and David's darling Shira. An Israeli pharmaceutical company, Teva, became the world's largest producer of generic drugs.

But terrorist attacks went on…and on: suicide bombings, stabbings, attacks on buses, in malls, in cafés. Five governments were elected; five governments fell. Targeted assassinations by the IDF became common; the world protested when civilians were killed during military actions; the euphemism "collateral damage" became familiar through the media. So did the Arab retaliation after each IDF air strike, another suicide bombing. Israeli children had cell phones in order to reach their parents if there were problems, and their friends for fun. Yet, most Israeli children grew up safe, succeeded in school, experienced true friendships, participated in football and basketball teams and individually in tennis and swimming, and were active members of secular or religious scout troops. Israeli parents and their children celebrated the holidays at home or abroad. And when they graduated from high school, Israeli youth – male and female – went into the IDF, with the majority of boys volunteering for combat units and the most dangerous missions anyone could imagine. The only ones who didn't go into the IDF were the *haredim*, the ultra-Orthodox young men. The Hofman family acknowledged Israel as a country of vast contradictions.

Chapter 5

When Dani was a precocious ten-year-old, Lise and David finally installed the long-anticipated in-ground swimming pool, and Lise set the rules: *No Use of the Pool if it was unsupervised by an Adult; No food or drink IN the pool; No pushing, no dunking, no rough play in the pool.* The Hofman home had always been a center for the gathering of friends and family, but now Lise thought it was more like the central bus-station with people always rushing in and out, phones ringing, pitchers of cold drinks constantly on the table, clothes tossed haphazardly around, laughter, tears or groans if someone tripped over someone else's shoes or if water polo became a little too rough for the younger players. And she loved every minute of it. Sometimes she stood at the picture window in her studio, paintbrush in hand, gazing at the pool and its inhabitants of the moment with love, ingesting the joy that she would later infuse in her paintings. But what she really loved most about the pool were her late-night swims alone with David – often naked. David had installed underwater lighting and they cavorted like dolphins when everyone else was asleep.

The years passed with *bat mitzvahs, bar mitzvahs*, parties, for every reason. There were birthdays and anniversaries; there were prizes to Lise whose work was extolled by art critics for its ingenuity; there were honors to Ephraim for a major scientific achievement and to David for another highly acclaimed book, this one on deconstructionism; there were promotions for Alon who became the head of cardiac surgery at Ichilov Hospital, and for Dina, the youngest assistant professor in Bar Ilan University's prestigious psychology department. There was a party to welcome new *olim* Richard and Anna, retirement banquets for David's parents, and a barbecue for Hoffman youngsters from America who came to study in Israel for a year or to join the IDF as lone soldiers.

There was also tragedy. Alon's parents were killed in a plane crash on their way back from a long-planned holiday in Thailand and India. Grandma Sara passed away in her sleep shortly before her 100th birthday.

One night, looking at the sad expression on Lise's lovely face, David said, "I know you'll rebuke the philosopher in me, my darling, but it's an occupational hazard. Sadness and loss are part of life. For you and me, the good has always outweighed the bad." He laughed. "Hey, listen to the cynic being an optimist!"

She sighed. "I won't rebuke you. You're right. Sometimes it just gets to me, the sensitive artist; it's my occupational hazard, I guess." David embraced her and said they would always get through their occupational hazards together.

◆ ◆ ◆

One by one, Lise and David's children graduated from high school and went into the IDF; Keren's basic training was delayed until November because she'd be going into *Hatzav*, a sub-group of the IDF's Central Intelligence Unit 8200, responsible for collecting and translating open-source intelligence (OSINT). All 18-21-year-olds serve in the Israeli army, and given their brief 2-3 years of mandatory service, recruits in *Hatzav* must have excellent spoken and written skills in English. They also have to learn quickly and even be able to teach themselves certain tasks. Keren fit the bill perfectly. "It's too bad there's no Alpine Unit in the IDF. With your prowess in ice-skating, you'd have been a natural!" Kobi teased. "And they would send you up north...far away from here!"

In the few months before her IDF induction, Keren worked in a computer lab at the Weizmann Institute, not in the biochemical division that was her grandfather's bailiwick. She loved the extremely complex tasks, especially figuring out the secret prime numbers being used in private key decryption in tandem with public key cryptography; in other words, finding a way to decode a message feasibly. After realizing she was Ephraim Hofman's granddaughter and how very bright she was, the senior lab technician teased, "A chip off the old block, or off the old bloke! Right?"

"Once removed!" came Keren's quick response.

She loved driving to and from Rehovot with her grandfather, chatting about scientific theories. She told him she wanted to study science in university, to follow in his footsteps. "With smaller feet... but not a smaller brain!" he joked.

Keren's IDF unit dealt with open-source information from radio, television, newspapers, the internet; they monitored and collected all data that was related to military intelligence and translated everything into Hebrew. Glilot, Keren's base, was in Herzliya, so close to home she went home to sleep in her own bed every night and reported for duty early the next morning. Of course, Lise and David approved of her unit, and her sleeping at home. An officer, who knew the type of activities she did at the Weizmann Institute, asked Keren to study in the Officers' Training course and remain in the IDF, but she wasn't interested in any type of military career. If she couldn't be an

Chapter 5

award-winning skater – she knew she wasn't good enough – she'd go into science, like her grandfather.

After they'd finished their army service and before their university studies, Keren and three close friends finalized plans for a "typical Israeli post-army trip". Before the IDF, they'd already decided on Thailand, Nepal and India; they all loved hiking and climbing in the Judean hills and the Golan, so 2 or 3 months of trekking in Asia was their plan, but they promised their parents they wouldn't even attempt to climb Mt. Everest. Shortly before the trip, David took Keren to the Carmel Market to buy a new rucksack and an anorak with a zip-in lining. Driving home, he said, "I know you'll call me a male chauvinist pig, but I'm really glad Omri's going with you. I know you, Tali and Nina are all strong, independent young women, but you're also lovely. Most men in the Far East aren't open-minded, so imagine what they'll think of a blonde, a redhead and a brunette – three gorgeous foreigners – wandering around by themselves. Girls on their own are harassed or far worse by men over there. Fortunately, no one seeing him would think even for a minute that Omri is gay, so as your father, let me say he's an excellent traveling companion for you three."

Keren bristled. "Why? Because he won't have sex with any of us? What's wrong with you? We've known him since nursery school, and we love him."

"You're misinterpreting my words, Keren. I don't care that he's gay. *Ema* and I have always liked him; so do Kobi and Yaniv, but not in a romantic way. We'd like Omri if he limped or stuttered or was blue with green stripes!" David stated. "I only meant that a strong, young man trained in the IDF can protect you, even with his life, should the need arise. As your father, knowing Omri is with you makes it much easier for me to accept you being so far away."

Keren smiled at her father. "Sorry, *Aba*. We're all very sensitive when it's about Omri. And I do know that his 'sexual orientation', as it is called today, doesn't mean anything negative to *Ema* and you."

In September, they flew to Bangkok via Frankfurt. The families of all four came to the airport, except Kobi who had recently been inducted into the IDF. David hugged and kissed his daughter and asked if she had her cellphone and the phone numbers of his colleagues in Bangkok and Delhi. And the Israeli Consul in Kathmandu, the son of *Savta*'s friend?"

"Yes, sir," she said with a cheeky little salute. "They're pinned in one of my bras. *Ema* wanted to paint the numbers on my stomach in indelible ink, but I told her that was absurd!" David was astonished at Lise's over-protectiveness for a moment, but then he realized she'd been teasing Keren, so he decided to go along with the joke. He said he thought it was a great idea and asked why she considered it absurd. She blinked and replied, "My bikini is really tiny and everyone would see the numbers. I would be mortified!"

"Why not wear a one-piece suit instead of that minuscule postage stamp you call a bikini?" he asked, tongue in cheek, but he couldn't suppress his laughter. "Saucy brat! That was an absolutely ridiculous suggestion, so I know *Ema* was only teasing." Keren laughed as well and kissed her father again. "I promise I won't lose the numbers, but I really hope we'll never need them." She hugged and kissed all of her family when their departure gate was posted on the computer screen in the flight lounge. As she started to walk to the boarding gate, Dani whispered that Keren shouldn't tell anyone if they did run into trouble because she wanted to do the same trip after she finished the army.

"I heard that," David said, "I don't know if we'll ever let you go; you're our baby and you've always been into some kind of mischief. It's one thing when you're home and we keep our eyes on you, but should we really let you loose on India? Notice that I said 'on' not 'in'?" He grinned at Keren over Dani's head.

"Oh *gimme* a break," Dani said to her father. And to Keren, "Remember that I want to take the very same trip in a few years!"

Keren stowed her luggage, fastened her seatbelt, and then remembered a note her brother Yaniv had stuffed in her pocket. "It's probably a joke," she said, but it was a note Kobi had written before he left for basic training:

> Be careful, Keren. I won't be a pilot for a while, so I won't be able to come and rescue you. Take good notes so I'll know where NOT to go when it's my turn to travel after the IDF. And please stay off Everest. It's no place for "girlie" girls. Besides, there's no ice-skating there. Enjoy, enjoy, enjoy! I love you all. Kobi

"Typical Kobi!" she laughed, as she passed the note to her friends. They had a five-hour stop in Frankfurt before the flight to Bangkok, so they walked around the airport shopping area and window-shopped in designer boutiques; the girls bought magazines and Omri purchased a costly underwater camera. Suddenly they heard an announcement on the loudspeaker: *"Achtung! Fräulein Keren Hofman, kommen Sie bitte an den Informations-schalter im Terminal 1 sofort!"* Then they heard it in

Chapter 5

English: *"Attention! Miss Keren Hofman, please come immediately to the Information desk in Terminal 1."* As they ran to the Information desk, Karen exclaimed, "OMG, I hope nothing's wrong. My parents, my grandparents, my brothers…!" Three blondes – an older woman and two younger ones, obviously twins – were standing at the Information desk. Keren stopped short, and Omri said that they looked just like Keren and her mom. Scared, Keren asked, "Aunt Marta, is everything OK?"

Embracing her, Marta said, "Of course everything's all right. Your mother told me you had a stopover on your way to Thailand, so we decided to surprise you. We've come to take you and your friends to dinner and to wish you *'Bon voyage'*." Keren introduced them to her friends and explained that Marta and her husband were physicians, as was Loren and Elli was a former champion gymnast. In a coffee shop in the departure lounge, the four Israelis devoured enormous hamburgers with chips, while the three German women ate salads.

"This may be our last decent meal," Omri said. Everyone laughed as Marta paid their bill and teased that she wasn't sure that the word 'decent' was suitable for such a cholesterol-filled meal, especially with two physicians and an athlete right there. But they were all young and would use up lots of energy in their hikes, so one 'last meal' wouldn't hurt. Their flight was announced and after hugs all around, Keren's relatives left, wishing them *'Gute Reise!'*.

Four exhausted travelers arrived in Bangkok 11 hours later. They checked into a youth hostel and then they went to a nearby Internet café to send e-mails to their families. For Lise and David, Keren's emails, phone calls and promises to share her journals with them were the "saving grace" of their first child's trip to the Far East. They knew Keren and her friends were excellent hikers and climbers, so they had few worries about that; nor did they think she would sample any of the vast variety of drugs available throughout that part of the world. Lise loved Keren's first email from Bangkok about "going outside the hostel and how her senses were immediately assaulted, not by the heat and humidity which were similar to Tel Aviv, but by the noise of *tuk-tuk* drivers loudly honking their horns and forcing everyone to jump out of their way, also similar to Tel Aviv traffic, except at home the drivers hooting at them were in cars. And the crowds! Saffron-robed monks rubbing shoulders with young girls in very short skirts who carried signs for shops making coats, shirts, shoes – in 24 hours! Carts selling mangosteens, rambutans, dragonfruit, and dreadful smelling durian – tropical fruits they had never seen or tasted – blocked their way! Garish neon signs were everywhere!" The next day she wrote they had "explored Bangkok's famous tourist sites and although the raucous capital was exotic, Bangkok wasn't their 'thing' and one day was enough for them, so they were going to Phuket the following morning." She sent photos of the *bach* in Phuket they shared with three New Zealanders, and of the "Kiwis" themselves, superb surfers who taught the Israelis how to *catch the curl!*" Lise emailed that Dani loved the photos of the 'gorgeous Kiwis' and hoped they'd still be there when it was her turn to travel! Keren responded with photos of white-water rafting, elephant-trekking, and Phuket's Old Town with its funky shops and colonial mansions. On their last day in Phuket, she wrote about snorkeling at "Banana Beach" and playing among the brightly colored fish in the crystal-clear water, and she sent Omri's photos of her riding a giant tortoise. David responded that he was looking forward to snorkeling there himself someday.

After a 10-hour bus trip, Keren sent a very brief email from Chiang Mai, but later she wrote how strange the city was, with ultra-modern hotels next door to Buddhist temples. She said Chiang Mai was full of wealthy tourists, including rude Israeli couples. She wrote that they had been invited to a party with lots of beer, lots of spicy snacks, lots of vulgar jokes in various languages; but when an Italian offered them "joints", they claimed an early pick-up the next day for a "3-day, 2-night, 1-mountain trek", and they left the party. In an email to her Aunt Dina, she wrote that they had tea in a remote hill-tribe village the government was trying to "integrate" into Thai society; and this would destroy the indigenous culture. She added that had she not been in the mountains of Thailand, she might have been in a Bedouin village in the Negev where "uprooting" the people's way of life was similar. Her last Chiang Mai e-mail described the *Loi Kratong* festival in honor of the Goddess of Water – that they worshipped her by tossing banana-leaf holders with candles into the water and by launching small hot-air balloons made of rice paper that disappeared into the sea; Keren said she loved this exotica.

The next day, they flew directly to Kathmandu. At the Israeli Embassy, they met Natan Ginsberg, the first consul; he said his mother, a friend of Keren's *savta*, had told him to expect them. They asked him about trekking, saying they weren't interested in climbing Everest but hadn't a clue about where to go. He suggested the Annapurna Circuit, 15-25 days of 'teahouse trekking', with lodges and food along the way, and a side-trip to the Annapurna Base Camp. Keren emailed her *savta* that when they asked Natan about a hostel

Chapter 5

where they could leave things during the trek, he laughed and said "my house". His wife Ronny was pregnant and a little lonely, so not only would she enjoy their company, but she'd be their guide in Kathmandu. And they could leave their bags. When Omri asked him if all Israeli Embassy people were so nice, or if this was because of Keren's *Savta*, Natan answered, "Both." He asked us if we knew about *Pesach* in Kathmandu when thousands of Israelis travelling in the Far East came to Nepal for the world's largest *seder*, so he and Ronny were used to entertaining Israelis then, but the rest of the year was pretty dull. We loved Ronny's guided tour of the exotic city, but the best part of the day was a leisurely dinner in their villa. Twenty-two days later, tired but exhilarated by their never-to-be-forgotten experience, they were back in Kathmandu, having completed both the Annapurna Circuit and the Base Camp, and having sent daily e-mails as well as many photos to their families.

After breakfast the next morning and before he left for the Embassy, Natan gave Keren his cellphone number and said, "Call if you need anything. *Shalom, chaverim. Lehit'ra'ot.*" Ronny drove them to the airport and they said goodbye, wishing her an easy birth. Then they flew to Delhi.

Delhi was noisy, crowded and dirty, with loose "sacred" cows messing the street as a rickety cab brought them to the Blue Triangle Hostel; they struggled to hold onto their luggage as hordes of people jostled them. The hostel, owned by the Young Women's Christian Association, was clean, open to everyone, conveniently located; it had internet, so they sent emails. Keren wrote that Tali told her parents she hated the way India smelled, but her friends reminded her that so many young Israelis loved India and she retorted that so many young Israelis loved the weird drugs they could buy there. Maybe it was something about Delhi or maybe it was just travel overload, but all of them emailed that they weren't excited about Delhi and it was strange that all the tours the desk clerk recommended were based on food – eating it, buying it, even cooking it. Since none of them liked Indian food, those tours literally weren't their "cup of tea"; nor did they want to see monuments or tombs because they were saving their enthusiasm for Agra and the Taj Mahal. They did walk through the silver market, but they didn't like the jewelry. At the wedding market, they giggled when they were told that a bride could rent an elaborate outfit if she couldn't afford to buy it – like Israeli brides! The only tour Keren detailed in her emails was "Street Life of Delhi". Their guide, Pravit Gupta, told them the area had once been inhabited by indigent children. As they listened, they realized he was telling them about his own life on the streets. When they asked, he said, "My story isn't unique. I'm from Benares. My family was very poor and after a terrible fight with my father, I ran away. I was 10-years-old and I hid under a seat in a tour bus that arrived in Delhi after ten hours; the driver saw me and called the police, but a kind woman told me to run and gave me enough rupees to survive at the bus station for a few days. My belongings were stolen the first night and I was desperate until a 'good' man gave me a hot meal at a *gurdwara*, and took me to a carpet factory where I slept, ate, and worked 16-18 hours each day for three years with several other 'slaves'. A tourist saw us one day and he reported the horror to the police. The premises were raided and the owner of the factory was ordered to release us at once or he would go to jail. We were freed and given food and shelter. I was sent to school and it was the beginning of my new life. Now I'm a social worker in this area." Keren wrote that after hearing his story, all of them gave him some money for his goal of restoring a 'real childhood' to the vagrant children living on the streets or as slaves by providing them with safe homes, education, and the kinds of benefits the four Israelis had always known. Keren and her friends thanked their parents for their wonderful childhoods.

They left Delhi for Agra very early the next morning, looking forward to their visit to the Taj Mahal. They had booked a "homestay", an Indian-style B&B recommended by friends. Keren called home later that evening and told Lise and David the homestay was delightful, as was Gayan Kapoor, the young owner. He made them leave everything in their rooms, even their cellphones, and after breakfast he sent them to the Taj Mahal by taxi. Polluting vehicles couldn't approach the Taj Mahal, so the driver stopped not far from the main entrance, *darwaza-irauza*. It was still early in the day and their first glimpse of the fairy-tale masterpiece was incredible; the light on its white marble façade gave the classic mausoleum a pink glow. Without cellphones, they had nothing to check and they walked through the Great Gate into the extraordinary beauty of the Taj Mahal; they gasped at the long pathways and the rectangular basin, at the two symmetrical minarets flanking the domed mausoleum on each side, so familiar from photos, yet seeming so new; they'd never seen anything like it and knew they never would again. Keren's email to Lise said, "We could take 1000 pictures, we could write 1000 words, or 10,000, and we still could never capture its sublime proportions, its perfect geometric patterns, its grandeur! We walked around for hours marveling at the Taj Mahal from every side and every angle, inside and out, avoiding tour groups with their guides spouting spiels in many languages. Finally, knowing we'd absorbed as much as possible, we left. Gayan said he didn't even have to ask because it was all there in our eyes; he told us we had to see the Taj Mahal at sunset from the spectacular but not very crowded garden opposite, Mehtab Bagh; we accepted his advice. Pink in the morning, the Taj Mahal was milky white as the sun set, and silver and gold as the moon rose. When we thanked Gayan for the Mehtab Bagh experience, he told us to go to bed, wake up early to watch dawn, a glorious pink and orange halo, coming up around the Taj Mahal." In her next email, Keren said "I wish I were an artist like you, *Ema*, with a great talent for color, so I could paint the Taj Mahal at different hours of the day, but I've never seen a painting or photo that captured it, so I'm sorry to say that I don't think even you can do it! Gayan said our last excursion to the Taj Mahal should be to the Black Taj! When we said we'd never heard of it and queried what it was, he laughed and told us the myth: 'Shah Jahan built the Taj Mahal for his third wife and he had planned a black mausoleum for himself, but he was murdered before it was built. There are ghostly black marble ruins in Mehtab Bagh but the only ones who can see them are those who really believe the story. A more plausible theory,' Gayan said, 'is that several black stones and the position of the moon and the Taj pool cause a dark reflection of the white mausoleum.' We didn't see the Black Taj!"

Gayan was going to Jaipur for business the next day and he said they could join him on the long drive; that way they wouldn't have to *'shlep'* their luggage by train. "That's the right word, isn't it?" he asked when he saw them grinning. "I learned it from Israelis who stayed with us a few months ago." Not only did Gayan drive them to Jaipur, but he also took them to a homestay owned by old friends. Keren emailed that they told him they didn't know how to thank him for his hospitality and suggestions about the Taj Mahal. "Send me Israelis like yourselves; you're what keeps us going. Enjoy the rest of your time in India."

But they didn't enjoy the rest of their time in India. In Jaipur, the "pink city", they went to Jantar Mantar Observatory, a collection of geometric instruments for predicting eclipses and tracking stars, with an enormous marble and bronze sundial as accurate as the world's standard clock in Greenwich, England. And they went to Hawa Mahal, an 18th century five-storey honeycomb red and pink sandstone palace. While they were looking up at the complex structure, three motorbikes, each holding two young men, approached them; one of the bikes forced Omri away from the girls and the men on the other two bikes grabbed the girls who tried to give them their bags, but the men didn't want the bags! They wanted the girls. Omri tried to get to them, punching the driver of the bike, but the bike knocked him down, backed up and hit him again and again. The girls' screams immediately brought people to their aid, and all three of the motorbikes raced away. Omri, unconscious, was lying on the ground; someone phoned the police and requested an ambulance. While one of the policemen who arrived at the scene took the accounts of the girls and the witnesses, Omri was placed on a stretcher and taken to a hospital. Then the other policeman drove the girls to the hospital where they were all checked by a doctor who said their bruises from the thugs were superficial. X-rays showed that Omri had a compound fracture and would be in a cast for at least six weeks While he was having a cast put on his broken leg, Keren called Natan Ginsberg and told him what had happened. She said all of them just wanted to go home and asked if he could help. "I have a friend in our embassy in Delhi. I'll call him and get back to you. In the meantime, you should phone your parents and tell them what happened. If I call, they'll panic; if you call, they'll know you're all right. Tell them Israel always takes care of our own, so we'll get you home soon, and safe!" All the girls were talking to their parents when Omri came out in a wheelchair a few minutes later, his left leg in a cast from toes to mid-thigh. He'd been given painkillers and wasn't himself, but they told him to call his parents so they'd know his injury wasn't life-threatening. As Keren was saying goodbye to her parents, a nurse came over and asked if she was Keren, there was a phone call for her at the desk. It was Natan. "I spoke to my friend, Uri Katz; he's already arranging a flight to Jaipur, but it will take a few hours. Do you want to stay at the hospital?" She said Omri knew how to use crutches, so they would go to the homestay and wait there. She thanked him for his help, and said she was so glad her *savta* knew his mother. They packed their things, including Omri's; traumatized, but thankful Omri's injury was not as serious as it might have been, they waited for Uri Katz. Three days later, after the Embassy convinced El Al to change their tickets, they left India, still in shock but happy to be going home. Four sets of parents met the exhausted travelers at the airport. After hugs and wishes of *"Refuah shlema!"* to Omri, the others left and Keren whispered to Omri, "Just think of the story we can tell our grandchildren! Those hoodlums almost killed you when you were saving us from being abducted or worse. You're my hero."

Keren refused to talk about Jaipur. She spoke about the treks, the

Chapter 5

awful way the Thais treated the hill-tribes in remote areas, all the fun they'd had with the Kiwis, the kindness of Natan and Ronny Ginsberg, Gayan Kapoor's homestay. She told them about tea-trekking in the Anapurna Circuit; she talked non-stop about the Taj Mahal. But she never mentioned Jaipur. Finally, David insisted she go with him to the Carmel Market to buy exotic spices. He parked their car and saw a look of panic on Keren's face as she glanced toward the crowded market; David led her to a table at an outdoor café at the entrance. He ordered soft drinks and said, "Keren, darling, you know you won't get past the trauma of Jaipur until you talk about it with a psychologist, or with Aunt Dina or with me. You know we won't judge. Maybe you should do what I did after the Yom Kippur War, write about it. That helped me so much and afterwards, I could talk about what happened. Before you left on the trip, I told you how pleased I was that Omri was going with all of you, that he might be excellent security for three very pretty young women traveling in India. And he was."

Keren began to cry. "I remember. You took me to buy a rucksack and an anorak. I also remember accusing you of being happy that Omri's gay and you wouldn't worry about us having sex. *Aba*, he saved us from being kidnapped, and the thugs attacked him! Two of them ran him down with their motorbike; he could have been killed, but he really fought. Natan, *Savta*'s friend's son, called someone in our embassy in Delhi and they convinced El Al to let us come home." She sobbed, "It was awful. It ruined the whole trip for me."

David took her hands and said quietly, "No, my darling, it was awful, but it didn't ruin the whole trip, even if that's how you feel now. Grandpa Richard told me Grandma Anna insisted on seeing 'Schindler's List' when it came to Denmark because she needed to know that some people working for the Nazis actually saved Jews. If you ask her today, she'll tell you she never saw the film. She totally erased it from her memory along with the possibility of 'good' Nazi supporters, because her experience was so traumatic. But today she talks easily about her early life in Holland, about her family, her husband and even about her baby. But she never talks about the Holocaust. What happened in Jaipur was awful, but all of you are OK. You'll never forget it, but in time the good memories, all the treks, all the people you met, the Taj Mahal, all of that will overshadow Jaipur. And you'll always have a wonderful friend named Omri." He squeezed her hands and kissed her on the tip of her nose.

Keren squeezed back. "When did you get so smart, *Aba*?" she asked.

"I was in such a bad place after the Yom Kippur War," he answered.

"What got me to a better place was facing the horrors, writing about them, knowing how many people I have in my life who love me, especially *Ema* and all my family. I lost old friends and comrades, but look at my life now. I have so much now, good memories and not only horrendous ones. And so much love, for Ema, for you, Kobi, Yaniv and Dani, for my whole family. So let's go buy those exotic spices; and you'll help me do some really fancy cooking."

At home, David took the spices into the kitchen, just as Lise came in from her studio, wiping her hands. She looked at him with questions in her eyes.

"She talked and she cried," he said. "I'll tell you about it later. OK?"

"I knew if anyone could get through to her, you'd be able to do it. Keren has always been a 'Daddy's Girl'!" she teased.

"Brat!" he said, swatting his wife lovingly on her rear!

◆ ◆ ◆

Keren went back to her Weizmann Institute lab until she began studying physics at Tel Aviv University. She rented a 4-bedroom partially furnished flat three blocks away from the campus; she shared it with her friend Tali and two other students. Her home was very close to the TAU campus, but since she'd lived at home during her army service, Keren wanted to live with friends.

Meanwhile, Kobi was living his childhood dream of flying, but he wasn't enjoying it as much as he'd expected. Athletic, with excellent grades and test scores, Kobi had been spotted by IDF recruiters as a potential fighter pilot while still in high school. When he explained his ambition to Lise and David, he said he knew that a pilot flying a single-seated combat aircraft faced many challenges from the moment a mission was assigned, to takeoff, to completing the mission, to landing his plane; he knew that he had to face those challenges alone and that the success of the mission rested solely on his shoulders. Both of his parents said they'd support his choices, whatever they were. He passed the 6-day Israeli Air Force *gibush* very easily, and he was inducted in September 1999 for the seven years of mandatory service for pilots. On his first day at Hatzerim Airbase, he was given not only all the requisite equipment but also the shortest haircut of his life. Despite not being happy about his buzzcut, he still breezed through all of his initial training, received an air crew pin, and made it into the combat pilot program. Before beginning the second training phase, however, he had a short break at home. While doing errands for Lise, the car was rammed in the back and Kobi's left elbow was

Chapter 5

slammed into the window; it was swollen and the pain was severe, but he assumed it was just a bruise because the car wasn't damaged. Ice reduced the swelling but the pain was severe; when he was checked by doctors at the base, X-rays revealed ulnar nerve entrapment. He was given anti-inflammatory medications and a padded brace to keep his elbow straight. He reported to his commanding officer who said, "Take a seat, Kobi. I have some bad news for you. I'm really sorry, but you can't continue training as a fighter pilot although you can remain in the IAF. You've been top of your group and it saddens me to lose you as a combat pilot, your ultimate dream. Still, becoming a navigator isn't such a significant setback. Don't be too disappointed."

"Thank you, sir," Kobi responded, trying not to sound despondent. But in his room, a crestfallen Kobi phoned home to tell them the bad news. Lise and David tried to bolster his spirit. "Kobi, remember how excited Gilad was last month when he talked about Unit 669?" Lise asked. Kobi replied that of course he remembered how much his closest friend loved his unit, as much as Kobi loved flight school. "Well, honey, maybe you should transfer into Unit 669," Lise said. "Don't say it's a stupid idea. Think about it." David added that they'd support him whatever he decided, and maybe he should talk to Dina, and she might be able help him get over what had to have been a major letdown.

"Maybe I'll talk to Uncle Alon and see if he thinks I can handle Unit 669's medical stuff…wait, that means I'm willing to think about it. Wow! I'm not wallowing in self-pity!" Kobi said. "And I know I always have your backing."

With two more days of sick leave, Kobi thought seriously about transferring to Unit 669. He could probably be a helicopter pilot and fly the Medevac units. Was he willing to be a medic? He'd only considered being a fighter pilot, and he knew very little about Unit 669 except its nickname – "the flying cats", with a green-eyed cat on the insignia. "OK, Hofman, it's time to find out if this can be good for you," he told himself as he made an appointment to see the CO.

The CO was surprised to see him again so soon. Kobi told him he was thinking about transferring to Unit 669. The CO said, "It seems to me, Kobi, that you always want to be in the heart of events. Our Medevac unit, the IDF Combat Search and Rescue extraction unit is heliborne, and subordinate to the Special Air Forces Command of the IAF; so it is considered one of the IDF's premier elite units. The training you've already had will exempt you from some required programs in helicopter training. Are you all right with this?"

"I think so, sir. I've loved every minute of what I was learning about flying before that accident. My best friend is in Unit 669 and it might really be right for me to be flying 'choppers! I also spoke to my uncle, a cardiologist, and he thinks I won't find learning the medical side of Unit 669 too difficult. Please tell me whom to contact to get this ball rolling…or, I should probably say, this bird flying again! Oops! To find out more about the flying cats, not birds?"

The CO laughed and gave him the phone number of Sergeant Shoshi, a Unit 669 recruiter. He said, "Good luck. Let me know when you're absolutely sure." Kobi said he would, saluted his commander, and left. In his room, he called the number and asked to speak to Sergeant Shoshi.

"Speaking," she said. "How can I help you?" Kobi explained the situation. He said his best friend was a cadet in Unit 669, and he spoke so highly of the unit that it might be a good fit for him. She said, "And you might be a good fit for us. I'll check you out. Do you know why we're called 669?"

Kobi answered. "It's for perfect vision which is also required for IAF pilot training. I have that. Both the doctor and my CO assured me that my medical profile is still 97. I was dropped from combat training because my elbow needs time for healing. Lost time is the problem, not fitness."

"OK, Kobi. I'll get back to you after I consult our commanding officers."

After hanging up the phone, Kobi took a deep breath. "You've really done it now, Hofman," he said to himself, laughing a little. "Digest it for a little while, as Aunt Dina would say, and then call home and the CO." The approval of his transfer came through and within two weeks, he was at Tel Nof for Unit 669 training; he was delighted to be on the same team as Gilad. And once again he quickly became the top cadet in the unit; he then went on to the paramedics' course. At their commencement ceremony, a special film of the new graduates performing rescue maneuvers such as rappelling down a mountain to evacuate an "injured soldier", of Kobi and three other medics jumping from a helicopter and skiing down Mt. Hermon in order to extricate a "trapped soldier", and of a few other very daring rescues was presented to their families and friends. Ted Hoffman and his son Ethan even came from Pittsburgh to congratulate Kobi on receiving his Unit 669 wings. The CO spoke directly to the assembled guests. "The young men in this unit never know what to expect," he said. "They're in the mess laughing with their friends one second, and the next, the siren

Chapter 5

goes off and everything's changed. They're running to a catastrophe, even if Israel's not in a military action at the moment: a train wreck, stranded hikers caught in a surge of water, an inexperienced skier trapped in a mini-avalanche. Unit 669 fortunately has a few expert skiers to handle that," he said, grinning at Kobi.

After becoming a "flying cat", Kobi completed the 18-month commander's training program, and after combat experience, he went on to the advanced commander's course, intensive, mission-based, with instruction in leadership and control methods for small-team rescue commanders. The demands on small-team commanders were great, including the ability to manage radio communications and issue orders simultaneously to pilots, ground forces, doctors, and their subordinate rescue soldiers; all of this was done from inside a helicopter on the way to the target and on the ground after landing. These difficult decisions could mean the difference between life and death, and must be made under fire and severe time pressure, often with imperfect information or no pre-mission preparation. Due to the emergency responder nature of the unit, the type of mission, time of day, and location could never be anticipated. Therefore, these commanders and their soldiers had to be perfect in all the specialties from their training (diving, rappelling, etc.), because there was no time to review them when the mission siren went off.

During his years as a "flying cat", Kobi commanded so many rescues; some were daring and difficult, some were fairly routine and quite easy. His personal injuries came not from the military but during vacations at home. Driving his grandparents to do some shopping before Yom Kippur in 2001, he had a small accident that required stitches in a long gash in his thigh; fortunately, the older couple escaped harm. Kobi's wound wasn't serious, but he was grounded for two weeks. Grandma Anna said she was grateful that she and Grandpa Richard hadn't been hurt, but she felt bad for Kobi; she laughed and said they all knew he had no *zitsfleysh*. Lise agreed, and knowing how he hated just to sit around doing nothing, she asked him to go to the airport to meet Alex Novak, a young man from Slovakia who was sponsored by Ted Hoffman's Jewish Federation of Pittsburgh, Alex would be joining the IDF after the holidays, probably in the special forces; he would be staying with them in Ramat Aviv until his formal induction. Given his official IDF security clearance, Kobi was allowed into the Arrivals area; holding Alex's name on a small sign, he was pleased when an athletic young man exited Passport Control and came directly to him. When Alex told him this was his first trip to Israel,

Kobi decided to give him a short tour of the highlights of Tel Aviv.

As everyone knew, the only thing that really bothered Kobi during his years as a "flying cat" was the inactivity between missions that gave the Search and Rescue Unit the silly nickname *"Shesh Besh Tesha"*, a pun on the number 669, *Shesh Shesh Tesha*, because the soldiers "wasted" a lot of their time playing *shesh besh*, a game similar to backgammon. His CO understood Kobi's lack of *zitsfleysh*, his inability to do nothing for long periods of time, and Kobi was given special assignments, training new recruits and devising new strategies for future missions. The CO urged him to continue as a career soldier after his required service ended, and he agreed. But his attitude toward the military in general changed in 2006 during the Second Lebanon War; he had led a few less than successful rescue missions; his small team rescued injured soldiers behind enemy lines and lifted several dead ones from a downed aircraft, three of Kobi's acquaintances among them. Like many Israelis, Kobi questioned that war and he decided to leave the IDF, knowing that his skills would open many different doors. He knew he could be called back for reserve duty at any time, but he also knew he really needed a new life with time to relax, not just to be off-duty. He needed time to play tennis or touch-football or pick-up basketball; he needed time to go to a concert or make love with one of the "hot chicks" in his life without always waiting to be called to an emergency rescue. He needed home cooking and lessons on how to do some cooking for himself, he needed a cool head and perhaps he needed a serious girlfriend, a "hot one" of course!

♦♦♦

In April 2000, a new IDF division was established, the Combat Intelligence Collection Corps, abbreviated as *Modash*; its purpose was to fulfill some of the former combat intelligence functions of the Directorate of Military Intelligence (AMAN, *Agaf Modi'in*). Yaniv "knew he was destined" to do his compulsory army service where he could contribute the most, and that had to be Unit 8200 (*Yehida Shmoneh-Matayim*), the cyber warfare branch of *Modash*. His *tironut* began in August 2001 at Mifrasit, the southern base of *Modash*. Lise was very weepy as she and David hugged Yaniv and left him at Tel HaShomer's *Bakum*. "Three to the IDF already, one out, two currently in, and another in two years. The IDF owes me a lot for having four children and a husband who was a hero in the paratroopers," she said as they walked back to the parking lot. Hugging her, David said all Israelis owe a lot to the IDF, too, as she well knew. If the IDF hadn't

Chapter 5

allowed him to go to Paris after the Yom Kippur War, he and Lise wouldn't have any children in the IDF because they probably would never have married and had four terrific kids! "You're so logical!" she teased, laughing. He also laughed and said she could blame that on him being a philosopher.

After the horrors of the 9/11 terrorist attacks on the United States, Yaniv knew *Modash* had been the right choice. All IDF Intelligence services would work day and night to help Israel's strongest ally in its war on terror, and Unit 8200 would need Yaniv's technical skills, but rather than Glilot, where Keren had served, he was sent to Urim, the main headquarters of Signal Intelligence (SIGINT), responsible not only for the collecting of signal intelligence but also for code decryption, evaluation of intelligence security planning, assessment of counter-intelligence policy and dissemination of intelligence to IDF branches and to the government. Israeli media claimed Unit 8200 provided more than half of AMAN's total data, and a British research institute head called Unit 8200 the world's preeminent technical intelligence agency, totally focused on what they saw and what they heard, conducting vital operations with tenacity and passion. However, neither the Israeli government nor the IDF confirmed Unit 8200's achievements or even its existence.

Soldiers in Unit 8200 always worked in pairs, and Yaniv's assigned partner was a new immigrant from Austria, a very recent convert named Gabriel Ben Shmuel, who had remarkable language skills: English, German, Urdu, Farsi, Turkish, and several others, but he lacked Yaniv's technical expertise. They were excellent partners and became good friends, eating meals together and sharing breaks. In perfect Hebrew without a foreign accent, Gabriel told Yaniv that he was illegitimate, that his birth name was Dominik Müller which he'd changed when he converted, that his Catholic school in Graz had expelled him and his mother had disowned him when he questioned Christian dogma, so he had gone to live with a remarkable rabbi and a few teenagers, and that he had converted to Judaism twice, first in Vienna and again at Kibbutz Sde Eliyahu. He told Yaniv that an IDF recruiter came to the Sde Eliyahu just days before he left and urged him to make *Aliyah* and join Unit 8200. He told Yaniv that his father was a philosophy professor in Iran, and thanks to the Rabbi, he had met his father, and later his grandmother, in a hotel in Zurich.

Yaniv told Gabriel that he believed in coincidence and asked if Gabriel did. "My Grandma Anna calls it *bashert*, a Yiddish word for 'destiny' or fate'. But to me it's all coincidence. Here's the first coincidence: my *Ema*, a well-known artist, was born in Germany but she was raised in Denmark, until she went to study art in Paris and met my *Aba*, a PhD student at the Sorbonne. My parents had two weddings; the first was in Paris and the second was in Tel Aviv after my *Ema* converted to Judaism only once, in Israel, even though she started the conversion process in Paris. Like yours, my father is a professor of philosophy; that's the second coincidence. You'll have to come home with me for Shabbat and meet everyone. Dani, my younger sister's very pretty and will instantly fall in love with you. Our house is a gathering place for family and friends from all over the world; my grandparents are usually there on Shabbat and you can ask them to tell you their stories that are full of coincidences. For example, both my Israeli and German grandfathers were at El Alamein during World War II, on opposite sides; my German grandpa deserted to the British and spent most of the war in a POW camp; that's coincidence number three. Wow," Yaniv added, "I don't think I've talked this much in a very long time."

Gabriel said, "All of this is extraordinary. And here's another coincidence if your *Ema* is Lise Hofman. I've seen several of her paintings; one is in the home of my 'remarkable rabbi' in Zurich, another one is in Vienna in the home of his good friends, and a painting of a Purim party is in the home of the Rabbi's son in Jerusalem. I can't wait to tell them I know the artist's son."

Yaniv laughed. "You see, coincidences upon coincidences. My *Ema*'s name is Lise, and after you come for Shabbat, you'll be able to tell all your friends that you met the artist, not just her son! I told you we were *bashert*."

In order to bolster Unit 8200's mastery of tactical intelligence and provide the United States with urgent data, the two young soldiers worked an enormous number of extra hours. They had no time off until they were finally given the Shabbat in October during *Sukkoth*, and they went to Yaniv's home in Ramat Aviv. When Yaniv opened the front door, they were immediately assailed by savory cooking aromas, raucous noise and much laughter. Gabriel asked, "Am I in Israel or in Austria? This is exactly what it was like Friday afternoons in the Rabbi's flat in Graz as we were getting ready for *shul*, with noise, laughter, and the delicious scent of Frau Sarah's tasty meals. Wow!" Yaniv started to tease Gabriel again about so many coincidences just as a beautiful barefoot woman with messy blonde hair came into the front hall.

She grabbed Yaniv in a hug, saying, "It's about time! Let me look

Chapter 5

at you, my love. Grandma Anna will say you're getting too skinny. Introduce me to your friend and then tell me those coincidences. Then, let's go outside."

Hugging her, Yaniv said, "*Ema*, meet Gabriel, my partner at Urim and my friend. Grandma Anna always says I'm too skinny, but this Shabbat I'll let her try to make me fat because her cooking's so much better than what they have the *chutzpah* to call food at Urim. You wouldn't believe how awful it is and sometimes Gabriel and I just have PB&J that we get at the kiosk or halvah on challah. You'll have to wait a few minutes to hear about the coincidences until we've stowed our gear in my room. Who's here? Grandma Anna and Grandpa Richard? *Savta* and *Saba*? Keren, Kobi and Dani? How about the new guy that Uncle Ted sent here? What's his name again? Alex?"

Ema? Gabriel couldn't get over his first sight of this gorgeous woman or that she was Yaniv's mother! He handed her the bouquet of flowers he'd bought at a local florist, and said, "It's a pleasure to meet you, Ma'am. One coincidence is that I've seen some of your fabulous paintings!"

"*Shalom*, Gabriel. Thank you for these gorgeous flowers! And please don't call me Ma'am! It makes me feel very old. My name's Lise, as you know since you've seen my paintings! Where did you see them?"

A tall young-looking man joined them in the hallway just then; he hugged Yaniv and shook Gabriel's hand, "I'm David, Yaniv's *Aba*. Welcome to 'The Hofman Holiday Madhouse'!" he said, laughing. "My wife already loves you because she always adores people who appreciate her work! Yaniv, place your bags on the stairs and we'll all go outside." Yaniv and Gabriel went with Lise and David. Gabriel was still astounded by his friend's 'young' parents.

"Our soldier's finally home," Lise called out as they walked out to the deck. "And he's brought us this very handsome young man whose name is Gabriel!"

David winked at his son and then said to Gabriel, "After I introduce you to everyone, I'll test you on all their names."

A very pretty young girl sitting on the floor with three other girls said, "He'll do that, too! I'm Dani, Yaniv's sister. And you are very handsome!"

Everyone laughed. Gabriel loved it all, the ambiance, so many people of all ages, such gaiety. When the two soldiers had been given some brownies and a cold drink, David introduced everyone to Gabriel, but that wasn't followed by a test.

Right after David said his name, a young man called Alex grinned at Gabriel and said, "I was also stunned a few days ago when I first met Lise. I couldn't even close my mouth! How could anyone so young and lovely be the mother of four grown-up kids? Or almost grown-up!" he said with a big smile at Dani. "It's not that my own mother in Slovakia isn't beautiful, young-looking and the mother of four grown-up kids! But Lise really is something else!"

By the time they went back to Urim after *Sukkoth*, Gabriel knew he'd never experienced a more enjoyable holiday, not even at the Rabbi's home. "In Graz, Frau Sarah's meals are comparable to your Grandma's and your *Savta*'s, but it's the people who made it incredible," he admitted to Yaniv, "All the talk, all the joking and teasing made it fabulous. Even going to synagogue for Shabbat services had been different than in Austria, although he enjoyed the way Dani flirted with him along the way, just as his friend Ruth used to tease him. But it was their home and all the people in it that made it so fabulous. Everyone had something to say in a noisy political debate and in appreciation of the heroism of the passengers on United flight 93; no one was left out. Lise asked Gabriel once again where he'd seen her paintings and when he said one was in Rabbi Breitling's Zurich home and another one was in his son Jakob's Jerusalem flat, Simon Gordon, a friend of David's from Harvard, stared at him and asked if he was talking about Rabbi Samuel Breitling.

"Yes," Gabriel said. "Rabbi and Rabbanit Breitling sort of adopted me after my school expelled me and my mother disowned me."

Simon said, "That boy's name wasn't Gabriel. Rabbi Breitling's an old friend from Camp Ramah in Massachusetts and I know both of his boys and his wife Deborah's whole family." Gabriel explained that his name in Austria had been Dominik Müller, but he changed it to Gabriel Ben Shmuel when he converted, to honor his spiritual father, Rabbi Samuel Breitling, Shmuel in Hebrew.

"Another one of those odd coincidences, *bro*," Yaniv said. That led to a long discussion about all kinds of coincidences. Gabriel was very attracted to Dani, Yaniv's young sister; she reminded him of his cheeky friend Ruth in Graz. He told himself that Dani was Yaniv's 'little' sister and only 16-years-old, so she was off-limits, no matter how much she liked to flirt with him. On the bus back to Urim, Gabriel couldn't stop talking about the fabulous weekend and all the fabulous food and all the really fabulous people. Yaniv joked, "My friend the linguist, are you having trouble with your vocabulary? You've used the word 'fabulous' at least a dozen times, Gabe! By the way, both my

Chapter 5

Ema and *Aba* said you're welcome, no, you're expected, at our house anytime. There are a lot of other 'fabulous' members of our family, and you should meet them. My Aunt Dina and Uncle Alon are 'fabulous', and so are their kids, Yoni and Yael. Kobi and Keren are both terrific, I mean 'fabulous', although they'll never hear me say that! And then there's Dani…" Yaniv stopped teasing when he noticed his friend blushing a little. *"Uh-oh!"* he thought, but he didn't say anything more, even knowing Gabriel and Dani into contact many times over the next couple of years whenever they came to Ramat Aviv.

Yaniv's world for the next two years centered around SIGINT, specifically the dissemination of vital information, about tactical and strategic intelligence and ongoing hostile activities to senior personnel and decision-makers through verbal briefings and intel bulletins. Everything technical to maintain SIGINT efficiency was performed by Unit 8200, much of it by Yaniv and a few others. Shortly before the end of his first year in *Modash*, Yaniv was told to report to his Commanding Officer. He was amazed when the CO asked him to consider staying on as a career officer. "With your very prodigious computer knowledge and vast technical skills, we'd hate to lose you when your compulsory service is over," the CO said. "The IDF will offer a lot to keep you. So think about going to Officer's Training. Talk to your parents about it, and let me know."

He told Lise and David that the IDF offered to pay for his BA wherever and whatever he wanted to study. "Do you honestly think that's necessary?" David asked, sounding a little worried. "It's great that they know how talented you are, something *Ema* and I've always known, but are you willing to stay in the IDF just because they would pay for your education, which is something *Ema* and I can easily do? You must have another reason. What is it?"

Yaniv said, "I think Officer's Training can help me become more assertive and more self-confident."

Lise burst out laughing, and said, "My darling second son, you may be less of a chatterbox and more introspective than your brother and sisters, but those of us who know you have always seen just how assertive you can be whenever it's really necessary! Don't you agree, David?"

David nodded. He repeated his question about Yaniv having another reason, and Yaniv replied quietly, "I really don't know what I want to do when I finish the IDF. I know I want to study, but I don't know what. Since I was very little, I've always liked history and geology and paleontology, but I'm also interested in politics. I know I should do something in technology or science, but what? I love computers, but I don't think I could work in high-tech. So maybe if I stay in the IDF a while longer, I'll figure out what I want to do with my life!"

"That makes sense, even if you're a bit confused now," David said. "You know we'll always back you. So become an officer and go on from there to whatever and wherever you choose!"

Yaniv told his CO he'd decided to attend Officer's Training, and Gabriel cheekily asked if that meant he'd have to salute Yaniv all the time. Less than two months later, Yaniv was sent to Camp Laskov for training in management and leadership. He remained in Unit 8200 for three more years, completing his service as a captain. His siblings and Gabriel teased him unmercifully about how assertive he had become, how good he was at bossing everyone. "Except *Ema*!" Yaniv countered. "We all know that she's the 'real' boss!"

Before beginning his interdisciplinary studies at IDC Herzliya, in computer science and conflict management in government, developing his interests in both technology and politics, Yaniv flew to the United States for a trip with his cousin Yoni, an MA student in Environmental Planning at the University of Colorado-Boulder. The two young men spent six weeks hiking, rock-climbing, and white-water rafting in the Grand Canyon, Zion National Park and Bryce Canyon in Utah, followed by a week in Yosemite Park in California, with its giant redwood trees, towering waterfalls and enormous granite cliffs; all of the vistas were familiar because of Ansel Adams' breathtaking photographs. In the Ansel Adams Gallery in Yosemite Village, Yaniv bought several books of the famed photographer's work for his parents and two prints for himself, a tunnel vista in Yosemite and one of Kings Canyon; they would hang proudly in his future home next to some of his *Ema*'s dazzling paintings. After Yosemite, the cousins went to San Francisco, where they enjoyed the sophistication and noise of a busy city; then they flew to Pittsburgh for their cousin Tammy's wedding.

♦ ♦ ♦

In 2003, it was Dani's turn to enter the IDF. While still in high school, she'd been evaluated by a team of IDF recruiters in written and spoken languages, public speaking, leadership and teamwork, even outdoor skills for a possible field position. All of the officers said her IQ, her knowledge about Israel, her ability to speak English, German and French, and her vivacious, even cheeky, personality, made her the perfect candidate for *Doveret Tzahal*. One recruiter joked that being "a gorgeous green-eyed blonde didn't hurt either!" When she heard that,

Chapter 5

Dani said it was too bad they wouldn't assign her to *Oketz* because she really loved dogs but had never owned one since one of her brothers was allergic to them. The officers laughed at her sauciness but didn't change their minds. She was assigned to the IDF Spokesperson's Unit.

Lise wasn't weepy this time when they said goodbye to Dani with hugs and kisses at *Bakum*. She said she knew that Dani's *tironut* was short, and *Doveret Zahal* was a non-combat unit; she added that maybe the IDF would instill a little self-restraint in their lovable but often cheeky younger daughter. She asked David if he recalled when he said she was a changeling. Walking with her to the parking lot, said, David replied that of course he remembered. "Our tiny daughter was having a very noisy tantrum that day and I was frustrated by her behavior. You said it was nothing more than 'artistic temperament' that she had inherited from you or maybe it was just capriciousness; and I laughed at you. But now I love her cheeky behavior and even her outlandishness. In the middle of my serious philosophical theorizing, she's very refreshing! And in some strange way, I think her boldness, or should I call it shamelessness, has helped me cope better with our tragic loss of sweet-natured Shira!"

Dani was in trouble only once during *tironut* when an officer overheard her telling a fellow recruit that Sergeant Chava was the only one who looked good in the shapeless olive-drab uniform because she was probably just as shapeless underneath; Dani's punishment for her "impertinence" was an extra 8 hours of guard duty. She told her parents that the "punishment didn't fit the crime" and was unfair because it was based on hearsay, but her parents said maybe she'd learn to think before she spoke. Dani said her parents were also being unfair and what she'd learned was to look around to see who was there before she said anything snide. After *tironut*, Dani was assigned to the Spokesperson's Public Affairs branch, to the unit responsible for all communications with the foreign press. She appeared in a few PR productions for the IDF and told her parents the Film Unit used her because she looked good in uniform; this time Lise and David agreed with her. Two months before the end of her compulsory military stint, and after a very effective briefing with a European delegation, the IDF's Spokesperson, a female Brigadier General, asked Dani if she would consider continuing her outstanding IDF service and going through Officers' Training. Dani thanked the superior officer for the compliment and queried cheekily if she would repeat what she'd said into Dani's phone because hearing that would make her parents proud. The Brigadier General wasn't impressed, and Dani didn't continue her IDF "career".

Maya Cohen, Aviva Rappoport, and Tamar Rejwan, Dani's closest friends, often discussed where all of them, including Dani, would go on their post-army trip. When the Far East was mentioned, Dani reminded them of the traumatic experience Keren had in India; all four young women acknowledged that they would like to see the Taj Mahal, but they weren't into trekking and didn't even want to think about attempts to "abduct" them, so they said "no" to Asia. They rejected Australia and New Zealand as being "too far away"; as for the States, Canada and Europe, "they'd been there, done that". So they decided on South America and Dani said, "Let's speak to Keren's boyfriend David; he's a med student at Tel Aviv U, but he spent his early years in Brazil where his father worked on special projects. David lived in his uncle's flat in Austria after his mother died. Gabriel, Yaniv's Unit 8200 friend, lived there too. Tamar, you remember Gabriel, don't you?" Dani asked, blushing a little. "David and Gabriel are like brothers; that's how we met him. I'm sure he'll help us plan a fabulous trip." Shortly before they finished the IDF and were at home, David came to the Hofmans to offer a few ideas, trying to keep the length of flights between points in the enormous continent to a minimum and all the girls took notes. He recommended flying to the States first for a few days to get over jet-lag, and then going to Ochos Rios, Jamaica; he told them about a phenomenal tour to reggae master Bob Marley's home first, then a real Caribbean jerk lunch, and afterwards, jumping into a lagoon under Dunn's Falls. From Jamaica, he said, they should go to Costa Rica, to Arenal Volcano which is still live but hasn't erupted for ages, and the area is awesome with rainforests, deep canyons, hot springs, hanging bridges. He would then fly to Buenos Aires, and after that to Chile, then to Peru and Machu Picchu and a short Amazon trip; he'd go to the Brazilian side of Iguassu Falls, then to Rio de Janeiro, and finally, come back home! All in all, two months or so. In fact, he said, he would someday like to do that same trip, or at least parts of it with Keren, who came out to the deck just then and asked if David was ready to go. "I am. Let's go to the Port. I'm thirsty and hungry. These girls didn't offer me a thing to eat or drink!" he said, grinning. "Dear ladies, surf the net and we'll discuss a full itinerary next time."

Dani tossed a napkin at David and said, laughing, "Ooh, such a liar, pants on fire! I offered you a snack, but you only wanted Grandma Anna's brownies and lemonade and we'd already finished them! Have fun in the Port. We'll all do our 'homework'. Until later, *'hasta la vista'*,

Chapter 5

'*au revoir*' and '*Ciao*'!"

As they left, David laughed and told Keren her sister was a "cute but cheeky brat!" Karen heartily agreed with his critique.

In the meantime, the four girls explored the internet and agreed on several sites, minus Bolivia because they all had promised their parents they'd avoid the notorious "death road", even though some thrill-crazy friends said it really was a terrific "rush". A few days later, they reviewed their "to do" lists with David and he helped them finalize their plans with flights, bus and train trips, hotels, B&Bs. He even explained the currency, *pesos* in Chile and Argentina, *reals* in Brazil, and *nuevo sols* in Peru. The night before her departure, Dani's entire family came to wish her "Bon Voyage". Alex was also there, excited about his own upcoming work-related trip to Australia. When Keren warned Dani about "macho Latinos and pretty foreigners", Dani retorted, "Alex, please buy me a koala; I'll buy you an armadillo that we'll use first against the Latino bullies!" Keren left the house without even saying goodbye to Dani. David left, too.

On May 2nd, the four young women flew to New York. At Maya's aunt's apartment in the "Big Apple", there was a telegram from Keren wishing all of them a great trip. After three days of shopping, one museum and a Broadway musical, they flew to Ocho Rios. They all kept in touch with their families via frequent e-mails. Dani said the resort was spectacular and they were thrilled by the sites David had recommended; they vowed to adhere to his itinerary. They flew to Costa Rica and a B&B owned by Israeli ex-pats. Only two kilometers from Arenal, they toured the volcano and tropical park, wide-eyed; their guide pointed out sloths clinging to trees and joked, "It's good that sloths don't have to go to school; they're so lazy they'd never get there on time!" After a day at hot springs and a Butterfly Regeneration site, they went to *Esterillos Oeste* with their B&B host; they surfed in the Pacific and rode horses on the beach; not on David's itinerary, but Dani emailed it was a side-trip they all loved.

Two days and seven hour later, four drowsy girls arrived in Buenos Aires but perked up, she wrote, at their hotel in the Palermo Soho *barrio*, a bohemian area with cobblestone streets, weekend craft fairs, chic boutiques, bistros and jazz clubs. At the craft fair, Dani bought Alex a tiny plush fairy armadillo; they named it "Antonio" for Banderas, and if "macho muchachos" came on to them, one of them shouted "Antonio! Help!" and the cowards would run away. She emailed photos of their group in the major sites in Argentina's cosmopolitan city, like *Casa Rosada*, the president's palace, where they imitated Madonna as Evita Perón on the balcony, waving to the adoring crowd. Wherever they went, they saw couples of all ages dancing the tango, so they found a flamboyant Rudolph Valentino impersonator who taught them the passionate dance and they sent their sexy photos home. After Buenos Aires, they spent a few days at a colonial *estancia* in the Pampas; they attended a polo match and, in 'gaucho gear' astride Criollo horses, participated in ranch activities with the *gauchos,* who later, after a barbecue of Argentina's famous *asado,*. performed equestrian stunts. Then they went to Córdoba, a mix of ritzy pubs and galleries of modern art next door to magnificent cathedrals and 17th-century Jesuit ruins.

On June 1st, they took a morning flight from Córdoba to Santiago, Chile, to the Bellavista, old artists' studios turned into a charming inn that Dani said Lise would love. Maria and Rubén, the owners, sent them to *Museo de la Moda*, a quirky display of fashions spanning three centuries, 19th century ball dresses with huge hoop skirts, World War II British and German uniforms, Madonna's conical bra designed by Jean Paul Gaultier, footballer Maradona's uniforms. Then Rubén took them to Xscape to rent skis for a trip to the Andes; he said if they waited to rent skis at the slopes, such *hermosa niñas* would be robbed by the resort's *banditos*. They toured Valparaiso, a 16th-century town built on 43 hills, with narrow winding streets and funiculars, and they went to Chile's wine area; Dani emailed it was hard to believe she strolled on a Pacific Ocean beach one day and would be skiing in the Andes the next. In Rubén's minibus, they drove 2-hours up to Portillo, the highest mountain in South America and the oldest ski area. Even though Israel was no winter "mecca", all four girls were expert skiers. After lunch, Maria and Rubén said *"Hasta la vista"* and the girls spent the afternoon skiing. The next morning they traveled up to the slopes via an elevator inside the hotel, and in the late afternoon, they flew back to Santiago by helicopter; they returned their ski equipment, and went "home" to the Bellavista for the night, exhausted, but eager to send emails about their fabulous experience. The next morning, a short flight brought them to Calama, where Mateo, the private guide provided by their hotel, drove them to Chaxa where whooshing sounds caused by air pushing off broad wings announced takeoffs and landings at very close range by a large flock of flamingos. After they photographed the unique sight, Mateo took them to the posh Awasi Hotel in San Pedro de Atacama, where they had a vegetarian cooking lesson with Chef Juan Pablo Mardones; in the evening, he winked at them from the Open Kitchen as he served the gourmet dinner

Chapter 5

they'd helped prepare. Then Mateo drove them to a 2-hour celestial exploration at the Ahlarkapin Observatory: they learned how to read a sky map and pinpoint constellations and stars; they saw Mars, Saturn, Virgo, and nebulae in vivid color, but the most incredible sight was the Boötid meteor shower; they were told it was pure luck that they happened to be there when the phenomenon occurred. Dani emailed "We've seen many images of Saturn's rings, but seeing them with my own eyes, even through a huge telescope, is something I'll never forget." The next day Mateo took them to Atacama, the driest desert on earth, so dry children living there have never seen rain, so dry NASA, the US space agency, chose it for research to detect life in the sterile environment of Mars. Later, Mateo photographed all of them standing under *Mano de Desierto*, an enormous sculpture of a hand, and then next to petroglyphs, rock paintings created 10,000 years earlier. They went shopping in the "pedestrian only" Avenida Caracoles and Dani bought small boxes with reproductions of petroglyphs, weightless vicuña shawls, and lapis lazuli earrings for her mother, Keren and herself. Before they left Awasi after another superb meal, Chef Juan gave Dani a flash drive with his recipes *"para su abuela, chica"*, for your grandma; Dani hugged him and said, "*Toda raba*, Juan. That's Hebrew for *muchas gracias*." In Santiago, she was happy to spend another night at the Bellavista before a 6:30 a.m. flight to Cuzco, Peru.

The concierge at their Cuzco hotel suggested a walking tour: *Qurikancha*, the most important Inca temple, dedicated to the Sun God, then after a steep climb, artisan workshops in *Barrio San Blas*. They couldn't resist happy hour in the Cross Keys, an English-style pub, where they met Canadian twins who were backpacking around the world with their Australian cousins. They told the girls about their rigorous 4-day trek to Machu Picchu and suggested the girls join them on an excursion to Lake Titicaca; one Aussie said the Israelis came from the land of the lowest place on earth, the Dead Sea, so they should see the world's highest lake. The girls agreed and they shared pub-grub and pints of Guinness. The next day, they met their new friends and flew to Juliaca Airport and Lake Titicaca; they cruised the lake and the unique Uros Floating Islands made of reeds. They went to the Coca Museum with its odd historical, medicinal and cultural exhibits of the coca plant and its uses; although the texts in English were dull, the old Coca-Cola ads and photographs were amusing. Dani sent a teasing email to David about this delightful non-itinerary side-trip.; The backpackers went on to Bolivia, joking that if they survived the "death road", they'd come to Israel someday. And then it was back to Cuzco for the girls; they booked a one-day trip to Machu Picchu and none of them felt guilty about not even trying the Inca Trail. Instead, they'd see the 15th-century Inca citadel without trekking. They boarded a train before dawn for a 2-hour ride through the mountains to *Aguas Calientes*, the small village at the base of Machu Picchu; then a bus shuttle to *Intipunku*, the Sun Gate. Given how many photos they'd seen and how much they knew about Israeli archaeology, they expected Machu Picchu to be anticlimactic, until their first look at the truly breathtaking site! They ascended the ancient stone "stairway to heaven" in 35 minutes and viewed the spectacular ancient grey stone city. Their guide told them Machu Picchu differed from all the other new wonders of the world in two ways: first, its mystery as nobody knew why it had been built and then abandoned, and second, its "unreachable" location which preserved its beauty. Dani wrote that among the 200+ buildings, they saw the Temple of the Sun, the Temple of the Condor and the Funerary Rock used for sacrifices. They posed for photos with their English-speaking guide, and returned to Cuzco. On the train, still awestruck, they emailed their families.

Their next stop was Lima; their original itinerary gave them only a few days, concentrating on the highlights: *El Malecón*, the six-mile stretch of parks along the cliffs above the Pacific Ocean in Miraflores, once an area of *quintas*, country farms, but now replaced by modern skyscrapers. They loved their pink adobe hotel, one of the last *quintas*, but were astounded to see a "Starbucks" sign on its façade but no coffee shop inside. At *Parque del Amor*, they saw the huge sculpture of a kissing couple, and the whimsical Gaudi-type seats with the names of famous lovers inscribed in the tiles. They went to the Larco Museum with its Inca mummies and erotic archaeological exhibits, not phallic symbols but clay pots portraying sexual acts, like Pompeii's frescoes or the *Kama Sutra*. Dani wrote that they were amused by the shocked expressions of other visitors. They went to *Plaza Mayor* at twilight when Lima burst into brilliant nightlife and they sampled *pisco sours*, the national cocktail. Taking the suggestion of their concierge, they flew to a UNESCO World Heritage Site, the Nazca Lines, ancient zoomorphic geoglyphs in a high, arid plateau 80 kilometers in length in the desert south of Lima; visible only from the air, the lines were created between 500 BCE and 500 CE and they had probably been naturally preserved due to the dryness and the windless climate, After the tour, when Jorge, their pilot-guide, was driving them to the *quinta*,

Chapter 5

Dani phoned her parents and exclaimed, "I don't want to leave Lima. I love it! What's so special about the Amazon jungle, Iguazu Falls, or Rio? I want to stay here, maybe forever!" Her friends laughed and reminded her that David's father expected to see them in Brazil in less than two weeks, so they'd be leaving Lima the next day to see "what's so special" about the Amazon jungle. As he said *"Vaya con Dios"*, Jorge told them the Amazon wasn't just special, it was magnificent, not like anything else they had ever seen or done. And he told Dani she would no longer wonder what was so special after swimming with pink dolphins! He promised she was really "gonna love it!" They flew to Iquitos early the next morning and were greeted by a local guide who helped them store most of their luggage in secure airport lockers and buy a few necessities, sunblock, insect repellent and anti-itch cream; a bit worried, they emailed home as they went on a 3-hour speedboat trip to Muyuna Lodge, a secluded, luxurious inn in the Amazon rainforest. Muyuna was perfect for travelers who weren't into trekking and camping outdoors. Dani and her friends did everything except fishing for piranha; daytime and nocturnal canoeing, taking photos of exotic fauna and flora, playing soccer with children in a local village. On their last morning, they went swimming with pink dolphins, the magical part of their Amazon trip. "Jorge was right," Dani said, "It isn't just special, it's absolutely *magnífico*!"

After returning to Iquitos, they flew to Foz do Iguaçu on the Brazilian side of the fabulous falls, to the Belmond Hotel das Cataratas. David had told them it was the only resort inside Iguassu Park, so its guests could explore the sites even when the park was closed; before going to their rooms, the girls went out for their first view of the majestic falls reflecting all the brilliant colors of the setting sun. Later, Dani emailed they'd received a discount at the luxurious hotel after a phone call to the manager from David's father, very well-known throughout Brazil for his engineering achievements. The following morning, a boat ride, a walkway allowing them to get close to the falls in rain ponchos, and helicopter flips over the falls offered unlimited opportunities to photograph Iguassu's splendor. At dinner in the veranda restaurant, they saw the cast of "Indiana Jones and the Kingdom of the Crystal Skull" which was being filmed at the falls. Needless to say, the girls didn't "waste" time on the falls that night; instead they gawked at Harrison Ford and Shia LaBeouf, but at the request of the maître d'hôtel, they didn't attempt to approach the actors for autographs, although Dani emailed that both Ford and LaBeouf winked at them.

Then they went to the Belmond Copacabana Palace in Rio de Janeiro. Their luxurious rooms with art deco fixtures overlooked the famous beach, and they emailed photos of the almost decadent splendor to their parents. Their went to Corcovado and "Christ the Redeemer", Rio's cultural icon, and saw Sugarloaf, the peak jutting out into the Atlantic Ocean. In the hotel boutique, they bought bikinis and went to the beach made famous by Antonio Carlo Jobim's song. But tall and tan and young and lovely as the Israeli girls were, nobody said "Ah-h!" Everyone was far too busy drinking icy beer or *cachaça*, or playing *footvolley*. Dani said, "I guess we're just not as pretty as the girl from Ipanema!" The only trouble the girls encountered on their entire trip happened on the white sands of Copacabana. As they were strolling, a few young men lolling on towels and smoking, whistled and catcalled; one snickered *"mi vida, mi princesa"* and another licked his lips lasciviously. The girls moved on quickly. Suddenly Maya felt a knife cutting through her money-belt and she was pushed to the ground; her leg hit the attacker sharply under his knee and he went down, but he stood up, dropped the belt and ran away. Another hoodlum shoved Dani face down in the sand and snatched her beach-bag. She yelled to Aviva and Tamar ahead of them, "Call Antonio!" but her assailant also ran away. Maya helped Dani to her feet as a lifeguard further down the beach blew his whistle and hurried to them, but both thugs had fled in the opposite direction. The girls said they'd been warned about snatch-and-grab-muggings in Rio, and their things contained only tissues and a magazine. The lifeguard told Maya she shouldn't have tried to fight back because *el ladrón* had a knife; he also told them to report the attack to hotel security. They did. The head of security said, "Stroll along the Promenade; that's like getting back on a horse after a fall. It's safe there." But they'd lost their appreciation for Rio, and wondered if they should email their families about the incident.

At the hotel, Dani had a message from David's father; she called him and when she told him about the misadventure, he said, "Thank God you weren't hurt. Try to enjoy the rest of your time in Rio; I'll see you soon." They didn't expect to see him quite so soon, but when they were going to dinner, a tall, well-dressed middle-aged man said, "*Shalom*, Dani. You're even prettier than the photo David sent me. After your experience today, I've decided to treat you to something special to prove that Brazil isn't all bad!" He was staying at the hotel for business, and he'd arranged for them to have dinner in Cipriani's, the hotel's famous restaurant. He ordered scotch for himself and

Chapter 5

champagne with fresh peach juice for the girls. He winked and said, "*L'Chaim!* Now let the fun begin!" In a unique culinary adventure, guests followed the chef who prepared various dishes inspired by that day's fresh ingredients. Dani and her friends were delighted with the lavish meal and the chef's explanations, and with Eli Rosenzweig. Later, he took them to *Boteco Belmonte*, a traditional mecca for *Cariocas*, a bar packed with young people, but the atmosphere was easygoing, with *caipirinha* or beer on tap. Eli told them the bar's motto was "No one is allowed to leave here sober!" After drinks, he asked if they'd changed their feelings about Rio; they said they liked it more, but as Dani emailed David, only because of Eli! Despite no hangovers, they spent their last day in Rio at the hotel, enjoying brunch near the pool, a massage at the spa, and a samba lesson.

Their 3-hour flight to Recife the next morning was pleasant, but when he saw their vast amount of luggage, Eli exclaimed, "Only women need so much! I'm flying to Israel first class next Tuesday, so give me anything you want to send back, and I'll give your things to David, although they'll take up half his flat! You'll sort it out when you get home." Aviva asked why he was so nice to them. He laughed and replied, "I'm a nice guy! Dani's family is wonderful to my son who's in love with Keren, so maybe we'll be *mishpocha* someday!" Eli's Land Rover was parked at the Recife airport and he drove them to Olinda, a suburb of Recife. His flat was small, so he'd booked them in *Pousada Sao Pedro*, a 200-year-old house converted into a luxurious hotel. Recife was a major tourist city with a vibrant culture, but it also had a very high crime rate, a serious problem for residents as well as visitors; that's why he wanted them in a *pousada* near his flat. He also said his driver would take them wherever they wanted to go. After they checked into the *pousada*, Eli took them to lunch in a charming house with a tiny funicular down to a garden restaurant. Dani emailed photos of the restaurant and funicular and said it was too bad they had nothing like it, or for that matter the *pousada*, in Israel. Then they drove into Recife to Eli's office and he introduced them to Chico, his driver, who asked if they wanted to see anything in particular, such as *Mirabilandia*, Recife's Disneyland? He wasn't disappointed when they vetoed that and said they also didn't want to see any churches or cathedrals. "*Bueno*," he said. "What about the oldest synagogue in the 'New World'?" Laughing at their obvious surprise, he said, "Actually that's tomorrow. The boss will tell you about it. For now, let me decide where to take four young Israeli beauties." They began their tour in *Recife Antigo*, the old port, at the central monument leading into a labyrinth of narrow streets to Eufrásio, the 17th-century Customs House converted into a glitzy mall. But they didn't want to shop, so they went to the old black slave market where its 16th century dungeons had also been turned into shops, and then to the colonial-era prison where convicts had languished until 1973 and was now a major cultural and art center. Dani emailed that it was "creepy" to think of buying anything in those places. The last tour was the unique Puppets Museum, the only place in America that still preserved *fantoxhada*, the art of making string and stick marionettes, *mano-molengos*, and *bonecos gigantes*. All of them emailed photos of the fascinating dolls, and Dani told Chico that the annual Puppet Festival in Israel was almost as old as the girls, and she had seen a puppet version of Maurice Sendak's "Where the Wild Things Are!"

At dinner that night in yet another garden bistro, the girls told Eli they were tired of restaurants, even excellent ones, and they'd really like to make a Jewish dinner for him Friday night. "I'll love that," he said, "but I have an alternative suggestion. Let's do your meal for lunch on Saturday; I have to fly to Brasilia tomorrow, so come with me and see Brazil's capital, an entire city built by one architect in the late 1950s; there's nothing like it anywhere. We'll be back for Shabbat services and a *Bat Mitzvah* at *Kahal Zur Israel*, the oldest synagogue. And Chico will buy everything you need for Saturday's lunch. So, are you in?"

The next day, they boarded his luxurious corporate Learjet, had breakfast on the plane, and cruised to Brasilia. Oscar Niemeyer's elegant and yet whimsical architecture, that embraced modernism with Brazilian sensuousness; it was stunning and they emailed photos. In the late afternoon, in Recife, they went to the *Kahal Zur Israel*'s museum in the old 17th century synagogue built by Portuguese Jews; the new synagogue was built in 2001. Eli told them Recife had been a Dutch colony in 1630 and the Jewish community flourished, but the Dutch were defeated by Portugal in 1654, and the Jews had a simple choice: convert, leave or die by fire. Twenty-four Jewish families, in Holland since the Inquisition and then in Brazil, fled north to New Amsterdam, Manhattan, and built a new synagogue; thus, the first synagogue in the Americas was *Kahal Zur Israel*. Despite other synagogues in Recife, *mitzvot* were celebrated in the old one because of its long connection to the Jewish history of Brazil. After the museum, they enjoyed Shabbat services and had dinner in an elegant restaurant with the *Bat Mitzvah* girl and her family, Eli's good friends. Later, Dani sent an email describing everything, from Brasilia to the history

Chapter 5

of Recife's Jews and *Kahal Zur Israel* to her grandparents and parents who were impressed with her vivid descriptions. Lise emailed that they loved the details…and Dani.

The girls arrived at Eli's flat early on Saturday. Everything awaited them in his spacious kitchen, and they laughed constantly while preparing a traditional meal; the only foreign element was Chilean wine that Eli said was better than Brazilian *vinho*. Dani said, "Grandma Anna will never believe we made such a fabulous Shabbat meal, even *her* brownies!" Maya had already taken photos and e-mailed them to David with loving regards from his dad. In the evening, Eli took them to a local pub known not for its drinks, but for the Brazilian dance *Forró*.

Their last day in Brazil was relaxed. They went to the *Sunday on the Street Fair* in *Recife Antigo*. The streets were closed for footvolley and basketball games, and many booths selling handicrafts and local foods. They even rented bicycles and rode the tree-lined Bike Lane from *Parque Dona Lindu* to *Parque Jaqueira*.

Monday morning, they checked out of the *pousada*, gave Eli two large suitcases to take to Israel, and boarded his company jet for the short flight to Fortaleza. It was hard to say thank you, *"Obrigado"*, and *"Shalom"* to Eli, but with hugs and kisses, they promised to see him in Israel. Then they began the 7-hour flight to the United States. It was the 4th of July, and their flight from Miami arrived in New York at 10:00 p.m. with Independence Day fireworks over New York harbor as they were landing; Dani emailed that it was a terrific welcome to America! In Manhattan, the apartment door was opened by Maya's parents who said they couldn't wait any longer to see her, so they came to New York. The other girls felt a little sad, but Aviva was flying home the next day; Tamar was going to visit family in Los Angeles, and Dani was going to Pittsburgh.

Chapter 6

Shani Hoffman met Dani at the Pittsburgh airport. On their way home she said, "Please stay until after Tammy's wedding; she'd love that. She'll be home in three weeks after all her finals at IDC. Then there'll be so much to do and so little time before the wedding. Your parents and grandparents, Dina and Alon, Yaniv and Yoni, of course, since they're already in the States, are all coming, and Kobi if he can. I don't think Keren or Yael will make it, a second MA in Copenhagen and medical school in Tel Aviv don't exactly allow them time to attend a wedding in America in August. Gadi, his parents and his best friend will get here around August 20th. Oh, Alex is coming, two days before the wedding. It's going to be really crazy here, so please stay."

"You've convinced me, Shani. But what will I do until Tammy gets home?"

"Ted will find things for you to do, and not just busy work! He'll put your IDF expertise to work. We also want to hear about your trip, the things you did, the people you met. I'm so envious. Ted says we'll travel when he retires, but by then we may be too old to do some of the things you and your friends did. Your mom said you even went piranha fishing in the Amazon! Ugh! But swimming with pink dolphins…that sounds terrific!"

Ted put Dani to work; she spoke about Israel almost every day for the next three weeks: to children in JCC day camps, to teenagers about joining the IDF as lone soldiers or studying in Israel's many programs for foreign students, to JCC seniors about "Golden Age" complexes, to United Jewish Appeal donors about Israel's security issues as well as Israel's special problems and needs in poverty-stricken areas. Ted was amazed that the funny little girl who'd been so unsure of her place among her high-achieving siblings, who often said or did outrageous things, had come so far; she was so confident, so knowledgeable, so eloquent, and yet still so cheeky in a charming way. He was so proud of her and couldn't wait to tell her parents all that she'd accomplished in Pittsburgh in only three weeks; he knew David and Lise would be as proud as he and Shani.

After Tammy came home at the end of July, Dani's time and effort went into helping with the wedding preparations. She went with Tammy for final fittings of her gown; on her laptop, Dani created an image of Tammy in her wedding gown so they could experiment with various styles of bridal bouquets. Tammy insisted on Dani being

Chapter 6

maid-of-honor, and Shani paid their exclusive designer to make a dress for Dani similar to those of the bridesmaids and in time for the wedding! At Sak's, Dani found outrageously expensive Jimmy Choo sandals that matched her dress, but since Shani paid for her dress, Dani could afford to buy the gorgeous shoes with their 5-inch stiletto heels.

Ted had rented a minibus to bring all the Hofman "guests" to Squirrel Hill, and Dani went to the airport with him. She was so happy to see her parents and grandparents, everyone; as they hugged and kissed, Lise looked at her closely and said how much she'd missed her darling Dani, who looked wonderful but a little tired, and a little thin. Dani laughed and said that was Grandma Anna's usual line, but she'd been so busy all over South America and then she told them about all the speaking she did for Ted's JCC kids and others that maybe she had lost a little weight. Then when Tammy came home, she became totally involved with the wedding plans. Dani told them she couldn't wait for them to see her absolutely gorgeous dress and shoes! Out of breath, she finally stopped talking. Hugging her tightly, David said, "You haven't changed one bit, my darling Dani! This is how I always love to see you. God, how I've missed you. It's so quiet with you, Keren and Yaniv away. Kobi and Alex have been around a little, and sometimes Gabriel and David R. Their friend Ruth made *Aliyah* last month, so they've also brought her to the house. But it's not the same as having *my* two girls at home! Now, my love, a moment of truth. Will the cost of your dress and designer shoes bankrupt me?"

She burst out laughing. "No, *Ab*a! Shani paid for my dress because I'm the maid-of-honor. So I spent all the rest of my travel money on my shoes!"

She then told her parents and grandparents they'd all be going to a fabulous "Jack-and-Jill" party three days before the big event! Gadi's family and his best man would arrive only a week before the wedding, so Tammy's brother Ethan and Dani decided against a stag-party and hen-night and planned an evening for everyone at *The Space Upstairs*, a performance art cabaret where artists would create a "live painting" of the engaged couple on a projected wedding cake. Originally, only the friends of the bride and groom were supposed to be there, but Dani wanted Lise to see the extravaganza; so we turned it into a pre-wedding party for all, including parents and grandparents. "But if I ever get married, I know exactly what I'll do. Elope! "Everyone laughed and her father said if she was the last of his kids to get married, he'd let her. No one could imagine that Dani would be the first of Lise and David's children to marry!

Dani grinned and said, "Good! Now sit back and relax. We're almost there! *Savta* and *Saba*, you'll have a chance to rest after the long flight. Yaniv and Yoni are at the house; they didn't come to the airport because Yaniv said I'd never let him get a word in, and he was right!" At Ted's home in Squirrel Hill, they had a superb reunion; Yaniv and Yoni had photographs and stories of their trip and Dani had innumerable photos on her laptop, from New York to Brazil: glowing like the phosphorescent fish in Jamaica's Luminous Lagoon, at the top of the stairway to heaven in Machu Picchu, on horseback in a gaucho outfit, on skis in the Andes, in rain ponchos at Iguazu falls, swimming with pink dolphins in the Amazon, but not piranha fishing, and many more. She told them that she absolutely adored David R's father who was remarkably kind to them in Brazil and all about the history of the synagogue in *Recife Antigo*; she told them about the pseudo-Valentino tango instructor in Buenos Aires; she told them about the extraordinary Nazca Lines, and finally she told them about the Jewish meal she and her friends cooked for David R's dad. Everyone was so bowled over by her recounting of the trip and all her photos that she didn't tell them about the unpleasant 'incident' in Rio. With tongue-in-cheek, at least slightly, Yaniv said "I can only tell you about the beauty, height and depth of the canyons in Utah, about El Capitan in Yosemite, and about our dismay when we saw so many homeless old veterans in San Francisco. Instead of personal photos, I'll show you the Ansel Adams prints I bought in Yosemite."

When Alex arrived, Dani opened the door and hugged him. He gave her the koala pendant with its emerald eyes he'd bought her in Australia, and she said, "It's absolutely gorgeous! I adore it! Wait right here just a minute." She raced upstairs. Two minutes later she descended the stairs like a princess, her blonde hair piled high on her head and her green eyes shining, with the koala pendant on her neck. She thrust a tiny pink armadillo into Alex's hands, and said, "This naughty thing was hiding in my luggage. I bet you thought I'd forget, didn't you? He's from Buenos Aires; we named him Antonio, for Banderas, such a handsome swashbuckler as Zorro. And how appropriate if you remember him in 'Evita'! Anyway, if 'macho muchachos' made sexist comments or harassed us in any way, one of us would yell 'Call Antonio!' and the idiotic jerks would run away. 'He' didn't help us on the Copacabana beach, but we survived a potentially ugly incident there. I'll tell you all about that later. In the meantime, I hope my big sister will get the joke about the armadillo! Now, where's your special koala? Kobi told Yaniv you'd been given one dressed like an Aussie. And that you bought hand-painted boomerangs! They'd better teach me how to throw it!"

Alex burst out laughing, almost dropping the tiny armadillo as he hugged her. "You're priceless, Dani, and sinful! I adore *you*! You haven't changed a bit, thank heavens! Your sauciness has always amused me, like my sister Paulina and Poppy, my cheeky little Aussie 'girlfriend', your *doppelganger*!"

"Impossible!" she pouted. "I'm one of a kind, so there's no way I can have a double, not in looks or in personality!" Pompously, she led him into the living room where everyone admired the green-eyed koala pendant that matched her eyes and, according to Shani, was the perfect necklace for her maid-of-honor dress.

As anticipated, the wedding of Tammy Hoffman and Gadi Schuster was a joyous event, and spectacular. To Alex's delight, Dani wore outfits in green or floral prints at all the festivities, so she could wear the pendant. Lise's wedding present to Tammy and Gadi was a *chuppah* in the colors of leaves changing in autumn, Tammy's wedding colors. Tammy and Gadi were thrilled and said the *chuppah* would hang above their bed wherever they lived, just like the one in Lise and David's bedroom, and in Dina and Alon's. The day after the wedding, they left for a honeymoon in New England; both of them would soon be going to graduate school, Tammy to Harvard and Gadi to M.I.T. They'd be moving to Cambridge after ten days. Of course, they took the *chuppah* with them.

Alex also left the next day; he went to Columbus, Ohio for two weeks with his old friends, and then he was going to Slovakia to visit his family. Two days later Kobi, whose last minute arrival for the wedding had been a surprise, went back to Israel and Unit 669. The others spent three relaxed days with Ted and Shani; their only activity being a visit to the beautiful botanical gardens and endangered plant conservatory in Schenley Park. Then, Lise and David went to Washington, D.C., with Aya and Ephraim, Yaniv and Dani for five days; the steamy heat of America's capital reminded them of Tel Aviv. Aya and Ephraim flew home via London and a few days in a cooler city, while the others rented a car and drove to Massachusetts to spend 10 days with their old friends. The school year was already underway there; Aliza was a *ganenet* in the Brookline JCC Preschool, and Gil was teaching at Harvard. Aliza told them a few JCC people had fond memories of cheeky Dani, who loved telling Aliza's children stories about her early years with their *Ema*, her beloved *metapelet*, even how, in her childish bloodthirsty way, she'd pictured Aliza lying bloody, maybe dead, in a street when she wasn't at home on New Year's Day. Lise, David, and Aliza all loved how Dani had blossomed into such a confident young woman who could laugh at herself and her early foibles. When Dani gave an evening talk at the JCC about the IDF, the *Consul* General of *Israel* to New England asked her to write an article for *The Jewish Advocate*, the oldest English-language Jewish newspaper in the United States; her parents were so proud of her latest achievements. David met with his Harvard colleagues, and explored Harvard's three amazing Art Museums with Lise. Yaniv also spent time in museums, the one at M.I.T. with its holography, robotics, and accounts of famous M.I.T. student pranks. At the John F. Kennedy Library, he pored over exhibits conveying the enthusiasm of America's 35th president for politics, and revealing how America had changed after JFK's young life was cut short by assassination, just as Israel changed after Prime Minister Rabin was murdered. All these exhibits reinforced Yaniv's decision to study both conflict management in government and Information Technology in the fall. Lise went to the Impressionist and Post-Impressionist collections at Boston's Museum of Fine Art, absorbing the brilliant use of color by the famed painters; she also went to ICA, the Institute of Contemporary Art, and was startled to see one of her own paintings in the Fineberg Hall of Emerging Artists; in speaking to Jill Medvedow, ICA's director, she learned that they had recently purchased the painting from Claude Aubry's Pierné Gallérie in Paris and ICA had been trying for weeks to contact Lise in Israel. Jill asked if she'd have time to give a lecture about Israeli art; Lise agreed if it could be arranged in three days. It was, and it was extremely well attended for an evening so hastily organized. Betty Gordon located paintings Lise had given to friends or sold at a JCC fundraiser and they were loaned to the ICA for Lise's talk. David, Yaniv and Dani reveled in Lise's triumph that evening, but they weren't surprised; they were astonished, however, when they saw Claude and Mignon in the audience. After kissing Lise on both cheeks, Claude said, "How could we miss this, *chérie*? Both your professional and family life began in my gallérie when David bought *Le Petit Sirène*. Mignon and I have been there for so many *moments le plus marquant* in your life, and even the painting here came from me in Paris. *N'est ce pas*? So, *bien entendu*, we also came."

Their ten days in Boston with all their friends were festive, but their return to Tel Aviv was not as joyous. As expected, Kobi met them at the airport, but Keren, totally unexpected, was with him, and she told them that Ephraim had undergone triple-bypass surgery two

Chapter 6

days earlier, but he was recuperating at Beilinson Hospital under the watchful eye of Alon. She said Dina had called her with the worrying news, and she'd immediately returned from Copenhagen with Richard and Anna who had been visiting. Keren was staying temporarily with *Savta* while *Saba* was in hospital. David insisted that Kobi drive them to Beilinson instead of home so he could see Ephraim for himself. Remembering his mother's breast cancer when he was on sabbatical at Harvard, David was upset that his parents always seemed to suffer major illnesses when he was away. He said he'd never go to the States again because disasters happened to his family here whenever he was there. Lise squeezed his hand and said, "Of course, my darling, you know these bad things happened because you were in America! They weren't 'disasters', since both ended on a positive note. Dina and Alon were only trying to protect you as there was nothing you could do, and professionals that they are, they are the best ones to help out. So, my dear husband the professor, you're too intelligent to wallow in guilt. Cheer up and then go cheer up your father!" As Kobi parked in the hospital lot, all four younger Hofmans agreed with Lise, and Keren, winking at her father, told him to remember that he once told her *Ema* was always right! David said he could acknowledge Lise's wisdom, but he didn't appreciate her sarcasm.

Rosh Hashanah began on the evening of October 3rd; Keren had returned to Copenhagen a week earlier. Since Ephraim was following a healthy diet, both grandmothers and, surprisingly, Dani prepared a few vegetarian recipes from the flash drive Chef Juan had given her in Chile. Grandma Anna and David did all the rest of the cooking for the holiday. In addition to all the grandparents and many family members, Gabriel and David R were invited; they brought Ruth, their beautiful, effervescent friend from the Rabbi's home in Graz. She was staying with David R since his flat was close to both the synagogue and the Hofmans' home; Gabriel bunked with Yaniv. Everyone liked the charming redhead, whose intense viewpoints and irreverent comments reminded all of them, even Dani, of Dani!

Gabriel told Lise and Yaniv he was so sorry Alex was in Slovakia with his family; he wanted to find a way to make Ruth happy with her life in Israel, and he was sure she and Alex were a good match, while Kobi and Ruth were destined just to be 'good friends'. Lise responded with a smile. "Alex will be here for *Sukkoth*, so we'll have a chance to check out your instincts, or maybe it's just 'wishful thinking'." Everyone and everything settled into their normal routines during *Yamim Noraim*, the "Days of Awe", the ten days between Rosh

Hashanah and Yom Kippur: Kobi went back to Unit 669; David prepared his lessons and started research for a new article his Harvard friends had requested; Lise experimented with new techniques, corresponding with Jill Medvedow, the ICA director. Both Gabriel and Dani pored through Hebrew University's *yedion*, choosing their programs for the coming year; and Yaniv reviewed his schedule at IDC, a fixed program. The three of them also found time for fun: water polo in the Hofman pool, a hike in the Galilee, and a few clubs in Tel Aviv's renovated port with David R and Ruth. They went to the *Shuk Hapishpushim* in Jaffa and haggled about a few pieces of furniture and a rug, not Persian as the dealer claimed, for Gabriel's flat in Jerusalem's French Hill, which he offered to share with Alex who had returned from Slovakia. So many people were in and out of the Hofman house for *Sukkoth* that Alex was reminded of his first arrival in Israel four years earlier. This time Yaniv, in Alex's own Jeep, had met him at the airport instead of Kobi; almost everyone was there: the entire family, except Keren who was in Copenhagen working on a second MA. Old and new friends like Dani's companions from her South American trip kept telling David R how much they adored his father. Ruth had accompanied Gabriel and David R to the Hofmans again, and noticing Alex frequently staring at Ruth and Ruth staring back at Alex, Gabriel whispered, "He's not a frog!" She laughed aloud, but refused to share the joke with Dani and Yaniv, even though they told her that wasn't fair. Lise nodded at Gabriel, leaving Dani and Yaniv even more confused. Gabriel talked to Dani's friend, Tamar Rejwan, whom he'd met the very first time he came to the Hofman's house with Yaniv; she had been sitting on the floor with Dani who'd flirted outrageously with him the entire weekend. Now, like Dani, Tamar was starting a BA at Hebrew University in Art History, with Political Science as her second major.

Gabriel, who still tried hard to hide his attraction to his best friend's little sister, liked the pretty brunette. When he discovered Tamar's family was Persian, like his family, but with relatives not just in Israel, but also in London, New York and California, unlike his family, he told her that his father had somehow gotten out of Iran with his mother, his wife, and his daughters, but their life in England as Iranian émigrés was far from easy. Tamar said she'd introduce Gabriel to her father, a professor of Jewish studies in SICSA, the Sassoon International Center for the Study of Antisemitism at Hebrew University; she was sure he would find a way to help Gabriel's family.

Meanwhile Alex, very attracted to Ruth, was reassured to see

Chapter 6

Gabriel's eyes on Tamar and Dani more than on Ruth; he hoped the relationship between Gabriel and the lovely redhead was just a brother-sister closeness from their teenage years in the Rabbi's home in Graz, and that he wouldn't be straying into proprietary territory if he asked her out. About a week after he'd settled in Gabriel's Jerusalem flat, Alex called Ruth and invited her out for dinner; she accepted but suggested a take-out meal and a tour of her studio. That was the beginning of a serious relationship; Lise and David liked Ruth and were pleased to see Alex, their "almost" son, in love. Ruth's jewelry was beginning to be noticed; she worked hard in her studio every day when Alex was in class or the library, and played hard or made love with Alex every night. They spent a lot of time during the first semester of the academic year with Gabriel and Tamar, his constant date. Dani never went out more than two or three times with any of the young men she dated; and even though both Ruth and Alex liked Tamar, they were delighted when Dani and Gabriel finally acknowledged their true feelings for each other and began a love affair as serious and committed as theirs. All four of them spent many Shabbats in Ramat Aviv with Dani's family. Although Alex spent almost every night at Ruth's and Dani slept with Gabriel every night in his flat or in her room in her parents' home, neither Alex nor Dani changed their official residence to their lovers' flats during that first year.

◆ ◆ ◆

On July 12, 2006, the day the Second Lebanon War began, Dani, Gabriel, Alex and Yaniv had completed almost all of their final exams. A week before the start of the war, Gabriel received a *tzav shmoneh*, summoning him to Unit 8200's command base at Urim. Hezbollah had fired rockets at northern Israeli towns, ambushed and kidnapped IDF soldiers; Gabriel was needed to translate Farsi codes and unusual online chatter in order to ascertain the depth of Iran's unprecedented military support for Hezbollah. Dani, Yaniv and Alex were all called to their units on July 12th; Dani conducted briefings with members of the foreign press, Yaniv's team at Urim corrected any errors they detected in the IAF's technical systems, Alex's *Sayeret Matkal* unit engaged Hezbollah's paramilitary forces in more than a few covert attacks, and Kobi's "flying cats" rescued many injured soldiers. Lise and David, all of the grandparents, and Ruth were glued to TV and radio, worrying about their loved ones, until the ceasefire on August 14th. Like most Israelis, the Hofman "extended family" had mixed feelings about this war; they believed there had not been a decisive victory.

A crestfallen Kobi decided to leave the IDF after 33 Israelis fell in 60 hours; Yaniv returned to IDC, knowing all IAF technical systems worked properly, but he was dispirited by serious failings in the deployment of ground troops. Dani, Gabriel and Alex, also depressed, returned to Hebrew University for their remaining exams. A few weeks later, when exam results were published, all of them had aced their final exams. That was when Dani informed her parents she was moving in with Gabriel; there were no arguments from her parents who loved Gabriel as one of their own. And Alex moved in with Ruth. For all of them, the next two years were a time of love, study, work, and family events.

In 2008, Lise and David planned an enormous barbecue in honor of the university achievements of their family members, and two "almost" family, Gabriel and Alex. When Alex told them he'd accepted a position as a military attaché in Washington, and that he and Ruth would be moving to the States in August, everyone was elated for them. Without saying a word to David, Lise announced, "We had a fantastic idea. Since everybody's already been invited, and I do mean everybody from all over the world, for the barbecue in mid-July, why not include another *simcha*: your wedding! Ruth and Alex were flabbergasted, and Ruth said nobody could plan a wedding in so little time. All of the Hofmans laughed, and David said if that was what she thought, then she didn't know Lise, their mothers, his daughters, his sister! Everyone nodded and high-fived Ruth, Alex and each other.

In the middle of July, the barbecue took place. Keren had returned from Denmark after her PhD dissertation was submitted; she hadn't received final approval, but no one doubted its acceptance. Yaniv had completed his BA at IDC Herzliya *cum laude*. Dani and Alex had graduated with honors from Hebrew University and "the outstanding MA graduate of 2008" was Gabriel. Kobi, just one year away from his degree at the Wingate Institute, had recently been accepted into Wingate's Sports Management honors program. Family and friends from around the world, and IDF comrades and officers devoured scrumptious food, played water polo, toasted the honorees with French champagne brought by Claude and Mignon, and partied all night. Alex's family came from Slovakia; Ted and Shani Hoffman from Pittsburgh with Alex's friend Rob Salter and his fiancée. Lise's mother and stepfather had come from Malmö to honor all their grandchildren, and Gabriel's father and his sister Darla came from LA. Most of the senior generation, including the local grandparents,

Chapter 6

Aya and Ephraim, Anna and Richard, enjoyed the food and drink on the deck. As for the younger people, Ruth was giddy after too many toasts and Alex teased that French champagne wasn't her drink. Only one awkward moment occurred during the entire event: arriving late, David R welcomed Keren back to Israel and then immediately went to the pool to congratulate Gabriel, Dani and Alex. Ruth, sitting on the edge of the pool with a few others, said that much as she loved David, he was an "idjit" and she'd like to toss him fully dressed into the pool. Alex asked why, and she said it was obvious that David was still in love with Keren and it was equally clear that she felt the same way. So, she added, she should also toss Keren into the pool. Alex warned, "Stay out of this, Ruth. They're adults and have to find their own way back to each other. Or not. Right, Kobes?" Barely paying attention because he was so amused by Paulina, Alex's witty and cheeky sister, Kobi just nodded. Before the special celebration ended, Alex presented an engagement ring from Tiffany's to his "tipsy tyrant of a fiancée, not a diamond, but a perfect square-cut emerald that he said matched her gorgeous green eyes.

Two days later, shortly before the wedding, Alex returned to the Hoffmans from an overnight tour with his sisters and Kobi, and he was stunned to see the Smythes, even Sir Andrew and Sylvia, sitting on the deck and chatting with Lise and David. Larry told Alex they couldn't *not* come to his wedding after they'd all survived the "Great Croc Attack". Poppy, now an exquisite but still cheeky beauty, reminded him he'd promised to introduce her to Paulina and Dani, so here she was.

Rabbi Jakob Breitling officiated at the wedding. Before he began, the older rabbi, Samuel Breitling, said how proud he was of Ruth, Gabriel and the other teens who'd grown up in his home in Graz, how pleased he was that Ruth was not only so successful in her career but that she'd also met Alex, her soulmate, and mostly how very delighted he was that the cheeky but insecure 15-year-old "*gingi*" he'd first met was now enveloped in so much love. Despite having been organized so quickly, the wedding was magnificent; Alex and Ruth, so thankful for their loving families and friends, especially Lise and David, were ready for their new life. Thirty days later, they moved to Washington.

That August, Dani and Gabriel moved to England for him to begin doctoral studies at Oxford. They found a small flat near the train station and Dani, who had a PR job at the Israeli Embassy, commuted to and from London four days a week. With everything in Oxford centered around the university, Gabriel also enjoyed his commute,

15-minutes on foot, to and from Balliol College. They lived frugally, not wanting to be dependent on either her family or his father; they would have accepted airfare from Dani's parents when the three-week conflict between Israel and the Palestinians, Operation Cast Lead, broke out, but they were already in Israel as it was Christmas break at Oxford; they both volunteered to join their units immediately, but were told by the IDF that they weren't needed right then. Alex wasn't needed either; the IDF said he was far more important for them in Washington. Both Yaniv and Kobi were mobilized, so the family again watched and worried until the brief, devastating war ended.

Gabriel had been offered a position as a teaching assistant in Balliol for his second year; his salary was sufficient to meet their basic needs, so Dani quit her Embassy job. In early October, she began an MA in Art History at the Courtauld Institute of Art, a division of London University. Because her BA grades in Art History at Hebrew U. had been high, Dani's only requirements were two seminars. Impressionism and Post-Impressionism; each seminar met only once a week, so she was able to do her reading and research in Oxford's library. During The Courtauld's orientation session on MA focus areas, Dani realized she was really interested in conservation of ancient mosaics and wall paintings; Gabriel teased her about "going ancient" so she wouldn't step on Lise's toes by specializing in contemporary art; Dani secretly admitted that he might be right. This focus presented Dani with a unique opportunity: to help save recently discovered mosaics near the Sea of Galilee. She'd always been a brilliant student, but Dani had never been so excited about her work. Knowing how much support she'd always given him, Gabriel was delighted for her, and once again Lise and David were so very proud of their younger daughter.

The next two years in Oxford passed quietly and quickly. Both Dani and Gabriel worked seriously on their research, but they also enjoyed visits from Lise and David, long walks along the Thames, and dinners in Holywell Manor, the medieval building that housed Balliol's graduate center. The first time they dined there, Dani said, "This beats shopping and cooking when there are so many other pleasures to enjoy, like making love with my soon-to-be husband!" Gabriel kissed his saucy fiancée as they raced home to make love.

In April 2011, Dani had been in Israel for a few weeks, completing her MA project on controlling the deterioration of the mosaics and wall paintings in the Galilee. Gabriel had accepted a tenure-track position at Tel Aviv University so she was also looking for an apartment. Equally important, she was finalizing the plans for an

Chapter 6

August wedding, but the minute she saw Gabriel at the airport when he arrived three days before Passover, she knew something was wrong. "What happened?" Dani asked after she kissed him. "Has an 'idiotic' professor rejected your dissertation?" He replied that Frederica, his mother, had sent him a long letter but he hadn't opened it because he wanted to read it together with people he loved. Dani said she would have read it at once, but they would wait until they got home; she drove as quickly as the law allowed. After everyone greeted Gabriel, they sat on the deck and he took the letter out of his pocket, opened it, unfolded five pages and read it aloud. His mother wrote about her shock on finding out that her mother was actually Jewish and that, therefore, so was she, and so was her son. She wrote how sorry she was that she learned all of this only after her father died. She wrote about her mother's tragic story, that her grandparents had been killed on Kristallnacht and her mother was adopted by Catholic neighbors and she eventually married their son. She wrote that her fear of her own father made her accept Dominik being expelled from school by Monsignor Dietrich and that same fear made her throw him out of their home and give the Rabbi custody of her son. She wrote that the Rabbi told her that he converted to Judaism and was now called Gabriel, that he had a lovely fiancée and a satisfying life and career, and that he was even in contact with his father. She wrote that she hoped he would eventually forgive her. Nobody said a word when Gabriel finished reading. He said, laughing a little cynically, "There are three additional pages. Documents. My mother is thorough and organized."

"She's hurting, Gabriel, honey," Lise said. "And so are you. You've both been hurting for so many years and maybe now's the time to let it go. It won't be easy to put everything behind you, but you should try. Meet her." David nodded, as did Yaniv, Kobi, and Lise's parents. Grandma Anna was weeping quietly and Dani, who'd been sitting very close to Gabriel the whole time, put her arms around him and kissed him.

"*Ema*'s right, Gabriel. Don't be cynical. Let's invite your mother to visit us in Oxford. *Saba* says Sholem Aleichem once wrote that 'if three people tell a man he's drunk, he should go to sleep'. You're not drunk, but seven people have told you to meet your mother. So do it! Now let's talk about something really important, our wedding!" Everyone laughed at Dani's cheeky comments, even Gabriel, and the tension in the room dissipated, as she'd intended.

Gabriel and Dani met his mother in Oxford three weeks later. At first there was a lot of silence, but finally Frederica said that she would try to call him Gabriel, even though it might take her a while to get used to it.

Gabriel responded with a small smile, "It took me some time, too." Slowly, the ice between Gabriel and his mother began to melt, mostly because of Dani's effervescence. After they walked his mother back to her B&B following dinner at Balliol and said a pleasant goodnight, they strolled to their flat, holding hands as was their custom, and Dani told him she liked his mother. "I always liked her, and not just because I loved my mother," he responded. "But it hurt so much when she threw me out and it will take me time to get past that, but I liked her a lot this evening." During his mother's four days in Oxford, Gabriel's PhD dissertation and Dani's MA paper were both approved with honors, and they even celebrated with his mother. Before she left, Gabriel was shocked to hear himself inviting his mother to their two graduation ceremonies, but he also told her that his father and grandmother would probably be there. She started crying and said meeting him again after so many years, and having him invite her to the celebrations, was a dream come true. She hadn't seen his father for thirty years, but she could handle meeting him if he could.

"It will give you the opportunity to meet all my family before you come to Israel in August for our wedding. And please, bring your mother." Dani tossed out the invitation casually, gripping Gabriel's hand. Frederica blinked, holding back tears; finally she said that she didn't know what to say!

Gabriel teased, "Just say 'Yes'! It's a 3-letter word, so simple even a linguist like you can say it!"

Everyone came for the two ceremonies: the 'pomp-and-circumstance' event at Oxford when Gabriel received his DPhil and two days later, in London, at the Royal Festival Hall, for Dani's smaller but no less gala commencement. His mother found Dani's family charming and appreciated the warmth of Gabriel's relationship with them; they found her equally charming and were so pleased that Gabriel and his mother had reconciled. When she wondered aloud if the two universities could accommodate so many family members; David heard her and joked, "I'm sure Oxford can, but we might have to capture and hold the London Eye hostage for Dani's graduation. We all love to party, so just wait until the wedding; Gabriel's friends and our family from all over the world will be there. We'll probably need a circus tent for that event!" Frederica was very grateful that after her disastrous treatment of him, her son had the good fortune to grow

Chapter 6

up with Rabbi Breitling's "family" in Graz and then to be so welcomed into Dani's loving family. She loved laughing with Dani's loving family, and Dani's loving family breathed a huge sigh of relief, as did their daughter and her fiancé, that the meeting between Gabriel's mother and father went well. Frederica knew she'd never used the word "loving" so much in her life.

◆ ◆ ◆

"Fantastic! Absolutely fabulous!" Those were the words everyone attending Dani and Gabriel's wedding said. The previous summer, with her parents, Dani and Gabriel had compared hotels and events venues in Tel Aviv and Jerusalem, and they booked Jerusalem's exquisite Mount Zion Hotel for Tuesday, the 18th of August, 2011. The 19th century hotel had unique features: a tiered Banquet Garden that could serve up to 500 guests, with a breathtaking view from every seat of biblical Hinnom Valley and the 16th century walls of the Old City from the Jaffa Gate and the Tower of David to the tall clock tower in the Dormition Abbey. Always cool in the evening, no matter how hot the day, and with no chance of rain, Jerusalem was ideal for an outdoor event in August. As soon as the date was set, Lise started planning a *chuppah*. Her own, still over the bed she shared with David, was geometrical, but for Dani and Gabriel she decided to make something unique, a patchwork quilt that would incorporate special moments in both their lives on the reverse side of a geometric *chuppah*. She chose photos and mementos: Dani as an infant with her green eyes wide open; Dani rolling around in autumn leaves in Brookline; Dani on her first bicycle with Kobi holding onto the seat; Dani lighting her JCC *chanukiah*; Dani skiing in Vermont as a child and later in the Andes; Dani, thumb in mouth, enthralled, while David read her a Beatrix Potter story; a red wool tassel from a hat Dani loved; a bit of navy satin from her Bat Mitzvah dress; Dani posing in her IDF uniform; Dani dancing the tango in Buenos Aires; Dani dressed like a gaucho on a Criollo horse. Sadly, the only photos Lise had of Gabriel were some that Deborah Breitling had sent, and a few taken in Israel: Gabriel wearing his first *kippa* and *tallit*; Gabriel standing on one leg, "No? Yes? No? Yes!" in a bubble above him; Gabriel stuffing a *sufgania* into his mouth with Ruth shaking her finger at him; Gabriel *leining Torah* with the Rabbi in his study; Gabriel at the sink in Graz with a dishtowel on his shoulder as he kissed Frau Sarah's cheek; Gabriel and Yaniv in their Unit 8200 uniforms; Gabriel handing Hebrew U's Outstanding Graduate of 2008 plaque and his diploma to his father; Gabriel with a few Qur'ans on his desk in Oxford. Lise had photos of Gabriel and Dani together: playing water polo; studying in the Bodleian Library; relaxing on the Arab rug in their Oxford flat; cheering Balliol's tortoise Rosa in her last very slow race; petting wild creatures in Cornwall's Screech Owl Sanctuary; on a window seat at Buckle Yeat, reading Beatrix Potter stories; looking at recipes with Grandma Anna; drinking champagne at Alex and Ruth's wedding. Lise knew the centerpiece of the quilt would be Dani and Gabriel up to their necks in bubbles and laughing in their huge clawfoot tub. After Gabriel reconciled with his mother, Lise called Frederica and asked if she had any mementos of Gabriel's early years. A package arrived two days later; photos of Gabriel as a baby in his mother's arms, Gabriel half-falling as he took his first step, Gabriel on a pony in Regents Park, Gabriel and his stepfather in Armenia on a see-saw, Gabriel scribbling words that he said were Chinese, Gabriel hugging a scruffy one-eyed camel; Gabriel in the national football jersey of Austria. And she sent Gabriel's bronzed baby shoes. Lise was delighted with all of these mementos. At the bottom of the package, she found a note from Frederica saying she had googled Lise and was deeply impressed; she loved the idea of the *chuppah* and knew she'd love seeing it in person someday. Lise said to David, "I think I'll like this Frederica."

David laughed. "My darling, you like anybody who appreciates your work." Lise playfully punched him in the arm, a habit she knew Dani had picked up.

She had to find a way to incorporate everything in a quilt; she experimented with photocopying the pictures and then silk-screening them on small squares of fabric, a time-consuming project, but eventually she was satisfied with the technique. Dani and Gabriel knew nothing about their extraordinary *chuppah*; the only ones who knew about it were David, Aya, Anna, Dina and Frederica. Lise also designed several wedding gowns, knowing that her mother-in-law's dressmaker would duplicate Dani's choice; she e-mailed the sketches to Dani and said they'd find the fabric on Dani's next visit. Lise's last surprise for them was the *ketubah*; she asked Gabriel to send her a list of what he wanted in the *ketubah* and told him she'd make it for the wedding; she didn't tell him that she would send the details to the artist-friend in Yafo who'd made her *ketubah*; her friend's calligraphy and illuminated borders rivaled those of Italian masters.

Family and friends from around the world came to Israel for the wedding: from Sweden, Denmark, Germany, Pittsburgh, Los Angeles, from Graz and Salzburg. Ruth and Alex came from

Chapter 6

Washington with their infant twins, and Eli Rosenzweig arrived from Brazil to see Gabriel, his son David's "brother", marry adorable Dani. The Breitlings were in Jerusalem, enjoying the summer with their grandchildren. Claude and Mignon, Chloe, Henri and Marcel, in David's words "*Our* French Connection" were at a charming hotel near the Jaffa Gate and Claude was already checking out Israeli artists. The Gordons, Aliza, Gil and their children, the Boston contingent, came together. Frederica had an amazing surprise for her mother and Gabriel: her brother. Following up on Gabriel's suggestion, she contacted the Graz Medical School and a retired professor told her he had sent her brother's transcripts to a medical school in Melbourne, Australia; he'd left Austria a few days after Frederica, changed his name from Friedrich Müller to Ted Miller and married a Jewish attorney. Their son and daughter, twins, would begin university studies in February and were active members of Habonim Dror, a Jewish youth movement worldwide and they were volunteers on a kibbutz and working with Israeli teenagers. Ted and his wife Judy were currently visiting them and touring Israel, just in time for the wedding and a grand reunion. Ted was thrilled to see his mother again, especially now that she was no longer a timid mouse-like creature, Ted was even pleased to meet Darian since his own alienation from everyone was the result of his father's horrendous treatment of Frederica. And, of course, it was a miracle to see his adored sister and meet his brilliant nephew.

The Hofman family arrived at the Mt. Zion Hotel a day before the event and an Israeli version of a rehearsal dinner that evening. Lise told everyone she'd booked the hotel's King David Hall because her husband was her personal "King David"; she also felt the stone walls and Middle Eastern décor offered a unique start to the wedding festivities. She claimed the dinner itself was a test to see if the food lived up to the standard of the samples they'd tasted when they booked the hotel; the meal was sumptuous. After dinner, the young men took Gabriel out for a pseudo-stag party in downtown Jerusalem; they drifted into clubs and bars but didn't find a place they liked; there was too much noise, too many young kids out for the evening, even a few drug-deals going on. Alex suggested *Tmol Shilshom*, a bookstore-café known for excellent coffee and cakes. Meanwhile, the girls had an informal hen-party for Dani near the pool. Older family members sat in a different area near the pool or went up to their rooms. When Keren noticed Dani yawning, she said in the 'big-sister voice' she'd used when Dani was tiny, "Time for 'beddy-bye', 'Danny-Tanny'!"

Lise grinned, Dani hugged Keren, said good night and went up to her room, all alone in a big bed, no Gabriel until the next night. An hour later, she heard a quiet tap on her door; Gabriel was there. He said, "We believe in coincidences, not superstitions. I can't sleep without you and we both need to be rested for tomorrow. I'll leave early; no one will know I've been here."

He didn't leave early, of course. After making love and falling asleep, the next thing they heard was much louder banging, and Lise saying, "Wake up, sleepyheads; there's a lot to do today, so let me in! Dani, please put on a robe and tell Gabriel to stay under the covers if he's naked!"

Gabriel half-choked, half-laughed at her words and said, "I'll be dressed by the time Dani opens the door." And he was, thus earning a loving hug from his soon-to-be mother-in-law.

"How did you know he was here, *Ema*?" Dani asked.

"*Aba* went to wake him and Yaniv, and your brother told him Gabriel hadn't come back to their room last night. But don't hit Yaniv for being a snitch! I knew Gabriel wasn't sleeping in a deck chair near the pool, so this room was the logical conclusion," Lise said, laughing. "Now get dressed and come downstairs for your 'last breakfast as free people'!"

"I don't think I've been a 'free person' since the first time Yaniv brought me home and I laid eyes on Dani after first having a 'crush' on you!" he told Lise, his arm around her and squeezing her shoulders softly. "Let's go. I'm so hungry I could eat a horse if it were kosher! Join us very soon, Dani my love!"

Gabriel and Dani's wedding day was gorgeous; so was the wedding. The only hitch was the difficulty Gabriel had breaking the glass; everyone laughed when he finally accomplished that feat. Jakob Breitling, now one of the main rabbis of Jerusalem's Yakar Center, officiated. The four poles supporting the *chuppah,* which Dani and Gabriel still hadn't seen, were held by Dani's uncle Jonas, her cousin Yoni, Aliza's husband Gil and Alex. Both Darian and David walked Gabriel up the aisle to the *chuppah*, where Yaniv, his best man, was standing. Then Keren, looking very beautiful, walked down the aisle and stood opposite Yaniv. Lise and Frederica, each holding a lighted candle in one hand and Dani's arm with the other, walked her around Gabriel seven times. Rabbi Breitling recited the *kiddushim,* the blessing for sharing a glass of wine and presenting the ring, followed by the reading of the *ketubah.* Lise's friend in Yafo had created a magnificent illuminated scroll, which included everything Gabriel wanted, many humorous: in case of divorce, the court would decide who owned the paintings Lise had given them or the six Beatrix Potter books purchased at Buckle Yeat, or the 30 screech owls Gabriel was sponsoring as a gift for his conservationist wife; the Rabbi laughed a few times as he read the *ketubah* aloud, as did Dani and the guests. They had thought carefully about the order of reciting the *sheva brachot*, the heart of any Jewish wedding. The older Rabbi Breitling was the first to be called. As he chanted *Barukh atah Adonai Eloheinu melekh haolam, bo'rei p'ri ha-gafen*, Gabriel smiled as he recalled his first Shabbat in the flat in Graz when the Rabbi recited the same blessing and Gabriel's "brother", David R, had explained the Hebrew words. Ephraim and Aya, Dani's grandparents were called to the *chuppah* to give the second blessing, followed by Grandpa Richard and Grandma Anna for the third. Kobi recited the fourth, and Dani's Aunt Dina and Uncle Alon chanted the fifth. The sixth one went to David R. Both Dani and Gabriel agreed that the seventh blessing should be sung by Karl Goldsmith because his trained voice would enhance the beauty of the longest *bracha*. And then it was the end of the ceremony. Gabriel found it difficult to stomp on the heavy glass wrapped in a slippery napkin. After numerous attempts, he finally succeeded, and to laughter and shouts of *"Mazal Tov"*, the Rabbi told Gabriel to kiss his bride; and then he invited everyone to join Dr. and Mrs. Ben Shmuel in the Banquet Garden for the reception and festivities.

Without telling anyone why, Lise and David stayed behind for a few minutes to detach the poles from the *chuppah* which they took downstairs to the Banquet Garden, where a member of the staff reversed it and spread it on a table. David then called Dani, Gabriel, and then the family and all the guests to view Lise's exquisite and unusual wall hanging. Dani burst into tears when she saw it. She said she thought her wedding gown and the *ketubah* were the most gorgeous things she'd ever seen, but this, this…she said she had no words! "I do," Gabriel said, echoing his earlier vow, but now it was barely more than a whisper. "We'd better never get divorced, my love, because you'll have the fight of your life over who gets this fabulous work of art, even though Lise is *your Ema*!" After his teasing words, he kissed Lise.

Everyone exclaimed at its uniqueness and then congratulated Lise on the extraordinary *chuppah*-cum-wall-hanging. Claude said he had to have one just like it for the gallérie in Paris. Hugging him and laughing, Lise told him it was such an enormous undertaking that she would only go through it again for the weddings of her other children.

Claude said maybe he'd be able to talk Dani and Gabriel into selling it to him for a really good price. David, standing next to Lise as she received so many accolades, smiled and said, "I don't think you'll be any more successful with them than you were in getting Richard to sell you the 'Little Mermaid' diptych or my sister Dina to part with *Le Petit Sirène*." Their French friend sighed and gave a Gallic shrug.

Non-stop dancing, interrupted only by a very funny skit put on by Gabriel's best friends and Dani's siblings, began. When some guests were ready to leave, David called all single women to come forward and Dani climbed to a higher tier in the Banquet Garden to throw her bouquet. She noticed where each girl was standing and, mentally focusing on her sister's position, tossed the bouquet backwards directly into Keren's hands. "You'll be next, Keren," Lise and David both said, and David added, "We'll be ready whenever you are, my love. Just give *Ema* time to make your *chuppah*." Both parents glanced at David R who wiggled his dark eyebrows like Groucho Marx and winked suggestively at a blushing Keren. Gabriel helped Dani down, and they went back to the dancing that would probably continue most of the night.

"You look absolutely knackered, my darling," David said to a yawning Lise a few minutes later. "And no wonder. No one's worked harder these last few months to make today a grand success than you, not even Dani. Let's just say goodnight to everyone, go to bed, and leave all this noise to the young people. After all, we're not 'young people' anymore."

"Speak for yourself, my darling David. I'm five years 'younger' than you, old man!" she teased, her smile followed by another even wider yawn. "OK, take me to bed, 'perchance to dream'!" They both slept late the next morning. Then, after showering together, Lise packed while David went to the manager's office to settle the outstanding charges and convey his thanks for a magnificent function. The manager smiled, "It was our pleasure, Professor Hofman. Any time you need another wedding or any type of celebration, please think of us. We all enjoyed the charming young people, such a beautiful bride and handsome groom! And that *chuppah*! Please tell your lovely wife if she wants to sell her work, our gift shop will be very happy to represent her." David smiled and said he'd tell her, but he didn't add that Lise was already famous worldwide. When he left the manager's office, David asked the desk clerk to prepare the bill and to have coffee and croissants sent up to his room.

Lise, wearing a long silk robe, opened the door, and a young waiter placed the tray he was carrying on a small table on the terrace. She signed the receipt and gave him a tip just as David walked in. "I ordered coffee and croissants for us. Come sit down." David burst out laughing as there was another knock on the door. "What's so funny?" she asked. "It's only breakfast."

"You'll see," he said, opening the door, still laughing. A pretty waitress came in and placed a tray on the desk. David said, "We may not be young any more, but you know what they say about great minds; we really do think alike! Shall we invite the kids to share our breakfast? Not Dani or Gabriel, of course! We should let them sleep, or…whatever!" Keren didn't answer the phone in her room, but Kobi and Yaniv joined them and as they enjoyed croissants and coffee, they rehashed all the highlights of the previous evening: the ceremony, the food, the music, the dancing, the guests and the general ambience. They all laughed when David told them the manager's offer to sell Lise's custom-made *chuppahs* in the hotel's gift shop. "I don't think he ever heard *Ema* called Lise, so he didn't know he was offering to represent an already famous artist. He had no idea of how much time and effort were involved in creating a *chuppah* like that. Making it for Dani and Gabriel was an act of love for *Ema*. So I'll tell you the same thing I told Keren last night. When you decide to get married, please give *Ema* enough time to make *chuppahs* for you, even though it won't be the incredible surprise that it was for Dani and Gabriel last night!"

Kobi and Yaniv helped carry the luggage to David's car while he went to check out; they were arguing about how to organize the suitcases and garment bags when he joined them. "I'll finish this. The correct way!" he told his sons, laughing. "We'll see you at Dina and Alon's barbecue tomorrow night." Kobi and Yaniv left, after hugging their *Aba* and kissing their *Ema*. As they drove home, David said, "Alone at last, my darling!" But they weren't really alone. There was only one *sheva brachot* party for Dani and Gabriel, the barbecue. But they had so many guests, family and friends from all over the world, that it was two full weeks before David collapsed on a lounge by the pool and said to Lise lying next to him, "Now I really can say 'Alone at last!' I love all of them, but thank heavens for peace and solitude!" Lise, already asleep, didn't respond.

◆ ◆ ◆

A year later, David went on sabbatical again, to Macquarie University in Australia. The academic year in the southern hemisphere is the reverse of the academic year in Israel: Semester 1 begins in late February and ends in June, Semester 2 runs from August to December. David and Lise went to Sydney in July 2012, for the 2nd semester; since he'd opted only for one session, David would teach two philosophy seminars, give a few lectures and collaborate with Neil Levy, a colleague, on an article. Both Lise and David had peppered Alex with endless questions about his time in Australia. With his help, they were able to rent a 3-bedroom house in The Rocks that belonged to a UTS professor on sabbatical in London, the brother of Julia Margolis, one of Alex's friends. The house had a superb view of the Harbour Bridge and the Sydney Opera House from the salon and their bedroom, and it was only a 20-minute drive to Macquarie. They loved being in the heart of a city that had so much to offer; yet shortly after settling in at the end of July, they went to New Zealand with Neil Levy and his wife. Lise couldn't make up her mind about what was more intriguing, the unusual flora and fauna on the two islands or the Maoris, but she knew she'd have unusual elements in her new paintings. Since David was free to travel after Semester 2 ended, they planned to tour Down Under with visiting family members; they had met the Smythes, Alex's Australian friends, when they came to Israel for his wedding, and they knew suggestions from them would be the best. David's parents arrived on December 2, summer in Australia; two weeks later, after David had submitted his students' grades, the four of them began touring the enormous continent. With advice from Liz Smythe, they revised the itinerary Alex had suggested, and they started with three days in Canberra and a detour to Wollongong just because they liked the name. Lise was absolutely astounded at the enormous collection in the capital's National Gallery: 160,000 works of Aboriginal art, Asian, European and American art as well as artefacts from Papua New Guinea and Micronesia. She knew it wasn't enough, but she and Aya spent two full days there while David and his father rented bicycles which they rode around the 11-kilometer artificial lake in the city center after a short visit to the NGA; on the second day, the two men went to the Centre for Biodiversity Research at the National Herbarium, and David almost lost Ephraim in the vast exhibits.

In Melbourne, the next major place on their tour, they stayed in the very odd Rialto, a combination of a 19th century neo-Gothic Venetian hotel built during Melbourne's Gold Rush and two ultra-modern towers with massive blue glass and mirrored facades that changed from dark blue during the day to brilliant gold at sunset. They invited Gabriel's uncle and aunt, Ted and Judy Miller, to dinner;

Chapter 6

it was an evening of exceptional food, very fine wine, and exhilarating conversation in the Alluvial Restaurant under the hotel's atrium. While David and his father viewed only aboriginal and Maori art in the National Gallery of Victoria, Lise, Aya and Judy, an attorney with clients in the art community, went to its impressive Impressionist and neo-Impressionist collections. Lise, laughing at her choice of exhibits, was also very impressed with the Australian Centre for Contemporary Art, ACCA, but she knew ICA, Boston's Institute of Contemporary Art, was far superior. All of them had fun feeding the penguins at SEALIFE Aquarium, and since they knew it was too hot to tour the Outback, they visited Crocodile Lair and saw "freshies" and "salties". To the horror of Lise and his parents, David chose to experience, not just watch, Shark Dive Xtreme. In full scuba gear, he came face-to-face with great whites and tiger sharks; Lise giggled that if they hadn't known where Kobi got his daredevil traits, they now knew! They had rejected a 3-day wine region tour; instead, they booked a 1-day trip in a hot air balloon floating 3,000 feet above Yarra Valley's wineries followed by wine-tasting in four of the most well-known vineyards. In general, Melbourne didn't fascinate them, except for the 88th floor of its tallest building, the Eureka Skydeck and The Edge, a large glass cube suspended 300 meters over the city, in which anyone who craved "living on the edge" could crawl across the floor to view the city from different and frightening perspectives.

From Melbourne they flew to Cairns; adhering to Alex's itinerary, they stayed in the Hilton Double Tree Hotel. It was bizarre to see a gigantic Christmas tree with tinsel and multi-colored balls in the hotel's lobby in mid-summer. In the restaurant overlooking the atrium, they laughed at a jovial Santa Claus with a white beard, red cap, and a very big belly wearing cutoffs; children in shorts and T-shirts were sitting on his lap, as he handed each one a present from the huge stack under the tropical trees. Shoppers with wrapped gifts raced in and out of stores on the Esplanade, carolers in shorts and pointed elves' shoes sang about the little drummer boy; the whole scene was surreal, so different from spectacular but cold and often snowy Christmas holidays Lise remembered in Copenhagen, Paris, Boston and New York. On Christmas Day, they went by catamaran to Fitzroy Island in the Great Barrier Reef, where they walked in the Rainforest and relaxed on the beach; after a sumptuous holiday buffet at the island hotel, they took a tour in a glass-bottom boat and explored the reef. Lise and David, in snorkeling gear, were awed at an enormous school of rainbow-hued tropical fish. On Boxing Day, they went to Kuranda for the phenomenal sights Alex had described: the Skyrail, Birdworld, the Doongal Arts & Artifacts Gallery, lunch in Frogs, although no one would eat Roo, Emu or Croc! When they returned to their hotel, there was a message to call Larry Smythe; he had a week off and would be happy to give them an Outback tour. He suggested meeting at Jabiru Safari Lodge in the Mareeba Savannah & Wetland Reserve, an hour west of Cairns and on the edge of the Outback. They would fly to Alice Springs and Ayers Rock (Uluru) with his friend Tony as guide, and they'd be back in Sydney for New Year's Eve. He said the Outback was surprisingly cool at the moment and they'd enjoy Uluru and the exotic features of the huge Northwest without suffocating; and with laughter in his voice, he promised they wouldn't be chased across a river by 'salties', an experience he knew Alex would never forget! David also laughed and said, "Salesman Smythe, we'll buy all your ideas, but you'll have to tell us the details about Alex's adventure with the 'salties' because he never did." The next few days were memorable, as were Larry and his friend Tony. On the 1st of January, Lise and David telephoned Alex and Ruth in Washington to wish them Happy New Year and tell them about their Outback excursion with his friends. Ruth said she was jealous and Alex promised he'd take her someday, but she'd have to stay away from the "salties"! David's parents enjoyed their remaining weeks in Australia at a more leisurely pace: theatre and opera at the famed Sydney Opera House, a hop on-hop off cruise, cafes, street performers in The Rocks, and a trip to the Powerhouse Science Museum in a converted electrical station; they went to Paddington Markets on Saturday and enjoyed the bizarre dog show Alex had described. Or sometimes they just relaxed on the balcony or in the swimming pool of the lovely house in The Rocks.

Sadly for Lise and David, his parents left on January 17th, taking a long way home with three weeks in China and Thailand. After they left, David focused on his article with Neil Levy, and Lise painted, merging elements from their tours; she was excited about the new colors and styles, but she also noticed that she was working at a much slower pace than usual. David teased that she had "morphed into a laid-back *Strayan*!" and Lise giggled. They'd planned to leave Australia in March and travel home the way his parents had, but with more time in China and a side-trip to India to the Taj Mahal. But before that, they anticipated a February visit from Kobi and Yaniv. At the airport, they were both astounded when Keren entered the arrivals hall with her brothers; Lise instantly spotted the gorgeous diamond and sapphire ring on Keren's left hand. "Ohmigod!" she exclaimed.

Chapter 6

"Why didn't you phone us?"

"It happened just last week," Keren responded, "and I wanted to tell you in person, so I swore everyone to secrecy. David is so sorry he couldn't come; he has some exams. The grandparents know. How could I not tell them! David's father, too. Now, turn around and close your eyes. There's another surprise, a big one." After a minute, she said, "OK, *Ema* and *Aba*, open your eyes!" Lise shrieked, almost collapsing in David's arms when she saw Dani and Gabriel standing with Keren, while Yaniv and Kobi stood there, grinning. Lise jumped away from David to hug the young couple; David said very quietly that he was very happy to see all of them, but *Ema* could have had a heart attack!

Kobi laughed, "We all missed you so much, but this was a 'Gotcha' moment and we couldn't pass it up. Besides," he added, "both of you are healthy as can be. So here we are, all together Down Under. Don't say you're not thrilled."

Lise recovered her composure quickly, and said, "Of course, we're thrilled. Let's go home and discuss everything that's going on, how long you can stay, what we should do. Omigod, you guys, I didn't realize until now how much I really missed all of you. Can everyone and the luggage fit in the car, David? I don't think so. Keren, Dani and I will go by taxi and you can take the boys and luggage." David agreed as Yaniv asked if they all remembered when he said that *Ema* was the 'real boss' in their family; clearly nothing had changed.

At the house, Lise assigned rooms and then kept looking at them, clapping her hands on her cheeks. "I can't believe you're all here. *Savta* and *Saba* left just a couple of weeks ago and they don't know about you and David, Keren. Do Dina and Alon know? Maybe we should call Dina and ask her to tell *Savta* and *Saba* to call us as soon as they get home so you can tell them, not Dina. Will you still be here? They'll be home by the 10th, so you'll be here unless you want to be with David on Valentine's Day. I'm talking too much, like Dani," she said, grinning at her younger daughter, "not letting any of you get a word in; but I'm just so excited! How long are all of you staying?"

Kobi and Yaniv said they planned to stay until the beginning of March, but Keren, Dani, and Gabriel were there for only two weeks. Alex's cheeky Aussie friend, Poppy Smythe, was studying aboriginal culture at Macquarie, pursuing her fascination with ancient peoples that had begun on the Outback trip with her family and Alex. She took the younger group to the vast campus; she and Dani discussed rock paintings and ancient mosaics, and Israeli and Australian conservation methods with experts Poppy knew; Gabriel met two Macquarie linguistics professors; Kobi inspected the Sport and Aquatic Centre, and Yaniv was awed by a research facility focusing on vertebrates and invertebrates in natural settings with minimal disruption to their normal habitat, Fauna Park. Keren toured Sydney University's Mass Spectrometry Laboratory, similar to Technion's and the Weizmann Institute's. In the evening, at the glass-walled Aria Restaurant overlooking Harbour Bridge, Poppy said her brother James wanted to know if Kobi and Yaniv would speak to his Special Ops (SASR) comrades about their IDF units, and then he would take them to Cairns and the Outback if they were available the last week of February when he had some time off. Both Kobi and Yaniv immediately agreed. "What about me? Why do they get to have all the fun?" Keren asked in a mock-petulant voice, knowing she, Dani and Gabriel would be home by then; Tel Aviv University's second semester began on February 24th and Gabriel would be teaching two classes. They spent most of their time in and around Sydney. Gabriel's uncle, aunt and cousins came from Melbourne for the weekend and they went to Paddington Market and laughed at the dog show, had milkshakes at the Max Brenner Chocolate Shop, took the Hop On-Hop Off cruise around the harbour, seeing all the major sites Alex had raved about. They enjoyed a 'barbie' at Julia Margolis's home, and a seafood buffet on a Sydney Harbour Lunch Cruise with Jazz; Lise and David informed them that as pleasurable as this cruise was, it couldn't compare to their two Bateaux Mouche dinner cruises on the Seine, the first the night they were engaged, and the second for their wedding lunch. In her usual effusive way, Dani told everyone she loved almost everything about Sydney, but Featherdale Park was her favorite, the ultimate hands-on wildlife experience: feeding kangaroos and wallabies and their joeys, holding baby spiny anteaters and tiny tiger quolls, being scared by huge 'salties', although a bit disappointing because Featherdale didn't have a platypus; but when they were eating lunch in the Billabong Café, two koalas sat at their table and took some food, even though it was against Australian law to feed them. Everyone in the café laughed when Dani said she assumed these koalas didn't know the law; she said this was the best activity, and besides, who really needed to see a platypus! Gabriel asked his saucy wife how this day compared to feeding the screech owls in Cornwall; she said it was even better!

In an SUV, they drove two hours west of Sydney to the Blue Mountains, a rugged region known for its dramatic scenery, steep cliffs, waterfalls, lush forests and villages dotted with galleries. In Katoomba, a quaint mining town, they stayed overnight at the luxurious Lilianfels Resort & Spa. After dinner, David, his sons and son-in-law played snooker while Lise and her daughters relaxed in the lounge, planning Keren's wedding and laughing at their men squabbling over snooker rules. The next morning, they took a private tour; Tommy, their guide, asked, "Do you want the standard tour or an amazing one with 'WHERE THE…HELL ARE WE! ADVENTURES'?" They opted for the wild tour, of course, and were jostled on unpaved roads off the beaten track, and away from crowds. Tommy told them "aboriginal legends" as they drove through thick eucalyptus forests and hidden valleys, and hiked high sandstone ridges to Echo Point Lookout to view incredible rock formations. From there, they went to the Jenolan Caves, one of the oldest limestone cave systems in the world, walking to the magnificent Grand Arch and marveling at the unearthly light in the tunnels, home to millions of glow-worms. They bushwalked to the spectacular Kanangra Walls, orange and grey sandstone cliffs towering above a gorge so deep that they couldn't see its floor, and stood beneath the cascading waterfalls that descended hundreds of feet to the valleys below. Yaniv said the vistas reminded him of canyons and cliffs he'd visited in Utah and Yosemite with Yoni, but Keren argued they were more like the sites in the Annapurna Circuit; ever the peacemaker, David, told them they were probably both right. They enjoyed seeing brush-tailed wallabies, quolls and, to Dani's delight, a platypus, all in their natural environment. Tommy said, "You aren't in Nepal or Utah or the Outback, but you are at the edge of a wilderness. Listen to the symphony of birds and breathe in the scented air." After a mesmerizing day, they thanked and tipped Tommy and took the short route to Sydney, stopping for burgers in The Rocks and then, exhausted, went 'home' to their beds.

Lise and David were a little sad when Keren, Dani and Gabriel left, but they knew they'd all be together in two months for Pesach. Kobi and Yaniv spent eleven more days Down Under, but six were in the north with James Smythe, who flew them to Alice Springs and Uluru and then further into the Outback for camping out and treks – although they claimed to be sorry that they weren't attacked by "salties" à la Alex. In Cairns, they surfed, scuba-dived at the Great Barrier Reef, rode the Skyrail, and bungee jumped with their new friend. In Sydney Lise and David found it hard to say farewell to their sons, but Kobi said, "To really misquote T.S. Eliot's 'Wasteland', 'March – I know he said April – isn't the cruelest month'; it will be here soon. We'll see you then."

When they'd arrived in Sydney in July, Lise and David had rented the house in The Rocks for 8 months; they'd intended to spend late March and April in China, Thailand and India. But the time with their family changed their minds, and they decided on three days in Bangkok, two days in Agra – and unwilling to be in a foreign country for a non-family Pesach *seder*, home by the end of March. Shortly after Kobi and Yaniv left, they packed and sent David's books and many of Lise's paintings to Israel; she was amazed at how much new work she'd done. She decided to give some paintings to local friends – to Neil Levy and a few of David's colleagues; to their Smythe friends; to their next-door neighbors in The Rocks who had become close friends – with Sally sharing a "cuppa" many mornings when she saw Lise through the window, and guarding the house when the Hofmans were touring. Lise made a special painting for Julia Margolis, who not only rented them her brother's house, but introduced them to Sydney's Jewish society. Lise gave her a Margolis family portrait; all her leftover supplies went to Sara, Julia's daughter, who was part of the Kaldor team, a ground-breaking art projects that had changed the total look of Sydney. Lise and David spent their last week in Australia enjoying the crisp, fresh air of early autumn, returning to sites previously visited and discovering new ones. Three nights before their departure, they hosted a cocktail party at the Museum of Contemporary Art. Lise presented Marge, MCA's director, who'd recently received an OBE from Queen Elizabeth, with a portrait Lise secretly painted. Marge was thrilled with the work and said if it weren't egotistical, she'd hang it in MCA's gallery of international contemporary artists. Lise laughed and told her to hang it in her office or home, but Neil Levy overheard and said he'd loan his Lise Hofman paintings for an exhibition if Marge wanted; she certainly did and other guests who'd received Lise's paintings also volunteered theirs. Marge told Lise she had no choice, she'd have to return to Sydney for the exhibit and bring some paintings for MCA's permanent collection. Marge said to David, "You must be so proud of your talented wife," but before he could respond, Lise said, "Just as I've always been so proud of his achievements!" The friends nearby laughed at the 'mutual admiration society' of the Israeli couple.

On the morning they left Australia, they gave the house keys to Julia with a cheque for the remaining months until her brother's return; Julia didn't want to accept the cheque but David insisted and said he'd cancel the cheque only if she found other renters for the lovely house. They turned in their leased car and flew out of Mascot International

Chapter 6

Airport on a Qantas flight to Bangkok. After checking into the ultra-luxurious Shangri-La Hotel, they showered, and had dinner in the hotel's Salathip Restaurant, Thai-style teak pavilions on the Chao Phraya River; after a superb meal, they enjoyed a performance of authentic Thai dance. As they left the exquisite restaurant, Lise sighed, "Not exactly where Keren and her friends stayed on their trip to Thailand!"

"No, but we also lived frugally as students in Paris – and even when we first moved to Tel Aviv? Only much later could we afford the big cars, a swimming pool, expensive restaurants, thanks to my beautiful wife's lucrative career!"

"Don't be so modest, my darling Professor Hofman. Your first book is still required reading in many universities around the world and you still receive royalty cheques!" she laughed. During their three days in Bangkok, they went to all the major sites, the Temple of the Emerald Buddha, and the adjoining Grand Palace; with so many tourists, David and Lise spent much of their time trying to avoid getting in people's photos, but they still enjoyed themselves. They weren't allowed to enter some buildings, e.g. the Royal Pantheon with statues of the first seven kings, or the two gilded pagodas flanking the Royal Pantheon with mythical demon creatures called *Yakshas*; or the impressive library built to protect major Buddhist scriptures and literature. Tourists were allowed inside the spacious reception room of the Grand Palace, the main site of "The King and I", which had not actually been filmed there and was still banned in Thailand because of inaccuracies in the story. Their last stop was the Queen Sirikit Textile Museum in the 1870 Finance Ministry, remodeled into a state-of-the-art museum with a library and a textile conservation laboratory; in spite of being very modern, the museum's past was still present in the original façade and internal architectural details. Finally, in total sensory overload after the splendors they'd seen, Lise and David went to the very noisy, very busy market across from the Palace, purchased a few purple mangosteens, furry red rambutans and rose-apples that looked like Israeli red peppers; they walked to a nearby park and practically collapsed on a bench, munching on tropical fruit and watching joggers and bike riders. Before returning to their hotel, they went to the highly recommended Platinum Mall, and David ordered a few Egyptian cotton shirts and a Savile Row suit that would be delivered to their hotel; Lise chose very colorful ultra-suede coats for herself, Keren and Dani, and several bolts of gorgeous Thai silk. At the hotel, they relaxed, swimming in the pool and having stone massages in the Spa. Later they opted for the international buffet on board the Shangri-La's private river cruise ship, the Horizon Cruise.

The next day they went to the temple containing the world's largest solid gold seated Buddha, five meters high, weighing five and a half tons. In the past, artisans hid golden Buddhas from invading armies by covering them with plaster; this one was discovered by accident when it was dropped and chipped, revealing the majestic Buddha under the plaster. They went to an Italian marble temple that looked very familiar because it had been the final elimination stop for contestants in "The Amazing Race 9"; a TV show they'd watched at home. Afterwards, they went to Chulalongkorn University where they lunched with two professors David knew from conferences. Founded in 1882 by Chulalongkorn (a.k.a. King Rama V), who'd established other schools that same year, saying *"All subjects, from our royal children to the very lowest commoners, will have the same opportunity to study."* Lise recalled how young Prince Chulalongkorn was influenced by Mrs. Anna, the teacher in "The King and I"; even if the film wasn't accurate, she really appreciated his interest in education. Later, they had dinner in the hotel's "authentic" Italian *trattoria*.

After breakfast the next morning, they left Bangkok and flew to Delhi, and then went by limousine to Agra, to the homestay where Keren and her friends had stayed. Greeted warmly by Gayan Kapoor who remembered the Israelis and was shocked when they told him what happened to Omri and the girls in Jaipur, he felt guilty because they'd accompanied him on the drive to that city. David reassured him that all the young Israelis were doing very well: Omri was a lawyer, Tali and Nina were teachers and working mothers with two children each, Keren was a physicist and they would soon be organizing her wedding. Gayan recalled that Keren had told him her mother was a very well-known artist but even she wouldn't be able to capture the magnificence of the Taj Mahal; Lise said with a wink that she'd try to prove her daughter wrong. That evening, Gayan and his wife Mishti took them to the Oberoi Amarvilas Hotel for dinner, at a candlelit table under the stars where they admired the soft silhouette of the Taj Mahal only 600 meters away. The next morning, they had their first close look at the famed mausoleum, its marble a milky white in the morning light. Like Keren and her friends, they spent hours wandering through the gardens, mesmerized by every angle of the stunning structure, its perfect proportions, its grandeur, its stone inlays, and its elaborate array of geometric patterns. In the afternoon sunlight, Lise thought the Taj Mahal glistened like diamonds against an opaque blue. The paradise garden, the water channel, the five fountains, the beauty of the dome and the four symmetrical minarets all created perfect harmony on the outside to balance the absolute serenity within. Somehow, Lise and David were able to leave after several hours; Lise admitted Keren was right, she'd never be able to capture the Taj Mahal on canvas; but David disagreed. He said, "Maybe not if the Taj Mahal is your focus, but you can paint people on the terrace of a restaurant viewing the Taj Mahal from the side, as we saw it last night." Lise told him she always knew he was a genius and, in her mind's eye, she began to envision several paintings. Gayan insisted they go again just before dusk when the orange, purple and pink rays of sunset were reflected in the marble and the water channel. From the garden opposite the mausoleum, Mehtab Bagh, the vista was spectacular and Lise, in total awe, whispered to David, "It's breathtaking, just like the Little Mermaid when I was five years old!" They stayed in Mehtab Bagh, holding hands, until the moon turned the luminous Taj Mahal both silver and gold, so magnificent that neither of them could find words to describe it. Back at the homestay, Gayan told them, as he'd told Keren and her friends, to go to bed in order to rise very early to watch the dawn coming up gloriously, a soft pink and orange halo around the Taj Mahal; then, he said, they'd be able to say they had seen it all. They took his advice and when they returned to the homestay for breakfast, Lise said she would have to find a way to incorporate the splendor of the Taj Mahal at the different hours of the day into her paintings. Before they left the homestay and their gracious hosts, Lise promised she would send them her paintings of the Taj Mahal at various times of the day and she expected to receive critiques. At noon they said thank you and goodbye to the Kapoors, and left for the three hour drive back to Delhi,. Then they flew to Mumbai, relaxed in the Hilton Mumbai near the airport, had a steak dinner at the Brasserie and boarded El Al flight #742 at 11:00 p.m. for the almost 8-hour flight to Tel Aviv. The only one who knew they were coming home that day was Kobi, and given his military clearance, he was inside the Arrivals Hall.

At home, they were so exhausted from so many hours of travel in one day, from Agra to Delhi to Mumbai and finally to Tel Aviv that, leaving their bags unopened on the floor in their room, they took a quick shower together and fell into bed to sleep until late in the afternoon. They awoke to the delicious aroma of coffee wafting from downstairs as they grinned at each other, slipped into jeans and T-shirts they'd found in their closet and walked downstairs barefoot to find Aya and Anna quietly preparing dinner as Ephraim and Richard sat out on the deck drinking coffee and playing chess. Aya poured mugs of coffee as Anna embraced them, "Such a surprise, my loves! Everyone will be coming to dinner to say 'Welcome home'. Now take your coffee and greet your dads. Aya and I will feed you soon!"

"Are we allowed to catch our breath?" David asked, laughing and hugging first Anna and then his mother, as Anna swatted him with her dishtowel. Lise picked up both mugs and tiptoed towards the two fathers so engrossed in their game they didn't even see her coming until she put down the mugs and caught their attention as she announced with a broad grin, "Thomas Wolfe was wrong. You can go home again – and it's really good to be here!"

Glossary

Prologue – German Words

Mutti – Mommy, affectionate term for Mother (*Mutter*)
Oma – Grandma (Großmutter)
bitte – please
Stasi – officially *Ministerium für Staatsicherheit* (Ministry of State Security), the secret police agency of the German Democratic Republic; one of the most hated and feared institutions of the East German communist government.
GDR – *Deutsche Demokratische Republik*, East Germany

Chapter 1 – Mostly French Words and Phrases

confiture de pêches – peach jam
c'est la tournée du patron – it must be on the house!
Jawohl mein schöne junge Frau! – Yes, my beautiful young woman!
La Rive Gauche – the left bank, actually the south side of the River Seine
bien sûr – of course
fiançailles – engagement
L'amour toujours! – Love always!

Chapter 2

joie de vivre – enjoyment of life, enthusiasm
shuk ha pishpeshim – flea market
haute couture and haute cuisine – French style high fashion and high-quality food
sous-chef – under-chef, second in command
gratis – free, without a charge or fee [Latin]
teken – a tenure-track, full salaried position

Chapter 3

Le Cordon Bleu – the famed French cooking school
Shalom Achshav – Peace Now
Intifada – uprising
buba – doll
brit milah – circumcision, the removal of part of the foreskin from a baby boy's penis.
sandak – godfather
mohel – a man, often a rabbi or a doctor, trained to perform the circumcision safely and according to *halakha*
Kohen – member of the priestly class
Laila tov! – Good night!
metapelet – caregiver
mitzvah – good deed
gan chova – kindergarten
Magen David Adom – emergency medical service, Israeli equivalent of the Red Cross

Glossary

Kupat Holim – health maintenance organization (HMO)

Chapter 4

ganenot – nursery school teachers
Hashomer Hatza'ir – Youth Guard, a secular Jewish youth movement
Eretz Yisrael – Land of Israel
Yishuv – the Jewish community in pre-State Palestine
Kristallnacht – Night of Broken Glass, November 9–10, 1938, when Nazis attacked Jews and ransacked property; the name refers ironically to broken glass in the streets.
Haganah – the military arm of the Jewish Agency
Galut – the Diaspora
Tipat Chalav – well-baby clinic; literally a drop of milk
Farhud – the pogrom or "violent dispossession" carried out against the Jewish population of Baghdad, Iraq on June 1-2, 1941
proteksia – having connections
déjà vu – a feeling of having already experienced the present situation
Adloyada – a parade held in Israel on the Jewish holiday of Purim.
glugg – mulled wine with cinnamon and raisins [German]
Law of Return – "Every Jew has the right to come to this country"; enacted into law by the Knesset, Israel's Parliament, on July 5, 1950
shiva – the week-long mourning period in Judaism
Pesach – Passover, 8-day holiday, commemorating the liberation of the Jews from slavery in ancient Egypt and their freedom as a nation under the leadership of Moses
seder – a ritual feast marking the beginning of *Pesach* (Passover)
Haggadah – the story of the Israelites' liberation from slavery in Egypt
Chad Gadya – a song with cumulative verses, about a small goat, similar in style to "The house that Jack built"
Ma nishtana – The Four Questions, focal point of the *seder*; the youngest child asks the questions and everyone answers; translated into 300 languages
afikoman – a half piece of matzo broken early in the *seder* and hidden by the leader; the child who "steals" is allowed to ask for special payment for its return
Magen David – 6-pointed Star of David
éminence grise – driving force, a powerful adviser who operates "behind the scenes" [French: literally, grey eminence]
chaver – friend
haredim – ultra-Orthodox Jews who reject all modern, secular culture

Chapter 5

Hatzav – a Unit 8200 sub-group for collecting signal intelligence (SIGINT)
"Gute Reise!" – "Bon voyage!"; "Have a good trip!" [German]
tuk-tuks – noisy 3-wheeled motorized rickshaws
bach – slang for seaside cottage in New Zealand and Australia

Glossary

catch the curl – surfing slang: stay close to the powerful part of the wave
Lehit'ra'ot – until we see you again
gurdwara – a Sikh place of worship with free meals for all poor people [Punjabi]
shlep – haul or carry something heavy [Yiddish]
Refuah shlema! – "Get well soon!"
Sheshbesh Tesha – a play of words [pun] on 669, *Shesh-shesh-tesha* in Hebrew; *sheshbesh* is a Middle East game similar to backgammon
zitsfleysh – inability to sit still and do nothing for a long period of time [Yiddish]
Yom HaMeah – trial day, to assign female IDF recruits to units suited to their skills
Doveret Tzahal – the IDF's Spokesperson's Unit
Oketz – the IDF elite canine unit
barrio – neighborhood [Spanish]
estancia – ranch [Spanish]
Museo de la Moda – Fashion Museum [Spanish]
hermosa – lovely [Spanish]
quintas – country farms [Spanish]
barranco – ravine [Spanish]
boteco – a bar [Portuguese]
Cariocas – Brazilians [Portuguese]
cachaça – a liquor made from distilled sugarcane [Portuguese]
caipirinha – *cachaça* with lime [Portuguese]
pousada – accommodation in a restored historical building [Portuguese]
fantoxhada – puppetry [Portuguese]
mano-molengos – hand-puppets [Portuguese]
bonecos gigantes – huge dolls for Carnaval (the week-long festivals 40 days before Easter, like Rio and Mardis Gras in New Orleans) [Portuguese]
Forró – music with various dance styles and musical beats [Portuguese]

Chapter 6

moments le plus marquant – highlights, striking moments [French]
N'est ce pas? – Isn't that so?
bien entendu – of course, naturally
yedion – academic course list
Shuk Hapishpushim – the Flea Market
tzav shmoneh – the IDF's emergency call-up order
trattoria – taverna or bistro, an informal Italian restaurant

– Tale Number 3 –
Alexander's Story
Prologue: January 1, 1993

"We are Jewish!" Lenka Marek announced at their festive New Year's lunch in Žilina. Some members of the family stopped sipping coffee and others almost choked on dessert or Slivovitz. Everyone looked shocked.

"What?" "No way!" "Is this a strange joke?" "How can that be?" "Why didn't you ever say anything before now?" "I don't believe it!" "Say it isn't so!" "Who really cares?" Denials flew around the table, disbelief voiced so loud it was almost impossible to discern who was uttering which words.

Johan Marek held up his hand. "Give us a few moments to explain. This morning *Babička* told you we had something important to tell you, and she said we'd only discuss it after lunch when the smaller children were playing elsewhere. We decided to tell you today because it isn't just the beginning of a new year, it's also a historic day, a new beginning for Slovakia and the Czech Republic. The newspapers and media are calling the dissolution of Czechoslovakia 'The Velvet Divorce'. I think it's a fitting name, and that's why we chose today to tell you, to make it a historic day for our family, but I really don't think it will change our lives very much. Lenka, my love?"

"Of course, I'll tell our story, Johan. You and Karel will be too emotional if you talk about what happened to your family. All of you know that Johan and I met as partisans, but I'm not sure you really know what the partisans did or very much about Slovakia's history at that time because nobody talks about it. I'm an old lady. Žofie, my dearest sister, was born 71 years ago in Bratislava, in 1922, and I was born a year later. At that time, Bratislava was an important center for European Jews; it had about 150,000 Jews, far more than Prague. Bratislava had major synagogues, *yeshivas*, great rabbis. Žilina also had many Jews and synagogues, but not like Bratislava. Some Jewish families were very religious, others were not. Our family wasn't. Žofie and I didn't go to a religious school, we didn't learn Hebrew, and we didn't even attend synagogue, but our Mama made sure we knew a little about Jewish traditions, and we celebrated the main holidays

– Passover and Hanukkah. I remember all the special food. And we had fun, didn't we?" Lenka asked, smiling at her sister seated a little way down the table. Žofie nodded.

Alex, Lenka's 14-year-old grandson, sat at the table fascinated, his hands cradling his chin. He asked quietly, "What about *Dedko*'s family?"

"*Dedko*'s family in Žilina was far more religious than ours. He had two brothers younger than Strýko Karel and himself, and two small sisters. His father, mother, brothers, sisters – all of them died during the war; *Dedko* and Karel were the only survivors, and we don't know what happened to the others," she said, her voice sad. "Now you must forgive me," she said, with a wink at her beloved grandson, "I retired a long time ago, but the teacher in me has to give you a history lesson about things that were never discussed in your schools. I apologize if it's boring."

Everyone smiled at her, although it was obvious that her son-in-law, Janek Novak, Alex's father, had already lost interest in the topic; he sat there sullenly, sipping his Slivovitz. "The story's long, but it will help you understand why we kept our religion from you until now. In 1938, Hitler and England's Prime Minister Chamberlain signed the Munich Agreement in order to save what they called "peace in our time", and Germany annexed the Sudetanland. Germany threatened to annex part of Slovakia as well and to allow the rest of it to be taken by Hungary or Poland unless Slovakia broke away from Czechoslovakia and declared total independence. In March 1939, Slovakia became the First Slovak Republic, Hitler's ally. Slovakia was a fascist clerical state, a puppet regime led by Jozef Tiso. Many Jews fled to Hungary, but most were sent to Nazi labor camps and to death camps. A few thousand Jews remained in work camps in Slovakia. Tiso claimed he saved 40,000 Jews during the war, but now we know it was only about 1,000. His regime was extremely cruel; almost 80% of the Jewish population, more than 110,000 people, including all of *Dedko*'s family, and some of my relatives, died. Not many people know that Jozef Tiso was the only European leader who actually paid the Nazis to get rid of 'his' Jews!" Lenka looked around the table. Most of the family were appalled by Slovakia's history, and perhaps also awed by her ability to explain in such detail. "Once a teacher, always a teacher," she shrugged.

Alex stood up, gave her a hug and kissed her cheek. "It wasn't boring at all, *Babička*. It was fascinating and awful at the same time! I'm interested in our family's history, even though some things were terrible. I want to know more and I love listening to you, so please tell us the rest of it," he said. His father was muttering under his breath and Alex knew it was about him; he was often at odds with his father, so he just said, "Please go on, *Babička*."

"Almost immediately after the so-called First Slovak Republic came into existence, anti-fascist partisan militias sprang up, eager to fight the Nazis and their Slovakian puppets," Lenka said. "Men and women – often just boys and girls – fought together in the ranks of the partisan units, Jews and Christians together. *Teta* Žofie was 17, I was 16 when we joined up; our unit carried out sabotage, trying to stop the deportations. We were idealists, dreaming of a free Slovakia. Some partisans sided with Russia's Stalin and eventually even joined communist partisans, but most of us just wanted freedom. *Dedko* and I met when we, with Žofie and Karel joined the Štefánik Brigade, the largest partisan unit, 1300 members. It was fiercely nationalistic, but it was tolerant about religion, with at least 300 Jewish partisans. One of our achievements was training the Nováky Brigade; it was a great accomplishment. Nováky Labor Camp was in a part of Slovakia with mostly miners and farmers who had no love for Tiso's pro-Nazi government, so with the help of local people, the Jewish inmates in Nováky Camp contacted us, and we joined them, to train them, but we never told them we were also Jewish. Why didn't we tell them, Johan? Žofie? Karel?" They didn't reply. Lenka said sadly, "I don't know why we never told them."

"At the end of the summer in 1944, it was clear the Russians were going to push the Nazis out of eastern and central Europe. After fierce partisan attacks against the Nazis, there was bloody retaliation and occupation, but in April 1945 the Soviet forces liberated Slovakia. Fearing an insurrection against them, Russia distrusted the partisans, so reunited Czechoslovakia became a member of the Warsaw Pact and it was under the thumb of the Soviet Union. Tiso was hanged for war crimes in 1947.

"While we lived under Communist control, *Dedko* and I knew it wasn't smart to let anyone know we were Jewish, particularly when Stalin was still alive. Many of the victims of Stalin's Great Purge in 1936-1937 were ethnic or religious Jews, but they weren't his specific target although some historians claim Stalin's fiercely anti-Semitic attitude was fueled by his long struggle against Leon Trotsky. During Stalin's meeting with Nazi Germany's foreign minister in 1939, Stalin promised von Ribbentrop he would end 'Jewish domination', especially that of the intelligentsia. To appease Hitler and let Nazi Germany know Russia was ready for non-aggression talks, Stalin directed

Vyacheslav Molotov, his Foreign Minister, to 'purge all Jews from his ministry'."

"Stalin didn't want to use the words 'deported' or 'exiled' during the war, so many Russian Jews were 'relocated' to Siberia, especially if they lived in regions vulnerable to Nazi invasion because of ethnic groups targeted for genocide. According to documented testimony, Stalin was sympathetic to Hitler's ideology and once actually said 'Gas chambers may sometimes be necessary!' In January 1953, the TASS information agency announced the unmasking of a conspiracy – the so-called 'doctor saboteurs' who covertly attempted to murder the Soviet leadership, even Stalin. Most of the accused were senior Jewish physicians from Moscow, who had allegedly confessed to carrying out horrible assassinations, including the poisoning of high-level Soviet citizens. All of the conspirators were accused of collaborating with Israel and acting on behalf of American and British intelligence services. A furious article, 'The Simple-minded and the Swindlers', appeared in *Pravda;* it featured characters with Jewish names – charlatans and villains who were naïvely trusted by the gullible Russian people. It was published in all the Warsaw Pact nations, including Czechoslovakia. What followed was a new wave of anti-Semitic hysteria, and a master plan by Stalin to send all Jews, not just the doctors, to Siberia. Many Jewish doctors were dismissed from their positions and arrested. Just a few weeks after Stalin's death, the new Soviet leadership stated lack of evidence and dropped the case against the doctors; soon afterwards, it was declared untrue. Stalin's successor, Nikita Khrushchev, openly stated that the 'doctors' plot was fabricated...a set-up by Stalin,' but he didn't have enough time to bring it to the ugly conclusion he envisioned, thus saving the doctors' lives. Khrushchev claimed Stalin had told Politburo members, 'You are all as blind as baby kittens. This country will perish because you do not know enough to recognize that the Jews are your enemies.' And, Khrushchev added, Stalin hinted to him a few times to find some new ways to incite anti-Semitism in Ukraine, Poland, Hungary and Czechoslovakia, saying, The good workers in all factories should be given clubs to beat the hell out of the Jews.' So, my dears, is it any wonder *Dedko,* Karel, Žofie and I didn't let anyone here know about our Jewish roots?"

"More than half a million Warsaw Pact forces invaded us with tanks to crush the so-called 'Prague Spring' in 1968; Alexander Dubček, for whom you are named, my darling Alex, tried to liberalize Czechoslovakia, and we held out for seven months. But then we became a federation: the Czech Socialist Republic and the Slovak Socialist

Prologue

Republic, which lasted until four years ago when Communism fell in the 'Velvet Revolution', and Dubček was reinstated until his recent death. Now we're separated from the Czechs again. As I said, until now it wasn't smart to let the Communists know we were Jewish, and that's why we never said anything. So, that's enough of the history lesson. Yes?"

Almost everyone was speechless. "Wow!" Alex said, stunned. "Can I ask a question, *Babička*? I remember your parents, but don't you know anything about *Dedko*'s family?"

"No," she said. "From what we found out from their neighbors, they were sent to transit camps in Poland, and then probably to Auschwitz; you know what happened there. My parents may have survived because no one knew they were Jewish; they were hard workers, generous and kind, so they were well-liked by our neighbors. Their life wasn't easy, but they survived the war somehow. Žofie and I went home to Bratislava, and *Dedko* and Karel went back to Žilina; they waited and waited, hoping their family was still alive, but no one came back. Their synagogue survived but there were no Jews to worship in it. Their family's home had been destroyed; so were the schools they'd attended as children. Finally, both *Dedko* and Karel realized there was nothing and no one for them in Žilina; so they came to live with our family in Bratislava."

Alex asked if there were records of what happened to Slovakia's Jews. Karel answered, "The Nazis loved to document all their heinous acts, and I'm sure Tizo's aides helped them, so there probably are records somewhere, but they have never been released. Maybe I'll go to Israel someday to check their archives; I've read that their records are incredible, very complete."

"Someday I'll go there to find out about your family," Alex said fiercely.

"That's enough, Alexander. You're not going to Israel," a scowling Janek said. "Let's discuss something else. All this about the Jews in Slovakia and their history is giving me a headache."

"It's not *their* history, Otec," Alex said. "It's *our* history."

Before Janek could rebuke his son, Helena, Alex's mother, looked at Lenka with a plea in her eyes. Lenka smiled. "I think we really have said enough for today. I know it's been a shock, but I agree with *Dedko*. I don't think our lives will change in any way." Johan, Karel and Žofie nodded.

"But it's already changed my life," Alex stated proudly. He raised his very small glass of Slivovitz and smiled at everyone, including his father. "*Na zdravie* and *Na slobodu,* and to the freedom to learn more about who we are." Everyone drank to freedom, but Alex's father did so reluctantly.

Chapter 1

1996 – 2001

Dedko's prediction proved correct; nothing really changed in the lives of the Mareks and Novaks. Adults worked and children played and went to school. To their benefit, Slovakia's economy advanced at an amazing rate, especially in Slovakia's flourishing automobile industry in Žilina. Johan, in his 70s, advised automotive engineers. As Slovakia prospered, so did the Marek and Novak families, with new marriages, more babies.

Alex was brilliant, popular, a champion chess player, president of the Žilina High School student government, and a star athlete in football and basketball. He graduated in 1996 and was immediately drafted into the military services, a mandatory 18 months for all Slovakian young men. His commanding officers, aware of Alex's intelligence and physical ability, recommended him for Slovakia's unit in UNFICYP, the UN Peacekeeping Forces in Cyprus. For Alex, coming from a landlocked Middle European state, Cyprus was an amazing experience; the troubled island located in the Mediterranean and lying east of Greece, south of Turkey, west of Syria, and north of Egypt, was only half an hour by air from Israel. At first, Alex was assigned to the UNFICYP base outside Nicosia, the capital of Cyprus; to Alex it was like any other big city, like Bratislava or Prague, but – unlike any other capital in the world – it was a divided city, with the southern part belonging to the Republic of Cyprus and the north to the Turkish Republic of Cyprus. When they had a day off, Alex and his UNFICYP friends went to Larnica or Limassol on the coast; with two days off, they went to Paphos, the mythical birthplace of Aphrodite, goddess of love. All the UNFICYP soldiers loved swimming in the warm water of the Mediterranean, Alex even more than the others. He claimed he could see across the sea to Israel, his ancestral homeland. After five months, his unit moved to Famagusta in the north, in the Turkish section; Alex was elated since Famagusta was on the coast and he could swim every day before or after his shift.

During his nine-month UNFICYP tour of duty, Alex witnessed the deep hatred between Greek Cypriots and Turkish Cypriots, two peoples forced to share the same land. It was probably similar to the enmity his grandparents had experienced in their partisan days. The UN's role was to maintain the status quo, to keep the buffer zones between the Greek and Turkish areas secure. During daily patrols and routine activities, Alex witnessed sabotage attempts and hostile attacks on the UN peacekeepers. His fellow UNFICYP soldiers were from many different countries: Canada, Argentina, Paraguay, Brazil, Chile, Austria, Croatia, Hungary, Serbia, the United Kingdom and even from China, but there was little or no animosity despite their obvious racial and religious differences; they only fought over whose football team was the best. They were all in Cyprus to do a job and Alex really enjoyed being in such a mixed group, in spite of the occasional danger. English was the "common language", even though it was often difficult to understand the heavy accents of some of his comrades, but the friendship among the peacekeepers was sincere, especially when they were off duty at the local tavernas or the clubs established many years earlier by the British, who still had bases on the island. On the beach or outside the tavernas they met local girls who constantly flirted with them, but the UN prohibited UNFICYP soldiers from dating local girls, even when off duty; besides, overprotective fathers or brothers were always standing nearby to intervene if the flirtation was reciprocated.

Alex was intrigued by the volatile and temperamental Greek and Turkish Cypriots, constantly erupting into hot-tempered squabbles, but cooling off was just as fast with a little UNFICYP intervention. He had read about the same kind of animosity across the Mediterranean Sea between Israelis and Arabs, but he also knew that the UN peacekeepers' role there was far more difficult, and – given the activism of terrorists – far more perilous than their role in Cyprus.

Upon his return to Slovakia, Alex's CO asked if he was interested in extending his service for another year and becoming a member of 5.PŠU. Since Alex hadn't yet decided what he wanted to study or do "when or if he grew up" – his father's words, 5.PŠU would give him more time to plan his future. And since 5.PŠU was based in Žilina, he could spend all his time off with his family. He knew 5.PŠU trained with the American 10th Special Forces in joint operations: parachuting together, experimenting with novel surveillance techniques, handling surreptitious demolitions, and practicing unusual field medicine procedures. Alex knew his UNFICYP experience in Cyprus plus 5.PŠU, and the new American friends he would make would serve him well whatever his career choices. After only a minute of thought, he accepted the 5.PŠU opportunity. His parents were delighted to have him so close to home, but they were worried about Alex delaying his education. His mother asked if the delay was because of fear, lack of ambition, or just uncertainty. "You're so bright, *miláčik*, and I don't

Chapter 1

believe you're afraid of anything. Is it that you still want to delve into family history?" He had told them about being so close to Israel and not being allowed by UNFICYP to go there even for a holiday. His father thought forbidding UN soldiers to visit a land even more war-torn than Cyprus was legitimate, and it annoyed him that Helena had brought up the sensitive topic again. Janek said, "We aren't actually Jewish, and Israel, ancient or modern, is not *our* homeland." Of course, however, since Lenka was Jewish, so were Helena and Alex, but both mother and son decided not to argue with him again on this subject.

In September 2000, after the end of all his military service – Slovakian, UNFICYP and 5.PŠU – Alex's parents threw a party attended by the family and many friends; his mother had also invited a few Americans from the 10th Special Forces to join the celebration. Sharing a beer with three of the Americans on the terrace of his parents' home, Alex asked when they were going home, and if anyone was Jewish. "We're being 'de-mobbed' in a few weeks, but why do you want to know if we're Jewish?" Rob Salter asked, a little angry. "Does it matter or make a difference in our friendship?"

Alex said, "Not to our friendship. I found out my family is Jewish only a few years ago and I don't know much about Judaism; in Žilina and even in Bratislava, it's hard to find out about Jews and Judaism or even what really happened to my grandfather's family during the Second World War. We have an old synagogue here in Žilina, but there are very few Jews and no rabbi. My father's dead-set against my going to Israel even for a short visit, so I thought I'd go to the United States, improve my English and learn about Judaism, and then come back home, maybe to teach English which isn't a priority here although it should be. In Cyprus it was clear to me one can't do much in today's world without knowing English. I learned a lot in Cyprus and with you guys, but my vocabulary is still not good except for slang and a lot of words I shouldn't use, and I hate reading books in translation. I'll need a sponsor to get a student visa to America, so if you know any Jews..."

Rob smiled. "It's OK, Alex, we know you're not prejudiced. I'm Jewish. My family lives in Ohio and my mom can probably help you follow your dream. When I get home, I'll ask her to send you a letter inviting you to stay with us and study at Ohio State University. That should help you get that visa." Alex grinned, delighted that Rob understood his goal. Thanking him with a slap on the shoulder, Alex went to get each of them another ale.

A month later, Alex still hadn't heard from Rob about the student visa. Disappointed, he thought, *"In all his excitement at being home, he probably forgot."* Alex was working in the office of an automobile factory in Žilina; the job was boring and he abhorred the lack of physical activity. He didn't have the training for a better position; and besides, it was only a stopgap job until he figured out what he really wanted to do. His father expected him to follow in his own and *Dedko*'s footsteps and study engineering, but Alex knew that wasn't the right profession for him. One evening, while drinking coffee with his mother and grandmother, he said, "I'm thinking of going to Comenius University. I can study English in the spring term, live with my Bratislava cousins, and save enough money to spend a month or two in Israel next summer. It's funny, but something inside me wants answers to the questions I have about Judaism. *Babička*, ever since you told us that we're Jewish, I've felt like there's a deep hole inside me and I need to fill it. That's why I dream about going to Israel."

His grandmother's eyes filled with tears and she said, "Don't ever give up your dreams, Alex. I'm sure your mother is as pleased as I that you're going to continue your education, and I know someday you'll go to Israel and fill that hole inside you with knowledge. But first, *miláčik*, fill the hole in your stomach with your mama's delicious cheesecake and then you can fill your head with thoughts of all the different things you'll learn in university!"

But before he put his plans to move to Bratislava into action, he received a letter from Rob's mother, inviting him to stay with the Salters and study at Ohio State University (OSU), starting the second semester of America's academic year in January 2001. Mrs. Salter's letter stated that their home in Columbus was very close to Ohio State and Alex could begin his studies as a non-matriculated foreign student. He was thrilled, as was his family; only his father thought going to university in America was total nonsense. Alex immediately answered Mrs. Salter, thanking her for the invitation. He was granted a non-immigrant student visa at the US embassy in Bratislava very quickly and he used his army savings to buy an airline ticket to New York.

He arrived in America three days before Christmas, and despite tourists overcrowding the city, through the Tourist Services at JFK airport, he found a room in an inexpensive hotel. Christmas in New York was exciting, full of brilliant lights and good cheer. For two days, Alex loved exploring the fabulous metropolis, but he realized New York was a very expensive city when he had to purchase a few necessities. Early on Sunday, the morning of Christmas Eve, he went to the Port

Chapter 1

Authority Bus Terminal, and bought a Greyhound Bus ticket to Columbus, Ohio. He'd sent Rob a letter saying he would arrive two days after Christmas, so he phoned about the change in plans before boarding the bus. No one answered, and he left a message on their answering machine. During a rest stop somewhere in Pennsylvania, Alex's wallet with all his cash was stolen, but fortunately, his passport and his other documents were hidden deep in his duffel bag.

Arriving in Columbus after the 13-hour trip, he was hungry and tired, but rather than using the last bit of money he found in the pocket of his jeans to buy a sandwich and coffee, he took a taxi from the bus depot to the Salter's house in an affluent neighborhood. Lights were on but no one responded to the door chimes, and Alex thought they might be watching TV and hadn't heard the bell. It was bitterly cold, so he picked up his heavy duffel bag and walked around the side of the house to the back door. He knocked several times, but it was no use. *"I guess they're out for the evening and I'll have to wait here until they come home,"* he thought. He took another warm sweater out of his duffel, put it on under his jacket and huddled down for what he hoped wouldn't be a long wait. Suddenly the lights went on next door; Alex jumped up but no one came out, so he sat down again. Less than a minute later, a uniformed policeman came around the back, flashing a light right in Alex's face, and an elderly woman wearing a long fur coat came out of the house next door. "Stand up, turn around and put your hands flat against the wall," the officer stated aggressively. "Who are you? What are you doing here on Christmas Eve? This lady heard you knocking on the Salters' door. She called 911 because she thinks you're trying to break in. Why are you still out here? Are you waiting for a partner to come with tools to disable the alarm system so you can burglarize the house?"

Frightened by this sudden shift in events, Alex stammered, losing even his basic knowledge of English, "I, uh, I'm not a thief. Rob Salter is, uh, my friend. I just came here from, uh, Slovakia. Wait a minute. I'll show you his mother's, uh, Mrs. Salter's letter, uh, inviting me. I wrote Rob that I would arrive two days from now, but, uh, maybe he didn't get, uh, my letter. I tried to phone him, uh, this morning. No one's here now, but there are, uh, lights. Will they be home, uh, soon? It's, uh, very cold out here."

"The whole family went to the Bahamas for two weeks as a surprise for Rob before he starts his university studies," the woman said. "They'll be home on January second. I've been collecting all their mail. Let's go inside where it's warm," she said, opening her door. While the policeman read the letter from Mrs. Salter and scrutinized the passport that Alex took out of his duffel, the woman filled a kettle and sifted through the Salters' mail. "Are you Alex Novak?" she asked, holding up a letter with a foreign stamp.

"Yes, ma'am," he said. Then, realizing what she'd said before, he turned very pale. "January second! Oh no! I don't know what to do. My wallet was stolen when the bus had a rest stop somewhere in Pennsylvania. I don't have any money. I don't know where I'll sleep or even where my parents can wire me some money."

The woman draped her coat over a chair and smiled at Alex. "They can send it to Western Union here in Columbus. My name is Miriam Green; the Salters are my very good friends. You'll stay here until they get back." Then she said to the policeman, "I'm sorry, officer, for calling in a false alarm on Christmas Eve. I think we've solved this young man's dilemma, don't you? At least let me give you a cup of coffee and some cookies. We always leave them for Santa on Christmas Eve!" she said, with a wink.

"No thanks, ma'am. I was just doing my job, and you were right to call. He could have been breaking in; Christmas Eve is a very busy night for the police. I'll head back to the precinct now and I hope that all our calls tonight turn out like this one," he said, handing Alex's papers back to him. Then he added with a grin and a twinkle in his eye, "Merry Christmas to all and to all a good night!" Mrs. Green laughed and told Alex that was a little joke; the officer was quoting a famous poem called 'The Night Before Christmas'. Alex was astounded. An American policeman hadn't given him a hard time although the start of their encounter was suspicious, and a total stranger had welcomed him into her home, and then the police officer left after making a joke. "Are all Americans like this? So friendly?" he asked.

"No, of course not," she said. "Your wallet was stolen! But it's Christmas Eve. The Salters know you, or at least Rob does, and that's good enough for me. I've got this big house and it's just me since my husband passed away; my daughter and my two sons live in their own homes with their families. So sit down, young man. I'll make you some sandwiches and a hot drink. I'm sure you're starving if your money was stolen on your way here!"

"Thank you, ma'am," Alex said courteously.

After he'd eaten the sandwiches and warmed up with a huge mug of tea, Mrs. Green made him call his parents to tell them about his "adventure" and where to wire the money. Then, while she was preparing the guest room for him, she said, "My family's Jewish, but

Chapter 1

we always get together for dinner on Christmas because schools, offices and businesses are all closed for the national holiday. I'll phone Danny, my son, tomorrow morning and tell him about tonight's excitement. He'll say I must bring you to his home so he can check you out. Danny's wife and daughter will be preparing the 'usual' feast, and you'll add something new – a different 'spice' – to our usual meal."

The following morning Mrs. Green told Danny that Alex was a charming young man and everyone would enjoy meeting him. "Uh-oh, Mom," Danny teased, "Are you flirting again?" They both laughed. When she ended the call, she told Alex he was definitely invited to the family dinner at Danny's home; Alex told her once again that he couldn't believe his good luck. He found the whole day amazing. All the Greens were really friendly, and he told them this dinner reminded him of family celebrations in Slovakia. He was embarrassed that he had no money to buy flowers, but his mother had promised she would wire some money through Western Union the next day, and he would make up for his lack of good manners another time. He was also worried that the Green family might not understand his English, but it was not a problem and they all were eager to hear about him, his family and life in Slovakia, his experience with the UN in Cyprus, and how he met Rob Salter. Jonathan, Danny's son, was a student at Ohio State and he offered to take Alex to OSU the next day although the university was officially closed until January 7th, when the new term would begin. Margie, one of Miriam Green's granddaughters, a pretty redhead, was a student at Antioch, another Ohio university. She invited Alex to be her special "date" at a New Year's Eve party, and Miriam said she wanted him to go with her to *shul*, their synagogue, on Friday night to meet the Rabbi and some special members of the congregation. Alex laughed, "Christmas dinner on Monday and a Jewish *shul* on Friday. What a week! What a country!"

The evening at the synagogue was as fortuitous for Alex as meeting Mrs. Green. He received several invitations after the service, including an offer to "fix him up" with an elderly woman's "beautiful" great-granddaughter! A well-dressed man handed him some money folded around a business card and said, "This is a loan, until you have enough money to enjoy America." At the end of the evening, Alex, awestruck, said, "I have no words for the kindness of the people here. With no money and Rob away, I was sure my time in America was over, so quick, and maybe I would be exported – no, deported – back to Slovakia. But I'm still here, and I've met so many new people, and it's all because of you. You, Mrs. Green, are wonderful!"

"Oh, go on with you!" she responded. "I've been a little bored since my husband of fifty years passed away two years ago. I'm happy my children and grandchildren have their own busy lives and still have some time for me. My son Danny may say I'm flirting with you but in my head and heart, I'm adopting you as another grandson. So from now on, we're family! And we'll keep you busy and entertained until your friend Rob gets home."

The time between Alex's arrival in Ohio and the Salters' return from the Caribbean passed quickly for Alex. He was comfortable in Miriam Green's home and he really enjoyed being with her grandchildren and their friends; he was more relaxed with the younger people and his command of English was more fluent. As promised, Jonathan took him to Ohio State University the day after Christmas. Alex was impressed with OSU's huge campus, and even more impressed when Jonathan said OSU's student enrollment was the second largest in America, only behind Boston which had about 30 colleges and universities. When they passed OSU's gymnasium and its skating rink, Jonathan asked, "Do you play any particular sports, Alex?"

"Football, of course," Alex replied. "But not your football. American football is a game I'll never understand, with all that padding and helmets!"

"We call your kind of football 'soccer'," Jonathan said.

"I know," Alex replied. "Rob and his Special Forces friends used to play something they called 'touch football'. I tried to play with them, but I never caught on to those rules. Our football's our national sport, so the American guys picked it up quickly from TV and local games, although they called it 'soccer'. In Slovakia we have a lot of mountains, so we do a lot of skiing. And we really have a lot of lakes, so I swim a lot. I loved swimming in the Mediterranean when I was stationed in Cyprus. The UNFICYP guys and I played a lot of basketball, just friendly and easy, not like a real sport…sort of like your touch football, I guess."

Jonathan said, "My brother, cousins, Rob and I and a couple of our other friends play 'pick-up' basketball whenever we get the chance. That's what we call it here, 'pick-up', with no refs, no set number of players, just anyone who's around. I'll see if we can put something together while you're here, and if we can get an indoor court since it's too cold to throw hoops at the park! Maybe our old high school or the synagogue."

"The *shul* has a basketball court?" Alex asked, astounded.

"Yeah! There's a gym on the lower level. Sports are really important

Chapter 1

in Ohio, especially at OSU, and a lot of kids from the synagogue go to OSU," Jonathan explained. "It's a Big Ten school, not like Harvard or Yale – the Ivy League – where academics are everything, but in the Midwest, from Pennsylvania to Nebraska, the Big Ten schools combine both athletics and academics. My dad, uncle, brother, cousins and I have season tickets for the Columbus hockey team. There's a game tomorrow night, the Blue Jackets against the Pittsburgh Penguins; hockey games are always sold out early in the season, but a lot of people are away now, like Rob, so you can take his seat if you like hockey. Hockey's very popular here, ever since American college guys beat the Russians in the Olympics; I think it was in 1980!"

Alex's head was spinning a little from Jonathan's narrative, but he said, "Hey. Beating Russia in hockey is something Slovakia likes to do, and we do it a lot! I play a little hockey, too. My sisters and I have been skating since we were about 4 years old. My grandmother taught us. She was a wonderful skater, but she says she's too old to skate now."

"My cousin Margie's a great skater," Jonathan said. "You can talk about it on New Year's Eve. How many sisters did you say you have?"

"Three," Alex responded. "One is my twin, Adriana; she's married and also has boy and girl twins. The other two, Nina and Paulina, are younger; Nina's studying architecture in university and Paulina's in high school."

The tired but tanned Salters returned from the Caribbean on the second of January; all of them, especially Rob and his mother, were stunned to find Alex comfortably ensconced as a guest in Miriam Green's house and to hear about the bus trip, the stolen wallet, the encounter with a police officer on Christmas Eve, and Alex's new acquaintances. "Miriam, why didn't you contact us?" Dorothy Salter asked. "You had our itinerary and our phone numbers. Rob and I would have flown home immediately."

"That's why I didn't call. I wouldn't dream of spoiling Rob's holiday treat; you know me better than that, Dorothy. Besides, would you have wanted to deprive me of my delightful guest? My granddaughter Margie's a little bit in love with Alex; of course, she's been in love three or four times this year. I took Alex to *shul* and introduced him to the Rabbi and several members, all of whom offered to adopt him, but I've already done that! Sarah Goldenthal wants him to marry her 'beautiful' great-granddaughter. Be prepared to do battle with me over where Alex will live, your house or mine," she added with a twinkle in her eyes. They all laughed; Alex, too, although he didn't catch the entire verbal exchange in English a bit too rapid for him to follow.

Alexander's Story

On Sunday, the Rabbi and several members of the Board of Congregation Tifereth Israel came to the Salters for lunch. Later, Dorothy Salter said she had to speak to him. "Alex, this is going to sound very strange, but we've been talking a lot about you for the last few days and I want you to know that we have only your best interests at heart. We think you should move to Pittsburgh. The Jewish community there is larger, wealthier, and – much as I hate to admit it – less provincial than ours; what I mean is that Pittsburgh is less 'small town' in their thinking and they can offer you so much more than our little community. If you're willing to move, I'll make some phone calls and we'll give you letters of introduction to the heads of the Jewish Federation, to the Jewish Community Center (JCC) leaders and to a few rabbis as well. We're not trying to get rid of you, but we know there are better opportunities for you in Pittsburgh. Of course, Miriam is distressed at the very idea of you leaving Columbus; she winked at her neighbor. But Pittsburgh isn't very far away, and you can visit us frequently."

Choked up by their concerns for him, Alex couldn't speak.

Rob said, "I'll miss you, mate, but as my Mom said, Pittsburgh's not that far from here. We'll see you all the time." Rob had already started OSU, but a few day later, when he was free, he drove Alex to Pittsburgh to prove that it wasn't far away; Alex came to Columbus many times in the seven months he lived in Pittsburgh. On that first trip, Rob showed him a little of the large city that bridged three rivers, and then he drove them to an elegant home in an upscale neighborhood called Squirrel Hill. When he rang the bell, Rob said, "This is my Aunt Susan's house. She said you can stay here as long as you want. You'll like my aunt, Uncle Henry and my cousins. So, let's go in. I'll introduce you and then I've gotta go. We'll talk again soon. OK?"

"I can't get over all this," Alex said, deep emotion in his voice. Just then the door was opened by an attractive woman, who resembled Rob's mother. "Welcome to Pittsburgh, Alex. I'm Susan Berger," she said, smiling as she shook his hand. Turning to her nephew with a hug and kiss, she added, "Hi, Rob. Look at your tan! I'm so jealous. I want a Caribbean holiday! I hope you'll stay for dinner. Don't say 'No'! My kids will be disappointed."

"I'm can't," he replied. "I have a lot or reading for a class tomorrow. So a quick cup of coffee and one of your fabulous brownies, and I'm gone!"

The two young men followed Susan into the house. "Just drop your coat and things here in the hall for now, Alex," she said. "Come into

Chapter 1

the kitchen for coffee and the brownies." After Rob left, Susan and Alex chatted for a few minutes and then she showed him a door in the kitchen that opened to a staircase down to a private apartment. "This is for you for as long as you need or want it. You'll have privacy when you need it, and company when you want it just by coming upstairs. I hope you'll be comfortable here. And if you need anything at all, please ask."

Once again Alex was astonished by the kindness of total strangers. The 3-room furnished apartment had a fully stocked kitchen with frozen meals carefully labeled in the refrigerator, a washing machine and dryer stacked in the corner; in addition to an attached bathroom, the bedroom had a double bed, two nightstands with lamps, a dresser, a large closet, and a bookstand with a number of volumes and a portable radio. The third room was small, a study with a deep armchair that looked comfortable, a desk, a computer and several books on a shelf above the desk. He noticed a VCR and a number of videotapes on a small cabinet opposite the armchair. While he was looking around, totally shocked, Susan apologized for the old computer, "We set up this apartment for my mother-in-law, but she decided to move to Florida with a friend. She doesn't know much about using a computer, so we gave her this old one. I'm sorry we haven't gotten around to buying a better one."

"This whole place is perfect, even the computer," Alex said. "I cannot believe I am not dreaming. I do not think even in a dream I could imagine how wonderful all the Greens, the Salters, and now you, are. Please, I know my English is not good, but I am so happy. Thank you, thank you. I cannot wait to write to my mother and grandmother about all this kindness."

"Rob told us your family was just as friendly and kind when he was in Slovakia – with homemade meals, a comfortable bed on his days off, and then there were your sisters…" Susan said with a wink. "In English, there's an old expression: 'turnabout is fair play', so this is our opportunity to thank your family for their kindness to Rob. And, whenever you want, please join us for meals. Tonight, of course. My husband and kids are all dying to meet you; but don't let my teenagers monopolize your time and keep you from doing what *you* want to do. Everyone will be home in an hour, so let's move your things in here now. Dinner's early tonight, at 6:00, so come then…or one of my boys will come down here and drag you upstairs," she joked.

The evening meal with Susan's family was congenial – delicious food, a lot of teasing and a lot of questions from her two sons and daughter about Alex's life in Slovakia, about his family, about sports he liked to play, about UNFICYP in Cyprus, about how he met Rob and about his training with the US Special Forces. Finally, Susan interrupted, "That's really enough, guys. Let Alex finish his dessert. No homework tonight?" The teens thanked Alex for his stories, asked to be excused, and then raced upstairs to their rooms.

"They're a bit overwhelming. Don't let them take advantage," Henry said.

"I think they're great," Alex said. "They remind me of my own family."

"I'll help Susan clear up," Henry said, "and then you'll have to excuse us. Both of us have meetings tonight." Henry Berger was an attorney and very involved in Pittsburgh municipal affairs and Jewish Federation activities; he said a large deficit had recently been found in the city's budget and he was called in as a consultant. Susan, also an attorney, was on their synagogue's Board of Trustees and they were meeting that evening. "So we'll just say *Welcome to Pittsburgh*. Settle in and make yourself comfortable."

"Please let me clean up. It's the least I can do after all your kindness and terrific company," Alex suggested, carrying a few plates into the kitchen.

"Don't be silly," Susan exclaimed. "Not on your first night here! Settle in first and then we'll see about letting you help. The kids usually do it, but they came home late today and had no time for homework before dinner. By the way, Daisy, a very nice woman, comes in three times a week to clean and do laundry, and she even cooks. You'll meet her tomorrow. The boys will probably invite you to watch the hockey game with them tonight when they've finished their homework. If it doesn't interest you, just ignore them. I've told them they always have to knock on your door; they can't just barge in on your privacy… because they might interrupt something with a young woman," she said, smiling. "So, 'bye for now."

Alex returned to the apartment, still overwhelmed by his good luck in America. He'd been so upset since his wallet was stolen; he'd thought he was penniless and on his own in the vast USA, frightened that he would have to go back home right away. But so many people had come through for him: Miriam Green and her family, Rob and Mrs. Salter and the Jewish community in Columbus. And now the Bergers in Pittsburgh. With a smile on his face, he sat down at the desk to write a long letter to his mother about the latest happenings and all the fabulous new people in his life, all these unbelievable Americans.

Chapter 1

His letters of introduction and some phone calls from Columbus brought Alex to the attention of some prominent members of the Pittsburgh Jewish community. At their meetings, Susan and Henry Berger had told friends and colleagues that Alex was staying with them, and Pittsburgh's large Jewish community immediately reached out to him with financial and educational aid. He studied English privately with a member of the synagogue, and in a language program at Pitt, the University of Pittsburgh, a short and pleasant walk or jog from the Bergers' home. Alex's aptitude for English staggered his instructors; one of them sponsored him in a 3-month special course at Carnegie-Mellon that granted a TESOL certificate, licensing him to teach English as a Foreign Language, which he intended to do in Slovakia. He also studied Judaism privately with Natalie Gold, an old friend of Rob's; she was in her final year at Pitt and then planned to move to Cincinnati, Ohio, to study at Hebrew Union College and become a rabbi, which she told Alex was allowed in Reform Judaism. Alex spent a lot of time at the JCC, the Jewish Community Center of Greater Pittsburgh, for lectures and social events; he met many influential members of the Jewish Federation of Pittsburgh. And amazingly, people seemed to like this young Slovakian man who was embracing Judaism; he emailed his mother, a math teacher, that his circle of friends of all ages had increased exponentially.

After six months of intensive studying and enjoying many new friends, Alex was both surprised and intrigued when three very influential members of the Jewish Federation – Manny Jacobson, Ben Wexler and Theodore Herzl Hoffman – invited him to lunch. Speaking for all three, although the others joined in from time to time, Ted Hoffman told Alex they all believed Israel was the core of Jewish identity as well as the unifying force for all Jewish communities in America. Furthermore, they were very impressed with Alex and everything he had achieved in his young life; they believed, given his deep interest in Judaism and his military experience with the UN in Cyprus and Slovakia's Special Forces, he could contribute a lot to Israel. And in turn, Israel could be an extraordinary experience for him. They wanted to sponsor him with airline flights and financial support if he joined the IDF, Israel's Defense Forces, and even a university degree, all with no strings if he was interested. Interested! Alex was completely flabbergasted; he told them he had wanted to go to Israel even for a short visit ever since he'd learned about his family's Jewish roots. He accepted their offer on the spot, but told them he really had to go home for a couple of months to be with his family;

his grandparents, who'd sparked his interest in Judaism, weren't getting any younger and he needed some time with them, with his parents, his sisters and his twin sister's twins. All his Jewish Federation "sponsors" agreed, and Alex flew to Slovakia at the end of August 2001.

Before he left, the Bergers gave him a farewell party. It wasn't a surprise party, but Alex was certainly surprised at the number of people who came: Rob and all the other Salters, Miriam Green and her sons Danny and Marv with a few of Miriam's grandchildren, several members of the Columbus synagogue. "We almost had to hire a bus because so many people wanted to come," Rob joked. Susan had invited Natalie, Jewish Federation members and their families, and a few of Alex's English instructors. Daisy attended as a guest, and friend, since Susan had outside catering for the party. It was a heart-warming send-off for Alex as he very sadly said goodbye to all his American friends who'd become another family. Miriam was the last to hug him. With tears in her eyes, she whispered, "Alex, remember, we really are your American family; we've all 'adopted' you. So don't forget us, and we'll never forget you." He hugged her, placing a soft kiss on her hair.

One of his most difficult goodbyes was to Natalie; no longer just teacher and student, they'd become lovers. They'd spent much of their free time at Pittsburgh's theatres and at concerts in Heinz Hall; Alex had even taught her to skate. She'd been accepted into the rabbinical program and was required to spend a year in Israel, so they looked forward to meeting again. Alex left the next day, hoping he'd see all these American friends again someday.

His mother and sisters were at the Bratislava airport. After many kisses and hugs, they carried his luggage to the car and drove to Žilina. His home town seemed claustrophobic, and Alex didn't know why. Like Pittsburgh, Žilina was at the juncture of three rivers. Like Pittsburgh, Žilina was very industrial with a fast-growing economy. But the similarities between the two cities ended there. Pittsburgh was glass and steel, with high-rising inner city buildings, spacious and attractive suburbs. Pittsburgh was a city with vast cultural offerings; in a word, it was sophisticated and Alex understood why it had been voted "America's most desirable place to live" a number of times. Žilina, on the other hand, was provincial, with low, old-fashioned buildings and little to offer culturally. Though he loved his family and was happy to see them, even his father, he felt a little uncomfortable in his old family home. Everyone loved all the small gifts he'd brought and hearing about his "adventures" in America; everyone enjoyed his stories. Everyone except his father. Alex helped

Chapter 1

his sisters with English; he even taught his niece and nephew a few words and expressions. His grandparents were getting older, but they were still vigorous and interested in everything he'd learned, and was still learning, about Judaism. They were astounded at the support and generosity of the Jewish community in America, especially the sponsorship and funds so Alex could live in Israel, join the Israeli army and study there afterwards.

Only his father was negative, grumbling about Alex selling his soul to the devil. Alex realized he'd have to leave Žilina sooner than he'd originally planned because he couldn't cope with his father's prejudices and outright cynicism. He knew his father was disappointed in his only son; his father had hoped Alex would study engineering, start a family with a local girl and carve a comfortable life for himself in Žilina. But Alex had learned that his life was his own, and it was his right to follow his own dreams, the dreams already on their way to being fulfilled thanks to his Pittsburgh benefactors.

Less than two weeks after Alex's return to Slovakia, on September 11th, he was as horrified as people all over the world at the devastation wreaked on New York City and Washington by the cataclysmic 9/11 terrorist attacks on the World Trade Center and the Pentagon. He was also very concerned about United Airlines Flight 93, the plane hijacked in New Jersey, and then brought down by its courageous passengers in a Pennsylvania field, only 60 miles away from Pittsburgh. He tried for days to call his Pittsburgh friends, but most of the phone lines to America were blocked. Finally, *Erev Rosh Hashanah* on the 17th of September, he was able to get through to Rob who told him none of his acquaintances had been on Flight 93, which had been destined for San Francisco. But the Salters did know a number of people who had died in the World Trade Center. Rob told him his Special Forces unit might be called into action if President Bush and Congress followed through on their plans for a War on Terror. He said he'd let everyone know Alex had called and he would keep him informed about how 9/11 affected everyone. Alex didn't know what else to say; he wished his friend *Shanah Tovah* and good luck. The quiet on both sides echoed across the phone lines and in their hearts long after they said goodbye.

On October 1st, Alex left for Israel; he was still quite disturbed about the friction between himself and his father, but he also knew Israel was really the right place for him. He had booked a 10:30 a.m. flight from Vienna's International Airport; knowing that El Al security for the flight to Tel Aviv would be intense, he left quite early with his sisters Nina and Paulina for the almost 3-hour drive from Žilina. They were all stunned to see their parents waiting in the departure lounge with Alex's twin sister Adriana and her twins. His voice shaking, Alex asked, "Is anything wrong? Are *Babička* and *Dedko* all right? How did you get here before us?"

"Calm down, Alex," his father replied. "Everyone's OK. My car is more powerful than Nina's; we passed you on the road and I was sure you'd seen us, but I'm glad we surprised you. Your mother and grandmother convinced me that I couldn't let you go to Israel with this tension between us. I really do love you and I know I can't mold you into my image of what you should be. I'm actually proud of your independence and what you have managed to do, even if I don't share your love of Judaism, but I'm not Jewish. That's your mother and you and your sisters, and my grandchildren, I guess. So we came to wish you *'Šťastnou cestu'* and to wish you well. Stay in touch and I hope we'll see you in the near future." Helena and the girls were weeping a little as they added their wishes to Janek's and kissed Alex goodbye. As he hugged his mother, he whispered, "Thank you so much, *Mamička, and tell Babička how much I love her and Dedko.* Reconciling with *Otec* means everything." His flight was announced then and Alex left, waving as he mouthed *"Dovidenia! Auf Wiedersehen!"*

Chapter 2

It was hot and humid when Alex arrived in Tel Aviv, like Pittsburgh in August – but it was October. He'd phoned Ted Hoffman's Israeli relatives with his flight number and time of arrival and a tall young man was in the arrivals hall of Ben-Gurion Airport holding a small cardboard sign with his name. "Hi, Alex. Welcome to Israel," he said in excellent English. "Uncle Ted told us to expect you, but he thought you'd be coming in a few weeks. He was here last week but still didn't know when you'd be arriving; so it's good that you called us. I'm glad you're here now because I'm in *Tzahal*, Israel's army; actually I'm in the Air Force, in Unit 669, our search-and-rescue unit. I had a small accident, so I'm grounded and at home until after *Sukkoth*. Uncle Ted told us a little about your military background and I really want to hear a lot more; so will my brother Yaniv. By the way, I'm Yaakov Hofman, but everyone calls me Kobi. And I'm talking too much. That's usually my little sister's domain."

"I'm glad to meet you, Kobi. Thanks for coming to get me," Alex said, shaking Kobi's hand. "My sisters also talk a lot. I don't know anyone in Tel Aviv. Ted's helped me so much and he told me a little about all of you."

"That's Ted!" Kobi responded. "He's not really our uncle but we all call him that. He's my dad's cousin, my dad's very rich American cousin! He's a great guy and we've spent a lot of time with him and his family, here and in the States. He's in Israel a lot because he's so involved in Jewish activities, AIPAC, Federation, other committees. He probably told you his daughter Tammy will be coming to Israel next year to study communications in the international program at IDC, the Interdisciplinary Center-Herzliya, which means not only will Ted show up often, but so will Aunt Shani and maybe my cousin Ethan. Have you met Shani? She and my mom are pals; they're both artists, but my mom sells her paintings while Shani gives hers away," he added, laughing. "Stop me if I'm giving away family secrets!"

By this time, they'd arrived at Kobi's automobile. As they were storing his luggage, Alex said, "No, this is great! I feel I'm getting to know you. And not only do I know Ted, but I also know Shani, Tammy and Ethan."

"Just wait until we're all together, if the IDF lets my brother Yaniv out for *Sukkoth*. Sometimes they keep soldiers in over holidays, in case there's any unrest. Yaniv's in Unit 8200 in *Modi'in*, Israel's Intelligence Corps; he's only been in a short time, but because of 9/11, Unit 8200 has to work very hard to share vital intelligence information with America, so Yaviv can't come home as often as he'd like. He's at the SIGINT base near Beersheva; where they collect signal intelligence, do code decryption and assessment of counter-intelligence and data security. Yaniv's a computer nerd, and he's so technology-savvy that Unit 8200 is perfect for him, and he's perfect for Unit 8200 since the horrors of 9/11, but he'll never hear me say that. Both of my sisters are at home; Keren's studying physics at Tel Aviv University where my dad works, but studies haven't begun yet so she's been working in a lab at the Weizmann Institute. Daniella's in her last year of high school. There'll be a lot of people at our house: both sets of grandparents, my two aunts and their families, and lots of friends, especially if Yaniv manages to get home. Dani's friends all have a crush on him, so they'll come over. Be prepared for lots of noise, and questions coming at you from all directions."

"That sounds like my family," Alex said, laughing, "although they don't know much about *Sukkoth*. We only found that we're Jewish a few years ago, after Communism collapsed, and Judaism isn't a big deal in Slovakia, especially in Žilina where my family lives. My grandfather was a professor at Žilina's technical university, and my father's also an engineer; my mother teaches mathematics at the university. My grandmother was a teacher and I think she still is – for our family. I have a twin sister who's married and has 3-year-old twins. And my two younger sisters are still in school; Nina is studying architecture in the university and Paulina, like your younger sister, is still in high school, and hoping someday to study cartooning in Paris. So now you know all about my family. Am I talking too much now?"

"No way!" Kobi said, "Our families seem to have a lot more in common than just Uncle Ted. My parents met in Paris; my mom was at Beaux-Arts, the big art college, and my dad was at the Sorbonne, working on a PhD in philosophy. My mom is from Denmark; she converted to Judaism and she really loves being Jewish, so we celebrate all the holidays like this one the right way because of her. You'll love my parents and my big sister. I'm not so sure about Dani, my little sister, because she's very fresh and can kill you with all her questions and her constant teasing, but although I would never admit it to her, I think she's really adorable!"

"I think I already love all of them!" Alex said enthusiastically.

Kobi burst out laughing. "Say that again after you've met all of them!"

The streets of Tel Aviv were crowded, too many cars, too many

Chapter 2

people rushing here and there before the beginning of *Sukkoth;* people were even jaywalking. Others were at the street cafes they passed on their way to the Hofman home in Ramat Aviv. Kobi admitted he'd detoured through Tel Aviv to give Alex his first view of the city that "never sleeps", according to its PR. From the little Alex could see from the car, Tel Aviv was busy, very noisy and, in a word, alive! In Ramat Aviv, Kobi pointed out the university, huge, modern, and closed. A few blocks away, Kobi said, "Here we are, the Hofman house." He parked the car and helped Alex with his luggage. "My parents bought this place so my Dad could walk or bike to work and Mom could have a studio in the back. For us kids, it was like growing up in *Gan Eden,* in Paradise!" He opened the door and called out, "Hello? *Ema?* We're here." An attractive dark-haired older woman came into the hall, wiping her hands on a dishtowel. He grabbed her towel, kissed her cheek and said, "Hi *'Nana Banana'*, meet Alex. Alex, this is Grandma Anna. She's a librarian from Denmark, but she and Grandpa live here now."

"Don't call me that silly name, Kobi. It's very nice to meet you, Alex," she said in perfect English. "We heard a lot about you from Ted when he was here for *Yom Kippur,* after all the horrible events on 9/11. By the way, I'm not really Kobi's grandmother; she lives in Sweden, but I am married to his grandfather. And I'm originally from Holland, not Denmark. Kobi, your mother's in the studio, of course, and she has the stereo on really loud, so she can't hear you; she said she had to add finishing touches to a painting. Your father and grandfather are in the study; I'm sure they didn't hear you because you know what happens when they start discussing philosophy and politics. I've started all the cooking for tonight, and I just sent Keren out to do some last-minute shopping; she'll be back soon. I have no idea where Dani is. With friends, I suppose. Yaniv might be here for a couple of days. Maybe not. If he can, he'll be home before dinner. I've given you the full rundown now, and I've probably overwhelmed Alex with much too much information. What does Dani call it? Oh yes, TMI. I'm going to the kitchen right now or we'll have burnt soup for dinner tonight!"

Kobi kissed Anna's cheek again and, laughing, said. "How can you burn soup, Nana? She always says that, Alex, but she's a fabulous cook. So's my *savta*, my other grandmother, the Israeli one. My sisters and my mom, on the other hand, when it comes to cooking... You'll see, or maybe I should say you'll choke." He heard a rustling sound and slight cough behind him.

"I heard that, Brother Jerk," a beautiful but frowning young woman said as she stepped fully inside, carrying a few grocery bags. "I haven't poisoned you yet, even when I tried! You must be Alex. I'm Keren, the older sister of this jerk. He really is a jerk, even if he is a commander in Unit 669! I'd offer you my hand and welcome you to this madhouse, but both hands are full. Kobi, take these groceries to grandma," she said, holding out the bags.

Kobi put down Alex's luggage and took the shopping bags from Keren. "Just a second, mate. My weakling of a sister needs help taking these tiny parcels to the kitchen. It's so far away she'd probably collapse on the way. I'll be right back."

"Hello, Keren. I really like the way everyone in this family teases each other," Alex said. "You sound like my sisters and me."

"You'll have to tell me all about them later, but I have to run now. Dani phoned and asked me to pick her up," Keren said as she went back outside.

Kobi came back and looked around. "Did she collapse outside the door?" he asked, laughing. "Let's put your gear in Yaniv's room. He'll bunk with me if he comes. My aunt and uncle from Frankfurt have the guest room."

"Don't put your brother out of his room," Alex said as he picked up his baggage and followed Kobi down the hall. "I can sleep anywhere, on a sofa, on the floor. Your family's absolutely amazing. It's so international."

"My *Ema*'s family," Kobi said. "*Aba*'s family is here or in the States."

As they passed an open door, the two men in the room stopped talking. The younger one said, "Kobi, put Alex's things in Yaniv's room. Come in, Alex. I'm David, Kobi's father, and this is Richard, my father-in-law."

"Wow! You look so much like Ted. For a moment I thought you were him," an astonished Alex said.

"Nah," David joked. "I'm better looking! When we were kids, here or if I was visiting in the States, we'd switch clothes and no one knew which was which until we started talking, and my Israeli accent gave me away!"

"You have an Israeli accent?" Alex asked. "I don't hear it."

"Neither do I," Richard said. "I'm the one with an accent. Your English is excellent, young man. Your accent, too. How's your Hebrew?"

A few minutes later, Kobi joined them; they were all talking when the most beautiful woman Alex had ever seen came into the room. Tall and slim, long blonde hair tied back with a twisted string, wearing

Chapter 2

jeans and a tee shirt, barefoot; she looked like Keren's older sister. Conversation came to a halt until David and Richard spoke at the same time. "You've a smudge of orange paint on your cheek, Lise," David said.

Richard added, "Orange is quite a good color on you, my dear!"

"I'd offer to kiss it off, my love," David quipped with a grin, "but you know I really hate the taste of acrylics."

"At least I washed my hands before I came to meet Alex, but I forgot my sandals." Holding out her hand to Alex, standing there agog, she said, "I'm Lise, Kobi's *Ema*. Welcome. It's so nice to have you here to share our happy holiday."

"You're Kobi's mother?" he stuttered. "You're so young!"

"And the mother of Keren, Yaniv and Daniella. And David's wife and Richard's daughter," Lise said, counting off each name on her slim fingers. "I'm not as young as you think...but thanks a lot for the compliment. My paint-smudged ego needed that." She turned to Kobi and inquired, "Did you put Alex in Yaniv's room? And how are you feeling, my love? Tell me quickly and then I'll go help Grandma Anna in the kitchen," she added with a grin, "so she won't burn the soup! Did Keren get back with the shopping?"

"I did put Alex in Yaniv's room, and Keren brought the shopping. It's in the kitchen, but she's off again to pick up Dani," he said, standing up to hug his mother and wipe off the smudge of paint on her cheek with a tissue. "The drive to the airport was easy, no pain in my leg. The smudge isn't very big. Besides, as Grandpa said, orange is a good color on you." Everyone laughed. Alex was enthralled with the warmth and love in this family; he knew he was fortunate to be with them at the start of his new life in Israel, if that's what it would be. He offered a silent thank you to Ted Hoffman.

Lise left the room, tossing her long hair and adding a teasing remark over her shoulder. "The rest of you should help Anna. Papa, you know you and David are better cooks than I. The best I can be is a pathetic *sous-chef*."

Richard smiled at his daughter, "Oh no! You know what they say about too many cooks spoiling the broth my wife's always threatening to burn. Besides, you've learned from some of the best cooks I know. So, we'll leave 'women's work' to the women," he joked as David punched him lightly on the shoulder and Lise tossed the cloth she'd been using to dry her hands at him. Kobi burst out laughing and Alex couldn't stop himself from joining in. Richard added, "I'd better be careful not to say anything so chauvinistic around Keren. What is it young people say today? Oh yes, she'll 'bust my chops' whatever that means!" Once again, everyone laughed.

The entire holiday, family only the first evening, passed the same way with laughter and teasing; on the other days, diverse people offered a truly international flavor, with family and friends constantly stopping by, food that was familiar to Alex sometimes and unusual at other times. All meals were eaten on the large deck off the kitchen, under a roof of branches and thatched leaves on its pergola, roll-up bamboo shades enclosing the huge windows down to the wood railing. "This is our pseudo-*sukkah*, like the hut where religious Jews eat, and many even sleep for a whole week in order to commemorate God's bounty when the Jews escaped from slavery in Egypt. You know the story, don't you, Alex?" Lise asked.

"Yes, ma'am," Alex replied. "I learned about all the Jewish holidays at the JCC in Pittsburgh."

"Please don't call me 'Ma'am'," she scolded. "First you tell me I look too young to be Kobi's mother, and now you call me 'Ma'am'! You can't have it both ways, Alex. So just call me Lise."

After sundown Tuesday night, *motzei chag*, the younger people went into Tel Aviv for some fun. Yaniv had to leave for his base early on Wednesday morning, less than an hour after they returned from clubbing. Both of his parents were awake to see him go; Lise pressed a box of brownies into his hand and said they were from Grandma Anna for the guys in his group. As Yaniv kissed her and hugged his dad; he said, "Next time I get home, I'll try to bring my partner at Urim, Gabriel. You'll really like him a lot, *Ema*. He loves your paintings. And that's such an 'in' with you!" he added, winking at his father. Yaniv very lightly punched Kobi's shoulder and said, "Take care, *achi*; no more accidents, please! Alex, I know I'll see you again, probably here. Good luck! I think you and *Tzahal* will be a very good fit."

Later that morning, after driving Yaniv to the bus station and they were all eating breakfast on the deck, David said, "Alex, it will be much easier to set up your meetings with Ted's *Tzahal* contacts after the end of this entire holiday. Half the country is either abroad during *Sukkoth*, or out camping somewhere; Israelis who are here work only half a day if they do any work at all this week. Lise has an exhibit coming up very soon, so we should all get out of her hair and let her work in peace. How would you like to see a bit of Israel with Kobi, me, and whoever else wants to come?"

"That would be fantastic," Alex responded, "if you have the time." Keren and Dani, Anna, Richard, and Lise's sister Marta and her husband, Philipp. joined them on the tour; in two cars, they spent the next three days visiting most of Israel's major tourist sites: Caesarea, Haifa, Tiberias, Safed, the Sea of Galilee, the Golan, Jerusalem. Alex began to understand Israel's history and achievements: the economy was based on high tech since Israel had no oil, no coal, no gold, no silver, and even most of its forests had been planted by people, not by nature, in what had once been desert. More than a quarter of a billion trees! Airplanes and automobiles, televisions, computers, and most other consumer products were imported. David told them Golda Meir, Israel's fourth prime minister, once said that Israel had only two natural resources, "sand and brains!" Alex began to understand Israel's problematic security needs: a country less than half the size of Slovakia, with 7 million people compared to 4.5 million, surrounded on all sides by enemies who envied it at the same time as they hated it. Alex began to understand that Israel had peace treaties with Egypt and Jordan, but they weren't friends or even allies. Alex began to understand why Israel's defense budget was more than 6% of its annual GDP while Slovakia's defense budget was only 2% of its GDP; he realized that was because Slovakia wasn't threatened by any of its neighbors. And Alex was really amazed that Jerusalem, despite being unrecognized as Israel's capital by the rest of world, protected the sites of all religions, Christian and Muslim as well as Jewish. He remembered what his grandmother had told him about Jewish synagogues and institutions in Bratislava and Žilina that had been destroyed not just by the Nazis but also by Slovakia's "legitimate" government, and only a few were restored under the Communists. After their five-day tour, Alex found himself enthralled by Israel and totally committed to what he already felt was his homeland.

Chapter 3

After *Simchat Torah*, the end of the *Sukkoth* holiday, Lise's sister Marta and her husband Philipp, both doctors, went home to Frankfurt, and Richard and Anna returned to their Tel Aviv apartment. David and Keren started preparing for the opening of the academic year at Tel Aviv University, and Dani went back to high school. Kobi had three more days at home before reporting to the hospital for his formal release; if all went well, he'd return to his base. After *Simchat Torah*, Alex called Ted Hoffman's *Tzahal* contact person and wasn't surprised to hear they'd been expecting his call; in his super-efficient way, when Ted was in Israel after 9/11, he'd told them about Alex's special qualifications. A preliminary meeting was arranged for the following day at 11:00; Alex was told to come to the main gate of *HaKirya*, the IDF headquarters on Kaplan Street, and to ask for Sergeant Sivan.

Security was tight when he arrived at the gate; one guard examined his credentials carefully and another made a phone call. Shortly afterwards, a pretty female soldier came to the gate, introduced herself as Sergeant Sivan and said she'd escort him to his meeting. He'd expected the meeting to be in *HaKirya*, but she removed her ID badge and took him across a footbridge into the Azrieli Center. In the Circular Building, they took an elevator to the 43rd floor, entered an unmarked room where another female soldier offered him coffee. The room was sparsely furnished, just a mid-size table, a few chairs, a picture of the Prime Minister on the wall and photos of stages in the construction of the Azrieli Center. Sivan said, "I'll leave you here, Alex. Good luck." Amazed at the security, efficiency, and the choice of meeting place, he laughed to himself, *"Everyone knows that the IDF is 'a lean, mean fighting machine', but its focus on secret locations is beyond belief!"*

He shouldn't have been surprised, even though he was, when an officer entered the room and asked for his credentials; he looked them over but asked no questions. Instead, he asked the female soldier to photocopy the documents; she went into a small room which, Alex had noted in a quick glance when she'd opened the door, contained a lot of office equipment. The officer poured coffee for himself and for Alex, sat down, and waited silently. When she returned with the copies, the officer smiled, gave Alex the original papers, and told him he'd be contacted about a formal meeting. Then he left without telling Alex his name. A little stunned by a meeting lasting barely 15 minutes,

Chapter 3

Alex said goodbye to the female soldier and also left, thinking, *"Oh well, it's not clear to me, but no one ever says the Israeli army doesn't know what it's doing!"* He wandered around the Azrieli Center for a little while and then took a cab back to the Hofmans. Lise met him at the door and said, "That was quick, but not as quick as *Tzahal*. They called a few minutes ago and said they want you to come there tomorrow at 10:00. The person who called said you should meet Sergeant Sivan in the building where today's meeting was held." Lise handed him a key and a note. She added, "This is the code for our alarm, so you can come and go without depending on someone being home. How did the meeting go?"

Alex thanked her and said, "I don't know how it went, because it lasted only 15 minutes. All they did was photocopy my passport and other papers. It wasn't even in *HaKirya;* it was in the Azrieli Center, which is impressive, by the way. Both the round building and the triangular one are taller than anything in Slovakia, although Pittsburgh has taller skyscrapers, like the U.S. Steel Building and the Mellon Center. It looks like Azrieli has started another building, but no one was working today." As she fixed sandwiches for them, Lise told him there'd been disputes about the third building and work had been suspended two years earlier, but they'll finish it someday. After lunch, Lise went to her studio, and Alex went to his room to read.

The next morning, he arrived at Azrieli before 10:00; Sivan walked into the building exactly on time. *"Military efficiency,"* Alex thought, greeting her. She took him to an unmarked room on the 37th floor, larger than the previous day's room, with a long rectangular table, seven chairs on one side, a yellow legal pad and a pen at each place, and one chair on the other side. He saw an open door leading into a fully equipped office with a coffee urn and cans of soft drinks on a small table. There were several photographs on the walls: Prime Minister Ariel Sharon, assassinated former Prime Minister Yitzhak Rabin in military uniform, photos of former IDF Chiefs of Staff, and pictures of what Alex assumed were early military bases. Sivan took a seat behind the rows at the table and told Alex to sit down; she added that she knew it looked like an interrogation room, but she couldn't do anything about that. Alex smiled. "This *is* an interrogation room; it's what I expected yesterday." A few minutes later, several officers entered, including the one from the previous day, who introduced himself as Erez. Alex didn't know why the insignia on each officer's uniform was a different color, as was the beret under the epaulet on his shoulder. Erez informed him that the others, whose names he didn't give, represented various IDF units: *Golani*, *Givati*, *Duvduvan*, *Egoz*, *Oketz* and *Aman*. Each officer had a folder containing Alex's CV and other documents, including his letters of recommendation. They questioned him about UNFICYP in Cyprus, about 5.PSU in Slovakia and about their training exercises with America's 10th Special Forces. They asked about his particular specialty; he said he'd been a demolitions expert. They asked if he knew that Israel and America cooperated in many military activities, and they asked if he knew that America had financed quite a lot of Israel's Research and Development of weapons, and subsidized major defense projects like the Merkava tank and the Lavi ground-attack aircraft. They asked if he knew that Israel was a participant in the special program that developed the F-35 Lightning II fighter, and they asked if he knew that America had offered Israel access to the F-22 Raptor program but Israel had turned it down because of its high cost. They asked if he knew that America and Israel cooperated on technology, notably the Arrow missile system and Nautilus, the High Energy Laser. They asked if he knew that America and Israel carried out biennial joint exercises called JUNIPER COBRA in order to test their inter-operational ability. In addition, they asked if he knew that Haifa was the main Mediterranean port of call for America's 6th Fleet. They asked if he knew that America had been storing military equipment in Israel since the 1990s. They even asked if he knew that Israel shared intelligence with America, and, in the wake of 9/11, the two nations had set up a joint anti-terrorist working group. Then, each one asked if he knew the specific mission of that officer's brigades; then each of them told him. Astonished at all the information they were sharing, even when framed as questions, Alex understood that *none of the information was "Top Secret" and they'd shared it with him for a reason, even if he didn't know what the reason was.*

Finally, after almost two hours, Erez asked if he had any questions. Alex replied, "I have a lot of questions, sir, but I really have to absorb all of this first." He hesitated for a moment, "Actually, I'd like to know why all of you gave me so much information, even if it was in the form of questions. I'm sure none of it was classified, but I still don't think it's really appropriate for me to ask a lot of questions now." Behind the officers, he saw Sivan silently applauding his response; he smiled at her. Erez asked if any brigade was of particular interest to him. "Yes, sir, a couple," Alex replied. "But again, I really have to absorb, or digest, all this before I can tell you which ones."

"In that case," Erez stated, "we're completing this session at 1200 hours." The other officers nodded or flicked thumbs upward; Erez

Chapter 3

added, "Think hard. Sivan will bring you to a meeting at 1400 hours. Shalom." All of them stood and left the room; two officers said they hoped to meet him again.

"Whew!" he said to Sivan as he stood up. "That was intense."

"Yes, but you handled it really well. They obviously approved, or Erez would not have invited you to another meeting later today. Let's grab lunch downstairs. We have to be at the entrance at 1315 hours."

An old blue sedan with a young woman driver in civilian clothing drew up to the curb just as Alex and Sivan exited the Azrieli Center. Alex sat in the back, thinking, and Sivan in front as they drove, talking to their driver about the heat and about new movies currently in Tel Aviv. They arrived in a nearby town, Petah Tikvah according to the road sign Alex had noticed, a minute before 2:00. With no security guards out front, the building looked just like an ordinary 8-storey apartment house. Sivan told the driver, "I'll be back soon, Chani." She pressed the number 6 on the intercom, said who she was, and after the buzzer allowed them to open the door, she escorted Alex to a third floor flat. When Erez answered her knock and opened the door, she said, "Shalom, Erez. Good luck, Alex." And she left.

This meeting was with Erez and two other officers, representing the IDF's most elite units: *Sayeret Matkal*, *Shayetet 13* and *Yehidat Shaldag*. Alex knew "*sayeret*" literally meant "reconnaissance unit", but in practice, these units specialized in commando and other special ops roles; training included advanced weapons, reconnaissance technology, and hand-to-hand combat. These were the units that interested Alex the most, and it seemed they were equally interested in him. Erez said these elite units performed the most important, and often the most secret, IDF missions. Their soldiers had more rigorous training than other units. Erez himself was from *Sayeret Matkal* which, he told Alex, was usually referred to just as "The Unit"; their work was highly classified, open only to the very best soldiers. Subordinate to AMAN, the Intelligence directorate, The Unit, had a large budget for the purchase of advanced weaponry. One of the other officers told him *Shayetet 13* was Israel's naval commando unit, equivalent to the US Navy SEALS; the third officer informed Alex that *Sayeret Shaldag* was the commando unit of the Israeli Air Force, specializing in target designation outside Israel, and often working undercover.

Alex was fascinated by the activities of all three units, but he knew he had to be totally honest, so he told them he wasn't qualified for *Shayetet 13* or *Shaldag*. "Slovakia is a land-locked country," he said, "and even though I was in Cyprus with UNFICYP, my maritime skills

Alexander's Story

are not up to *Shayetet 13* standards." The officers noted his comments in their folders. He hesitated for a moment, but then he told them he'd had almost no airborne training and was nervous about parachuting, so he couldn't be in *Shaldag*. Finally, he said it would be an honor to be in *Sayeret Matkal* if they accepted him. As he finished speaking, there was a knock on the door and an American officer, Major Andy Johnson, who as Captain AJ, had been CO of the US 10th Special Forces in Slovakia when 5.PŠU held joint exercises with the Americans, entered the room. Alex was stunned. Captain AJ saw his shock and told him the 10th was co-training with Israelis and he'd been invited to this meeting. AJ told the Israeli officers that Alex had superior leadership qualities. "But," he added, "if he has told you that he's apprehensive about parachuting, it's because one of his closest childhood friends was killed due to a faulty chute. Nevertheless, Alex completed his parachute training very successfully. If you want my recommendation, you've got it." Captain AJ stood; the officers thanked him and saluted. He tapped Alex lightly on the shoulder and said, "Good luck, Alex. They're lucky to have you."

As the meeting was ending, the *Shaldag* officer asked Alex if knew what Kobi Hofman did in the IDF. Alex said he knew Kobi was in Unit 669, the Search-and-Rescue unit, but he didn't know about any of their missions. He smiled and said he knew 6:6 referred to perfect vision, and 9 meant the 9 lives of a cat, but he didn't know exactly what Unit 669 did. The officers laughed, and one said 669 even has a green-eyed cat on their insignia, and they're called the *Flying Cats*. Erez added, "They're also called '*Sheshbesh Tesha*' instead of '*Shesh-shesh-tesha*' because they spend their time between missions playing *sheshbesh*. Thank you for your honesty, Alex. You'll hear from us soon. Chani's here. She'll take you to the Hofmans. Shalom."

When Alex left the meeting room, he drew his first really deep breath of the afternoon and wondered if he had a future in the IDF. He saw the blue car outside the building and sat down in the passenger seat. "Have you been waiting long?" he asked Chani, "Not really," she said. "Besides, this is my job. So let's hope we don't have a lot of traffic on the way to Ramat Aviv."

The Hofman's door opened before Alex took the key out of his pocket, and Kobi said, "You look drained. Was it awful?"

"No," Alex answered. "It was exhilarating! In the morning, I met officers from special units, even *Oketz*. In the afternoon, it was officers from the top *Sayerets*. All of them, a.m. and p.m., told me about their specific programs. I told them I can't be in *Shayetet 13* or *Shaldag*

Chapter 3

because I don't have all the right skills, but I'd be honored to be in *Sayeret Matkal*. I don't know if I'll be accepted. Then Andy Johnson, CO of the US 10th Special Forces when my 5.PŠU trained with them, came in. He's here for joint exercises with the Israelis and he gave me a great recommendation. By the way, the *Shaldag* officer asked if I know what you do in Unit 669 and I said all I know is that you're in Unit 669 and what the numbers mean. And that's the truth."

"They're sneaky; they probably wanted to know if you can keep secrets," Kobi said. "So why do you look shattered? Hungry? *Ema* said dinner will be a little late, so help yourself to whatever you want in the fridge."

Alex laughed. "I'm 'shattered' because of the female driver who brought me home; I didn't think we'd get here in one piece. And I'm always hungry. I'll grab a snack. As for secrets, what secrets? You haven't told me a thing."

Kobi laughed. "I shudder to think of next year when Dani learns to drive. We'll all have to stay off the roads, and probably off the sidewalks, too!"

"Stop it!" Alex groaned. "You adore her, and she's so well-coordinated she'll probably be the best driver in the family. Oh wait, that's you, the one your mother calls 'the daredevil who's taken years off her life'!"

Alex was unusually quiet that evening, thinking a lot. The next morning, he received a phone call telling him to report to the Petah Tikvah apartment at 1200 hours. *"Hmm,"* he thought, *"Interesting that they said 'report'."*

Erez buzzed him in. Another officer was at the table, and Alex assumed he was from *Sayeret Matkal*, although he didn't see a red beret. "Shalom," the other officer said, "I'm Major Sefi, Erez's CO. He's told me about you and I read your file, but I'd like to hear about your training in Cyprus and with the American 10th. Then we'll see if you're acceptable for The Unit."

Alex told them with a smile that it was difficult for him to discuss 5.PŠU because most of the training was top-secret, but since he hoped to get into an Israeli top-secret unit, he knew he could count on the discretion of these officers vis-à-vis the information he was sharing with them. Erez grinned, but Sefi remained taciturn. Alex said 5.PŠU was divided into six companies with 400 men: four reconnaissance units, one signal unit and one support unit. Each reconnaissance unit had 10-man teams subdivided into smaller units in communications, camouflage/small weapons, demolitions/heavy weapons, medicine;

he'd been in camouflage and small weapons, although he was trained in all the other areas. 5.PŠU regularly trained with NATO special ops units, including the Americans and the French; he'd worked with the Americans based in Žilina, his hometown which, he flashed a grin, was very convenient for R & R. He said since the creation of 5.PŠU in 1994, they'd adopted NATO Special Forces techniques and equipment. When he finished speaking, he knew they'd already known everything as there were pages and pages about his Slovakian military experience in his file and both officers had read them. He was sure, after Ted Hoffman's initial call, Israeli intelligence had ferreted out all the details of his life.

He wondered if he was being paranoid, but they'd asked more questions about his experience in UNFICYP in Cyprus than about his time in 5.PŠU other than its setup. He told them the U.N. Security Council had adopted special methods for UNFICYP to maintain the ceasefire on the divided island: the peacekeepers supervised the deployment of both the Turkish Cypriot forces and the Cyprus National Guard, and they controlled the integrity of the buffer zone between the areas under control of the opposing sides. When he was in Cyprus, UNFICYP investigated and countered any violations of the ceasefire and the military status quo. He said the buffer zone remained calm and there'd been a decrease in violations during the last half of his stay, in spite of two bombings and four unsuccessful attacks against UNFICYP.

When Sefi asked about his grandparents' experiences as partisans during World War II and how they'd managed under Communism, Alex knew he'd been thoroughly vetted. When asked how he felt about finding out he was Jewish, he said it had been an earth-shaking experience, although he'd been only 14-years-old when his grandparents revealed the secret. He added, "I know it sounds strange, but I felt like a very deep hole somewhere inside me was beginning to close; I wanted to learn more and more about Judaism. I don't really know why, because he's never been anti-Semitic, but my father was furious about our family being Jewish and my interest in the religion; a chasm opened between us before I went to America to study. I hoped things would improve while I was away, but when I returned from Pittsburgh, he didn't even want to hear about my experiences or what I'd learned. One day he overheard me telling my sisters I was sorry I hadn't had a Bar Mitzvah, and he just exploded; I was afraid he'd have a heart attack or a stroke. His extreme anger and our alienation were the reason I came to Israel earlier than I'd originally planned, but he

Chapter 3

came to the airport in Vienna when I left." Looking a little sad, he said, "When I was a little boy, I adored my father, but then things began to change… So I'm glad he came to the airport to apologize and we can talk again without fighting about my life and the choices I've made."

Sefi said, "Let's take a short break, half an hour max. Sivan's here with sandwiches and coffee." Alex left the room and there she was, sitting at a table in the kitchen, typing away on her laptop. Her phone rang, and after answering, she said, "Sefi says we should eat, and you should come back in 20 minutes. You look a little deflated. I know I shouldn't ask, but how did it go?" When he said he thought it went OK with Erez but wasn't sure about Sefi, she told him she'd never seen Sefi crack a smile and yet the guys in The Unit loved him, so just relax and, as the Americans say, go with the flow. Smiling, he told her he really hoped he'd see her again…often.

Back in the other room, Erez asked if Sivan had said anything. "She told me she'd never seen Major Sefi smile but the guys in The Unit love him."

Erez grinned at Sefi and said, "Too true!"

Sefi, of course, didn't smile; he just opened Alex's file and turned to a page covered in Hebrew handwriting. He looked directly into Alex's eyes and said, "We're going to offer you the chance to be in The Unit. Normally you'd start with a one-day try-out to determine if you're fit to join, but given your experience, you can skip it. Instead, from next Sunday, you'll have to do *Gibush*, the selection camp for potential recruits: four sleepless days. American recruits have compared it to Parris Island, which they've said is 'affectionately' known as the 'Marine Torture Chamber'. You, like all other recruits, will be constantly monitored by doctors and psychologists. If you have the stamina to make it through, you will have a shorter training period than the others because of your experience. We know any information we tell you won't leave this room, so you should know The Unit's structure has been heavily influenced by the UK's SAS; we frequently train with them, but we also have joint exercises with France's GIGN, Germany's GSG-9, and America's Delta Force which has a very distinct character. So, are you interested?"

"Am I interested? It's exactly what I want!" Alex exclaimed, grinning from ear-to-ear. "I was afraid you wouldn't take me because I'm too old. You can trust me to keep quiet. Where do I have to go? And when?"

"First let's see if you make it through *Gibush*," Sefi grunted. "It will take place 'somewhere in Israel' so report to the Ashdod railroad station at 0530 hours sharp on Sunday." He closed the file and prepared to leave.

Erez flicked a cheeky half-salute at Sefi and said, "Ciao, Sefi." Then he shook Alex's hand, "Good luck, Alex. I hope you make it. I'll like working with you." Alex's didn't stop grinning as he thanked Erez for his support.

"Is Sivan still here?" he asked.

"No," Erez said. "She went back to *HaKiryah*. I'll call a taxi for you."

"Too bad," Alex said. "I would've liked to share my excitement with her. Guess it'll have to wait until I'm at the Hofmans. Wow, I want to celebrate!" He shook Erez's hand again as the officer left, and Alex waited for his taxi.

When he knocked, Lise opened the door. "Where's your key?" she asked, smiling. "I can tell you're excited. Today's meeting was really good?"

"Good," he exclaimed. "It was fantastic! I'm going to *Gibush* starting Sunday and then, if I make it through that, I'm in!"

"Congratulations," she said, hugging him. "I'm sure the interview was difficult and I'm as proud of you as I'd be of my own children."

Alex still found it hard to think of Lise as the mother of four grown-up or almost grown-up children, but he appreciated her support, and the hug. He said to himself, *"Watch it! Don't let yourself have a big crush on Lise even though she's so beautiful. Think about Sivan instead, or Keren, or Sayeret Matkal and the Gibush."* Aloud he said, "I'm going to email my mom to let her know what's happening, a little of what's happening. And Ted!"

"Good idea," she said. "Try to get a little rest. You've been too excited for the last few days and haven't slept very much. I've almost finished a special painting I want everyone to see. Papa and Anna will be here for dinner tonight, so we'll have a great meal. And wine. We'll celebrate!"

He was just finishing his last email when Kobi popped in, holding two diet-Cokes. "I just came home. One of these is for you," he said, handing Alex a can. "Now, tell me all about it, or as much as you can tell me."

"I'm in. At least I think I am. I have *Gibush* on Sunday. If I live through that," he laughed, "I'll get a red beret and I'll be in *Sayeret Matkal*."

"You'll make it!" Kobi assured him. "I just picked up Grandpa and Nana Anna and she's already in the kitchen starting your celebration

Chapter 3

meal and my 'last supper'! For a librarian, she certainly likes to cook. I'll have to tease her about spending a lot of her time in the library reading cookbooks!"

"She's a librarian? And what's this about your 'last supper'?" Alex queried. "And I know she doesn't like being called 'Nana Anna'."

"I call her 'Nana Anna' when I feel like teasing her because she hates it; usually I call her Grandma Anna. She was a librarian; that's how she met Grandpa; both of them were studying for their MAs at the university in Copenhagen. Tomorrow I'll be a 'Flying Cat' again, but the food on my base stinks! So tonight, Grandma Anna's fabulous cooking is *my* last supper until I'm home again." Kobi was in a good mood, as was Alex, and the two of them were almost sick with laughter when Dani came home and stopped near the door. Her grandfather's arm hugged her shoulder loosely.

"Grandpa says it's been awfully noisy in here for the last couple of hours. Please share the joke; I've had a very bad day!" Dani moaned.

Kobi grinned at his little sister. "How bad a day can it be in high school? Wait until you're in the IDF; then you'll know what 'a bad day' means."

"Boys, boys!" Richard said pointedly. "Stop acting like 10-year-olds and teasing the girl the minute she gets home! Anna says dinner will be ready in ten minutes. David's home and Keren's on her way. I've been ordered to tell you to wash up…and Dani probably wants me to tell you to shut up!" The boys laughed and Richard and Dani left the doorway, grinning.

Dinner was fun as well as delicious, but Alex already knew dinner at the Hofman home was always fun as well as delicious. Anna was a gourmet chef and everyone was delighted when she cooked, although both Lise and David weren't bad either when they worked together. Hofman kids teased each other, their parents, their grandparents, guests. With so much obvious good humor, Alex found himself relaxing and enjoying life with them.

David asked him about the meeting. Alex grinned, "I'm in!" Lise smiled and said she hadn't said anything because it was his right to tell everyone.

"*Matkal?*" Dani shrieked. "I'll finally have a brother with a red beret!"

"I'm not your brother," Alex teased, "but you remind me of Paulina, my sister. You sound like her… except for the different language, of course!"

"And Paulina's probably as much of a *nudnik*," Kobi added. Dani threw her napkin at Kobi across the table and said to Alex, "You might as well be one of my brothers. You're just like them…speak about being annoying!"

Lise frowned at her younger daughter and said, "Verbal fooling is fine, Dani. But I don't allow anyone to throw food or napkins at dinner."

Reprimanded and not happy about it, Dani apologized to her brother but added, "He started it!" Before her mother could say anything, Dani asked to be excused because she had a major homework assignment to start. "I'll see you before you go home, Grandma, Grandpa. Like always, it was a great dinner, Grandma." With those words, she dashed upstairs to her room."

"Come back down for a minute," Lise said, surprising her daughter. "I want everyone to see a painting I've just finished." They crowded into her studio, a square room with windows all around. Lise lowered all the blinds, even on the skylight, and said, "It won't show at its best at night, but I think you'll like it." She uncovered a huge canvas almost the length of the studio. They all gasped at a painting of their lunch in the *Sukkah*, with branches and leaves on the ceiling, food piled high. Everyone was there, family and friends, every face delineated, every mouth smiling or talking. In the studio, there was total silence. "Well?" Lise finally asked.

"It's breathtaking!" her father and Anna said simultaneously. David just grabbed her and held on tight. "It's absolutely magnificent!" he said, "Your best work ever!" And Dani added, "Leonardo da Vinci was nothing if you compare him to my *Ema*!" They all laughed at her cheeky comment and tried to get closer to the painting.

"Is it dry? Can I touch my face?" Alex asked in awe. Lise nodded.

After a while, Dani went back upstairs to her homework and the others sat on the deck off the kitchen, within sight of the painting, drinking coffee, talking about the painting and offering a caffeine toast first to Lise for her brilliant achievement and then to Alex's potential appointment to *Sayeret Matkal*. After Keren and the grandparents left, Kobi said to Alex, "I've got to leave really early tomorrow morning, so no clubs tonight and there's nothing on TV, so how about letting me trounce you in chess?"

"In your dreams!" Alex replied, "I'm on to your ploys, so let's see who trounces who…er, whom!"

After three games, one win each and one draw, Kobi said, "I've had it, man. If I don't get some shut-eye, they'll put me back on sick leave! Ugh! There's no way I'll let them drum me out of the *Cats* to

Chapter 3

something 'lesser' like The Unit!" He winked and gave Alex a brief bear-hug. "You'll do great next week at *Gibush*. You'll be the 'old man' in the bunch; the others are all 18 or so except the instructors who'll try to scare the shit out of you. But you've been there, done that and tougher stuff, you've got experience, so you'll make it. We all think so. My family has good instincts about who can do what in the Israeli army. My dad was kind of a hero in the paratroopers in both the 6-Day War and the Yom Kippur War, but he won't talk about it at all. The philosopher, you know. My mom gets all teary about the 1973 war; they were already married but she was in Paris and he was here and they didn't see each other for four months. Dad's parents were both in the *Hagana* before there was a state of Israel, and before that *Saba* was in the Jewish Brigade fighting with the Brits against the Nazis. That's funny in a way because before the Jewish Brigade, *Saba* enlisted in the British Army's Palestine Buffs and both he and *Ema*'s father, were at El Alamein. But they were on opposite sides. Grandpa Richard was German but he was anti-Nazi so they sent him to Dachau concentration camp for a couple of years to try to brainwash him, and then to Rommel's *AfrikaKorps*, but he deserted to the Brits and spent the rest of the war as a POW..." Kobi broke off, yawning.

"Wow!" Alex said, "And I thought my grandparents' experiences as partisans during the war were fascinating!"

"If you want to know more, ask my *Saba*. He'll tell you." Kobi yawned again and went to his room, flicking a backhanded salute at Alex.

Saturday night Alex said his 'goodbyes' and 'thank-yous' to the Hofmans and went to bed at 11. Lise hugged him and said, "Just leave all your things; don't even try to pack them. You'll be back on Thursday...victorious!" Both Lise and David wished him good luck.

He was awake at 4:00 a.m. *"I've got to remember to say 0400 hours,"* he told himself silently. After dressing, he crept downstairs to make a cup of instant coffee. At 4:20, David came down and said, "Let's go to Ashdod."

"You don't have to drive me, sir. I was just about to call a taxi."

"No need. I'm already up and dressed; I want to take you there in person! Besides, Lise insisted that I do this. And don't call me 'sir'. My wife doesn't like to be called 'Ma'am' and I'm not 'Sir'. I'm 'David'," he said, chuckling.

Alex started to say "OK, s..." and then caught himself, "OK, David." He grinned and, as usual, was amazed at the generosity of the Hofman family.

The streets were quiet and they arrived in Ashdod even before 5:00 a.m. A few young recruits were waiting with parents and friends. David said he'd wait until Alex was on the bus. "Lise's orders, of course!" he quipped.

A bus painted with camouflage designs pulled up at 0515 hours. A gruff sergeant stated, "We leave at 0530. Anyone not on the bus then is out!" The recruits hugged their families, and boarded. As Alex moved toward the bus, David gave him a bear-hug and said the red beret was a *fait accompli*!

The *'gibushim'* were taken somewhere south of Ashdod; Alex found out later the base was Nitzanim. They received army fatigues, an M16 rifle and a kit-bag full of what seemed to Alex like cast-off Army goods: a canteen and a many-pocketed vest, along with a two-man tent and pegs. They were allowed to wear their own shoes although their other clothes were bagged and taken away until the *Gibush* was completed. When they were suited up, they waited…and they waited. They received brief medical check-ups and were given clearance; then they waited for four hours in the blazing sun, doing nothing. *Manot Krav*, combat rations were handed out; somehow the MREs would become more edible as the week wore on, not because the food in the *manot krav* improved, but because the *gibushim* were hungrier.

By 1500 hours, they'd been organized into 20-man squads for the next two days; 250 participants started the *Gibush*, but at least 25% would be eliminated by the officers at the end of the second day, and many others would drop out on their own for medical or psychological reasons. Alex was amazed at his *déjà-vu*; not one new experience, just tedious and a bit off-center. At 1600 hours, an officer younger than Alex explained the "rules and regulations" of *Gibush*. Then, wearing all their equipment, Alex's squad followed four officers toward sand dunes where they began a sprinting drill with rifles in hand. They sprinted from dune to dune, some very steep, for an hour with no break. Alex was relieved both David and Kobi had told him to wear hiking boots instead of running shoes; at least his shoes didn't fill up with sand during these sprints. There were 20 dunes, and although it wasn't known at the time, this was the "torture chamber" for tough drills twice each day for the next four days. After sprinting up and down one very steep dune 15 times, they moved to crawling down the dune. At first that was strenuous because Alex hadn't done any crawling for a long time and it demanded the use of every muscle in his body, but after a while the skill came back. By the time the first drill session ended, Alex was exhilarated more than exhausted, but

Chapter 3

some of the young *gibushim*, who'd started out highly motivated and cheerful, looked totally drained, and depressed.

After that first session, the squads returned to the base camp, sweaty and sandy, set up their tents and fell into them; they couldn't shower and slept in their fatigues. A siren woke them at 0400 and it was back to the dunes, sprinting and crawling with 20-kilo sacks of sand on their backs along with their rifles and other gear. On the third morning, they filled out questionnaires about the drills and ranked the others in their squads. Alex, 23 years old, was called "the old man" by his group; some of them asked how he'd ranked them, but he wouldn't comment. Later, all of them were interviewed by the officers. And then they waited and waited – to be sent home or assigned to another squad. Five from each squad were sent home; Alex was assigned to a new squad with 15 *gibushim* and six officers whose role was to make the next two days even more hellish than the first two.

Some drills were merely difficult, while others were strange, even a bit crazy, to Alex; he knew some were impossible given the constraint of time, but he did what he was told. In one drill, instructors set up pull-up bars to see how many pull-ups and chin-ups a recruit could do before he gave up; Alex easily won that one. They had pseudo-fights: two recruits standing face-to-face in circles drawn in the sand, trying to push the other one out of the circle without boxing or judo or any of the martial arts; the winner was the last one standing. Alex didn't win but he came close. Sometimes they were asked trivia questions during physical drills: Who is the president of India? How many stripes does the Australian flag have? Alex grinned when they asked for Slovakia's capital. They were given articles about political issues during lunch, *Manot Krav* of course; several hours later they were asked to summarize the issues verbally. They had to respond as a group or privately about hypothetical missions gone wrong. In the midst of one sprint, Alex's squad had to pick a topic out of a beret and choose someone to speak about it in front of the instructors; naturally, his squad chose "the old man." The topic was NATO; Alex spoke with confidence, even though he wasn't sure of all the Hebrew terms. Then they continued their sprint. Once they had to sketch two maps in the sand, Israel and the *Gibush* base, a simple task for Alex. The instructors demonstrated how to break an M16 apart and then put it back together; they timed how quickly the recruits could do the same. That task was not a problem for Alex. There were "team challenges"; in a complex one, Alex's squad was split into two teams and told to get everyone plus a heavily weighted stretcher to the opposite side of a log without walking on it, over it or even touching it; if anyone did, there was a punishment sprint and they'd have to start again; only one person, chosen by the instructors, was allowed to speak. Even though Alex wasn't allowed to speak, by using a stick to draw a picture in the dirt, he "told" his team to dig a tunnel under the log, wide enough for them to crawl through; his team won. No team was able to complete some challenges, even if a squad member like Alex knew exactly what to do; unlike his young team, he knew the purpose of these tasks was to see how they responded to the challenge, who came up with innovative solutions, who was a leader… and who acted like a jackass or crybaby.

Late Wednesday night, after they'd completed the last drills, they filled out another questionnaire, were interviewed again…and that was it! *Gibush* was finished. Thursday they were awakened as usual at 0430, collapsed the tents and cleaned the base, showered for what felt like hours and changed back into their own clothing; then they waited for six hours for the results. Alex passed. They were bused back to Ashdod where the mother of a boy who'd also passed was waiting at her car, and she gave Alex a lift to Tel Aviv. A very tired, but at least very clean, Alex returned to the Hofmans. He was excited despite his exhaustion and he was so looking forward to telling all of them he would be in The Unit, *Sayeret Matkal*.

Lise opened the door and told him there had just been a phone call from a Lieutenant Erez and Alex was to report to Petah Tikvah at 0900 hours on Sunday. "I gather that you passed," she said. "I can tell just by your smile. Come in and relax. David and the girls will be home soon and our parents will come over later and I'm sure Kobi and Yaniv will call. All of them will want to know. Maybe you should call or email your family. And Ted. You must be starving; you've lost a bit of weight. Hey, I'm not giving you time to relax, but I'm thrilled for you. So let's go have a drink and a snack, and you can send your emails in a little while."

When David, Keren and Dani came in a short time later, they were all so happy for Alex. Lise greeted her family and said to David, "Look how thin Alex is after the horror they call food in *Gibush*, those Meals-Ready-to-Eat. I've defrosted steaks and put some baking potatoes in the oven; we've also got corn, so please heat up the grill, my love. Keren and Dani, one of you should make a salad and the other should set the table. We have ice cream for dessert. I have brushes and a palette to wash and then I'll help you." She breezed out back to her studio.

"Sometimes she's like a whirlwind or one of your *Gibush* instructors, Alex," David said with a smile, "I feel I should salute her! Yet we all do

Chapter 3

what she wants us to do, and usually when she wants us to do it!"

"What can I do to help?" Alex asked.

"Come help me with the fire and tell me the things about the *Gibush* you don't want the girls to hear," David said. Alex laughed and went out to the deck with him, carrying some of the food. David changed the subject. "You know you'll get a red beret, like mine from the paratroopers, don't you?"

"I do now," Alex admitted. "And if I hadn't known, Dani said something about your red beret last week when Kobi and I were teasing her."

When the fire was going nicely, David called Keren and asked her for the potatoes. She brought them out and grumbled a bit, although her father knew she was good-natured and was only teasing about all the women in the house except her mother doing all the work around there. She went back inside to finish "women's work". David put the potatoes and corn on the grill and said, "OK, Alex, come clean. How tough was it?"

Alex answered, "Not as bad as I expected. Some drills were tough, some were stupid and some were impossible. I'm so glad you and Kobi told me to wear hiking boots instead of running shoes. I've never seen so much sand in my life, maybe only in that film about Lawrence of Arabia. And the flies! A few of the kids couldn't take the sand and the flies. Or the *Manot Krav*. My squad called me "the old man" and some instructors were younger than me. I already knew some drills and I helped the young guys with them. A few of the drills were just stupid. The kids couldn't understand why they gave us no time to do some impossible tasks; they didn't realize they were testing us to see how we reacted under pressure. Living in the same filthy clothes for four days, sleeping only a few hours here and there, I've done that before, but I felt sorry for some of those kids who want to be in The Unit so much but they would never last. Didn't Kobi and Yaniv want to wear red berets? To be Paratroopers like their hero dad?"

"I'm no hero! Kobi's always wanted to fly. When he was five, he climbed to the top of his closet and tried; he broke his collarbone. In his *Gibush*, he made it to combat pilot training, but transferred to 669 after an accident and he's happy there, with a blue-green beret. Yaniv's always been cerebral, a computer nerd, so he's perfect for *Modi'in*'s Unit 8200 and *Modi'in*'s perfect for him," David said.

"They say apples don't fall far from the tree and even if their berets aren't red, their commitment to *Tzahal* is as strong as yours," Alex said, smiling.

"Thanks," David said. "But, in truth, my father's grandchildren seem to have his fascination with science, especially Keren. And surprisingly, Kobi enjoyed his training as a medic; of course, since that comes together with flying a chopper, how could it miss? Yaniv's so smart, but not particularly philosophical except when he's talking about coincidences. And Dani, the only one of our children with a little of Lise's artistic talent, doesn't have the drive to develop her flair and complete art projects the way Lise does. Dani doesn't make little sketches whenever she has a pencil in her hand; I doubt she'll ever do anything in art. But she's young, so we won't push her; we'll support her in anything she wants to do."

"I think your father's grandchildren are all very bright and will do really well in whatever they choose. Like their parents," Alex said sincerely.

Lise came out of her studio and onto the deck, interrupting them without a moment's pause. "*Clean hands at last, thank God almighty, clean hands at last*! My apologies to Martin Luther King for misquoting him! Clean hands and an empty tummy! Are the steaks ready? I thought we'd eat out here, but I guess the girls felt chilly and they set the table in the dining room. Is there something for me to take inside? And what's that I overheard Alex saying about 'like their parents'? Who's like their parents?"

A few minutes later, they were all eating what for Alex was his first real meal in days. Just as they finished and David was bringing ice cream to the table, both sets of grandparents came in. "I've brought *tarte aux pommes*," Anna said, "and it's still hot. Oh good, David, we've got ice cream!"

"And we brought a good bottle of wine," Aya added. "We've come for just a few minutes to let Alex know we are very proud of him."

"I don't know what to say," Alex said, emotion cracking his voice. "My family in Slovakia couldn't have made this evening better."

"There. You said it," Lise responded. "I told you we already think of you as family." After they all toasted Alex's success and devoured Anna's pie smothered in ice cream, the two older couples were ready to leave. "I'm stuffed," Lise said. "Tomorrow's diet time!" Everyone scattered, Keren to drive the grandparents and herself home, Dani to do homework, David and Lise to finish straightening the kitchen, and Alex to a real bed for the first time in days after a few emails and telephone calls.

Chapter 4

On Sunday morning, Sivan congratulated Alex on becoming part of The Unit as she drove him to Petah Tikvah. Four *Sayeret Matkal* officers were seated at the table: Erez, Sefi, and two others, Avram and Benny.

Sefi said, "Good morning, Alex. I'll come right to the point. You know The Unit's normal training period is 28-30 months, with heavy emphasis on small arms, martial arts, camouflage, navigation and other skills for survival behind enemy lines. You already have many of those skills. In fact," he said with the first smile the others had ever seen, "I heard you disassembled and re-assembled an M16 faster than the instructors, even faster than I can do it. And, without speaking, you found a novel way of telling your squad to dig a tunnel. So, given your skills, we devised a special training program for you: 4-5 months, mostly in the Paratroopers' basic training base." Alex was flabbergasted that such close tabs had been kept on him during *Gibush* with everything being reported to The Unit's top brass.

"You'll be sent to different groups of trainees based on their programs. The first segment, two weeks at the IDF Parachuting School, will start next Sunday; then you'll do a five-week CT, a counter-terror course in the IDF Counter-Terror Warfare School, followed by some additional CT training in The Unit. The rest, about two months or a bit longer, will be navigation-and-orienteering and long-range reconnaissance patrol training, crucial in The Unit. While navigation training in other IDF units is done in pairs for safety reasons, *Sayeret Matkal* conducts solo long-range navigation. When you've finished everything, you'll still have to complete the 120-kilometer march to receive your beret. You'll probably be assigned to Unit 269, responsible for counter-terrorism activities outside Israel; if so, you'll work with the Special Forces of other countries, particularly the US, but not the 10th; this time it will be Delta forces or Navy SEALs. When you've completed everything, your work will be as a liaison with other Special Forces."

Captain Avram spoke for the first time. "Because you're a *chayal boded* with no family in Israel, we've asked Chaim Satloff, a former officer in The Unit, who lives on a kibbutz quite near the Paratrooper base to invite you to his kibbutz when you're free on Shabbat; his wife Lotti is Czech. We know the Hofmans are your good friends, but the kibbutz is closer to the base."

Erez said, "All uniforms and gear will be issued next Sunday at

0800 hours when you report to the base. They'll also give you a shorter haircut, not that yours is long. Welcome to The Unit, soldier. Any questions?"

"No sir. Thanks. I'm just looking forward to being in The Unit."

When the officers left the room, Alex felt like doing a jig in the air, even though he'd never done a jig before. *"Do I even know what a jig is?"* he wondered. Instead he went out to the kitchen and asked Sivan to join him for a cup of coffee. She agreed, logged out her computer and plugged in the kettle. While they were drinking their coffee, Alex asked her if she'd be interested in going out with him when he had free time, but she informed him she was seriously involved with someone; however, if she were free…. She smiled. Alex said, a bit sadly. "Oh well, win some, lose some. I hope he deserves you. You're a beautiful and rather irresistible young woman."

♦ ♦ ♦

Early Sunday morning, Alex reported to the Parachute Training School at Tel Nof. He received uniforms and a key to his assigned room, and then went to the camp barber for a short haircut. Fully dressed in uniform and boots which still needed to be broken in, he went to the opening session: 30 recruits and 5 instructors (3 male, 2 female), all of them younger than Alex except Yaakov, the CO who looked at the eager recruits sitting in orderly rows before him, and said, "Imagine standing at the open door of a plane thousands of feet in the air, and preparing to jump out. You're scared, and this will not be the only time, but every paratrooper about to leap from a plane must overcome that fear; to feel fear is natural, but paratroopers learn to leave fear behind them. Jumping out of the plane is the first part; more important is what happens when you land. You might be cut off from the others and can't see them on the ground. You might end up fighting the enemy; therefore, we train you in spatial relations and teach you to take initiative, and we make sure you can fight effectively after landing. The Paratroopers airdrop all the equipment needed for sustained operations in enemy territory – in padded bundles, even heavy vehicles. And now that I've really scared you," he grinned at the young faces, "I'll finish by saying the best part of a jump is the contrast between the aircraft's noise before you jump and the quiet after your parachute opens. Good luck, soldiers."

Training included everything: how to board, how to land correctly, what to think about on the way down, when to open the spare parachute, how not to break your leg, and how to relax before jumping.

Chapter 4

The instructors treated the training seriously and orders were given in a singsong cadence that the young soldiers mimicked; Alex sometimes joined in their fun. Ultimately, he decided that humor might be his best defense against the constant fear resulting from his friend's tragic death. Alex realized the rationale behind many drills was to master the technique so the body would react without thinking; he knew this was particularly important for him given the issues he'd never come to terms with. The first time Alex jumped from a C-130 Hercules at 500 meters, he said to himself, *"You can do this, Novak, you can do this. You can land and you won't die. Just keep your feet together and you can do this now."* He knew that his fear came from lack of control; not jumping was not an option for any of them and they all were afraid as the ground rushed ever closer. Alex, as the oldest, stood up to be the first to fly out into space the moment the side doors of the aircraft were opened and the wind rushed in. That was the moment fear took over; with both of his hands clamped on the sides of the plane, one foot forward, his throat dry, he hesitated. "Jump!" came the command and a pat – or a push – on the back. He jumped. For a second, he was disoriented; then his parachute opened. He looked up, saw the white canopy above him, and thanked the Lord and the parachute for doing what was expected of them. He was also aware of silence, the glorious quiet the CO had mentioned. Alex floated effortlessly through the sky and then suddenly the wonder of it was forgotten as the ground came closer. *"Feet together, feet together,"* he reminded himself. And he was down, the wind dragging his parachute a short way along the dune. He had overcome his fear and executed an almost perfect landing on his first jump, his toes touching before his body rolled over to the side. At the end of parachute training, all those who had completed the program were awarded silver wings. The CO said, "This course is sometimes said to serve the combat spirit more than operational capability, because it requires both physical and mental effort. To jump out of a plane is to act contrary to the human urge to defend itself, and that requires immense power. You're completely alone; it's not possible to try again. From the moment you leave the plane, you're on your own and the knowledge and skills you acquired during training are in your own hands. You're to be commended for all you accomplished in two weeks." When Alex's turn came, the CO said to him, "I'm giving you the wings I received when I completed this course."

"Why?" Alex stammered. "What did I do?"

"You jumped five times with only a small parachute. I know it was hard after losing a good friend back home. I hope you now know there's nothing you can't do; these jumps will always be a part of you and who you are."

Shaking hands with the CO, Alex promised to be worthy of such trust.

Tel Nof wasn't that far away from Ramat Aviv, so Alex hitched a ride to the Hofmans for the weekend. David was delighted to see him, but he was in the midst of writing an article and was expecting a conference call. Lise came out of her studio, hugged him without touching because of the blue paint on her fingers, and immediately led him to the kitchen for something to eat and drink. "Food first, then I want to hear all about parachuting."

"Yes, Mother," he joked.

"Am I really that bad?" she asked.

"Yes, but I love it," he responded. "You make me feel like I'm home."

"So how was it?" she persisted, handing him a tall glass of iced tea and a plate of delicious home-made brownies. She noticed his expression and said, "Not my doing. Grandma Anna's. Now details of the jumping."

Alex said, "Classes were fine, but I was terrified the first time I jumped. The CO gave me his own wings at the ceremony; he said he knew I'd lost my friend in a jump gone bad, and this was hard for me. I was speechless."

Lise took a napkin and grabbed a brownie off his plate. After stuffing half of it into her mouth, she said, "Alex, my 'almost son', everyone who comes in contact with you is impressed with the things that you're able to do. I'm not surprised about the wings. I'm in the midst of a painting, so what do you want to do now? Rest? Read? Watch TV? The house is yours…"

After a weekend of food and fun, on Sunday Alex reported to the IDF Counter-Terrorism Warfare School and was assigned to a room with twelve trainees. While he was changing into a black t-shirt, two young men came in, wearing shirts with the US Navy SEALs insignia. Alex shook hands with Marc and Adam and told them he'd been in the Slovakian Special Forces and trained with the US 10th Special Forces prior to moving to Israel. When they asked about his excellent command of English, he told them about living in Pittsburgh. Marc said he was from Philadelphia and Adam was from California; fearing they wouldn't understand some Hebrew explanations, they were happy to be in the course with Alex. However, in the first session, all the instructors wore t-shirts with English writing, not Hebrew; the trainees were told joint training was so common because most IDF

Chapter 4

special ops personnel speak English, making everything easier.

The intense 5-week course was divided into several phases:
- Weapons, standard types and special ones;
- *Krav Maga* with one goal, to disarm and incapacitate the enemy quickly by any means, unlike the other martial arts which depend on philosophy;
- Rappelling and fast rope descent from a moving helicopter, for hostage rescue;
- Takeover and Engagement rescues;
- Camouflage;
- Close Quarter Battle training with primary and secondary weapons for assaults on multiple rooms; and finally,
- One day of training with IDF's K-9 unit, with Belgian Shepherds, mid-sized dogs large enough to attack an enemy but small enough to be picked up by their handlers to help extract hostages from fortified buildings seized by terrorists.

Alex was amazed at the school's simulation facilities with unique videos and modular CQB sites: full-size models of buses, trains and airplanes for hostage rescue training. With so much to learn and so little time, he spent Shabbat reading and studying. On the third Saturday, one of the instructors asked Alex if he'd like to go to the "city that never sleeps" with Marc and Adam. They drove to the Tel Aviv Port, had dinner in one of its restaurants and even went to a few clubs. Back at the base, they all agreed it had been a very welcome break from the intensity and pressure of the program.

A final exercise took place in the last week: a complex hostage rescue scenario to plan and execute an assault; a few of the trainees were an entry team and the others were terrorists and hostages. The role-playing not only boosted their confidence but also provided them with a wider perspective on hostage rescue operations and even gave them insight into the mind of a terrorist/kidnapper. To make the exercise seem realistic, they used paintball guns and *simunition*. At the end, Alex received a CT certificate and a report card, and he was given a one-week vacation before he had to report to the paratroopers training base in the Jordan Valley. Lise and Dani came to take him home, and they drove the US Navy SEALs into Tel Aviv, with Dani flirting the entire way. Both SEALs promised to stay in touch with Alex and hoped they'd come back to Israel someday on vacation. They told Dani she was adorable, but far too young for them; behind Dani's back, Lise silently thanked the two young Americans. At home, Lise said, "Alex, you look absolutely 'knackered', I think that's the correct word. Why don't you go for a swim? You know our pool is heated so we can use it all year. This week you'll have the guest room instead of Yaniv's room because we've no out-of-towners! Hallelujah! I say that as I'm working like mad for an exhibit that's opening very soon. You, of course, are not a guest. You're family! I've no idea who'll be here for dinner, but we'll do something good."

Dani winked at Alex. "Catch your breath, big brother who will soon be wearing a red beret. She's on a roll. It happens whenever she's getting close to exhibit time. We've all learned to live with it…and with her!" All three of them laughed at Dani's cheeky remarks, and then went to follow their own pursuits: Alex to stow his gear and head to the swimming pool, Dani to get a soft drink and finish her homework, Lise to do some finishing touches on the new paintings for her coming exhibit in the Helena Rubinstein Pavilion, next door to Habima Theatre, and part of the Tel Aviv Museum. Alex knew the centerpiece would be her huge painting of the extended Hofman family lunch on *Sukkoth*, and he hoped the critics would love it as much as he did. He enjoyed his week off, swimming in the Hofman's pool, reading books he hadn't had time for up till then, relaxing with Kobi and Yaniv and Yaniv's friend Gabriel when they all had time off, clubbing in Tel Aviv with Keren and her friends, learning several basic recipes from Grandma Anna, sharing military stories with David, and even teasing Dani about her little "crush" on the US Navy SEALs Marc and Adam. He'd noted signs of attraction between Dani and Gabriel, but she seemed interested in every male and he attributed that to her age, remembering the same expressions on his sister Paulina. Because Lise was so pressured about her exhibit, no one saw much of her, but everyone tried to offer their support through peace and quiet in the house; almost the only sound was the stereo Lise played in her studio and hushed voices in the kitchen as they prepared meals. Alex was sorry he probably wouldn't be released to attend the opening of her exhibition.

To get an early start for his arrival at the Paratrooper base in the Jordan Valley, Alex had booked a room at *Beit Hachayal*, the Jerusalem hostel for IDF soldiers for the last night of his *chofesh*. After breakfast the next day, the soldier on duty at the desk told him an officer who was being driven to the Jordan Valley had offered Alex a lift. On the way to the base, Alex saw a sign for Kibbutz Tirat Zvi, the home of Chaim Satloff, the former *Sayeret Matkal* officer he'd been told about during his last interview for The Unit.

At the base, he was assigned to a large barracks and then summoned to a meeting with the CO who told him he'd immediately begin two weeks of navigation-orienteering training, and then he'd move on to six weeks of long-range reconnaissance patrol in a small group; he'd train with both the Paratroopers' elite *Egoz* unit and *Sayeret Matkal*, and possibly with special ops forces from the US. European Command. Alex found the training in navigation-orienteering simple as he'd always had an excellent sense of direction; his *Babička* called it an "internal compass". With either a map or a compass, he had always found his way in unfamiliar territory, but the IDF focused on two different techniques: (1) dead reckoning or locating a polar coordinate on a map and then on the ground; and (2) terrain association by comparing what was expected from a map and what was actually on the ground, and making adjustments based on special features such as shape and elevations of the slopes, steepness, hydrography and vegetation. The ultimate test of this training was in the field; Alex found those experiences fairly simple and surprisingly enjoyable.

Two nights before the last navigation-orienteering session, he called the Satloffs and asked if he could spend Shabbat at their kibbutz; Lotti said he was most welcome. He hitched a ride to the kibbutz Friday afternoon and was directed to the Satloff's small house; Chaim told him he'd be in one of the cottages they kept for volunteers, but they would see him at the synagogue and in the dining hall for meals. Alex thought the accommodation was a bit strange, but he was exhausted Friday night and went to asleep shortly after dinner; when he awoke in the morning, he noticed his duffel was open. His wallet was on the floor and although his IDs and IDF bank card were still there, all his cash was gone. He remembered reading about Yogi Berra, an American baseball player known for fracturing the English language, and he frowned as he quoted Yogi's famous line "It's déjà vu all over again!" In other words, *"Welcome back to Pennsylvania!"* He said to himself, *"If I have another weekend off, I'll find some way to get to the Hofmans!"* After the Shabbat morning services, he told Lotti and Chaim about the theft, and they expressed shock, but he knew that they didn't believe him; the Satloffs and the kibbutz manager were not willing to acknowledge that a volunteer they had known for months would steal from a soldier who was a stranger. Nevertheless, Chaim told Alex he would drive him back to the base after Shabbat. As Susan Berger, his Pittsburgh hostess, would have said, Alex was not a "happy camper," but he tried to put another unhappy incident behind him by telling himself there are good people and bad everywhere, even in Israel, even in a kibbutz.

In Alex's mind, long-range reconnaissance patrol evoked images of war movies he'd seen, like US Rangers in Vietnam creeping behind enemy lines to ambush the Viet Cong. He knew US Special Ops were experts in Long Range Recon Patrol and he wanted to learn their techniques and tactics. To be able to move deep into enemy territory totally undetected, to accomplish the mission and get back alive was a vital military strategy; it was the focus of four weeks of training with experienced *Egoz* instructors: marksmanship and the use of sniper equipment and procedures, e.g. stalking and collecting battlefield intelligence. They had to come within 300 meters of spotters in a tactical vehicle and shoot at the driver or passenger without being seen; and they had to hit targets 800 meters away. They were taught to blend in with the surrounding environment by wearing the appropriate camouflage. Not far from Eilat, they had one week of intensive instruction in combat diving and submarine exfiltration or infiltration, working with *Shayetet 13*, Israel's naval commandos. One expert said, "You can't just fall out of a plane, pull your 'chute and think everything's OK. You've got to go sub-surface holding your breath, lose the 'chute and then resurface in the correct location to do the mission." Alex wasn't surprised that he didn't panic when he jumped out of the helicopter into deep water; he knew his 'chute would function properly.

After so many weeks of preparation, they took part in a joint IDF and US military exercise: Alex and other trainees in The Unit as well as more than 100 *Egoz* soldiers were Israel's participants; the Americans were 150 select forces from the 173rd Airborne Brigade Combat Team based in Italy who'd arrived at Ben Gurion Airport with assault rifles, 7.62 mm machine guns, sniper rifles, and personal combat gear. The two forces tested all their skills shoulder to shoulder in "invasions" into urban warfare training centers simulating villages with armed enemy militants; they practiced taking over enemy controlled territory in other villages. All orders on the radio channels were in English, but the safety guidelines were the Israeli ones. Only blanks were fired outside the shooting ranges because of the much more stringent IDF safety protocols; therefore, to institute a live fire effect, the IDF used pyrotechnics. An *Egoz* officer said, "We all learned a lot." Alex agreed.

The final challenge of Alex's training was the *Masa Kumta*, the Beret March. In *Sayeret Matkal*, this was a 4-day, 120 km march in full gear, through any kind of weather and all kinds of terrain, finishing at Masada where they'd receive their red berets. They began in the evening, continued through the night and into the next day; fatigue

Chapter 4

set in as the sun rose, but undeterred by the pain, they pushed on, still in full gear. Alex was hot and tired, but he tried to overcome his exhaustion by helping others, bearing in mind The Unit's motto: "Who Dares, Wins" and by adhering to the *Tzahal* code: never leave a man behind. In the Judean Hills, not far from their final goal, their commanders stopped them, but not for a break. One officer said, "Nothing invigorates a tired body quite like doing pushups in full gear!" Finally at Masada, they cleaned up as much as possible, and after a last check, they were ready, and proud, to receive the red berets. Veterans and current members of *Sayeret Matkal*, including Erez and Sefi, attended the ceremony, as did the Chief of General Staff who arrived by helicopter to the cheers of the men; the Brigade Commander welcomed all of them to Israel's most elite unit, congratulated them and wished them good luck. He spoke to them about disturbing changes in the Arab world and how these might have an effect on The Unit's future missions. After handing each soldier his red beret, he reminded them that they're not allowed to wear The Unit's emblem in public to maintain secrecy. Both Erez and Sefi congratulated Alex and the training CO beckoned him to meet The Unit's highest-ranking officer who smiled and said, "Alex, you've been outstanding through these months of intense training. Therefore, I'm really pleased to give you a few days off to unwind and get your head around everything. You'll soon receive orders about where and when to report." He shook Alex's hand, and added, "Good luck, son. Wear your red beret with pride!" Exultant, Alex saluted him.

From Masada, Alex returned to Jerusalem overnight to think about all he'd experienced. He decided on a swim in *Beit Hachayal*'s pool, a decent meal, and then emailing his parents, the Hofmans and Ted Hoffman about his future. As he was finally drifting off to sleep, he said to himself, *"Who would have believed on New Year's Day in 1993, when Babička and Dedko told the family we're Jewish, that I'd be where I am, a member of Israel's counter-espionage reconnaissance unit, in only 9 years!"* The next day, Alex went to Ramat Aviv to spend the few days of his needed break with the Israelis he loved the most: Lise and David and their family. Of course, they'd arranged a small celebration in his honor on the weekend and hoped Kobi, Yaniv and Gabriel would come for Shabbat. But first, they had a more intimate dinner of just family, including Lise's and David's parents. When Alex asked Lise about her exhibit, before she could say a word, Keren handed him the rave reviews: one said Lise Hofman's work was "innovative and brilliant", another focused on her unusual "sense of color" and a third claimed "she raised the use of acrylics to a new high". Every review praised "Extended Family at Sukkoth" and her rare ability to "make every person on her canvas alive." Alex went to her exhibit the next day.

Chapter 5

As The Unit's liaison with international counter-terrorism forces until February 2005, Alex spent most of the next two-and-a-half years abroad, with the British Army's Special Air Service, SAS, whose motto "Who Dares, Wins" had been adopted by *Sayeret Matkal*; he worke*d* with France's GIGN, Gendarmerie Intervention Group, with Germany's KSK, *Kommando Spezialkräfte*, with Canada's Joint Task Force 2, JTF2. But the bulk of his liaison was with Delta Force, the US Army's 1st Special Operational Detachment. Alex loved what he was doing, but he often felt deeply lonely. He really missed his family, although he'd spent two weeks at home in 2003, amazed at how much his niece and nephew had grown and worried about how much his grandparents had aged. Of course, he also missed his "Israeli family", although email allowed him to be in touch with them often. Lise and David had become closer than just friends, and he loved Dani like another younger sister. Kobi, Yaniv, and Gabriel, Yaniv's IDF buddy, were his "brothers", as close as Rob Salter. He'd even tried to think of Keren, who was almost as beautiful as her mother, in a romantic way, but it didn't work; she was "another sister" and it seemed incestuous. When he was in Israel for short periods of time between assignments, he stayed with the Hofmans. Because they needed a guest suite for their many visitors from abroad and with Keren living in a flat near Tel Aviv University, Lise and David redid her room as a haven for Alex. He was dumbfounded when he saw it; Lise hugged him and said, "I told you a long time ago that you're a member of our family. We all love you." It seemed very strange to be in the United States and not spend much time with his American friends, although both Rob Salter and Jonathan Green spent a long weekend with him at Fort Bragg, North Carolina, when he taught *Krav Maga* to the Delta Forces. He spent Thanksgiving in 2003 with Ted Hoffman and his family as well as the Bergers and other friends from the Pittsburgh JCC; he went to Columbus for a Christmas reunion with the Greens and his Ohio friends. He really missed Natalie Gold and their loving relationship, but when Rob told him she'd recently married another rabbinical student, he was pleased for her.

A few days after returning to Israel in 2005, Alex met with The Unit's CO and a few other officers. When they asked him to remain in the IDF as a career, his response was odd. "I once read a story called *A Man without a Country,* and in a way, that's how I sometimes feel. That man denounced his country and was punished by living on navy ships for the rest of his life, never allowed to set foot in his country. I left Slovakia when I was 21 and lived in America for a few months. Then I came to Israel, made *Aliyah* and joined The Unit. *Tzahal* has sent me all over, to the States, Canada, France, England, Germany, and someone recently said there might be an Australian course. Really? The Unit's been a marvelous experience, but I feel I have no roots, no permanent home. Three weeks here, a month there, and then a few weeks somewhere else. I know I can be called into *Milu'im* at any time, but I honestly feel I'd like to stay in one place, Israel, at least for quite a while. I'd like to study in university for a degree. I hope I'm not a disappointment to you; I'm so grateful for everything The Unit has given me…but I'm 26 years old, have no degree, no profession. So…"

His CO interrupted, "It's OK, Alex. We understand. Those of us born here or who came as children have a history with this country, families, the people we grew up with, the schools we attended, the clubs we joined, the IDF. And we have homes to go to when we can. I know the Hofmans have been a superb substitute family, but they're not the same as your real mom and dad, your grandparents, your siblings. I'm pleased you aren't thinking about going back to Slovakia, and you believe that Israel should be your home. So what now? Israeli universities begin the academic year after all the *chagim*; that's the end of October this year, and now it's only February. Would you consider staying in The Unit as a paid instructor for another few months? You're already a lieutenant and after working with special forces in so many countries, your expertise would be invaluable for new recruits, and even for veterans in The Unit. Don't answer now. Think about it." He grinned at Alex and added, "And if you're interested, since we share "Who Dares, Wins" with Australia as well as with the Brits, we could definitely arrange something with their SASR, Special Air Service Regiment, if you want to get out of Israel again during the next few months!"

Alex took their offer. One of his very first actions after agreeing to stay in the IDF until mid-August was to purchase a 2003 red Jeep Wrangler with fairly low mileage and only a few dents, enabling him to go wherever he and the IDF wanted him to go. Kobi, Yaniv, Gabriel, and David helped him hammer out all the dents; with so many workers and a lot of laughter, they finished quickly and the jeep looked brand new, so the afternoon ended with a pick-up basketball game followed by a swim in the Hofman's pool. Later they were joined by Lise, Dani, David's sister Dina and her husband for an impromptu barbecue, with Maccabee beer and superb Yarden wines. As he relaxed

Chapter 5

on the deck, Alex looked around at everyone and lifted his glass, "It's so good to be home! *L'chaim!*" he said. Lise squeezed his hand as she echoed, *"L'chaim!"*

Alex's first IDF assignment was in March, a four-day *Gibush* for *Garin Mahal*; this *Gibush* was specifically for *Shayetet 13*, Israel's Navy SEALs, and for 669, the Elite Search and Rescue Unit. The IDF wanted to know if any of the Lone Soldiers from abroad are qualified to serve in those special forces. As an instructor, Alex knew he had to be tough, but he remembered how difficult those days had been for some young men in *Gibush* with him less than four years earlier, and he tried to be supportive. All the training was in Hebrew to ascertain the foreign trainees' language skills, and some of *Tzahal*'s most elite forces would prepare, and test, these future soldiers step-by-step, physically and, more importantly, mentally for *Shayetet 13* and Unit 669. Many exercises and drills took place in the Mediterranean: swimming 100 meters in each direction followed by the same swim again, blindfolded; dismantling a rifle under water; diving 5 meters to extract a ring; swimming with minimal breathing. Of those who started, half would be released after two days; of the remaining *gibushim*, less than one-third would pass and go on to full boot camp. One of the *Shayetet 13* instructors called the dropouts "whining little mama's boys" but Alex knew many of them were just scared kids on their own in a foreign country. One named Guy who didn't make the final cut told Alex he heard *Gibush* was "Israel's Parris Island with man-eating crocodiles as instructors", but to him it was really more like a medieval torture chamber complete with the Rack and the Iron Lady! Alex didn't respond, but inwardly felt sorry for this young man who'd wanted to call himself an Israeli SEAL. He told Guy and the others who hadn't been accepted into *Shayetet 13*, they might still be able to serve in another special forces unit, like *Egoz*, *Duvdevan* or *Oketz* if they passed an interview with that unit's commanding officer. Alex was pleased when some young men immediately told him they would apply to other units.

His next assignment, two weeks before Passover, was a special 5-day training exercise with 50 members of Germany's counter-terrorism unit, *Grenzschutzgruppe 9 der Bundespolizei*, GSG-9, formed after the dismal failure to rescue 11 Israeli athletes who were hostages and then murdered in the 1972 Munich Olympics. The GSG 9 soldiers were eager to learn new rescue techniques from "the world's best special ops forces" and how to seize, destroy, disrupt, capture, exploit, or damage terrorist targets. Alex had worked with German soldiers in

NATO's International Security Assistance Force. But he'd never seen anything like the enthusiasm of the GSG 9 group about being in Israel; on the bus to the Counter-Terrorism Warfare School, several young men openly admitted that their grandfathers had supported Hitler. They were deeply ashamed of their grandfathers who'd been members of the *Wehrmacht*, or worse, of the *Waffen-SS* or the *Gestapo*, responsible for the atrocities of the Holocaust. Alex and Aryeh, the other training instructor, didn't know how to react to the guilt of these young Germans, but at the Warfare School, Colonel G, the high-ranking officer who greeted them in excellent German, said, "You have no reason to feel responsible for the actions of your grandparents; you weren't even born. Think about where you are now and what you're doing. Hitler didn't win! Israel's here to stay and we're quite successful. So let's work together in this training program to prevent another Holocaust from ever happening again. Alex's grandparents were Slovakian partisans in the war, so maybe they extracted a price from the Nazis. Now, work hard with Alex and Aryeh and you will participate in a remarkable exercise. *Willkommen und Viel Glück!*"

Two days after saying *shalom* to the GSG 9 soldiers, Alex was in another *Gibush*, a joint tryout for Israeli youngsters who wanted to be in *Sayeret Matkal, Sheldag* and Unit 669. The *Gibush* with 250 men and 25 officers started in Nitzanim in a *sharav*, or *khamsin*; the humidity dropped to almost nothing and by noon it was more than 36 degrees Centigrade. Alex knew it would be extremely difficult for many *gibushim*; on the other hand, if they passed *Gibush* under these conditions, they'd succeed in Special Ops. After waiting in the hot sun for hours and eating their first MREs, the *gibushim* were taken to the sandy dunes for the sprinting, crawling, and team drills that were repeated again and again. Unit 669 required additional exercises to teach rescue operations in water and Kobi joined them as an instructor for one day; none of the *gibushim* or officers objected to going into the cool Mediterranean Sea for those water exercises. Fortunately, the *sharav* ended after two days and it was easier for participants and instructors to complete *Gibush* without the intense heat, sand and flies. The ones who passed were congratulated and told they'd begin *tironut* after *Pesach*. Alex, relieved that this difficult *Gibush* during a *sharav* was over, looked forward to enjoying the *Pesach* break in Ramat Aviv.

When he parked his Jeep in the Hofman's driveway and carried his duffel bag to the front door, he was surprised when it opened even before he could ring the bell. Then he was speechless when he realized the person standing in the open doorway was his mother. She pulled

Chapter 5

him inside in a huge bear-hug, and said, "I've been watching for your car. Ted Hoffman arranged this for you, and as a vacation in Israel for us." Over his mother's shoulder, he saw his father and his grandparents in the hallway.

"Oh my God!" he spluttered. "Are you really here or am I dreaming after four days of an exercise from hell?" He realized he wasn't dreaming when his *Babička* hugged and kissed him, followed by *Dedko* and then his father.

Hearing the commotion, Lise came in from the deck, followed by Ted. "Surprised, Alex?" Lise asked. "Come out to the deck for a real visit. Kobi knew about this but he was sworn to secrecy during your joint *Gibush*."

On the deck, Alex said, with tears in his eyes, "I don't know what to say. I'm not usually speechless, but I never expected this." He looked at Ted and said, "You know you're the best. Right? Actually," he said, "I'm sorry to say you're next in line behind the Israeli Hofmans, Lise, David, their kids!"

"How can you say that, Alex?" his father asked in Slovakian. "Mr. Hoffman has done so much. He arranged this for us and won't let me pay him back."

Ted, sitting between his wife Shani and Lise, his arms around both their shoulders, smiled at Alex's father and said, "I don't speak Slovakian, Janek, but I know what you said, and it's OK. This is special for Alex, but I also know how important Lise, David and their kids are to him. I'm the one who sent him to them." Everyone relaxed with Ted's comments, including Janek.

Alex, sitting between his mother and grandmother, wondered who else would join them. Just as the doorbell rang, Shani asked, "How bad was the *Gibush*? Sand everywhere and it was so hot here! Not like April at all…"

"It was awful!" Alex answered, as David and Keren came out to the deck, with Lise's and David's parents, everyone carrying a casserole or bag.

"What was 'awful'?" Keren inquired.

"*Gibush*," Alex said. "I felt so sorry for those kids. It was hot and windy on the dunes; sand got into hair, eyes, tents, food, everything. They were so tired. This *Gibush* was for Unit 669, *Matkal* and *Shaldag*, so whenever we had swimming drills, everyone, including us instructors, was happy to jump into the sea! *Gibush* under such conditions helped us select the very best recruits for those forces. Speaking of 669, will Kobi be joining us?"

"Tomorrow, just before Shabbat," David answered. "Yaniv and Gabriel will come as well. And Gabriel's other buddy from Austria, David R. My sister Dina, her husband Alon and their kids will also be here. And even though she's almost 20, Dani's still the youngest, so I guess she'll ask the Four Questions Saturday night at the Seder or maybe we'll all do them. She's on her way home right now from Tiberias with Tammy and Ethan. They're Ted and Shani's children," he added, for Alex's family.

"We know all about Hoffman with two 'fs' and one 'n', Hofman with one 'f' and one 'n', and Hoffmann with two 'fs' and two 'ns'! So many ways to spell the same name!" Alex's mother said. "What your families have all done for Alex is remarkable! But so many people tomorrow for the *Seder*; we can have ours at the hotel. I'm sure we can still arrange a table."

"Absolutely not!" Lise exclaimed. "A long time ago. I told Alex he's not a guest, he's family. So the four of you are family, too. All over the world, Jewish families get together for the *Seder*. And," she added with a grin, "in Israel we only have one *Seder*. Most of the food's done, thanks to Anna and Aya with a little help from David and me; those casseroles and bags they brought in were for the *Seder*, and Dina will bring other things tomorrow. So we're all set, and there's no way on earth we'd let you experience your first Israeli *Seder* at an impersonal hotel with strangers. I'm sure the Hilton's food would be great, but ours will be better. Ours will be sensational!"

As Lise predicted, their *Seder* the next evening was superb. She'd told everyone to enjoy a snack because it would be late before their meal was served, and the delectable aromas wafting from the kitchen to the deck would make everyone hungry. The table was grand, set for 24, a wineglass and *Haggada*h at every place, candles, flowers strewn across the elegant tablecloth. Bowls of peeled hard-boiled eggs and tiny pitchers of salted water sat on the table, along with small dishes of *charoset* and plates of celery and sliced potatoes. There was wine, red and white, sweet and dry. The entire Seder would be in English to make it easy for Alex's family; if it was in Hebrew, they'd have to read everything in translation. Joking, David said they should all read fast because English is much longer than Hebrew, and he'd like to eat the fabulous food at a reasonable hour. David conducted the Seder with a little help from his religious cousin Ted, and from Gabriel and David R. who'd spent their teenage years in the home of an Austrian rabbi, and from Alex who'd studied Judaism in Ted's JCC in Pittsburgh. He told Alex's family *seder* means "order" and they'd follow standard order.

Chapter 5

When they came to *Mah Nishtana*, the four questions traditionally asked by the youngest child, David said, "There's no youngest child here tonight. Since Lise and I have four children, each one of them will ask one question, starting with our youngest, Danielle."

Dani said, "At least, *Aba*, you didn't say I'm the 'one who doesn't know how to ask'! Oh, that comes later."

Alex said to his parents, "I told you she's cheeky, just like Paulina." Even Dani laughed. She probably would have tossed her napkin at him, but she glanced across the table and saw her mother's frown.

Finally, it was time for the festive meal. It was festive and traditional as well as fabulous: gefilte fish; chicken soup that "Nana Anna didn't burn!" Kobi teased; salads; brisket in gravy and roast chicken; roasted potatoes and potato *kugel*; a sweet potato-carrot-prune-raisin *tzimmes*; asparagus and green beans; sparkling soda, soft drinks. When everyone was stuffed and groaning, David thanked the cooks and announced it was time to eat the *afikoman*, which he'd hidden at the back of his chair earlier. Ted recalled how Kobi and Ethan had found it at their *seder* in Pittsburgh so many years earlier, and how the boys had demanded a ransom, not a reward: a remote-control plane for Kobi and a microscope for Ethan. David gave a piece of the *afikomen* to everyone, and said, "Since we had no children demanding a reward, or a ransom for the *afikomen*, and since we're all full after far too much food, Lise and I have decided to make a donation in the names of all of you here at our *Seder* to Leket, the network that provides food to Israel's poor. Does everyone agree?" Around the table, he saw nods and smiles.

Lise then said, "A piece of *matzah*, even the *afikomen*, is a pretty sad dessert, so let's get back to the *Seder* and after some singing, we'll bring out the fancy desserts." After the third of the four required glasses of wine, Aya, Anna and Lenka, the grandmothers, said they were old and feeling tipsy, so they shouldn't keep drinking. Helena said she was a grandmother, too, and didn't think she was old, but she also felt she shouldn't drink more wine. "Nonsense," all the husbands scoffed, as they poured the fourth glass for everyone. "The wine's good and we'll all probably sleep very well."

The *Seder* ended with the traditional Jewish prayer of hope: "*L'shanah haba'ah b'Yerushalayim!* Next year in Jerusalem!" Lise said, "All leftovers are in the fridge and the dishwasher has already worked overtime tonight, so anything else can wait until tomorrow. Anybody want to join me for a hike to work off calories?" When she had no takers and Alex said he'd drive his family to the Hilton and Keren said she'd drive her grandparents home and David Rosenzweig said he'd walk, but only the three blocks to his flat, Lise said, "OK. To misquote a famous poem, 'Merry *Pesach* to all and to all a good night'!" But a few minutes later, sharing a lounger near the pool with David, she said, "Let's unwind, my darling, not by taking a long walk but in what's always been one of our favorite ways, skinny-dipping!"

David laughed, immediately kicked off his shoes and started stripping. "Last one in is…" but stopped speaking when Lise's colorful dress landed on his head. They heard Alex come back, and David called out, "Join us in the pool," but Alex noticed clothing strewn carelessly around the deck and realized everyone except Lise and David had retired to their beds. He just waved and tiptoed upstairs to his room without saying a word.

◆ ◆ ◆

Ted had hired a private tourist guide with a minibus to give Alex's family a special tour of Israel, and Alex appreciated the opportunity to spend that time with his family. One day they went to the historic ruins in Caesaria and then had lunch in Zichron Yaakov, a picturesque town. Then they drove up to the grottoes in Rosh Hanikra on the Lebanese border. Another day was spent in Jerusalem but the capital was so filled with holiday tourists, local as well as foreign, it was difficult even to get near the major sites. In the evenings, if it had been a long day of touring, they ate supper with Lise and David, first consuming all the *Seder* leftovers, then doing a little simple cooking; on other evenings, they went to one of the many Tel Aviv or Herzliya restaurants open during the holidays. Sometimes the American Hoffmans and Israeli Hofmans joined the minibus tours; sometimes Alex's grandparents thought that day's scheduled tour was too strenuous and they opted to spend the day with Anna and Richard at their Tel Aviv home, or strolling on the nearby promenade along the Mediterranean seashore from north Tel Aviv to Old Yafo, or just enjoying coffee and pastries at one of the many cafés on the route. Looking at the unusually peaceful sea one afternoon, Lenka remembered that Alex had told them how he had often looked across the Mediterranean towards Israel when he was in Cyprus and that he had longed to visit his ancestral homeland, but it was forbidden to UN peacekeepers. Anna said, "But just look at your wonderful grandson now. We want him to stay in Israel, find a nice girl and raise a family here. At one time, we hoped he and Keren would get together, but they're like brother and sister. Sad, because you know we all love him, don't you?"

Chapter 5

Alex was sad when his family's visit ended a few days after *Pesach*; he'd been granted four extra days of vacation to spend with them. Touring his beloved Israel with his parents and grandparents, listening to his mother's accounts of the antics of his mischievous niece and nephew, and catching up with his sisters' activities had been extraordinary. He knew his adored grandparents were getting on in years, but they were still so interested in everything going on, still open to every new experience, still generous to everyone they encountered; and he really enjoyed watching the friendship that developed among the elderly couples. But to him, perhaps the most special moment of this holiday was his father apologizing for giving him a hard time about everything, about going to America and wanting to learn about his Jewish roots instead of studying engineering and working with him in the automobile factory in Žilina. His father said although he would never be a practicing Jew, he appreciated the religion, its history and all the Jewish people he had met, and he wanted Alex to know he was so proud of how much his son had accomplished in Slovakia, in the US and in Israel. Alex was almost able to recapture his childhood love and hero worship for his father. At the airport, it was a very sad moment for all of them, but they promised to meet again soon, either in Slovakia or in Israel.

When Alex reported to The Unit, driving there directly from the airport, the CO said, "Even though you're just back from the *Pesach* break, Alex, I know your work up to now has been very intense, so how would you like a trip to Australia? They want *Krav Maga* for their special forces, and we both know how very good you are at that. With your knowledge of English, you'll have no trouble with their accents and very weird slang. Do you need some time to think about it?"

Alex responded, "No, sir. I'd be delighted to go. When would I leave?"

"A week from today, Wednesday, May 11th, at 2230 hours, on an El-Al flight to Bangkok with a brief stop in Vienna, arriving at 1330 hours, 1730 hours Bangkok time; then you'll have an almost 10-hour flight to Sydney on Qantas or Cathay. With several time changes and given the length of your flights, I hope you can sleep on a plane. I know the Aussies will allow you some time to settle in. You'll be based in Potts Point, a suburb of Sydney, near the headquarters and training center of SOCOM, Australia's Special Operations Command. You'll train two or three special ops groups, working with the 1st Commando Regiment, a unit based in Sydney, and with SASR, the Special Air

Alexander's Story

Service Regiment based in Perth, but I don't know anything about the third, or even if there is a third group. The distances in Australia are enormous so if you want to go to the Outback or the rest of the country, we might be able to give you a few extra days. How does that sound?"

"It sounds great, sir. I'd really like to do some diving at the Great Barrier Reef, but just getting to see some of the Aussie wildlife, kangaroos and koalas, but not crocodiles I hope, will be terrific. Since I'll arrive in Sydney on Thursday, or maybe it will be Friday, would it be possible to report to SOCOM on the following Monday, the 16th? That way I can check into a hotel, catch up on sleep, and be ready, in *Tzahal* fighting form, to work."

"That makes sense. I'll get in touch with SOCOM and tell them to expect you on the 16th. Go home, get your gear together, and be at B-G at 2030 hours Wednesday." He handed Alex the SOCOM contact numbers and added, "It's winter in Australia now. Enjoy yourself and good luck."

Alex said, "Thank you, sir", saluted the CO and left. He couldn't wait to tell the Hofmans where he'd be going for the next month. Driving there, he realized he'd been given the perfect way to deal with any residual sadness after saying goodbye to his parents and grandparents. Smiling, he thought, *Leave it to The Unit to come through for me once again!*

The Hofmans were delighted for him; Aya, Ephraim, Anna and Richard, the grandparents, were all coming for dinner that night because Dani had completed her army service and would be leaving the next day with three friends for a post-IDF trip, 2 months in South America and a few weeks in the States. When Alex told them about his trip to Australia for work, Lise asked if he could put her in his duffel and smuggle her aboard? David said he was considering a sabbatical Down Under, and he asked Alex to check out Macquarie University, but only if he had the time. Kobi and Yaniv told him they were green with envy and to think of them when he was surfing at Bondi Beach; in his typical way, Kobi said Unit 669 wouldn't rescue him if he wiped out at Bondi. Keren, a recent *summa cum laude* MA graduate in molecular physics from the Weizmann, was nervously awaiting acceptance letters for a PhD from Copenhagen's Niels Bohr Institute or Berlin's Max Planck Institute. She wished him a colossal trip to a great place, and then, having had a very bad experience herself in India with three friends, gave Dani "big-sister" advice about the dangers in chauvinistic, male-dominated countries for pretty girls. Dani ignored

Chapter 5

her sister, turned to Alex and said in her usual cheeky way, "Bring me a koala, *big brother*, and I'll bring you an armadillo," and added, smirking at her sister, "after we've used it to protect us from those big, bad bullies!" The grandparents hugged Dani and wished her "Bon Voyage!" As a silent and annoyed Keren left the house to drive her grandparents home, she whispered to Alex they'd all wish *him* "Bon Voyage" on Shabbat.

The next day, he started putting together his gear for the Australian trip. He searched the Internet about May-June weather in Sydney, Uluru and Cairns, and noted that he'd need only a light jacket in addition to his IDF uniforms, without The Unit's insignia, of course, and jeans, T-shirts, three sweaters and something for Shabbat, knowing he could buy anything else in Sydney. At the Azrieli Mall, he purchased a new Apple iPhone, an iBook laptop, and a Nikon "Point-and-Shoot" digital camera almost as small as a credit card. Since these last three items had taken a considerable "bite" out of his savings, Alex declared himself *"ready to take on Australia and the Aussies with Krav Maga!"* Knowing SOCOM would provide housing after the 16th, he went online and found "Blue Parrot Backpackers", a hostel in Potts Point, SOCOM's location, and although he loved the name, it only had shared dorm facilities, and Alex knew he would really need a private room and bath after the long flights from Tel Aviv to Sydney. So he reserved an available room with a queen-size bed and private bath for three nights at the Sydney Harbour YHA-the Rocks.

David insisted on driving him to the airport, saying, "Kobi picked you up at Ben-Gurion when you first came to Israel and I, the elder Hofman in this family, will escort you out, even though it's only for a fairly short trip this time!" Alex agreed as long as they used his Jeep and David let him pay for the gas; David agreed to the Jeep but not the gas. Lise chimed in. "I'll be a back-seat driver with yet another Hofman 'cowboy' the whole way, so your 'baby', I mean your Jeep, will be in pristine condition until you're home." David punched Lise very lightly on her arm, and asked Alex, "Have you ever wondered where Kobi and Dani got their cheekiness?" After a brief farewell, a bear-hug from David and kisses from Lise at the departure area, Alex was on his way to Australia.

Chapter 6

Arriving at Sydney Airport at 8:00 p.m. on Thursday, not Friday; Alex was exhausted after 27 hours en route, so although YHA – the Rocks was within easy walking distance of the railroad station, he opted to go to the hostel by taxi. On the 14-kilometer drive to the hostel, he could barely keep his eyes open and he noticed only the Opera House and the Harbour Bridge. After checking in, he took a quick shower, collapsed totally naked on the clean and comfortable bed, and slept for 10 hours. In the morning, dressed in jeans and a sweater, he stopped at the YHA's front desk and told the very pretty clerk, "Stacy Brell" according to her nameplate, that he was starving and asked where to go for breakfast. She told him to step right outside and he'd find several cafés, but one of the best for breakfast was The Baker's Oven on George Street, a short walk from YHA. Alex found the cafe and ordered their Big Breakfast and a Cafe Latte. He'd taken tourist brochures and a map of the city from a rack near the entrance of the hostel, and while he was waiting for his breakfast, he looked through them. Full of food and full of energy after his meal, Alex decided to "play tourist". He started by walking all around The Rocks with its interesting history: for hundreds of years prior to the arrival of Europeans, Aboriginal clans lived in The Rocks. Alex knew punishment for crimes in Britain in the 17th to 19th centuries was often "transportation" to the New World rather than incarceration, to Georgia in America or to Australia, where the land itself was an outdoor jail; the earliest maps showed no prison buildings and convicts themselves built wood and mud camps that warped and shrank or collapsed in heavy rain. George Street was visible on a 1791 map, but it was a map from 1802 that showed 70 huts, two windmills for grinding grain, a church, military barracks and a wharf. Having toured far more ancient Israeli sites, Alex didn't think it necessary to go into the 100 heritage sites in The Rocks. So he walked to Cumberland Street and the Harbour Bridge Climb Visitors Centre. Athletic and fit, Alex opted for the shorter but far more strenuous Bridge Climb; securely clipped into a safety wire, he climbed the steady incline of 1002 steep steps up the arches of the bridge, traversed catwalks and ladders all the way to the 134-meter summit. At the top, not only did he admire the superb panoramic view of Sydney and its surroundings, but he pulled his tiny Nikon out of his pocket and took photographs of the "sails" of the Sydney Opera House to the east and the majestic Blue Mountains in the distance to the west. Alex had read that before

Chapter 6

he became well-known as *Crocodile Dundee*, Paul Hogan had worked as a maintenance rigger on the 134-meter tall Harbour Bridge; in the famous ledge scene in *Dundee II*, he drew on his real life experiences of stopping people who were trying to jump to their deaths from the bridge.

Still "playing tourist", Alex decided to enjoy the hop-on hop-off harbour cruise and boarded a ferry at Circular Quay. He hopped off to explore the glorious Opera House, and then boarded another ferry to Taronga Zoo. He was fascinated by Australia's amazing and exotic wildlife, more than 2,900 native animals, and captivated by the zoo-keepers' free talks. He was tired, or jet-lagged, and back at Darling Harbour, he didn't visit the Aquarium or the Maritime Museum. Instead, he took a cab to Macquarrie University so he'd be able to tell David about it. He walked around the huge campus, saw ultramodern buildings on 126 hectares of rolling hills and natural bushland. With about the same number of students as Tel Aviv University, he talked to a few and then went back to The Rocks, where he wandered around the picturesque area of trendy shops and cafes along cobbled streets. He had dinner at Zia Pina on George Street where he took the waiter's suggestion and had *Il Brodetto*, a magnificent meal of Australian barramundi, clams, king prawns, mussels and crostini plus Little Creatures Pale Ale, an oddly named Australian beer. Walking back to YHA, Alex knew he was not only stuffed after the amazing meal and ale, but also enchanted with Australia. He went up to the roof to chill out with another beer; a couple of young Aussies asked if he was a Yank and when he told them he was Israeli, they said they were *gobsmacked*. One of them, Jed, said, "We're from Darwin, up north, not a *Big Smoke* like Sydney. I've met a few Israelis backpacking around the Outback, but never one who speaks like a Yank. So, mate, how about joining us for a *cold one* at the oldest pub in the Rocks and then tellin' us whatcha doin' here Down Under?"

"Sorry, guys. I'm really knackered tonight after playing tourist too much today and too much traveling yesterday. But if you're here tomorrow, I'm sure I'll be up for pub grub and a cold one at that old pub!" Alex said.

"Not to worry. We'll catch you on the morrow for a pub crawl. G'night!"

The next morning, Stacy sent him to Pancakes on the Rocks, where Alex enjoyed another Aussie breakfast. It wasn't warm enough for surfing, so he went back to the Taronga Zoo for several hours, including a ride on the Sky Safari to view the enormous size of the zoo and the special enclosures for Asian elephants, apes, gorillas and the big cats. Then he took the hop-on-hop-off cruise to the Royal Botanic Garden; on 30 hectares, it was divided into four major areas, the Lower Gardens with the Band Lawn, ponds, an Oriental garden, a lodge and a pavilion; the Middle Gardens with more than a million preserved flora of the world; the Palace Rose with its unrivaled Rose Garden and the Conservatorium of Music; and the Bennelong Precinct containing Government House, the Parade Ground and the Native Rockery. Inside each area, there were many smaller gardens and after walking around for what seemed like hours, Alex was a little discombobulated but he finally found the Palm Grove Centre, had a drink in the café and purchased some postcards. Afterwards he took another hop-on-hop-off boat to Fort Denison, formerly a penal site and fortress on a very small island; it had Australia's only Martello tower. Alex had read James Joyce's *Ulysses* with its opening scene in a Martello tower in Dublin, and he was delighted finally to see one in person; it was a defensive round fort with thick walls resistant to cannon fire, its 12-meter height ideal for a heavy artillery piece on the flat roof, and able to fire in a 360° circle. With many new developments in artillery, Fort Denison was already obsolete by the time the Martello tower was built; the only guns still there were three 8-inch muzzle-loading cannons that couldn't be removed because passages within the tower were too narrow. Alex really looked forward to telling his friends in the IDF about this military oddity.

At YHA, he showered and went up to the roof to wait for Jed and Cal, the Aussies he'd met the previous evening. Jim, an American, joined them and they went to the riotously popular Lord Nelson Brewery Hotel, known as the oldest licensed pub in Sydney since the actual oldest one had closed during an epidemic. The four young men feasted on the unique offerings in the famed restaurant; Alex and the Yank decided to try something totally Aussie: ostrich steak tartare with quail eggs. The Aussies were stunned, and Cal laughed, "For an Israeli and a Yank, you two blokes are real gutsy!" They ended their meal with a tasting party of six house-brewed ales. Alex hadn't done much drinking since Cyprus and his UNFICYP buddies, but he really enjoyed the crowded pub and the Aussies; he loved their accents and slang even if it took him a while to understand that "coldie" and "amber fluid" both meant beer, and "a butcher" was a small glass of beer. Still, on the way back to the hostel, he said to himself, *"Surfing tomorrow, so no more amber fluid or coldies, Alex; you need a clear head when you work with Australian Special Ops!"*

Chapter 6

After breakfast on Sunday, hoping it would be warm enough to surf, he took the hop-on-hop-off bus to Bondi Beach. There, he rented a wetsuit, a surfboard, a towel, and a locker to store his things. Locker key on his wrist, he went to the area between red and yellow flags indicating where surfers could avoid the worst rips and holes. Alex had learned to surf in Cyprus and occasionally surfed in Tel Aviv, but the Mediterranean Sea was nothing like Bondi Beach and the ironically misnamed Pacific Ocean with its enormous swells. He kept wiping out within seconds after standing on his board, but he was an excellent swimmer and didn't need rescuing. After about an hour, feeling he'd had enough exercise for the day, Alex changed back into his own things and returned the wetsuit and board; then he took the hop-on bus back to Circular Quay. He walked around, window-shopped, and bought a few gifts: tiny plush kangaroos for his niece and nephew, a koala pendant in gold with emerald eyes for Dani; he wondered if she'd remember to bring him an armadillo of some kind from Argentina. Back at the hostel, he wrote and posted cards to his family and friends; then he telephoned his contact at SOCOM and arranged for a pick-up at 0730 hours. He spent the rest of the afternoon planning *Krav Maga* workouts for the Aussies.

He was about to go back to his room when Stacy caught up with him and said, "I finished my shift, but I'm not ready to go home. Mind if I join you?" Alex smiled, pleased to have an unexpected companion. Not having eaten lunch, Alex was hungry and asked her where to go for dinner and if she'd like to join him. She recommended Mr. Wong's; when they arrived, she said he'd probably enjoy sitting at the counter and looking into the open kitchen. They both appreciated watching the Chinese chefs quickly preparing dishes for the large crowd of diners; they finished their meal with dishes of green tea, mango and lychee ice cream. Alex laughed at the colorful dessert, and said, "But no fortune cookies!" Australian restaurants didn't offer the crisp dough tidbit with its paper prophecy and Stacy laughed at the odd messages Alex said he'd found in the so-called Chinese eateries in America. Stuffed, they wandered around The Rocks for an hour before strolling to Stacy's flat close to the YHA; she invited him in. Stacy's roommate, Ivy, also a student at McQuarrie with a part-time job at YHA, was awake, so they drank wine that the girls called *plonk* and joked for a while until Ivy went to bed. Stacy wanted him to stay, but Alex said that he had a very early pick-up the next morning. They kissed for a few minutes and then, reluctantly, Alex went to the YHA to pack his gear and have a good night's rest.

At 0715, when Alex came down to the lobby, an attractive young woman in a Women's Royal Australian Air Force, WRAAF, uniform was already waiting He checked out and picked up his gear as she led the way to a Land Rover parked at the entrance. "I'm Caro, by the way. Let's go to Potts Point. My dad, the CO of SOCOM, hopes you haven't *bogged into brekkie* yet," she said. "He'll meet us at *the diner* for some *tucker, a fry-up* and *a tall Joe*, to plan your schedule for the courses. Is that *good onya*, mate?"

Alex stared at her as if she were speaking Greek. She laughed and said, "If you want it in American English, I said my dad hopes you haven't eaten breakfast yet, and he'll meet us in the dining hall and you'll probably have bacon and eggs and coffee, and then plan the schedule. Is that satisfactory?"

Alex grinned. "Believe it or not, I did catch some of that, but I'm looking forward to going back home with some more 'Ozzie' slang! Israelis know 'barbie' isn't the doll, and you boil water in a 'billy'. We know some of the words in 'Waltzing Matilda' and *Crocodile Dundee*'s still a popular film!"

At SOCOM headquarters a few minutes later, Caro parked the SUV and took Alex to the dining hall where her father was waiting. They saluted the officer who returned their salutes and said, "*Ta*, Caro. See you later." Then he turned to Alex and said "G'day, Lieutenant. I'm Colonel Markham. Sit down and we'll have some breakfast and work out the training schedules. I think some of the women on our staff, even Caro, would like to learn *Krav Maga*; I've had a few complaints about sexual harassment and we've even had a couple of allegations of rape. Can you teach self-defense to *sheilas*?"

"I can teach girls as well, sir, and I won't be overly gentle with them. In fact, I'm already sorry for any guy stupid enough to tangle with them."

"*Ripper*," the Colonel laughed. "That means 'great' in Aussie. After we eat, I'll show you around the base and take you to the gym we're using for your courses. You'll bunk in Victoria Barracks in Paddington, eight or ten minutes from here. It's the 1st Commando Regiment headquarters. One of the men will take you after today's session. If that's *good onya*, let's go."

The next two weeks seemed to fly by. The sessions were in a large gym with mats all over the floor. During Week One, regular and reserve soldiers of the 1st Commando Regiment worked daily for six hours, with two half-hour breaks in which to cool down and hydrate with bottled water. All of the men were physically fit,

Chapter 6

so each session was rigorous and rewarding. Alex explained, "*Krav Maga* means 'Contact Combat' in Hebrew. It's not based on oriental philosophy like most other martial arts; the only goal of *Krav Maga* is to disarm, incapacitate and even maim the enemy quickly by all and any means." Alex insisted on the men wearing helmets and heavy padding during practice because *Krav Maga* was brutal, combining all the nastiest elements of the other martial arts. He demonstrated the techniques against an enemy's most vulnerable points, and he made trainees practice attacking their opponent's eyes, throat, neck, ribs, fingers, groin, liver, solar plexus, knees, feet. *Krav Maga* also required simultaneously studying their surroundings while dealing with the threat in order to locate possible escape routes, additional attackers, and objects to defend or help in the attack. Alex emphasized the need to understand the vicinity, the psychology behind the enemy confrontation, and potential threats prior to the actual attack. With minimum force and by not following completely through on the dangerous techniques that might injure them, he showed them the quickest movements for maximum damage to the assailant, like breaking his arm, dislocating his kneecap, perforating his eardrum, and knocking him out. The Aussies, even the Colonel, were impressed with *Krav Maga* and especially with Alex as their very professional and straightforward instructor.

In the afternoons, Alex worked for two hours with a few women soldiers and civilian employees of SOCOM. He told them *Krav Maga* was perfect for women because it didn't rely on brute strength, and it was easy to learn. He also told them *Krav Maga* encouraged women to avoid confrontation, but if it was impossible or unsafe, a woman should finish a fight as quickly as possible. He said, "I'm going to throw you right in, so find a partner and you'll learn how to defend yourself against all kinds of attacks and how to counteract those attacks quickly. First, introduce yourself to me and then I need a volunteer who's been attacked in the past." The women introduced themselves, giggled, and Sally, a petite military driver, volunteered to be his "victim". She explained why she'd signed up to learn *Krav Maga* in two words: "Boob grab!" She was walking to her vehicle one night when a big man grabbed her around the chest. She'd kicked and pushed him and when her screams attracted attention, he finally ran away; but she knew that had he not stopped, she would not have been able to fight him off.

Alex whispered in her ear, "You're never going to be a victim again." He told her what to do, and within 10 seconds, she floored him. "It isn't exactly *Krav Maga*," he said, "but young women can be easily attacked, so always carry your keys in your hand not your handbags when you're alone; you can thrust them into an assailant's eyes if attacked." In the next class, he taught them a technique known as a 'powerslap'. "Don't wait for your assailant to hit you," Alex said. "Get him talking and while he is, you've got the perfect opportunity to perforate his eardrum by slapping him hard. Believe me, he will go down in severe pain. Then it's up to you to injure him permanently or notify the authorities. But never forget to consider all the consequences."

After the first session, Julia Margolis, a civilian employee, told him she lived in Paddington and would give him a lift to the barracks. He thanked her and took his gear. Julia told him her family was Jewish and she invited him to have dinner with them on Friday night. "I have twins, boy and girl, and they'll be thrilled to meet a 'real' Israeli soldier," she said. "They attend a Jewish school and anything you can tell them about the Israeli army will make them celebrities. You know teens love that." Of course, Alex agreed.

The minute he stepped inside the barracks, he was greeted by a number of men from that morning's class. Charlie, who seemed to be the leader of the group, said, "How'd it go with the *sheilas*? Better than with the *blokes*, I'll bet. We hope you like Thai chow, 'cause the students are *shouting* the teacher tonight." Each night, groups of 6, 8, even 12, took him out! Alex had never been offered so much beer in his life, but he usually passed on more than one drink; he mostly enjoyed the camaraderie of the Aussies.

On Tuesday, he called Stacy and asked to see her that evening after her shift; she instantly agreed. Alex stopped by his room in the barracks to get a clean uniform and a few condoms. In a cab on the way to Stacy's flat, he phoned Julia and asked her to pick him up the next morning at the YHA. The second Stacy opened the door, they were sharing what she later called *real pash*, and raced to her bedroom where they made love long into the night. Just before he left very early the next morning to meet Julia at the YHA, Stacy asked, "Tonight?" He agreed and she told him to leave the uniform he'd arrived in and she'd have it cleaned. That led to another *real pash*, and he walked to the YHA, smiling broadly.

When the guys suggested real American cheeseburgers on Friday night to celebrate the end of the program, Alex asked for a raincheck, saying he was sorry but he'd accepted an invitation to a Shabbat dinner. "With Julia's family?" Charlie asked. Alex nodded and Charlie

Chapter 6

added, "She's *ripper* and her husband and kids are *ace*! I'll drive you there." Alex laughed and said he'd actually understood what Charlie said, even *ripper* and *ace*! Then he asked where he could buy flowers for Shabbat? Earlier that afternoon when he'd finished the last session of *Krav Maga* for women, Gwen, a redhead who'd been blatantly flirting with Alex from the beginning of the program, came over to him while he was stowing equipment and invited him to her place later for a celebratory finish to the course, but with a different kind of tangling. Alex looked at her and gently told her that he already had plans for that night, and that he was seriously involved with someone else.

She said, "I know all Israeli guys cheat on their wives and girlfriends. Besides, I want to 'do' you in order to add an Israeli to my very long list of lovers!" Despite her cheeky remark, Alex knew she was really annoyed.

◆ ◆ ◆

Before Charlie dropped him off at Julia's home, Alex put on the *kippah* he'd packed in his gear. When Julia opened the door, he saw four teenagers waiting to greet him, instead of two. She thanked him for the flowers and introduced her husband Hal and her two children, Sara and Michael. "These other two are friends from their school, Jeremy and Shelley. Michael said no one had believed them when they said an Israeli soldier was coming for dinner tonight, so my kids invited 'witnesses'. I hope you don't mind. Come in and take a seat. I have to put these lovely flowers in water and finish a couple of things for dinner. Hal, please help me."

The four teens and Alex sat down in the lounge. Jeremy asked, "Why aren't you in uniform? And where's your gun? I'll bet you're a fake, not even a real Israeli soldier."

Alex smiled at Jeremy and said, "It's not appropriate to wear a *Tzahal* uniform on Shabbat except on base. I didn't bring my weapon because I'm not in Australia as a soldier. I'm here to teach the Israeli martial art, *Krav Maga*. Mrs. Margolis has been one of the students in my class."

Julia's husband came into the lounge then and said, "Alex, we heard what Jeremy said and I'm sorry. Jeremy, you've been extremely rude to a guest in my home and that's not allowed. So you now have a choice. You apologize to Lieutenant Novak or you go home right this minute. As for you, my dear children, I'm ashamed of both of you. Why didn't you stop Jeremy when he was insulting a guest in our home?"

All four teens were embarrassed by Hal's reprimand, and very red-faced, Jeremy mumbled, "I'm sorry, Alex, er-Lieutenant. I don't know what got into me. I want to stay, Mr. Margolis. I promise I won't be rude again."

Alex smiled at the teens and said, "I accept your apology, Jeremy. What is it you Aussies say? Oh yes, *'fair dinkum'*!"

Julia called everyone to the beautifully set table then, and the rest of the evening passed agreeably. After a tasty meal, a few *zemirot* and the *birkat hamaizon*, Alex thanked Julia, "I felt like I was at home." Hal drove Alex to YHA-the Rocks where Stacy was just finishing her shift. As they walked to her flat, he told her about the events of the evening at Julia's house and the impudent teenager. She told him she had both Saturday and Sunday off, but she had two exams in the coming week and although she thought she'd have to study on Sunday, it had been quiet during her shift and she was prepared for both exams, so they could spend both days together if he wanted. At her flat, they drove each other to the point of madness as they made love again and again, showered together, and slept entwined in each other's arms for a few hours. On Saturday, they took a cab to Paddington Markets, stopping at the Not Just Coffee café for breakfast. Alex was intrigued with the weird names of some menu items; Stacy ordered a *"Wakey Brekky"* and Alex had a "Messy Mexican Mashup", but the only signs of Mexico were a few bits of jalapeño pepper and a taco. They explored Paddington, an arts and crafts market with 150 stalls of fashions and accessories, jewelry, sweet smelling soaps, candles, and many other items. Alex found it even more charming than London's famous Portobello Road that he'd visited on a work stint in the UK, although much of the charm was his companion, he admitted to himself. A billboard at the entrance showed the location of the stalls and explained the mission of the Eddie Dixon Centre: buying a product from Paddington not only supported local designers, but also contributed to the providing of warm meals, clothing and shelter for the disadvantaged and homeless people of Sydney. After reading the billboard, Alex said, "That's great. Let's buy something for you and me, and maybe a few small toys for my niece and nephew, or gifts for my Israeli family, and we'll be doing a good deed at the same time." He was pleased when he found a book about the unusual animals and birds of Australia, a hand-painted scarf in colors Lise liked, another for Keren and one for Stacy which he didn't say was for her, and a fine Merino wool 'jumper' in pale green for himself,; Stacy hadn't bought anything for herself, but she helped him choose his other purchases. At 2:00, they attended the free Paddington Markets Dog Show where 100 dogs competed not only for usual titles like "Best in Show" but also quirky titles like "Best Dressed Dog", "Best Dressed Dog and Human", "Best Old Dog and Human", "Best Trick Dog" and "Cutest Child with Puppy". They hadn't planned to stay for the entire show, but Alex didn't remember ever laughing as hard as they did at the antics of some of the dogs and owners. Afterwards, they wandered along the stalls again and Alex bought Stacy an amethyst bracelet that he said was like the unusual color of her eyes. When Paddington was about to close, he spotted a Max Brenner Chocolate Bar a few steps away. Since they'd eaten *brekkie* many hours earlier, he insisted they indulge themselves in their decadent delights, icy shakes with Bailey's Irish Cream and fudge ice cream called "choctails" and chocolate waffles for two with fruits of the forest. He told Stacy about the two Israelis who combined their names, Max Fichtman and Oded Brenner, and created this international chocolate empire. After their 'sugar high', Alex gave Stacy the scarf. "But you already bought me a gorgeous bracelet," she said.

"And this also matches your eyes," he said. "I wanted to buy it for you as soon as I saw it, so just say *'Thank you, Alex'*!" She did and surprised him with a kiss. Sunday was a day of total relaxation. They had brunch with Ivy and her boyfriend Matt, and then they strolled around the Rocks, enjoying the sunshine, people-watching, and the unusual aborigine art in the Spirit Gallery. Entertained by street performers: didgeridoo players, a few "living statues" who had painted themselves gold or silver, a classical violinist who they thought good enough for a major orchestra, and a group of very young, oddly dressed break-dancers, they then went for a casual hamburger dinner. Alex said, "I have to go back to the Barracks soon. Tomorrow's students are coming in from Perth and I have to meet them tonight. Matt said he'd drive me, so let's go." They walked back to Stacy's flat and Alex collected his things. He kissed Stacy for a few minutes and said, "This weekend's been super and I'm sorry to leave, but I've no choice. I'll see you again soon, if not tomorrow night, then Tuesday. Good luck on your exams." He said goodbye to Ivy and left with Matt.

◆ ◆ ◆

Alex's second week, with SASR, the Special Air Service Regiment from Perth, was a repeat of the first week with very fit, athletic young men, eager to learn the famed Israeli martial art. The only surprise was another group of young women who wanted to learn *Krav Maga*; they'd heard from the first group that it wasn't difficult, and learning how a 55 kilogram female could deliver a stunning blow and knock out a 100 kilogram assailant was something they all wanted to do. No one "came on" to him like Gwen, and he was free to spend several nights with Stacy; a few times he had dinner with the men from both SASR and the 1st Command, even American food. In the States he'd heard about Philadelphia cheesesteaks but he'd never been able to eat one because all his friends ate only kosher food; he'd also heard of chili cheese fries but hadn't eaten those either, so going for an American meal was as much a treat for Alex as the camaraderie of his companions. He and Stacy went out to dinner twice, first to a French bistro where they ate escargots; Alex joked that both of them had to eat the garlicky snails or they'd never be able to kiss. They drank too much Pinot Noir, not as good as the *plonk* Ivy and Stacy gave him at their place, she teased. For their second dinner, Stacy took him to the restaurant on the 36th floor of the spectacular Shangri-La Hotel, where they dined on Great Southern lamb, and this time shared a half bottle of Sauvignon Blanc; Alex thought the view of the harbour from the restaurant's floor to ceiling windows was far more impressive, and far less expensive, than the food. At the end of the *Krav Maga* training program, both the SASR unit and the 1st Commando trainees insisted on a farewell dinner in another Paddington restaurant; the owners closed the Sports Bar to other guests for the large military group, including Colonel Markham, and even Julia and Hal Margolis. Charley told Alex they all knew he had a girlfriend and he suggested Alex invite her. The colonel thanked Alex for an exhilarating and significant training program and told him a letter of commendation would soon be sent from Australia's SOCOM to Israel's IDF. Alex was extremely moved as he stood and said, "I was only doing my job, but there's something I want to say, so please forgive me if I'm *not the full quid* as I try to *give a burl* on a few bits of *strine*. *Cobbers, diggers, blokes* and *sheilas*, this has been an absolute *rip snorter* for me. Work has never been as *bonzer* as it's been with you, I should say because of you. I'm *gobsmacked* at how much I'll miss you *'hoons'*! I'll never forget you. *Holy dooley*, I did it! I've learned *strine*! *Ta*!" Alex sat down to wild shouts, applause and laughter.

Taking the lead as usual, Charley said, "*Good onya*, mate. You gave us a lot of *flat out yakka*, but you weren't the only teacher in our *Mickey Mouse* program; we *larrikins* of *The Lucky Country* taught you how to *jabber* in *strine*! We won't forget ya either, Alex. And we have a little something for you, thanks to Julia and Lilianne, the best techie at SOCOM, so ya won't forget us." He handed Alex an album with

Chapter 6

snapshots of the trainees doing *Krav Maga* and group shots of all of them with Alex photo-shopped into each photo. He gave Alex a wrapped package and said, "Ya gotta undo this one!" Alex tore off the wrappings and found a cheeky-looking koala, about 40 centimeters high, wearing Aussie camouflage and a wide-brimmed bush hat. He was astounded; all he could say, in English, not *strine*, was "Wow! This little Aussie's amazing!" The party came to an end with hugs from all, and a playful *Krav Maga* knockdown from Charley.

As Alex and Stacy were leaving, Colonel Markham came to shake hands and said, "I know you want to go to the Great Barrier Reef, Alex. A couple of SOCOM officers are flying to Townsville tomorrow by helicopter; it's a 5-hour flight and Townsville's 350 kilometers south of Cairns. You can fly to Cairns from there, or go by bus. It's worth five hours of your time to see the Queensland coast, lush rainforests and golden savannahs. I sound like a tour guide, but… there's room on the 'chopper if you can be at SOCOM at 0630 hours. Thanks for all your hard work. Alex. G'bye and good luck."

In the taxi on the way to her flat in The Rocks, Stacy said, "I knew you were here for something important, but I never knew how important! I'm even more impressed than I was before." They talked late into the night and then made love for what both of them knew would be the last time. Early in the morning, Alex kissed a tearful Stacy long and hard, and then took a cab to SOCOM for the flight to Townsville. The helicopter was a noisy Airbus six-seater; the officers, Major Larry Smythe and Captain Reggie Seaburn, were busy after an initial chat with Alex, so he busied himself on his laptop, looking into sites worth seeing in Cairns. They disembarked in Townsville at 1330 hours and Major Smythe said, "Alex, I hope you don't mind if I call you Alex, and you should call me Larry. I have meetings here until Monday night and then I'll be on holiday for a few days. My older son is flying my Cessna here and then to Cairns on Tuesday to meet my wife, daughter and my aunt and uncle who are visiting from England. They've been in Cairns for several days but they've never been to the Outback. Both my sons are planning on a few days of diving with friends, so I'm flying the rest of us out of Cairns on Wednesday morning. My plane can seat six and if you've finished sightseeing in Cairns, you're welcome to join us. A good friend of mine, Tony Benson, owns a tourist company that's part of the Lonely Planet chain and he does tours of Uluru, also known as Ayers Rock. His 3-day trip is incredible; I know that from personal experience with my own family and Tony, you camp in swags around campfires; everything, even showers, are provided. The tour starts in Uluru and ends in Alice Springs and you'll see Uluru from all sides. Tony's groups don't actually climb Uluru because it belongs to the local Aborigines; Tony respects them and they don't want people climbing Uluru. But you go to Kata Tjuta, the Olga Mountains, and they're much higher than Uluru, and, for someone as fit as you, those climbs in and around 36 domed rocks, are fabulous. You also go to Kings Canyon in Watarrka National Park with amazing walls of red rock, water holes and gorges in the Aboriginal homeland; you'll have unforgettable memories of the Outback. Have I sold you on it? Believe me, my friend doesn't give me a commission, but from what Colonel Markham has said, I think you'd love it. Here's my mobile number. Call me on Tuesday and I'll set it up."

Alex was completely quiet for a few moments. *"Australians, at least the ones I've met, are as friendly and helpful as all my Pittsburgh friends,"* he said to himself. Aloud he said, "I don't have to think about it, sir, er, Larry. I'm in! Thanks so much. But I do have a question. The tourist info I have isn't very clear and I don't know if I should stay here in Townsville and go to the Great Barrier Reef from here or from Cairns. Any advice?"

"It depends on your skills. My sons are advanced divers and they prefer Cairns. There are day-tours for neophytes. Are you an experienced diver? If you just want a tour on a glass-bottom boat, both cities are fine. Personally, I think Heron Island has the best reefs but getting there's a hassle on a 2-day 'live-aboard' boat. Have I helped you make a choice?"

"Yes, sir, er, Larry. I'll go to Cairns today."

The two men shook hands and Larry said, "Have fun in Cairns, and we'll talk Tuesday night." After first taking the major to his meeting, his driver took Alex to the bus depot. The bus to Cairns wasn't crowded and Alex sat up front. Tim, the driver, was as friendly and chatty as most Aussies. When Alex said he was from Israel, Tim said he was a Christian and he'd always dreamed of visiting the Holy Land. Tim pointed out major highlights along the 450-kilometer Great Green Way, and Alex found the coastal rainforest with its unusual flora and waterfalls gorgeous. They passed kangaroos and wallabies all along the route, until they stopped for a 20-minute break at Mission Beach, an unspoiled paradise of golden, sandy beaches midway between Townsville and Cairns. Alex hadn't eaten much since the previous night, so in appreciation for Tim being his personal tour guide, and because of intense hunger pangs, he bought both of

Chapter 6

them fabulous fish and chips at Tusker's Tuckerbox on the beach. By the time they reached Cairns, Alex was exhausted from the farewell party, making love with Stacy almost all night long, the long flight to Townsville, and a captivating but very long bus ride to Cairns, so he was longing for a long night of sleep. He'd asked Tim, a Cairns resident, about hotels and wasn't surprised when the Aussie offered his own house, but Alex declined. Tim recommended the Double Tree on the Esplanade, close to the beach, probably with vacancies because May and June are off-season. At the depot, Tim pointed him in the direction of the Esplanade; Alex bought a bottle of water and a candy bar, walked to the hotel, and registered. In his room's huge en-suite bathroom, he showered and then fell onto the bed and into a deep sleep. In the morning, refreshed, he drank the bottle of water while viewing boats going out to the reefs; then he went down to the hotel's restaurant that overlooked an interior rainforest atrium. Like Israeli hotels, the vast breakfast buffet was part of the cost of his room; but unlike Israeli hotels, this hotel offered sausage and bacon in addition to the usual eggs, pancakes and fruit. Then he asked the concierge about tours; he explained that he'd spent most of the previous day traveling and needed to do something outdoors, and the obliging concierge suggested parasailing, jet skiing or bungee jumping. Hackett Bungee Towers were the world's first bungee jumps built on purpose, and the one in the rainforest near Cairns was a significant site for "adrenaline junkie" thrills; Alex chose that one. The concierge made arrangements for a coach to take Alex with a few other "courageous souls" to the gorgeous location, 20 minutes outside the city, with fantastic views out to the Great Barrier Reef. He had to sign a legal waiver releasing the company from any liability in case of an accident but he'd read that Hackett had a million safe jumps in their 20-year history. As he climbed the tower stairs, Alex freed his mind for a "death-defying" jump and remembered his first parachute jump. At the top of the 50-meter tower, the crew strapped him in a harness, checked the rubber bands tied to his ankles and explained the safety rules. And just as there'd been nowhere to go but forward at the open door of the Israeli C130 plane, Alex counted to three and jumped. He remembered the plummeting feeling in his stomach during the 4-second free fall and the quiet after his parachute opened; now he had four seconds of free fall and then he dangled up and down, up and down. It was fun! When the dangling slowed, a staff member at the bottom waved to the staff up top to lower the rubber band, and Alex landed slowly on his back on a soft raft. He jumped two more times and then received a Bungee T-Shirt with a cute cartoon of a dangling sneaker, a "brave sole", a certificate that he jumped successfully and photographs of his three bungee jumps. On the way back to the hotel, Alex felt his first day in Cairns had been fabulous. At the hotel, he asked the concierge about a trip to the Great Barrier Reefs the next day. Alex said he dived but wasn't an expert, and the concierge recommended TUSA Dive, a company serving both experienced divers and people with little diving experience; Alex booked the excursion and was told to bring *swimmers*, a towel, and a credit card or cash for any onboard expenses. He then spent the rest of the afternoon swimming in the salt-water Esplanade Lagoon, quite safe from jellyfish, marine stingers and crocodiles, and then in the hotel's fresh-water pool. Later he sent emails to Slovakia and Israel before walking down the Esplanade to have dinner in a quirky bistro known for its Brazilian-style BBQ. As he ordered a Mexican Corona beer, local diners at a nearby table asked if he was anti-Aussie ale. He reassured the chauvinists that he liked Cooper's and Little Creatures Pale, but since he was eating Western hemisphere BBQ, he thought it fitting to drink Western beer; the Aussies laughed, said "*Good onya,* mate" and invited him to join them. They spent the evening chatting and joking until the restaurant's early closing time at 9:30.

Early Monday morning, after breakfast in the atrium, Alex walked to the TUSA pier; before he left, he took a few photos of the raintree garden. He'd changed the battery in his camera and since it was only slightly larger than a credit card, and since the concierge had told him to bring a credit card on the diving tour, he hoped the Nikon was as waterproof as they claimed and he'd be able to take underwater photos. Boarding TUSA Dive's custom reef craft, Alex noted that the boat had been designed for ultimate comfort, and with only 25 passengers, it would be a unique adventure. TUSA not only provided all snorkeling and diving equipment from masks to wristwatch-type dive computers, but morning tea with sugary and savory pastries, and gourmet hot and cold buffet lunches later in the day. Shortly after everyone was seated in the lounge, drinking tea and eating pastries, the crew presented a video describing the Great Barrier Reef as a breeding area for humpback whales migrating from the Antarctic and as the natural habitat of numerous endangered species, including the Dugong Sea Cow, and some species of giant turtles; the Great Barrier Reef had been listed as a World Heritage Site by UNESCO in 1981 in recognition of its ecosystem. Always conscious of the need to protect the environment, Alex was pleased TUSA Dive was an ecotourism operator, committed to respecting and contributing to the preservation of the flora and fauna as well as the coral of the reefs. All TUSA snorkeling tours were guided by the crew, and even certified divers had to be accompanied by the experienced crew as they explored the vast coral gardens, caverns, walls and isolated pinnacles. The skipper told them their sites on this cruise, Cod Hole and Pixie Pinnacle, were two of the best diving sites in the world, made famous by Sir David Attenborough, the English naturalist; he said Sir David's favorite *bommies*, slang for areas of large waves breaking over submerged rock shelves, were incredible. In the IDF, Alex had scuba dived in Eilat and he'd brought his certification card so he could do three dives and use his tiny camera for photographs of the coral and some of the 1500 different species of tropical fish inhabiting the reefs: bright yellow Butterfly Fish; orange Clown Fish familiar to every child as Disney's Nemo; brilliant Damselfish and Surgeonfish in all the colors of the spectrum, and to Alex's delight, a non-aggressive white-tipped shark. He hoped his underwater photos would reflect the amazing diversity of the Reef's marine life. After his three dives, Alex had an onboard fresh-water shower, followed by a cup of excellent coffee. On his return to Cairns, he knew it had been a thrilling experience to explore part of the world's largest coral reef system. Later, as he ate a light meal in the hotel, still elated by his day, he realized while he ate alone in the beautiful atrium that he missed Stacy. *"I'd love to call her, but I can't be selfish. It wouldn't be fair to either of us because there's no way we can build a future together."* He sighed, took his digital camera out of his shirt pocket, and gazing at the unique images stored in his tiny camera, once again said a silent "thank you" to his CO in The Unit for setting up this phenomenal Down Under experience. *"And,"* he reminded himself, *"Wonder of wonders! My unforgettable junket isn't over yet!"* The next day he'd ride the Rainforest Skyrail and then go with Larry Smythe and his family to the place the Aussies call *Never Never*, the Outback, and after camping at Uluru, to Melbourne for a couple of days. And then home! *"Interesting!"* he thought. *"Israel really is my home!"*

On Tuesday morning, Alex walked to the train station and boarded the Kuranda Scenic Railway for a spectacular journey on the 120-year-old line still considered an engineering feat of enormous magnitude. Although many tourists opted for a Gold Class carriage with its luxurious lounge chairs, he enjoyed the old world charm of traveling for an hour and 45 minutes in an authentic timber carriage as it slowly meandered past dense rainforest, steep ravines and picturesque waterfalls. Rising from sea level to 328 meters, the railway wound through 15 hand-carved tunnels, across a giant bridge, past the spectacular Barron Falls and finally into Kuranda, a unique rainforest village. Fortunately, the journey included English commentary on each site and passengers received a souvenir card with the history of the railway and a map of Kuranda. In the city, Alex visited the butterfly aviary, enchanted by the aerial dynamics of these wonders of nature; since he was wearing a red T-shirt, many enormous-winged insects fluttered all over him. His next stop was the Heritage Markets; he browsed around stalls and galleries, and then, in the middle of the Markets, chanced on Birdworld, a sanctuary with waterfalls and exotic plants replicating the natural habitats of 80 species of Australia's most precious birds such as cheeky rainbow lorikeets, cute pink galah cockatoos, and the endangered and stately cassowary; in other words, all around him he saw species from the world's vanishing rainforests.

When a brilliantly hued rainbow bee-eater landed on one shoulder and a large-billed kookaburra on the other, Alex asked a young man holding two professional cameras to take a photo of him and the two birds; hesitantly he handed over his tiny Nikon, hoping the slight movement wouldn't make the birds fly off, but they didn't move. He and Sid, a professional photographer from Canada, were astonished when a peacock spread its awesome tail next to Alex and a huge cassowary with black plumage, blue facial skin and a bright yellow neck came to stand on his other side. After shooting several photos of Alex and the birds with the Nikon, Sid uncapped his single-reflex digital camera and starting taking photos. The whirring noise frightened the cassowary and it nipped the tail of the peacock; it strutted away arrogantly, but the kookaburra and the rainbow bee-eater didn't move until Alex started walking. Alex invited Sid to have lunch with him; they went to Frogs, the most popular restaurant in the Kuranda Markets where they both ordered James Squire Nine Tales Amber, and Alex laughed at yet another Aussie beer with an odd name. They laughed at the silly antics of the two birds and talked about what each of them did at home; each of them was intrigued by the other's work and what had brought them to Australia. Sid had heard of *Krav Maga* but had never seen it, so he'd look into it back in Toronto. Alex said he'd look for Sid's photos of endangered Australian wildlife in a future issue of *National Geographic;* Sid laughed and said Alex might see a photo of himself because the cassowary attacking the peacock with Alex in his red shirt standing between the two big birds and with two small birds perched on his shoulders was the kind of

Chapter 6

photo that his editor loved. After lunch, they shook hands, exchanged email addresses and each went his own way.

Alex's last stop was Doongal Aboriginal Arts & Artefacts Gallery, with a stunning collection of bark, cross-hatch, dot-and-leaf paintings, string art, symbolic weavings and decorated boomerangs and didgeridoos, most of it by indigenous artists, descendants of the original inhabitants of the area. The director of the gallery told Alex that the Aborigines had no written language, and their laws, stories and even social mannerisms, were passed on through song, dance and drawings, like African griots. Many drawings were in caves and rock faces and on the inside of bark from trees. For this reason the value and significance of their art was priceless, representing the last generations to have lived a semi-nomadic traditional lifestyle. Original artwork in the gallery was way beyond Alex's budget, but he did purchase three hand-crafted wooden boomerangs, weighing 100 grams each, richly painted with humorous themes and symbolic shapes. He bought one for his niece and nephew, and the others for Kobi and Yaniv. In the nearby Hidden Words Bookshop, he bought an Australian cookbook for Anna and a few books about Aboriginal art and theory for Lise, David and himself. Then he walked to the terminal and boarded the Skyrail Cableway for his return trip to Cairns; the 7.5-kilometer Skyrail, with its 6-person gondola gliding only meters above the rainforest was the perfect way to end his stay in Cairns. At the first station, he transferred to another gondola which descended through the canopy layers deep in the forest to the second station, 545 meters above sea level. A third gondola brought him to the disembarkation point where a bus took him the 15-minute return trip to Cairns.

At the hotel, he called Larry Smythe to find out what time they'd leave the next day. "Hi Alex," the major said, "How about joining us for dinner? My sons would like to meet you. We're at the Shangri-La in The Marina, an easy walk from your hotel; if your answer is 'Yes', tell me you eat prawns, lobster, all that stuff. You'll like my aunt and uncle; she's very gracious, and he's an adventurer: a mountaineer, a daredevil. And I have another idea; so we'll see if you're up for a special adventure. We'll see you at 6:30?"

Alex laughed. "All I can say is 'Yes', 'Yes', 'Yes' and 'Yes'! Yes, I'll join you for dinner. Yes, I love lobster and prawns, and Yes, I'll enjoy meeting your sons and your daredevil uncle and Yes, I'm up for a new adventure. Of course, now I'm also very curious. So I'll see you soon. Thank you, sir."

After showering, Alex dressed in well-pressed black jeans and his tweed sports jacket. He slipped the tie he'd brought for Shabbat into his pocket, hoping he wouldn't need it but just in case there was a dress code at the luxurious Shangri-La. He asked the desk clerk if the Shangri-La was at the same marina as TUSA Dives, and then walked down the Esplanade to the hotel. Major Smythe was sitting at a table in the lobby with a distinguished older man and two young men in their twenties, all drinking whiskey or ale; the major beckoned Alex over and he joined them. "Welcome, Alex. Let me introduce you," the major said, "Sir Andrew Smythe, James, Ryan, meet Lieutenant Alex Novak of the Israeli Special Forces." After they all shook hands, the major said, "Sit down, all of you. Alex, call me Larry, and tell me what you'd like to drink." Alex, of course, opted for ale.

They chatted for several minutes about diving in the Great Barrier Reefs, the rainforests, the scenic railway, bungee jumping, and *Krav Maga* versus Karate. James told Alex he'd graduated from the University of Sydney with a BA in Chemical Engineering and had been accepted into the SASR the previous day. When Alex congratulated him, James said, "You'll have to come back in a couple of years to teach *Krav Maga* to my unit, maybe next time in SASR's home in Perth." Conversation flowed freely; just when Alex was talking about Australia's impressive ecosystem and efforts to protect endangered wildlife, three generations of very attractive, very well-dressed females joined them. Larry introduced Alex to Sir Andrew's wife, Sylvia, his wife Elizabeth, and his daughter Poppy who cheekily said their dinner reservation was for 6:45 and they'd better go there at once! On the way to the restaurant, Larry said, "Everyone will say it's *chutzpah*," he grinned at Alex as he mispronounced the well-known Hebrew word, "but since I know everyone eats seafood, I boldly ordered our entire meal!" Seated at a round table overlooking the waterfront, munching on a salad and garlicky ciabatta and sipping a prize-winning Yarra Valley chablis, Alex was dumbfounded as four waiters rolled several carts with seafood towers of grilled oysters, langoustines, lobster, calamari, red claw crabs and king prawns, served with cocktail sauce, Moroccan *chermoula* and mayonnaise dipping sauces. When Alex admitted he'd never seen anything like all this, Larry said, "This is the signature dish of the Shangri-La and why I chose to eat here tonight."

During the lavish meal, Alex asked about Sir Andrew's experiences in mountaineering. He replied, "It's in the blood, my boy. Or maybe I should say adventure is in the Smythe family's blood. My grandfather, Frank. S. Smythe, was an author and botanist, but he's probably remembered mostly for mountaineering in both the Alps and the

Chapter 6

Himalayas; he discovered two new routes on Mont Blanc but twice in the 1930s attempted unsuccessfully to scale Everest. Reginald Smythe, my father, climbed Everest in the 1970s and joined Sir Edmund Hillary in two Antarctica climbs, Mt. Herschel and Brewer Peak. Dylan, my son, climbed Everest with Sir Edmund's son Peter two years ago. I've also scaled Everest and I joined CBE Neville Shulman on Mt. Kilimanjaro, Ngga Pulu in Papua New Guinea, and Mt. Aragats in the Armenian Caucasus. So you see why I say adventure is in the Smythe family blood! Sylvia, my wife, is a well-known essayist and photographer, and she's climbed a few mountains herself. And look at Larry's family: he can fly anything with two wings, and James is already flying the Cessna. But even better, both James and Ryan were on Australia's Olympics diving team in Athens last year; Ryan trains with silver and bronze winner Matt Helm, and I bet he'll be on the podium in China in 2008, not just on the 'boards. And 'pretty Poppy', she's only 14, but she dives as well and maybe better than her brothers, and her backstroke is so incredible that I'm sure she'll swim and dive in China. And Liz. She also swims, but absolutely her most exciting adventures are in the excellent children's books she writes."

Alex was speechless after Sir Andrew's long list; all he could utter was "Wow!" He said "I know my Israeli 'family' is also extraordinary: a world-famous artist, a war-hero philosophy professor and author, a prize-winning biochemist, top-notch IDF personnel. And my 'real' family in Slovakia are engineers and teachers. But this family! Wow again!"

Sir Andrew said, "There's nothing wrong with your two 'families', lad. And I understand from Larry you're not too shabby: UN peacekeepers and Israel's top special ops. Don't ever sell yourself or your family short!"

Sylvia Smythe smiled at Alex and added, "A few years ago, we toured Israel, but Andrew didn't scale mountains there; instead he climbed… What is it called? Oh yes, the snake path at Masada while I took the cable car. We loved Israel, but I didn't love trying to swim in the Dead Sea; I couldn't even float normally as the water kept pushing me up. I had a small cut on my leg and the sting from the salty water was awful."

"It's a required experience for everyone who goes to Israel to try and swim in the Dead Sea," Alex said, "It's quite an experience; I mean not being able to swim, not the salt-water sting."

After dessert, Larry said, "Don't you want to know my proposition, Alex? You said you were very curious. And don't you dare call me 'sir'!"

"Yes, Larry," Alex said in a 'tongue-in-cheek' way. "I really, really want to know what your proposition is, Larry!"

"*Good onya*. Andrew and Sylvia aren't in Australia to climb mountains as there's really no peak high enough for our intrepid mountaineer. Sylvia's been asked to do a book on cave painting around the world. She's already written articles and taken photos of France's famous cave art and Spain's. She's also written about the Bhimbetka rock shelters in India where the paintings date back about 30,000 years ago, she said. But she's never been in the caves in Australia or the Horn of Africa, and that's what her publisher wants: a panoramic history of rock art. Before Cairns, Andrew and Sylvia were in Brisbane and the Whitsunday Islands and she photographed some recently found cave paintings. Now we're planning to explore the caves in the Outback, you're more than welcome to join us. I can fly you to Uluru, a little more than two hours from here. Or you can come to Darwin with us, see the cave art and I'll get you to Uluru four days from now. What do you say?"

"I'd like to say I'm in, sir, er, Larry. I bought two books on Aborigine art, but they only had vague photos of cave art. Seeing them in person would be fantastic, but I'm booked from Melbourne to Bangkok on Monday and then to Tel Aviv on Tuesday. I don't think I can change my reservations."

"You can't but I can!" Larry Smythe boasted. "SOCOM perks, Alex! We have certain special privileges, and I'll use them."

"Wow! *Omigod*, if you can, that's sensational," Alex said with a wide grin. "I don't know what to say!"

"A simple *'Ta!'* will do, but to Andrew and Sylvia because you'll be their guest on this adventure. I'll call Tony and tell him you'll be in Uluru next Sunday. Lieutenant Novak, we'll be leaving for Darwin tomorrow at 0930 hours. Meet us at the airport a few minutes earlier in the area for private planes." He smiled at Alex and said, "Don't you dare salute me!"

James, Ryan and Poppy walked with Alex back to his hotel. Poppy kept moving closer and closer to Alex as they strolled along the Esplanade and whispering that she couldn't wait to be alone with him in Darwin. Both of her brothers overheard and noticed that their little sister had developed a big crush on the handsome Israeli. Ryan leaned toward Alex and said quietly, "We'll tease her out of it later!" Alex smiled and said he could handle it.

"Handle what?" Poppy asked.

"You, of course," her brother James said, grinning.

Chapter 6

Wednesday morning, after his final buffet breakfast in Cairns, Alex left a tip for the busboy who'd served him every morning, and then checked out. He took a cab to the airport and was amazed to see how many planes were in the reserved area. He saw Larry doing the safety check of his Cessna and directed the cab driver to the plane. Looking up, Larry said, "G'day, Alex. I can change your flights; I have the number in my mobile and we just have to call later this morning to confirm what you want. You can fly out of Melbourne on Saturday, June 11th at 1515 hours on Thai Air, arriving in Bangkok at 2145 hours. Then on Sunday at 0010 hours on El Al to Tel Aviv, arriving in Israel at 0700. OR, and this is a big "OR", you can forget about Melbourne, stay with us in the Top Land, go camping at Uluru, and then fly to Bangkok from Darwin. To me, one big city is just like any other big city; Melbourne has some things worth seeing, but nothing you haven't seen except Yarra, the wine country, about an hour away. I know Israel has great wines, so what's so special about grapes? With us, you'll be going to Darwin, and to Kakadu National Park, a number of sites in Arnhemland and the Kimberley to see fabled rock caves, wildlands and wildlife. In the short time I've gotten to know you, I think this is more your thing than a big city and a tour of vineyards. But it's up to you, Alex."

"Then it's the Top End, Larry. As you said, a big city is a big city, and good as Yarra wines may be, I'm more into Aussie ale. From everything I've heard and read, the Outback is awesome! So, thanks so much."

"Hey, we like you. Poppy a little too much, but we can deal with that. So, *good onya*, mate. Let's go over to the flight office and I'll make those calls." Within 20 minutes, all of Alex's flights and overnight reservations had been changed, from Alice Springs to Darwin on Friday evening at 1930 hours for overnight, then a flight to Bangkok at 0600 Saturday morning, arriving in Bangkok at 1240 after a short stop in Singapore to switch planes. His El Al flight would depart just after midnight and he'd arrive in Tel Aviv at 0700 on Sunday, June 12th. Larry said, "Because you're military, all of your baggage will be forwarded to El Al with no need to claim it and go through the annoying check-in again! If you're conscious after the early flight and all the different time zones, and if you've never been in Bangkok, it's worth taking advantage of your early arrival to see the Royal Palace and the Wat Traimit Temple's gold statue of Buddha." Alex was impressed with all the strings the SOCOM officer was able to pull. He thanked him again and sent an email to the Hofmans to let them know when he'd be back in Israel.

They went back to the Cessna and Larry continued his pre-flight check and said. "Climb aboard now, Alex. The others will be here soon." When the rest of their party arrived, Poppy said she wanted to sit next to Alex, but her father said, "No way, poppet. You'll sit next to your Mum because Alex is sitting with me. I think the Yanks call that 'riding shotgun'. Isn't that right, Alex?" Two and a half hours after take-off, they arrived in Darwin and were escorted to their parking spot where two Land Rovers with military drivers were waiting. Both drivers saluted the major, and then one of the soldiers, said, "It's good to see you again, sir. Here are the Rover's keys. We'll take the luggage and then head to base. Which hotel, sir? The Double Tree?"

Sylvia had booked two suites, each with two bedrooms, a sitting room and a balcony, at the Hilton Double Tree, where Larry and his family stayed when they were in Darwin. At the luxurious hotel, fifteen minutes from the airport, Larry said, "You get the second bedroom in Andrew's suite, Alex, and Poppy, of course, will be with us. Let's unpack, then have some lunch near the pool. Then, Andrew, you and I can go to the Military Museum." When Poppy said she also wanted to go, her father said, "I hate to say 'No' to you, my darling daughter, but 'No'!"

"You're being mean, Daddy. Why? Because you don't want me to spend time with Alex? Why not?" she asked, with a pout on her very pretty face.

Larry kissed his daughter and said, "That's part of the reason, my poppet. He's too old for you, he lives thousands of miles away, he's going back to Israel soon, and he has a girlfriend at home. Besides, last year you visited the Military Museum with me and you thought it was boring. And the most important reason, Headmaster Bradley granted permission for you to miss school days because your mother told him about Aunt Sylvia's project and he decided that since you're such an excellent student, you can present an oral report on rock painting to your class. So, be my delightful girl, swim, and then sit with Sylvia and your Mum to plan our visits to the caves. OK?"

"OK," she said, still pouting. "I wanted Alex to tell me about Israel."

"Saucy little minx!" Larry said, laughing as he hugged her and tickled her under the chin. "I'll buy you a book or two about Israel."

After lunch, Larry drove them to the East Point Military Museum, later renamed the Darwin Military Museum, the DMM. At the main gate, he and Alex both showed their Military IDs; the two soldiers on

Chapter 6

duty saluted them and passed them through. The 4-acre DMM had been established in 1960 by the Royal Australian Artillery Association to present Darwin's history in the Second World War. One exhibit, "Australians under Attack" was in the original concrete bunker used for their anti-aircraft guns. The DMM's war memorabilia included Australian, US Navy, Army and Air Force uniforms, weapons, vehicles, medals; it was housed in what had been the most heavily fortified part of Australia during the war; the DMM even had an Imperial Japanese Navy submarine half-submerged in the harbor. Larry pointed out the most honored icon, the framed badly damaged 12th Squadron flag that had been flying over the RAAF Base on February 19, 1942, when Japan bombed the city 64 times. 188 Japanese aircraft attacked at 0958; then, in a second raid at midday, 54 aircraft attacked, resulting in the death of at least 1000 people. The Japanese aircraft-carrier-borne forces that bombed Darwin were the same forces that launched the surprise attack on America at Pearl Harbor on December 7, 1941; they dropped more bombs on Darwin than on Pearl Harbor. In 1943, at the peak of the war, 110,000 armed forces were based in Darwin. Larry said General Douglas MacArthur launched his campaign to liberate the Philippines from the Japanese from this very same Darwin base. Alex photographed some of the DMM's exhibits and took a few brochures. He told Larry and Andrew that his IDF comrades would be fascinated, since Israel also had several military museums: the IDF History Museum depicting the actions of the underground organizations during the British Mandate up to modern IDF combat activities; the Palmach Museum on the contribution of the pre-state Haganah to Israel's creation; the Israeli Air Force Museum at Hatzerim Airbase with a variety of IAF and foreign aircraft, including anti-aircraft arms; Latrun's Armored Corps Memorial for fallen soldiers, and one of the largest tank museums in the world; and then, of course, there was Mount Herzl, the national military cemetery, but also the burial place of many of Israel's national leaders. Sir Andrew said he'd visited Mt. Herzl, the Palmach Museum and Latrun and he had been very impressed; driving back to the hotel, Larry said he hoped to visit the Israeli museums someday, maybe with Poppy, he added with a grin.

Following the schedule worked out by Sylvia and Elizabeth, they left early the next morning on the first leg of their excursions to the Aboriginal cave paintings of the Northern Territory. With a thermos of coffee and a cooler of food, they were at the airport as the sun was rising. Forty minutes after take-off, they landed in Jabiru, a small town in Kakadu National Park. Two cabins at Davidson's Arnhemland Safari Lodge had been booked by Sylvia's publisher, and an 8-seater Land Rover was waiting for them with Bob Yunipingu, an experienced guide from an indigenous clan. Access to Arnhemland was restricted and required a permit from the Northern Land Council as it was private Aboriginal territory; a research permit had been faxed to the Lodge. They asked Bob to go directly to Borradaile, considered one of the best cave art sites in the world. Sylvia told them that the history of Australia's earliest people, hunter-gatherers, was recorded in the art in Borradaile rock shelters: tens of thousands of years in an area still teeming with crocodiles. She said all French people are so proud of their cultural identity in Lascaux's and Chauvet's caves dating back 20,000 years, but Australia's 100,000 incredibly diverse and complex sites are unknown to most Australians. She winked at Poppy, and the cheeky teenager blushed. At Borradaile, they walked into the sandstone escarpments that had been hollowed out by the sea, a labyrinth of caves ideal for human occupancy and a perfect "canvas" for Aboriginal artists. With vegetable dyes, charcoal and clay, unknown artists had filled the walls with vast images in different styles; there were primitive stick figures and "X-ray" paintings showing the internal organs and anatomical features of kangaroos, fish, and humans. The highlight of Boradaile was a platform under an arched roof, with an overlay of fantastic art, the history of the indigenous population and the evolution of their artistic styles, dating back 45,000 years: totemic figures symbolizing different clans; exquisitely drawn animals, fish and birds; children playing with crude balls or looped string; and even some paintings depicting climate change, such as a boy pulling a huge fish out of a river or a skeletal man in a desolate area of dead trees. There was a man with a long pigtail standing near a ship and men on horseback wearing hats and holding rifles, images possibly representing foreigners from China or Europe. Tasmanian tigers, the largest known carnivorous marsupial, had been extinct for thousands of years, but there were some on Boradaile's walls, attesting to the antiquity of the site. On the floor, they saw glass shards once used to sharpen spears, and they saw burial sites wedged in the cave's ledges where the skulls of ancestors were guardian spirits watching everything. Sylvia enchanted her audience, even the Aboriginal guide, as she described the longest artistic heritage on Earth. Bob said this richness and diversity distinguished the caves in Borradaile from the rest of Kakadu; the park was a treasure trove of Aboriginal rock art, but Borradaile was a hands-on experience for history buffs because

Chapter 6

nowhere else could tourists pick up the blade of a spear from the cave floor. "I'm going to have such a 'fab' report," Poppy said. "Thank you so much, Aunt Sylvia, and Bob. And thanks, Mum, for letting me skip school for this. What did you think of the rock art, Alex?"

"Like everyone else, I've never seen anything like it," Alex replied. "The history in Israel and the Middle East is very long, with ancient art in Egypt, like the pyramids, the Sphinx and the temples, but there's nothing like these cave paintings. I can hardly catch my breath. Thank you, Sylvia. And thank you, Larry, for the opportunity to share this." After lunch, they drove to a Kakadu region called the Easy Alligator. At Bob's prodding, they climbed to the top of Ubirr Rock for a panoramic view of the floodplains and cliff-like plateaus. Bob said Ubirr's "Rainbow Serpent Gallery" had traditionally been a women-only sacred site, but it was now open to tourists, and Sylvia told them the legend of *Garranga'rreli*, the Rainbow Serpent. She told them tribal elders said *Garranga'rreli* had visited the spot on her journey across Australia during "The Dreamings", a mythical period with a beginning but no end, when the natural environment was born, shaped and humanized by fantasy creatures. As *Garranga'rreli* crossed the land, she "sang" plants, animals, and people into existence. This "songline" was still considered a sacred pathway by the indigenous people of Northern Australia.

When they left Ubirr, Bob said it was worth their time and effort to take a Yellow Water cruise through the *billabong*, home to magpie geese, funny-looking jabirus, crocodiles, and many others. Just before sunset, the boat anchored in still water among pink lilies and all the boisterous travelers aboard fell silent, their laughter extinguished by the spectacle. Alex with his tiny Nikon and everyone else with a camera, professional or amateur, tried to capture the brilliant pinks, oranges, reds and purples of the sunset. Then they drove back to Davidson's Safari Lodge for showers, dinner and a relaxed evening. Poppy fell asleep against her father's shoulder the minute they were in the Land Rover. Sylvia said quietly, "It was a long day, but great for my book. I'm so glad all of you, especially our sleeping flower and you, Alex, were here with us." The exhausted group, even Bob who said Sylvia taught him things he hadn't known about his own people, agreed that the tour was worth every minute. Alex told Sylvia he looked forward to buying her book. "I'll send you an autographed copy, luv," she said.

In the dining room, Max Davidson, their host, told them the area around Borradaile was still owned by its traditional custodians, whose inhabitation dated back 50,000 years; he'd been granted honorary custodial status when he built the Lodge and therefore, although Arnhemland was alcohol free, Max's well-stocked bar was licensed. Poppy was tired and announced she wanted to go to sleep; she started to ask Alex to walk her back to the cabin, but Larry said, "We're two doors away, sweetheart. You'll be safe. G'night." The flirtatious teenager gave in reluctantly, and went to bed.

The next morning Bob drove them to Injalak Hill in Gumbalyana. He said the Gumbalyana people were members of three *kunmokurrkurrs*, all speaking Kunwinjku, an Aboriginal dialect. Contemporary artists were encouraged to depict the myths and spirit creatures of stories such as "The Dreamings". Injalak images were carbon-dated more than 35,000 years ago. Sylvia told them Injalak's rock art documented the daily life of the *Bininj Gun-Wok* people, revolving around a 6-season calendar. In the paintings, dragonflies above water revealed the abundance of fish in *bangkerreng;* bush tucker was another subject and could still be seen in the art in Injalak's Arts and Craft Centre. Viewing a few fairy-like creatures in some paintings, Poppy asked her aunt to tell them about these fairies or whatever they were. Sylvia said, "I'd love to, but let's sit down." Outside, sitting on rocks, Sylvia said, "According to legend, these characters, *Mimihs,* with elongated bodies so thin they might break if caught in a high wind, were the original spirit beings of the Aborigines. To avoid their bodies breaking, they lived in rock crevices and were rarely, if ever, seen by humans, like the leprechauns in Ireland. *Mimihs*, however, were obviously seen in Injalak art. In addition to rituals and song and dance, the small but dynamic *Mimihs* taught the *bininjs* survival skills: how to hunt, how to use fire and how to cook kangaroo and crocodile meat. Some elders claimed *Mimihs,* if they were approached the wrong way, were dangerous; they shrieked, kicked, slapped, even smashed racket-like objects on people, causing injury. *Mimihs,* good and evil, were depicted in paintings 50,000 to 20,000 years ago." Sylvia's listeners were mesmerized; finally, Poppy said she would never want to meet one of those "screaming *mimis*" on a dark street, and everyone burst out laughing.

Their next site was Burrungui, originally Nourlangie Rock, traditional home of the Gundjeihmi-speaking people, who claimed they were created during "The Dreamings". Amazing wall art illustrated figures like a female spirit with four arms, but Burrungui's paintings had to contend with natural threats to their survival, water, nests of wasp, and tourists. Custodians built shelters around the outcroppings with signs explaining the importance of preserving these

Chapter 6

treasures. In one shelter, they saw paintings of tall men in headdresses with boomerangs and spears, and a white two-masted sailing ship with an anchor, possibly a reference to early Europeans. Unfortunately, with so many books about Burrungui rock art, tourists had stolen and even destroyed Aboriginal treasures. Standing in front of one of the sheltered outcroppings, Poppy said, "Aunt Sylvia, look! Dolphins! And 'screaming mimis' in very funny dresses!" Sylvia congratulated Poppy on her excellent observation skills and said, "With short beaks, those dolphins are probably porpoises; scientists say porpoises have been in these oceans for 40 million years. I think the *Mimhi*-like figures are in ceremonial dress, but I don't know what kind. I'm so proud of you, Poppy, and I'm sure your Mum is, too."

Poppy laughed. "Daddy, Uncle Andrew and Alex are silly for not coming inside. I can't wait to tell them what I 'discovered'. Daddy will be so proud of me, too, and not just for winning medals in swimming!" Liz asked Bob to take a picture of Poppy with her 'discoveries'. Afterwards, the tired group returned to the Lodge and went swimming for an hour; Larry told Poppy he wasn't proud of her only for her swimming medals and he couldn't wait to see the photos of her special 'dolphins' and 'screaming mimis'. Later, Poppy was thrilled to hear Larry bragging to Max Davidson about his daughter's 'discoveries'. The older couples retired to their cabins, but Poppy and Alex stayed in the Lounge chatting, and in Poppy's case, flirting, with a group of young Canadians touring Australia's wildlands instead of the wildlands of North America.

On the way to their cabins, Sylvia said, "Let's sit on the veranda. I have a proposition and, if you agree, we'll change our itinerary. Gentlemen, after two days of climbing in and out of rock caves and listening to endless stories, I think you're bored with rock art. I have a commitment, but you don't. We're in the glorious Outback, and tomorrow we're flying to Kimberley's million-acre El Questro Station; we can see the homestead on Saturday and Sunday. Larry, you said you can fly us to Cockburn Range, over the waterfalls and caverns that are accessible only by air; you said you've been there and it's indescribable; I think we should do it. We can check into the Homestead in the morning, ask a ranger all about its history and original pioneers. Then, we can do the air tour of the Cockburns, and fly over Bungle Bungles to see the sandstone beehive domes. Sunday we can take the Chamberlain Gorge Cruise in a dinghy with a mast, and sail on the 3 km waterhole accessible only by boat, to view the cheeky spinnerfish, Mareeba rock-wallabies, and the freshwater crocodiles, the 'freshies'.

We can even go to Zebedee Springs and dip our feet in the rocky thermal pools. At dusk, we'll relax, indulge in fruit and wine while we enjoy the dazzling colors of the Kimberley shimmering on the cliffs. So what do you think of my plans? Sound good?" They agreed instantly, and Andrew said his wife was not only beautiful, but she also had a great mind for detail. "Thank you, darling, but here's the real reason for this itinerary," Sylvia said. "Poppy and Lizzie will go with me to see more rock art on Monday and Tuesday, but the three of you, including Alex of course, can forget rock painting and enjoy Kimberley's wilderness; you can explore the gorges, hike the famous cliffs and lookouts, even go horseback riding or fishing. I'll leave for Hall's Creek early Monday morning with Liz and Poppy. Poppy was allowed to come on this trip because of rock art, so she'll come with me to complete her report. Also, I'm not sure she should trek Kimberley with the 'gentlemen'. What do you think, Lizzie?"

Liz instantly agreed to let the men "bond" in the wilderness. She said she already had ideas for her next children's book from Sylvia's fantastic stories. Andrew sighed. "My darling, I'm willing to accompany you anywhere, to caves, to the opera, even to the moon. But exploring the Kimberley would be fabulous. So the men and women will go separate ways for a couple of days. Oh, here come Poppy and Alex. We'll tell Alex. And Lizzie, you and Larry can break the sad news about leaving Alex to Poppy. Goodnight."

On Saturday and Sunday, they adhered to Sylvia's plan from beginning to end, although she felt a little guilty about Larry doing so much flying. But he said, "Today was fine my dear. You know I love to fly. And tomorrow will be totally relaxing: a good cruise, good food, good wine, good family, and a new good friend." They teased him about his 'good' vocabulary. Monday, the men had breakfast, said goodbye to the ladies and began a two-hour horseback trek around Saddleback Ridge and Moonshine Creek. Then they went by helicopter to Amaroo Falls, one of the highest waterfalls in the Station; the ranger-pilot said it was a view of El Questro from a different vantage point and a way to discover Kimberley's vast wildlife; the 360° panorama of El Questro's endless landscape was astonishing. Alex took photograph after photograph from every angle; he told them growing up in a landlocked country of 49,000 square kilometers, and living in Israel only a little more than 20,000, made it impossible for him to get his mind around the size of the Outback. 6.5 million square kilometers and so huge that people traveled everywhere by plane or helicopter. After lunch, they skinny-dipped in the isolated

Chapter 6

splendor of Amaroo and flew back to the Station. They dined on steaks so enormous and grilled so rare that they knew Sylvia and Liz would call their meal "instant heart attack"! Later, they relaxed in the Lounge, with 30-year-old single malt Scotch for Andrew and Larry, and another oddly named ale, Granite Belt Brewery's "Irish Red" for Alex When they'd inquired about the Tuesday excursion, they were told that El Questro rangers led arduous treks to different gorges each day, followed by lunch and an invigorating swim in a pristine waterhole. The three of them opted for the bone-rattling drive on the Chamberlain River track that dropped steeply to the riverbed and then ended in Explosion Gorge, where a boat zigzagged around sandstone escarpments to Pentecost River. They ate their lunch in the small boat, and afterwards hiked to a remote fishing area. At the Pentecost River crossing, a 4-wheel vehicle was waiting; the ranger said they were lucky because they'd be able to cross despite the river's two hazards: the water level sometimes so deep that vehicles couldn't traverse the river which was infested with the other hazard, hundreds of "salties", saltwater crocodiles, the largest living reptile. The Jeep ventured into the "not too deep" river but about halfway across, the ranger started driving as fast as possible to avoid the snapping jaws of the salties trying to grab the vehicle's tires. Safely on the other side, everyone drew a deep breath, and the ranger said, "We pay those salties to attack our Jeeps so that tourists have a great story to tell when they get home!" His passengers laughed and relaxed a little. Then they drove to Branco's Lookout for the breathtaking view of the setting sun casting dazzling streaks across the Cockburn Range in the background. Back at the Homestead, they relaxed with a few *coldies*, a perfect end to an unforgettable day. When they were finishing their starter course in the dining room, their three ladies came in, smiled, and Liz said, "We're back. We didn't know where you were, but the server in the Lounge said he saw the three of you staggering in this direction!" Andrew kissed Sylvia, Larry hugged his wife and daughter, and Alex said hi.

Larry said, "We didn't drink that much, two ales each, but it was quite a day. Let's move to a larger table." Poppy glared at the fish platters a waiter was carefully carrying, and asked if they'd spent the whole day fishing and if their dinner was the fish they'd caught. Her father answered, "No, poppet. Yesterday we went horseback riding and today we were almost 'eaten' by 'salties'. So, check the menu and order your meal. Then tell us what you saw and later we'll tell you all about the 'croc incident'."

Poppy said, "We saw the Wandjina paintings. I know I was really little, but I remember the opening of the 2000 Sydney Olympics, the dancing and smoke. Do you remember, Daddy? It was the story of the Wandjinas and it was wonderful; today we met the man who designed it. We stayed at the Mangrove Hotel in Broome last night; it's on the bay, but it has two pools and I swam in both! This morning we went to Gantheaume Point; the tide was very low and we saw dinosaur footprints 130 million years old! Mum said some prints were cut out of the ground and stolen, but they've been put back. I don't know how they could do that, not the stealing, but putting them back in the sea so we can see them. Anyway, it was fantastic and I can't wait to tell all my friends." Liz said Poppy was so excited she was telling everything in the wrong order, so they should eat and then the 'survivors' could tell them about the 'croc incident'.

In the Lounge, over coffee and triple scoops of ice cream for Poppy, Sylvia gave them a recap of their trip. "We flew to the Bradshaw Paintings; they're long-bodied, graceful humans and they show us what the Guion people believed, how they adjusted to changing climate conditions and how they lived. The Wandjina sites were very different and undoubtedly the highlight for me; 200,000 square kilometers in the Kimberley, their culture dating back at least 60,000 years but probably even older. It was mind-boggling. Aboriginal people treat Wandjina sites with respect and caution, and even approach them with fear; they don't stay at the sites very long because they believe the Wandjina are still there and they don't want to anger them. They really believe Wandjinas brought rain to the Kimberley, and the Aborigines refresh the Wandjina images each year to ensure the return of the rains and fertility. We went to Munurru, site of the earliest images; as we drew near, our pilot Kevin began to call out to the resident spirits in his language, his deep voice asking again and again for permission from those spirits for us to visit the site. And almost immediately, we saw them, a line of Wandjina spirits along the base of the site. Perhaps what is most interesting is the way the Wandjinas are depicted, with white faces, large black eyes, no mouth, and a big head with a halo. Poppy said they looked like aliens, and Kevin agreed. Maybe he was merely teasing Poppy, but he said ancient writings suggest extraterrestrial beings visited Earth thousands of years ago and had direct contact with the Wandjinas. Some Aboriginal clans believe the aliens had a role in "The Dreaming", and that is reflected in the creation stories of certain clans. If their sites are disturbed, the Wandjinas consider it a crime and they can punish those who break their laws with floods, lightning and even with cyclones. After that

Chapter 6

riveting exposure to the Wandjina culture, we flew to Broome. This morning, we took the side-trip Poppy mentioned, to Gantheaume Point to see the dinosaur footprints. Then we flew to Derby.

At the Mowanjum Art & Culture Centre; we met Donny Woolagoodja, the designer of the colossal highlight of the opening ceremony of Sydney's Olympics. As a child, Donny watched his clan's elders painting Wandjinas and learned about "The Dreamings"; he became an extraordinary Aborigine artist. His father was one of the last lore and medicine men of the Wororra people, and after his father's death, Donny became responsible for passing on its cultural traditions to new generations. From there, we saw one of the unique sites along the Gibb River Road, a huge limestone rock straddling the water; called *Bandangnan*, 'boss-man rock' by the locals, it's in charge of Wandjina Gorge. Our final stop was yet another gorge, further down Gibb River, with extensive art, though much of it has faded through natural decay. Fortunately, it's not an easy site to reach and relatively few people visit it, so there wasn't any evidence of deliberate damage. Then we flew here. I'm happy to be 'home' and now I'll stop talking. Please tell us about the 'croc incident'. What happened? Are you all OK?"

Andrew said they were all fine and gave them his very brief version of "The Occurrence at Pentecost River Crossing", how the ranger drove as fast as possible to escape from the enormous "salties" nipping at the Jeep's tires. "I won't tell you we weren't scared because the jaws of those 'suckers' are huge and a few of them were really close. On the other side of the river, our driver told us El Questro pays those crocs to go after Jeeps and Land Rovers so tourists have a terrific story to tell when they get home. We knew, pun intended, his story was a '*crock*', but we laughed and were happy to come back here. Still, I'll admit each of us did drink a couple of ales."

"Wow! I wish I'd been there." Poppy said, yawning. "No, I wouldn't have missed today for anything. I can't wait to tell all my friends about the aliens who came to earth and met the Aborigines, and about my 'discovery', about everything. When are we going home, Daddy? Tomorrow?"

Larry answered, "Actually, luv, we're going home on Saturday. I'm flying Alex to Ayers Rock tomorrow morning. We're leaving very early because it's a four-hour flight and we have to meet Tony at Uluru air-strip at 11:45. You can come, Poppy, if you go to bed right now. OK?" She said goodnight to everyone and went to the cabin. Larry smiled at Alex and said, "I guess we know what she wants. Leave your

Alexander's Story

luggage here, Alex, except what you need at Uluru, and we'll bring it to Darwin. Now, I'm knackered, too, so I'll see all of you tomorrow. G'night." In the morning Larry, Alex, Andrew and Poppy met for breakfast, and then went to the air-strip. Alex's backpack held the things he'd need for the 3-day trip, including his tiny Nikon. After Larry's check of the Cessna, they flew to Ayers Rock with Alex "riding shotgun". At Kata Tjuta, the Ayers Rock airstrip, Tony was waiting. Larry chatted with his old friend for a couple of minutes, and Andrew wished Alex a really great time; Poppy hugged Alex, knowing her father disapproved. Alex returned her hug and whispered, "It's OK, Poppy. You remind me so much of my sister, Paulina, and Dani, my Israeli 'almost sister'; both of them are also huggers. G'bye for now. I'll see you Friday evening in Darwin."

Tony and Alex drove to Ayers Rock Resort, Uluru's service village, to meet the other members of their tour group. Their first destination was the awe-inspiring Uluru, Australia's renowned natural landmark and the world's largest rock. Tony told them they couldn't climb it because the Aboriginal custodians objected, and he respected their feelings, but they could hike 10-kilometers around Uluru and detour to the snake-like grooves of Mutitjulu Waterhole. Tony said, "Almost everyone thinks Uluru is just a large orange rock giving the Outback a strange silhouette, but they don't know anything about the area. Despite all the dust, there are valleys, trails and other peaks with bursts of greenery against the arid desert background. Mutitjulu's an odd shaped water-filled hole, but it's so much more than just a hole filled with water; not only does it provide water, it's home to almost 300 people. In less than four hours, the group completed the Uluru and Mutitjulu hike and then drove to the edge of Kantju Gorge with its vertical walls, and total peacefulness, to see the flora and fauna of the area and to enjoy the colorful sunset before driving to Ayers Rock Campground with toilets and showers, and to their own *swags*. The tired group cooked dinner over a campfire and opted for an early night. Day 2 began after Uluru's dazzling sunrise: then Tony took them to the Valley of the Winds with its awe-inspiring views. A Canadian hiker said she felt the same spiritualism she had experienced in a sanctuary of British Columbia's indigenous people, the Haida. Alex nodded, remembering how he'd felt when he came to his ancestral homeland for the first time. As they were hiking, Tony handed out small bags of bush tucker, bush carrots; bush tomatoes called desert raisins; bush plums that weren't plums; a purple Emu apple with a large stone-like seed; and a quandong, a red native peach. After hearing a lecture about

Chapter 6

the Anangu version of "The Dreamings", they drove to The Olgas, 36 impressive domes, less known but 200 meters higher than Uluru, its neighbor. Tony gave them a choice: to climb Mount Olga, or to take the 2.6-kilometer Walpa Gorge walk; Alex climbed. Just before twilight, they went to a lookout point for yet another brilliant sunset. They spent the night at Kings Creek Station, a working cattle ranch with campground facilities. On Day 3, they woke before dawn to drive to Kings Canyon for one of the highlights of the tour, observing how the perpendicular red rock walls in the huge gorge changed color as the sun rose. After a sunrise breakfast, they climbed 500 stone stairs to the top of the cliffs, 600 meters above sea level, and embarked on the challenging Kings Canyon Rim Walk, skirting the edge of the canyon. Lying on their bellies on the narrow path, the hikers carefully peered down into the gorge more than 150 meters below. They hiked the Rim Walk in single file and in one direction, clockwise, for safety, but it felt weird with no one coming the other way. Further along the trail, they walked into the midst of the striped bee-hive domes of the "Lost City", weathered rocks resembling the ruins of an ancient city. Another kilometer further, they descended wooden stairs to the lush "Garden of Eden", a waterhole and conservation site, a refuge for 600 species of unique flora and fauna. Then they ascended the South Wall Return to the parking lot and drove to Kings Canyon Resort. Tony offered them a camel ride before heading to "civilization" in Alice Springs, but they declined and chose the 3-hour drive in his air-conditioned mini-van. Alex's flight to Darwin was at 5:00, so after saying goodbye to his fellow campers and Tony, he showered and changed into almost clean clothes. At 7:15, he arrived in Darwin on the first leg of his trip back to Israel and was delighted to find Larry and Poppy waiting to welcome him.

 On the short drive to the hotel, Poppy told him of the things she'd seen on their family trip to Uluru with Tony and asked if Alex's trip was the same; he teased that it was even better. Alex was surprised again to see Andrew, Sylvia and Liz drinking pre-dinner cocktails in the lobby and waiting for him. Liz handed him a key, and said, "Why don't you go to the room, drop your stuff with all the rest of your baggage, and meet us here in ten for your farewell dinner?" In clean jeans and T-shirt, Alex joined the Smythe family, these generous, caring people he'd come to love during their week together in the phenomenal Outback, for dinner. When they were seated and looking at their menus, Poppy said, "Daddy bought me a book all about Israel. You should order prawns or scallops because you can't get seafood in Israel." Alex laughed and said he'd take her advice, but didn't tell her about all the places in Israel that serve non-kosher food. As they finished their meal, their waiter set a chocolate cake with small Australian and Israeli flags and *"Hooroo, mate"* piped in blue and white frosting. Alex blinked, so moved he could barely speak. In her cheeky manner, Poppy said, "Just say *'Ta'* and *'good onya'*!" Everyone laughed at her nonsense and started talking at once. Before she said goodnight, Poppy kissed Alex on both cheeks and whispered, "I'll see you in Israel someday and you'll introduce me to both your 'sisters'!" Alex hugged her and told her he was looking forward to that visit.

At 4:45 the next morning, when Alex came downstairs for a taxi to the airport, Larry was waiting instead. He punched Alex lightly on the shoulder as he said, "You told my son James you'd come back to instruct his SASR team in *Krav Maga*. I'll hold you to it! *Hooroo!* And *Shalom*, Alex."

Alex gave Larry a brief bear-hug and said, "*Lehit'ra'ot*, that's Hebrew for *'hasta la vista'* or *'auf wiedersehen'*!" He got into the cab, a little shocked by the tears he felt in his eyes. The flight to Bangkok and his brief visits to the tourist sites Larry had recommended seemed rather anticlimactic after six incredible weeks Down Under. He knew he would always remember the warmth and friendship of the Aussies who not only made his trip fantastic, but also taught him a lot of new slang!

When his flight landed in Israel at 7:00 the next morning and he passed through Passport Control, Alex was astounded again, to see David and Kobi waiting for him, with Kobi holding a small sign obviously painted by Lisa:

They'd pulled IDF strings to wait in the airport's huge arrivals hall instead of greeting Alex in the large crowd outside. Both of them embraced Alex in the Hofman traditional group hug, and David said, "Welcome home, Alex. We really missed you. Lise's waiting at home with breakfast, and I wouldn't be surprised if our parents are there, with Anna cooking, of course, although Lise does a good breakfast. We can't wait to hear all about Australia and the people you met. And the Outback! Wow!"

Without giving Alex a chance to say a word, Kobi said, "You look

Chapter 6

wiped out, *bro*. But after such long flights and so many zones, who could blame you! My CO let me off, or out, until mid-week, so we'll have loads of time to catch up after you get over jet-lag and culture shock, and then you can spill everything: SOCOM, SASR, diving at the Reef, the Outback, and a *Sheila* named Stacy! *B'seder*?"

"*Good onya, mate! Ohmigod!* It's so good to be home, and to see you guys!" They collected Alex's luggage, and he said, "I was so busy and it was so far away, like Peter Pan's *'Neverland'*. I didn't even realize how much I missed you until now. The Aussies I met are great people, but you're my family. I've spent so many of the last few years abroad: Cyprus, America, France, the UK, Slovakia with my family, and now Australia, but Israel's my home and I just want to stay here, to put down some roots, to study in university, and to do some serious as well as fun things with people I love, in Israel!" Alex stopped, shocked at the emotional outburst, normally so unlike him.

David and Kobi stared at him. Then David said with a grin, "Wow! We won't make you repeat what you just said at home, but Lise and Anna would have loved to hear you. Let's go to your Jeep. Yeah, we drove it here! Let's get you home for food and sleep. Then we'll talk, after you unwind a little." Half an hour later, they pulled into the driveway, and Lise, Anna and Richard raced out to hug Alex simultaneously. They spoke simultaneously as well. Lise said, "It's so good to see you, luv. Welcome home." Anna said, "Come inside and sit down, dear. I made your favorite waffles and we have maple syrup from Canada! "And Richard said, "Let the boy breathe. He's dead on his feet! "

David and Kobi burst out laughing as they carried Alex's luggage inside, and Lise pulled Alex out to the deck. "This is like one of those zany Marx Brothers comedies!" Kobi said, "Let's just sit down and eat. Alex is exhausted and we should let him get some sleep. We can hear about Australia tonight." He sat down, picked up a pitcher and poured some orange juice for himself and Alex, while David quietly applauded him. Kobi asked, "Are you sure you want a cup of coffee, Alex? It might keep you awake. "

"Nothing will keep me awake at this point," Alex said, yawning. "I think it was yesterday at 6:00 a.m. when I left Darwin. Then I had about 10 hours in Bangkok before my El Al flight. Every place was a different time zone and I was too wired to sleep on the flight. So I've no idea of how long I've been awake. I'd like to eat a couple of waffles, drink the juice, have that coffee, and then hit the sack! Is that OK? "

As he was walking upstairs, David said, "Alex, try not to sleep too long now. If you sleep just long enough to take the edge off your fatigue, you'll be able to sleep tonight and acclimate yourself to Israel time. If you want, I'll wake you in five or six hours. "Alex nodded as he walked into his room and fell onto his bed. He awoke a few hours later, slightly disoriented; the clock on the table next to his bed displayed "15:45". He heard some noise outside, but headed to the bathroom. After showering, he put on a pair of cutoffs and a T-shirt he found in his closet and went downstairs, barefoot.

Lise and Keren were chatting out on the deck, while David and Kobi were swimming. Keren jumped up and kissed him. "Welcome home. How was it? Fascinating? Especially the Reef? Did you climb Ayers Rock? Kobi says you have a beautiful girlfriend. Who is she and what does she do? Are the people in Australia as nice as everyone says? Did you see kangaroos or koalas or crocodiles? And why did you sneak up on *Ema* and me just now like a thief in the night? Where are your shoes?"

"You sound more like Dani than Keren. Whichever darling daughter you are, please give him a chance to answer those questions one at a time. I'm sure we'll hear about everything when Alex is ready."

He sat down and started counting off his answers on his fingers. "It was great and definitely fascinating. The Reef was incredible and you'll see my underwater photos later. I didn't climb Ayers Rock because Uluru, that's what the Aussies call it, belongs to the Aborigines and they don't want outsiders climbing all over it, but I did climb The Olgas which are nearby and higher than Uluru. I dated a lovely girl named Stacy a few times; she's fun to be with but she isn't Jewish and she isn't interested in leaving Sydney, so it was a very short but very pleasurable romance. All the Aussies I met were great, but they're not *my Hofmans*. I saw 'roos, and joeys, wallabies and wombats, koalas, emus and a nasty cassowary, giant turtles and even a platypus; I didn't see any *bunyips* but Poppy saw 'screaming *mimis*', 'aliens', 'dolphins' and dinosaur footprints in the Outback. Larry, Sir Andrew and I were almost 'attacked' by a mob of 'salties', enormous saltwater crocs. My sneakers are a real mess and I couldn't find my flip-flops, so that's why I'm barefoot and I didn't sneak up on you. Any more questions, my dear?"

Keren just sat there with her mouth wide open, and Lise said, "That's put you in your place, my darling daughter! Very well done, Alex. I was really impressed and I guess you're not suffering from jet lag. Everyone will want to know what happened with those crocodiles, so don't even begin to tell us now. Unless you want to join David

Chapter 6

and Kobi in the pool, relax and I'll tell you what's been happening here." Lise started counting with her fingers and continued, "You've seen Kobi and you can ask him anything you want to know yourself. Yaniv is thriving in Unit 8200, and I think he's even learning some of Gabriel's weird languages, like Urdu or maybe Farsi. Dani is having a blast in South America. And yes, Keren, she and her friends are being very careful about their contact with 'chauvinist Latinos'. They've just been in Machu Picchu and they may be flying to Bolivia tomorrow; all four girls have promised us not to go near the infamous 'death road', but should we believe them? David Rosenzweig knows their itinerary better than I do, and he thinks they're OK. Now for the most special news. Keren has been accepted for her PhD by both the Neils Bohr and Max Planck Institutes, and she's decided to go to Copenhagen, which is great because my brother and his family live there, and she already knows the city since we've all been there many times. Everyone's really excited for her except David R who hates her being away for a long time while he's stuck here, his words, not mine, with an internship and then a residency. *My* David is collaborating with an American colleague on a new book, and I have a few new commissions. My parents are fine, as you saw for yourself this morning, if you could actually 'see' anything this morning. So are David's parents. Whew! That was exhausting, so I'm going for a swim. By the way, your CO called. I told him you were fast asleep and he said he doesn't want to talk to you or see you until Wednesday. He also said he received an incredible letter, again his words, not mine, from the CO in Sydney, a Colonel Markham."

Keren said, "You know, *Ema*, I could have told Alex about Copenhagen myself. And I don't know if I'm ready to talk to anyone about *my* David. I really like him, but my PhD is very important. And I really want to do it in Copenhagen, so David and I have a lot of problems…"

"It's all right, Keren. I understand, not that my relationship with Stacy was anything like yours with David R. But I liked her a lot and I miss her. By the way, Lise, I learned that impressive 'counting trick' from you the very first day I met you. Oh, I bought you and David a book about Aboriginal rock art, but the photos don't do the paintings justice. I'll tell you, maybe tomorrow, about the days in the Outback when my friends and I saw some of the remarkable sites and I learned some of their legends. But now I also really need to swim a little."

Within a few minutes, everyone was in the pool, tossing a yellow water polo ball from person to person. Later, Alex unpacked and brought the gifts from his SOCOM students and the ones he'd bought for the family out to the deck, explaining a bit about each. Everyone was charmed by the stuffed koala wearing Aussie camouflage and a bush hat, and David appreciated the Macquarie brochures, but said it would be hard for Lise and him to be on sabbatical so far away from Israel when they had kids in the IDF. Both Lise and Keren loved the Paddington Markets scarves, and everyone laughed when he told them about the crazy dog show; they were impressed when he told them Paddington Markets is the sole source of funding for meals for Sydney's homeless people, and how that reminded him of Lise and David's *afikomen* donation to Leket at *Pesach*. He showed them the tiny enamel koala with emerald eyes holding a pale green jade eucalyptus, his gift for Dani who'd asked him to bring her a koala, but stated he'd never give her 'his' koala. Kobi was really pleased with the boomerangs and bush hats Alex had purchased in Kuranda. While Kobi was figuring out how to throw the hand-painted weapon so it would return to him, Alex said, "As the older brother, Kobes, choose the one you want, but the other one's for Yaniv, and you can't change if yours doesn't come back the way the manual says it should."

Keren commented, "He's become so bossy, hasn't he?" Kobi agreed, but added he was sure Alex was so bossy because he'd been very busy 'bossing' Aussie Special Ops officers. Keren laughed and said, "I guess that's as good a reason as any! Is that why you're so bossy now, Alex?"

Alex didn't respond; instead he told them he'd purchased several books in the Hidden Words Bookshop in Kuranda, near Cairns: a few on Aborigine rock painting and mythology for Lise and David and himself; a book about Australian racism and the segregation of the Aborigines and developments in Aboriginal education, especially science, for Ephraim and Aya; Australia during World War II for Richard, and a cookbook on unique Aussie foods for Anna. He also had several books for his sister's children, and he'd found three special books for Gabriel in the bookshop: a preliminary edition of the Bible translated into *Kriol*, an Aboriginal pidgin; and since no one had yet translated the Qur'an into *Kriol*, he bought a Qur'an in *Tuvulu*, a Polynesian language; and a dictionary of Aboriginal languages, *Walmajarri, Burarra, Kriol, Gurindji*, and many others. And he'd even found a book on infrared spectroscopy for Keren. Larry Smythe had arranged "military shipment" of the books to Israel via DHL and Alex expected them to arrive the following day. He said he hoped Lise's and David's parents and Gabriel would come to get their books, and Lise joked that they'd all come anyway. Alex said he really wanted to

Chapter 6

tell them all about the Smythe family and everything they'd done for him in the last week, and he also wanted to 'bore' them with all his photos. "But, I'm fading really fast," he said, yawning, "I guess my jet lag is kicking in again, so I'll say *G'night*. I'll see you all tomorrow."

When he awoke on Monday, Alex couldn't believe how rested he felt. *"My jet lag has disappeared?"* he said to himself just as Kobi knocked on the door and came in with a mug of coffee for Alex and asked if he was over the jet lag. "I hope so," Alex replied, "I have lots to tell you and a ton of photos, but I won't really know about the jet lag until tonight or if I zonk out again later today! Anyway, *g'day, mate!*"

"Boker tov to you, too, bro'. Hey, can you teach me some Aussie talk? It's so weird and I love hearing it. Let's grab breakfast and then toss *my* boomerang around a bit, if *you* can catch it!" Kobi said, grinning.

Alex laughed, *"Grouse, cobber!* In *Straya*, they say *bog into brekkie*, so I'll just *siphon the python*, something that's never to be said to *sheilas* 'cause it's *barra*. I'll yank on *stubbies* and a *Mickey Mouse* T-shirt, and we're *good to go*. As for *strine*, it's *yakka yakka* but you're not *drongo* or *bludge*, so let's *avago! Apples?* I need some *dardy runners*, so let's *lob* to Azrieli this *arvo* and I'll *shout* for *tucker*. A *sanger*, a *coldie* or a *fizzie*, not a *mystery bag. Fathom that nark?* If *yep, good on ya!*" [See Glossary] As Alex disappeared in the direction of the bathroom, Kobi fell back onto his friend's unmade bed and couldn't stop laughing.

While the two young men were enjoying their *brekkie*, Kobi said that Alex's return from Down Under was making his own forced "holiday at home" a better distraction than he'd expected. He told Alex he'd led his 669 squad in a difficult rescue with friendly fire and casualties, and after official debriefing, the full squad had received a week's leave. When Kobi and Alex returned from the Azrieli mall, David said a DHL package of books was on the deck. While Kobi was throwing his boomerang and practicing how to catch it on its return, Alex opened the package and found a note from James Smythe:

> Hey, Alex.
> If you're reading this, your packet has arrived. Dad says not to feel guilty about DHL flying your package to Israel free; SOCOM gives DHL a lot of business, and they owe us. Looking forward to seeing you for Krav Maga in a couple of years.
> James.

Alex put away his own books and the ones for his niece and nephew; then he transferred the best photographs from his digital camera to his laptop computer so he'd be able to show them to the family later, and went downstairs to offer his help. Both Lise and David were involved with commissions and approaching deadlines; so Anna's early morning call to let them know the grandparents would prepare a simple evening meal was truly appreciated. She said the only thing to be done was to fire up the grill at 6:30 p.m. And since both older couples wanted to hear about Alex's Australian adventures, Keren had agreed to pick up her grandparents and all the food on her way home from work. When Alex came into the kitchen, everyone was there and everything seemed ready. He heard Puccini's Tosca, loud as usual, blaring from the stereo in Lise's studio while she was probably washing her brushes and her hands; Anna and Aya were in the kitchen putting the finishing touches on dinner and humming along with the opera; on the deck, the grill was heating up and Keren was setting the table, glancing outside frequently to the backyard where Kobi was flaunting his prowess with the boomerang to his father, grandfathers, David R, Gabriel who'd come from Jerusalem, and Yaniv who'd wangled a 48-hour pass by lying to his CO about his "brother" being attacked in Australia! Feeling extremely content, Alex smiled and remembered Judy Garland's last lines in The Wizard of Oz: "Home! And you're all here! I'm not going to leave here ever, ever again, because I love you all! And, oh, Auntie Em, there's no place like home!"

After dinner, everyone relaxed on the deck with wine or soft drinks; Lise and Keren modeled their scarves and Kobi, Yaniv and Gabriel sported their Aussie bush hats. Earlier, David and Kobi had driven to Urim to pick up Yaniv, and the three of them went to David's department to borrow a device called a "Barca" which would reflect Alex's photos on a large screen. After Yaniv set up the Barca and screen, Alex opened his laptop to a photo of Sydney's landmark Opera House. He gave them the books he'd purchased with brief explanations about each. Richard, leafing through his book about the Japanese attacks on Darwin during World War II, said, "This is brilliant, Alex, but you didn't have to waste your hard-earned money on us."

Alex replied, "Yes, sir, I did. All of you have come to mean so much to me during the last four years and I sometimes have to find a way to show you. Besides, the money wasn't a waste or even hard-earned. Since I'm no longer officially in *Tzahal*, my salary is so much higher than an ordinary soldier's. And the Aussie Special Forces not

Chapter 6

only paid for my flights to and from Australia; they also paid me for the *Krav Maga* sessions, extra for the classes for women. They even provided housing for the two weeks of the course. I didn't even pay for the DHL delivery of your books. Listen to the note I found in the package." Alex pulled it out and read it to them.

Keren asked, "Who's James? Who's his father? Is this related to almost being eaten by crocs? You told *Ema* and me you'd tell us later, so now it's a day later, and we've been very patient!" Keren exclaimed.

As everyone looked at Alex, shocked at Keren's words about a crocodile attack, Alex said, "OK. I'll tell you everything out of order. My two weeks in Sydney, the Special Forces (SOCOM) trainees, Stacy, Shabbat dinner at Julia's house with cheeky teenagers, Cairns and diving at the Great Barrier Reef and all the early photos later if you're not bored by then. First, I'll tell you all about my 'all-expenses-paid' trips to the Outback and Uluru, Ayers Rock, and the Smythe family. They're extraordinary 'tall poppies,' which means high achievers in Aussie slang," but it's usually said derisively, although that's not the case with the Smythes. He showed them his photos from the Shangri-La Hotel in Cairns and told them about Larry and his career in SOCOM, about Larry's wife Liz who writes children's stories, about his sons, James and Ryan, who are on Australia's Olympic diving teams, about James who at 21 is licensed to fly a Cessna, and about Poppy, Larry's 14-year-old cheeky and flirtatious daughter who reminded him so much of Dani and his youngest sister, Paulina and was also an Olympics-level swimmer. He told them about Sir Andrew Smythe, the mountaineer, and his wife Sylvia who was writing a book about rock art all over the world, the reason they were travelling in the Outback with its remarkable Aborigine rock art sites. And, of course, he told them about the 'croc incident', the wild ride across the river crossing while a mob of ferocious saltwater crocodiles tried to grab the wheels of their Jeep, and how, once they were safely on the other side, the ranger who drove them joked about paying the crocs to attack SUVs so tourists would have a great story to tell at home. Showing them his hastily taken photos of the 'salties' surrounding the Jeep and nipping the wheels, Alex ended his tale.

Everyone was speechless, mesmerized until David said the ranger was right; it was a great story! "And you tell it really well," Aya said. "Have you ever considered going into teaching or writing after the army? You're a natural."

"Thanks, *Savta* Aya," he responded. "You know my grandparents were both teachers, and my mother still is. I enjoyed teaching English in Slovakia and I've thought about it, but not English. You know I'm starting Hebrew U. after *Sukkoth*, so I'll make some career decisions then…although I'll admit the Aussie 'tall poppies' and all their accomplishments intimidate me a little."

Lise jumped up and spoke, sounding a bit angry. "Are you bonkers, my dear Alex? I know you're not…what is that word Kobi said you taught him? Oh, yes, *drongo*, stupid! If you stayed in The Unit, you'd be a major or higher in no time! As for 'tall poppies', think about how your grandparents survived the war, or my father, or Anna. Think about what David's parents did in the Haganah, or what David did in two Israeli wars. Think about how many difficulties Gabriel has overcome and about his father's experiences; think about how many Israeli lives Kobi and Yaniv have saved in the IDF. And think about how Keren climbed Annapurna and will soon climb 'another mountain' in Copenhagen, a PhD mountain. Think about Dani; oh, I don't want to think 'my foolish girl' and her friends might be driving the "death road" in Bolivia right now! So think about yourself and all you have accomplished in only 26 years!"

"*Kol ha k'vod*, Lise," David said. "You sounded just like a Mama Bear defending her family. Female bears attack their own cubs, playfully of course, when they're doing something wrong, so I guess Alex is one of your cubs! I agree with you, by the way, as I'm sure everyone does. So please sit down, take a deep breath and then drink some wine. Also, by the way, you didn't tell Alex to think about *your* achievements!" He looked at Alex and said, "You know she's proud of you, so think about all of that later. Now, if you don't mind, please show us the rest of your photos, starting with Sydney Harbour Bridge because I have to return the Barca tomorrow." Alex returned to his laptop with quiet murmurs of "Hear! Hear!" in the background.

After enjoying all of Alex's photos and explanations, Keren said, "You know, Alex, if you choose not to teach, you could become a wildlife photographer even though you said all you had to do was Point-and-Shoot! Or, if all else fails, a personal shopper choosing fabulous gifts like the ones you brought us. As they all said goodnight, everyone thought her teasing words were the perfect ending to an entertaining and stimulating evening.

On Wednesday, June 15th, a little more than a month after leaving for Australia, Alex reported to The Unit. His CO was there with two other officers, one from The Unit and the other an attorney from IDF's Military Advocate General, which surprised Alex but didn't worry him as he knew he'd done nothing wrong. All of them congratulated

Chapter 6

him on his work in Australia; his CO told him the letter from Colonel Markham, SOCOM's chief, would be added to Alex's permanent file. It said he'd been brilliant and they hoped Alex would come again to teach additional *Krav Maga* sessions. The CO then told him there was another letter from the SOCOM director. A young woman, a girl named Gwen, had accused Alex first of sexual harassment and then of rape. However, they'd interviewed the other women in the course, and all of them said Gwen was extremely provocative, constantly "coming on" to Alex who always ignored her seduction attempts. SOCOM's investigation into the charges further revealed that she claimed the rape had occurred on the night of the last class of the program when Alex was at a farewell dinner with his trainees and Colonel Markham, a dinner Gwen had not attended. She then changed her story and said it happened the next day, but SOCOM's chief stated that Alex had gone home with his girlfriend and then left Sydney for Cairns very early the next morning and hadn't returned to Sydney at all. For serious but false accusations against a foreign officer, Gwen was dishonorably discharged from the WRAACs and a full reprimand was permanently added to her file. The MAG attorney assured Alex they'd only wanted him to be aware of the outrageous accusations and nothing would ever be known outside this office. After the MAG attorney left, the CO looked at Alex and said, "OK, all that nonsense is out of the way, so let's talk about your responsibilities for the next two months unless you're willing to extend your time in the IDF, even re-enlist. Any chance?"

Alex replied, "No, sir. I really want to start university. If nothing else, the time in Australia showed me I like teaching. So, I'll think seriously about that when I'm at Hebrew U. and figure out what I want to teach. In the meantime, I'm yours until mid-August. Do you have anything specific in mind?"

"Actually I do; I should say *we* do," the CO said, finally acknowledging the other officer seated near his desk. "I didn't introduce you two earlier. This is Colonel Shmueli from the IDF Manpower Directorate. Given your obvious success with SOCOM, the colonel would like you to write a new manual for *Krav Maga*, with instructions about how to teach it. The IDF's current handbook and teaching guidelines aren't very effective; we need something much better. If you're willing to do this, we'd like to organize practice teaching with your methodology for *Krav Maga* instructors in all units. Are you interested?"

"Very interested, sir, but I have several questions. In which language, English or Hebrew? Where would I work and when do I start? Is there a deadline? What will happen if I can't complete the manual in time?"

Colonel Shmueli responded. "Alex, those aren't real problems. You can write it in the language you're most comfortable using, English or Hebrew; eventually we'll want it in both. I'll arrange an office for you in *HaKirya* and you'll have both secretarial and translation help. There's no official final date, but of course I hope you'll complete it as soon as possible, partly because I really want to set up those practice teaching sessions to see how your methods work and to evaluate them with other instructors. If we run over into October, I hope you'll be willing to continue on a part-time basis. OK? If your answer is 'Yes', you'll start at *HaKirya* on June 20th. I'll need three work days between now and then to find you a room in the Manpower Directorate and hire your staff."

Alex said, "Very definitely OK, sir. This is new and exciting for me, but I can't tell you yet which language I'll use. I have to start writing and then I'll decide. What time should I be at *HaKirya* on the 20th? And my staff?"

"0900 hours, Lieutenant Novak. I'll meet you at the main gate with an ID badge and your official documents. Then I'll escort you to your office and introduce you to the staff. In the meantime…shalom, Alex."

"Thank you, sir." Alex said, standing up. He saluted Colonel Shmueli who also stood, shook hands with The Unit's CO and left.

"You can sit down, Alex, for a minute," his CO said, smiling. "I just want you to know I'm pleased you've decided to accept this project; I'm sure you'll succeed in this as you've succeeded in everything you've done in *Tzahal*. I'm just sorry you're not going to stay on in The Unit. Now get out of here. Shalom." Alex saluted the CO and he left.

When he returned to Ramat Aviv, he went to the kitchen for a drink and noticed a paint-smudged Lise sitting on the deck, her long bare legs curled beneath her, a pitcher of iced tea on the nearby table and a tall glass in her hand. "Hi," she said, "I'm taking a break to 'hydrate', the new buzzword, telling people they must drink a lot in the summer? So 'hydrate', Alex. Have iced tea and tell me about the extreme challenge they offered you."

Laughing, Alex said, "Hi yourself. You look about 16 sitting that way, with paint on your nose. I'll get a glass and then, if you have a few minutes, there's something I want to talk to you about." After he brought out a glass and filled it with tea, Alex sat down opposite her while Lise sat up straight with her hands folded in her lap, staring

Chapter 6

at him. Alex laughed again. "You still look like a 16-year-old, but now like a teenager waiting to be reprimanded by the principal. No reprimand, Lise, and I'm no principal. What I am is an overpaid employee of the IDF and a freeloader. I'm living in your house totally free, contributing nothing. What I'm asking you and David to do is to let me pay some kind of rent, at least until I move to Jerusalem. Please don't say 'No'. Say you'll think about it because right now I feel like a 'moocher', another buzzword, and that doesn't sit right with me at all. As for the new challenge, well, starting next Monday, I'll be going to *HaKirya* every day, to the Manpower Department, to write a new manual about *Krav Maga* with instructions and methods for teaching it. That's a challenge, because I've never done that kind of writing. But I think I'll like it. What do you think?"

"I know you'll do a really great job. Now I'd better get back to my 'job' or my painting won't be great! And OK, David and I will think about your request."

The next few weeks passed smoothly. Lise and David agreed to let Alex pay minimal rent, and he found it easy to work on the *Krav Maga* manual in his quiet office in *HaKirya;* he wrote in English and then worked closely on the Hebrew version with Sergeant Efrat, an extremely bright young woman. She was born in Israel but completed high school in the United States when her father was one of the IDF's military attachés at the Israeli Embassy in Washington; when her family returned to Israel, the IDF acquired a superb English-Hebrew translator and Alex benefitted from her expertise. He completed the manual in both English and Hebrew exactly on time, before the end of July. Then he worked with four practice groups using the Hebrew version of the manual during the first two weeks of August; after reviewing and incorporating the feedback from the instructors in the practice groups, he finished all of the revisions in both languages on the 19th of August. He knew he'd pushed himself extremely hard to complete the manual, but he also knew he always worked best under pressure; so he thought the manual in both languages was excellent, but he'd have to wait for the opinions of the IDF brass. He wanted to go to Tammy Hoffman's wedding in Pittsburgh on August 28th and he'd have to leave no later than the 25th, and then he'd try to spend some time with his friends in Columbus. Colonel Shmueli didn't disappoint; he read the manuals quickly and was satisfied with the final versions in both languages, congratulating Alex for his superb work and thanking Efrat for her contribution. When he said goodbye to Alex, the colonel expressed his sadness, as both a member of the

Manpower Directorate and as a former paratrooper, that a "major asset" was leaving *Tzahal*. Alex said he wasn't really leaving because he knew he'd be returning for *milu'im* and the colonel just smiled; neither of them could possibly know Alex would be called back less than a year later.

When Alex packed his things and left his almost empty office for the last time, before Shabbat on the 19th, he felt it was a profoundly anticlimactic ending to a significant stage of his life: four intense years of anticipation, strategic training, surreptitious maneuvers, wonderful comradeship, unique experiences, frequent exhilaration and frequent exhaustion, all in The Unit, IDF's Special Forces. *"But,"* he said to himself as he drove home to Ramat Aviv, *"Every time one door closes, a window opens. And for me that window will be Hebrew University after the holidays."* He wondered if that sentence was only a cliché or if it was from the Bible. As he approached the house, he saw Gabriel's car at the curb, and thought, *"Terrific, I'll ask him about that door-window thing! Gabriel really knows the Scriptures."* He went into the kitchen to get something to drink and saw only Grandma Anna there, preparing their evening meal. He sneaked up and kissed her noisily on the back of her neck. She laughed without turning around, and said. "Hi, Alex. I really needed that!"

"How did you know it was me?" he asked.

"Go out to the deck," she replied. "Kobi and Gabriel are out there fooling around with those boomerangs you brought. David will be here any sec' to help me because we have a mob for Shabbat, to celebrate your release from *Tzahal*. And David would never kiss me like that, so it had to be you!"

"Why not Grandpa Richard or Lise?" he continued.

"Because he knows I'd toss what was in my hand at him and it's a knife. Besides, he only does things like that at home," she said, putting down the knife, turning and hugging him. "Lise's too much of a lady, at least with me. I don't know where she and Richard are, so go join the boys outside."

Drinking his Coke straight out of the can, he did. And then he almost choked with laughter as Kobi and Gabriel bet on which boomerang had the better return. He joked, "OK, guys. Throw them again and I'll be the judge." He kept on laughing as each tried to bribe him to choose his boomerang.

Aya and Ephraim as well as Dina, Alon, Yael, and David R joined them. As usual at the Hofmans, Shabbat was fun-filled, with superb food, lots of laughter and love, even though everyone said how much

Chapter 6

Keren, Yaniv, Dani and Yoni were missed on family occasions. Anna said wistfully they'd be seeing them soon at the wedding, or at least most of them. "Come as well, you and Richard," both Lise and David said at the same time.

"Thanks, but no thanks," Anna replied. "I'm not being rude. Richard and I both think someone has to stay here to watch the *store*. Besides, we're also looking forward to a trip to Denmark after Sukkot, and we'll see Keren, Jonas, his family, and all our old friends. By the way, Alex, you should take the koala necklace you bought Dani to Pittsburgh and maybe she'll wear it at the wedding. It will look wonderful with her big green eyes!"

A few days later, they flew to Pittsburgh, except Kobi who didn't know if he'd be able to go, but he surprised everyone by arriving the day before the wedding. On the plane, David joked that they could have chartered their own plane with so many Hofmans aboard! When Alex frowned, David added, "Cool it, Novak, you know you're an 'honorary Hofman'!" Alex wasn't surprised to see Dani waiting for them at the Pittsburgh airport with Ted Hoffman, but he was astonished to also see Rob Salter and Miriam Green. Ted had rented a minibus to take the guests and all their luggage to his home in Squirrel Hill, but Alex chose to ride with Rob and Mrs. Green and hear about them and their families.

At Ted and Shani's home, Alex opened the carry-on bag he'd brought in from Rob's car and gave Dani the koala pendant with its emerald eyes. She hugged him. "I absolutely positively love it! Wait right here just a minute," she said, running up the stairs. Two minutes later she descended the stairs regally, her long blonde hair piled high on her head, her green eyes shining, and the koala pendant on her neck. She thrust a tiny pink fairy armadillo into Alex's hands, and said, "This naughty little thing was hiding in my luggage. He's from a Buenos Aires street fair; we named him Antonio, for Banderas, of course, such a swashbuckler as Zorro; when any of those 'macho muchachos' my sister worried about made sexist comments, one of us would yell 'Call Antonio!' and those idiotic jerks would run away. I hope my big sister gets the joke! I bet you thought I'd forget, didn't you? Where's *your* koala? Yaniv said you got one, and it was in Australian camouflage!"

Alex burst out laughing, almost dropping the tiny toy. He hugged her and said, "God how I've missed you, Dani. You're priceless, and sinful! I adore you! Your sauciness always amuses me, just like my sister Paulina and Poppy, my cheeky little 'Aussie' girlfriend, your *doppelganger*!"

"Impossible!" she pouted. "I'm one of a kind, so there's no way I have a double, not in looks or in personality!" They went into the living room so the entire family could admire her koala necklace.

Just as everyone had anticipated, the wedding of Tammy Hoffman and Gadi Schuster was a joyous event. Throughout all of the festivities, Alex was delighted to see Dani wearing outfits in green or floral prints with a lot of green so she could show off the pendant. The day after the wedding, Alex went to Columbus, Ohio, to spend two weeks with his special friends, an extremely enjoyable respite with people who meant so much to him.

Chapter 7

On September 12th, three weeks before Rosh Hashana, Alex flew from Pittsburgh to Slovakia for five weeks. So much was happening in the family and he realized he couldn't have chosen a more appropriate time. *Dedko* had suffered a mild heart attack, but he was recovering; *Babička* joked that she was a very old lady and *Dedko* was "running her ragged" with his demands all day long, for newspaper, for tea. Alex assured his beloved grandmother that he'd take over all the chores while he was in Žilina. The rest of his family was fine. His twin sister, Adriana, had just completed an MA in public health nursing and her husband, Denys, had recently been promoted to director of the engineering division of Kia Motors. They had purchased a 3-bedroom cottage with a large backyard just a few streets away from his parents and grandparents; his niece and nephew, Sasha and Jiří, had grown so much since the last time Alex had seen them and were doing extremely well in school, both speaking and reading English almost fluently. His parents were healthy and delighted to see him again after their *Pesach* reunion in Israel; his mother had a full teaching load and his father was the head of another major unit in the automobile factory, so Alex's help with his elderly grandparents was obviously appreciated. His sister Nina was newly engaged to another architect in the firm where she worked; Alex rejoiced in their obvious love, although he teased them unmercifully about what would happen if they had to compete for a new project. A local satiric TV program had purchased two scripts written by Paulina, his cheeky little sister, even though she was still in university, and the whole family was very proud of her. Alex told them about his remarkable "work-and-fun" trip to Australia; he even related the crocodile incident with humor. He showed them his photos and told them about the *Krav Maga* manual, his last task for the IDF. "What now, Alex?" his father asked kindly, totally without the rancor that had dominated their old discussions. Alex said he knew he was at another crossroads in his life, and he was looking forward to moving to Jerusalem to study at Hebrew University; after that, he'd see where this new path led. The five weeks passed too quickly and he savored every minute spent with the family he loved so much; at the end of his too brief vacation, everyone, including *Babička* and *Dedko*, escorted him to the airport, where they hugged and kissed him and wished him well on his return to Israel.

So many people were at the Hofmans during *Sukkoth*, family, friends, even friends of friends, and Alex was reminded of the same holiday four years earlier when he'd first arrived in Israel. Yaniv, driving Alex's Jeep, met him at the airport instead of Kobi, and Keren was still in Copenhagen working on a PhD instead of teasing her brothers, but everyone else who'd been there that first *Sukkoth*, Lise and David, Kobi, Dani, both sets of grandparents, David's sister and her family, even Yoni, Ted, Shani and Ethan Hoffman, aunts, uncles, cousins. And new friends, some of Kobi's Unit 669 comrades, and Dani's companions on her post-IDF South American trip which had been exciting even though the girls had kept their promise to their parents and hadn't driven down Bolivia's infamous "death road". Gabriel, Yaniv's Unit 8200 partner was there with two of his old friends from Austria, David R, the medical student Alex had met many times, and Ruth, a jewelry designer, who'd recently made *Aliyah*. Alex was instantly attracted to the beautiful redhead and hoped the obvious closeness he noted between Gabriel and Ruth was just a brother-sister relationship left over from their teenage years in the Rabbi's home. Seeing Gabriel's eyes frequently straying to Dani and her friend Tamar reassured Alex that he wouldn't be straying into proprietary territory if he asked Ruth out.

Gabriel had a 2-bedroom apartment in French Hill, not far from Mt. Scopus; it was empty after a failed relationship, and after Ruth, who'd been staying with him when she first came to Jerusalem, moved to her own flat near her studio in Katamon. He invited Alex to share the flat and the rent when Alex started his studies at Hebrew University, HU. Not wanting to live in dorms with students so much younger than himself, Alex instantly agreed; he was pleased that it was easy to find parking for his Jeep in French Hill; he was also pleased that HU's Mt. Scopus campus was within easy walking distance of Gabriel's flat. Alex had enrolled in two *chugim*, academic areas of study, Political Science and Jewish Studies. After proficiency tests, and with his certificate as a teacher of English as a Foreign Language as well as his experience in the IDF, Alex was exempt from required courses in Reading Comprehension in both English and Hebrew. He found the lectures he was required or opted to take thought-provoking, and neither the amount of bibliography nor the required term papers were too taxing. In fact, in some of his free time, he attended other classes and symposiums at the university, asking challenging questions and meeting some of the brilliant international scholars connected to Hebrew U.

About a week after he settled in Jerusalem, he called Ruth and invited her out for dinner; she accepted but suggested a take-out meal

Chapter 7

and a tour of her studio. That was the beginning of what became a deep and committed relationship; both of them admitted having had other romantic liaisons but neither of them had ever fallen so completely in love. Ruth's unique jewelry was beginning to be noticed and many Jerusalem shops asked her for completed products. She worked very hard in her studio every day and played very hard or made love with Alex every night. They also spent free time with Gabriel and Tamar during the first semester of HU's academic year. Just as it would have worried him if his sister Paulina flitted from man to man, so it bothered Alex that Dani never seemed to go out more than two or three times with any of the young men she dated. During the second semester, both Alex and Ruth were delighted, and relieved, when Dani and Gabriel finally acknowledged their feelings for each other and began a committed relationship of their own. The four of them spent many Shabbats and all holidays with Dani's family in Ramat Aviv, and some Shabbats with Jakob and Rebecca in Jerusalem. Although Alex spent almost every night in Ruth's apartment and Dani slept with Gabriel every night in his flat, neither of them formally changed their official residence that first year.

Alex, Gabriel and Dani had completed a few final exams in June and early July before all of them were called into *milu'im* after rockets fired by Hezbollah at northern Israel and ambushes resulted in the death of five IDF soldiers and the kidnapping of two others. Gabriel was called to Unit 8200's command base at Urim a week before the Second Lebanon War began; Alex and Yaniv were called in two days later, and Dani on July 12th, the first day. Gabriel translated hundreds of Farsi codes and online chatter in order to ascertain the depth of Iran's unprecedented military support for Hezbollah, while Yaniv corrected errors he detected in the IAF's technical systems. Alex and The Unit engaged Hezbollah's paramilitary forces in more than a few covert attacks, and Dani held briefings with members of the foreign press covering the war. Like most Israelis at home, Lise and David, the grandparents, and Ruth, were glued to TV and radio as they worried about their loved ones, until the ceasefire on August 14th. Despite the relative brevity of the Second Lebanese War, 165 Israelis had been killed, including 44 civilians; 1250 soldiers had been injured as well as 1384 civilians, and almost 4000 rockets had been fired at Israel. Like almost all Israelis, the Hofman "extended family" had mixed feelings about this war, convinced that no one had actually won. Following the war, Kobi decided to leave the IDF, and Dani, Gabriel and Alex, all slightly depressed, returned to Hebrew U and Yaniv to IDC to take their remaining final exams. Alex's spirits were buoyed when, upon returning to the flat in Jerusalem, he found emails expressing concern and support from his family in Slovakia, Rob Salter, the Green family, Susan Berger and many other Pittsburgh friends, Special Ops comrades from Germany, the UK, Italy and France as well as SOCOM trainees and the Smythe family. There was one from Poppy that had him chuckling as he read it, the cheeky teenager having written, "Text me the minute you're home. I won't sleep a wink until I know you're absolutely OK!" He immediately responded, stating he was fine, she should sleep well, and he was still holding her to the promise to visit him in Israel!

A few weeks later, Alex, Gabriel and Dani were astounded when the results of their final exams were published, and they'd aced all of them. That was when Alex moved into Ruth's apartment, and Dani informed her parents she was moving in with Gabriel. There were no arguments from Lise and David who loved Gabriel as one of their own, and Ruth almost as much because she clearly made Alex so very happy. After what he called his "earthly possessions" had been transferred from Gabriel's flat to Ruth's, Alex talked Ruth into taking a 2-week vacation. He was anxious to see his family, especially his grandparents, and he really wanted them to meet Ruth. They flew to Slovakia for a week, staying with his parents but spending time with the entire family. Everyone was charmed by Ruth and amazed at her talent; Jiří announced he was in love with Uncle Alex's girlfriend, the "prettiest redhead in the world", and Sasha said she was in love, too, with the beautiful bracelets Ruth had given her and with Ruth's lessons on how to make jewelry. At the end of the first week, his grandmother hugged Alex and whispered, "Finally, my dearest Alex, you have everything I've always hoped for! Enjoy it all, your lovely Ruth, your education, your life in Israel!"

Their second week was a real vacation for Alex and Ruth, on a Greek cruise with Alex's twin sister and her husband. As his sisters Nina and Paulina were driving them to the airport for the flight to Athens, he said he was worried that *Babička* and *Dedko* were becoming very frail and the recent death of Karel, *Dedko*'s brother, was weighing heavily on both of them. Ruth said even though she'd just met them for the first time, she understood what Alex meant, but she also thought his visit had given them a boost as well as something to look forward to, like a wedding, and while she knew it was egotistical to say it in such a way, it was the truth; Alex's sisters and his brother-in-law agreed. When they arrived in Athens, the two couples boarded

Chapter 7

the "Azamara Journey", a cruise ship for a 7-night voyage visiting Mykonos, Santorini, Kos and Rhodes. Their cabins were small but luxurious, the gourmet food superb but far too rich for diet-conscious Ruth and Adriana; with overnight stays and late departures, their time in the four ports was sufficient for sightseeing and shopping, but all of them agreed the most significant feature of the trip was the remarkable reunion of the Novak twins and the conviviality between the couples. Alex and Ruth said their goodbyes to Adriana and Denys in Rhodes and flew directly to Israel; they were absolutely stunned to see Gabriel and Dani waiting for them.

◆ ◆ ◆

Two weeks before he completed his degree from Hebrew University in 2008, Alex received a telephone call from his former CO in The Unit. The officer said, "Shalom, Alex. I know it's probably a bit premature for congratulations, but that's not why I'm calling. If you can find some time in the next few days to come to the base, we have a special proposition for you. Please try."

"Shalom to you, too sir," Alex said and then added to himself, *"Uh-oh, what could they possibly have in store for me this time?"* Later, when he and Ruth were finally in bed, he said quietly, "I'm not sure I even want to know what they want to offer me, but I owe The Unit so much that I have to go. Come with me. Now, my darling Ruth, let's see if we can have a private pre-graduation celebration!" Ruth laughed as she kissed him. A few days later, Alex drove to The Unit's base with Ruth. When they were escorted into the conference room, Alex saw a few familiar faces: Erez, Sefi and Avram; each of them had been promoted in the interim years since Alex had last seen them. Despite being a civilian, he saluted them. There were two strangers in the room as well, and the CO introduced them as Foreign Ministry employees. After shaking hands with the two men, Alex addressed the CO, "I brought Ruth, my fiancée, sir, because I don't know what your proposition is, but it is might affect her life, too. I hope that's OK."

"It's fine, Alex. I know the two of you are engaged, and if you accept our offer, it certainly will impact Ruth's life. Please, both of you, sit down,. Here's the proposition. Very soon we'll need a new assistant military attaché at our embassy in Washington. We need someone with IDF experience, preferably from the special forces and, in my opinion, from The Unit. We need someone who has worked with international special forces. We need someone who knows Israeli history as well as the political and military situations here, in

Gaza and the West Bank and the Middle East in general. We need someone who understands conflict management. We need someone who knows the workings of Hezbollah and Hamas. We need someone with an excellent command of the English language. And given the rise of terrorism worldwide, we need someone who knows how to share our expertise with the Americans. In other words, Alex, we need you. You meet all of the criteria, and I don't know anyone else who does. I don't have to go through each element individually; I've already told the Foreign Ministry people everything I know about you. As to the position, it's at least a three-year commitment, but possibly much longer. If you accept our offer, you can also study for an MA at Georgetown University. Washington is a very expensive city and most of our embassy personnel live in nearby Maryland or Virginia. But if you want to enroll in Georgetown, we can probably arrange an apartment or small house in Georgetown, a 15-20 minute ride from the Embassy or in Cleveland Park which is closer. Are you interested? If you have any questions, ask. Please consider this offer. Talk it over and let me know when you've made a decision."

Alex said, "It's a phenomenal opportunity, sir. Thank you for considering me. We'll consider it, and I'll get back to you as soon as possible, sir."

Out in the hall, Ruth and Alex looked at each other and both of them said

"Wow!" Alex said, "What do you really think?"

Ruth smiled. "I think you should take it. It's perfect for you, and with a Georgetown MA to boot! I can work anywhere, as long as I can set up a studio and buy supplies. I can ship finished products to my Israeli dealers. Besides, I've always wanted to live in the United States! So I think you should knock on that conference room door right now and say 'Yes!' to the CO and the Foreign Ministry guys."

Alex knocked on the door, and Erez opened it. He grinned at Alex and Ruth, turned to the others and said, "I told you he'd accept the position. I know him and I knew this was an offer he couldn't refuse!"

"But I do have one condition before I agree completely," Alex said. "We must have a flat with a studio for Ruth to create her jewelry. She's very well known now and she must be able to work."

"No problem at all," the CO said with a smile. "My wife and daughters love your jewelry, Ruth. They have a lot, and it's cost me a pretty penny!"

Back in their apartment in Jerusalem, Alex locked the door and locked Ruth in his arms, kissing her. Laughing, he said, "I can't get

Chapter 7

over it! What luck! A great job! An MA at Georgetown! And the most important luck of all, my gorgeous redhead, all of it with you! Let's get married soon!" Too overcome to speak, Ruth just nodded and kissed him again and again. Between kisses, Alex added, "I'm hungry, but let's feed the *other* hunger first, and then call the Hofmans. We can celebrate with food and wine later." Ruth nodded again as, laughing, she led him to their bedroom.

All of the Hofmans were thrilled for them. After digesting the news, Lise said, *"Motzei Shabbat* we'll plan a wedding." After a celebratory Shabbat lunch only with the family, Lise grinned at Alex and said, "David had a great idea. We've already invited everybody, and I mean everybody from all over the world, for an enormous barbecue in mid-August in honor of all our 'tall poppies' and their graduations! So let's add another *simcha*, your wedding!" Of course she hadn't mentioned "his" idea to David earlier, but he nodded in agreement.

Alex and Ruth were flabbergasted; and she said nobody could plan a wedding in six weeks. All the Hofmans laughed, and David said, "If that's what you think, Ruth, you don't know Lise, our mothers, our daughters, my sister!" Everyone smiled and high-fived Ruth, Alex and each other. Lise telephoned Dina and told her they needed her; then she told the men to "disappear" so the women could get right to work. Online, Ruth found a Vera Wang wedding gown with a plunging neckline that "demanded" an emerald necklace and earrings; Aya said her dressmaker would be able to copy it. When Ruth said she didn't have the "proper emeralds" for the jewelry, Lise told her Ted Hoffman would be in Israel the following week and he could bring whatever Ruth ordered from the New York Diamond Exchange. Lise proposed building a small but sturdy wooden bridge over their swimming pool to be strewn with flowers for the ceremony, but she made Ruth swear to keep everything a secret from Alex. She also promised Ruth a special wedding gift, a one-of-a-kind "Lise Original" *chuppah*. She and Dani helped Ruth design wedding invitations and Dina promised to have them printed in two days. Ruth's head was spinning before the men returned from their impromptu pick-up basketball game at Dina and Alon's home. Everything for the wedding was planned: the wooden bridge, the flowers, the catering, the chairs and tables, and flowery green dresses for Ruth's attendants, Dani, Keren, Alex's twin sister Adriana, Rebecca Breitling, and Alex's niece Sasha. Everything would be ordered the next day, including tuxedos for Alex, Kobi, Yaniv, Rob Salter, Gabriel and Jiri, Alex's nephew. As they drove back to Jerusalem after the weekend, Alex asked Ruth if she was all right; he said he'd never seen her so quiet. She laughed and said, "I'm exhausted. You've always told me how incredible the Hofmans are, and I've seen it myself, but Lise's like a 'whirling dervish'! Everything's planned, and we're getting married in 6 weeks, my darling!"

In mid-August, Lise and David hosted an enormous barbecue in honor of family members, including honorary ones. Keren's PhD dissertation had been submitted and, although not yet definitively approved, no one at all doubted its acceptance, so she had returned from Copenhagen. Yaniv had received his BA in information technology and conflict management from IDC Herzliya *cum laude*, and both Alex and Dani had graduated from Hebrew University with honors. Gabriel, upon receiving his Master's Degree at a commencement ceremony for MA and PhD students, had been recognized as the outstanding 2008 graduate of Hebrew University. Kobi, who'd left Unit 669 in 2006 after the war, was only a year away from completing his degree, at the Zinman College of Physical Education and Sport Sciences at The Wingate Institute, and he'd recently been accepted into a prestigious honors specialization program at Wingate, Sports Management. Hundreds of guests, family, friends, IDF comrades and officers, toasted all the graduates or – as Lise joked – Alex's 'tall poppies', with French champagne brought to Israel by Claude and Mignon, Lise and David's friends from their university years in Paris. They enjoyed fabulous food, swam and played water polo, and partied almost the whole night. All of Alex's family had come from Slovakia along with his American "family" from Pittsburgh and Columbus, and Ruth and Gabriel's "family" from Austria. Lise's mother and stepfather had come from Sweden to celebrate with all their grandchildren, and Gabriel's father and his sister Darla arrived from LA; all the senior guests, including Yaniv and Dani's local grandparents, Aya and Ephraim, Richard and Anna, were enjoying the party from the deck. Ruth was giddy with the number of people toasting all of them, and Alex said she was giggling because she'd had too much French champagne. There was only one awkward moment, when David R welcomed Keren back to Israel and then walked away to congratulate Gabriel, Dani, Yaniv and Alex. Sitting near the edge of the pool with them and with Kobi and Paulina, Ruth told Alex that much as she loved David R, he was an 'idjit' and she should toss him fully dressed into the pool. When Alex asked why, she said it was obvious: David's feelings for Keren were as strong as ever and it was equally clear Keren felt the same way, so maybe she should toss Keren into the pool as well. Alex said, "Please stay out of it, Ruth. They're adults and will

Chapter 7

have to find their own way back to each other, or not. Right, Kobes?" Kobi, laughing at Paulina's witty ripostes, now understood why Alex had always compared his cheeky sister Dani to Paulina, and he just nodded. Before the evening ended, Alex surprised his "tipsy tyrannical love" with an emerald ring from Tiffany's, which Ted brought to Israel; Alex said it matched Ruth's gorgeous green eyes perfectly.

Two days later, after touring parts of Israel with family and a few foreign visitors, Alex received several surprises. Not only was he stunned when he saw the bridge over the pool, but he was astounded to see the Smythes, including Sir Andrew and Sylvia, sitting on the deck and chatting with Lise and David, along with Ruth and a few other relatives. Laughing, Larry told an amazed Alex he and Andrew couldn't *not* come after surviving the famous "croc attack" with Alex, and the other Smythes, except James who was on SASR maneuvres, were "stowaways". Poppy, who'd grown up into an exquisite but still cheeky beauty, kissed Alex on both cheeks and reminded him that he'd promised to introduce her to Dani and Paulina, his "sisters".

Only two hours later, Alex's father and David escorted a still somewhat dazed Alex, who'd showered and donned the tux, to Lise's elegant emerald green and white *chuppah* held aloft on the flower-adorned bridge by Yaniv, Gabriel, Rob Salter and Alex's brother-in-law Denys; he stood there with Kobi as his best man and one of his principal witnesses, as Dani, Keren, Rebecca and Adriana walked onto the bridge. He was awestruck as his bride, breathtaking in her copy of a Vera Wang gown and emerald jewelry, was led to the *chuppah* by his niece Sasha scattering flower petals. Then, accompanied by Lise and Frau Sarah, Ruth winked saucily at him as they circled him seven times. Both Rabbis Samuel and Jakob Breitling, officiated, with the older Rabbi Breitling saying a few words about how proud he was of Ruth who'd grown up in his home, how pleased he was that she was not only very successful in her career but that she'd also met Alex, her extraordinary soon-to-be husband, and mostly how delighted he was that the talented, cheeky but insecure 15-year-old *"gingi"* he'd first met was now surrounded by so much love. Then Alex's nephew, Jiri, handed Rabbi Jakob Breitling the rings he'd carried very carefully, and the wedding proceeded until Alex stomped forcefully on the glass and all the guests shouted *"Mazal Tov"*. The wedding, so quickly and so impressively organized, had been splendid. Alex and Ruth, thankful for such loving families and friends, were totally content as they anticipated a new life.

Twenty-two days later, they arrived in Washington. The Israeli

Embassy hadn't yet arranged an apartment for them, so they were temporarily booked into the Embassy Suites-Chevy Chase Pavilion, not far from the Embassy. As an *Olah Chadasha*, Ruth had purchased her flat with the Jewish Agency's help and her quite remarkable earnings when the owner decided to sell it, but she still had a substantial mortgage. They hadn't yet found a tenant who satisfied Ruth, so while she was packing jewelry supplies and personal things to be sent to Washington and Alex was packing books and other items to be stored in Ruth's studio, she suggested Alex go to Washington alone, find them a place, and she'd follow. His instant reply was "No Way!" Rebecca Breitling, helping them pack, said she and Jakob would interview potential tenants. On their way to the airport, Alex received a telephone call from a secretary at the Israeli Embassy who said she might have a house for them in Georgetown. "I'll email you photos of it," she offered, but Alex responded that they'd be in D.C. the next day and he'd call her from their hotel. "OK. Call me at 364-5500, extension 343 or just ask for Noa. *N'see'a tova!*" she said and ended the call. Two days later, they saw the house on M Street; it was perfect, a charming 4-storey row house, narrow, with a small patio and garden in the backyard, and an empty but finished basement Ruth could use as a studio. Sam Diamond, the owner, was a professor at Georgetown who'd accepted a 3-year contract in PEPS, a special Hebrew University program combining Philosophy, Economics and Political Science; his gay partner, Rami Yacovi, an Israeli cinematographer, was anxious to find work and a nice place to live. When Alex and Ruth burst out laughing, the others looked at them as if they'd gone crazy until Alex told them he'd recently graduated from Hebrew U. with a degree in Political Science and knew all the staff in PEPS, and Ruth told them about her flat in Old Katamon, even showing them a few photos. Within an hour, an informal contract for an exchange of residences had been written and signed, hands had been shaken, and all four of them were drinking mint juleps on the patio and planning their mutual moves over the next two weeks. Before going back to the hotel, Alex and Ruth held hands and walked around the delightful neighborhood and nearby Georgetown U. campus. Then they took a taxi back to the hotel, asking the driver to pass by the Israeli Embassy so Alex could see how long it would actually take to get from the house to the embassy; they sent flowers to Noa in appreciation for finding the house for them and told her she'd be one of their first guests. Then, noting the 7-hour difference between Washington and Jerusalem time, they sent an email to Rebecca informing her their flat was rented.

Chapter 7

Their first year in Washington passed quickly, and successfully, for both of them. Alex got on well with Sallai Meridor, Israel's ambassador, and all the Embassy staff. His job became increasingly important given the ever accelerating number of incidents by Al Qaeda-related terrorists and other Islamic militants. When a war between Palestinians in the Gaza Strip and Israel, "Operation Cast Lead", a three-week conflict from December 2008 to January 2009 broke out, Alex offered to return to The Unit at once, but his CO told him he was more valuable in Washington at that time. Alex met frequently with US officials to discuss ways of anticipating and dealing with terrorist attacks, especially Al Qaeda-related incidents.

He also began an MA program at Georgetown, challenging but not too difficult. Meanwhile, not only was Ruth working on new jewelry designs, but she also created unusual wedding rings for Alex and herself. They spent the long Thanksgiving weekend in Pittsburgh with Ted and Shani Hoffman who'd also invited Alex's "American family", the Greens, Salters and Bergers. Shani said Thanksgiving was the festival of Macy's famous parade, food, football, football and more football. Ruth was fascinated by this American festival, and claimed she felt she was back in Israel with the other Hofmans, whose home was always crowded with family, friends, fun and food, food and more food. Shani said to Ruth, "Definitely fun, and family forever, in America and in Israel."

In August 2010, Ruth gave birth to Lauren and Jonathan, another set of twins in the Marek-Novak clan. And in the summer of 2011, they brought their family to the Israeli Hofmans for Dani and Gabriel's wedding and then vacationed in Žilina so Alex's family could enjoy spoiling this new set of twins.

Glossary

Chapter 1 – Mostly Slovakian and/or Czech

Babička – Grandmother
Dedko – Grandfather
Strýko – Uncle
Teta – aunt
Yeshivot – religious schools for Jewish boys [Hebrew]
Otec – father
"Na zdravie" – "To your health"
"Na slobodu" – "To freedom"
5. PŠU (5. Pluk špeciálneho určenia) – 5th Special Purpose Regiment, based in Žilina, the Slovakian Armed Forces counter-terrorism and special operations unit
miláčik – sweetheart, honey
Erev Rosh Hashanah – the day before the Jewish New Year [Hebrew]

Chapter 2

Šťastnou cestu' – 'Bon voyage'
Mamička – Mom, affectionate term for Mother *(Matka)*
Ocko – Dad, Papa, affectionate term for Father *(Otec)*
"Dovidenia!" – Until we meet again: *Auf wiedersehen! Arrivederci! Lehit'ra'ot!*

Chapter 3

HaKirya – the area in central Tel Aviv, containing the headquarters of *Tzahal*
Tzahal – (acronym), *Tzva Haganah Le'Yisrael*, Israel Defense Forces (IDF)
achi – my brother
Golani and *Givati* – Infantry brigades
Aman – Military Intelligence Directorate
Duvduvan – Paratrooper counter-terrorism unit
Egoz and *Oketz* – reconnaissance units, *Oketz* is a canine unit
Sayeret Matkal (Unit 767) – the IDF's main special operations-commando unit, mainly used to obtain strategic intelligence behind enemy lines
Shayetet 13 – Israel's naval commando unit, equivalent to US Navy SEALS, responsible among other things for maritime hostage-rescue missions
Sayeret Shaldag – Israel's Air Force commandos, specializing in reconnaissance and target designation outside Israel's borders, often undercover
nudnik – pest, a pain in the butt   [Yiddish slang]
gibushim – recruits undergoing the selection process
fait accompli – a decision already been made, a 'done deal'

Glossary

Manot Krav – combat rations. MREs (Meals Ready to Eat), bread, tuna, grape leaves filled with something, olives, ketchup, mustard, and tinned pineapple
tarte aux pommes – apple pie

Chapter 4

chayal boded – lone soldier]
Krav Maga – brutal, aggressive contact combat combining nasty elements of other martial arts, without the oriental philosophy of the other martial arts
simunition – non-lethal training ammunition
chofesh – vacation, freedom or free time
Beit Hachayal – a free hostel for IDF soldiers

Chapter 5

Kommando Spezialkräfte (KSK) – German Special Commando Forces
Garin Mahal – lone soldiers from abroad living in Israel for less than 18 months
Grenzschutzgruppe 9 der Bundespolizei – Border Protection Group 9 of the Police
Wehrmacht – united armed forces of Nazi Germany
Waffen-SS – armed wing of Hitler's *Schutzstaffel* paramilitary "protectors"
Gestapo (Geheime Staatspolizei) – Nazi secret police
Willkommen und Viel Glück! – Welcome and Good Luck! [German]
sharav [Hebrew], or ***khamsin*** [Arabic]– the dry, hot, sandy, wind blowing in from the south with a speed up to 140 kilometers per hour, coming from North Africa and carrying great quantities of sand and dust from the deserts

Chapter 6

Australian slang: ***gobsmacked*** – shocked; ***Big Smoke*** – a large city; ***cold one*** – beer; ***plonk*** – cheap wine; ***sheilas*** – girls; ***shout*** – treat; ***ripper*** – great; ***ace*** – excellent; ***fair dinkum*** – absolutely true; ***fair dinkum blitzed*** – truly emotional; ***not the full quid*** – not too intelligent; ***give a burl*** – take a chance; ***Ozzy strine*** – Australian words and accent; ***cobbers*** – good friends; ***diggers*** – soldiers; ***rip snorter*** – a great experience; ***bonzer*** – terrific; ***hoons*** – hooligans; ***Holy dooley!*** – good grief! ***Ta*** – thanks; ***flat out yakka*** – hard work; ***Mickey Mouse*** – excellent; ***larrikins*** – pranksters; ***The Lucky Country*** – Australia, of course; ***jabber*** – talk in *strine*; ***swimmers*** – a bathing suit; ***billabong*** – a stagnant pond left behind after a river changes course
kunmokurrkurrs – clans   [Aboriginal]
bangkerreng – the wet season   [Aboriginal]
Mimihs – fairy-like spirits, often bad-tempered   [Aboriginal]
bininj – the Aboriginal people   [Aboriginal]

Glossary

crock – nonsense   [British slang]
swags – canvas sleeping compartments sometimes called "backpack beds"
Hooroo! – goodbye, but its literal meaning is "heaps"   [Australian slang]
bunyips – mythological creatures   [Australian slang]
b'seder – OK, all right: literally, in order   [Hebrew]

Alex's 'fooling-around' speech to Kobi: "***Grouse, cobber*** (Great, my friend)! In ***Straya*** (Australia) they say ***bog into brekkie*** (eat breakfast), so I'll ***siphon the python*** (use the toilet) – not to be said to ***sheilas*** (girls), it's ***barra*** (vulgar). I'll yank on a pair of ***stubbies*** (shorts) and a ***Mickey Mouse*** (nice) T-shirt and we're ***good to go*** (ready). As for ***strine*** (slang), it's ***yakka yakka*** (hard work) but you're not ***drongo*** (stupid) or ***bludge*** (lazy), so ***avago*** (try)! ***Apples?*** (OK?) I need ***dardy runners*** (good trainers), so this ***arvo*** (p.m.) let's ***lob*** (drop in) at Azrieli, and I'll ***shout*** (treat) for ***tucker*** (food) – a ***sanger*** (sandwich), a ***coldie*** (beer) or a ***fizzie*** (soda), not a ***mystery bag*** (sausage in a roll). ***Fathom that nark*** (understand that nonsense)? If ***yep*** (yes), ***good on ya*** (well done)!"

Chapter 7

simcha – happy event or occasion
gingi – redhead
"N'see'ya tova!" – Have a good trip!

Epilogue

Israel's first prime minister, David Ben Gurion, considered the IDF an ideal melting pot, bringing together soldiers of every background, European, North African, American, Ashkenazi, Sephardic; religious, non-religious; every socio-economic level. And so it was for the major characters in these stories; Gabriel and Alex were brought together with Lise's children through the IDF. During the next few years, the vagaries and happenings, the consistencies and inconsistencies of life, especially life in Israel, occurred in the lives of the Hofman family and those closest to them.

There were marriages. There were children and grandchildren. There were family deaths and other tragedies. There were promotions and achievements. There were scandals and corruption in Israel. There was BDS and there were worldwide efforts to delegitimize Israel. There was war. There was terrorism. But there were also medical, economic and technological breakthroughs.

◆◆◆

And somehow, despite the sadness and the nation's problems, the fear and the despair and the loss, there was always love and joy and pride and loyalty and responsibility and a sense of fun as well as purpose and contentment, and always lots of good food and laughter among the members of the very large and extended Hofman-Hoffman-Hoffmann family.

www.ingramcontent.com/pod-product-compliance
Lightning Source LLC
Chambersburg PA
CBHW071647160426
43195CB00012B/1380